T3-BGW-228

SpringerWienNewYork

Horst Sondermann

Photoshop® in Architectural Graphics

SpringerWienNewYork

Prof. Arch. Horst Sondermann
Faculty of Architecture and Design
HFT Stuttgart
Schellingstr. 24, 70174 Stuttgart

Printed in Austria
SpringerWienNewYork is a part of Springer Science+Business Media
springer.at

Layout and Cover Design: Horst Sondermann
Typesetting in Tasse Regular Wide and Bold Wide
Translation from German into English: George Morton, Stuttgart
Printing and binding: Holzhausen Druck & Medien GmbH., 1140 Vienna, Austria

Printed on acid-free and chlorine-free bleached paper
SPIN: 12030606

Library of Congress Control Number: 2008943077

With 1000 colored Figures

ISBN 978-3-211-71591-8 SpringerWienNewYork

Table of Contents

Introduction

Photoshop® by Adobe Systems Inc. is the global market leader among image-processing applications.

Besides the "classical" fields of application in photography, graphics and web design, it plays an important role in 3-D modelling, both in the creation of textures and in the post-production of rendered still images.

In the context of architectural graphics, one can say that Photoshop® is used in nearly every workflow phase, e.g. for creating picture footage for plan layouts, bitmap textures for use on virtual models or assembling photographed and rendered picture components.

Given this popular and refined software's omnipresence, it is rather surprising that among numerous Photoshop® books there is no particular manual for architects, interior designers, screen- and production designers.

This book tries to close the gap, and to answer some typical questions concerning the use of Photoshop® in architectural graphics.

To filter out what is usable and comprehensible for students and professionals from the wealth of possibilities the application offers, I have both consulted the current specialist literature and in particular concentrated on the things which are discussed during lessons.

I neither could nor wished to go into topics like color management, which go far beyond practical day-to-day use.
For such themes there is sufficient exhaustive specialist literature which you should consult as required.

Yet, while working on this book, I realized that there is much more to show (in my Mac there is still some material which I developed for this but for which there was no space in this book) – we shall see if there is a chance to introduce it in a second volume.

It seems to me appropriate at this point to make a few remarks about the specialist terms I have used.

First of all, I presume that you use a mouse with at least two keys, thus the frequent references to the context menu reached by right-clicking.

If you work with a single-key mouse or a trackpad there is, depending on the operating system, a modification key for simulating the right-click : on the Mac keyboard it is the CTRL key.

Moreover, I use the term CTRL for the most important command key; Mac-users then know that on their keyboard it is the Apple or Command key.

PC-users are quite simply in the majority (still), and the idea was to save space when writing.

The Shift key should be familiar, the Option key is referred to as Alt throughout the book.

Please forgive my preference for keyboard shortcuts; the work is quite simply done faster when one knows them. I have, however, tried to name the associated menu commands as much as possible.

And now I wish you much fun, and also energy, when working through the tutorials.

1

Photoshop® and Bridge® – Workspace and File Management

At the risk of boring you, I should like at the start to discuss the interface of Photoshop® and such related topics as navigation and shortcuts (experience shows that some of these are not known, or at least not commonly used).

Please bear in mind that in what follows we will always talk about the current version, CS3 Extended.

Open file 01_pplatz.jpg. Probably you will come across the first stumbling-block at this point; it is not your chic Photoshop® which opens but a spartanly-equipped utility application of your operating system (Preview on the Mac or Windows Picture and Fax Viewer on a PC).

In this case your operating system simply does not yet know that it must open Photoshop® for JPG files.
You can either solve the problem spon-

2

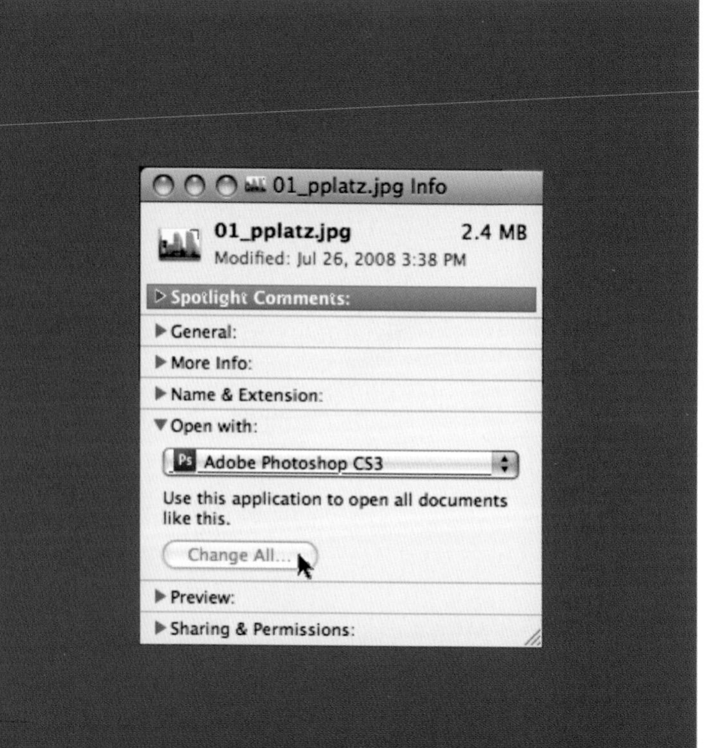

View Window Help

Proof Setup ▶
Proof Colors ⌘Y
Gamut Warning ⇧⌘Y
Pixel Aspect Ratio Correction
32-bit Preview Options...

Zoom In ⌘+
Zoom Out ⌘−
Fit on Screen ⌘0
Actual Pixels ⌥⌘0
Print Size

Screen Mode ▶
- Standard Screen Mode
- ✓ Maximized Screen Mode
- Full Screen Mode With Menu
- Full Screen Mode

✓ Extras ⌘H
Show ▶

Rulers ⌘R

Workspace ▼

taneously by clicking on the file symbol with the right mouse key, and choosing Photoshop® via the command Open with...; or systematically, by calling up the information about this file (Get Info, also found by right-clicking) and instructing that Photoshop® should always be used for files of this type (ill.2)

Now to Photoshop® – the Standard Workspace shows the image in 1/3 of its proper size, in the so called Maximized Screen Mode (ill.1)
Should you wish to view it in the familiar "window look", just select the command Screen Mode – Standard Screen Mode (Ill.3) from the View menu.

Alternatively you can press F; every time you do this the image appears in a different mode, or on a different background; on one occasion even the menu bar disappears (Full Screen Mode).

If you now press the Tab key, all the palettes disappear too, and the image can be admired alone on a black background, even full-screen if you press CTRL-0 (ill.4).

Press Tab again, so that your palettes reappear, and F once, so that you see the image in the so called Maximized Screen Mode (don´t worry, nobody remembers these terms; I only use them so that you can check in the View menu whether you have chosen the same as I have).

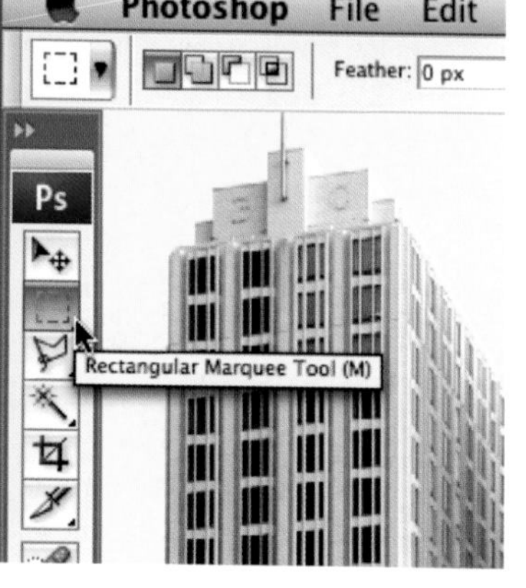

5

6

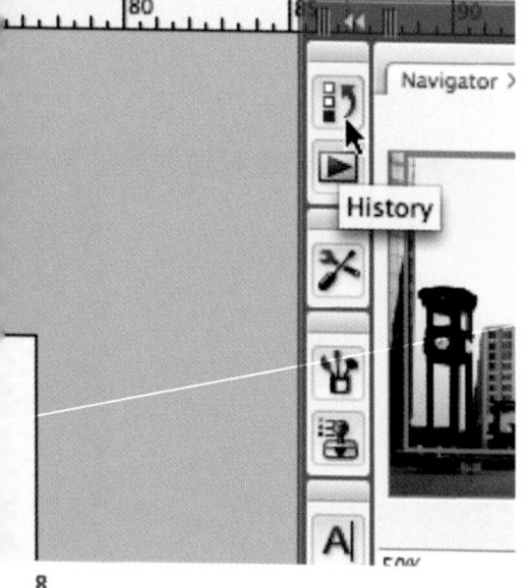

7

8

9

As you can see, a tool is active at the moment (the Rectangular Marquee tool, ill.5) – a good chance to show you how to navigate in your image, independently of the tool selected.

Your most pressing need is usually to see your image enlarged, so you can work more exactly, or conversely reduced again, or complete, in order to take an overall look at it.
The latter works with CTRL-0 (see above); you will see your image as large as your screen and the space between the palettes allows (in Full Screen Mode Photoshop® does not take the palettes into consideration).

Press CTRL-+ or CTRL-- to reduce or enlarge the image.
This also works when you are using a tool such as the Polygonal Lasso. The disadvantage is that you thereby have no control over the visible clipping.

If that is what you want, hold down CTRL-Space; with the magnifying glass you now see instead of the cursor of your active tool, you can draw a rectangle, which then appears enlarged.

An additional press of the Alt key shows you the minus lens, which enables you to reduce, but without the possibility to deciding on a clipping, so it is no better than CTRL--.

When enlarging, parts of the image eventually move outside the window, i.e. you may have to move the clipping to see other image areas.

Simply hold down Space, and the hand icon indicates that you can now move the clipping by clicking and dragging.

In the Tool bar, there are also tools available for these tricks which allow you to view your image enlarged, reduced, or in a certain clipping (ill.6).

Based on the above, you will surely realize that they will never be needed, especially because you would then have to deselect your active tool, with which you are working.

Don´t forget; CTRL-0 puts the image back to maximum size, and should you wish to see it 100%, here is another shortcut: CTRL-Alt-0.

So much for navigation, now to the creation of your workspace.

You have probably already realized that your image window and the palettes around it "stick" to each other; you can,for example, click on the gap between the image and the right-hand palettes and drag to the left, thus enabling the extension of the palettes (the image window then correspondingly reduces, but this only occurs in Maximized Screen Mode, ill.7)

Some palettes are reduced to an icon, e.g. the History palette (ill.8;- what it is will be revealed later).

Click on it and it is displayed normally; a click on the double arrow shrinks it to icon size again. (ill.9)

OK, you already know that you can stick the palettes together as you want, but nonetheless I would urge you to personalize your Photoshop® workspace rather than just accepting the default.

You can take any palette, even those in miniature shape, at its tab (ill.10) or its icon miniature (ill.11), and drag it out of its palette group to somewhere else on your workspace, e.g. when you are fed up with only being able to see a few of your many layers at the same time (from another example: ill.12).

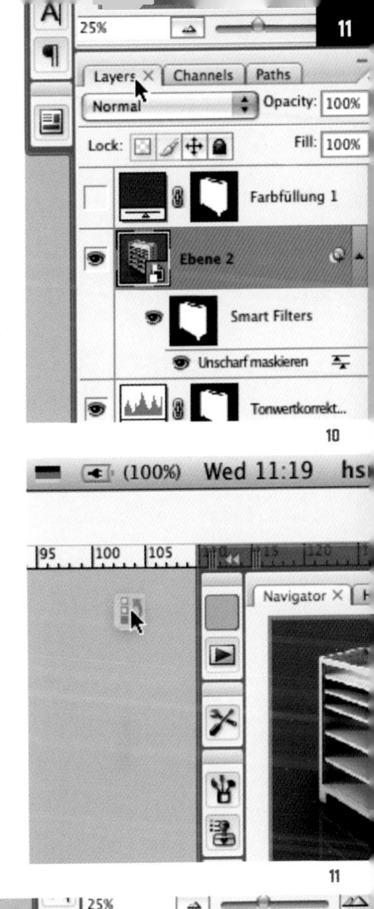

10

11

12

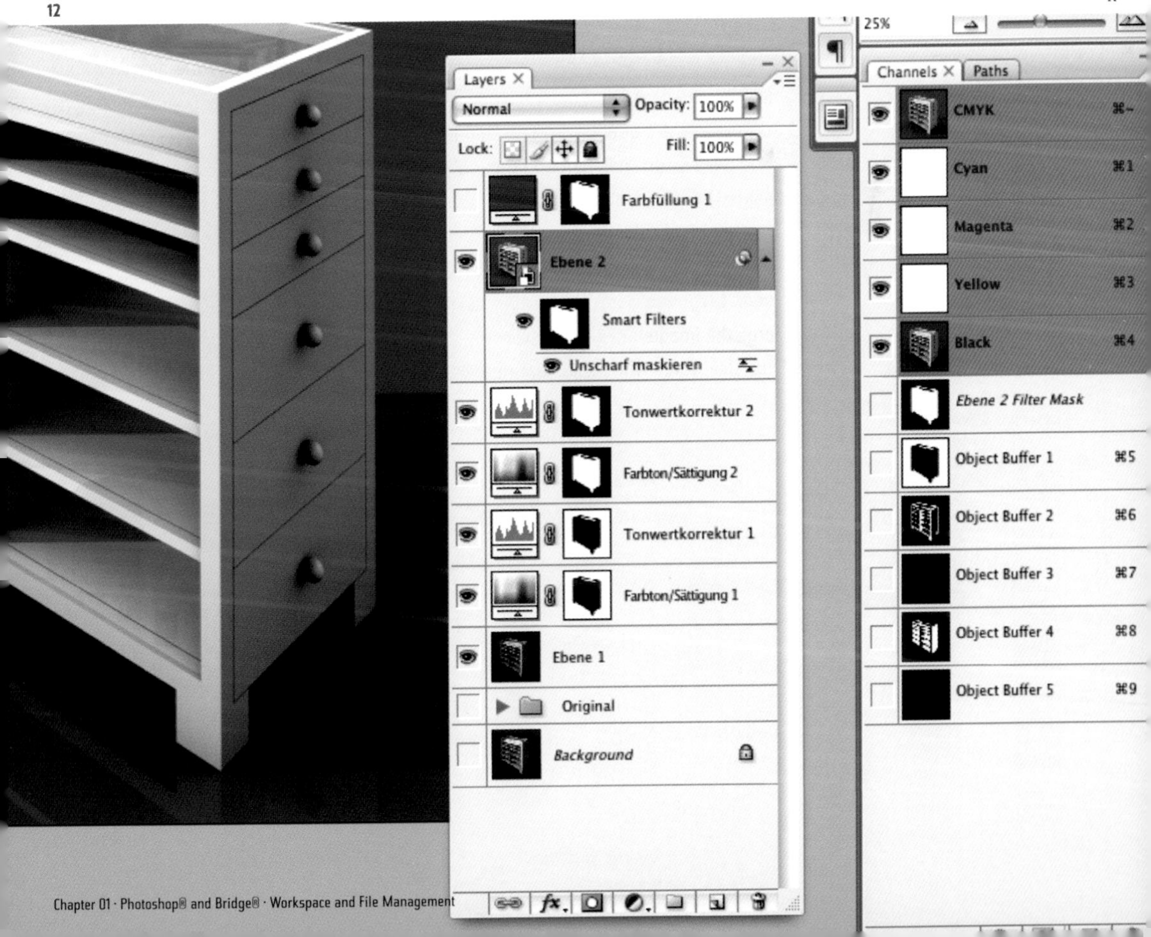

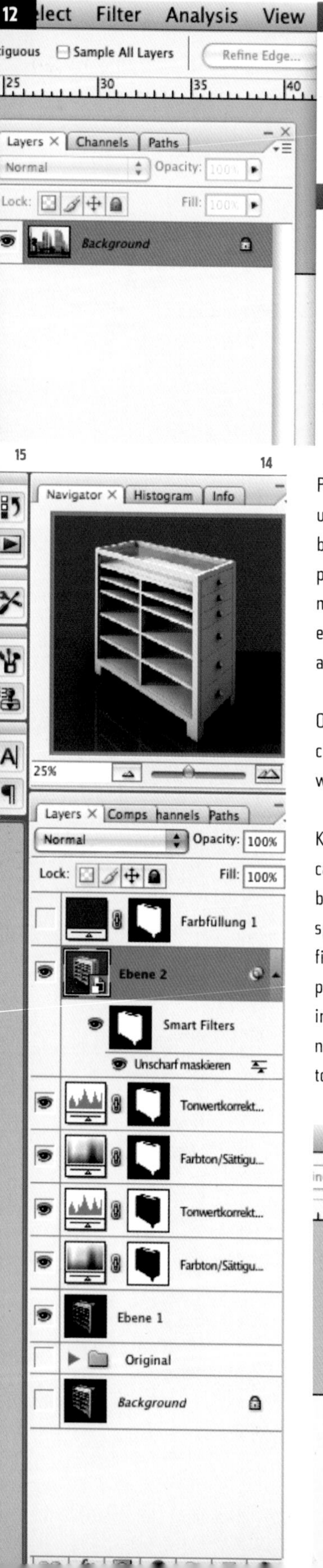

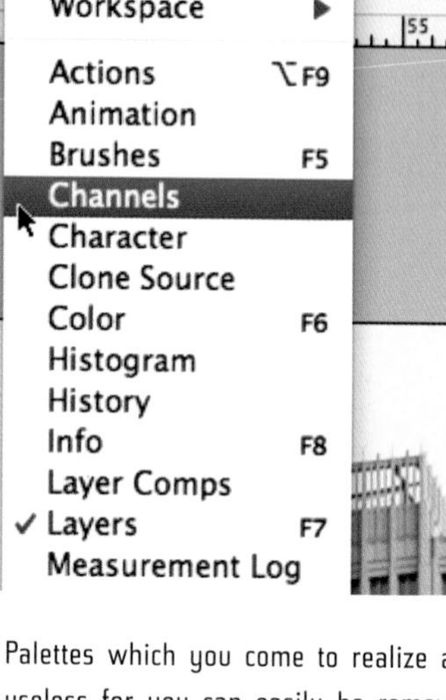

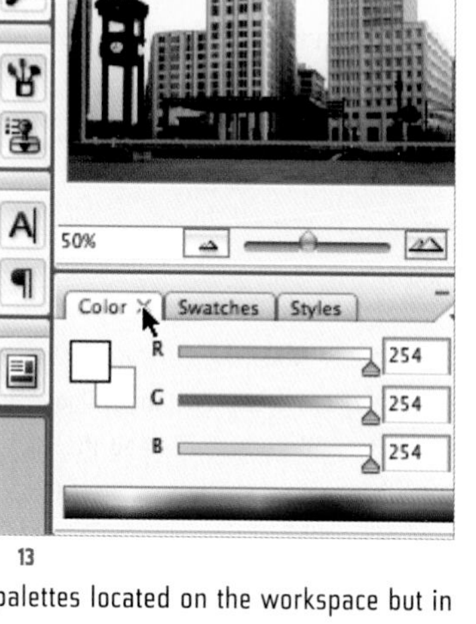

15

14

13

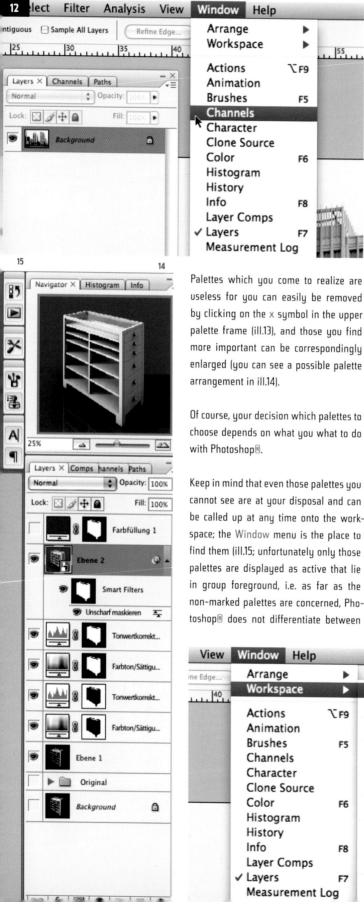

Palettes which you come to realize are useless for you can easily be removed by clicking on the x symbol in the upper palette frame (ill.13), and those you find more important can be correspondingly enlarged (you can see a possible palette arrangement in ill.14).

Of course, your decision which palettes to choose depends on what you what to do with Photoshop®.

Keep in mind that even those palettes you cannot see are at your disposal and can be called up at any time onto the workspace; the Window menu is the place to find them (ill.15; unfortunately only those palettes are displayed as active that lie in group foreground, i.e. as far as the non-marked palettes are concerned, Photoshop® does not differentiate between palettes located on the workspace but in group background, e.g. the Channel palette, and palettes not to be found on the workspace at all).

Be that as it may; when you have decided that your palette arrangement suits your workflow ideally, you can save it as a so called workspace ((Window menu – Workspace – Save Workspace, ill.16; if you activate the Keyboard Shortcuts option the current shortcut set, which you have presumably not altered, is simultaneously saved too in "your" workspace, ill.17)

At this point you may wish to view the other, already configured workspaces, in particular the one which shows you the new features of Photoshop® CS3 Extended in the form of color-marked menu items (Window menu – Workspace

16

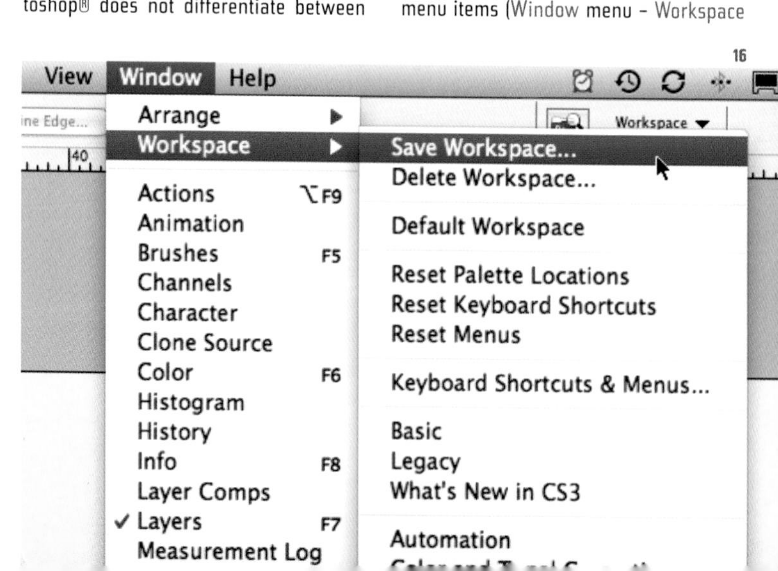

– What's New in CS3, ill.18); Photoshop´s alert message should simply be answered with Yes (ill.19).

Now look at the individual menus, or at their sub-menus (ill.20), and see what is new.

You can have the colored menu items for your workspace too; you may also hide menu items if you never need the corresponding commands (e.g. some of the filters). You will find the corresponding settings right at the bottom of the Edit menu, at Menus command.

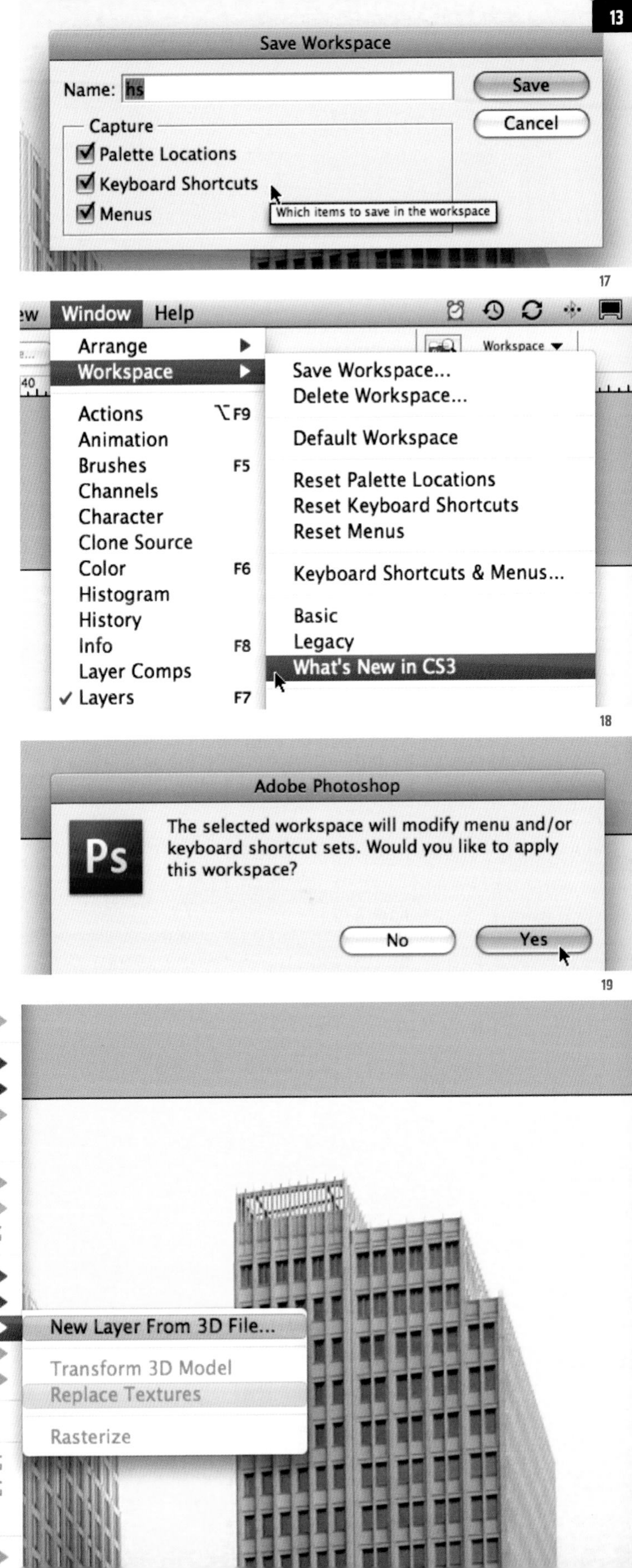

17

18

19

20

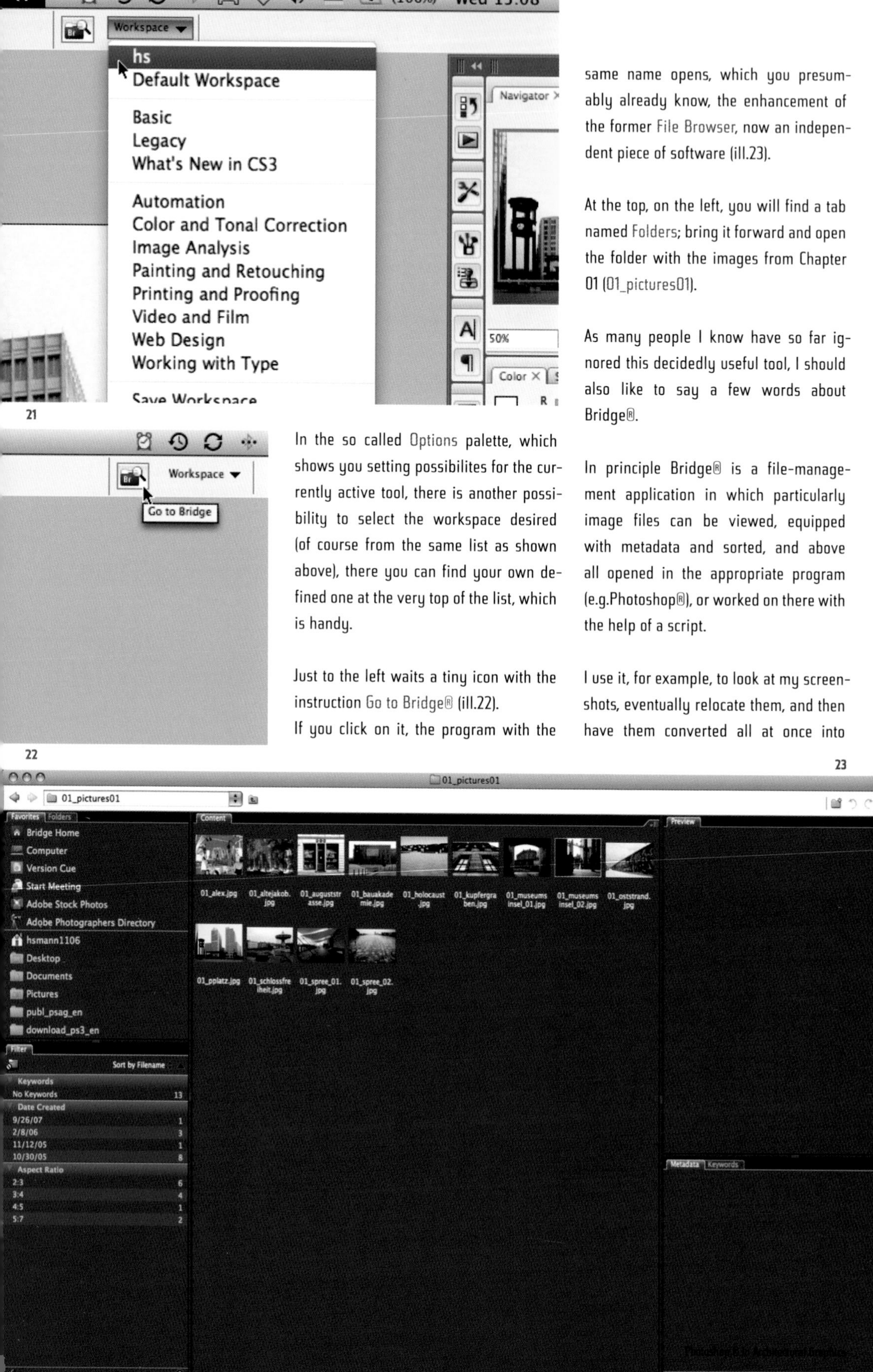

21

22

23

In the so called Options palette, which shows you setting possibilites for the currently active tool, there is another possibility to select the workspace desired (of course from the same list as shown above), there you can find your own defined one at the very top of the list, which is handy.

Just to the left waits a tiny icon with the instruction Go to Bridge® (ill.22).
If you click on it, the program with the same name opens, which you presumably already know, the enhancement of the former File Browser, now an independent piece of software (ill.23).

At the top, on the left, you will find a tab named Folders; bring it forward and open the folder with the images from Chapter 01 (01_pictures01).

As many people I know have so far ignored this decidedly useful tool, I should also like to say a few words about Bridge®.

In principle Bridge® is a file-management application in which particularly image files can be viewed, equipped with metadata and sorted, and above all opened in the appropriate program (e.g.Photoshop®), or worked on there with the help of a script.

I use it, for example, to look at my screenshots, eventually relocate them, and then have them converted all at once into

CMYK in Photoshop®, sharpen them and save them as a copy in a new folder.

Bridge® can, however, not only show „normal" image files, but also PDF files, Illustrator® files und even Quicktime films; you may play them within Bridge® (ill.24), and you can browse through multi-page PDFs. (ill.25).

Bridge® contains a brilliant tool with which you can losslessly correct images, even RAW files from your digital camera (but also JPEGs), and after that open them in Photoshop®, even several simultaneously with the same adjustments.

For this, click on one or more images in your collection and select from the File menu Open in Camera Raw (ill.26), then the corresponding window appears, in which you can correct and work on the image just as you wish (ill.27).

24

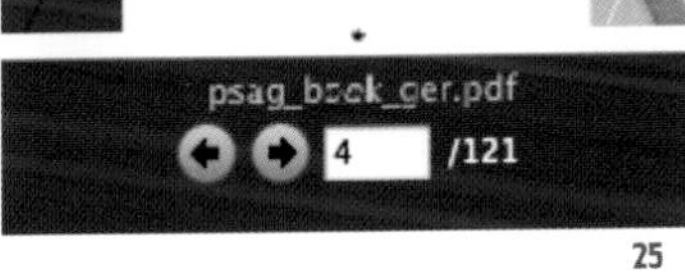

25

26

27

01_pplatz.jpg

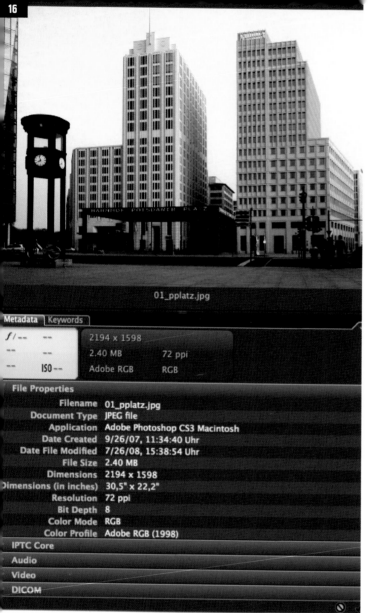

Metadata | Keywords

2194 x 1598
2.40 MB 72 ppi
Adobe RGB RGB

File Properties

Filename	01_pplatz.jpg
Document Type	JPEG file
Application	Adobe Photoshop CS3 Macintosh
Date Created	9/26/07, 11:34:40 Uhr
Date File Modified	7/26/08, 15:38:54 Uhr
File Size	2.40 MB
Dimensions	2194 x 1598
Dimensions (in inches)	30,5" x 22,2"
Resolution	72 ppi
Bit Depth	8
Color Mode	RGB
Color Profile	Adobe RGB (1998)

IPTC Core
Audio
Video
DICOM

29

auakademie.jpg 01_holocaust.jpg 01_kupfergraben.jpg

28

Just play around a bit with the adjustments. When you have concluded this with Done, you will see that a small icon is sticking to the image miniature, indicating that you have worked on the image (ill.28).

Bear in mind that the image has not really been altered; you must imagine the processing more like a layer lying over the image. Thus you can change your adjustments or restore the default settings at any time.

In Bridge® you may move the window frames too and so create your own workspace, which you can save. I will not go into this, however, since it basically works as described for Photoshop®.

Take a look at the palettes on the right in the middle with the names Metadata and File Properties (ill.29): in Metadata you see two numbers which display the size of the image in pixels (in the example:

30

2194 x 1598), the file size, the resolution and the color mode.

Under File Properties you can also see the Name and the File Format, its Creation Date, the Bit Depth (see chapter 03) and the embedded color profile.

What you can do especially well in Bridge® is rename your files; in addition you can transfer them at the same time to some other, suitable place on your hard disk.

Select the files you wish to rename and move (in our example, for the sake of simplicity, all of them ill.30)
.Then select the command Batch Rename from the Tools menu (ill.31), and take a cool look at the dialog that opens up (ill.32).

First of all you can decide if you want to rename the images in the folder available, or play safe and save them as a copy somewhere else. (e.g. if you are dealing with images from your camera chip).
In the middle of the dialog you can create the new name of the files; in my example it is a piece of text (berlin), followed by a two-digit number beginning with 1 (a little tip; before you rename everything you can rearrange the images in the Bridge® window with your mouse if you dislike the sequence).

Should more name components occur to you, click on one of the plus-signs on the right. For your security you will see a preview of your new file name displayed below.

Label Tools Window Help
Batch Rename... ⇧⌘R
Device Central...
Create Metadata Template...
Edit Metadata Template
Append Metadata
Replace Metadata
Cache
Photoshop
Illustrator
InDesign
Start Meeting...
Photoshop Services
01_pictures01
01_holocaust.jpg
01_kupfergraben.jpg
01_spree_02.jpg

31

32

Batch Rename
Destination Folder
Rename in same folder
Move to other folder
Copy to other folder
Browse... /Users/hsmann1106/Desktop/psd_temp
New Filenames
Text berlin_
Sequence Number 1 Two Digits
Options
Preserve current filename in XMP Metadata
Compatibility: Windows Mac OS Unix
Preview
Current filename: 01_alex.jpg
New filename: berlin_01.jpg
13 files will be renamed
Rename
Cancel

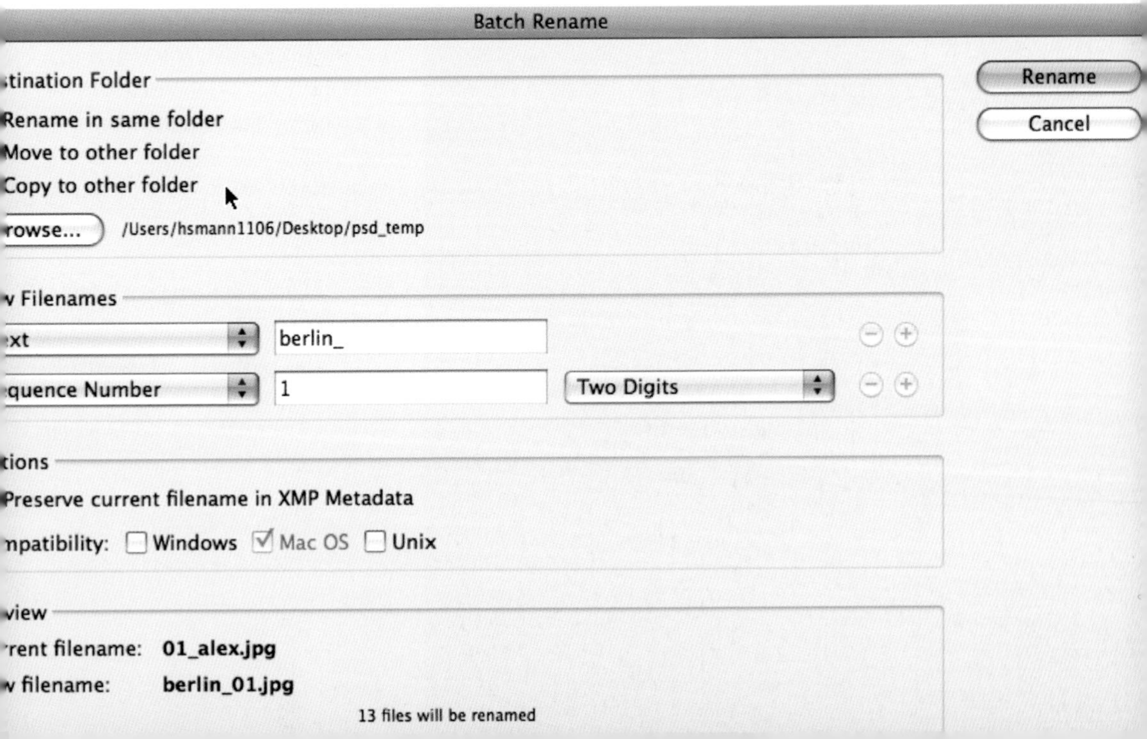

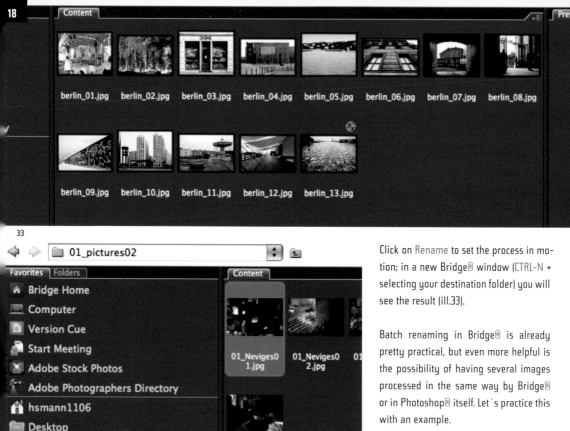

33

34

35

Click on Rename to set the process in motion; in a new Bridge® window (CTRL-N + selecting your destination folder) you will see the result (ill.33).

Batch renaming in Bridge® is already pretty practical, but even more helpful is the possibility of having several images processed in the same way by Bridge® or in Photoshop® itself. Let´s practice this with an example.

In Bridge®, open the folder 01_images02 (ill.34). If you click on one of the images you will see, bottom-right, that we have an image with the pixel size 2400 x 1600 (ill.35).

We will now convert all these images into Black & White, reduce their image size and save them in compressed format. We will apply the necessary adjustments on one image, record the process, and leave Photoshop® to edit the rest of the images automatically.

Open the first of the images by double-clicking on its miniature in Bridge®. In Photoshop®, open the Actions palette (ill.36); in the palette you will see a list of action sets, normally only one with the name Default Actions.

First of all define a new set, by clicking on the corresponding button in the lower frame of the

Actions palette (Create new set, ill.37). Give it the name animation (ill.38) und confirm with OK.

Your new set is activated in the Actions palette; now start a new action by clicking on the button Create new action at the bottom frame of the Action palette (ill.39). give this a name too (W_1024), because we will, among other things, reduce the image width to 1024 pixels (ill.40).

As soon as you have pressed the Record button, Photoshop® awaits your action. You can see from the red dot in the lower frame of the Actions palette that record-

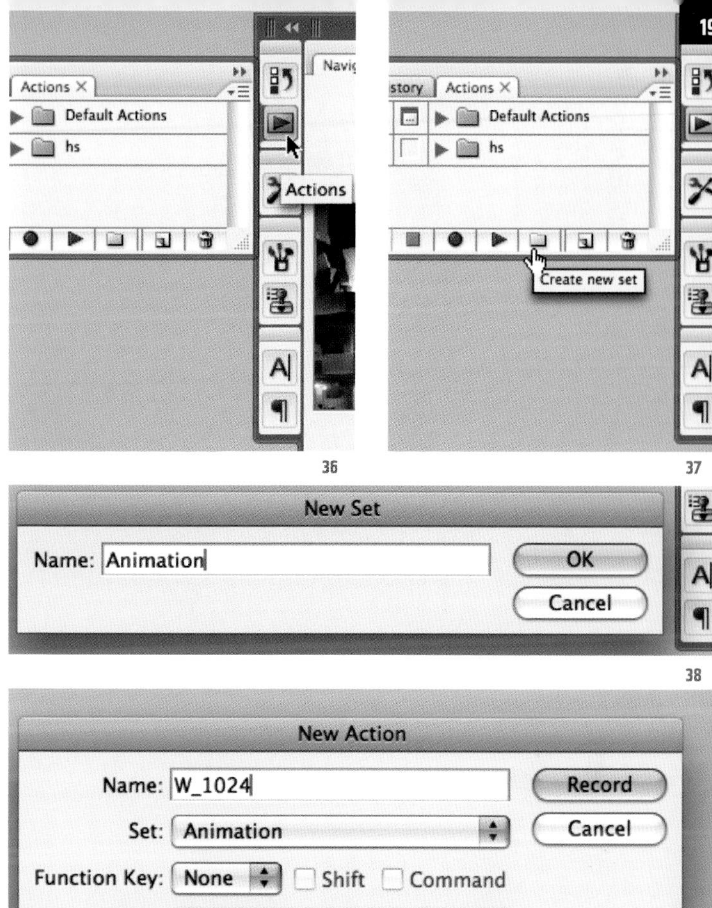

36

37

38

40

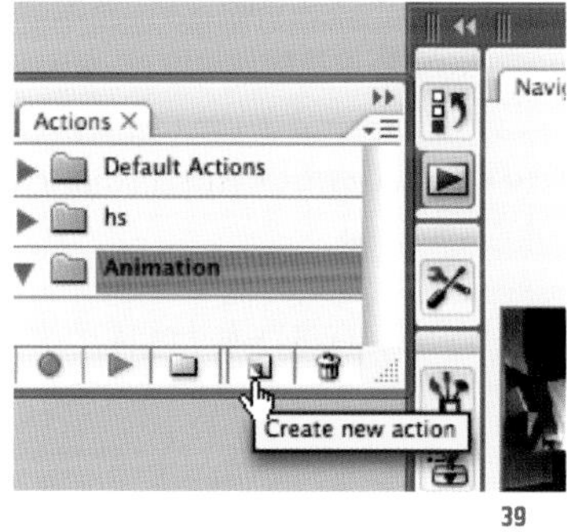

39

ing is taking place (ill.41). But don´t worry. Photoshop® only records your adjustments; how much time you need for them is irrelevant.

In the first step, convert the image into Black & White, with the help of an adjustment layer which you can select from the corresponding menu at the bottom frame of the Layers palette (ill.42).

This function allows you to convert a color image losslessly into Black & White.

42

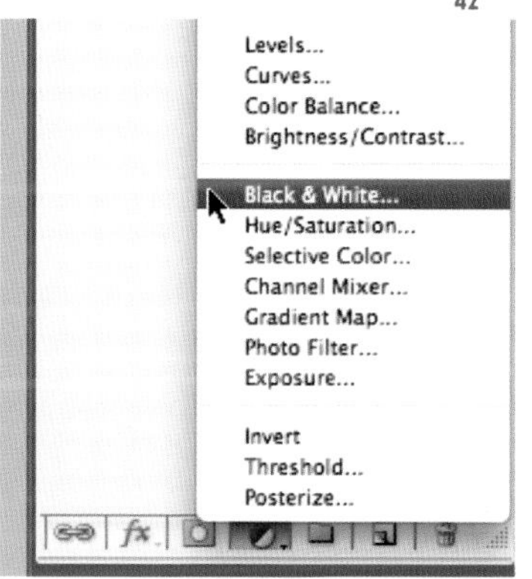

41

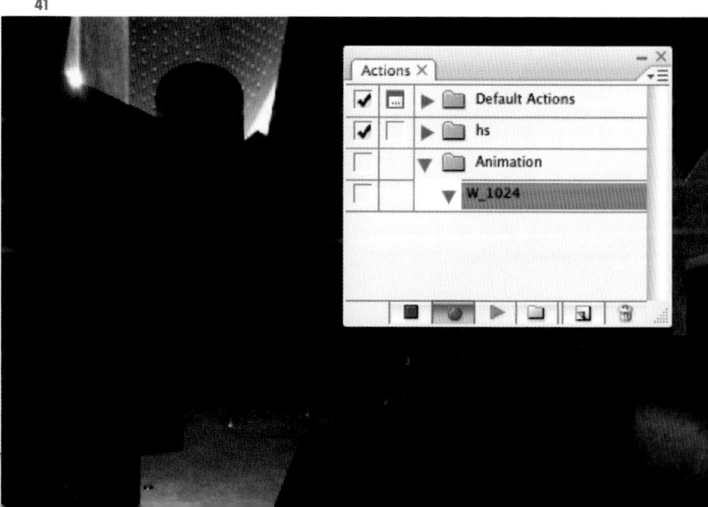

43

Black & White 1
Solid Color...
Gradient...
Pattern...
Levels...
Curves...
Color Balance...
Brightness/Contrast...
Black & White...
Hue/Saturation...
Selective Color...
Channel Mixer...
Gradient Map...
Photo Filter...
Exposure...
Invert
Threshold...
Posterize...

44

In the adjustment dialog of the Black & White layer, select the Preset Yellow filter. As the original is rather yellow, tending towards red, it remains relatively bright during the transformation via Yellow filter (ill.43).

But while you´re here, try out the other presets, or play around with the controls. If you´re satisfied, confirm with OK.

As a second thing, you´ll perform an Auto Levels adjustment.
Although this has no significant effect on this specific image, it may show positive results for the other images, on which the same correction will later be exerted via automatic processing.

So, select the adjustment layer Levels from the corresponding menu of the Layers palette (ill.44); in the adjustment dialog just press the button Auto and confirm with OK (ill.45).

To be able to use a filter next, copy all your layers onto a new one.
Make sure all the layers are turned visible and that the uppermost is activated, and press Shift-Alt-CTRL-E (ill.46).

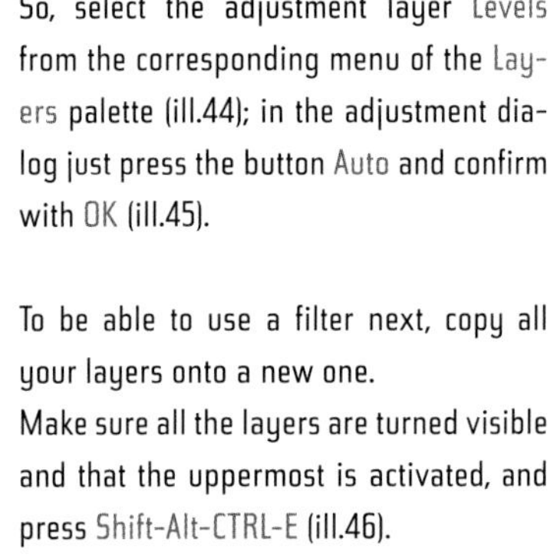

45

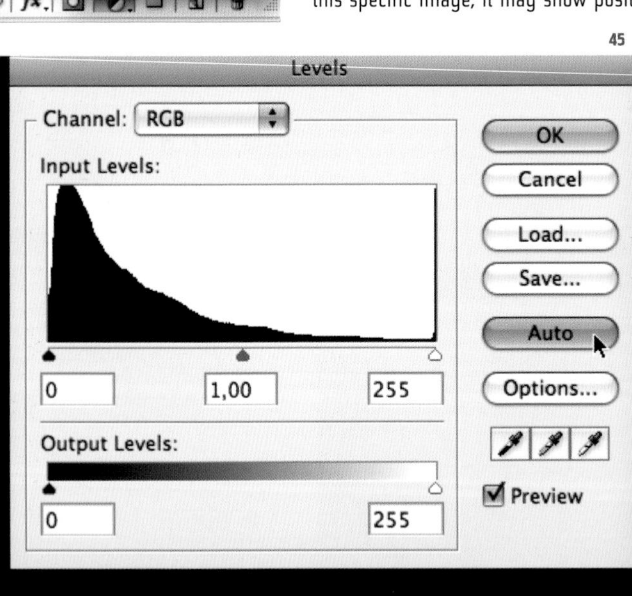

46

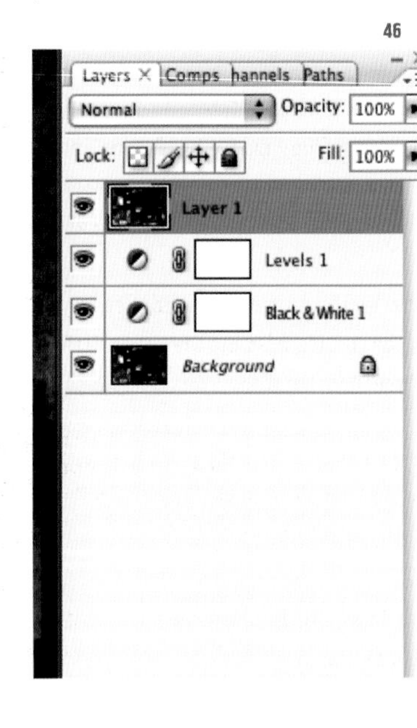

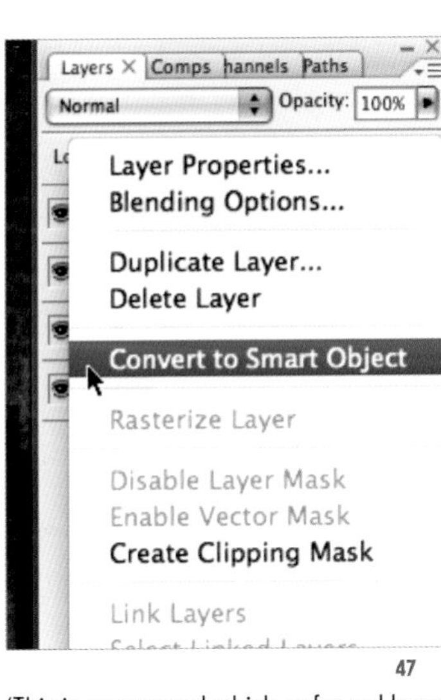

47

(This is a command which as far as I know doesn´t appear in any menu, and which combines all the visible layers in a new one; in this respect it´s an extension of the command Merge Visible, Shift-CTRL-E.)

You´ll now use a sharpening filter on this new layer.

This is possible without losses, if you convert the layer beforehand into a so called Smart Object (by a right-click on the layer entry and by selecting the corresponding option from the context menu, which then opens (ill.47).

.

Pick the Sharpen filter Unsharp Mask (from the Filter menu, ill.48), and in the adjustment dialog, set the Amount to 100% and the Radius to 2 pixels (ill.49).

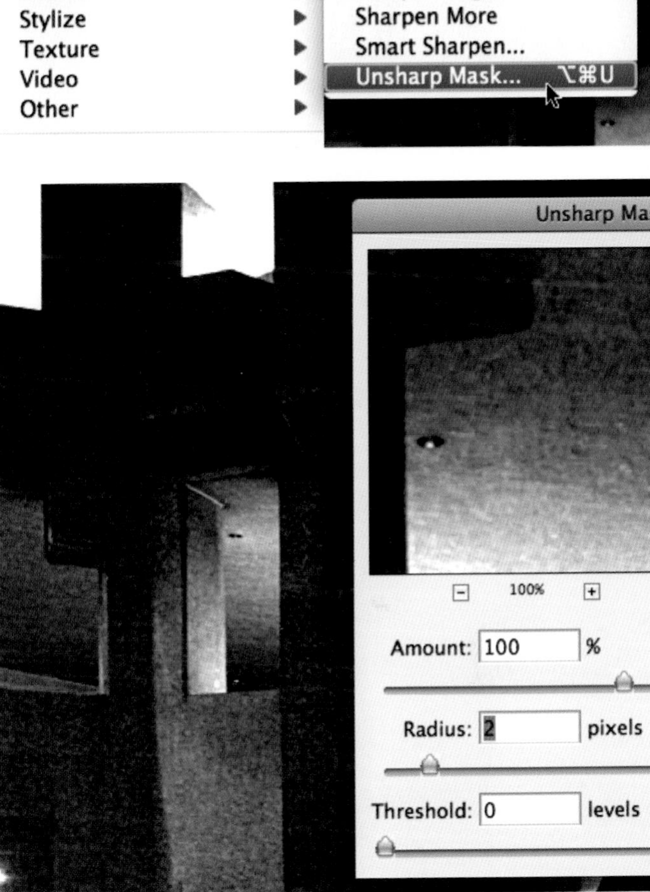

48

49

Now you´re almost finished. Reduce the image size by selecting the corresponding command from the Image menu (ill.50).

In the adjustment dialog, enter value 1024 for Width (be careful the units on the right are pixels! ill.51).

The Constrain Proportions option should also be checked.

50

51

53

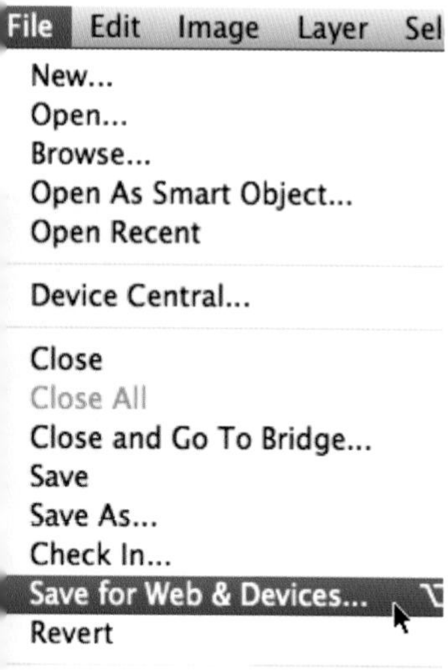

52

54

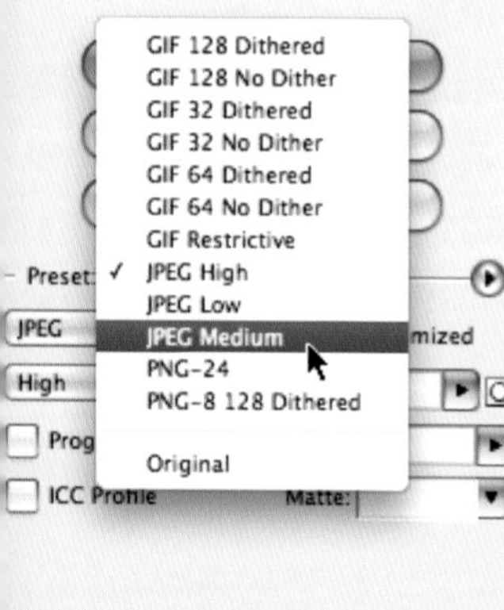

Finally, you should save the file in a format that demands as little disk space as possible. This is best done with the command Save for Web & Devices from the File menu (ill.52).

The window which then opens should show your image twice; if not, click at the top on the tab 2-up (ill.53).

On the left you can see your original image; on the right the version which is created in the file format selected on the right. Here, eventual quality losses can be observed.
On the right side, JPEG high is the default preset. Here, select from the menu the preset JPEG Medium (ill.54).

I don´t want to go into detail at this stage about how the quality selected (which further to the right can be set steplessly) affects the image and its size.
Just check yourself; the resulting file size will be displayed below the right-hand image in accordance with the settings you've chosen.

At this point, let´s stay with the JPEG Medium preset.
Click top right on Save, and you can enter the file name und destination.
I advise you to create your own folder at this stage, so that the saved copy doesn´t conflict with your original (ill.55; my folder is named Frames).

With that, saving with the adjustments you´ve performed is finished.
You should now close your original, without saving the changes. The edited copy has been, after all, saved in the new folder.

The time has now come to finish recording. To do this, click on the left button at the bottom frame of the Actions palette (Il.56).

So, now you´ll want to reap the benefits of your preparatory work. In Bridge®, select all the images apart from the one you´ve already worked on (ill.57).

Also in Bridge®, select the command

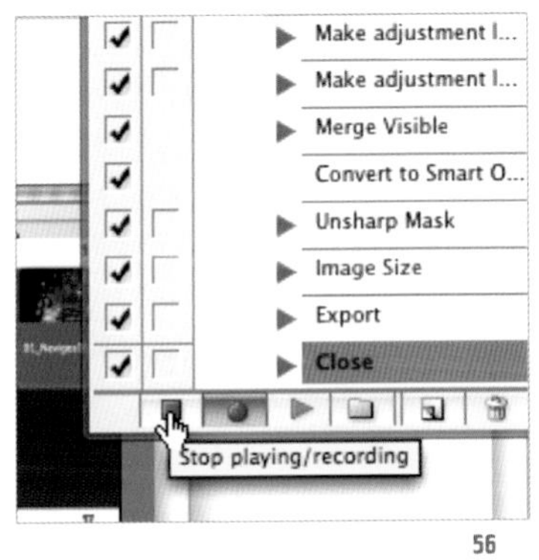

56

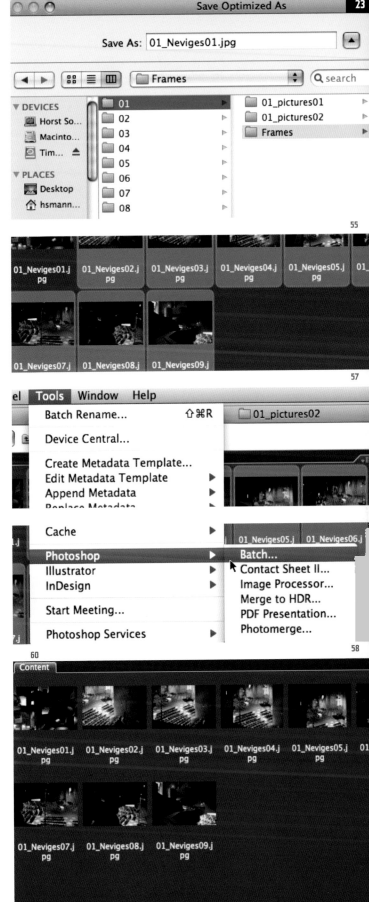

55

57

58

Batch from the Photoshop submenu of the Tool menu (ill.58).

In the adjustment dialog, you´ll see that Bridge® kindly displays your latest recorded script from your newly defined set (ill.59); Bridge should be selected as Source (meaning the images selected in the Bridge® window).

You don´t need to give a Destination, as it´s already set in the recording (your new folder).

Confirm with OK, and Photoshop® opens your images in sequence, processes them in accordance with your scripted specifications and saves them in the new folder, where you can admire them after batch-processing has finished (ill.60).

With that, this introduction is complete; in what follows, the emphasis will be on solving concrete tasks.

59

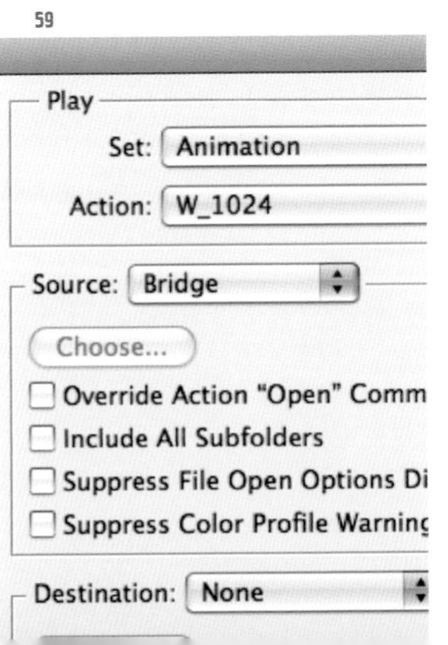

60

Paint and Drawing Tools · Selections, Channels, Masks

Now, to get you into work, I´d like to acquaint you with Photoshop®´s most important tools; first of all let's have a look at the paint and drawing tools.
Most of all you will need the Brush, more often than you might think, especially for working on selection and layer masks.

To get to know the most important tools of your tool palette, first create a new, empty Photoshop® file: File menu – New (CTRL-N, ill.2).

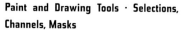

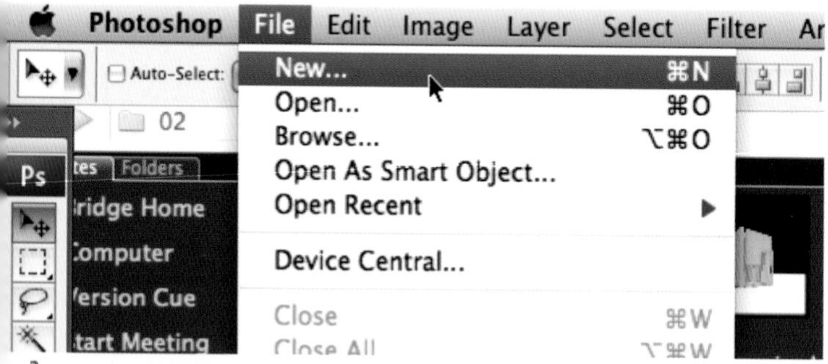

2

3

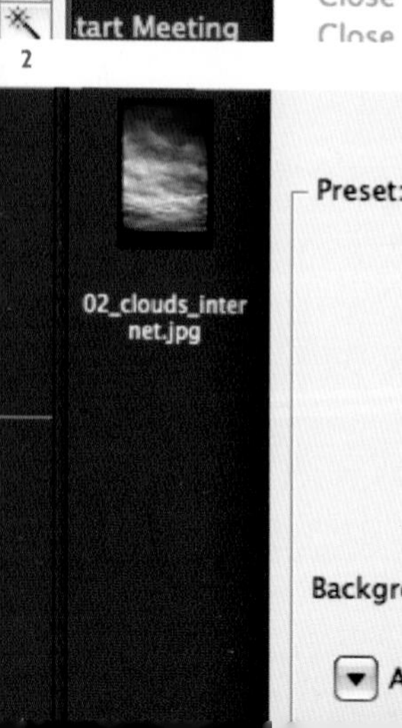

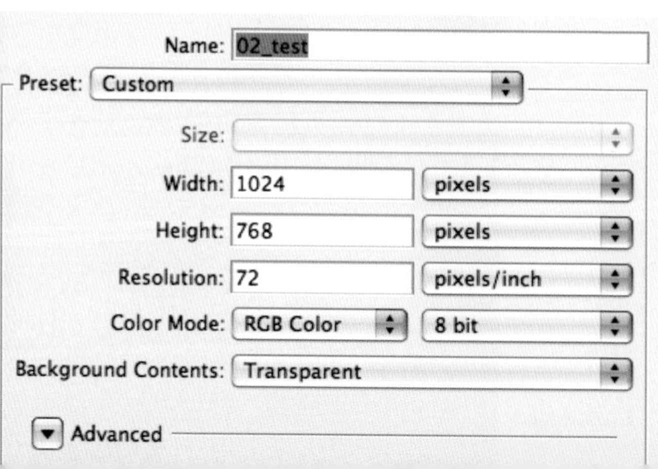

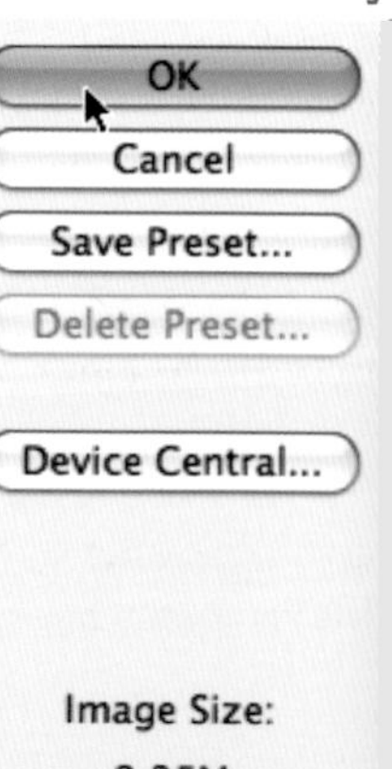

In the adjustment dialog which then opens (ill.3), you are allowed to set up the image's size and quality.

Enter the most important thing, Width and Height, in pixels (1024 x 768; if other units are displayed for Width and Height, select pixels from the pulldown menus located on the right).

The Resolution should be 72 pixels/inch, the Color Mode RGB, the Depth 8 Bit, and Background Contents should be Transparent.

Just set up these things as I´ve suggested; I´ll explain in the next chapters what the individual adjustments mean. For now, let´s get familiar with the tools.

In the Layers palette bottom right (ill.4) you´ll see that your document consists of one empty layer; the chessboard pattern is the background of Photoshop®. The fact that you can see it means that there are no image pixels so far.

Take a look at the bottom end of your Tool bar.
There you´ll see two small squares, one above the other, which depict the foreground (top left) and background colors (bottom right, ill.5). We´ll see later what this is about.

First of all change them to Black and White, if they aren´t already, by pressing D on your keyboard (alternatively, click on the small Black & White symbol); the foreground color should be Black, press X if it isn´t (you may also change the foreground and background colors by clicking on the small, crooked double-arrow).

Now press Alt-Backspace, and you´ll see your image, empty so far, filled with the foreground color Black.

Press CTRL-Z to redo this, then CTRL-Backspace to fill it with the background color White.

Redo this second action again, and press Shift-Backspace – a dialog opens in which you can decide the fill-color yourself, e.g. here you can select Black or White, if your foreground and background colors happen not to be, or also Gray.

There are also patterns available to fill your image; just select the corresponding entry from the pulldown list (ill.6); you can now click on the small arrow beside Custom Pattern, to get to a selection of patterns.(ill.7).

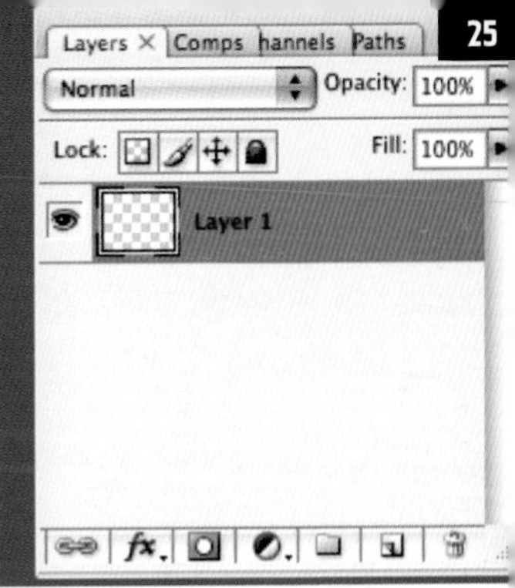

4

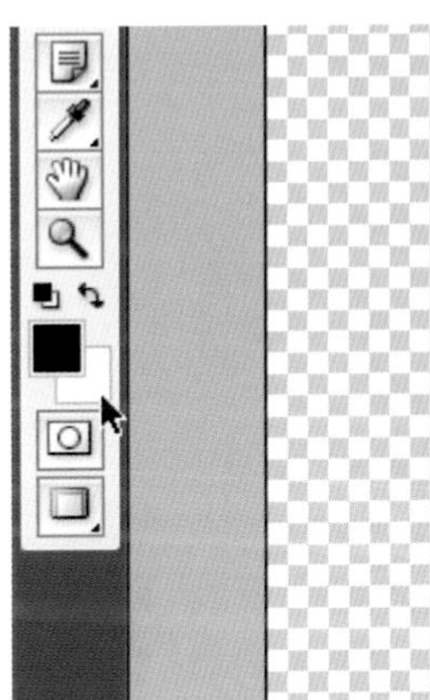

5

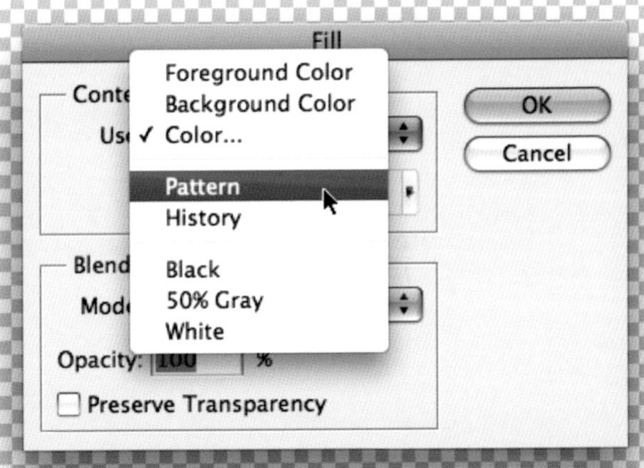

6

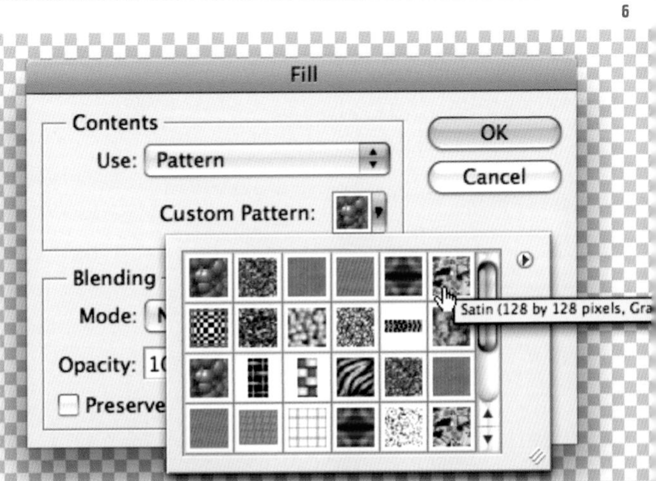

7

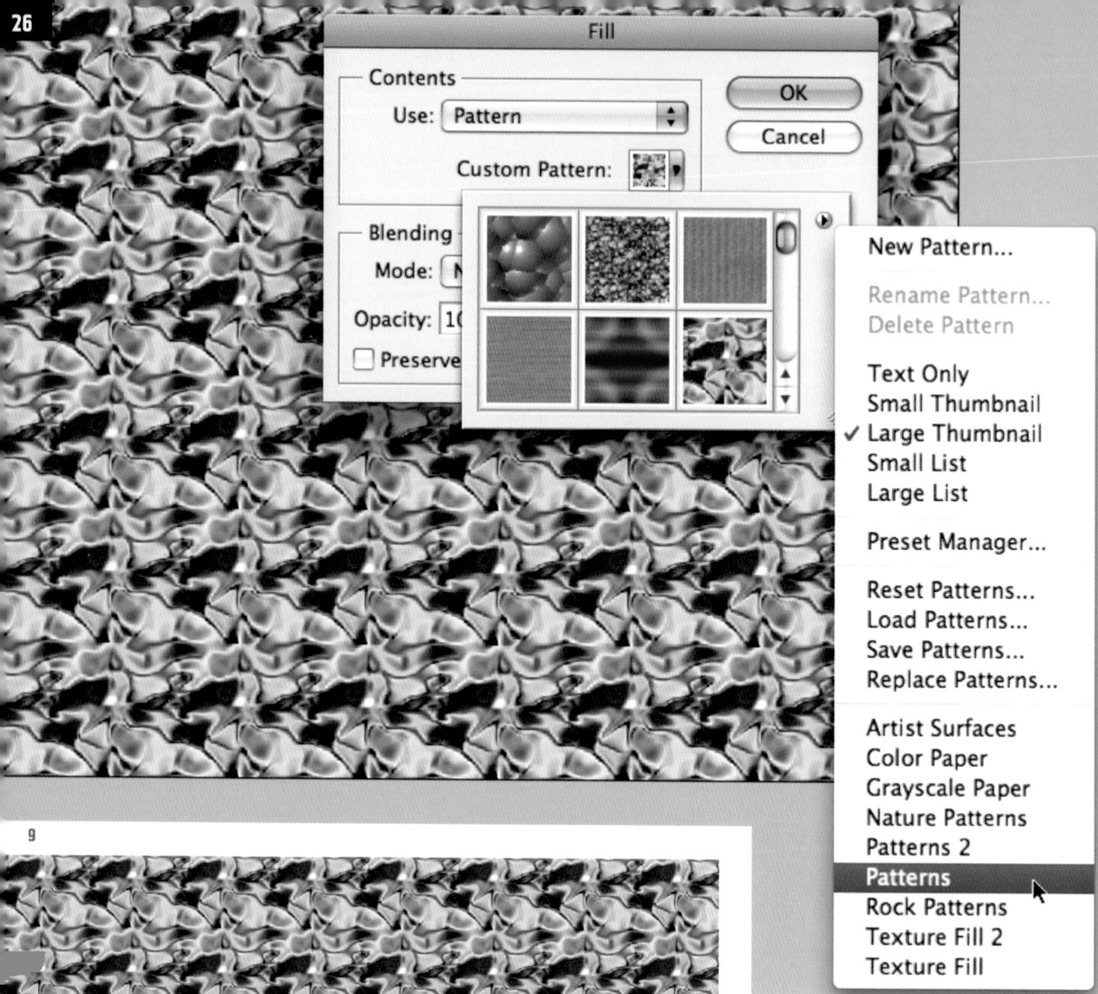

9

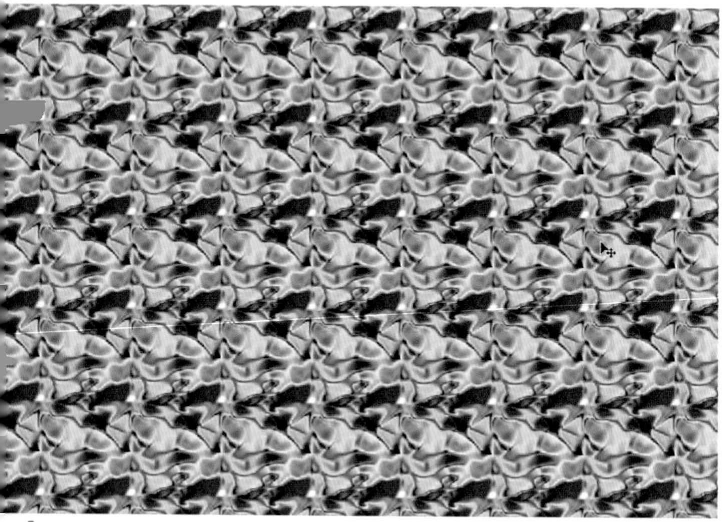

8

10

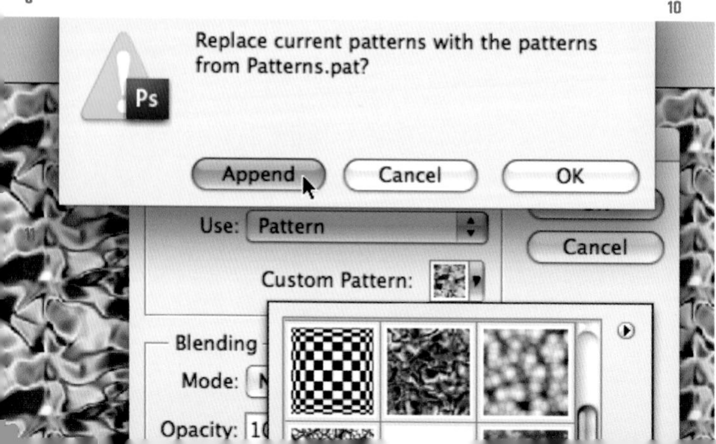

Choose one, confirm with OK, and your image will be filled with the pattern – the basic module is clearly much smaller than your image, and is therefore tiled (a technical term for image repetition as in the example shown, ill.8).

Maybe you think you´ll never need these patterns, but there are some that appear more suitable for use in architectural graphics than the few you can see.

Open the Pattern menu again and click on the little arrow on the right, from the pull-down menu which then appears, select one of the other pattern libraries listed below (in my example Patterns, ill.9).

Instead of your present patterns being replaced by the new collection, you will rather Append them (ill.10). Now the new ones appear in subsequence to your default patterns.

Now for example select Fractures (ill.11), and confirm with OK. The result looks far less tiled, and you can imagine how the image can be used for surface textures together with a few filters and color overlays (ill.12).

So much for the possibilities of filling an empty layer fast with color, or with a pattern.

Make a note of the shortcuts (see above.); OK, there is of course a menu command which corresponds to Shift-Backspace (Edit menu: Fill, ill.13), but if you want to work quickly, it´s simply faster with the key shortcuts

Press Alt-Backspace, to replace your pattern by Black.

Now you´ll get to know the paint tool, which you use most often if you want to change your selections "by hand", or your masks (we´ll come to that, don´t worry).

You can use the Brush tool to apply foreground color, or replace it by the background color, simply by toggling the two preset colors via the X key.

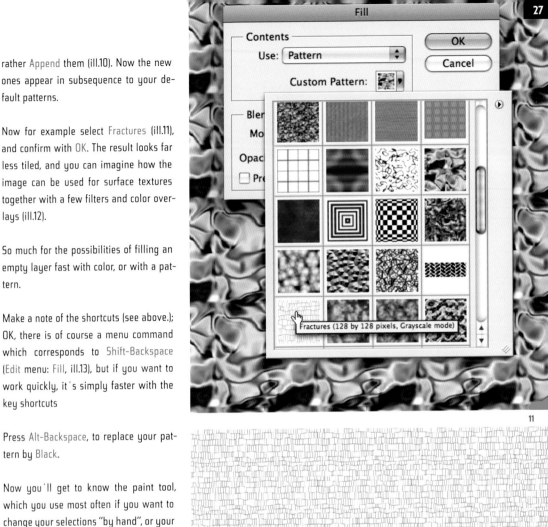

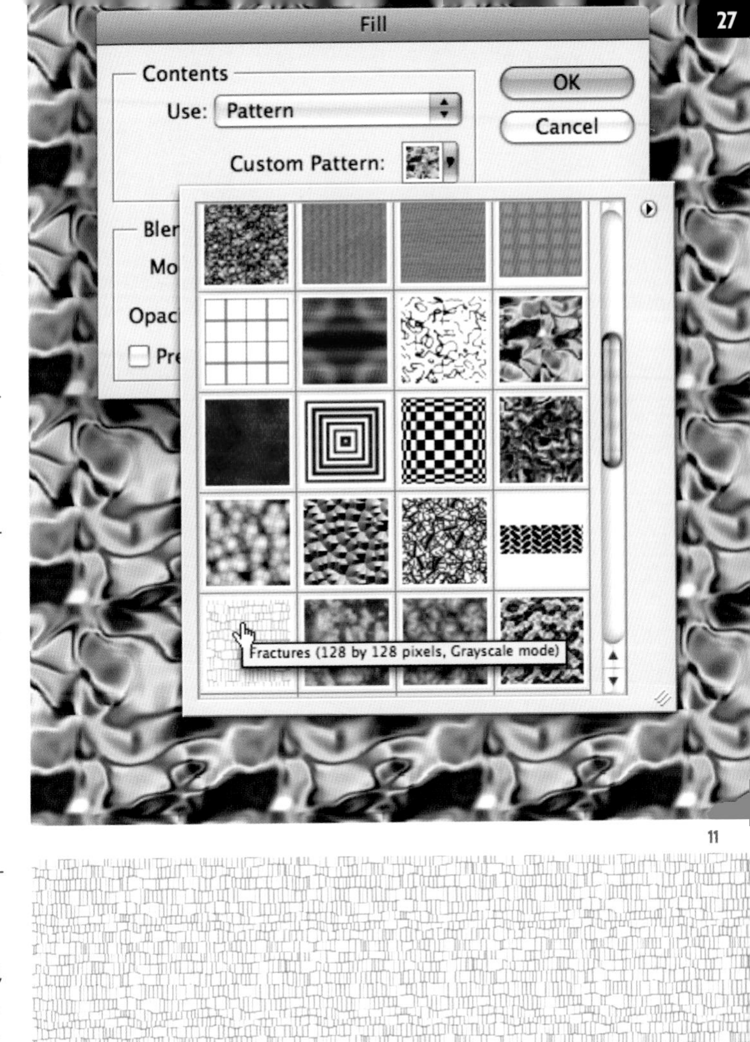

11

12

13

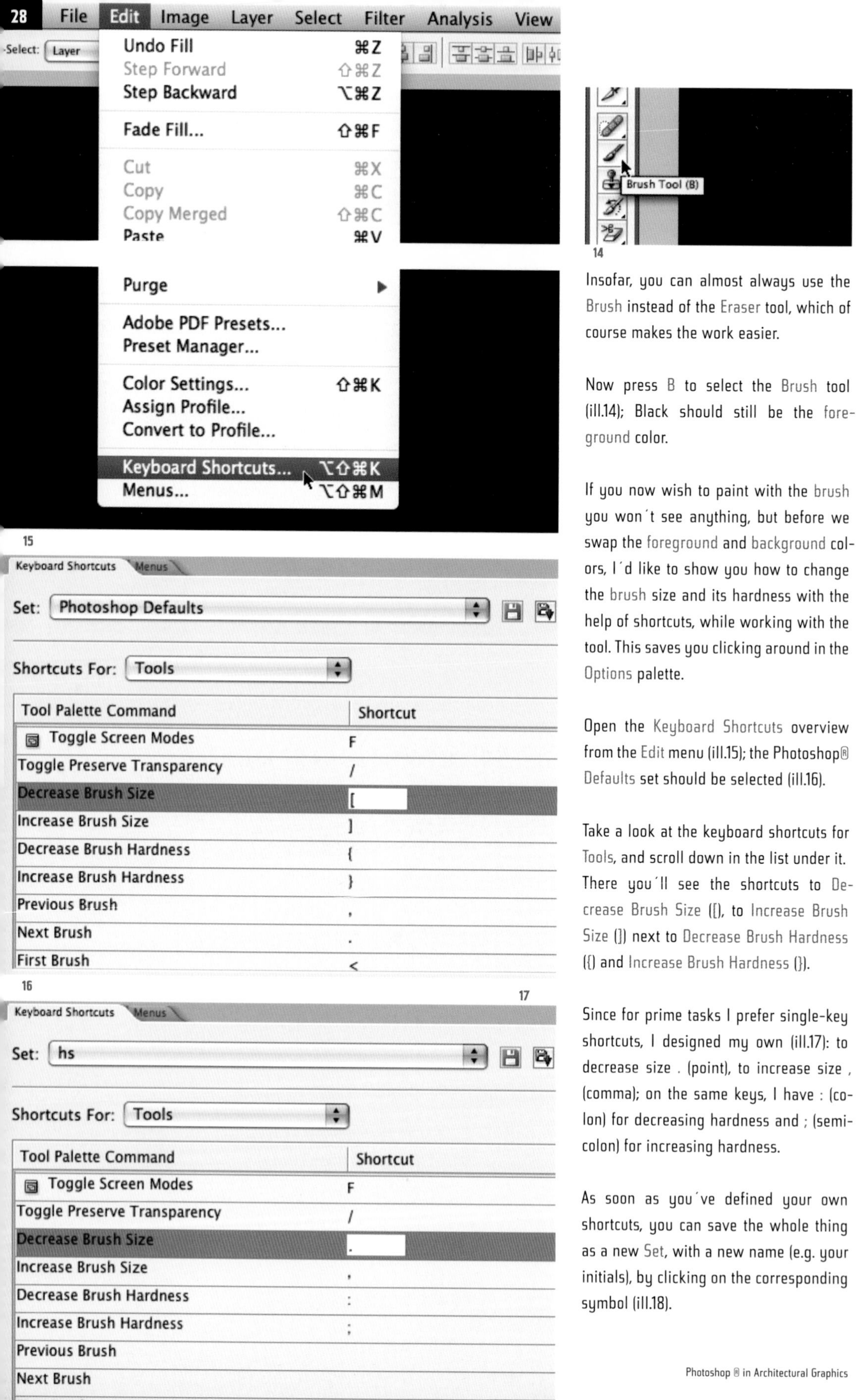

14

15

16

17

Insofar, you can almost always use the Brush instead of the Eraser tool, which of course makes the work easier.

Now press B to select the Brush tool (ill.14); Black should still be the foreground color.

If you now wish to paint with the brush you won´t see anything, but before we swap the foreground and background colors, I´d like to show you how to change the brush size and its hardness with the help of shortcuts, while working with the tool. This saves you clicking around in the Options palette.

Open the Keyboard Shortcuts overview from the Edit menu (ill.15); the Photoshop® Defaults set should be selected (ill.16).

Take a look at the keyboard shortcuts for Tools, and scroll down in the list under it. There you´ll see the shortcuts to Decrease Brush Size ([), to Increase Brush Size (]) next to Decrease Brush Hardness ({) and Increase Brush Hardness (}).

Since for prime tasks I prefer single-key shortcuts, I designed my own (ill.17): to decrease size . (point), to increase size , (comma); on the same keys, I have : (colon) for decreasing hardness and ; (semicolon) for increasing hardness.

As soon as you´ve defined your own shortcuts, you can save the whole thing as a new Set, with a new name (e.g. your initials), by clicking on the corresponding symbol (ill.18).

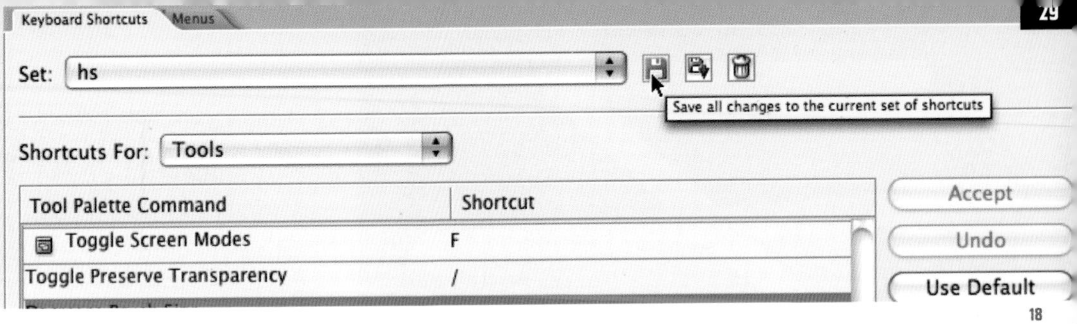

18

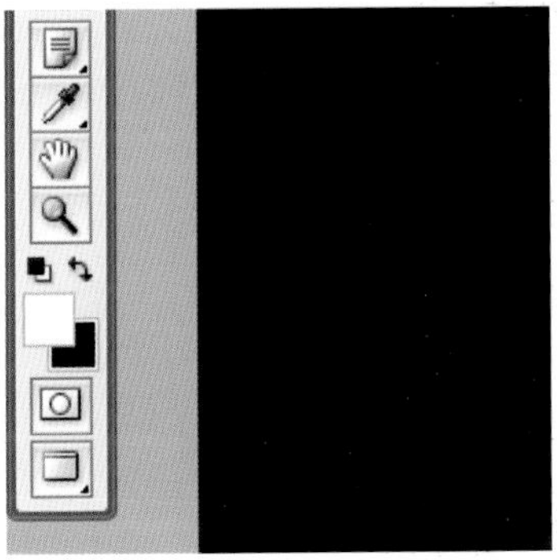

19

Now just paint along a little on your black canvas, using your four keys to vary the stroke – but first of all swap the foreground and background colors by means of the X key, so that you can paint with White (ill.19).

20

21

You´ll see a few results in ill.20 (notice that even very large brush sizes are possible). Swap the colors with X and paint with Black for a change (ill.21).

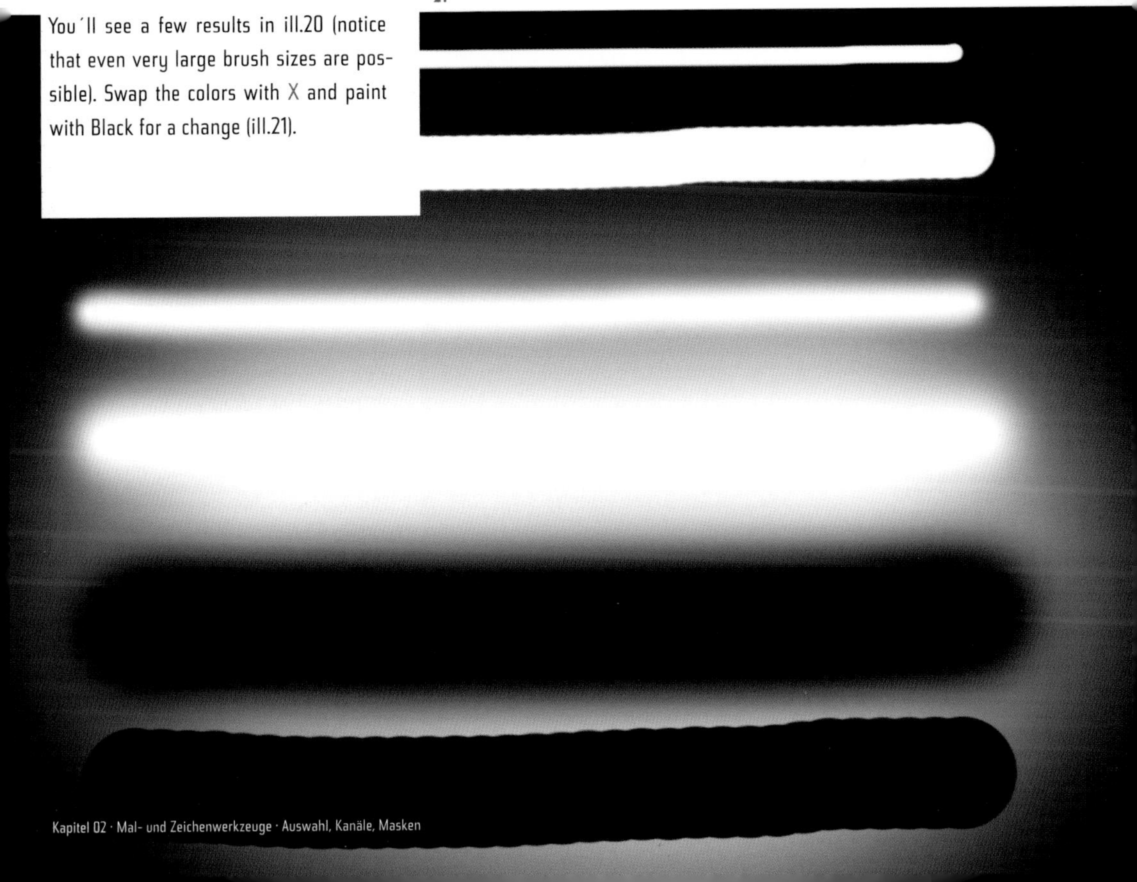

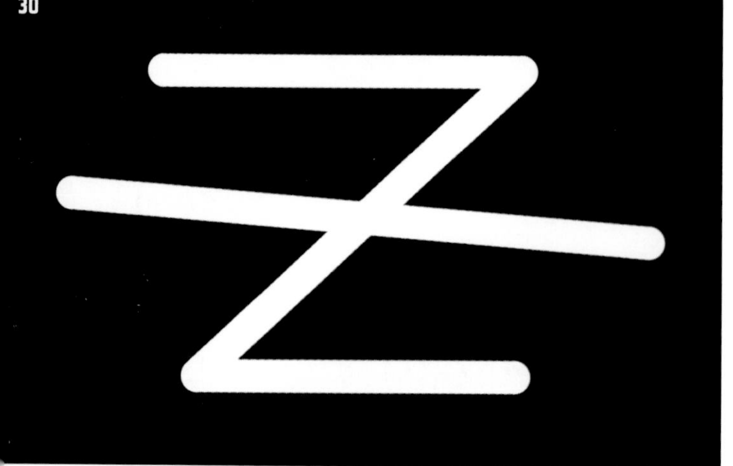

22

As soon as you click anywhere without pressing the Shift key, a new line begins.

The whole thing works at any angle you want, not only at specific ones, as we know from Shift-lock in CAAD applications (ill.22).

Fill again with Black, to try out something different (for this, CTRL-Backspace should work, because Black should actually

You really should know another trick, especially if you´re involved with architectural graphics: with this quaint, seemingly so inaccurate tool, you can also produce absolutely straight lines – to do this, don´t drag the mouse but place a line's start and end points via mouse-clicks, holding down the Shift key during the second one.

First fill your image area with Black again (if it´s still the foreground color, by Alt-Backspace), and get going; one click for the first blot, then a second with the Shift key held down, and Photoshop® connects the two with a straight interpolation between them.
With a third Shift-click, you can produce another line connecting to it's predecessor, and so on.

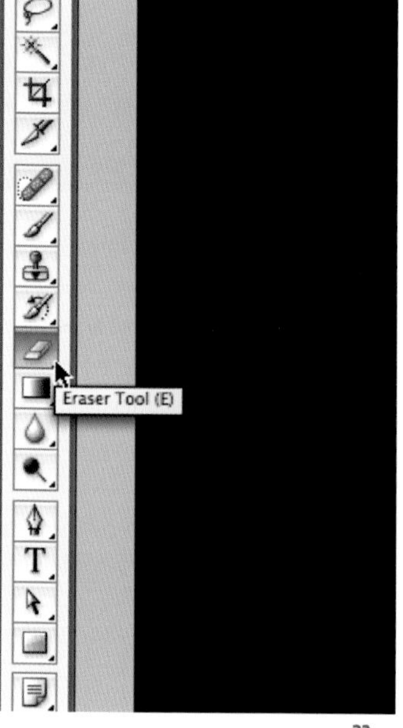

23

be the background color). Then pick the Eraser tool (ill.23).
Note that for the eraser, Brush Mode is selected (above in the Options palette).

Now paint with it, also using your shortcuts for thinner, thicker, harder and softer (ill.24) – as you´ll see, this tool removes the color completely, and Photoshop´s background becomes visible.
Even the eraser can be used in straight lines, as we´ve already seen with the brush, and in just as gigantic dimensions.

Now fill the canvas with Black again, and paint a few straight bars with the Brush

24

tool (if you hold the Shift key down when dragging the mouse, the lines are painted exactly horizontally, ill.25).

Now try out how to clone image parts with the Clone Stamp tool; select it (S for Stamp, or Shift-S if one of the other retouch tools is at the front, ill.26).

Increase the tool size, using the corresponding keyboard shortcut, so that the circle is larger than the width of your line group (ill.27).

Make sure that the circle is over a complete part of the line group (the one you want to clone, preferably centered), and click once with the Alt key held down. With this, you have copied the image contents within the circle, and can now paste it to the right, to lengthen the lines.

Here the first click is especially important, so that your lines are not crooked. When you managed to hit the correct position, drag the mouse to the right with the Shift key held down, and your lines will grow longer acordingly (ill.28).

Please don´t despair; the Clone Stamp tool doesn´t make accurate work all that easy, but with a little practice it should work.

A further tool you really should know about is the Pen, with which you can draw vector shapes that can be transformed into normal pixel selections. Most important, the Pen tool allows you to select image areas with curved edges easily.

25

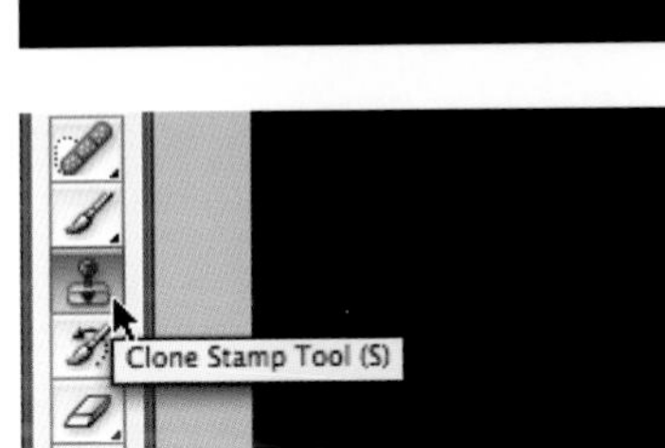

26

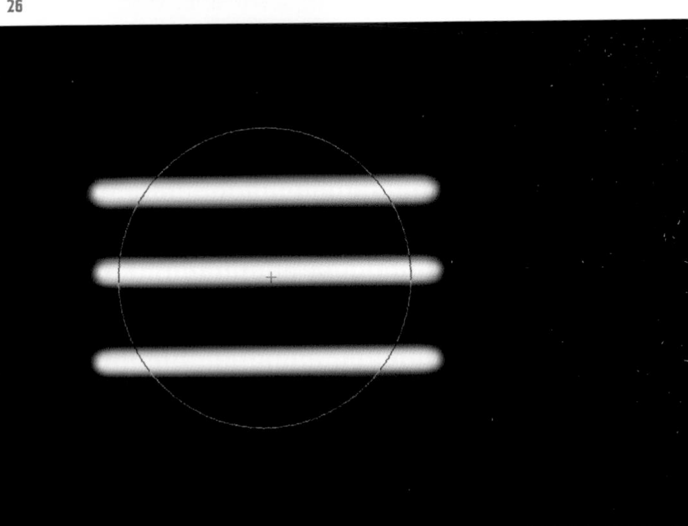

27

28

29 30 31 32 33 34 35 36

Now for a change, fill your canvas with Gray (Shift-Backspace with the corresponding option, ill.29).

Pick the Pen tool in the Tool bar, or alternatively use P (or Shift-P, if it isn´t at the front of the group, ill.30).

Before you get going, make sure you carry out the appropriate adjustments above in the Options palette.

In the first place you want to create a so called Shape Layer with the pen (more about that later, ill.31), then you´d really also like to use the „genuine" Pen tool and not the Freeform type (ill.32).

What´s more, before that you want to decide on the color to be created within the line shape to be drawn (ill.33) – if it shouldn´t be White, simply click on the little color icon, and choose another (I for example decided on a light Blue. ill.34).

Now just click some points into your image (ill.35). When you hold down the mouse key after the click and drag a little, a curved point is created (ill.36).

A last click on the first point of the series

closes the shape (the so called path) for the time being (ill.37).
You may modify this figure, e.g. with the Direct Selection tool (A, ill.38).

Select the tool, and click twice on one of the corners to move it to another location (ill.39).
If you click on two points with the Shift key held down, so both are marked, you can move the whole line between them (ill.40).

There is even more you can do – pick the Convert Point tool from where you´ve just selected the Pen (ill.41).

With this tool you can now convert corners of the shape you´ve drawn into curve points. Click on a corner, hold down the mouse key, and drag (ill.42).

Using the same tool, you can rotate (ill.43) and scale the tangent halves (ill.44).

If you´d like the shape even more complex, add a point at the place you want (Add Anchor Point tool, ill.45 and 46).

Should you wish to rotate both tangents together, you need the Direct Selection tool again (A, ill.47).

A look at the Layers palette shows you that Photoshop® has created a new layer, the so called Shape layer, which is basically a layer-wide color area limited by a vector mask (the figure you´ve drawn).

The color of the layer (and thus your shape) can be changed at any time by double-clicking on the layer´s miniature (ill.48).

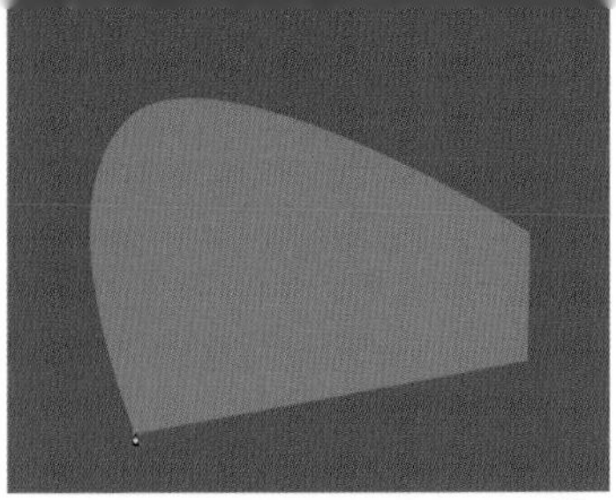

37

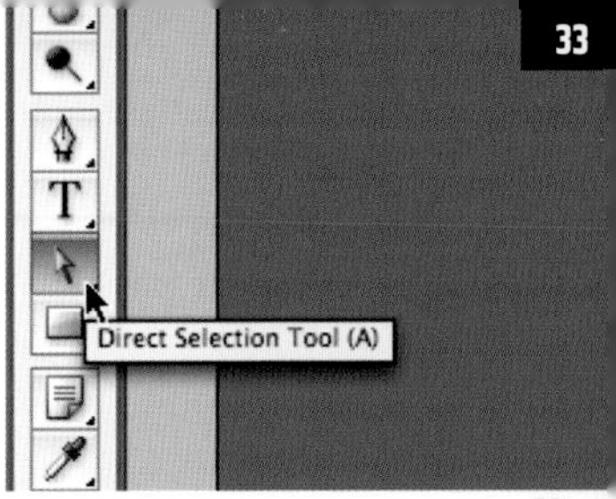

Direct Selection Tool (A)

38

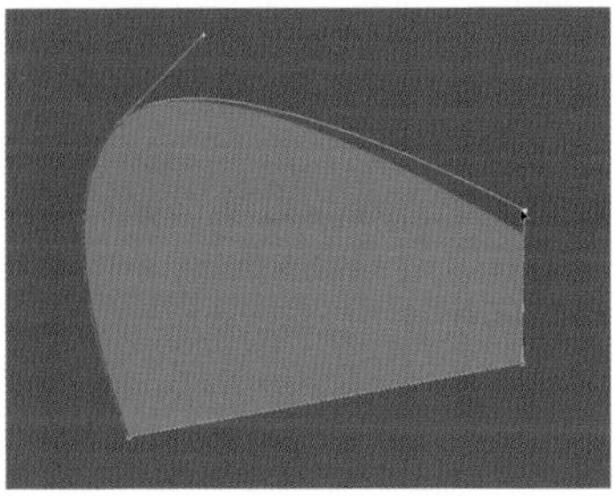

39

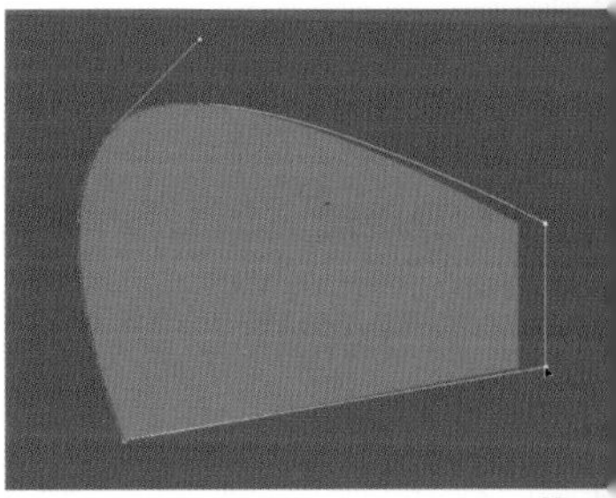

40

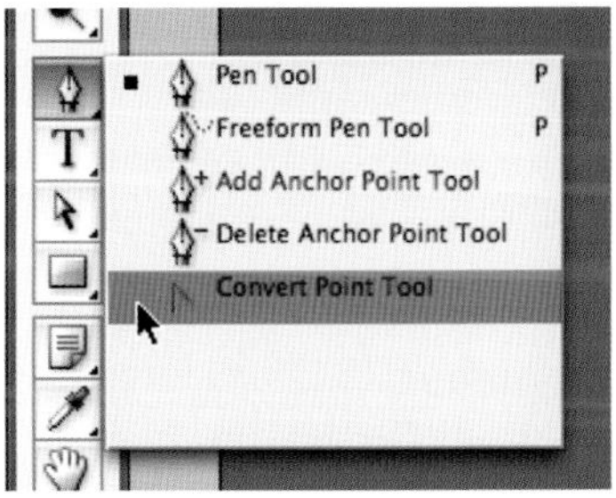

Pen Tool P
Freeform Pen Tool P
Add Anchor Point Tool
Delete Anchor Point Tool
Convert Point Tool

41

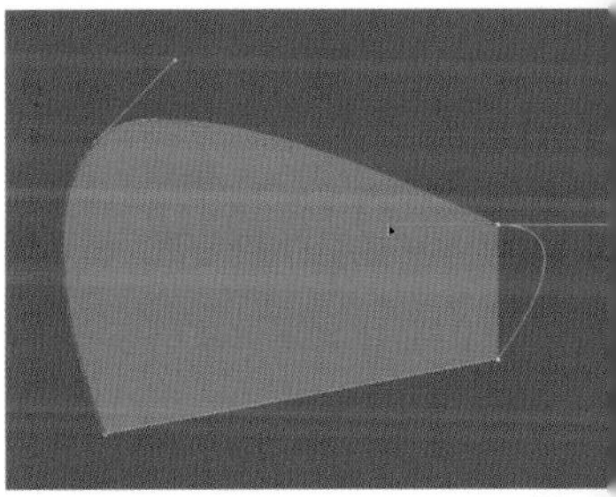

42

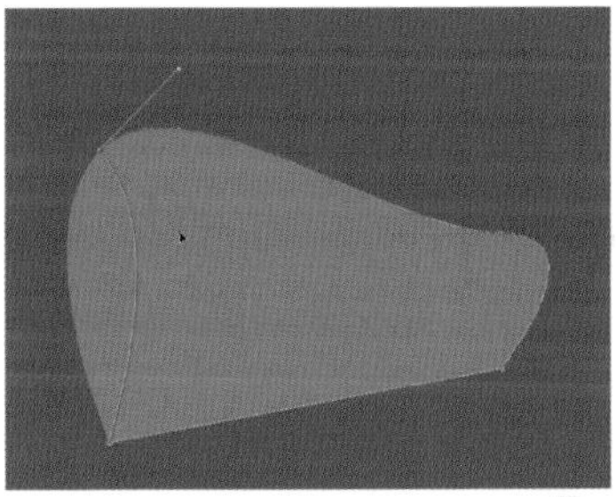

43

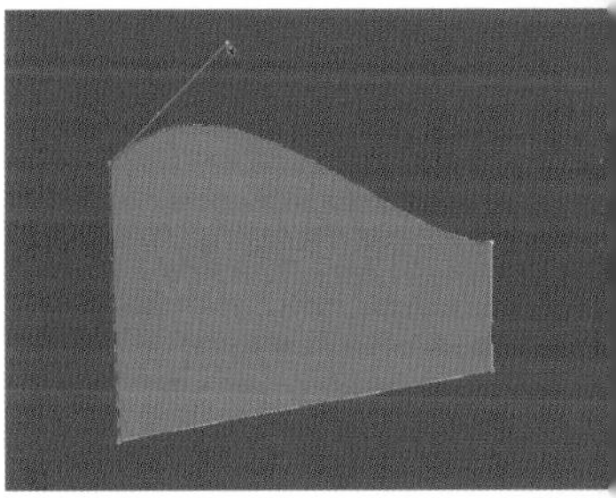

44

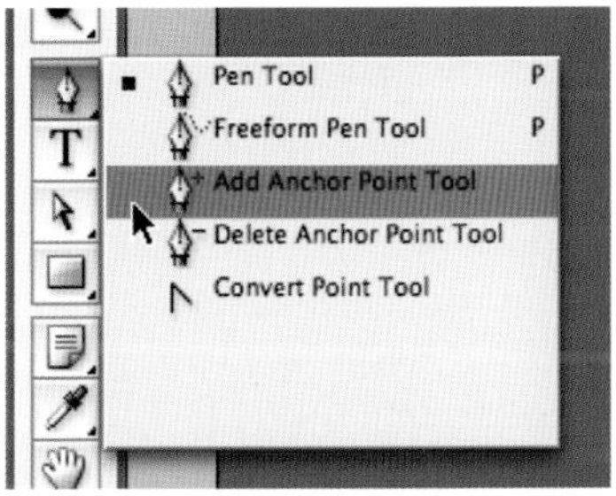

Pen Tool P
Freeform Pen Tool P
Add Anchor Point Tool
Delete Anchor Point Tool
Convert Point Tool

45

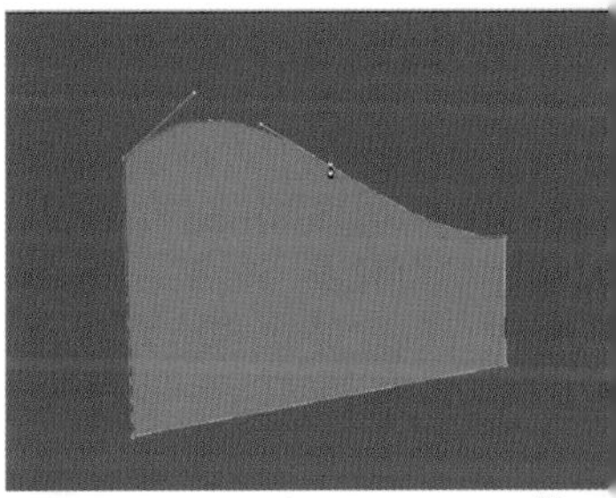

46

47

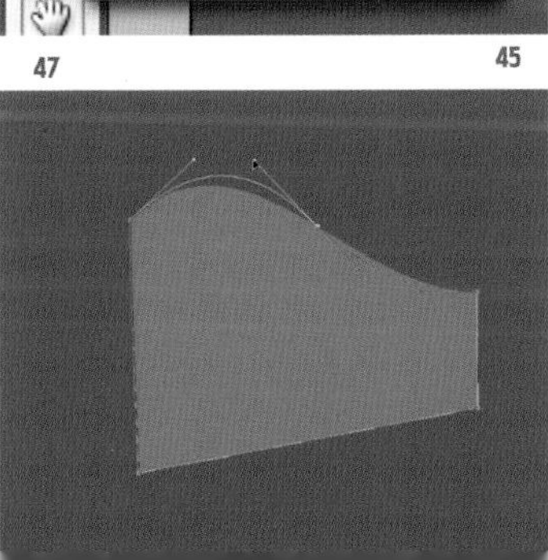

48

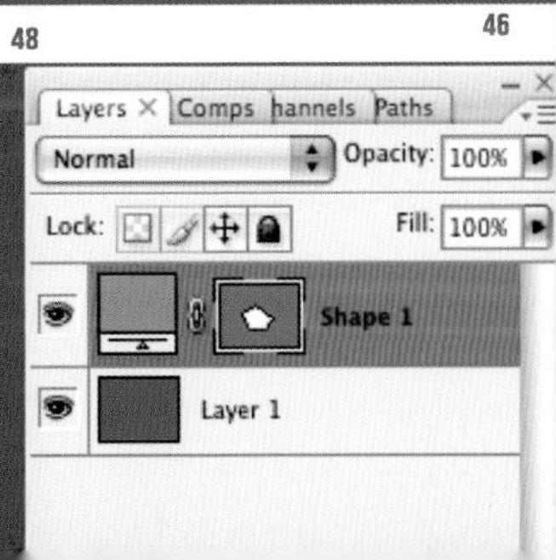

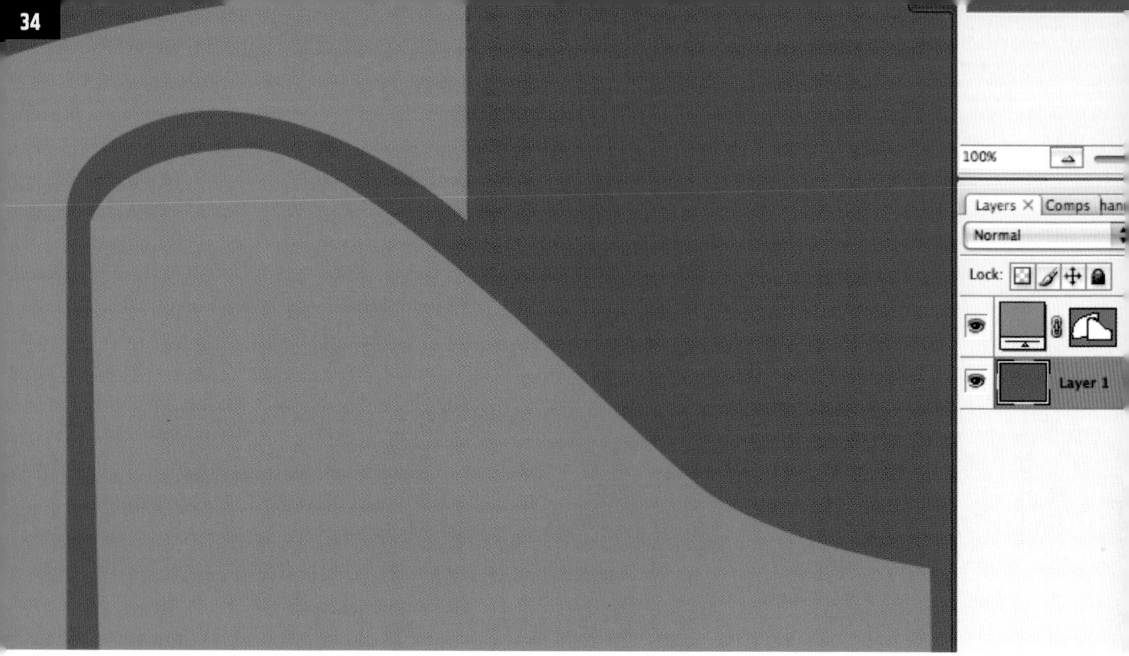

50

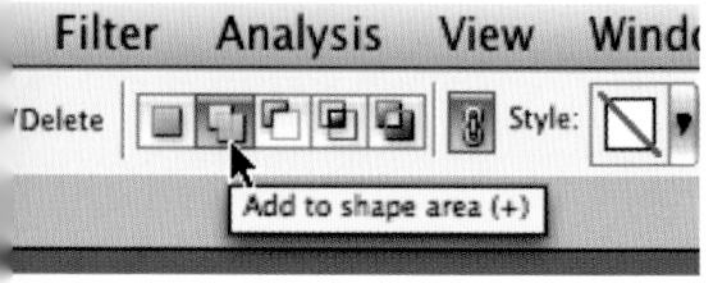

49

If you now want to draw yet another path selection with the Pen tool on the same layer (perhaps because you want the same color for both) you can do it, but make sure the corresponding option is activated in the Options palette (ill.49).

In the first place click on the vector mask miniature once, to deactivate the first path, then again, to make it editable again. By doing this you make sure that all points and tangents are deselected.

After drawing you can see the change in the mask miniature of the layer (ill.50; if it hasn´t worked properly, Photoshop® has created a new layer for the second figure).

By the way - clicking on the mask miniature of the shape layer with the CTRL key held down allows you to load the shape as a pixel selection (ill.51).
I´d rather not go into this at this stage, but you should be aware that it also works in reverse; a pixel selection can be transformed into a vector path, with a corresponding command from the Paths palette menu.

You can also cut holes in your shape by

51

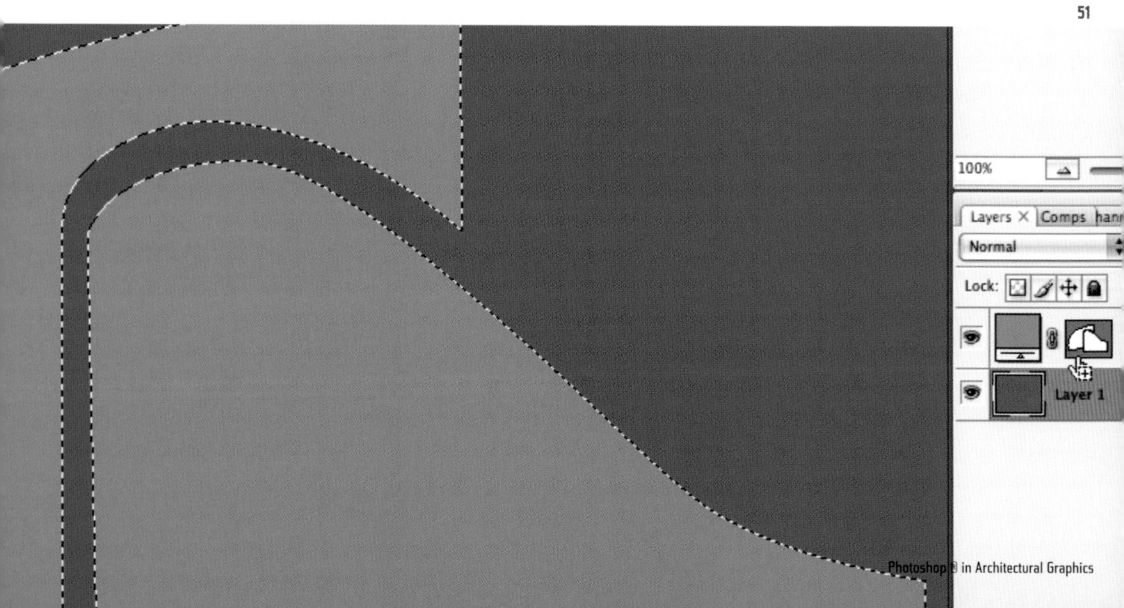

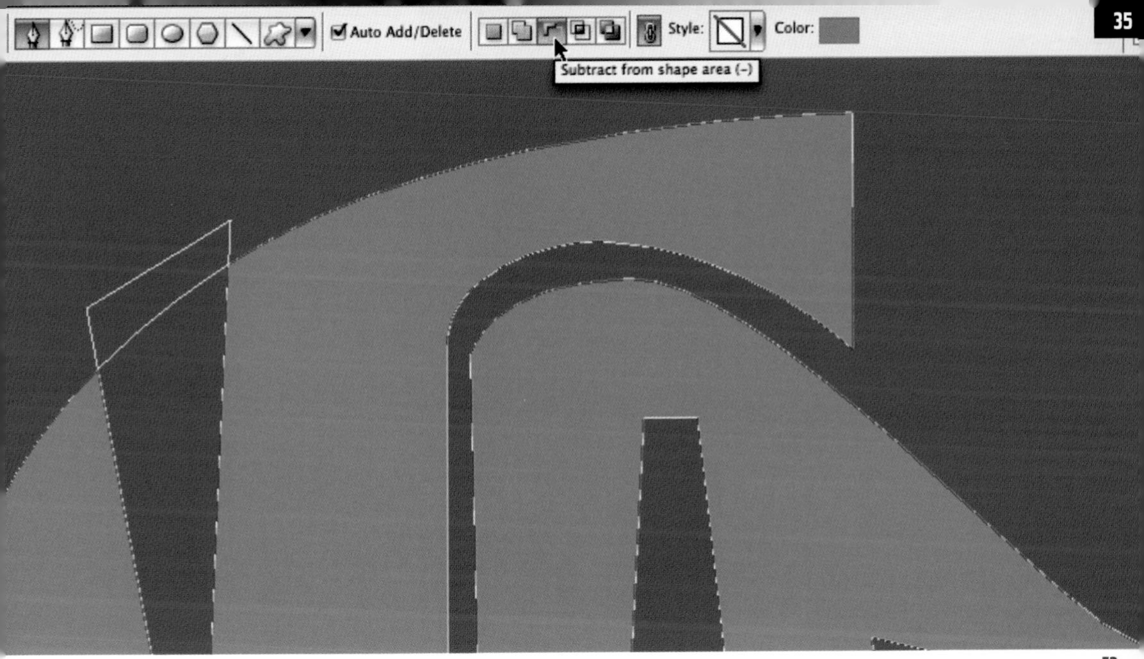

52

simply using the Subtract from shape area option (ill.52).
Keep in mind that to do so, you should deactivate your path again, as shown above, via two single clicks on the vector mask miniature.

By clicking on the mask miniature of the shape layer, you can see the figure without the boundary lines (ill.53).

If you want to assign an overall edge double-click on the layer entry in the Layers palette (not on the layer or mask miniature!), so that the adjustment dialog for the Layer Styles opens. Click bottom left in the list on the word Stroke, and choose the appropriate adjustments on the right (ill.54).

We´re now finished with the paint and drawing tools for the moment, so let´s take a look at the subject of selections, channels and masks.

53

54

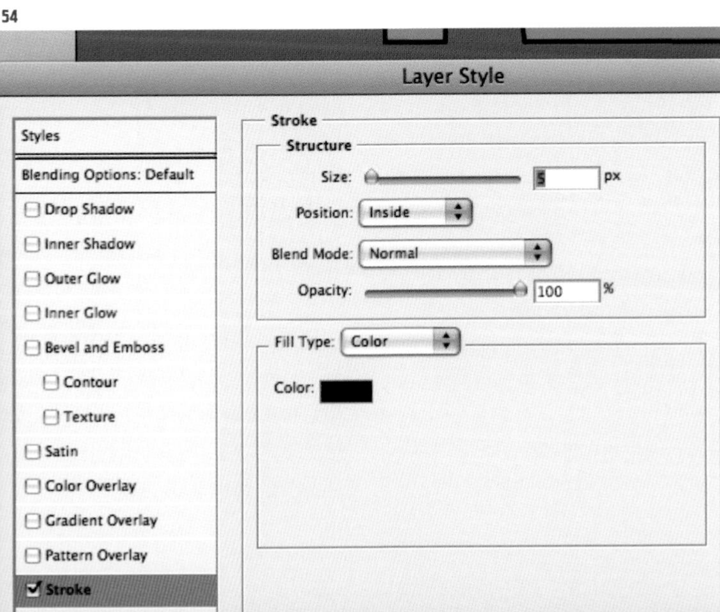

54

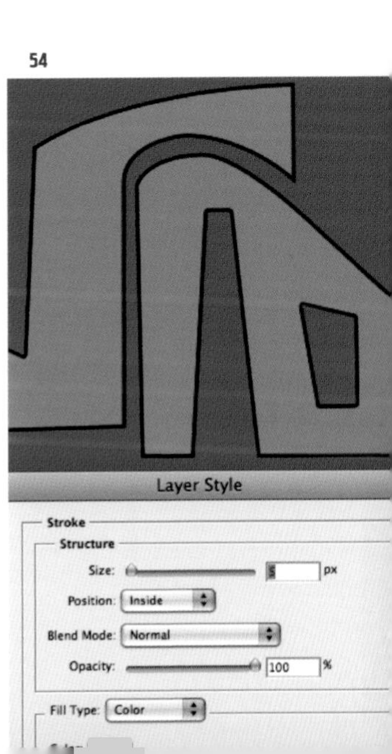

56

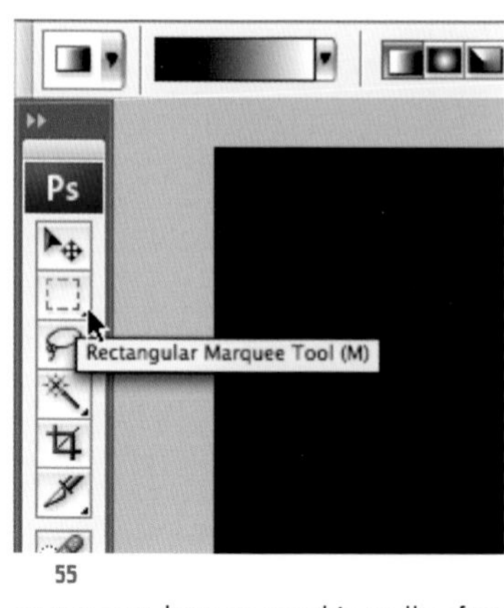

55

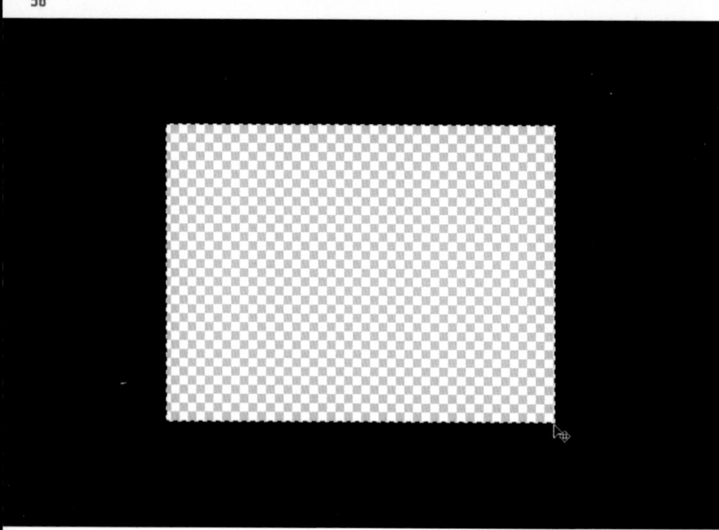

57

58

59

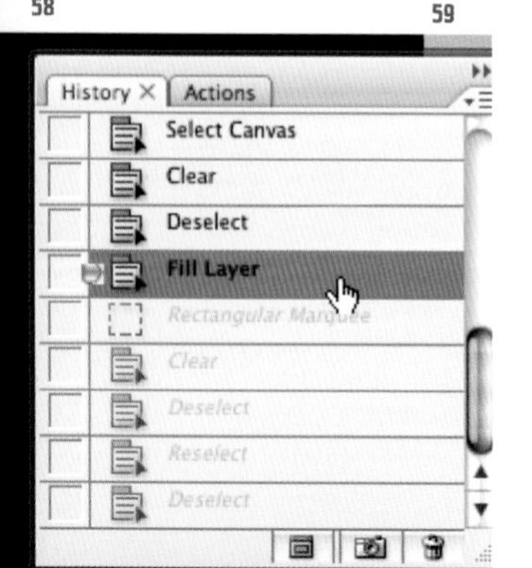

Delete your shape layer, and fill the canvas with Black again.
Select the Rectangular Marquee tool (ill.55) and drag a rectangle over your black canvas, with the mouse key held down (ill.56).

Press Backspace to delete the selected area to make Photoshop®'s background appear.
The black pixels selected have disappeared (ill.57).

The selection (which looks like a line of ants) can still be seen. To continue working, you usually have to get rid of these; for this there´s a menu command (Select menu - Deselect, ill.58).
Please note, however, the shortcut CTRL-D, as you now have to use this really often, and you don´t want to be clicking around in a menu all the time.

Selections, no matter which tool produced them, are basically always handled similarly, so at this point I´d like to go into a few aspects in detail.

Redo your last steps till you see the entire black canvas again, without a hole and without selection "ants", by pressing Alt-CTRL-Z several times (in other applications CTRL-Z is all you need for doing this, whereas in Photoshop® you can only redo the last step).

Alternatively, you can also click on the entry Fill in the History palette.
That was the step when you filled the area with Black (ill.59).

The History palette lists the last steps in more or less understandable terms, so that you can return to any state of your editing.

The number of work-steps saved is preset at 20 and can be changed in Photoshop® Preferences (ill.60).

So, now everything´s black again. Make sure that the Rectangular Marquee tool is selected, and then look at the Options palette at the upper screen border, where

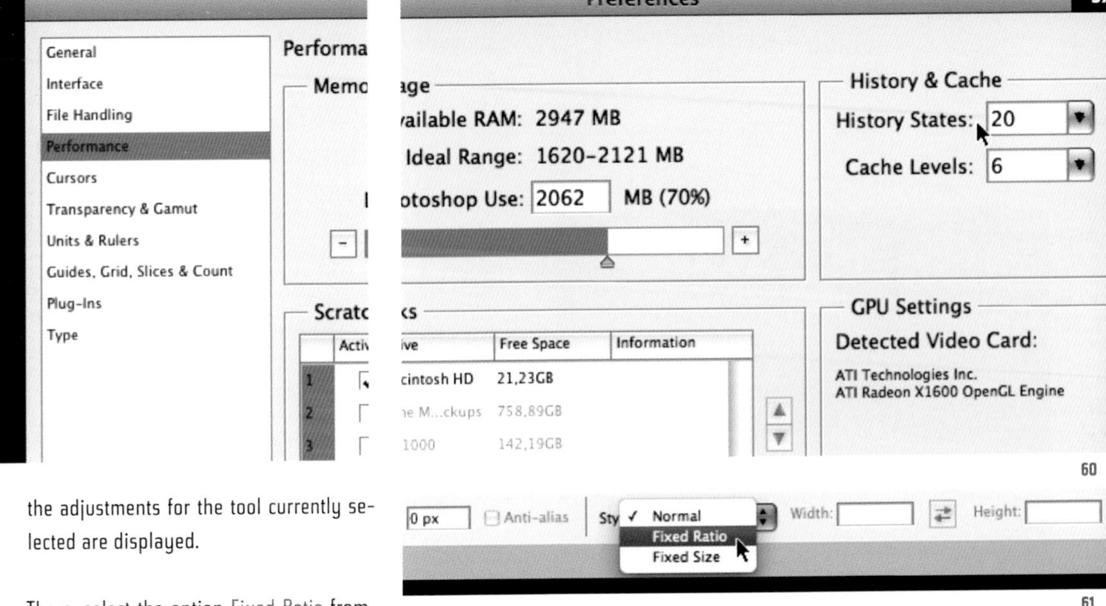

60

the adjustments for the tool currently selected are displayed.

There, select the option Fixed Ratio from the pulldown menu named Style (ill.61), then you can enter factors for Width and Height (ill.62).

If you draw the selection with these settings defined, the rectangle will always show the same proportion (ill.63).

Eventually you need a smooth selection edge, or you have to contract or expand the selected area – click in the Options palette again, on Refine Edge (ill.64).

An adjustment dialog opens (ill.65) – handily, there´s a preview which shows you in advance the result of the adjustments you choose.

In the icon array below, click on the second from the right, and you´ll see your selected area on a white background.

As you can see in the preview, your selection is slightly feathered (1 pixel), and the corners are chamfered with a Radius of 3 pixels.

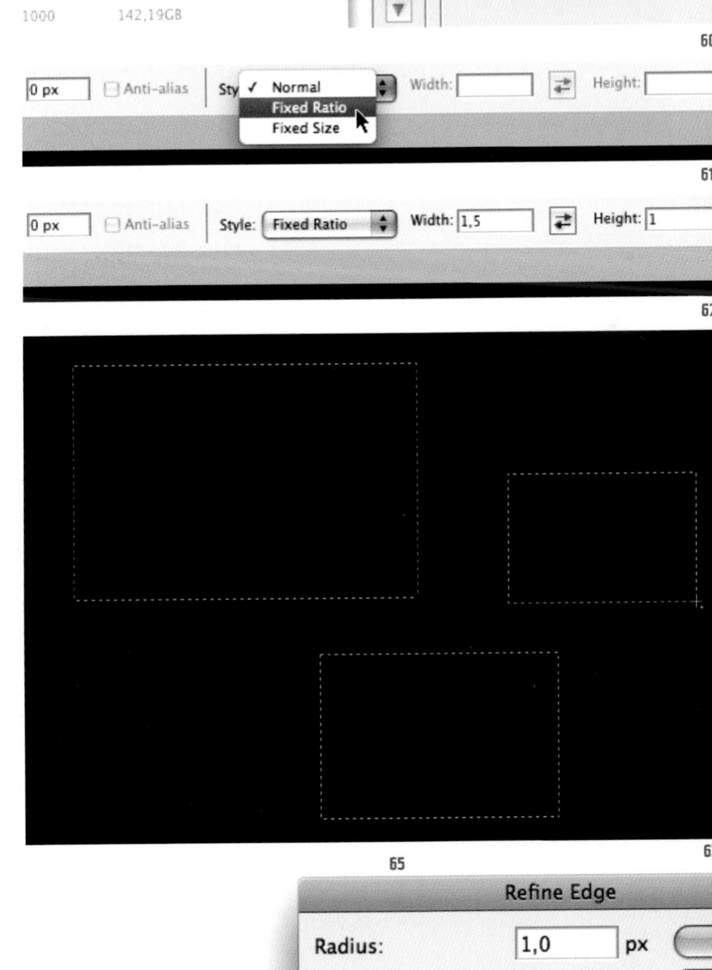

61

62

63

64

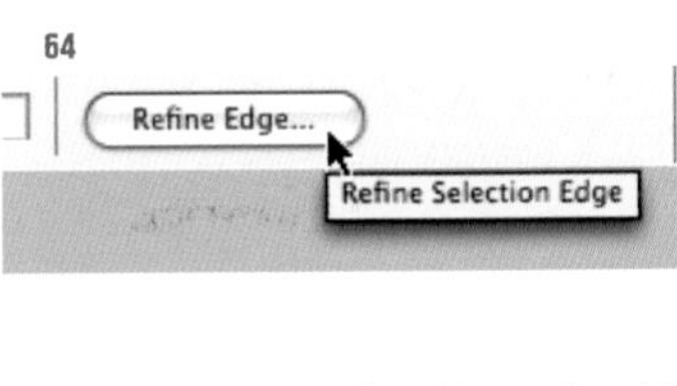

65

Refine Edge

Radius: 1,0 px

Contrast: 0 %

Smooth: 3

Feather: 1,0 px

Contract/Expand: 0 %

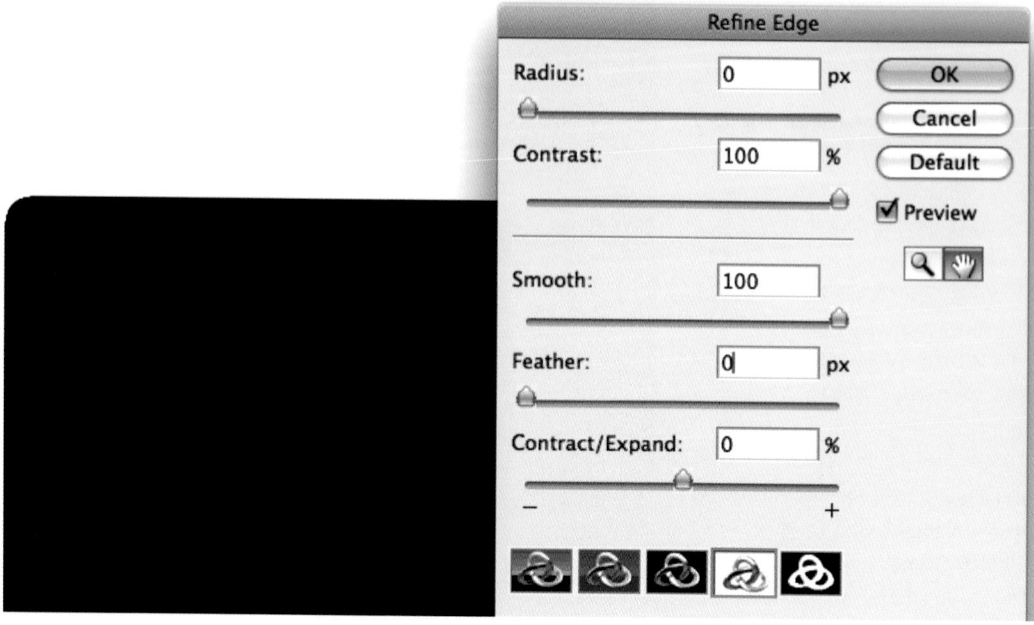

Refine Edge
Radius: 0 px
OK
Cancel
Default
Contrast: 100 %
Preview
Smooth: 100
Feather: 0 px
Contract/Expand: 0 %
− +

66

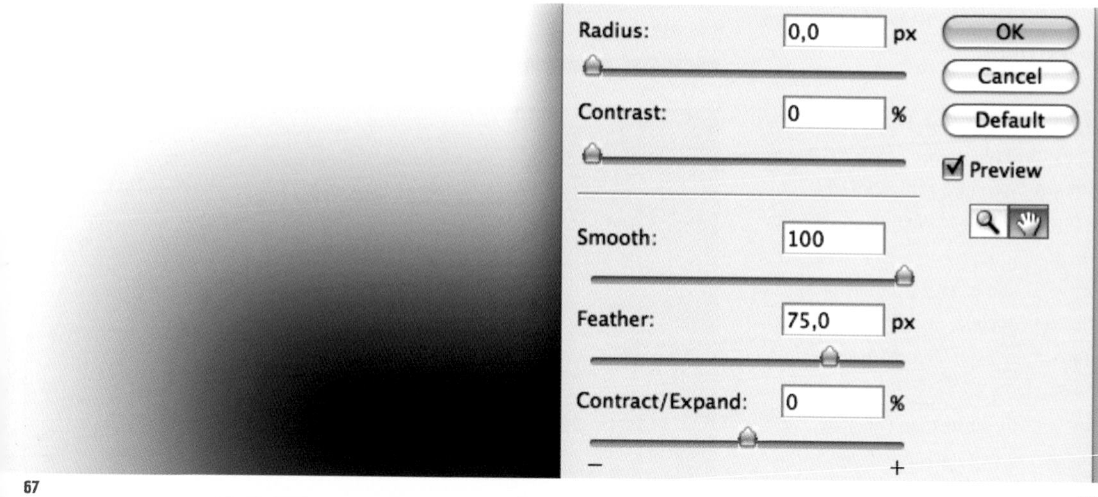

Radius: 0,0 px
OK
Cancel
Default
Contrast: 0 %
Preview
Smooth: 100
Feather: 75,0 px
Contract/Expand: 0 %
− +

67

68

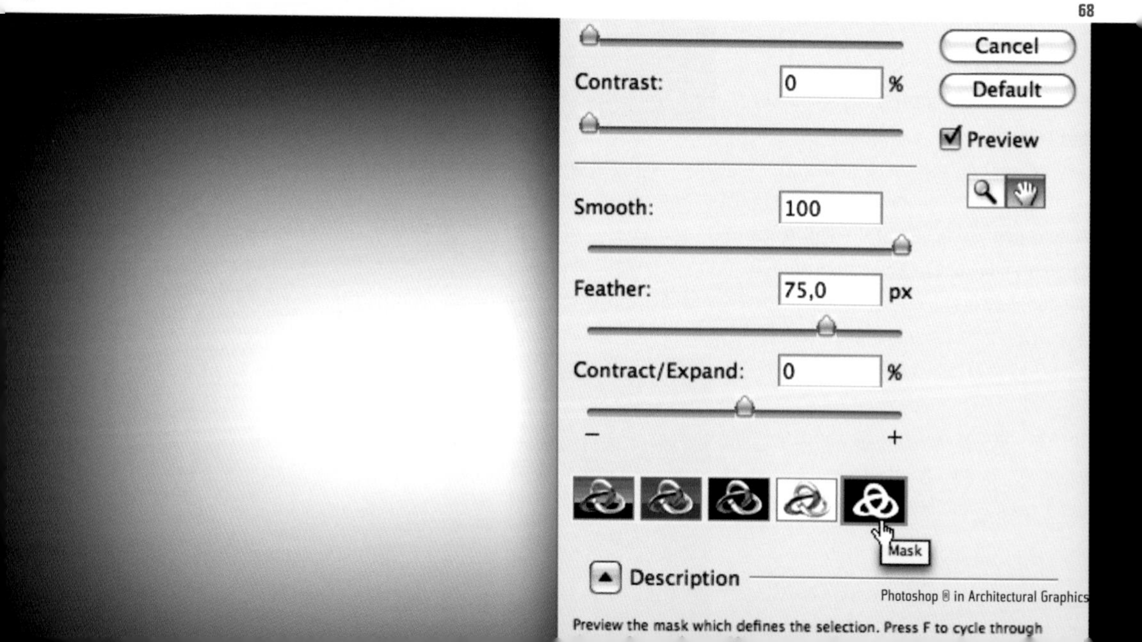

Cancel
Default
Contrast: 0 %
Preview
Smooth: 100
Feather: 75,0 px
Contract/Expand: 0 %
− +
Mask
Description
Preview the mask which defines the selection. Press F to cycle through

Now enter a value of 100 for Radius and Contrast, and set everything else to 0 (ill.66).
Your selection is completely sharpened, and the corners are chamfered.

Now give the selection a rather smooth edge (Feather=75, ill.67), and reduce Radius and Contrast again to 0 – the result looks completely different.

If you change the preview mode to Mask (ill.68), you´ll see your selection inverted, just like it would look as a mask (a subject I´ll come to later).
Now confirm the Refine Edge dialog with OK, and delete the selection – the result is a smooth-edged, oval hole in your black canvas (ill.69).

To understand the selection's mask charcter, create a new layer under your present one filled with color; you'll see it through the oval opening in the upper layer.

You can create a new layer in different ways. Press Shift-Alt-CTRL-N, and you get a new layer inserted over the existing one without further notice; if you leave out the Alt key, you are allowed to give your new layer a suitable name (ill.70).

Usually, this is the best way to have a new layer, as it works with keyboard shortcuts.

In this specific case, however, I´d like to show you the second-best strategy, since we do want to have a new layer under the existing one (as I´ve mentioned above, new layers are normally placed over the last active one).

For this, click on the corresponding icon at the bottom frame of the Layers palette (ill.71) – the equivalent of the key command Shift-Alt-CTRL-N (see above).

At the same time, however, press the CTRL key, and the new layer is indeed placed under our perforated layer.

At any rate there´s now a new, empty layer lying under the layer with the smooth-edged hole.
Please fill this new layer with a color of your choice, using Shift-Backspace (ill.72).

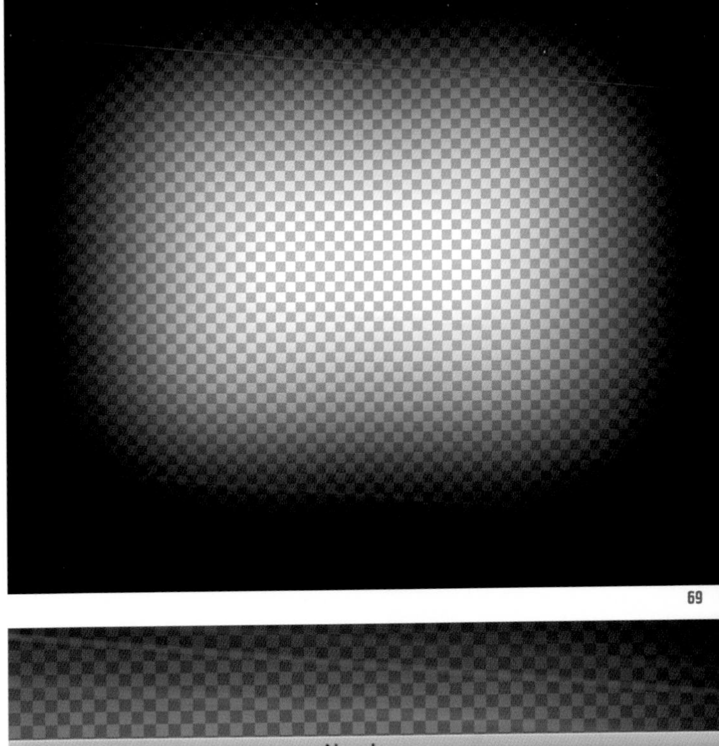

69

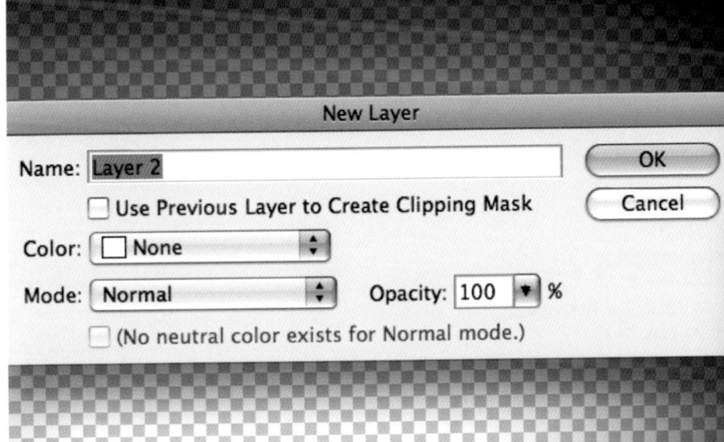

70

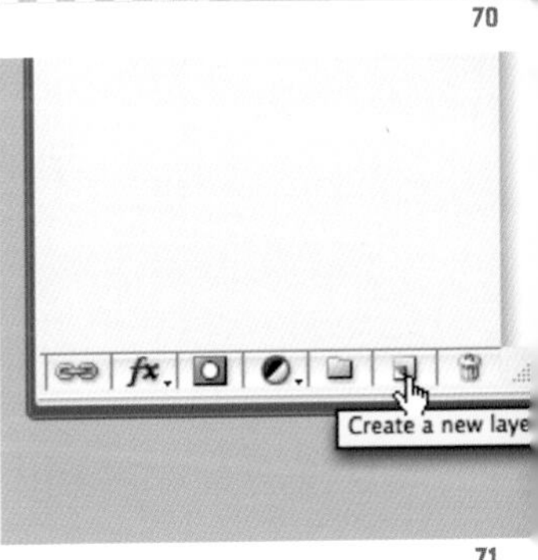

71

72

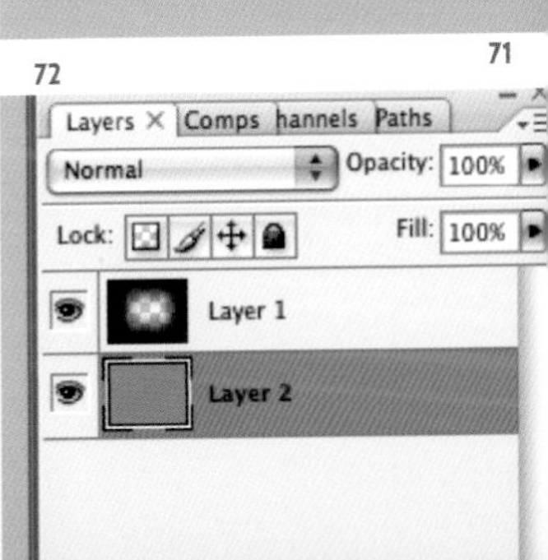

73

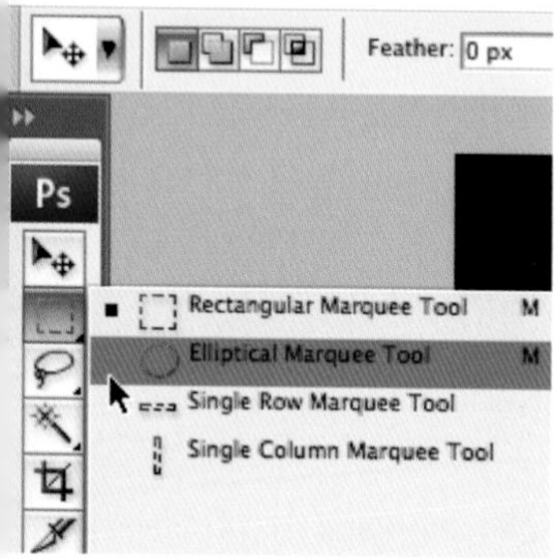

74

When viewing the result (ill.73), keep in mind that this feathered, oval spot has emerged from a normal rectangular selection only by edge-refinement adjustments.

Now there are a few more tricks concerning selections. For these you can simply use your file, as we won´t be changing the image.

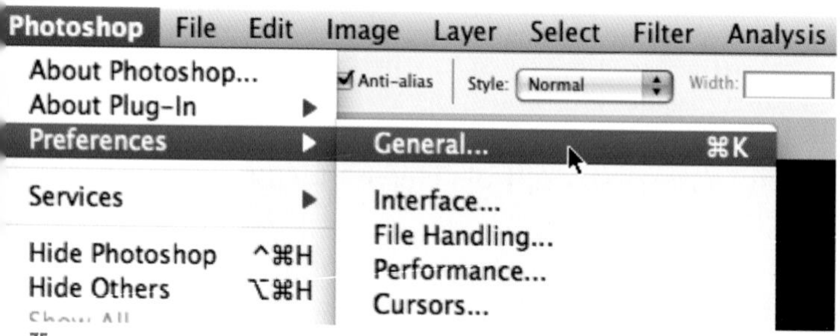

First of all select the Rectangular Marquee tool again, and hold down the Shift key when drawing the selection frame; the rectangle keeps a square proportion. The same is true for the Elliptical Marquee tool, hidden behind the rectangle in the Tool bar (ill.74); if you use this to draw a selection and simultaneously press the Shift key, the ellipse becomes a circle.

As you can also see in ill.74, there´s a shortcut for choosing the Rectangular and Elliptical Marquee tool (M), but how do you decide which of the two to get with it?

Just take a look at Photoshop® Preferences (MacOS: Photoshop menu - Preferences - General, ill.75; in the Windows version the Preferences are to be found at the bottom of the Edit menu).

There you´ll see, on the right, an option named Use Shift Key for Tool Switch - this should be checked (ill.76). Confirm with OK.

Now press the Shift key, plus M several times (it´s the shortcut for the Rectangular Marquee tool).
As you can see in the Tool bar, you thereby alternate between the Rectangular and Elliptical Marquee.

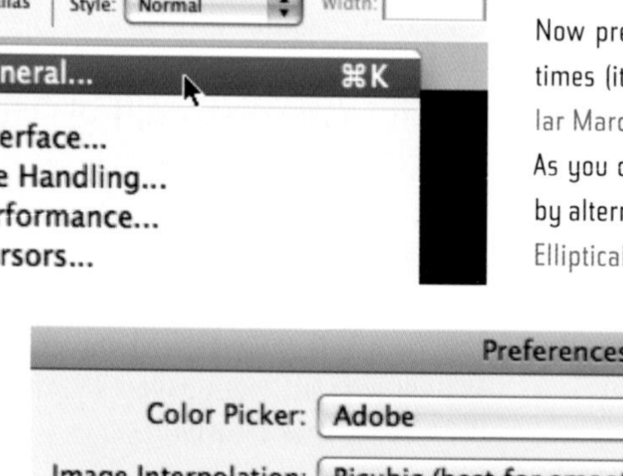

75

76

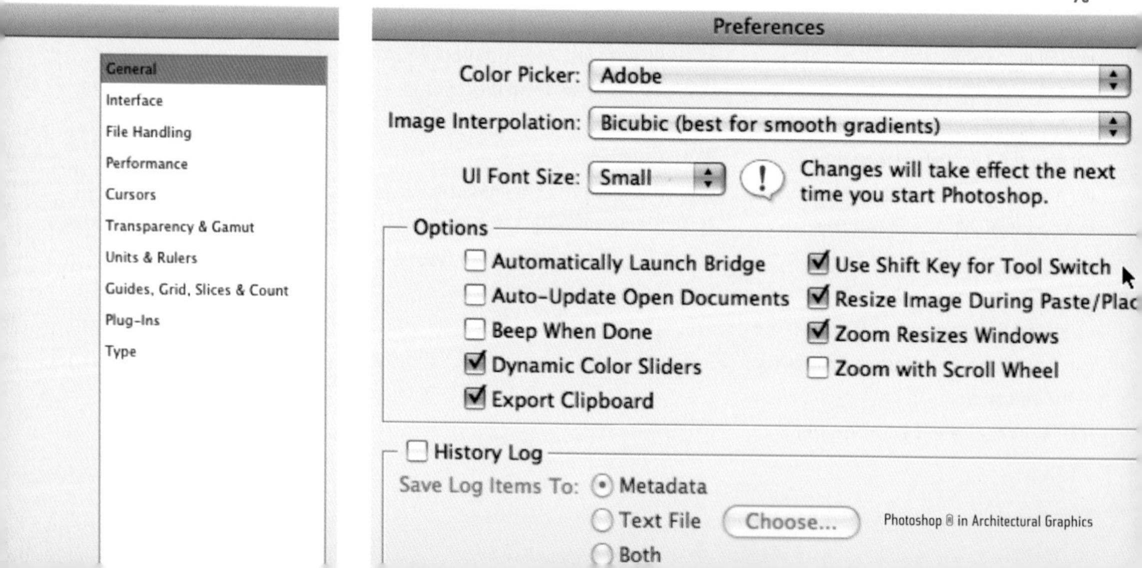

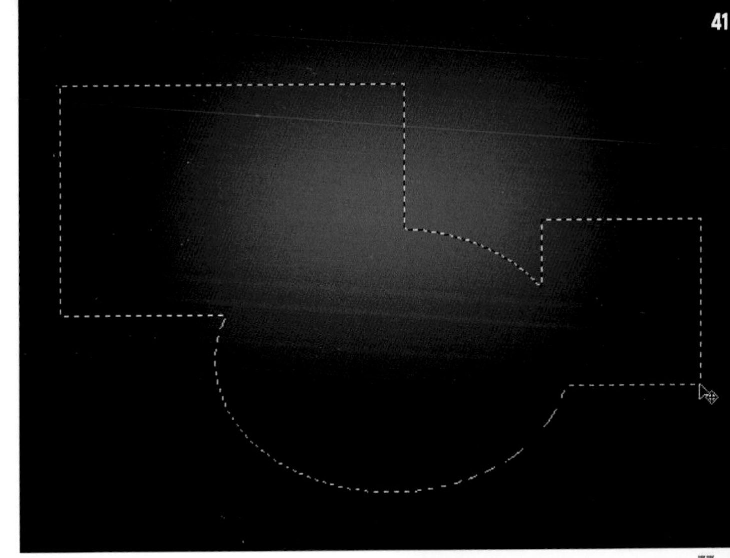

77

The Rectangular Marquee tool isn´t as simple as you might think at first, especially if you consider the possibilities of edge refining (see above).

With selections, no matter which tool produced them, even more can be carried out.

Draw a selection again (no matter whether it´s rectangular or elliptical) - don´t release the mouse, but press Space with your left hand, and you can move the selection marquee drawn so far.
Release Space again, and you can finish drawing the selection.

While drawing, you can also press the Shift key, then it becomes quadratic or circular (see above).

Press CTRL-D, to get rid of the selection ants.

Now start a selection again, but this time with the Alt key held down.
You´ll see that the selection is now drawn from it's center (marked by your first click).This usually makes sense if you have to select circular image areas.

So, you´ve now drawn a selection, and want to select further image areas in addition? By default, this does not work, as a new selection generally replaces the preceding one.

However, if you press the Shift key before clicking the next selection will be added, even when you change the selection tool, or its type (ill.77).

As you know, pressing the Shift key while using the Rectangular Marquee tool normally results in the square or circle shape.

This is not the case if you press Shift before the first click of your subsequent selection - release the Shift key as soon as you´ve begun drawing your additional selection, and if you press it again, you will again force your added selection area into square or circle shape.

Subtracting works similarly to adding.
This time press the Alt key, if you want to subtract something from an existing selection with a further one (ill.78).

To boot, you may create intersections by pressing Shift and Alt.

Furtheron, you may modify the shape of a selection you've already created, via the command Transform Selection (Select menu, ill.79); make sure to have an active selection, and choose this command - now you can scale, rotate, distort or flip your selection, just check the right-click context menu for all the alternatives (ill.80 and 81).

If you find that your selection is transformed correctly, press Return, to conclude the transformation of the selection (ill.82).

Should it occur to you that you´d really rather not change the selection, just press the Escape key.

78

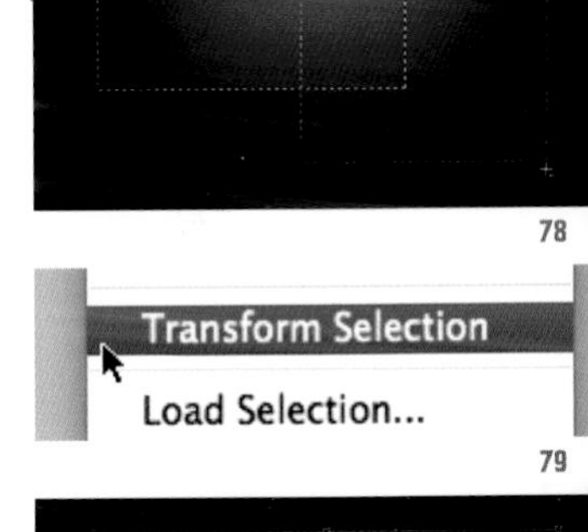

79

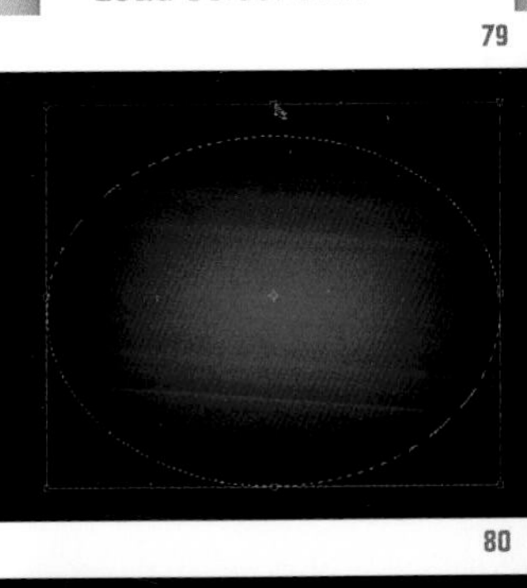

80

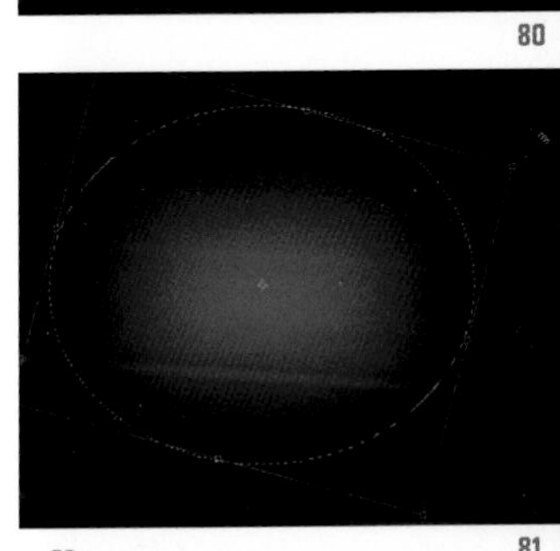

82

81

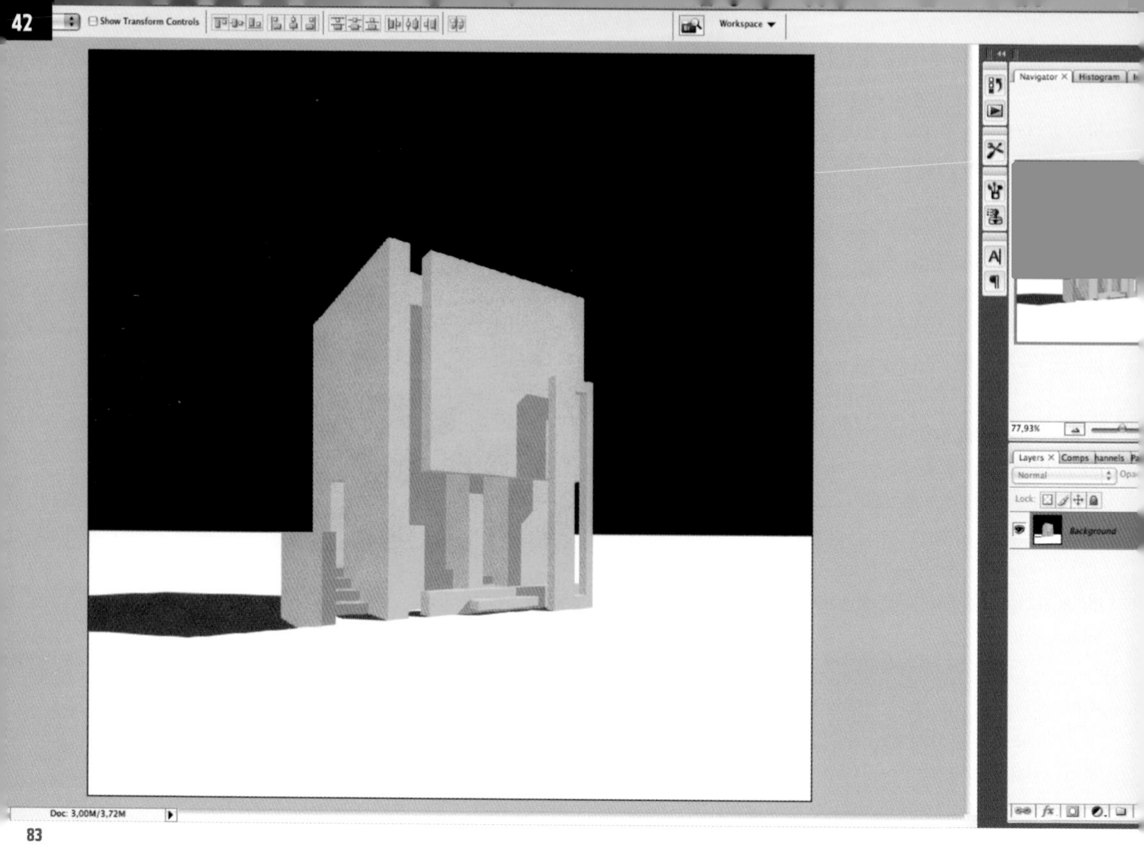

83

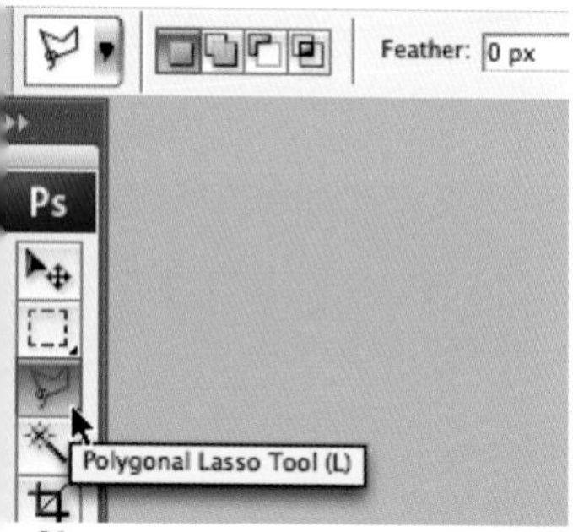

84

Now to a further selection tool; please open the file 02_terragni.psd (ill.83).

Let's assume you want to assign a different color to the building – in the first place, you have to select the according faces.

Activate the so called Polygonal Lasso (the tool directly under the Rectangular Marquee tool, ill.84); if you see something different there, because here too several tools are hidden behind one icon, press Shift, and keep pressing L till the one you want appears.

Now try to draw a polygonal selection around the house with a sequence of clicks.

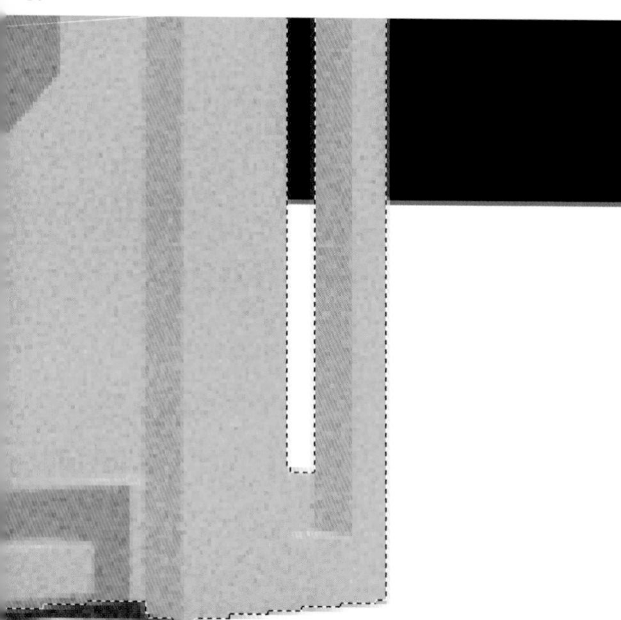

85

Do you want to zoom in while clicking, to be able to work more exactly?
Consider my tips from the first chapter – for zooming in or out, you don´t have to deselect your Lasso tool and choose the Zoom tool instead.

No – just press CTRL-Space to see the zoom cursor, use it to draw the clipping rectangle you want to see enlarged, release CTRL-Space, and keep on lasso-clicking.

If you need to move the image clipping, stay with the Polygonal Lasso, but this

time press your Space bar - you can now move the image clipping with the little hand cursor.
(If you move your Lasso tool towards one of the window borders while clicking, the clipping will move by itself, but rather fast - avoid the rush, and stick to the Space-bar shortcut).

In this example, as in most architectural graphics, you often have to draw selection edges exactly vertically or horizontally - to do this, just press the Shift key.

If you´ve clicked wrong, press Backspace to reverse the click. You can do this several times, until you´re back at the beginning.

After completing your selection, you will want to subtract the hole bottom right, through which you see sky and floor - hold down the Alt key before beginning to select the hole area too with the Polygonal Lasso - a small minus symbol beside the lasso cursor indicates that you are now removing parts of the existing selection (ill.85; you only need to press the Alt key for the first click, then you can release it).

If you´ve done everything right, the selection is finished (ill.86).
Just imagine what you could do with the selected image part; use a filter, alter the color, lighten or darken the image, increase contrast, etc.

Remember that the process of selecting has involved a bit of work.
It would certainly be handy if you could save this selection, to be able to access it again whenever you want.

This is possible, of course, via the corresponding command Save Selection from the Select menu (ill.87).

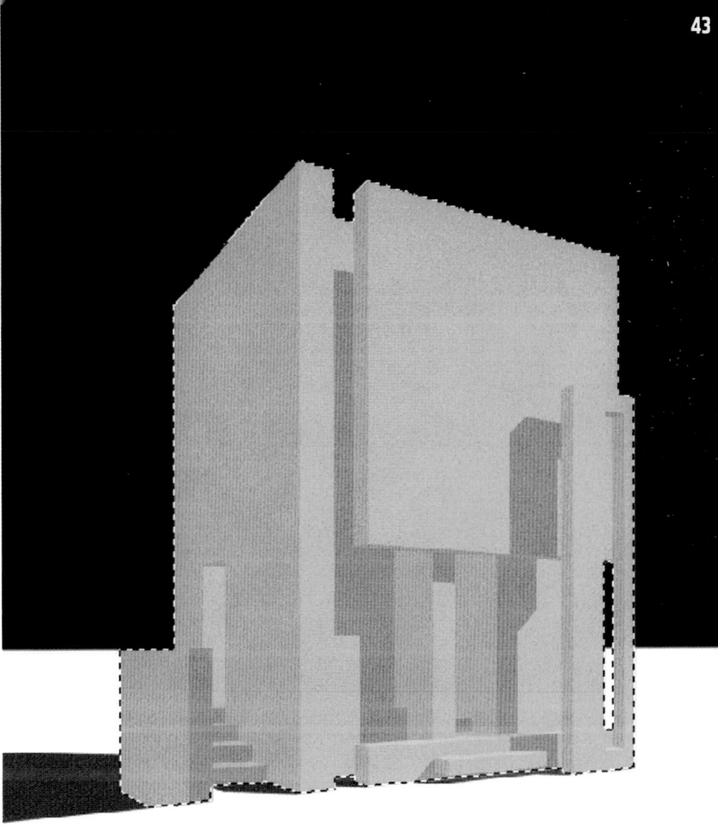

86

Note that in the adjustment dialog, that New is selected for Channel (channel is the technical term Photoshop® uses for a saved selection, ill.88), and enter something suitable as the name, e.g. building. Confirm with OK.

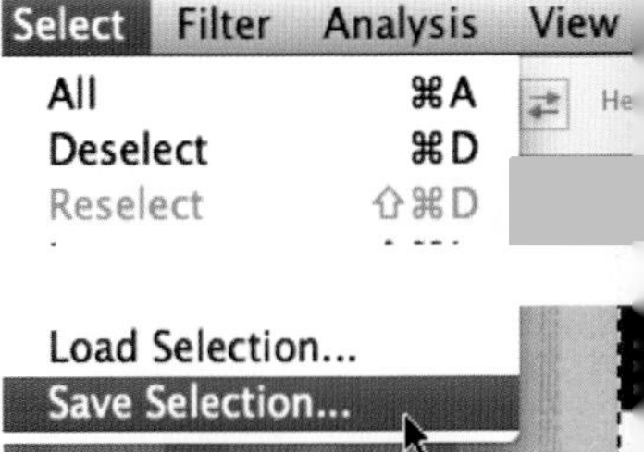

87

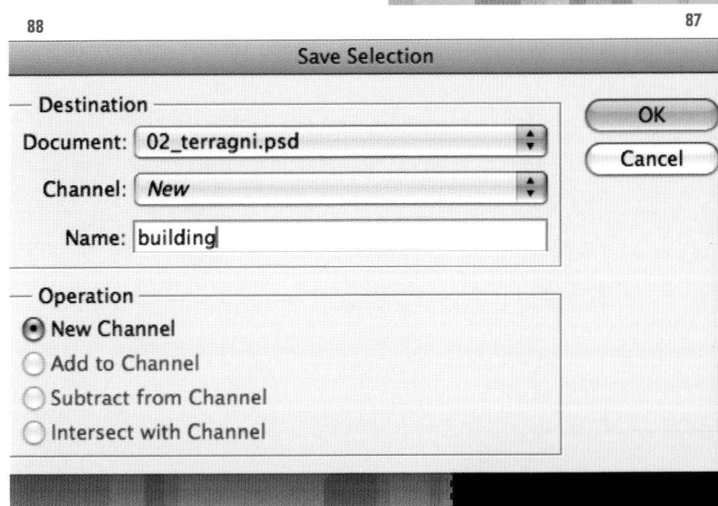

88

89

90

92

Now where has Photoshop® put your selection ? Check in the Channels palette.

There you´ll see under your RGB color channels, that make up your image, a new channel showing the selection in the form of a black-and-white image (ill.89; click on the channel to see it alone).

As you see, the selected area is white, the rest black. From this channel you can recover your selection at any time.

Before switching back to the Layers palette, you must reactivate the RGB channels by any means (clicking on the uppermost is all you need to do, ill.90).

Let´s now assume you´ve cancelled your selection by mistake, or you realize later that you need it again.
Just select Load Selection (Select menu, ill.91) and from the Channel pulldown menu the entry building (or whatever you´ve called your selection, ill.92).
Confirm with OK, and your ants are back again.

To learn what you can do with such a selection, we´ll undertake a short visit to color
adjustment.
Make sure your selection is on screen,

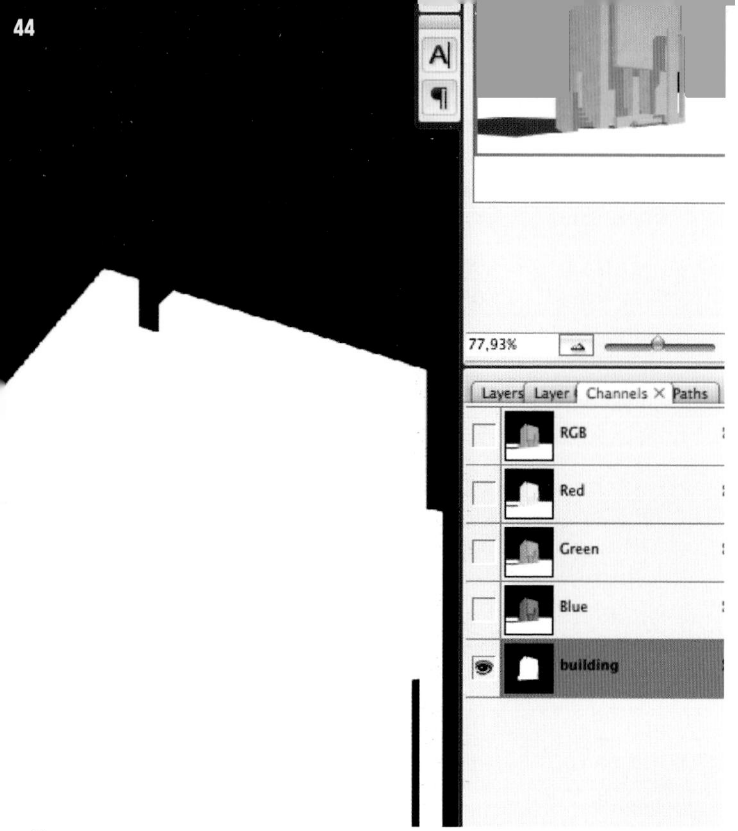

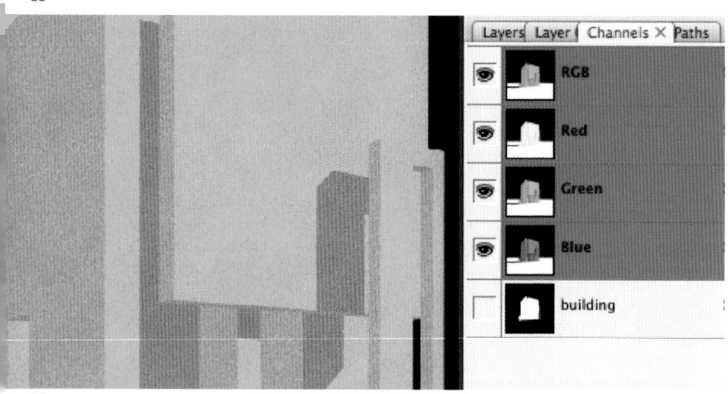

91

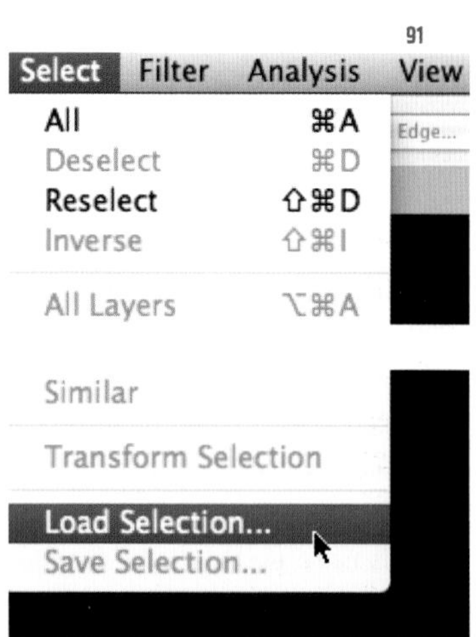

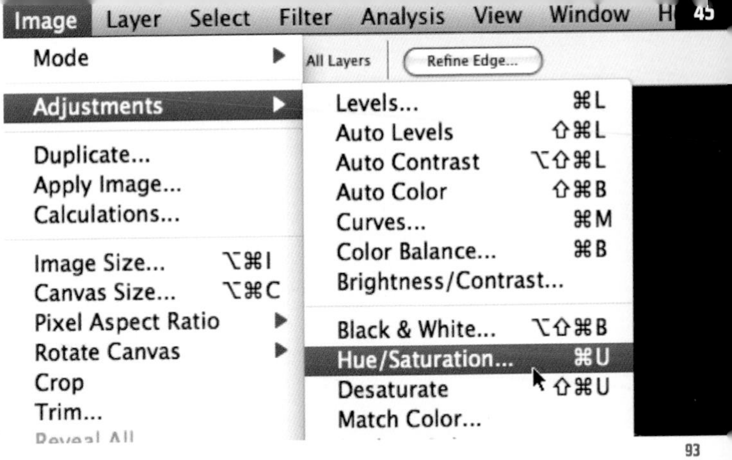

and select the adustment tool Hue/Saturation (Image menu: Adjustments, ill.93).

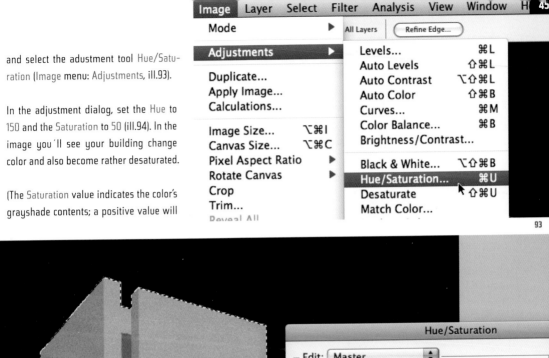

In the adjustment dialog, set the Hue to 150 and the Saturation to 50 (ill.94). In the image you´ll see your building change color and also become rather desaturated.

(The Saturation value indicates the color's grayshade contents; a positive value will reduce gray, a negative value will enhance it.)
Confirm with OK.

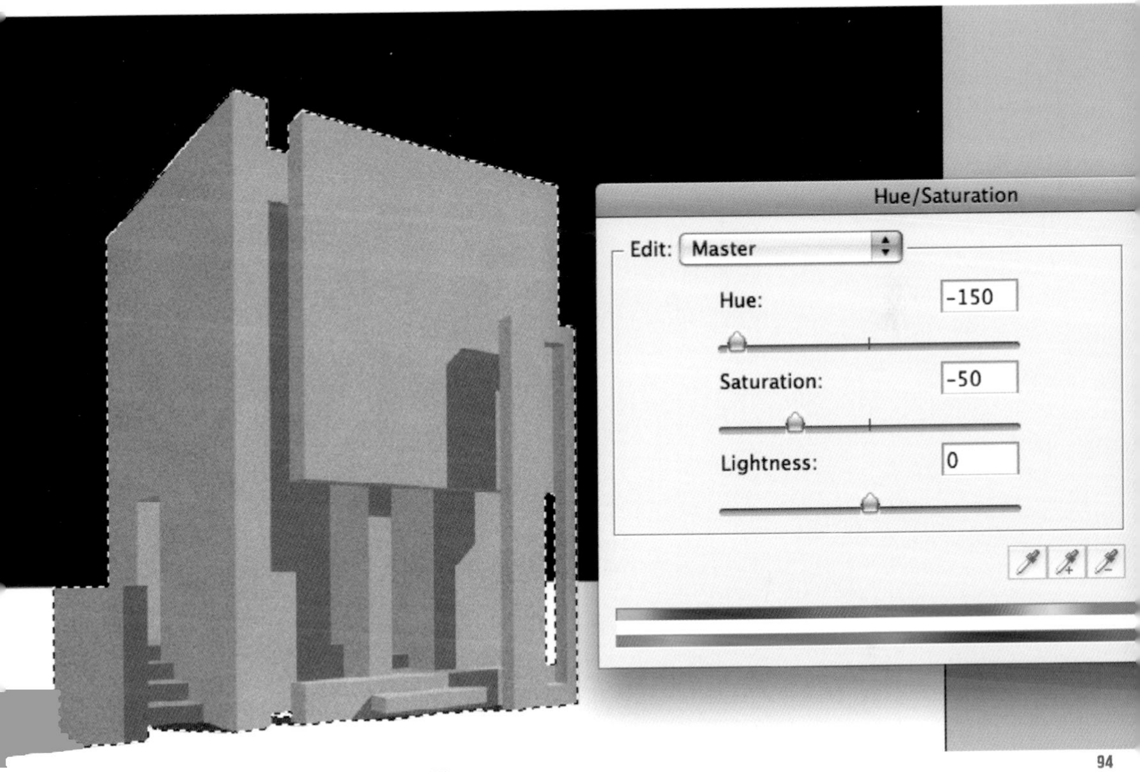

93

94

95

In addition you will use a filter; if you have an active selection, filtering will only affect the selected area.

Your selection should still be active, otherwise you´ll have to load it (see above) – then select the Sharpen filter with the ominous name Unsharp Mask from the Filter menu (ill.95).

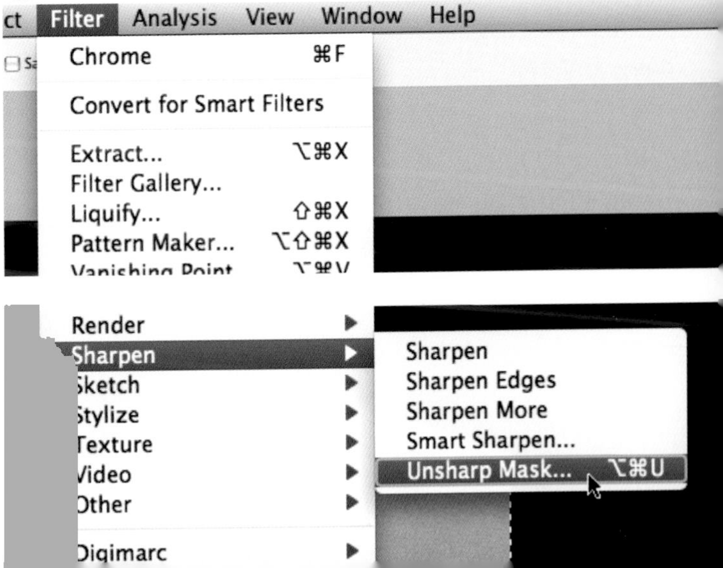

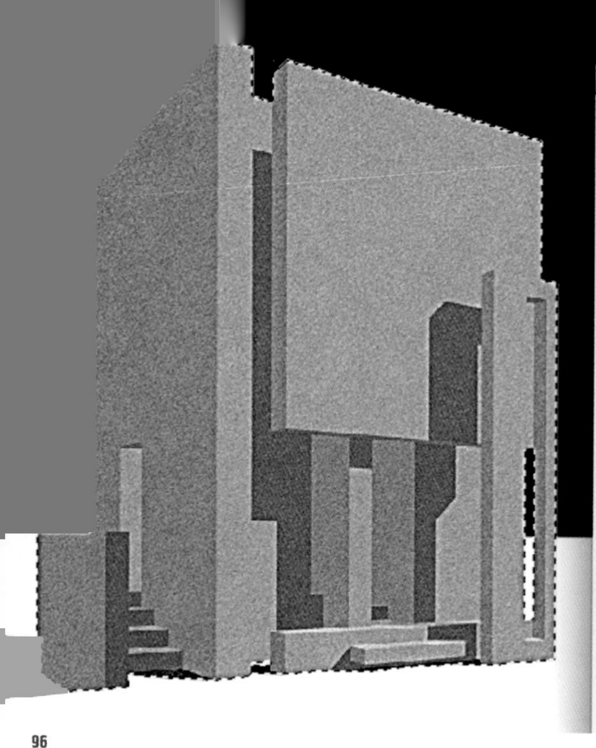

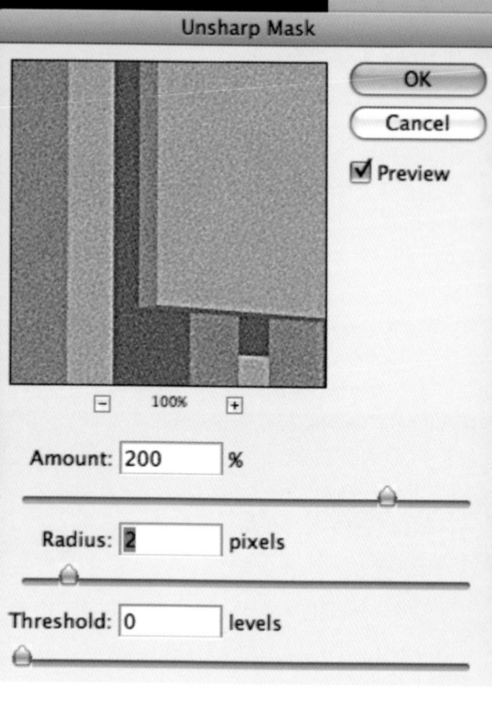

96

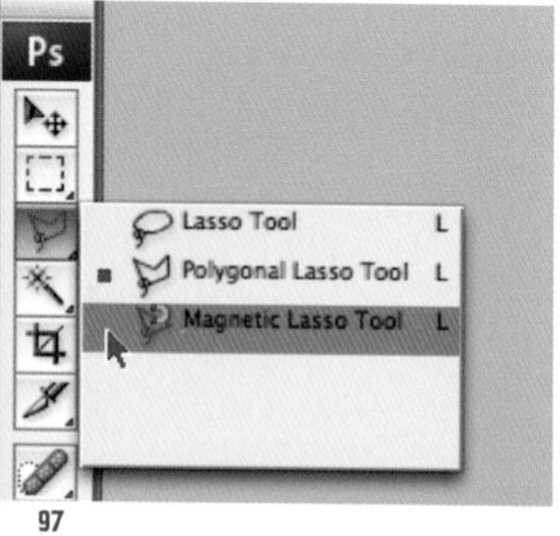

97

98

For the adjustments, select Amount = 200 and Radius = 2,0 (ill.96).

In the image you´ll see that the grain already present becomes much stronger in the selected image area.

Also try out the two other colleagues from the lasso fraction.

The simple lasso probably strikes you as somewhat inexact, but the result can be trimmed a lot via the Refine-Edge operation, like any selection.

The Magnetic Lasso tool offers to trace contours without constant clicking, taking into account the contrast between image areas, whose amount may be adjusted (ill.97).

Now to the last important selection tool in the Tool bar, the Magic Wand.

Please open the image 02_tree.psd; you see a black tree on a colored background (ill.98).
The first thing we usually want to do with a tree is to clip it, i.e. to separate it from its background, so that we can insert it in an architectural graphics.

This is normally extremely tedious, because the leafy, branching outline of a tree is hard to select.

What´s more, trees have "holes" through

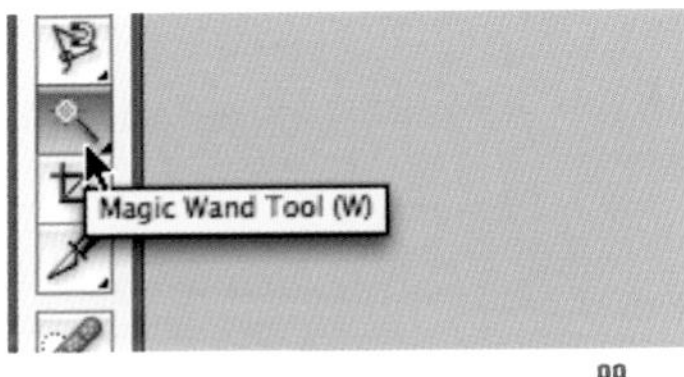

99

100

101

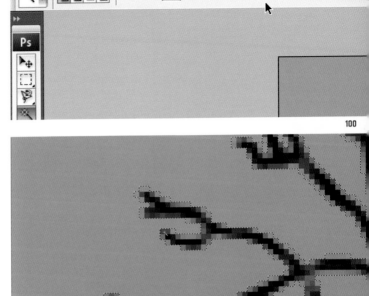

which the background is visible; that makes them even more difficult to handle than, say, human figures or haircuts.

In this case however, the situation is rather comfortable, as the tree clearly does nowhere resemble the background colors.

This is of course not typical, but good for practising with the Magic Wand tool.

Select it (W or Shift-W; not to be confused with the Quick Selection tool, ill.99).

Look at the Options palette above, and you should see the Tolerance value set to 1. You should deactivate the option Contiguous (ill.100).

The magic wand enables you to select image areas with similar colors based on the very pixel you click with it – you can decide just how similar it should be via the Tolerance value you enter in the Options palette.

With a colored background whose hue isn´t present in the image area you want to clip, the lowest possible value of 1 is suitable – the selected color range is thus very narrow.

With the Magic Wand tool, click onto the blue background – it seems properly selected.

To check, zoom in to the tree, and you´ll see that even pixels whose colors vary slightly are not included in the selection (ill.101; if it should look different to you, use the feature Refine Edge, and here Contract/Expand).

Zoom out again, and click onto the image's floor area – but hold down the Shift key, so the new selection will be added to the existing one (ill.102).

Back to the little task we´ve given ourselves. You want to clip the tree, what use is the background selection?

Now, you could delete it, but then the tree would be isolated.

It´s more elegant to invert the selection, then you´ve selected your tree instead of the background, and can transport it to a new layer, which has the advantage that your background is kept.

This inversion would also be practical if you wanted to correct the tree's luminance, or simply color it.

So, select Inverse (Select menu, ill.103), now the tree is selected instead of the background –

102

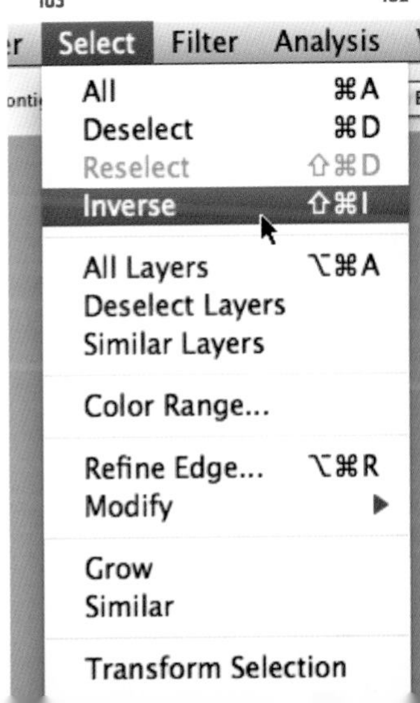

103

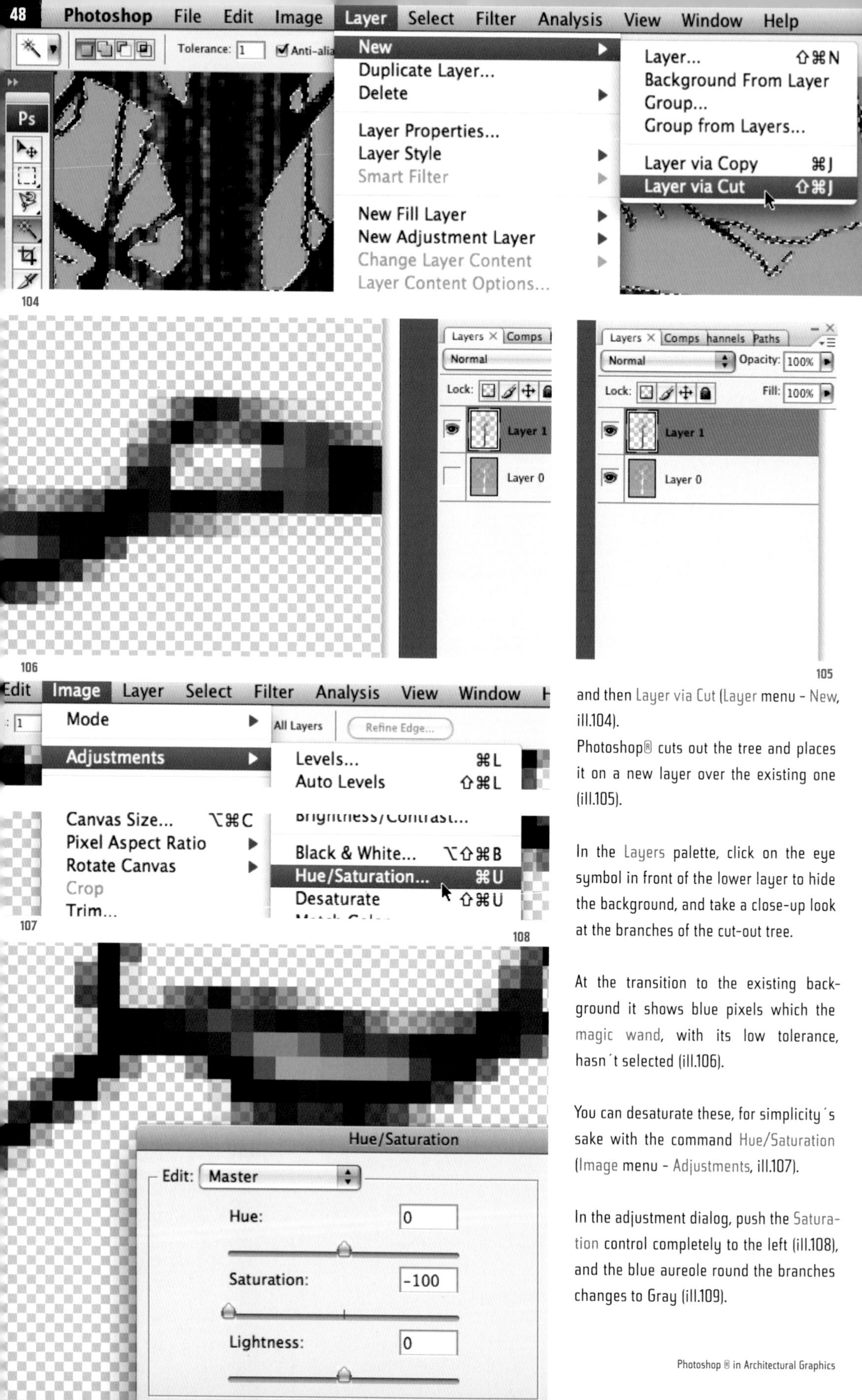

104

106

105

107

108

and then Layer via Cut (Layer menu - New, ill.104).

Photoshop® cuts out the tree and places it on a new layer over the existing one (ill.105).

In the Layers palette, click on the eye symbol in front of the lower layer to hide the background, and take a close-up look at the branches of the cut-out tree.

At the transition to the existing background it shows blue pixels which the magic wand, with its low tolerance, hasn´t selected (ill.106).

You can desaturate these, for simplicity´s sake with the command Hue/Saturation (Image menu - Adjustments, ill.107).

In the adjustment dialog, push the Saturation control completely to the left (ill.108), and the blue aureole round the branches changes to Gray (ill.109).

109

111

110

Hide the upper layer, and reveal the lower one.
Zoom in anywhere at the clipping edge, and you´ll see that you really have cut out your tree completely (ill.110).

Remember the shortcuts for the three selection tool types we´ve discussed: M for the Marquee tool, L for the lasso, W for the magic wand - or Shift-M, L or W respectively, to select within the particular group.

Just as important is the shortcut for deselecting: CTRL-D.

Ok, so much for the selection tools offered in the Tool bar. There are a lot more possibilities of selecting something, but they don´t work simply with a tool like the ones described above.

In the following chapters we´ll get familiar with some of them.

To conclude, I´d like to confront you with the mask subject, with whose help you can hide image areas on a layer, or limit the effect of an adjustment layer on parts of the layer.

Open the file 02_clouds_internet.jpg (ill.111), which comes from www.wolkenatlas.de.

I´d like to show you how to modify this image using layers creatively.

For an example, let's assign it a color gradient, with the blue fading upwards into red.
To do this, we need a second layer showing the image in red, and a cross fade between the two layers.

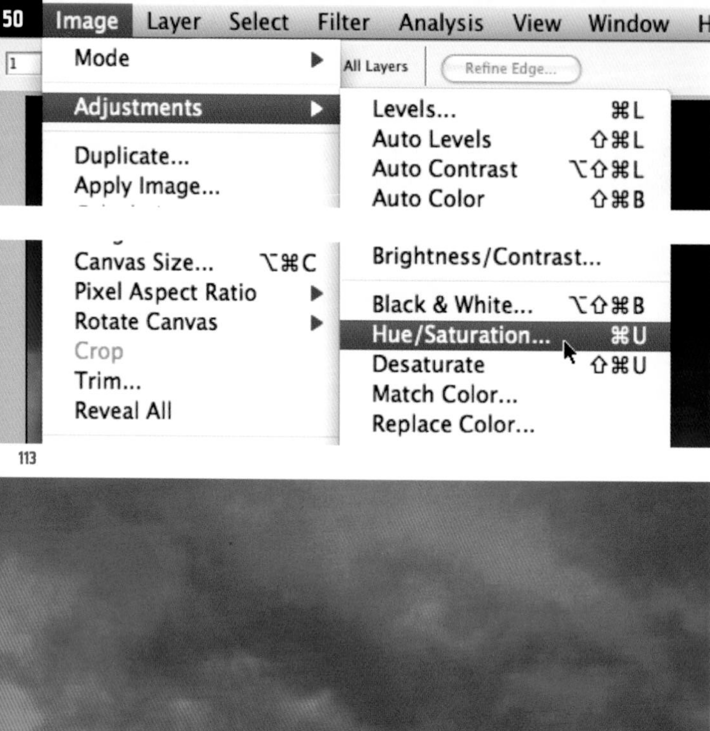

113

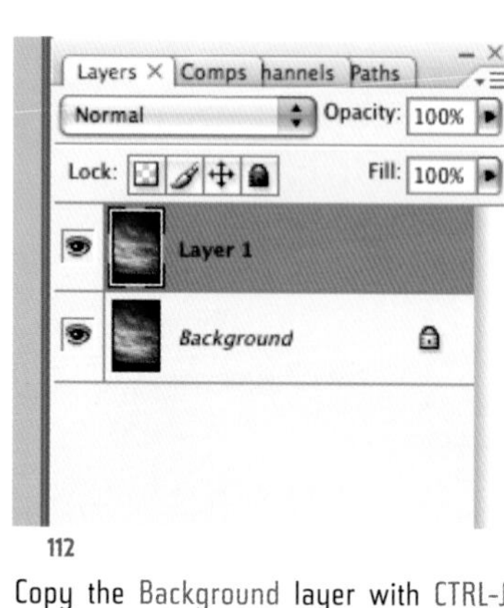

112

Copy the Background layer with CTRL-J (ill.112). You´ll now change its color, and then crossfade the two layers (the one with the original colors and the one with the altered ones) into each other via a layer mask.

The upper layer is active – select the adjustment command Hue/Saturation from the Image menu (ill.113).

In the adjustment dialog which opens, move the Hue control (for Edit, Master is selected,

meaning that you will change all image pixels, not only those from a specified color range, ill.114).

As you can see, I´ve set the control to the value +135.

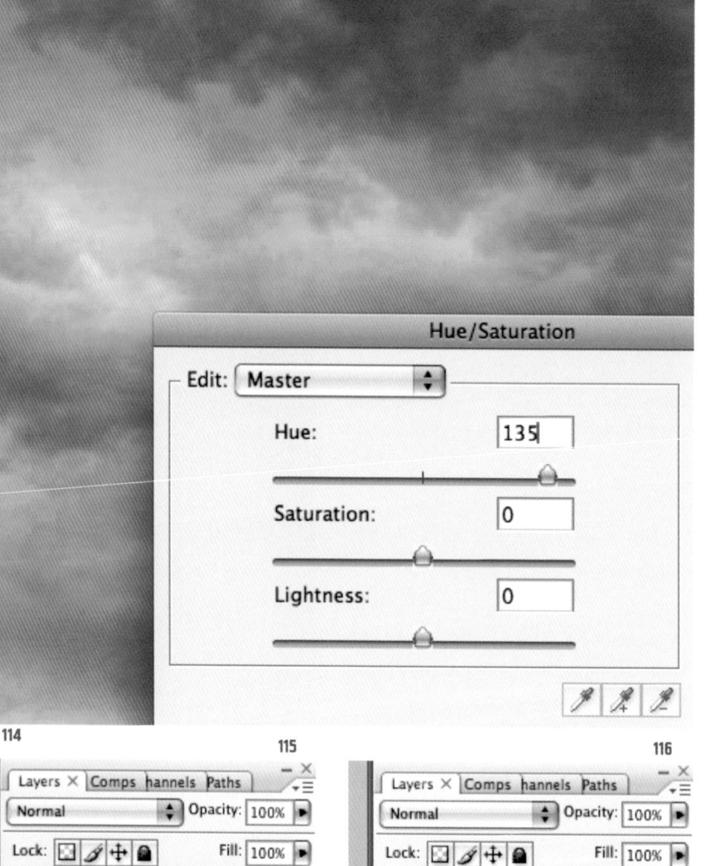

114

115

116

Now it´s time to insert a mask. We´ll assign it to the upper layer, to hide parts of it's image contents and vice versa make the corresponding areas of the underlying layer visible again.

Make sure the upper layer is activated, and click on the small circular button on the bottom frame of the Layers palette. This corresponds to the command Layer – Layer mask – Reveal all (ill.115).

In the Layers palette, beside the miniature of the upper image layer, you´ll see a further icon in the form of a white rectangle. It´s the symbol of your new layer

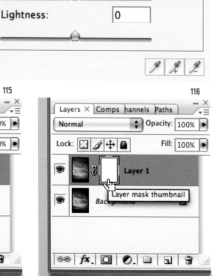

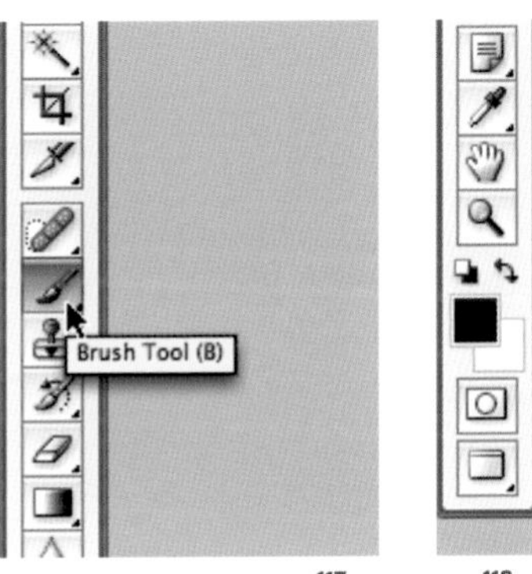

117 118

119

mask, empty right now (=white) indicating the layer is not yet masked, or to put it differently, the empty mask still leaves all of the upper layer visible (ill.116).

Ensure that this mask miniature is activated, which is indicated by its doubled frame.

You can now paint in the mask with Gray and Black – everything not white in the mask is more or less faded out, depending on the Gray shade.
What´s black in the mask is completely faded out.

Grab the Brush tool (B, ill.117) and make Black the foreground color (D, or D and X, ill.118).

Paint around with it in your image; since the mask is activated, you don´t see black dots in the image, but your lower layer revealed in the overpainted parts (ill.119).

In the mask miniature of the Layers palette you see, very small, what you´ve just painted. (ill.120).

I think the basic principles of layer masking have become clear by now.

To refine the masking effect, you´ll now replace what you´ve just painted by a Black-and-White gradient, to achieve the desired cross-fade between the lower and upper layers.

Select the Gradient tool (G, ill.121) and click on the small gradient miniature above in the Options palette, to choose the desired color range (ill.122).

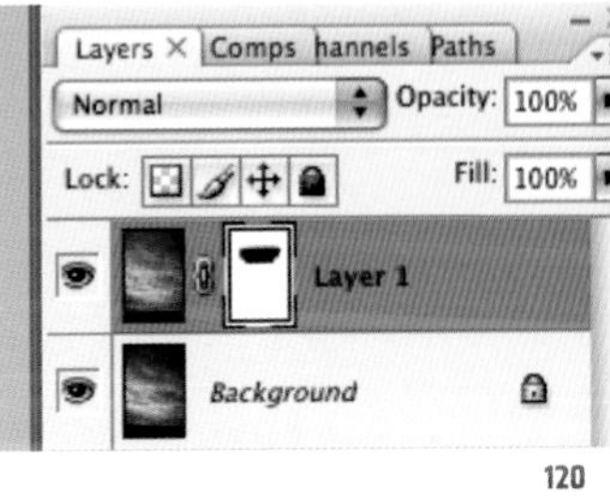

120

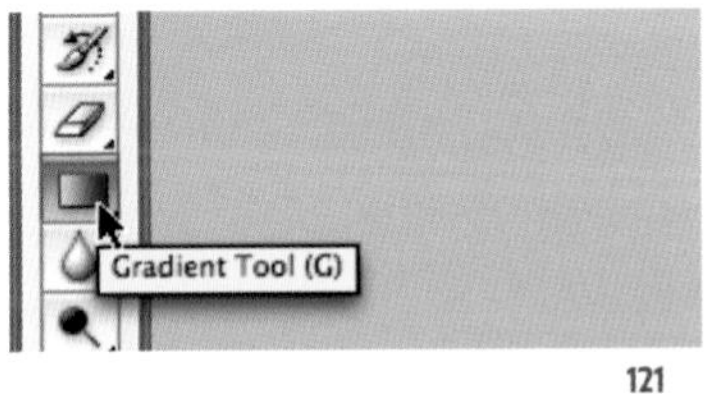

121

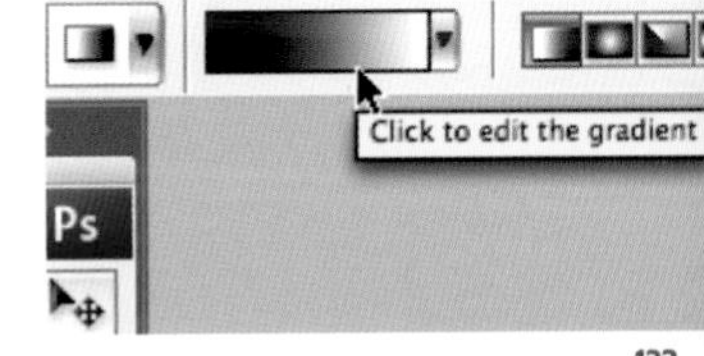

122

123

In the window that opens, click on Black, White in the array of Presets (ill.123). Confirm with OK.

Also make sure that in the Options palette the Linear Gradient is selected; it should be checked anyway as default (ill.124). For safety´s sake, check again in the Layers palette whether the mask is still activated for editing. If necessary, click again on its miniature (ill.125).

124

125

126

Now draw a gradient over your image from bottom to top with the mouse held down (you can hold down the Shift key, so that the movement is absolutely vertical (ill.126).

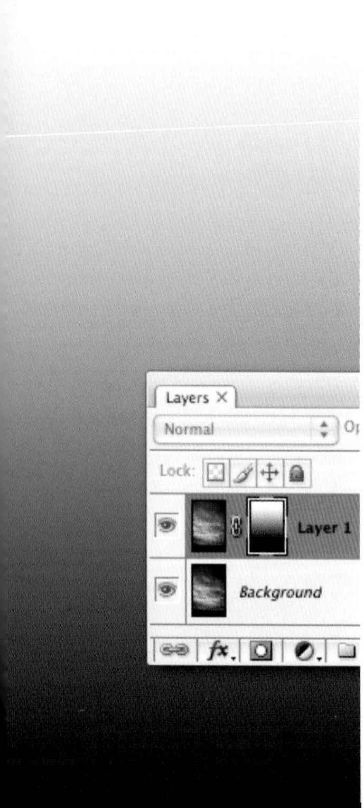

In the image you should now see a gradient-shaped transition between the lower and upper layers, and in the Layers palette the Black-and-White gradient in the mask miniature (ill.127).

If you wish to see the mask image large for once, just click on the mask miniature with the Alt key held down (ill.128). A click on the eye symbol of the masked layer shows you the actual image again.

A click on the mask miniature with pressed Shift key deactivates the mask (ill.129).

When using masks, always ensure that in a layer coming along with a mask, you can work on either the image or the mask, depending which of the two miniatures is selected.

Till now you can also move the two together, the image and the mask, as

127

128

129

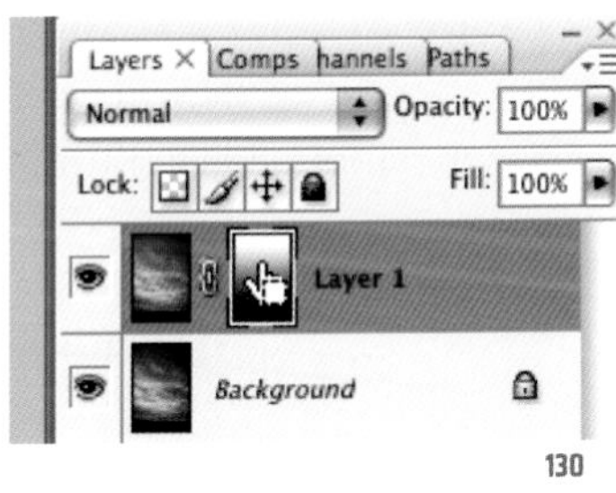

130

they´re linked with each other. If you want to avoid this, click on the small chain symbol between the miniatures to make it disappear, then they can be moved separately.

Finally, an important tip. You can load the mask content as a selection, by CTRL-clicking on the mask miniature (ill.130) - in the image you´ll see that only the upper half of the image seems to be selected (ill.131).

That´s deceptive; Photoshop® changes the grayscale image into a gradient selection, in which the black area of the mask isn´t selceted at all,the white area completely and the grayscale gradient in-between according to its Gray value between 0% (Black) and 100 % (White).

The fact that the ants only circle the upper half is because they are only shown for the part which is brighter than 50% Black. In this case, however, Photoshop® kindly draws this phenomenon to your attention.

So now you can be confident that you´re dealing with a gradient selection, even if it doesn´t look like one. You´ll now learn how you can achieve "instant"-masking of a new layer, with the help of such a hovering selection.

Let´s suppose you´d like to have it even darker in the upper image part, just select a Levels adjustment layer by clicking on the according button at the bottom frame of the Layers palette (ill.132).

131

In the adjustment dialog, push the right White control to the left, to the beginning of your histogram range (ill.133); push the Gray control to the right to shade the image (in my case 0.50).

While adjusting, you´ll notice that the change doesn´t affect the image evenly, but the way we want: strong at the top, weak at the bottom.
This is due to the mask, which was produced for this layer too, with the assistance of the selection just generated (ill.134).

By the way, you´ve learned something helpful on this occasion. Selections can be generated not only from channels but also from layer masks.

In the latter case, you don´t fetch your selection ants by the command Load Selection, but by a CTRL-click on the mask miniature.

132

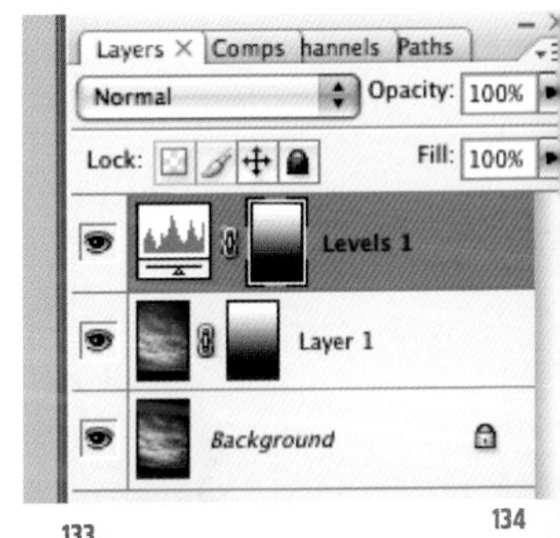

134

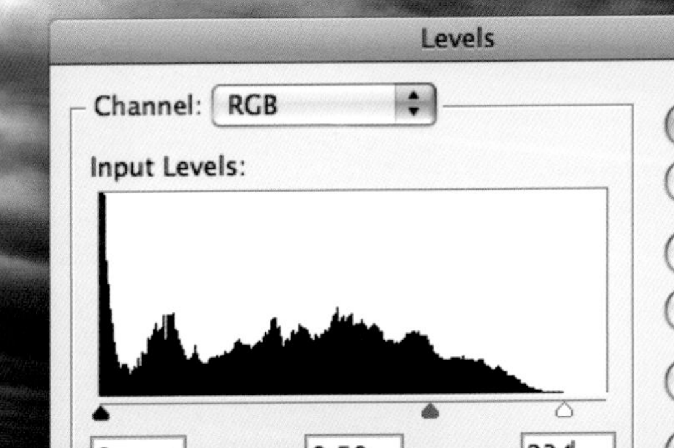

133

1

2

Edit Image Layer Select Filter Analysis View Window

Mode
Adjustments
Duplicate...
Apply Image...
Calculations...
Image Size... ⌥⌘I
Canvas Size... ⌥⌘C
Pixel Aspect Ratio
Rotate Canvas
Crop
Trim...
Reveal All
Variables
Apply Data Set...

Bitmap
Grayscale
Duotone
Indexed Color...
✓ RGB Color
CMYK Color
Lab Color
Multichannel
✓ 8 Bits/Channel
16 Bits/Channel
32 Bits/Channel
Color Table...

Dither

RGB and CMYK

At this point I´d like to bother you with a subject which might strike you as a bit prim, but which plays an important part in production.

Maybe you already know about the difference between **RGB** and CMYK color spaces, but there´s no harm in restating the significance and the technical pitfalls of color management, of course in a context which is digestible for architects and the likes of us.

You´ll find out things which go beyond this, and which can´t be described here, in the extensive specialist literature.

In general, images only to be presented on screen (e.g. in a PowerPoint presentation), can remain in the RGB space, while all images to be printed (whether from Photoshop® or embedded in a PDF), have finally to be converted into CMYK mode.
A professional printshop, or in my case a publisher, simply doesn´t accept RGB data, no matter how hidden.

The reason is simple: printer colors can only reproduce part of the color spectrum that is available on screens. So every printer driver converts the colors that reach beyond the CMYK space, on the basis of rather opaque criteria, into other, printable colors.
The result is often disappointing.

From the foregoing, you probably conclude that the RGB mode has advantages over the CMYK mode, which is correct, because many tools in Photoshop®, e.g. a lot of the filters, are only available for RGB images.

We´ll come to that later, but first let´s take a look at the whole thing in detail.

First of all, please start Photoshop® and open the file sophienhoefe.psd.

You´ll see a photo of the neon-tube installation in a passage of Berlin´s Sophienhoefe (a suite of courtyards in Sophienstrasse, ill.1).

Bear in mind that the image on your screen looks different than in the illustration, the reason being that the image for the bookprint had of course to be converted into CMYK.

This is now my dilemma during the whole chapter: I´m talking about RGB images, and in the corresponding illustrations you see CMYK. So take a very close look in each case at the illustration numbering, and orientate by what you see on your screen.

Now select the command Mode from the Image menu. As you´ll see, the image now appears in RGB mode (ill.2).

Now select CMYK Color at the same place (ill.3).
As you see, the colors of your image change.
If you press CTRL-Z a few times, you can alternate between RGB and CMYK, and recognize the diffences better. (That´s the advantage of Photoshop®´s speciality of being able to redo just one step with CTRL-Z). For the moment, leave the image in CMYK mode.

Open the Filter menu. You´ll see that some filters are displayed gray, meaning they´re not available in CMYK mode (ill.4).

There are more functions not available in CMYK mode, but as you normally stay in RGB mode till conversion, there´s no need to worry about that.

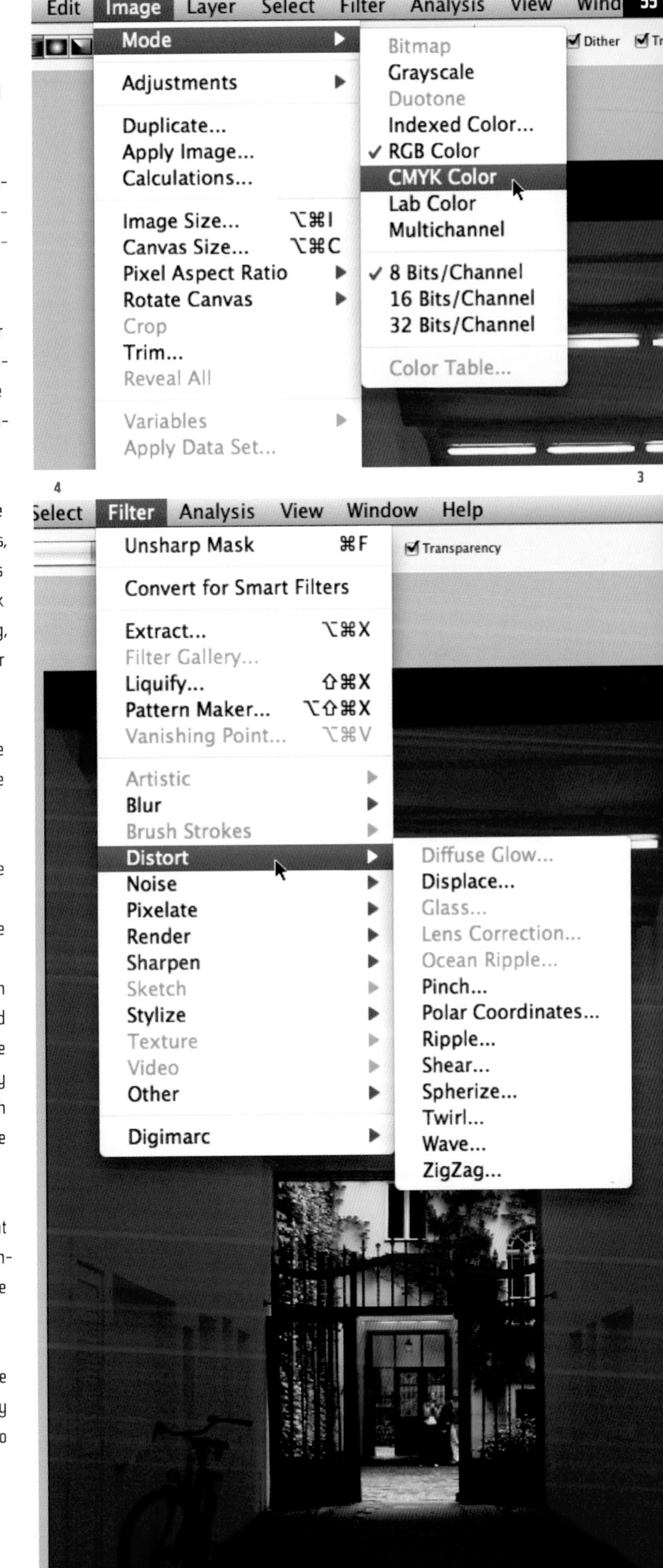

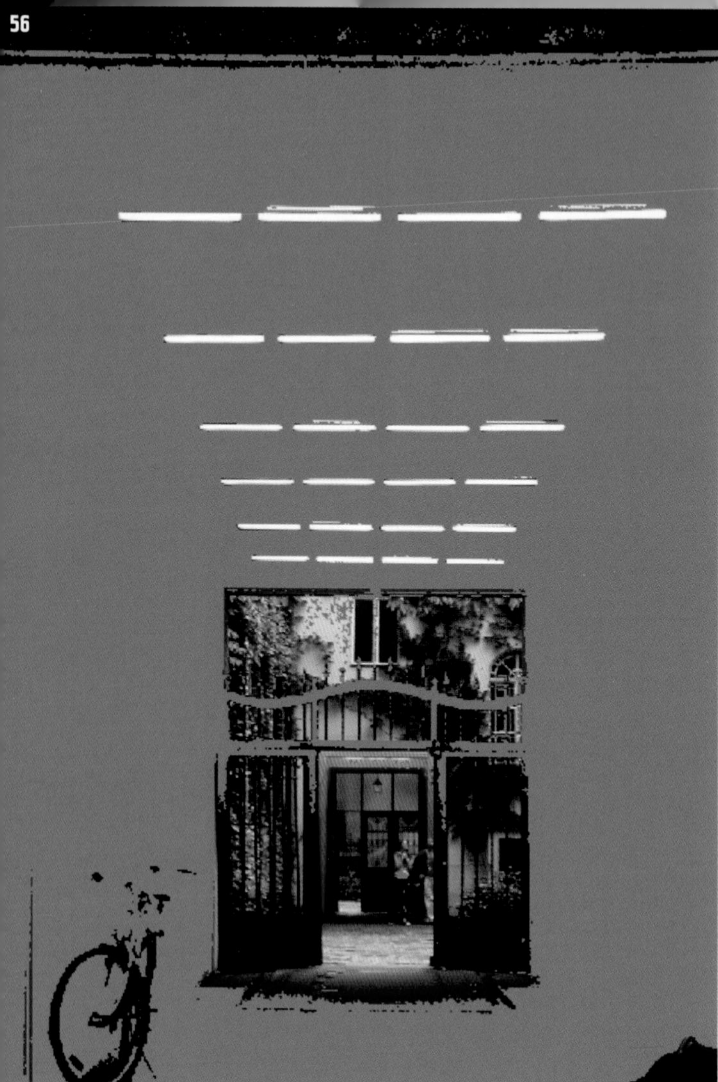

5

View Window Help
Proof Setup ▶
Proof Colors ⌘Y
Gamut Warning ⇧⌘Y
Pixel Aspect Ratio Correction
32-bit Preview Options...
Zoom In ⌘+
Zoom Out ⌘−
Fit on Screen ⌘0
Actual Pixels ⌥⌘0

6

Navigator	Histogram	Info	
R: 98		C: 74!	
G: 57		M: 74!	
B: 255		Y: 0!	
		K: 0!	
8-bit		8-bit	
X: 9,82		W:	
Y: 3,94		H:	

Doc: 8,85M/8,85M

Click and drag to move layer or selection constrained to 45 degree increments.

7

Switch back to RGB mode, either by simply pressing CTRL-Z or, if necessary, Alt-CTRL-Z (Step Backward) several times, and then select the command Gamut Warning from the View menu (ill.5). Photoshop® then marks in gray all the color areas that will change when converting to CMYK (ill.6).
You´ll notice that almost the whole image is affected, i.e. the whole area showing the shining blue.

Select the command again, to cancel the mark, then move your mouse cursor over the critical image areas, and check in the Info palette (ill.7). If you can see an exclamation mark behind a CMYK value, the RGB value which you currently are on with your cursor can´t be depicted directly in CMYK.

Now´s the right time to confront you with a bit of theory about the color spaces (you can read in Wikipedia about things that interest you beyond my scant information).

RGB stands for Red, Green and Blue, the three primary colors, from which all the colors in the RGB color scheme are composed. A mix of equal proportions produces a neutral Gray; if all three colors are represented 100%, the mix appears as White; if none of the three colors is present, Black is created.

The RGB space represents the additive light color space, i.e. the spectrum that in particular sunlight produces (in whose White all colors are of course also contained), to a slightly lesser extent artificial lighting, and especially our screens.

CMYK stands for Cyan, Magenta, Yellow and Key (Key corresponds to Black). This color space basically represents the color spectrum which can be depicted in process-color printing (offset printing, but more often inkjet print).

It´s based on the subtractive color scheme, in which the colors are created because some of the colors contained in light are swallowed by ink or printing color; thus visible color appears a relict after certain parts of the light color spectrum have been absorbed.

The color composition proceeds in exactly the opposite way from the RGB color scheme: Cyan,
Magenta, Yellow and Key (Black) together, all with 100% color application, produce Black. If, on the other hand, no colors are

applied (application 0%), the white paper remains visible. (Which means you ought to realize that the lightest color of the print is determined by the paper color).

Theoretically, Black isn´t necessary in this color scheme, but in practice it is, because with it the color application can be reduced. Instead of producing a Black with 100% Cyan, Magenta and Yellow respectively (which would mean three color layers with a total of 300% color amount), the 3 can be replaced by 100% Black.

Usually the color hue's gray component is in particular replaced by a corresponding black component (the so called achromatic setup).

The RGB scheme can, depending on the device (screen, camera chip, scanner sensor), appear in a differentially large color range, and this is exactly how the CMYK scheme behaves, where the size of the color space depends on the output device and the kind of paper.

That´s why there are so called color profiles, little add-on files in which corresponding device colors are allocated to the original colors, in tabular form.

Without my going into this subject in detail, it should be borne in mind that the CMYK mode always depicts fewer colors than the RGB scheme.

You can see this graphically in ill.8, where in a diagram the CMYK is depicted in front of the RGB space (gray). (What you see in the illustration is the window of Apple's ColorSync utility).

8

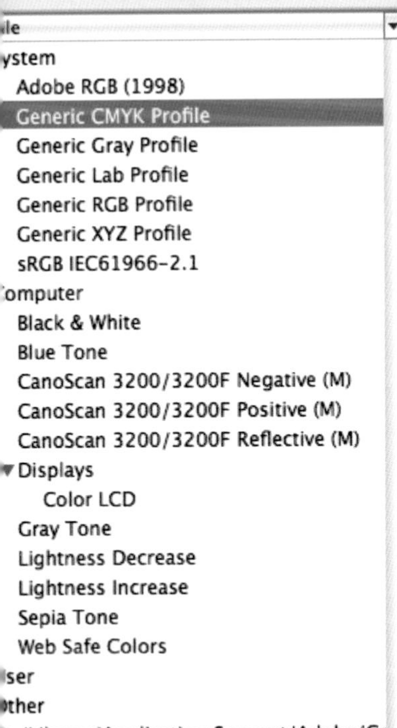

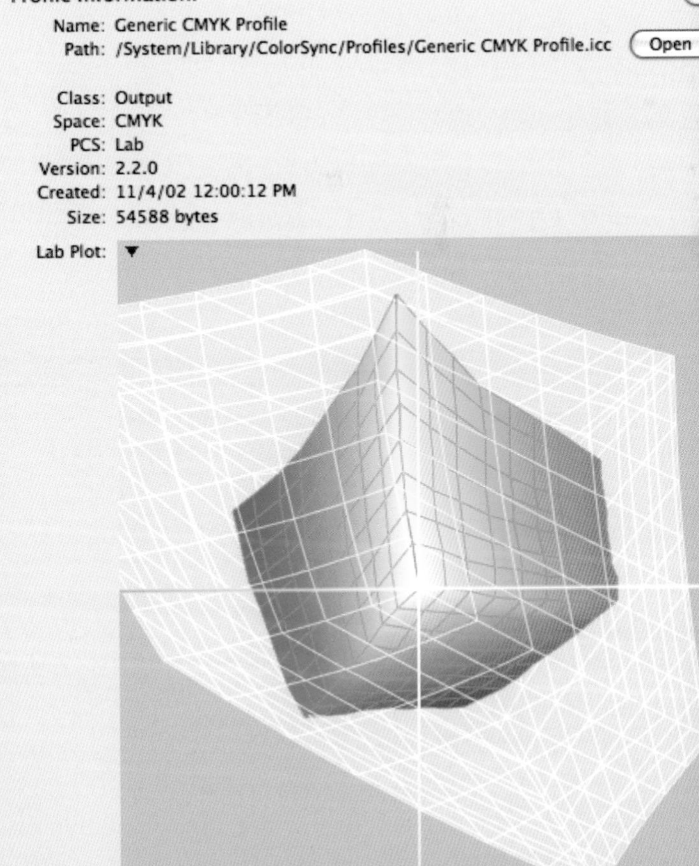

9

So, what does this mean for our work in Photoshop®? It means the whole range of tools which Photoshop® has ready for image processing is only available to you in RGB mode, and that means you should keep every image as long as possible in it.

Not until printing is planned (or more generally, not until processing is finished and the file is integrated in a print layout), should you convert the image into CMYK (quite simply like you did before, via change of mode).

This action is also termed separation, because the color information is divided into the four process colors. For this, in offset printing, say four printing plates are created. Mind you that separation always follows criteria which you can influence by deciding on a specific CMYK space.

Back to our image. Let´s assume you now wish to insert it into a print layout, by placing it, for example, in an InDesign® file. Your aim is to preserve the shining Blue of your RGB image as good as possible.

Make sure your image is still (or again) in RGB mode. If necessary, check Image - Mode, or press the F key till you see the image in the "normal" window display, then the mode information will be displayed in the window title (ill.9). If you can still see the gray mask of your gamut warning, deactivate it (View menu).

Now select the command Proof Colors from the same menu (ill.10). This feature provides a preview of your image's CMYK layout, while in fact the image remains in RGB mode.

The result of the simulated separation (CMYK-conversion) is, as you´ve just seen, deflating. In what follows, the idea is to make the best of it. A first step is to fine-tune the adjustments on whose basis the image is converted.

To do this select Proof Setup - Custom from the View menu (ill.11). A window opens in which you can carry out adjustments (ill.12).

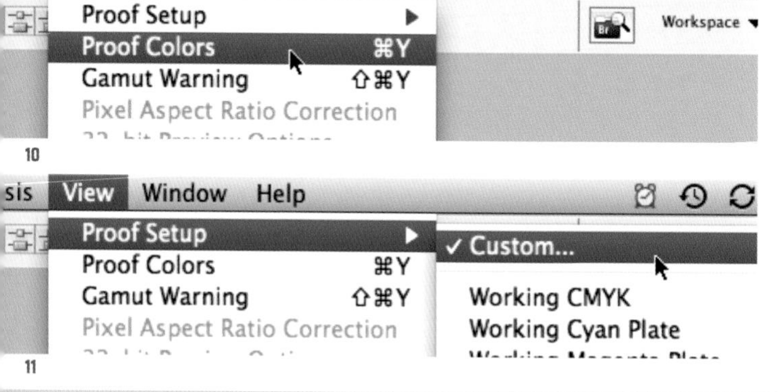

10

11

12

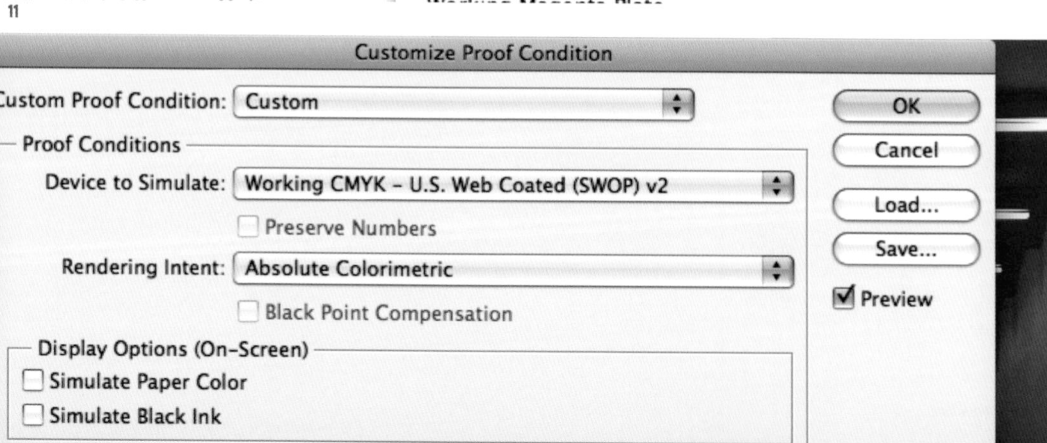

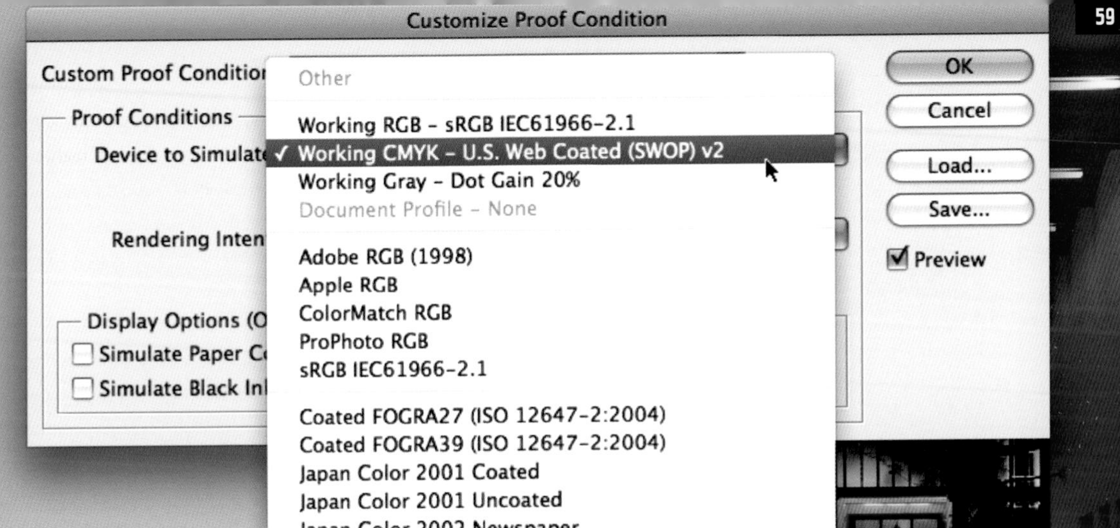

13

For the Device to Simulate option you´ll find a generous choice of color space alternatives, both for RGB and for CMYK (ill.13). Select (or leave in place) Working CMYK – U.S. Web Coated (SWOP) v2.

As you´ll see in your list, the color space types for your printer are also depicted (if you´ve already installed one or more). Take a cool look at the result of these options.

The Rendering Intent option is important, as here you decide on the basis of which criteria Photoshop® converts the RGB colors which are not presentable with CMYK. Test the four options; I´ve left it at Absolute Colorimetric, because here the result seems to me the most differentiated (ill.14). If you´re interested in the intent options but don´t really understand the words Perceptual, Saturation, Relative and Absolute Colorimetric, look them up in Photoshop® Help. I´m content here with deciding on the basis of visual impression.

If you´d like to see how the whole thing will look in print, set a check at the option Simulate Paper Color.
The image becomes generally grayer, which indicates you have to set the colors a bit stronger to compensate (ill.15).

Confirm with OK and press CTRL-Y to switch off the digital proof. You now see the image in the RGB original again; the difference between RGB and CMYK is, with this image, quite serious.

Activate the digital proof again (CTRL-Y).

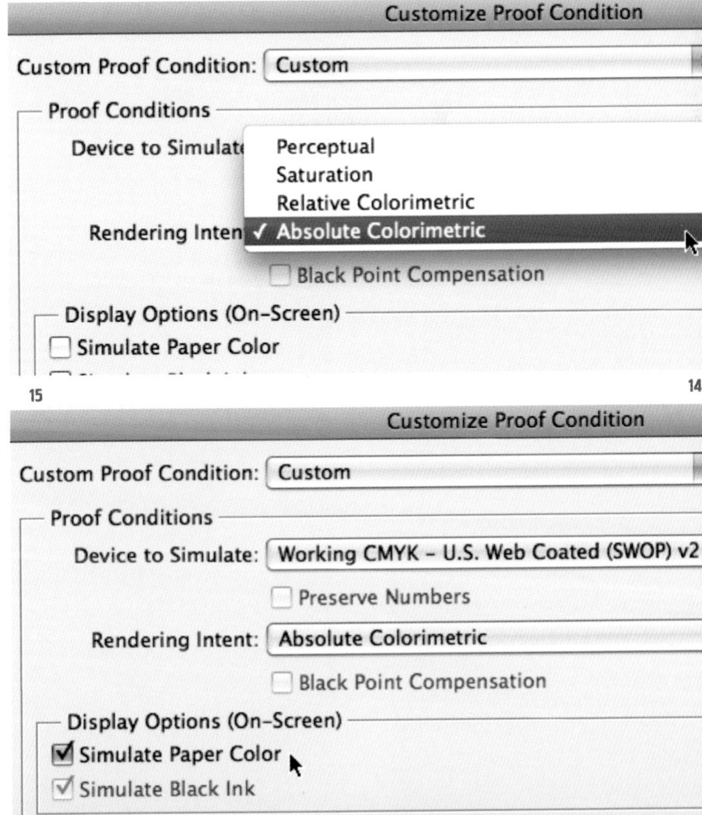

14

15

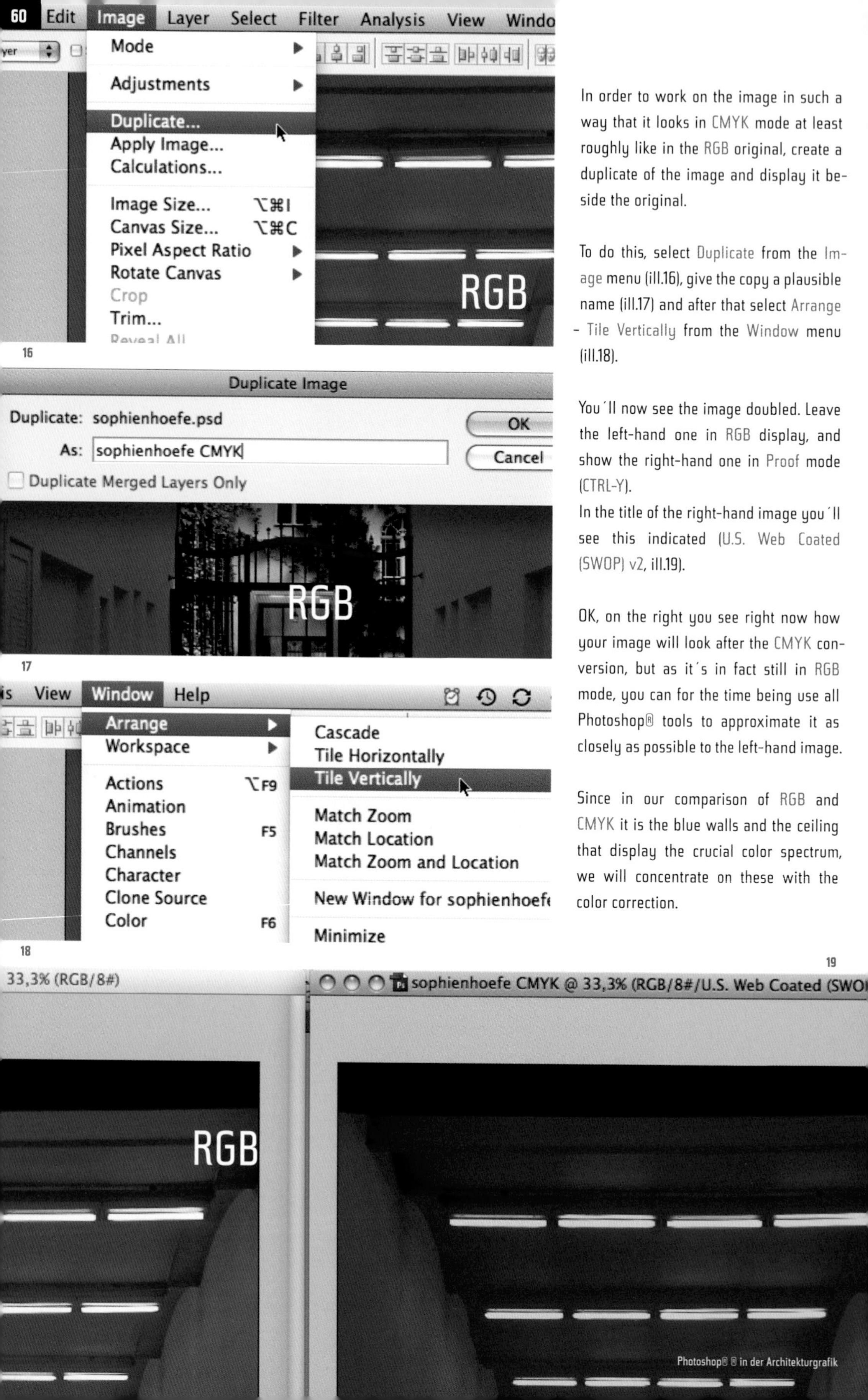

16

17

18

19

In order to work on the image in such a way that it looks in CMYK mode at least roughly like in the RGB original, create a duplicate of the image and display it beside the original.

To do this, select Duplicate from the Image menu (ill.16), give the copy a plausible name (ill.17) and after that select Arrange - Tile Vertically from the Window menu (ill.18).

You´ll now see the image doubled. Leave the left-hand one in RGB display, and show the right-hand one in Proof mode (CTRL-Y).
In the title of the right-hand image you´ll see this indicated (U.S. Web Coated (SWOP) v2, ill.19).

OK, on the right you see right now how your image will look after the CMYK conversion, but as it´s in fact still in RGB mode, you can for the time being use all Photoshop® tools to approximate it as closely as possible to the left-hand image.

Since in our comparison of RGB and CMYK it is the blue walls and the ceiling that display the crucial color spectrum, we will concentrate on these with the color correction.

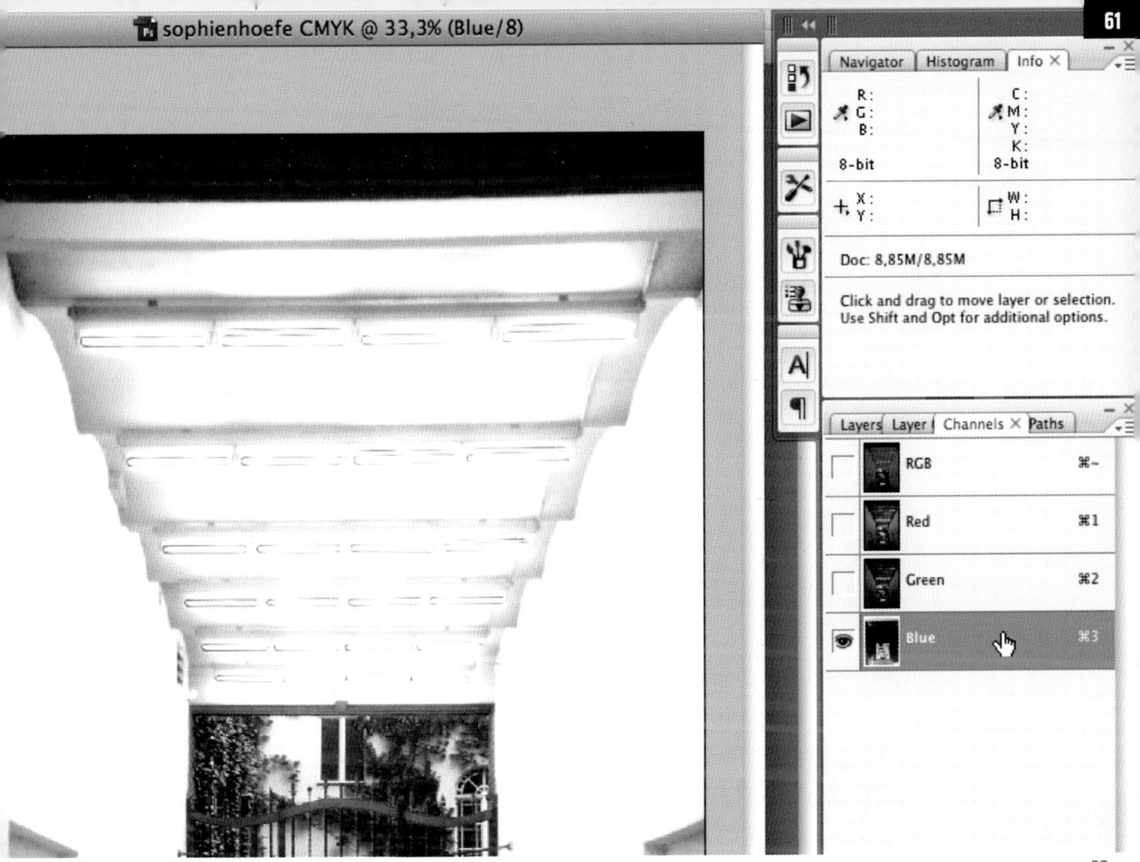

20

Thus, it makes sense to first apply a mask to keep the rest of the image from being modified. For selection, we choose a view which shows the greatest possible contrast between the walls plus ceiling and the rest of the image: we find it in the Blue Channel (ill.20).

Press F twice to display the image isolated on a gray background (this is the equivalent of the menu command View - Screen Mode - Full Screen Mode With Menu Bar).

This way you can navigate best when creating the selection. First select the ground and the court background with the Polygonal Lasso (tool selection via L, maybe several times with Shift-L, till the polygonal lasso is available). Ignore the bicycle on the left for the moment.

When your selection is done, select the foremost part of the ceiling too; in the original image it´s dark.

Hold down the Shift key for the first click of your additional selection, so that your selection already created in the lower part of the image doesn´t disappear.

Now you´re finished with your mask, apart from the bicycle (ill.21; here the selection is displayed in mask mode via the Q-key).

21

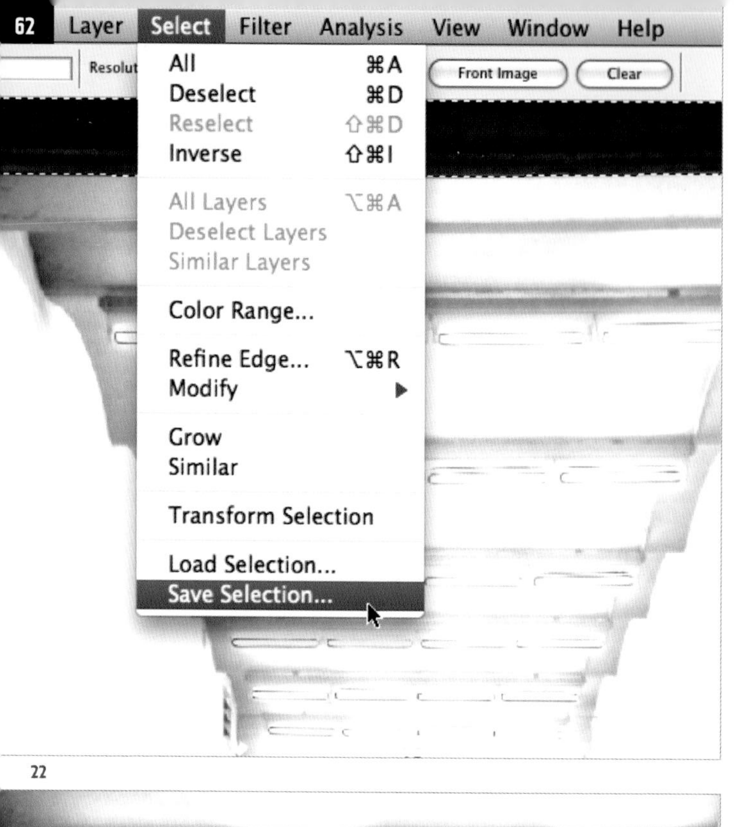

22

Save Selection
Destination
Document: sophienhoefe CMYK
Channel: New
Name: court
Operation
New Channel
OK
Cancel

23

Now please save this selection, so that you can concentrate on the bicycle. Should you also have activated the mask mode, press Q again, since you may only save a selection in "ant" mode.

Then choose Save Selection from the Select menu (ill.22), and in the adjustment dialog decide for some traceable name for the selection saved (e.g. court, ill.23). Confirm with OK, and deselect via CTRL-D.

Now to the bicycle. Select it as well, and then add this new selection to the one saved.

For selecting the bike, the Quick Selection tool is rather suitable (it´s hidden behind the Magic Wand tool we already know). With the Shift key held down, press W till this tool is available (ill.24), and up in the Options palette set the brush size to 6 pixels width (ill.25).

Zoom in on the bicycle (CTRL-Space) and begin "painting" over it with the tooltip of your Quick Selection tool.

It doesn´t matter if you hit areas which don´t belong to it; press the Alt key from time to time, and paint over or click on these places so that they´re removed from the selection again (you remember

25

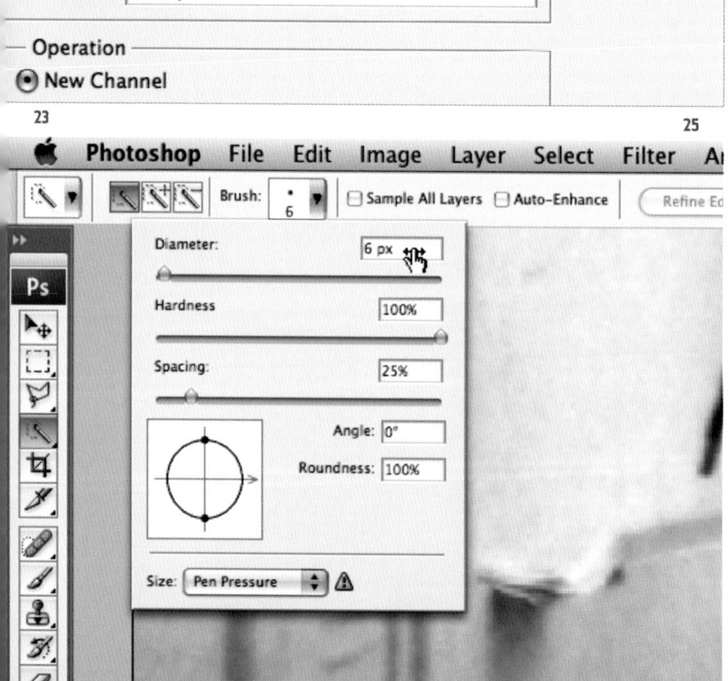

24

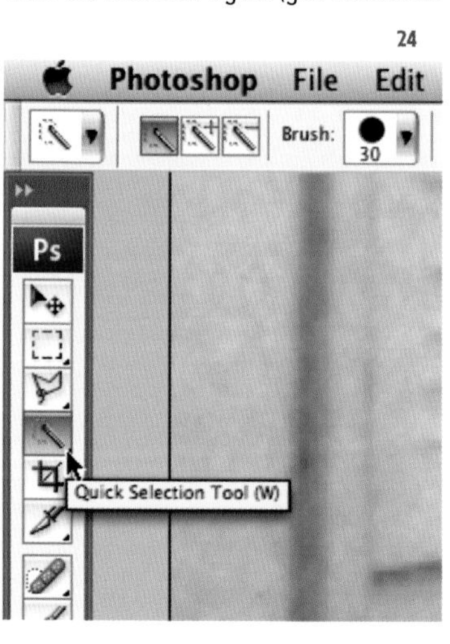

from Chapter 02 that you can remove selection areas with the Alt key held down). If you feel that you can´t improve your selection with the Quick Selection tool any more, activate the mask mode (Q-key, ill.26).

The places which don´t yet look perfect (e.g. the lower part of the front tire), can now be repaired with the Brush tool.

Select this (B, ill.27), and think about what you want to do now.
If you want to remove surplus selection areas, you have to apply mask color, i.e. paint with Black (which automatically turns Red in mask mode).

So make sure the foreground color is Black (to play safe, press the D-key to set the foreground and background color to Black-and White, then the X-key till Black is the foreground color (ill.28).

Set the brush size so that you can work well with it on the filigree bicycle, and paint over the places which are not to be selected.

If you´d like to extend the selection at other places, press X so that White is the foreground color, and paint over the corresponding places.

26

You may wish to change the brush size eventually, so remember the apt keyboard shortcuts (see chapter 2).

When you´re finished, leave mask mode (Q) so you can see the ants selection again, and save the bicycle selection.

Choose Save Selection again from the Select menu, choose the Channel you created before (in my case court) and check the Operation Add to Channel (ill.29). Confirm with OK.

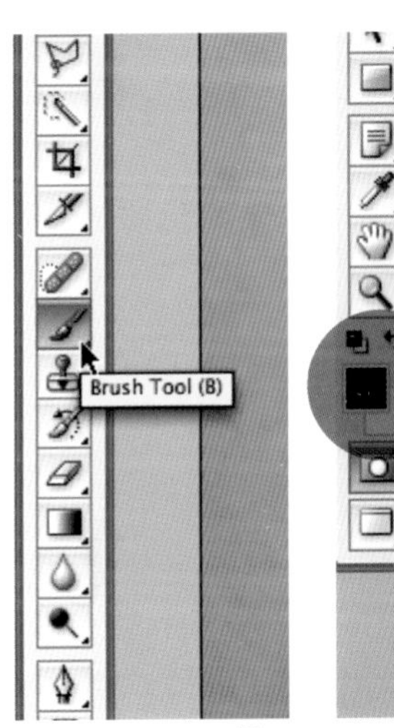

27

28

29

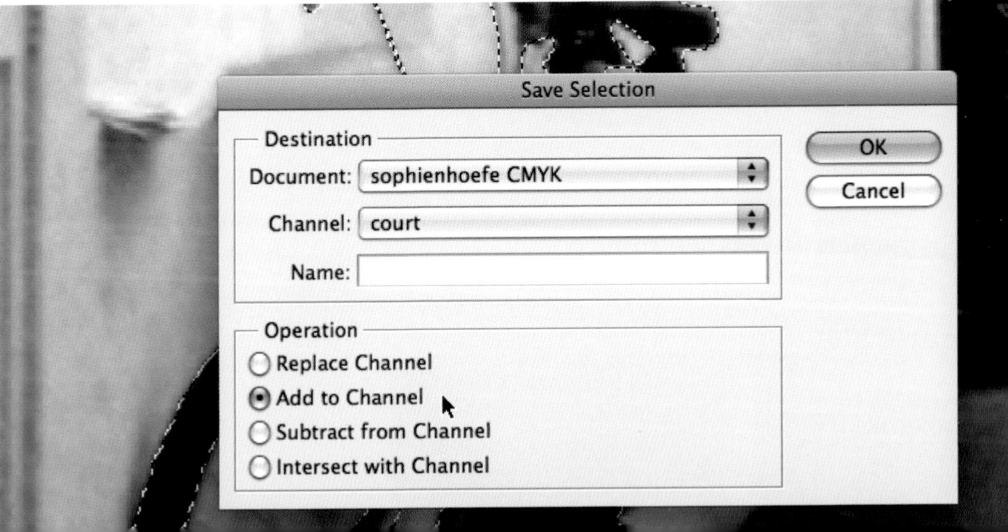

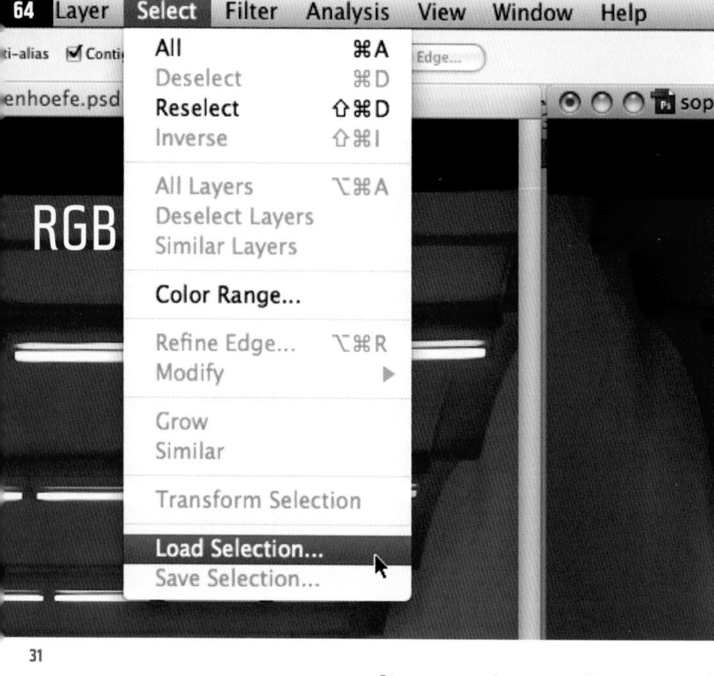

31

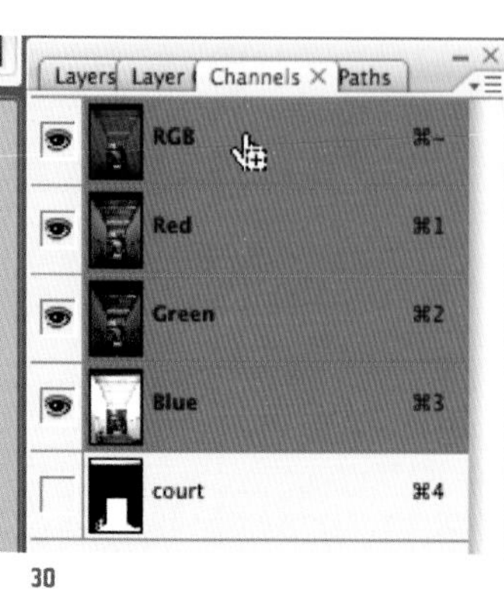

30

Since now, at last, you will want to work on the image, you must by all means reactivate the normal channel display.
Click on the RGB channel in the Channels palette to do this (ill.30).

By the way, at the very bottom you see your selection displayed as a new channel. But now switch to the Layers palette again.

You want to improve the color balance of the image under CMYK conditions so much that it corresponds to that of the RGB image - be aware that a 1:1-restoration won´t be possible. You saw a good while ago that the RGB values of the blue areas are not presentable with CMYK colors (ill.7).

Depending how good your printer is (if it can, for example, print with more than four colors), you can at best achieve an approximation to the original state; in our case a standardized profile for process printing is selected as a CMYK profile, for safety´s sake (see Proof Setup, ill.12).

It makes sense anyway that you learn about the color which predominates in the critical areas, so you can perform accurate adjustments.

One possibility for this is the Info palette; if you move the mouse cursor over the image, you´ll see that, of the RGB values, the Blue almost everywhere shows the maximum value.
So it´s probably sensible to concentrate on that during the adjustment.

Reload your selection (Selection - Load Selection, ill.31), select the Channel court (ill.32), and check the option Invert.
You´ll see that now the whole critical area is selected.

Now play around a bit with the adjustment tool Hue/Saturation, using it via an adjustment layer.

32

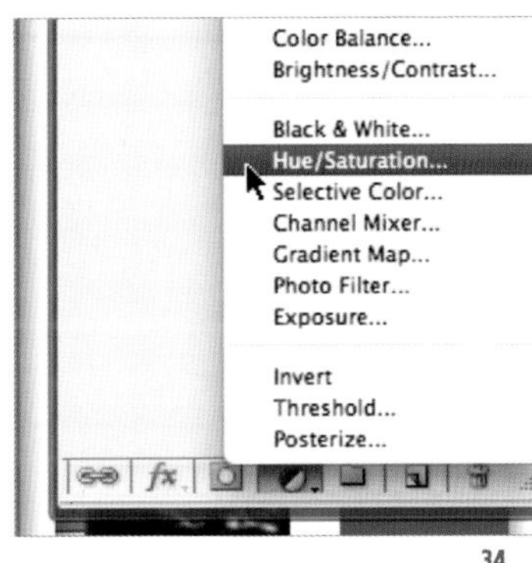

34

At the bottom frame of the Layers palette, click on the corresponding button (ill.33) and select from the popup menu the corresponding entry (ill.34).

In the adjustment dialog, select the Blues from the Edit pulldown, and move the Saturation control fully to the left (ill.35).

As you see, the critical image area turns completely Gray, which confirms our previous observation that Blue is the dominant color in the area, and also that we´re dealing almost continually with pure Blue (without a Gray percentage), since if you pull the Saturation control fully to the right, the image hardly changes (ill.36).

33

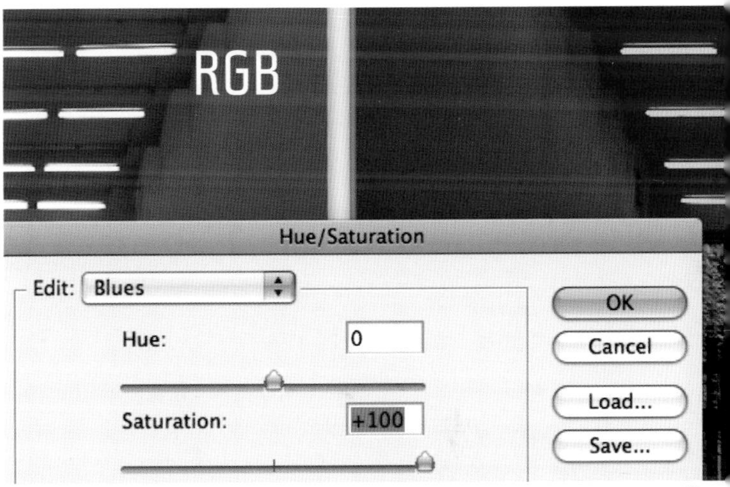

36

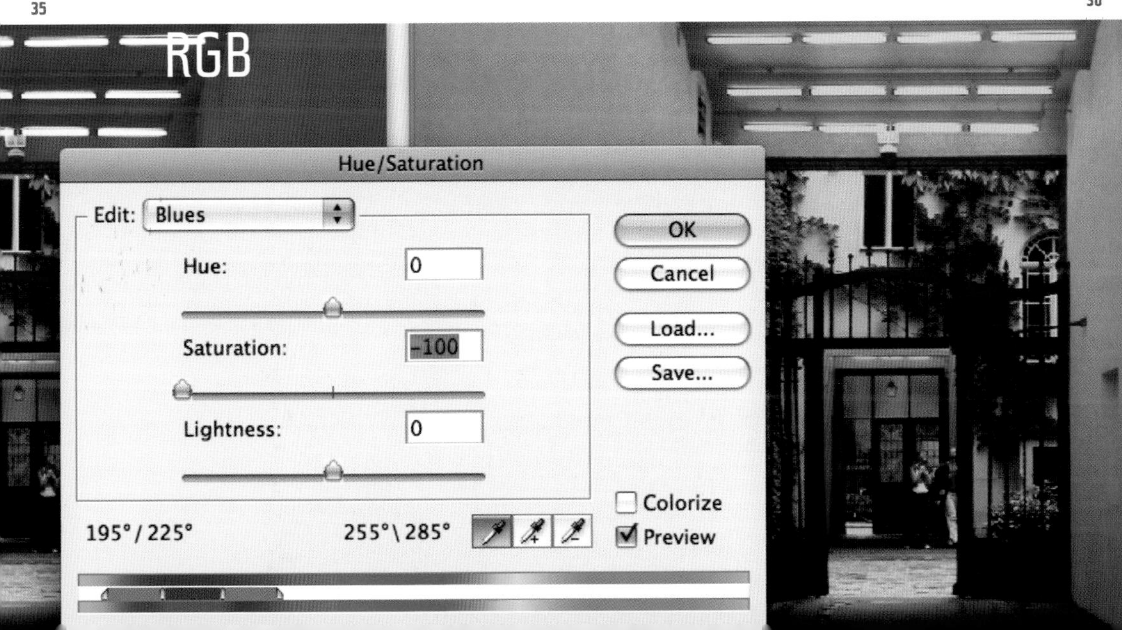

35

38

37

So it looks as if we can´t get any further at this point, and even a levels adjustment doesn´t really help, as we´ll now see.

Discard the Hue/Saturation adjustment (your selection being still active), and pick the Levels tool from the same adjustment layer menu of the Layers palette (ill.37).

Here too, concentrate on the blue content (Channel: Blue, ill.38), move the Black control to the right (e.g. to the value 75), and the mean value control to the left to brighten the Blue (say, to 2).

With this adjustment too, no similarity will come up with your shining RGB original.
Play around at leisure in the other channels Green and Red too (ill.39 and 40).

It just doesn´t work this way, so cancel the Levels adjustment as well.

You probably guess that there´s no way you can keep the color of the RGB image with the CMYK conversion.

39

40

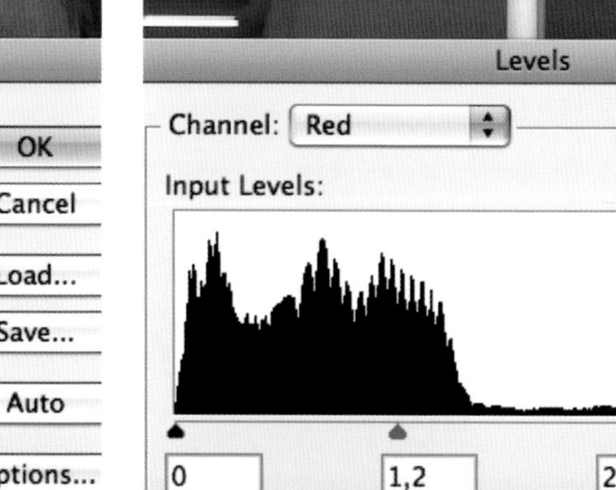

All you can do is achieve a variant which resembles the original image.

To get at least a little more range, change to the 32-Bits mode (Image – Mode – 32Bits/Channel, ill.41).

If you have another adjustment layer in the file, apart from the Background layer, a question comes from Photoshop®; answer it with Don't Flatten (ill.42).

You have to reactivate the CMYK Simulation (View – Proof Colors).

Pick the adjustment layer Hue/Saturation again – as you see in the corresponding popup menu of the Layers palette, the number of adjustment layers available in 32-Bits mode is strictly limited (ill.43).

To edit, select the Blues again and move the Saturation control fully to the right.

You´ll see a great change (ill.44). Obviously the color range in 32-Bits mode is clearly bigger.

Before we go on, I´d first like to acquaint you with some basic facts about the so called color depth.

41

42

43

44

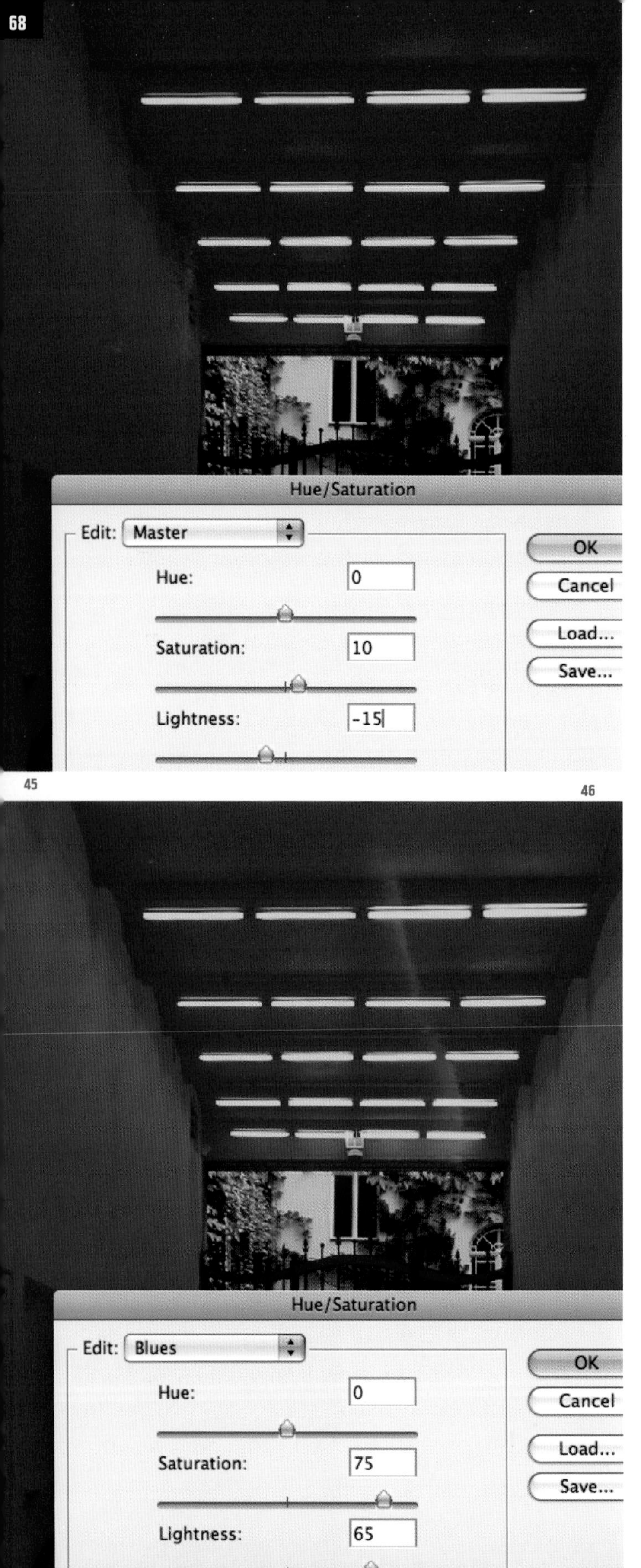

45

46

Normally the images you work with in Photoshop® have an information depth of 8 Bits per pixel (with grayscale images) or 24 bits per pixel (with RGB images, each of the three color channels has a depth of 8 bits).

This means that a grayscale image pixel can display (28=) 256 different values, an RGB pixel on the other hand (224=) 16,777,216. That sounds a lot, but it by no means covers the dynamic color spectrum of reality.

However, it is of course sensible to work with such a reduced color range in digital image processing, as this way the disk usage of your image files ranges within manageable limits.

The 32-Bits mode is not normal; it helps to create and work on so called HDR images, whose main feature is a significantly higher color range. At 32 bits color depth per channel a pixel can have, in one color channel alone, (232=) 4,294,967,296 brightness values, the complete color spectrum in 32-bits mode thus allows 4,294,967,296 x 4,294,967,296 x 4,294,967,296 different values.

Fortunately, the disk usage only quadruples this way (8 : 32). However, not all the filters work (despite RGB mode), and as we´ve already seen, not all the adjustment tools.

The attempt to adapt the colors of the digitally proofed RGB image in your sample image in such a way that it still resembles to some extent the original image in its bright RGB colors, was frustrating. Your freedom of action with 8 bits color depth is in this case all too restricted. A trip to the 32-Bits space should give us a few more possibilities to freshen up the image´s colors, and when we´re finished,

47

we can of course reconvert it again to the familiar 8-Bits space.

Back to our image. Click on the layers miniature of the Hue/Saturation adjustment layer you´ve just created, to reach your adjustments (if the window isn´t still open anyway).

Make sure that at the top of the window Master is selected for editing (so you can access the complete color spectrum of the image, ill.45), and set the following values: Saturation:10, Lightness:-15, leave the Hue at 0.

Then for editing select the Blues (the dominant color in our problem area, ill.46), and here set the Saturation to 75 and the Lightness to 65, again leaving the Hue value at 0.

Confirm your Hue/Saturation adjustment with OK, and continue with a Levels adjustment (ill.47).

In the adjustment dialog, deal first with the whole RGB channel (ill.48), setting the Black value to 5 and the White value to 165.

In the Red channel, change the mean value to 0.70 and the White value to 215 (ill.49). In the Green channel only adjust the White value, to 215 (ill.50).

Leave the Blue channel unchanged, and finally confirm the Levels adjustment with OK.

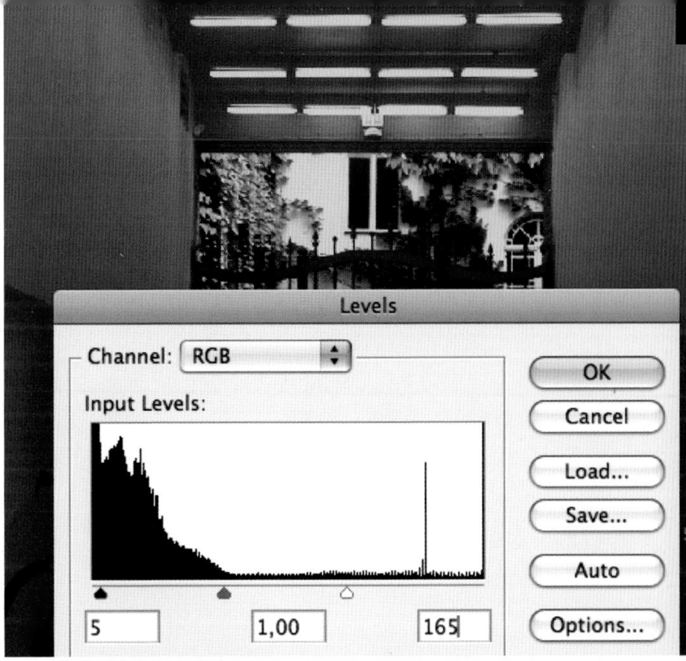

51

48

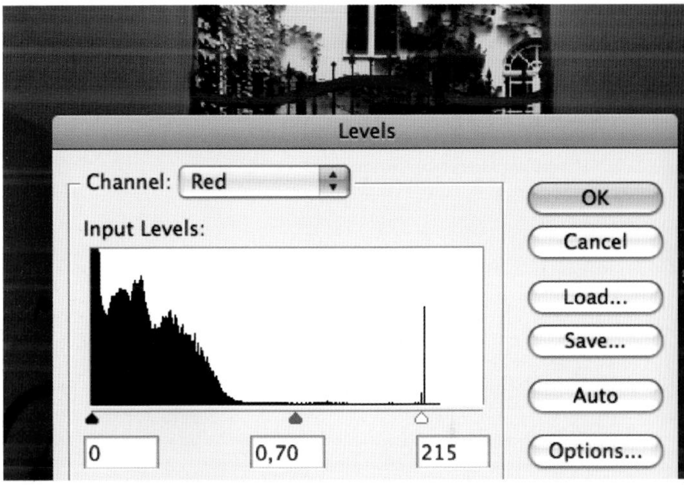

52

50

49

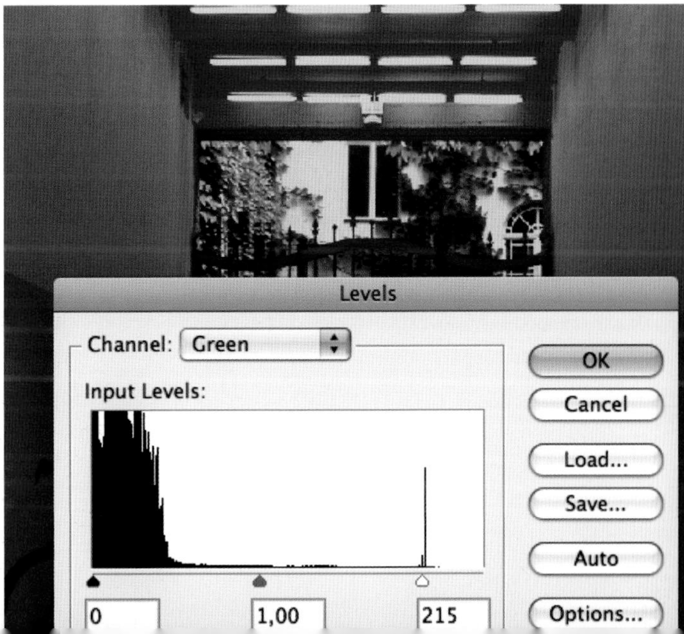

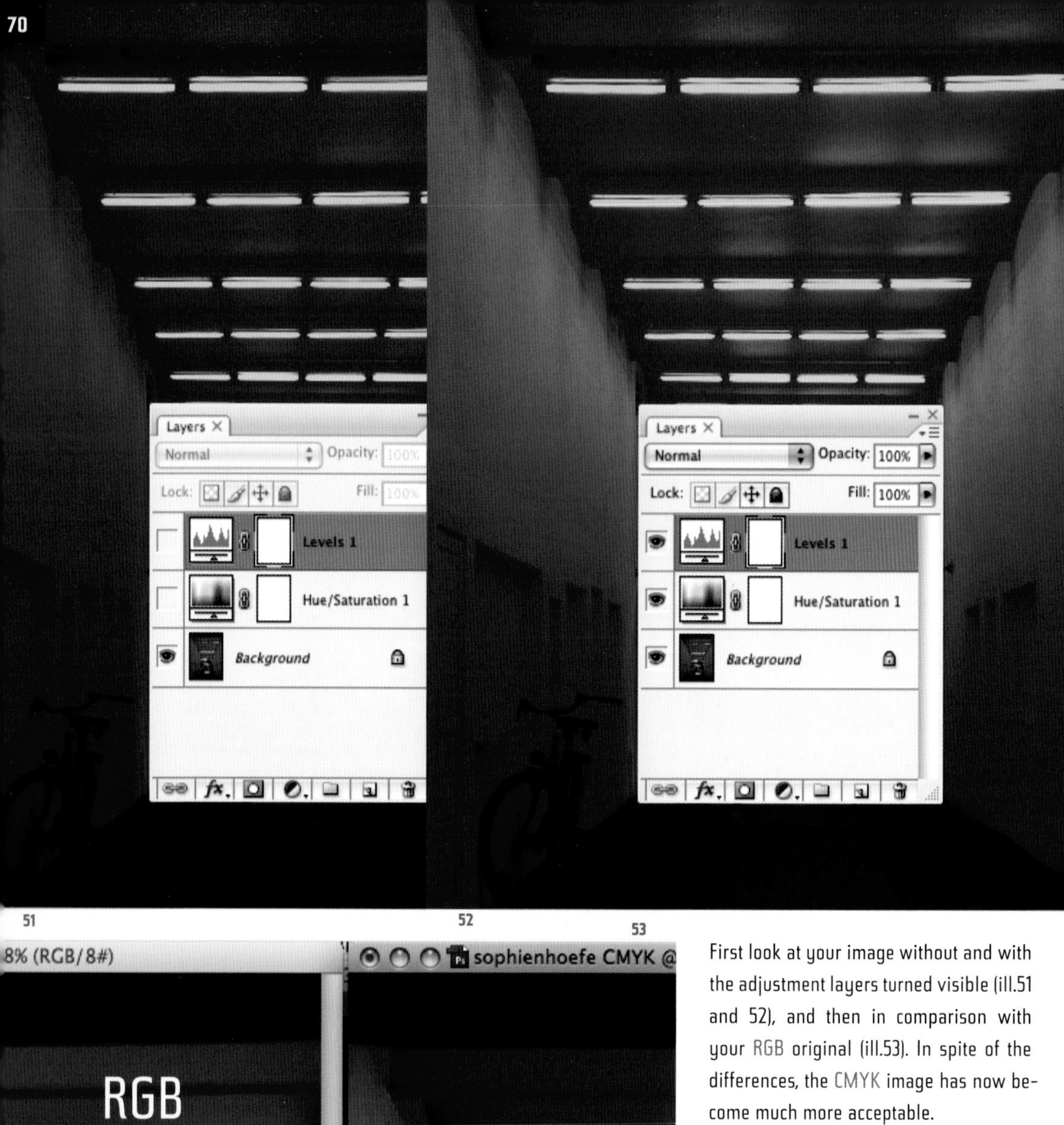

51

52

53

8% (RGB/8#)

sophienhoefe CMYK @

RGB

First look at your image without and with the adjustment layers turned visible (ill.51 and 52), and then in comparison with your RGB original (ill.53). In spite of the differences, the CMYK image has now become much more acceptable.

Earlier in the chapter we created a selection for the image area which isn´t dominated by the tricky Blues. We used it as a mask for the adjustment experiments we carried out in 8-Bits mode.
Now, working in 32-Bits mode, we´ve ignored the fact that the floor and the court image area have nothing to do with the Blue adaptation, but it´s time to take a look at this.
Click on your Hue/Saturation adjustment layer in the Layers palette, so that it´s activated and its layer mask can be worked on (ill.54).

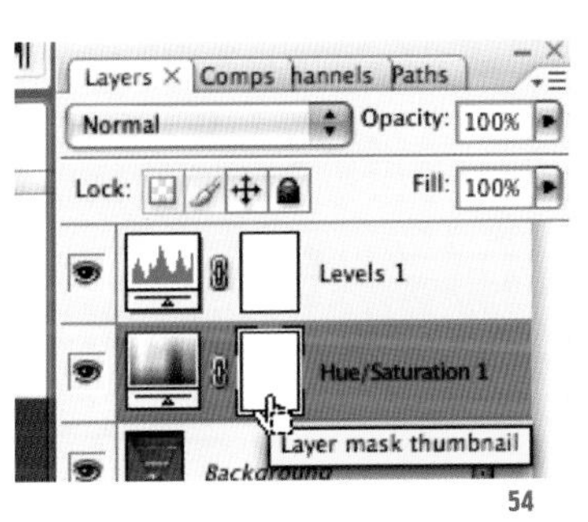

54

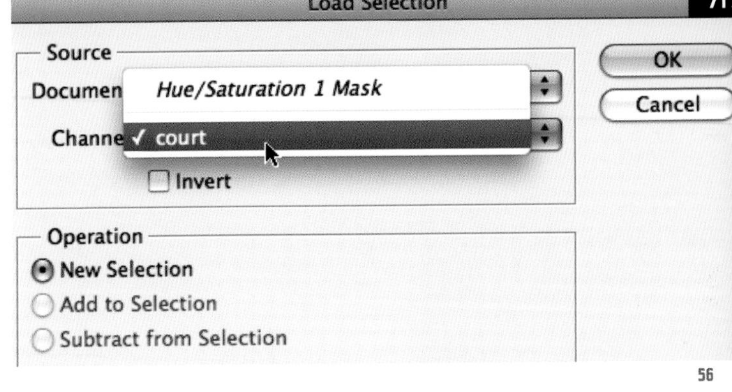

56

Load your saved selection (Selection – Load Selection – Channel:court, ill.55 and 56).

Now you can fill this with Black. To be on the safe side for this, press Shift-Backspace and select Black as the fill color (Use: Black). Confirm with OK.

In the Layers palette now select the Levels adjustment layer (ill.57; you´ll already see the new mask miniature of the underlying adjustment layer).

The selection is still active, or you choose Reselect from the Select menu – on the mask of the Levels layer, fill the selection area with Black too, again with Shift-Backspace.

Even the image areas which aren´t blue should undergo a Levels adjustment. Make sure that your
selection stands as before, and add a new Levels adjustment layer (this is automatically masked).

In the adjustment dialog, set for the RGB channel the mean value to 1.25 and the White value to 235 (ill.58). In the Red channel change the mean value to 0.90 and the White value to 220 (ill.59).

55

57

58

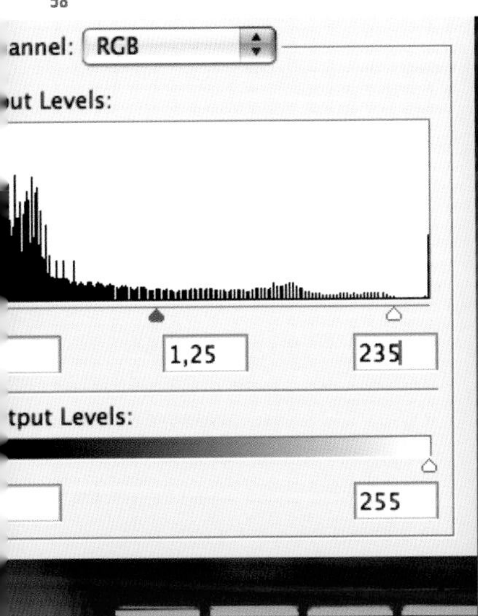

59

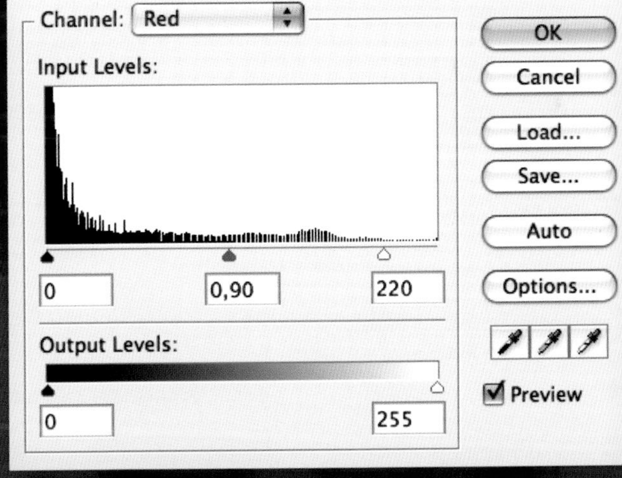

GB

61

62

63

64

60

In the Layers palette you´ll now see three adjustment layers with their mask miniatures (ill.60).

Our excursion into 32-Bits mode is now ended. To reconvert the image into an 8-Bits image, you first have to flatten the layers into one, otherwise unwanted exposure changes arise on converting. Select the corresponding command from the menu of the Layers palette (ill.61).

The conversion takes place quite disdainfully again in the Image menu (Mode - 8-Bits/Channel, ill.62). Answer the adjustment dialog with the default values (ill.63).

Now try out another filter: Diffuse Glow, which can be found among the Distort filters in the Filter menu (ill.64). But wait! Don´t just use it now on your only layer. After all, the image has already taken quite a lot of work.

Exit the filter, and copy your Background layer (CTRL-J).

To use your filter losslessly, turn the new layer in a so called Smart Object (right-click on the layer entry in the Layers palette - Convert to Smart Object, ill.65).

In the Layers palette you´ll see that your new layer has received a rather different icon (ill.66); you can now use filters on this without the image contents of the layer being affected.

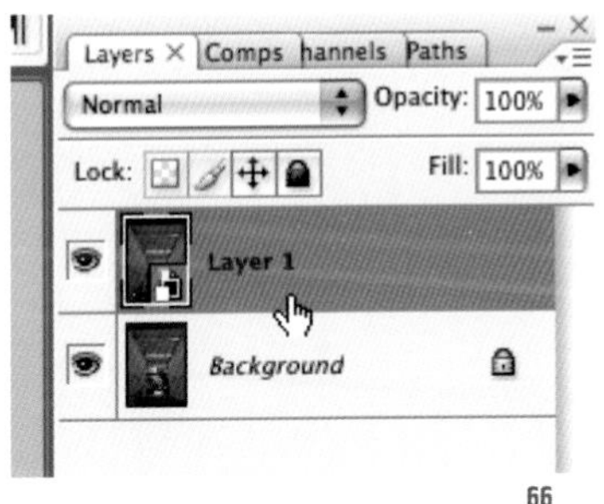

66

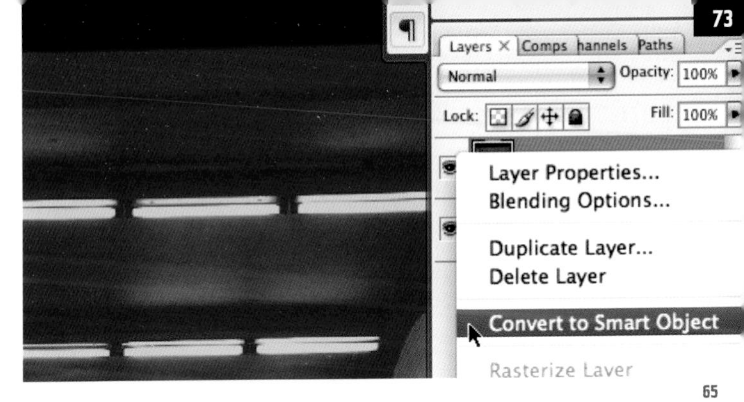

65

When preparing to use the filter Diffuse Glow, ensure that the background color is White.
This is most easily done by pressing the D key and if necessary the X key (ill.67).

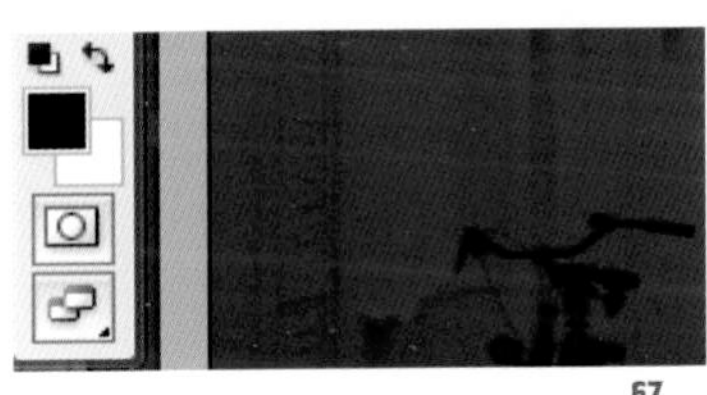

67

Now select the filter Diffuse Glow again. A sub-application opens, the so called Filter Gallery.
When you´ve got there, first press CTRL-0 to see your image in full (ill.68).

Then undertake the appropriate adjustments on the right: Graininess=0, Glow Amount=2, Clear Amount=16 (ill.69). Confirm with OK.

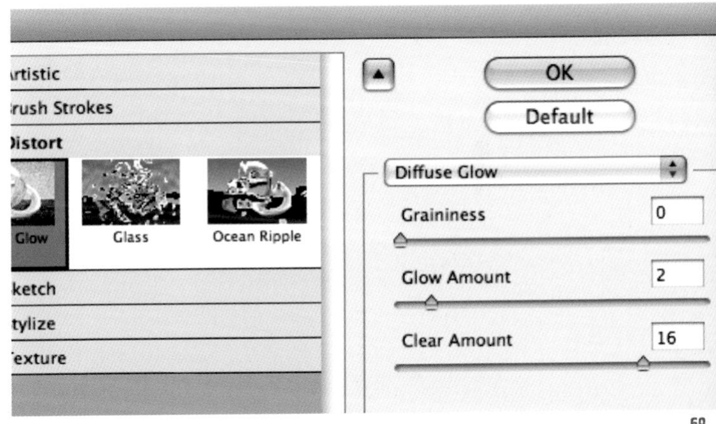

69

68

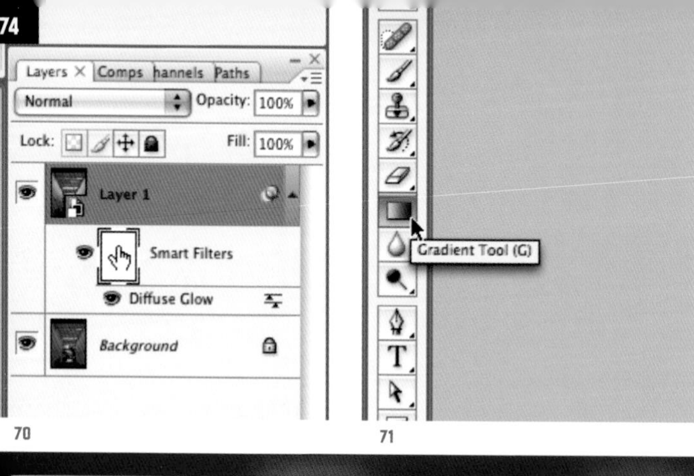

70

71

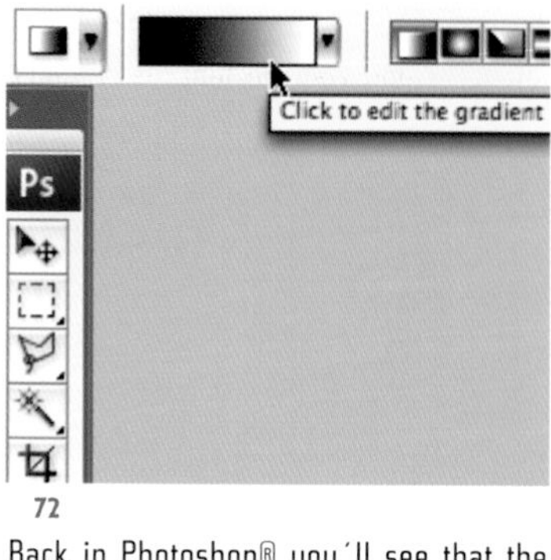

72

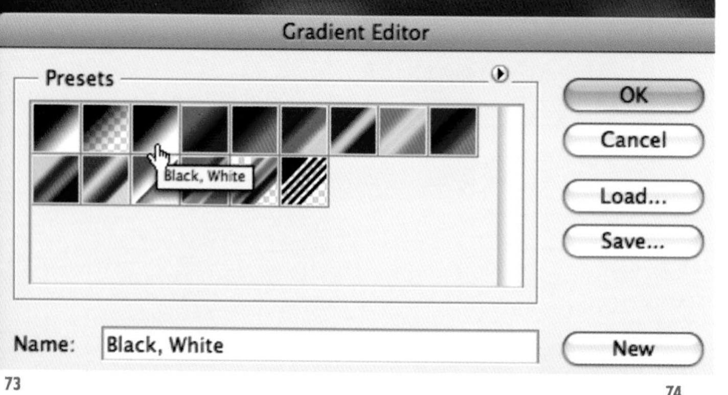

73

74

Back in Photoshop® you´ll see that the filter has greatly brightened your image, especially in the upper wall areas. If you wish to confine the filter effect to the lower image area, a gradient mask is available.

Look in the Layers palette; the filter has nestled itself like an adjustment layer beneath the Smart Object, and above it you can see an empty mask which you can use for your purposes (ill.70).

Click on its miniature, in order to insert a gradient; select the according tool (G, ill.71), and click up in the Options palette on the gradient icon (ill.72). From the gradient assortment, pick the Black, White gradient (ill.73). Confirm with OK.

Now, in your image, draw a vertical line from the top (just above the blue area) till near the bottom (ill.74). You see that the upper image area appears darker again; in the Layers palette the mask displays the gradient as a miniature (ill.75).

If you want to study the filter effect, hide and show the filter a few times, by

75

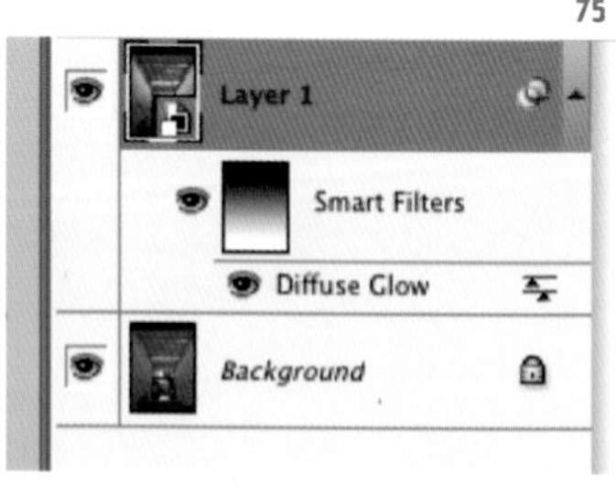

clicking on its eye symbol in the Layers palette. If you want to tune its settings, double-click on its entry, then the Filter Gallery opens again.

One detail is missing: the filter is only to affect the blue image area, not the rest. Here you can once again make use of your saved selection.

Load it (from the Select menu), and click again on the mask miniature of your filter in the Layers palette (which so far shows the gradient just created).

Press Shift-Backspace to select the fill color, decide for Black (it should still be selected from before), and confirm with OK.

Your mask miniature shows you that in addition to the gradient the selected area is black – so here the filter has no effect. If you want to see your mask as a real image, click on its miniature while pressing the Alt key (ill.76) – another Alt-click reveals your picture again.

The problem with a CMYK conversion only arises if you wish to use the image in a print layout.
Part of preparing printing is also to sharpen the image, which for simplicity´s sake you also do in your smart layer, though then the sharpening only affects the blue area.

Check that your Layer 1 is selected in the palette, and select from the Filter menu, section Sharpen, the filter Unsharp Mask (ill.77).

Set somewhat stronger values if you like, e.g. Amount=150 and Radius=2pixels (ill.78). If you click the preview on and off, you can already recognize the change, especially in the area of the window embrasures front-left. Confirm with OK, and the filter now also appears stacked in the Layers palette, directly over the filter Diffuse Glow.

So, that was it. Your image doesn´t look exactly like the RGB original, and that wasn´t to be expected.

However, not every image is so dominated by colors which are not depictable in CMYK.

For your own projects, allow by all means time for having to experiment a bit with the color adjustments before you´re satisfied.

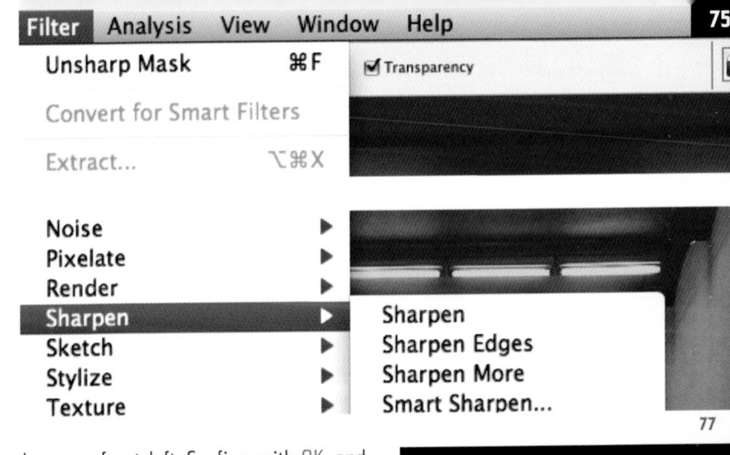

77

76

79

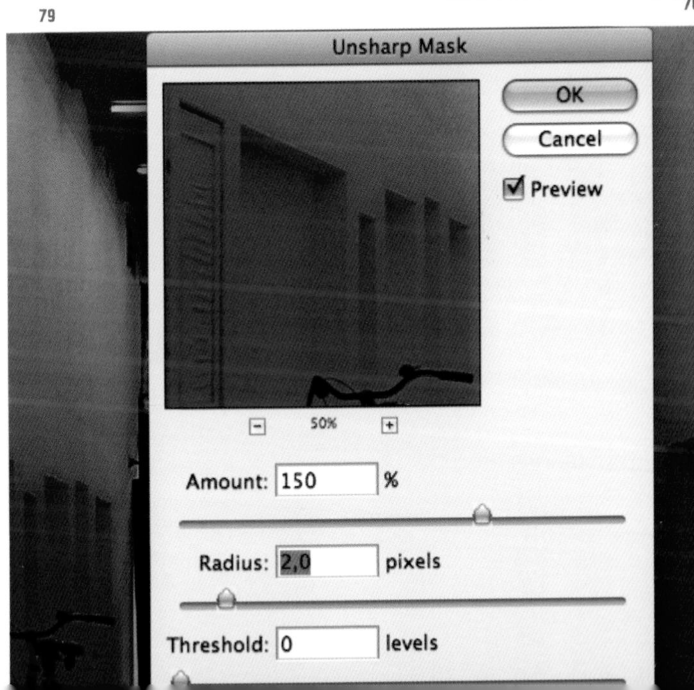

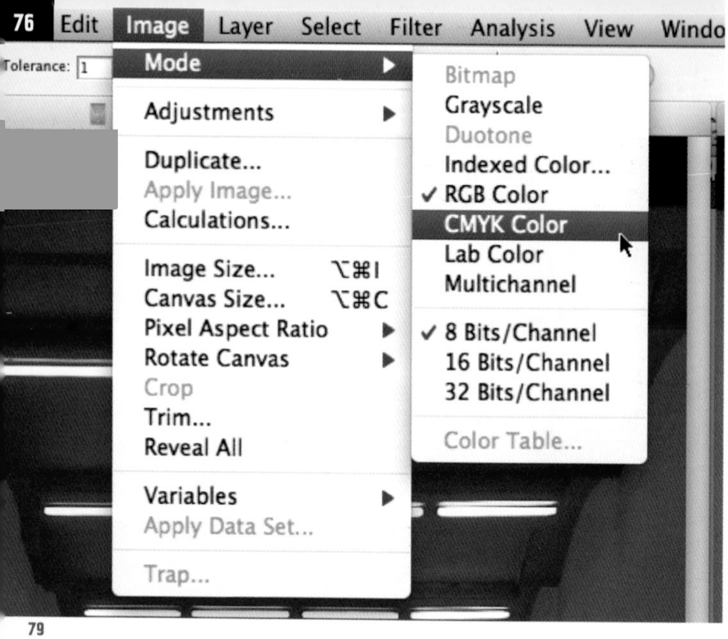

79

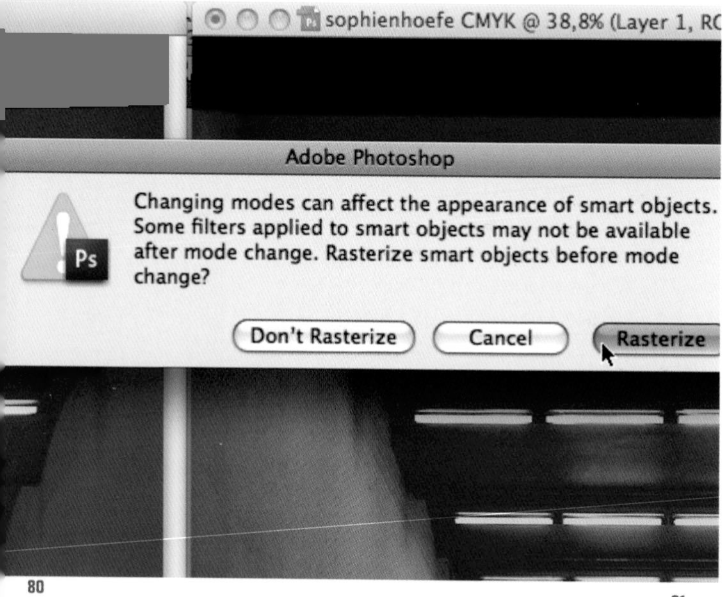

80

81

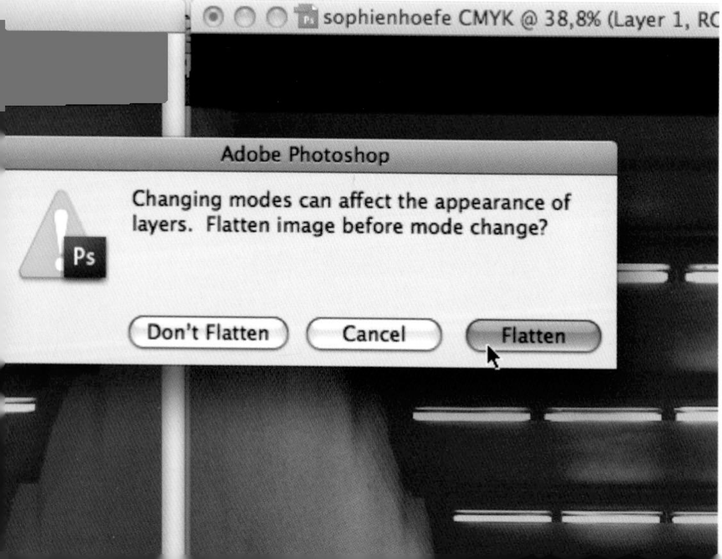

Finally, really convert the image into CMYK; this mode change too takes place in the Image menu (ill.79).

Sadly, not all filters work in the CMYK space, which is why Photoshop® asks you whether you want to rasterize the"useless" smart objects, i.e. irrevocably integrate them into the image's pixel structure. Confirm this question with Rasterize (ill.80).

Then Photoshop® asks you whether you want to merge the layers. Since smart objects don´t work in CMYK anyway, confirm with the option Flatten (ill.81).

And so your image is converted. But on no account get rid of your RGB original, as it shows the original colors.

Even though conversion into CMYK has some frustrating aspects, there´s no way round factoring these into your workflow if you´re preparing print layouts.
Print shops don´t usually accept files with RGB data, or don´t rework them, not even when you think you´ve hidden them via embedding in an InDesign® file plus PDF export.

Yet it´s also important for you that your images emerge from the printer correctly.

82

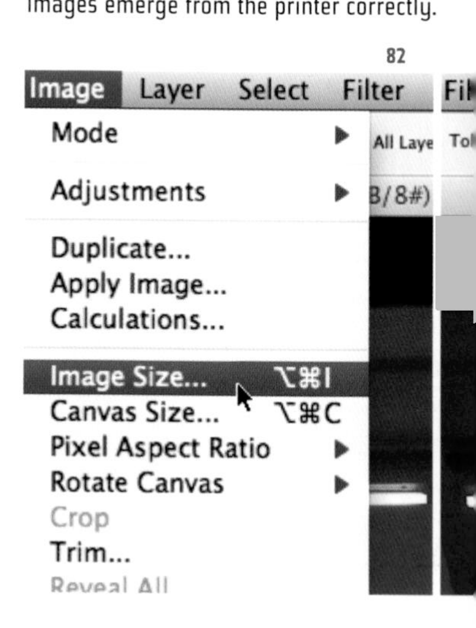

In our example, the result would probably have been rather surprising for you without a prior CMYK conversion and post-processing.

Lastly, a few more words on the subject of color mode and file size (see also p.68): if you select the command Image Size from the Image menu (ill.82), you can read the file size right at the top in the window that opens, as it is given due to the pixels structure (Pixels Dimensions; the additional demand for storage space by additional layers is not taken into account at this point, which means that the displayed value isn´t always the final size).
As you see, the RGB file (ill.83) is smaller than the CMYK one (ill.84; more exactly, it takes up 3/4 of the disk space of the otherwise equally big CMYK file. This is because an RGB image has three color channels but a CMYK one has four, the memory requirements for each channel being the same.
If you transfer the RGB image into Grayscale mode (ill.85 and 86), the file size shrinks to one-third, as there´s only the one Gray channel left (ill.87). You can take advantage of this, for example when scanning Black-and-White images, as you can allow yourself a higher resolution in Grayscale mode.

83

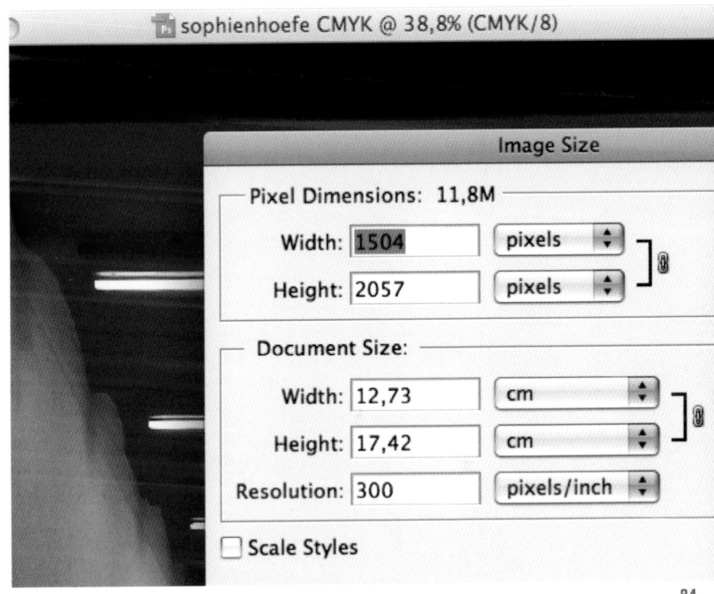

84

86

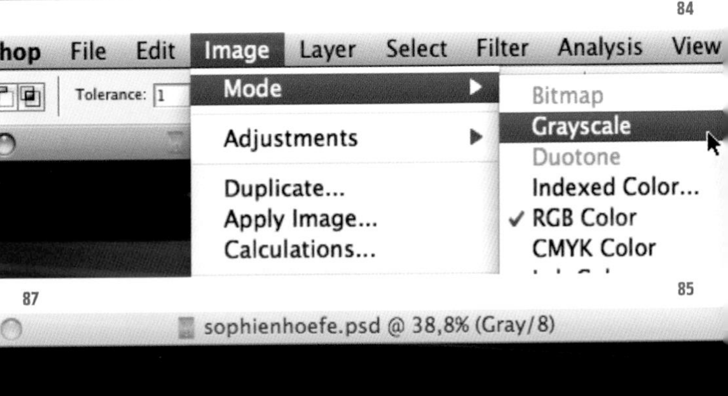

85

87

sophienhoefe.psd @ 38,8% (Gray/8)
Image Size
Pixel Dimensions: 2,95M
Width: 1504 pixels

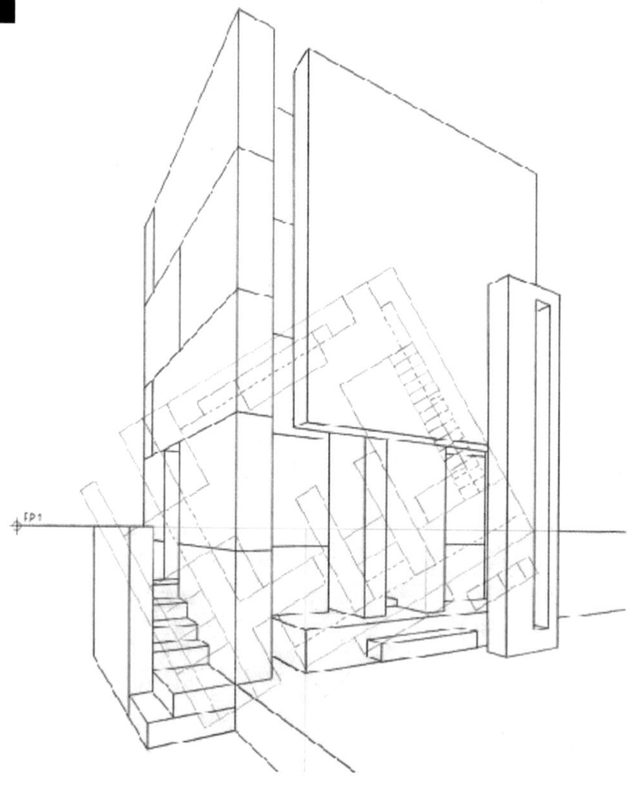

1

Pencil Drawing

In this chapter you´ll learn how to refine a scanned pencil drawing with a few Photoshop® feature.
Among other things, the Vanishing-Point filter and the Quick Selection tool will be used, plus once again, of course, adjustment layers, masks and Smart Objects.

Please open file 04_terragni_pencil.psd (ill.1), which shows the hand-drawn perspective of a non-realised project by Guiseppe Terragni: the Tomba Mambretti. At the end of our efforts the drawing will look like illustration 2. But, one step at a time.

First of all I´ll show you how to enhance the drawing itself very quickly, with the aid of some adjustment layers.

The first tool to provide interesting effects on such a gray-shaded pencil drawing is the so called Gradient Map.
Here, a gradient of your choice is merged with the drawing, so that the color of one

2

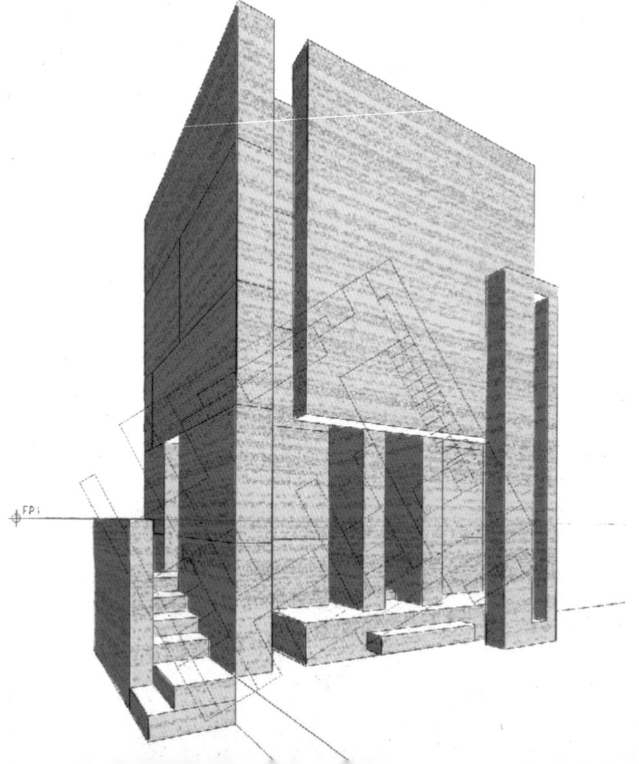

3

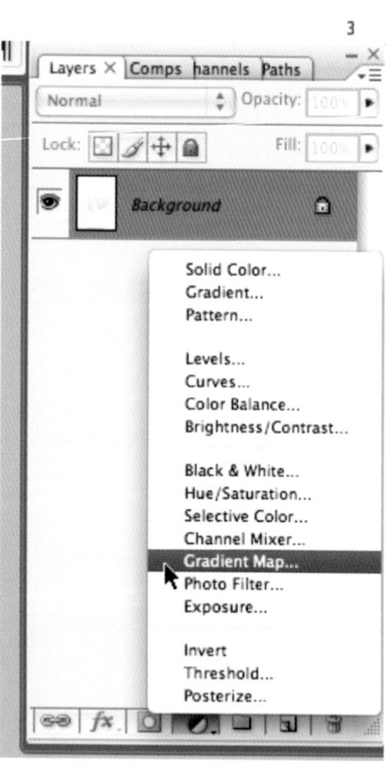

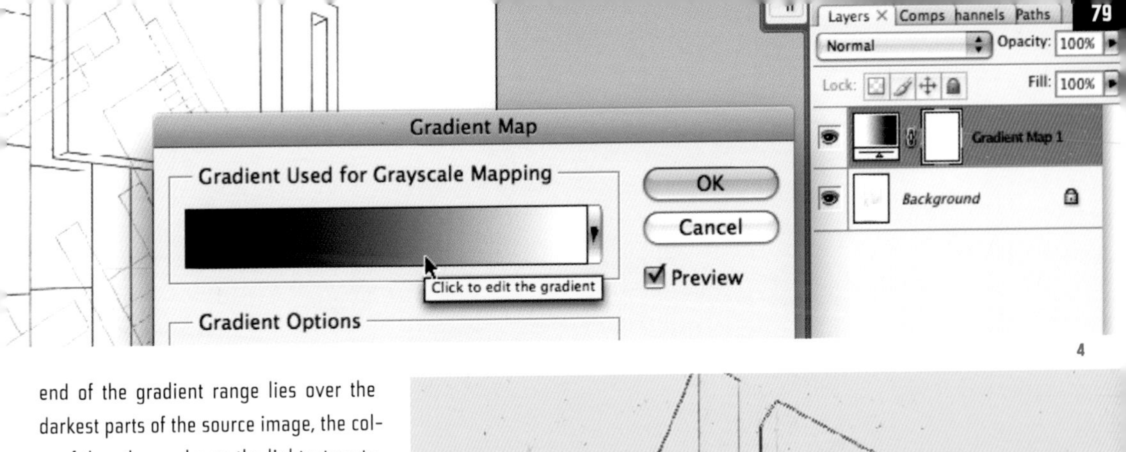

4

end of the gradient range lies over the darkest parts of the source image, the color of the other end over the lightest parts. The rest is distributed accordingly over the mid-range hues.

So, place an adjustment layer for such a Gradient Map over your Background layer (from the corresponding menu at the bottom frame of the Layers palette, ill.3).

In the adjustment dialog which opens, please click on the gradient miniature (ill.4), and from the assortment select the Copper gradient (ill.5).

Click on OK in both windows; your drawing now looks roughly like a Leonardo da Vinci (ill.6).

5

6

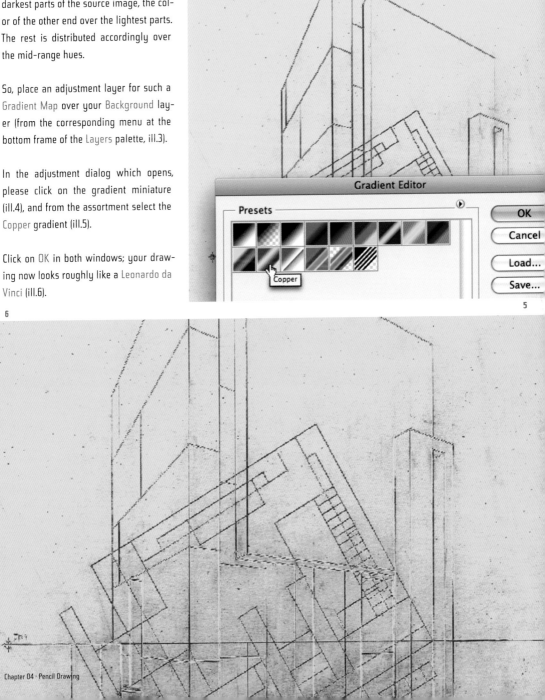

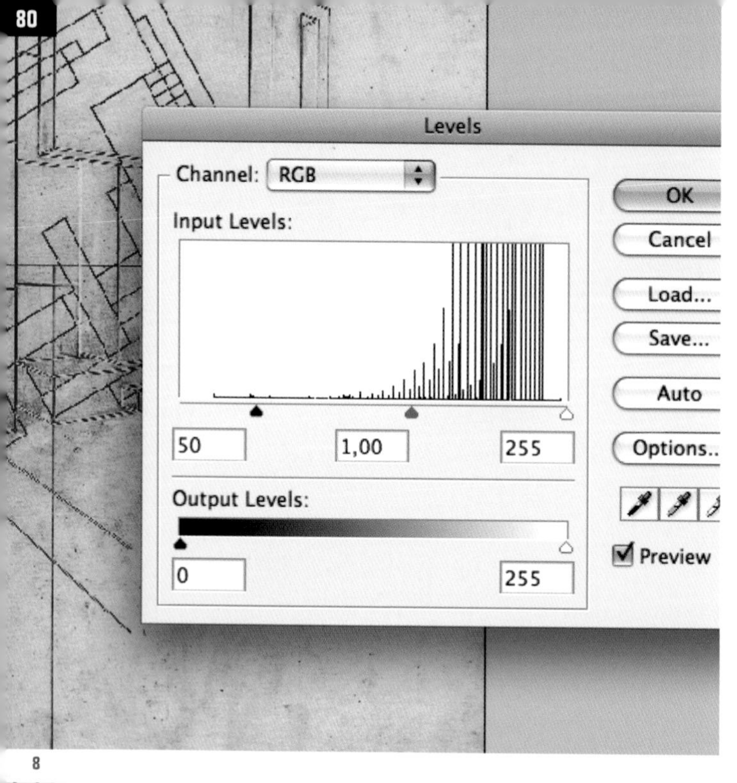

8

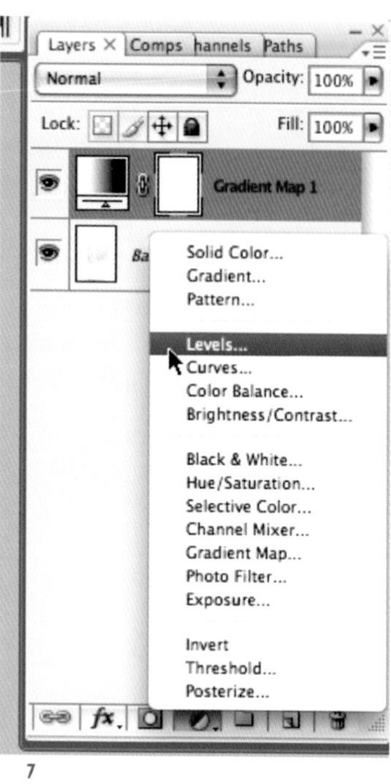

7

Now strengthen the contrast by using a Levels adjustment layer (ill.7).
For the RGB channel, set the left control to 50 (ill.8), and for the Red channel the Gray control to 0.80 (ill.9). Confirm with OK.

Finally (at least for the moment) make a negative from it, with the adjustment layer Invert (ill.10).
Your image now looks like a chalkboard drawing (ill.11).

As you can see it´s relatively simple, with the help of the corresponding image adaptations used as adjustment layers, to

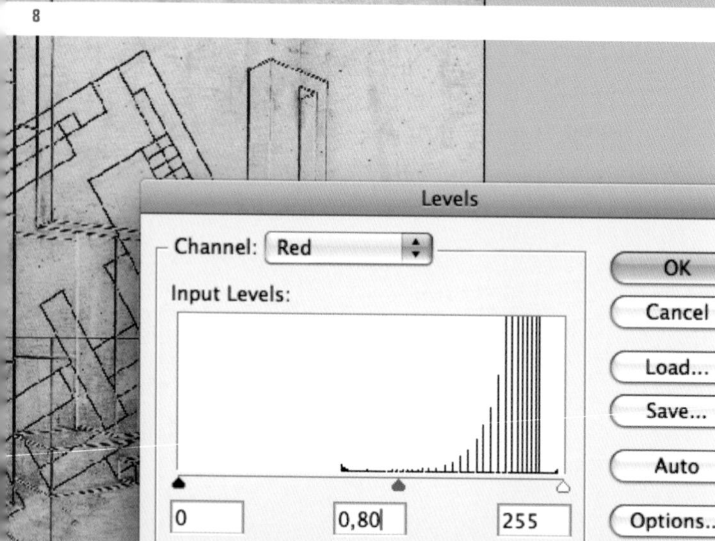

9

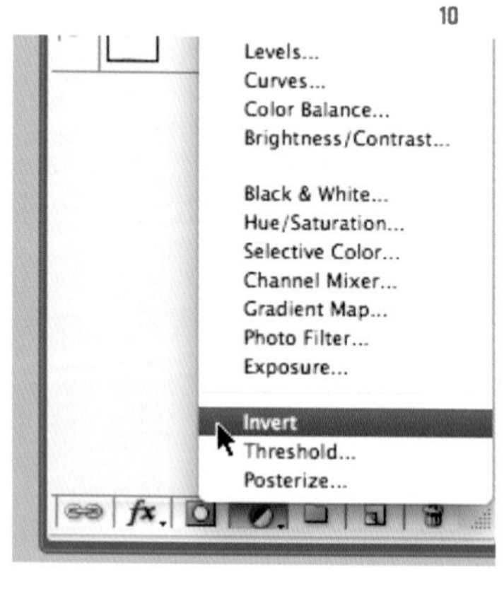

10

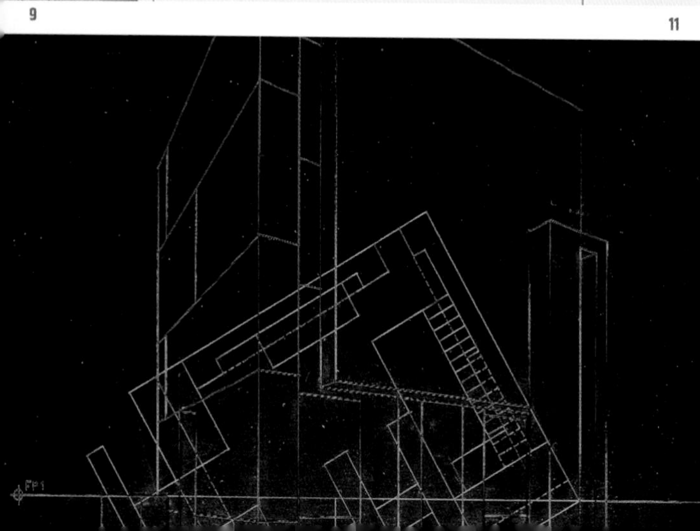

11

produce strong modifications in a pencil drawing.

In what follows, however, we want to do something different: texture the building via simple means.

So, please hide the three adjustment layers now, and copy the Background layer with the command CTRL-J (ill.12). This new layer should also be active.

First the drawing has to be colored, with a masked Solid Color layer.

Place one of these; it´s in the same menu as the adjustment layers we´ve just used (ill.13). Set all the RGB values to 220 (ill.14).

Please set the blending mode of the new color layer which is to lie over the image layer to Multiply, so you can see the pencil drawing under it. (ill.15).

Now color the mask of this color layer completely black, so that the gray color of the layer is invisible.

After that, select step-by-step the areas in the image which are to be colored gray, and fill these places in the mask with White.

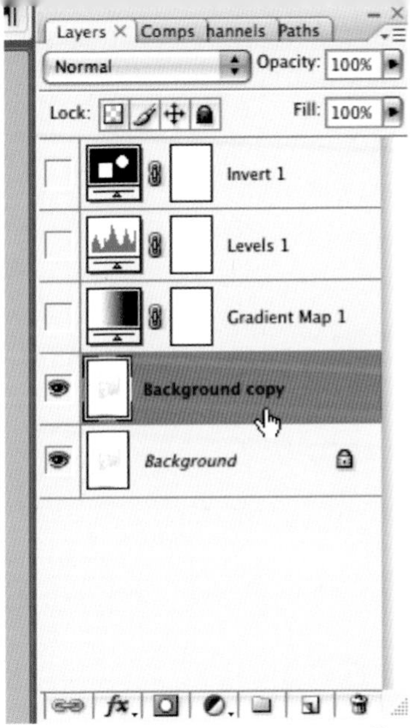

12

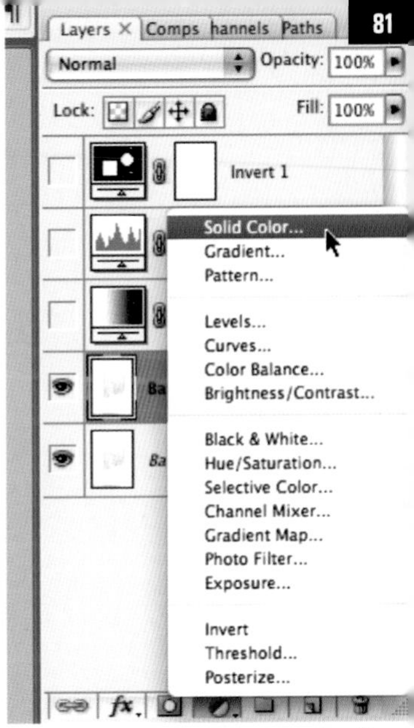

13

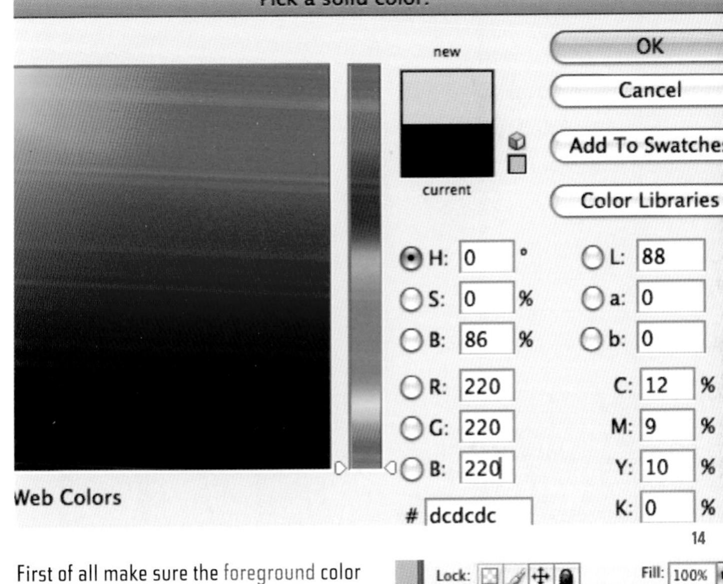

14

15

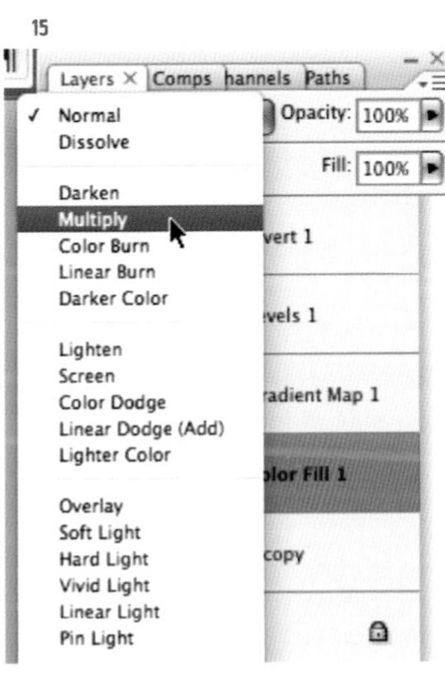

First of all make sure the foreground color is Black and the background White (ill.16). Press key D (Black-White) if necessary, and maybe X (to swap the foreground and background colors).

Now that Black is the foreground color, please click on the mask miniature of the color layer (ill.17) and press Alt-Backspace so that this mask is filled with Black.

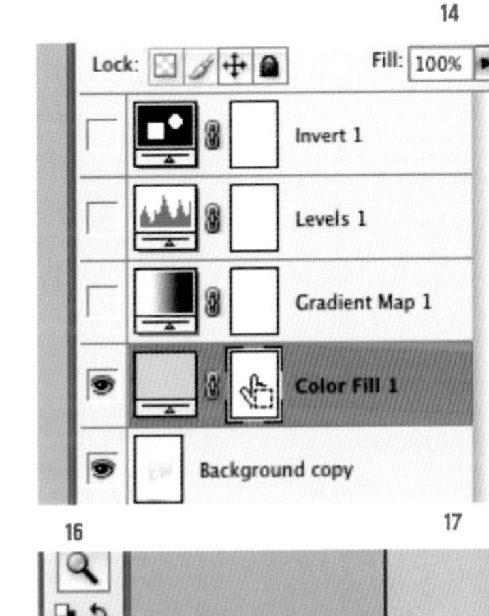

16

17

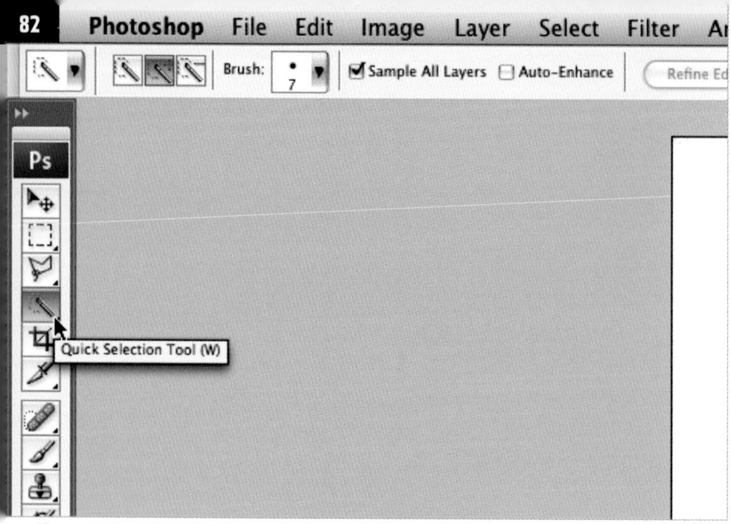

18

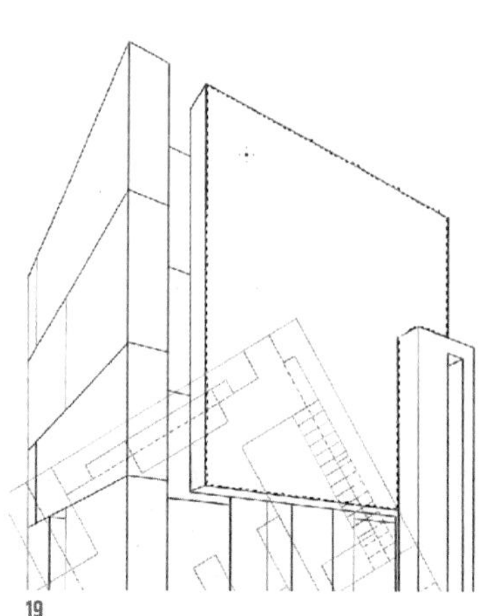

19

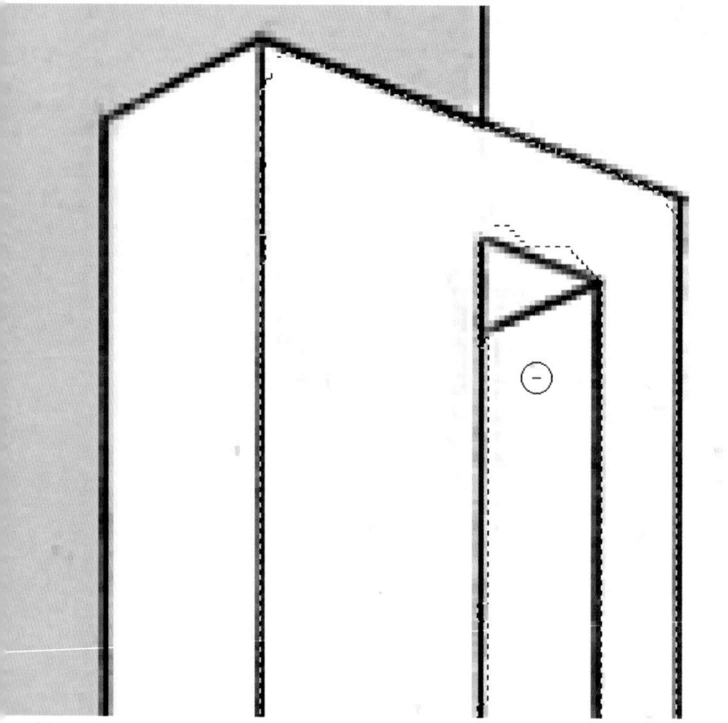

20

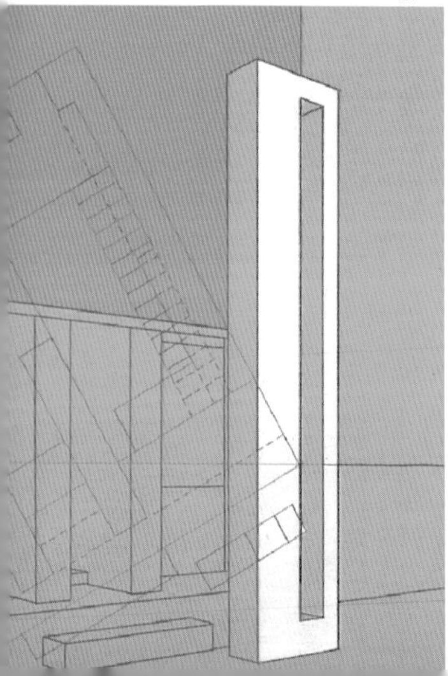

21

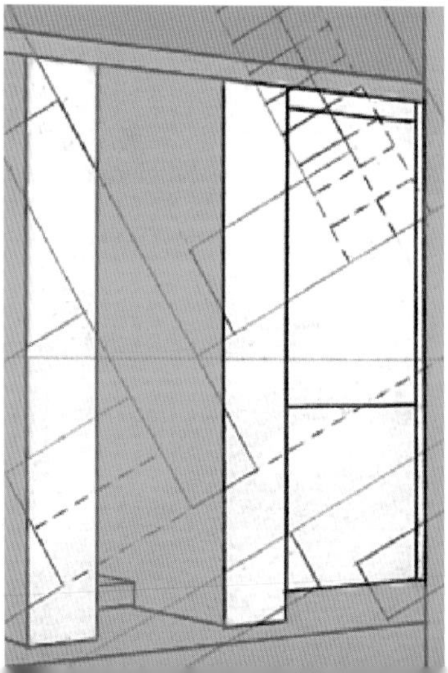

22

Select the Quick Selection tool from the Tool bar (it´s maybe hidden behind the Magic Wand; press Shift-W till you see it, ill.18).

You can now paint selections with this tool.
Click on one of the surfaces of the building facing you, and move the tool cursor inside this area until it´s completely selected (ill.19).
You can also let go the mouse and click again on a point not yet selected with this tool, the selection areas are added by default.

If, on the other hand, you wish to remove something from a selection, press the Alt key for the first click of the subtract selection (ill.20).

When you´ve selected a manageable area (as can be seen in ill.19), click on the mask miniature of the color layer, which is of course completely black so far, and press CTRL-Backspace.
The part selected is filled with White in the mask (the background color), and in the image you can see that the area selected is now colored with the Gray of the color layer (ill.20).

Now continue the same way, selecting further surfaces facing you.

For this you don´t need to activate the image layer to create your selections, as for the Quick Selection tool the option Sample All Layers is crossed (see ill.18).

As I´ve said, if you want to remove something from a selection, press the Alt key for the next brush stroke with the Quick Selection tool (ill.20).

To check if the selection is correct, press the Q key from time to time, and the non-selected part is then shown colored red (Ills.21 and 22).

Keep going like this, limiting yourself to manageable areas, before filling the selection in the mask with White.
The final result should look like in ill.23.

Click once on the mask miniature with the Alt key held down, and you´ll see the mask in the image as a Black-and-White picture (ill.24).
With its minor inaccuracies, it corresponds quite well to the manual character of a pencil drawing (ill.25).

Now you´ll add a hatching to the surfaces, using the Vanishing Point filter.

First of all, however, you have to create such a hatching, conveniently in a separate file.

First check how large your current image is, in order to calculate the size of the hatching image.

To do this, select the command Image Size from the Image menu (ill.26), and take a look at the Pixel Dimensions.

The image is roughly 1200 pixels wide, which means it would be good if the hatching graphics were about 600 pixels square.

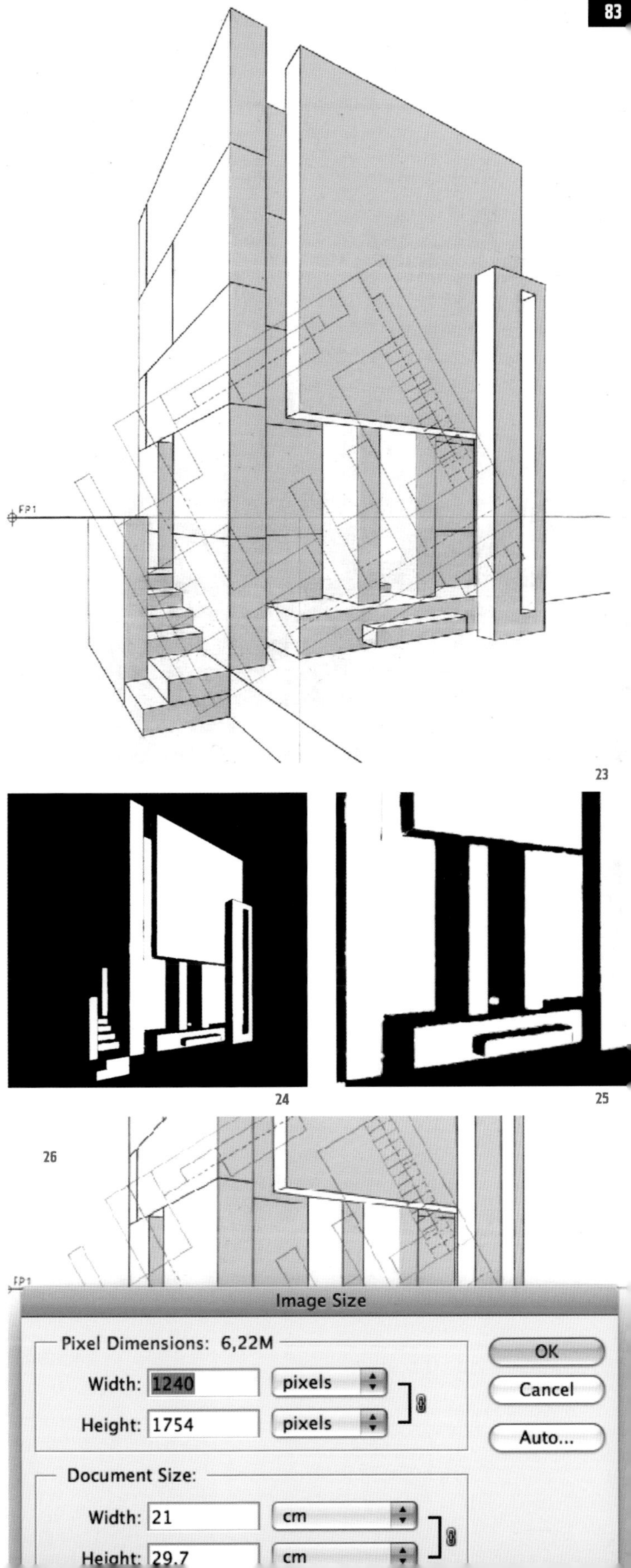

23

24

25

26

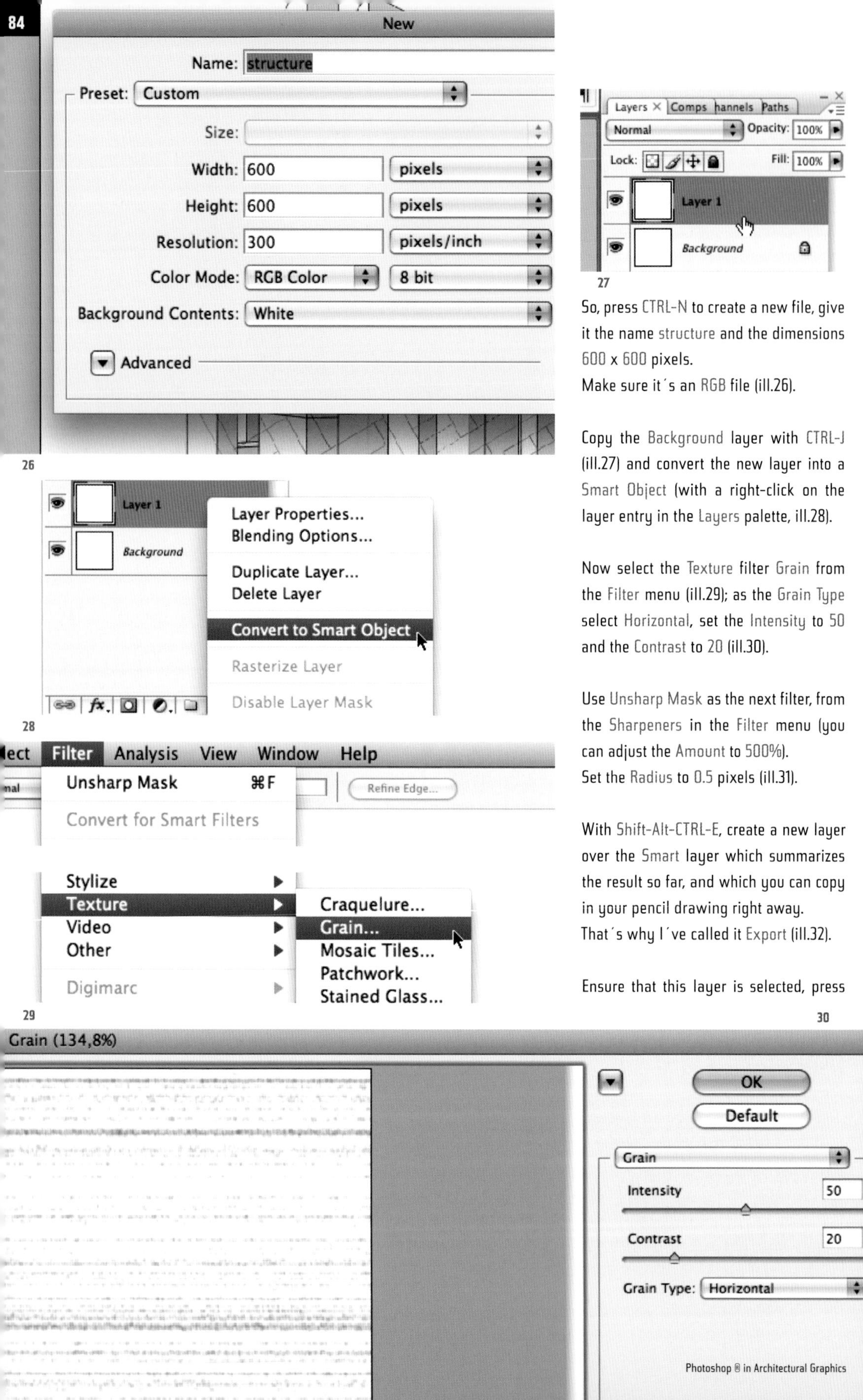

26

27

28

29

30

So, press CTRL-N to create a new file, give it the name structure and the dimensions 600 x 600 pixels.
Make sure it´s an RGB file (ill.26).

Copy the Background layer with CTRL-J (ill.27) and convert the new layer into a Smart Object (with a right-click on the layer entry in the Layers palette, ill.28).

Now select the Texture filter Grain from the Filter menu (ill.29); as the Grain Type select Horizontal, set the Intensity to 50 and the Contrast to 20 (ill.30).

Use Unsharp Mask as the next filter, from the Sharpeners in the Filter menu (you can adjust the Amount to 500%).
Set the Radius to 0.5 pixels (ill.31).

With Shift-Alt-CTRL-E, create a new layer over the Smart layer which summarizes the result so far, and which you can copy in your pencil drawing right away.
That´s why I´ve called it Export (ill.32).

Ensure that this layer is selected, press

32

CTRL-A (Select - All) and after that CTRL-C (Edit - Copy).

Now change back to the pencil drawing. Add a new, empty image layer there over the gray color layer (using the small icon next to the trash symbol at the bottom frame of the Layers palette, ill.33).

Then select Vanishing Point from the Filter menu (ill.34).

In the window which opens, you can draw a perspective polygon (a so called plane), which you can then fill with the hatching in such a way that the hatching takes on the perspective of your plane.

The Create Plane tool is already selected by default (ill.35), and with its help produce click-wise a polygon that covers the whole front surface of the building (ill.36).

35

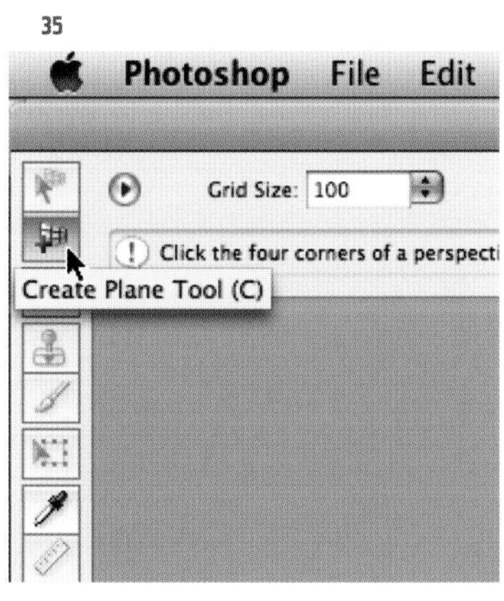

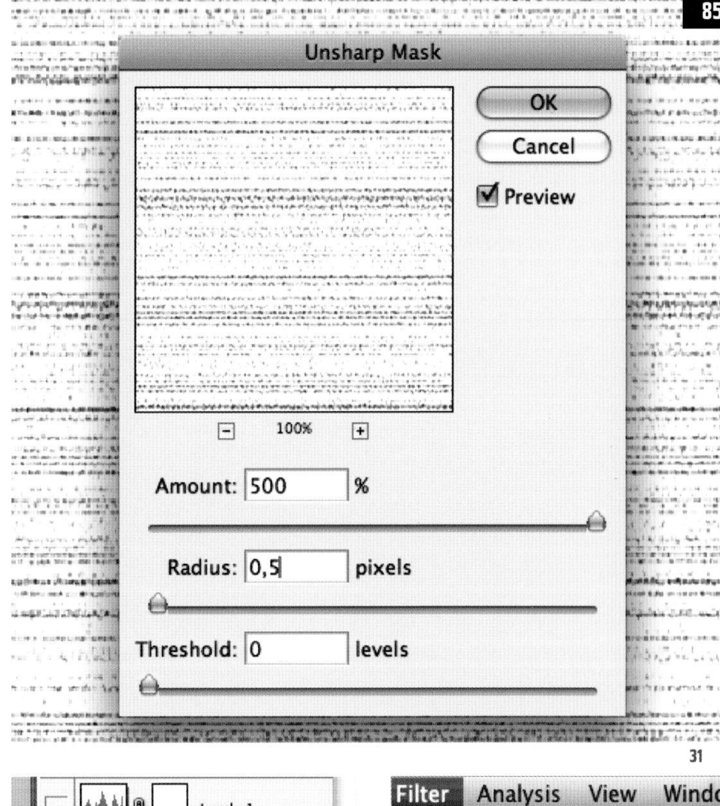

31

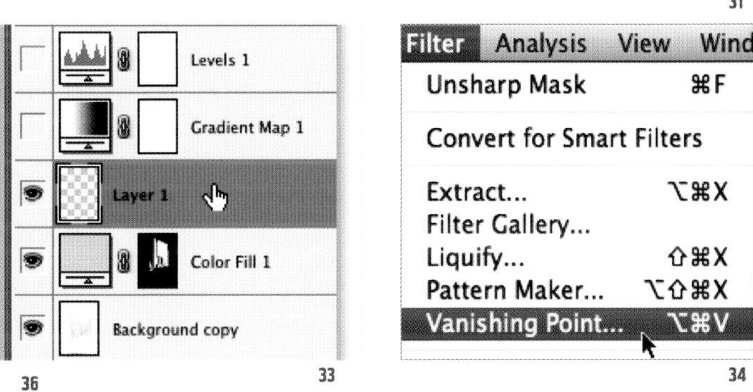

36 33 34

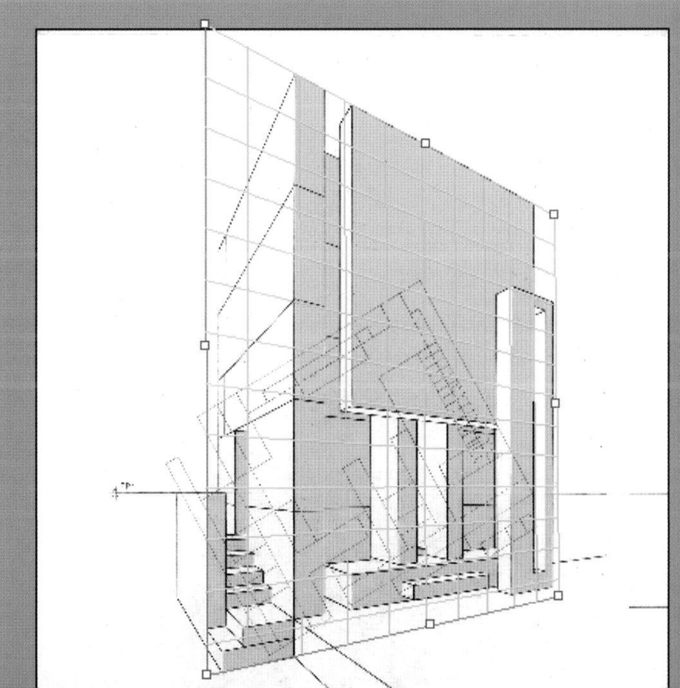

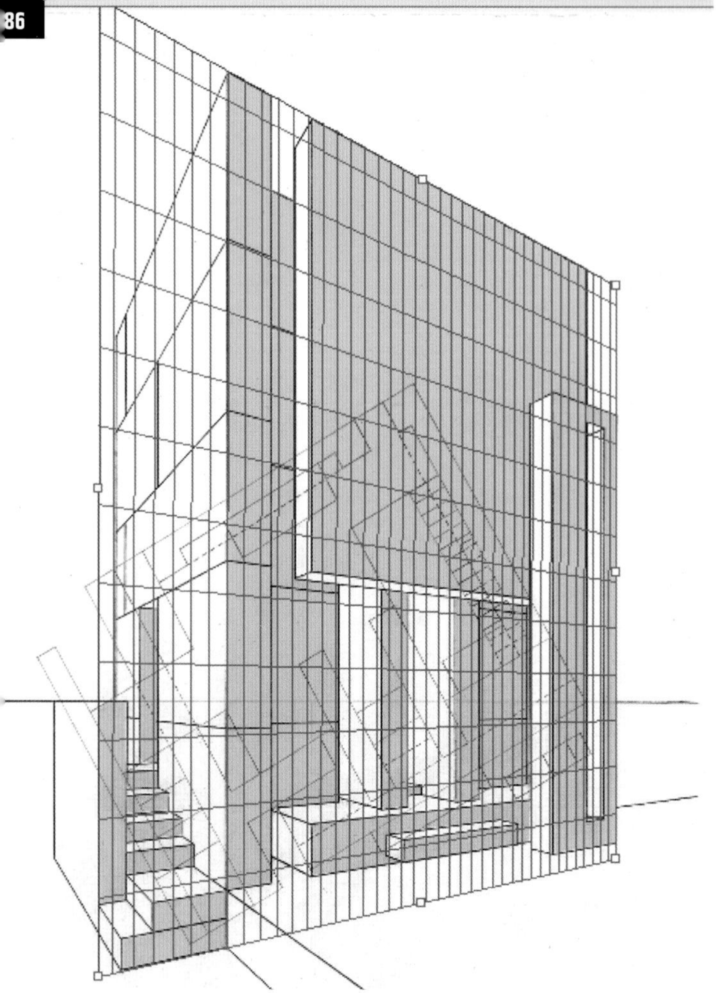

38

39

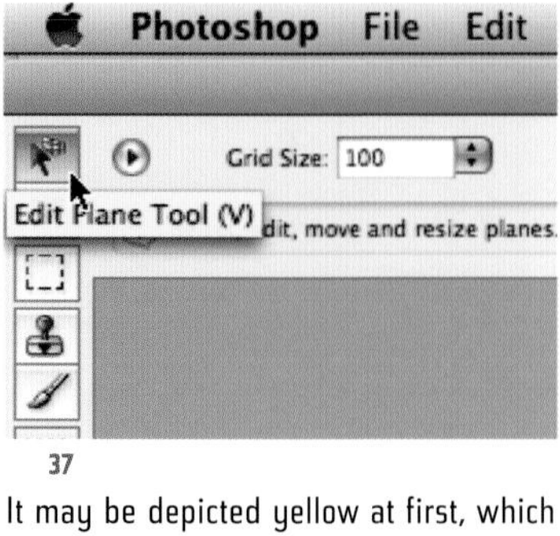

37

It may be depicted yellow at first, which means that the perspective is not yet recognized as correct (ill.36).

In this case, and also to make the drawing somewhat more precise, pick the Edit Plane tool (ill.37) and move the corner points to the right place.

If you do it correctly, the perspective grid is depicted blue (ill.38).

Incidentally, in this window you can also zoom into the drawing with CTRL-Space and out with CTRL-Alt-Space.

When the grid is ready, press CTRL-V to paste in the hatching you´ve just copied. At first it´s placed top left in the image (ill.39).

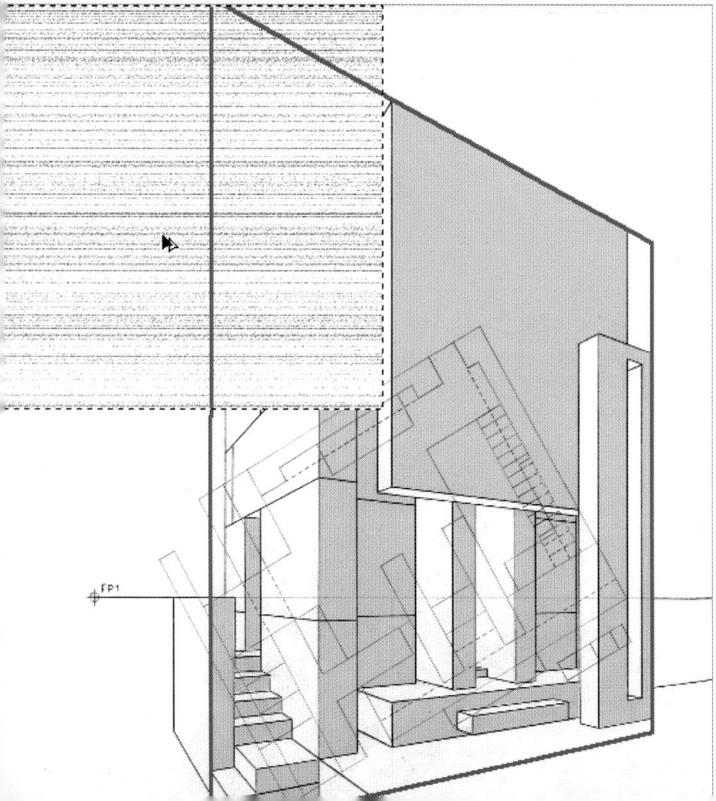

If CTRL-V doesn´t work, break off, change again to the file structure, make sure the Export layer is selected, repeat CTRL-A and CTRL-C, and try it again in the pencil file.
The perspective frame can still be seen.

So, if you see the hatching in the top-left corner of your filter window, grab it with the mouse and drag it onto the perspective frame.

As soon as you move your hatching over the polygon, it snaps into the plane's perspective (ill.40).

Release the mouse button if the hatching

40

41

slightly overlaps a side of the polygon, and press CTRL-T to scale it.

Drag all four sides so far that they protrude a little over the margin of the perspective frame (ill.41).

Confirm with OK, and the hatching is now part of the drawing image, in the right perspective (ill.42).

Now switch the blending mode of the layer to Multiply, to be able to see the pencil drawing under it again (ill.43).

42

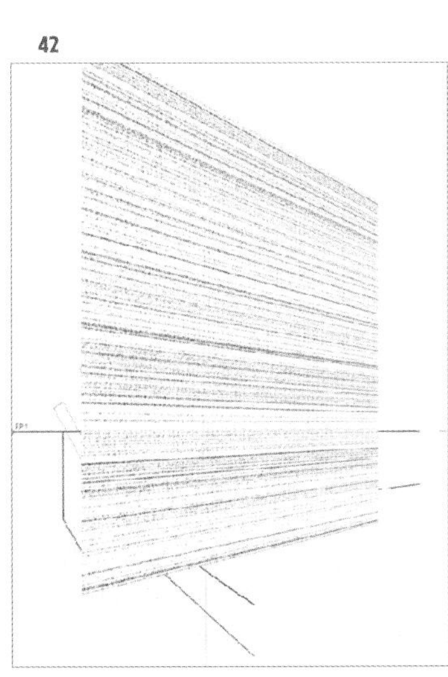

43

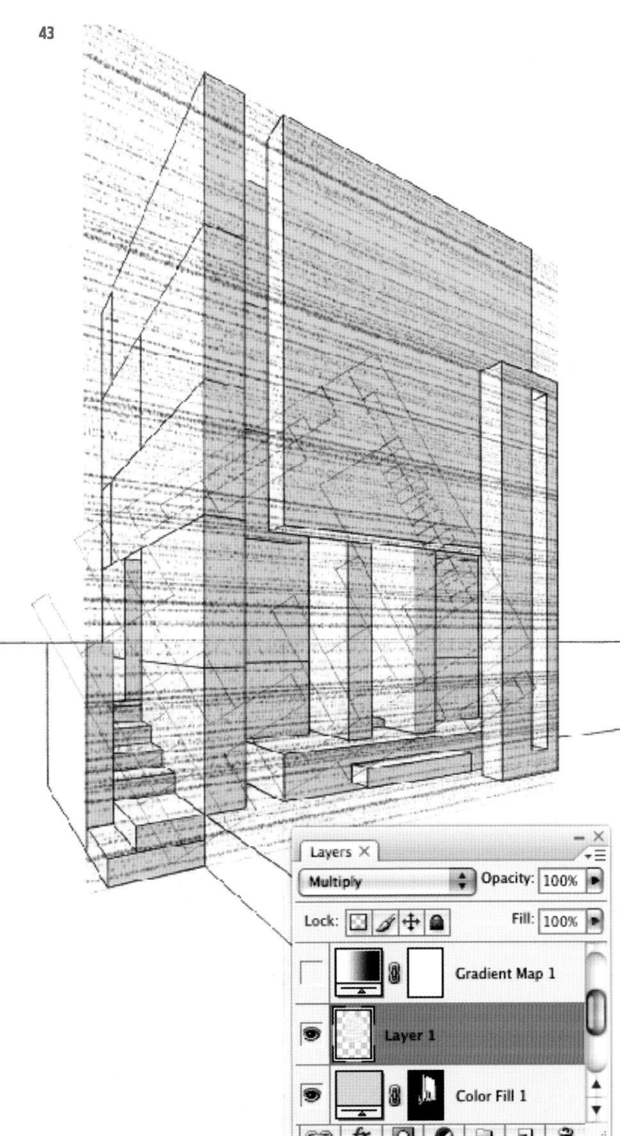

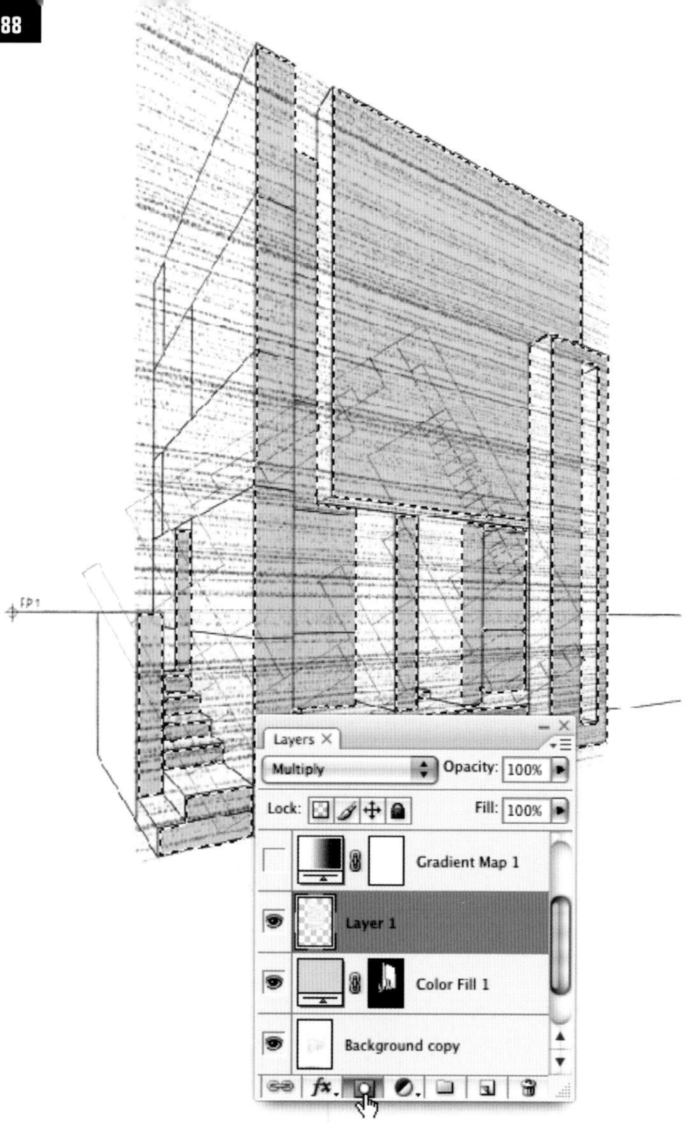

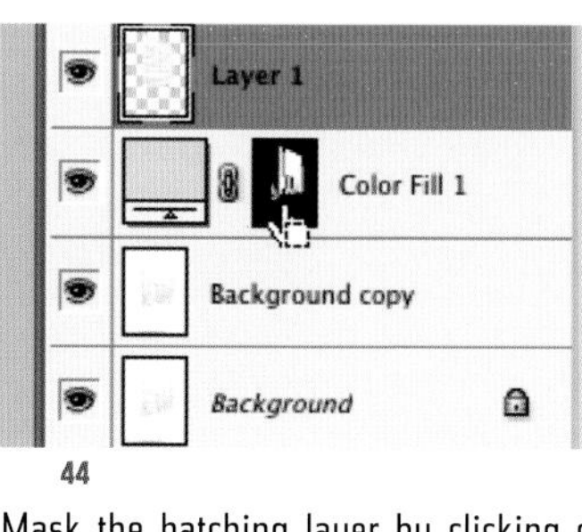

44

Mask the hatching layer by clicking on the mask miniature of the color layer with the CTRL key held down, to load its content as a selection (ill.44), and then allocate a mask to the layer with the hatching via clicking on the third icon from the left at the bottom frame of the Layers palette, ill.45).

Now the hatching can only be seen on the surfaces colored gray (ill.46).

You´ll now repeat all this for the building surfaces pointing to the left, first coloring with a (darker) shade of gray, and then placing a perspectively aligned hatching.

First to the color layer: insert a second one over the copy of the Background layer (Solid Color, ill.47).
Here select a darker shade of gray (R, G, B = 150, ill.48).

45

46

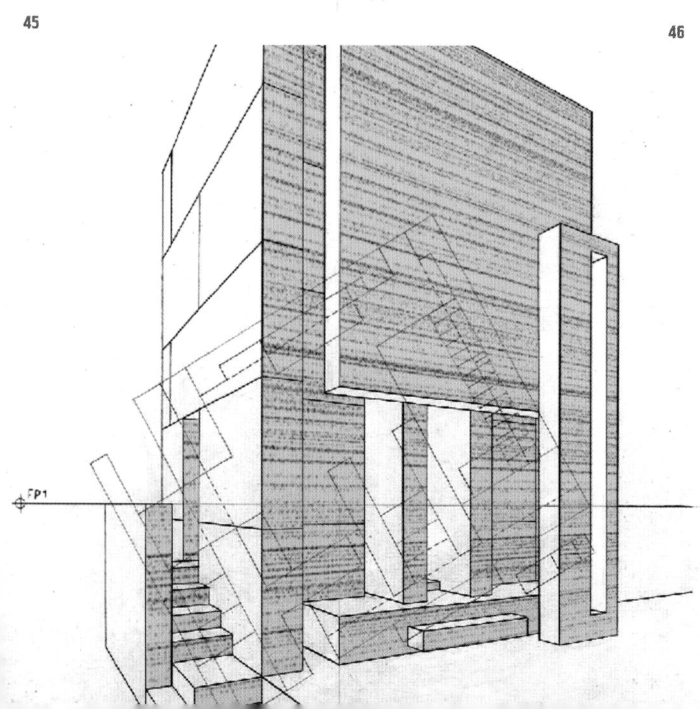

47

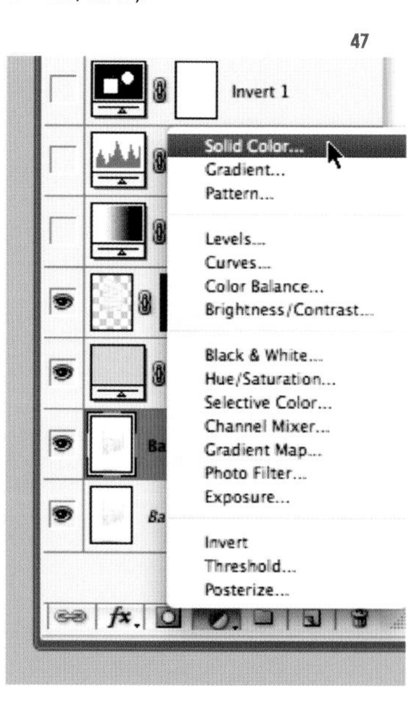

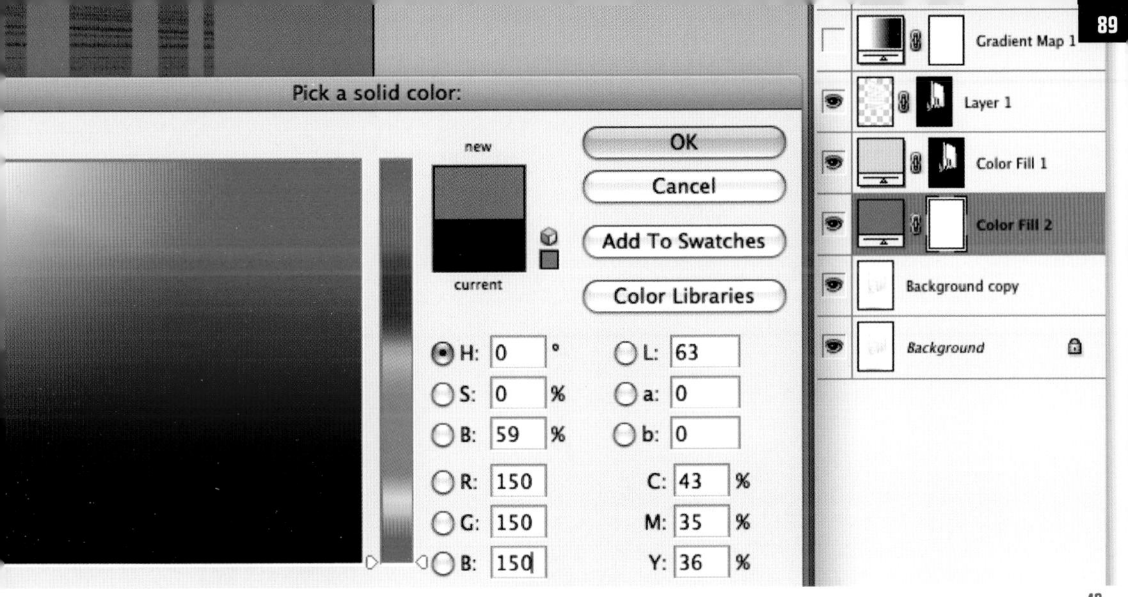

48

Ensure that the mask of this new layer is activated for working on, and fill it with Black again (Alt-Backspace if Black is the foreground color, and CTRL-Backspace if it´s the background one).

Grab the Quick Selection tool again (W or Shift-W, ill.18) and select, one after the other, manageable parts of the building surfaces pointing to the left.

Again keep in mind that with this tool you add selection areas by default with every stroke, and that you have to press the Alt key if you wish to remove parts of a selection.

Here too, press Q from time to time, to check the quality of your selections.

Every time you´ve selected a sufficient area, fill the mask of the new color layer with White, but be absolutely sure that for this the mask miniature of the color layer really is clicked on.

When you´re finished, your image should look like in ill.49 (the hatching layer is hidden here).

49

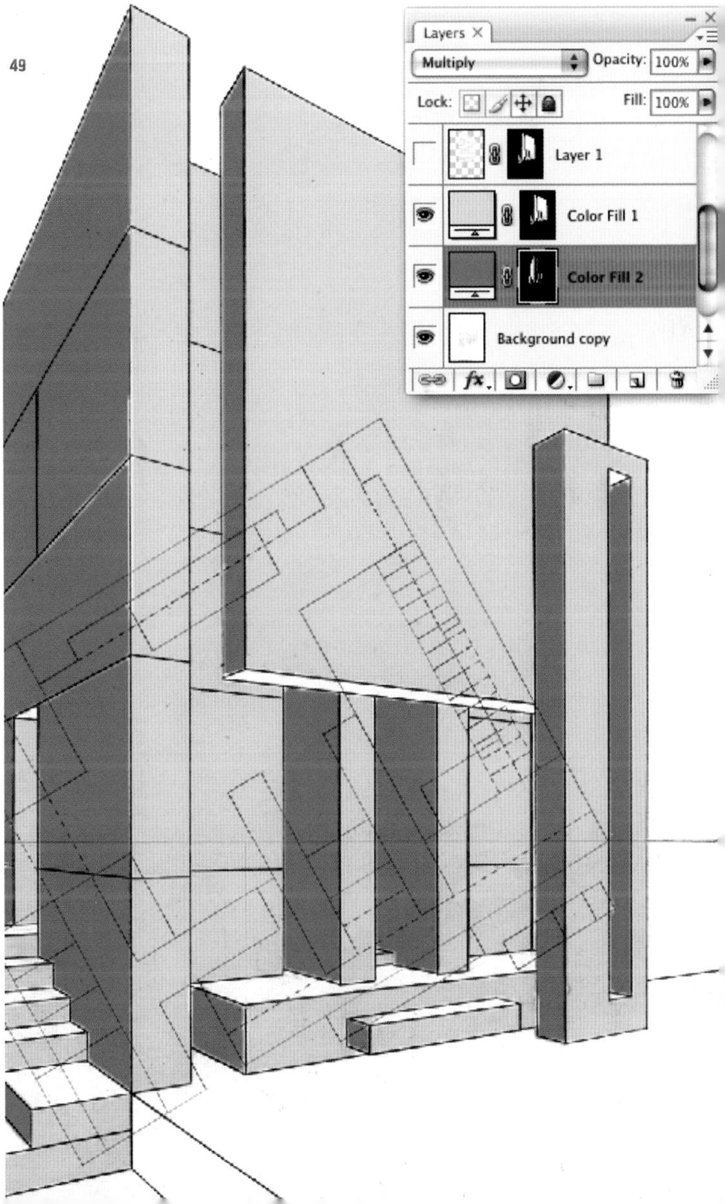

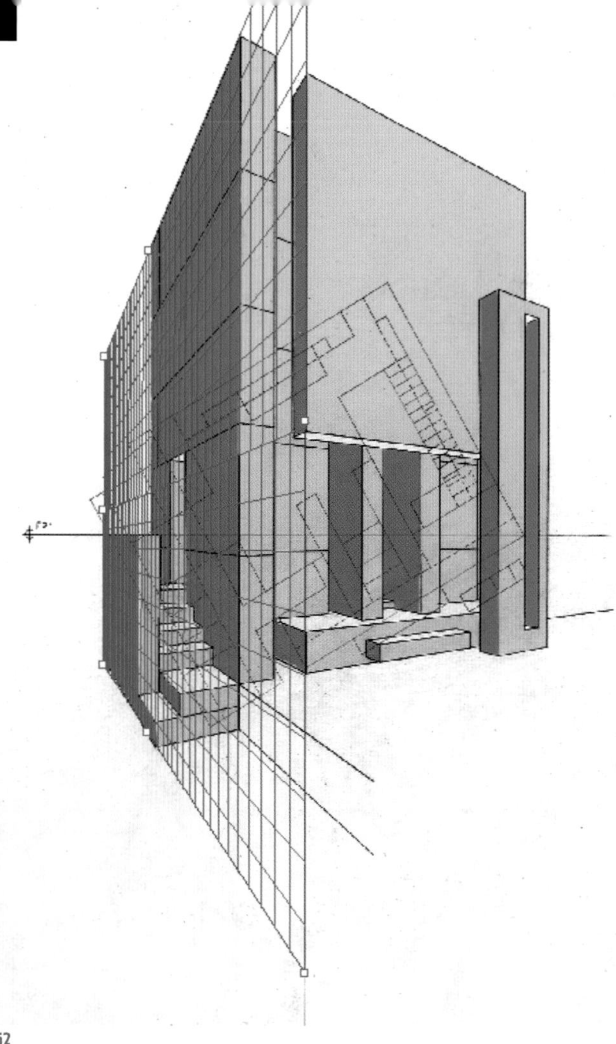

52

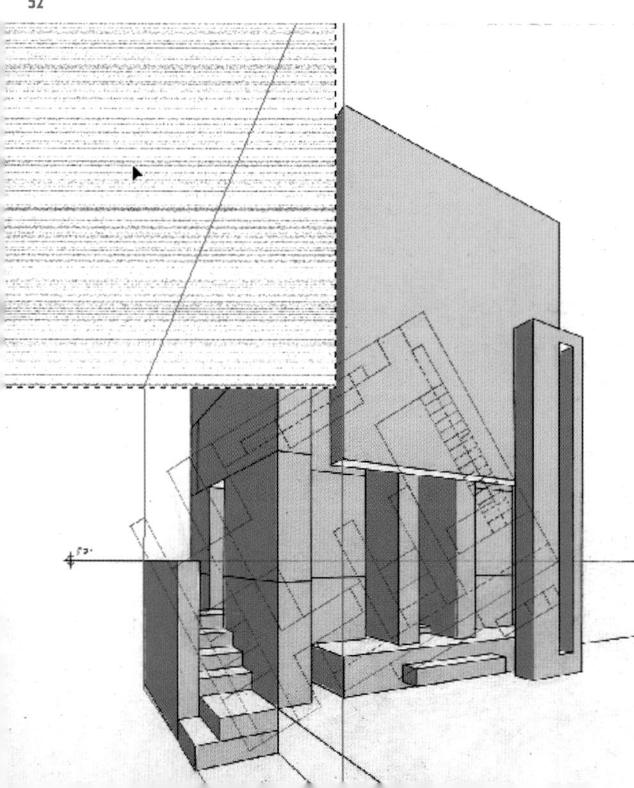

53

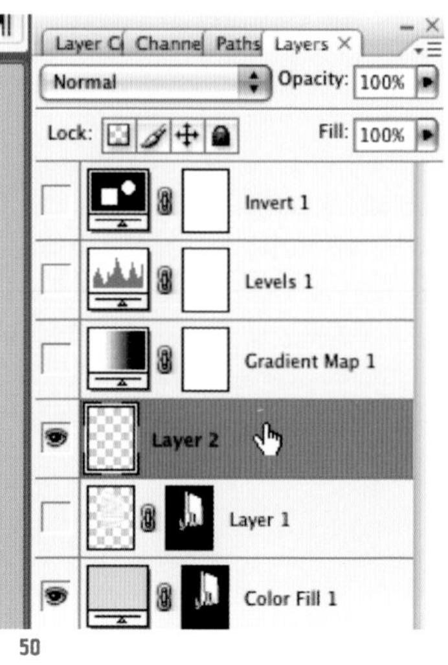

50

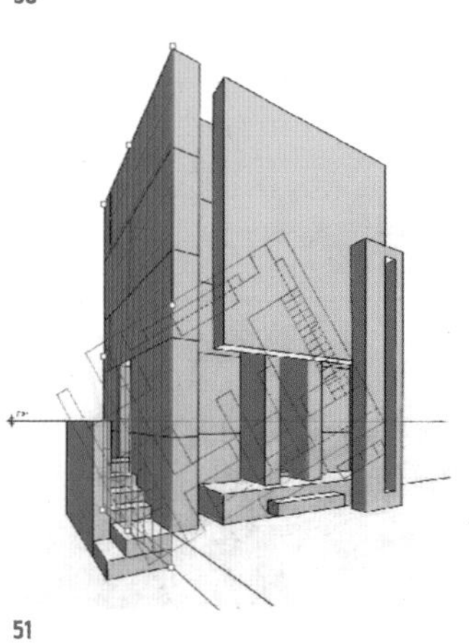

51

Now let´s deal with the hatching for the left-hand surfaces; it´s best if you work in two planes, so that the perspective augmentation for the areas on the right doesn´t turn out all too strong. First create a new empty layer, over the layer showing the first hatching (ill.50)

Change to your hatching file and copy the contents of the uppermost layer again.
In the pencil file, call up a new window of the Vanishing Point filter again (Filter menu) and draw a new plane as shown in ill.51.

Enlarge the polygon with the Edit Plane tool to the backmost edge and forward to the place shown in ill.52; at the top and the bottom the polygon should end with

the building. If the polygon grid is depicted yellow again
(i.e. the perspective isn´t "right" yet), correct the position of the corner points till the grid appears blue.

Press CTRL-V so that the hatching appears in the top-left corner of the image again (ill.53), and from there drag it onto the perspective polygon till it´s perspectively aligned (ill.54). Press CTRL-T again and drag the hatching over all the edges of the blue perspective polygon (ill.55).

Back in the image, also set the blending mode of this new layer to Multiply (ill.56).

With the CTRL key held down, click on the mask miniature of the lower color layer (the one which controls the coloring of the left-hand surfaces, ill.57), so that you see a hovering selection of the left-hand facade surfaces, and add a mask to the new hatching layer (which should be active for this purpose) by clicking on the corresponding icon at the bottom frame of the Layers palette (ill.58).

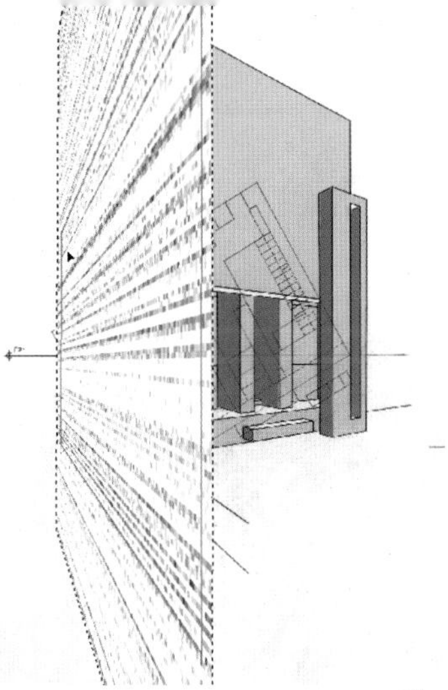

54

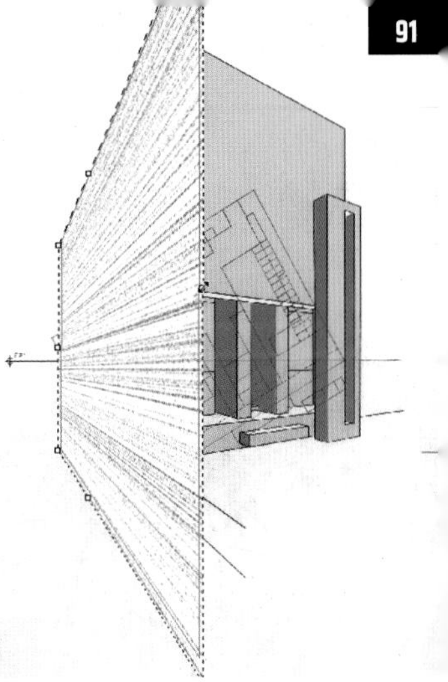

55

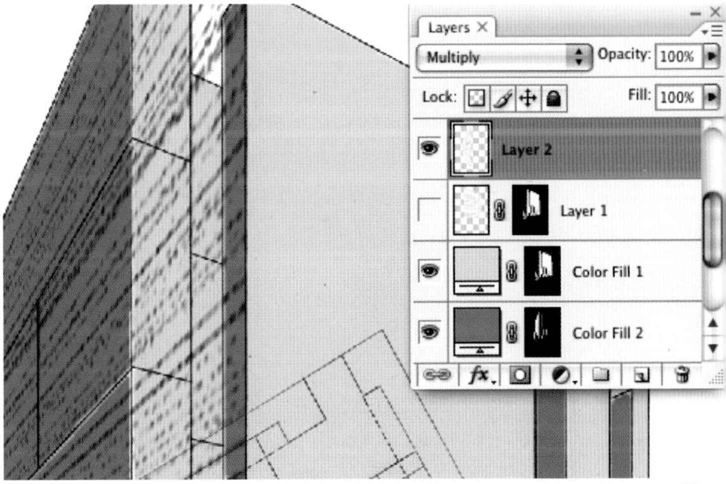

56

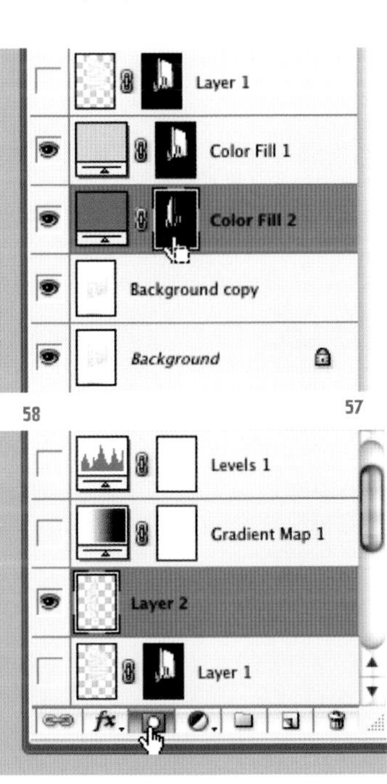

58 57

59

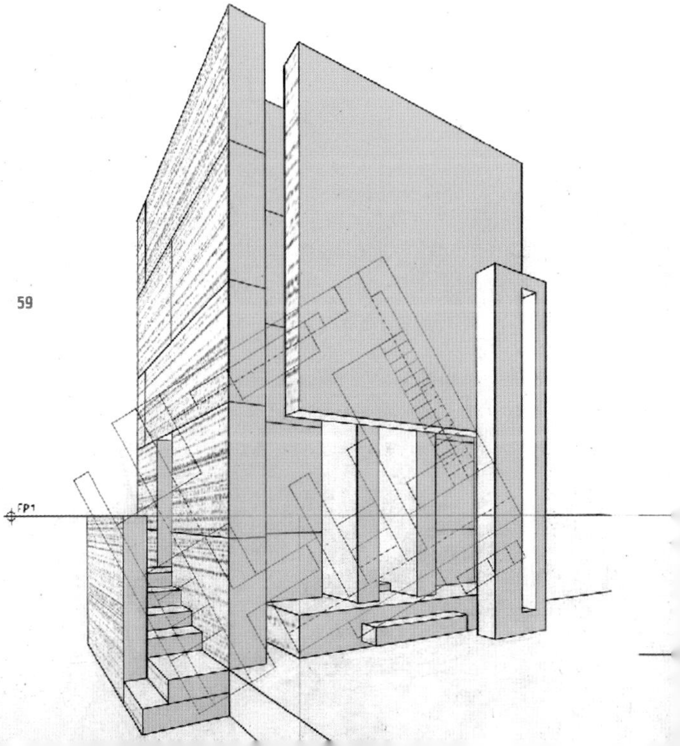

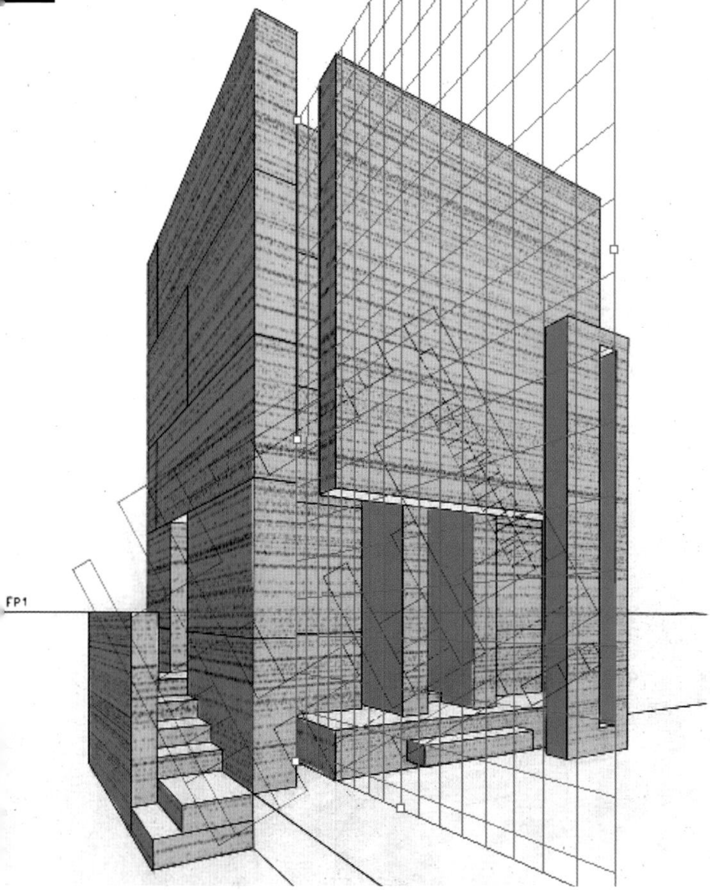

FP1

62

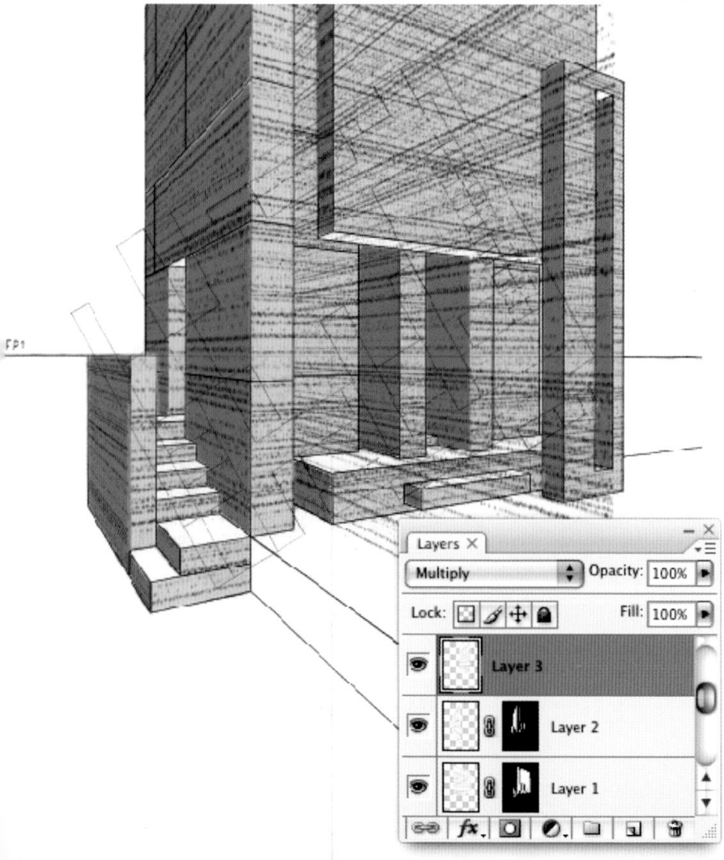

64

FP1

Layers
Multiply
Opacity: 100%
Lock:
Fill: 100%
Layer 3
Layer 2
Layer 1

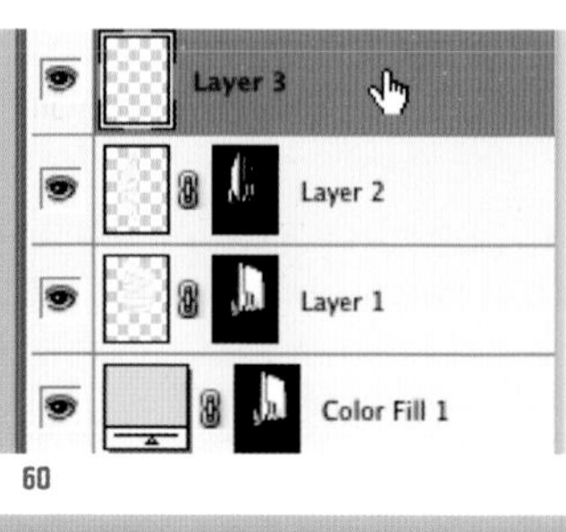

60

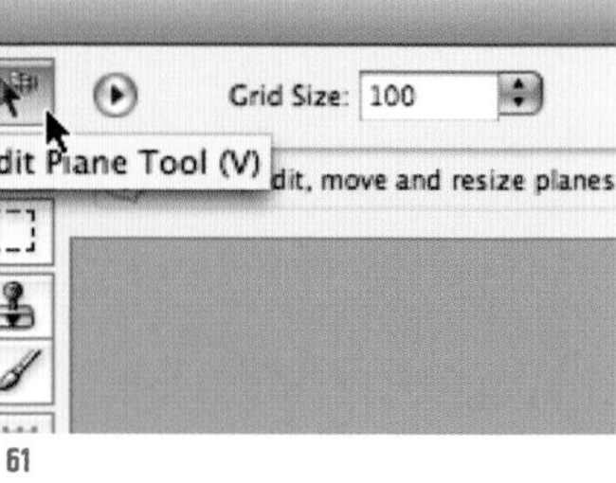

61

A part of the building's surfaces pointing left is now overlaid with the hatching (ill.59).

You´ll now "hatch" the remaining surfaces pointing left. Create another, third image layer over the one last placed (Shift-CTRL-N, ill.60), and switch again into the window of the Vanishing Point filter (Filter menu).

There you already have a plane displaying the apt perspective, but using the Edit Plane tool (ill.61) you should move and adjust it (ill.62).

63

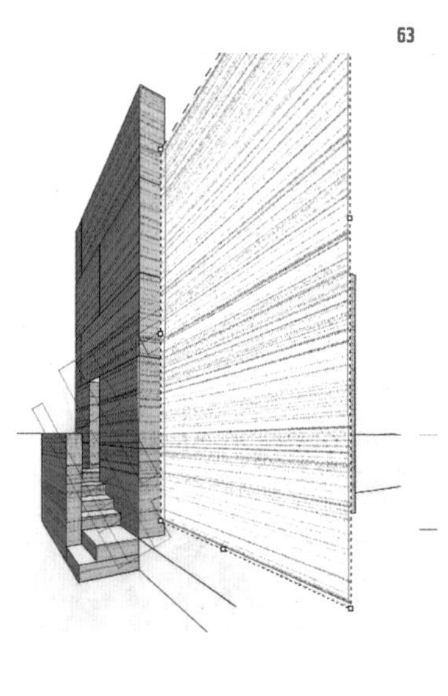

Insert the hatching again (CTRL-V; the hatching should still be in the clipboard, if not, you´ll just have to select it in the hatching file again), drag it onto the perspective polygon and adjust it via CTRL-T (ill.63).

Back in the image, also set the third hatching layer to Multiply (ill.64), again take the mask of the darker color layer as the selection into the image (by a CTRL-click on its miniature, ill.65) and thus allocate a mask to the active Layer 3 (by clicking on the corresponding icon at the bottom frame of the Layers palette, ill.66).

Show all three hatching layers, and admire the result of your work (ill.67).

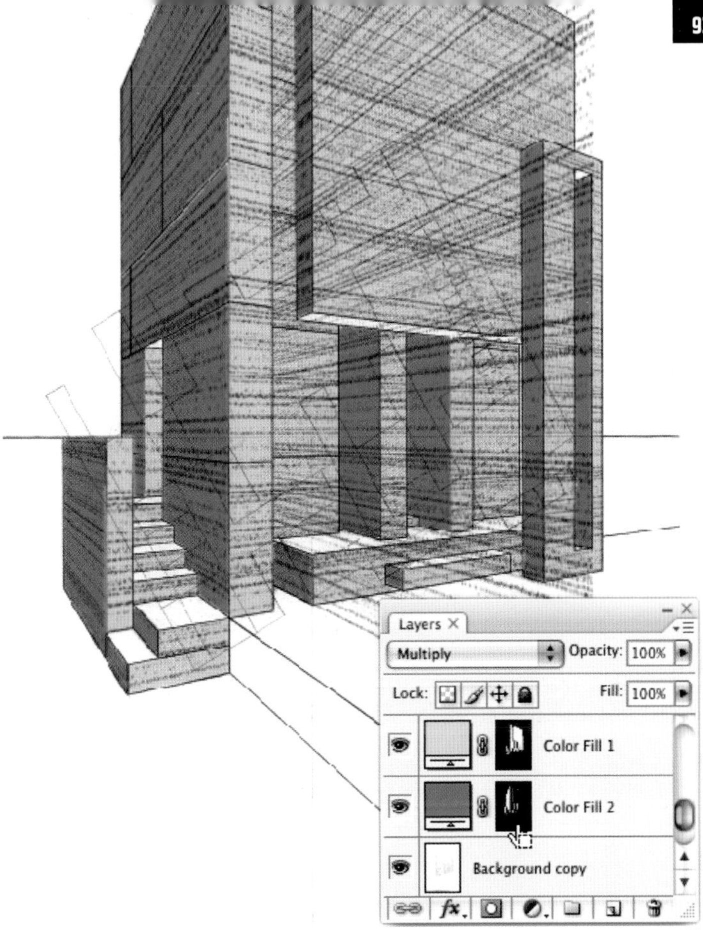

65

66

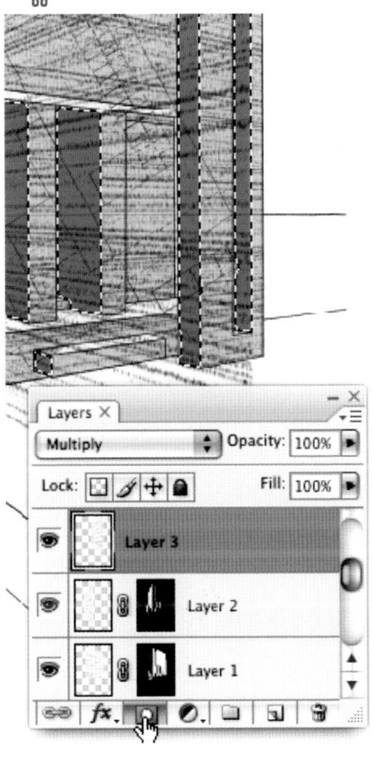

67

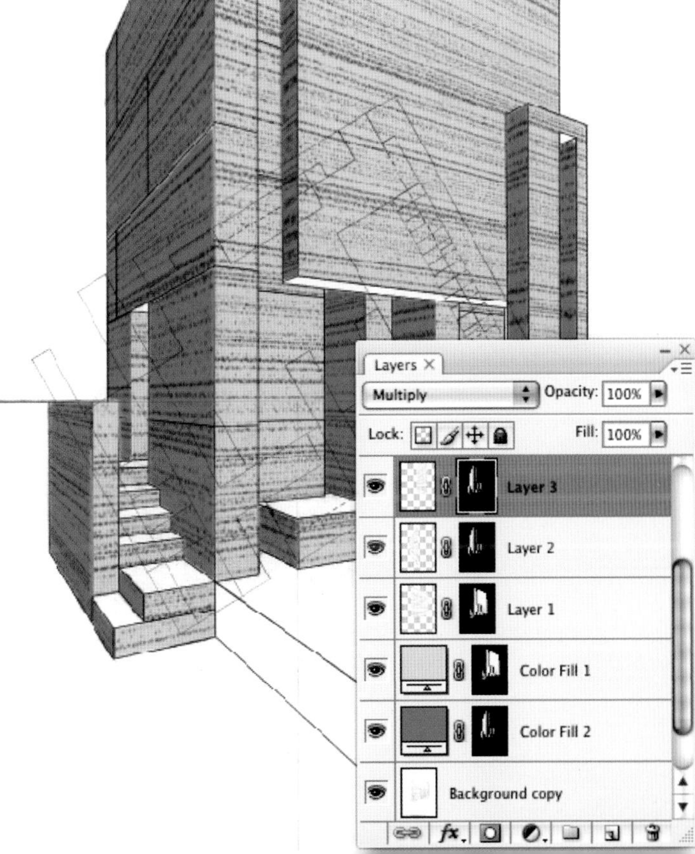

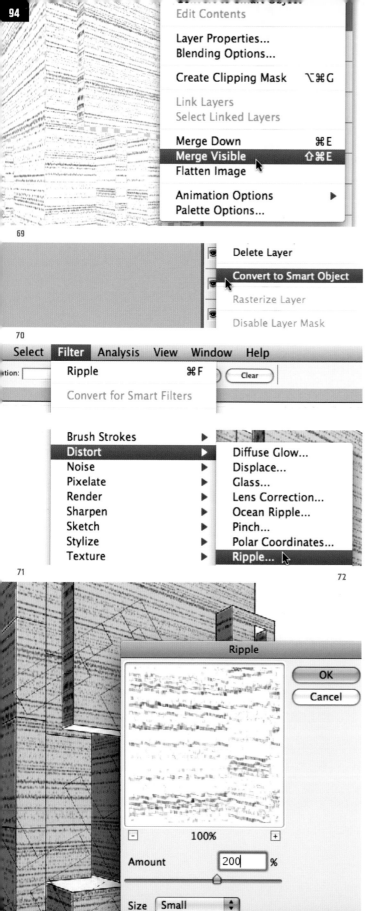

69

70

71

72

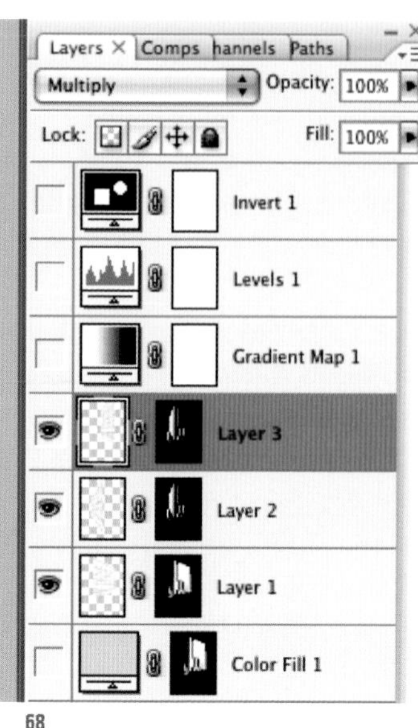

68

Make sure all the other layers are hidden (ill.68), and select the command Merge Visible from the menu of the Layers palette (ill.69).
It´s simply unnecessary for your further work that the hatchings are spread over three layers. You can call the resulting layer hatching.

Convert this layer into a Smart Object, so you can use a few filters easily.
For this, click with the right-hand mouse button on the layer entry and select the corresponding command from the context menu (ill.70).

Then pick the Distort filter Ripple from the Filter menu (ill.71), set its Amount to 200 and the Size to Small (ill.72).

To thin out the hatching image a bit, call up the Layer Style adjustment dialog for this Smart layer by double-clicking it (ill.73).

In the lower area of the adjustment dialog, move the left-hand blend control for this layer to the right, until its value is shown as 190.
With the preview active, you can observe

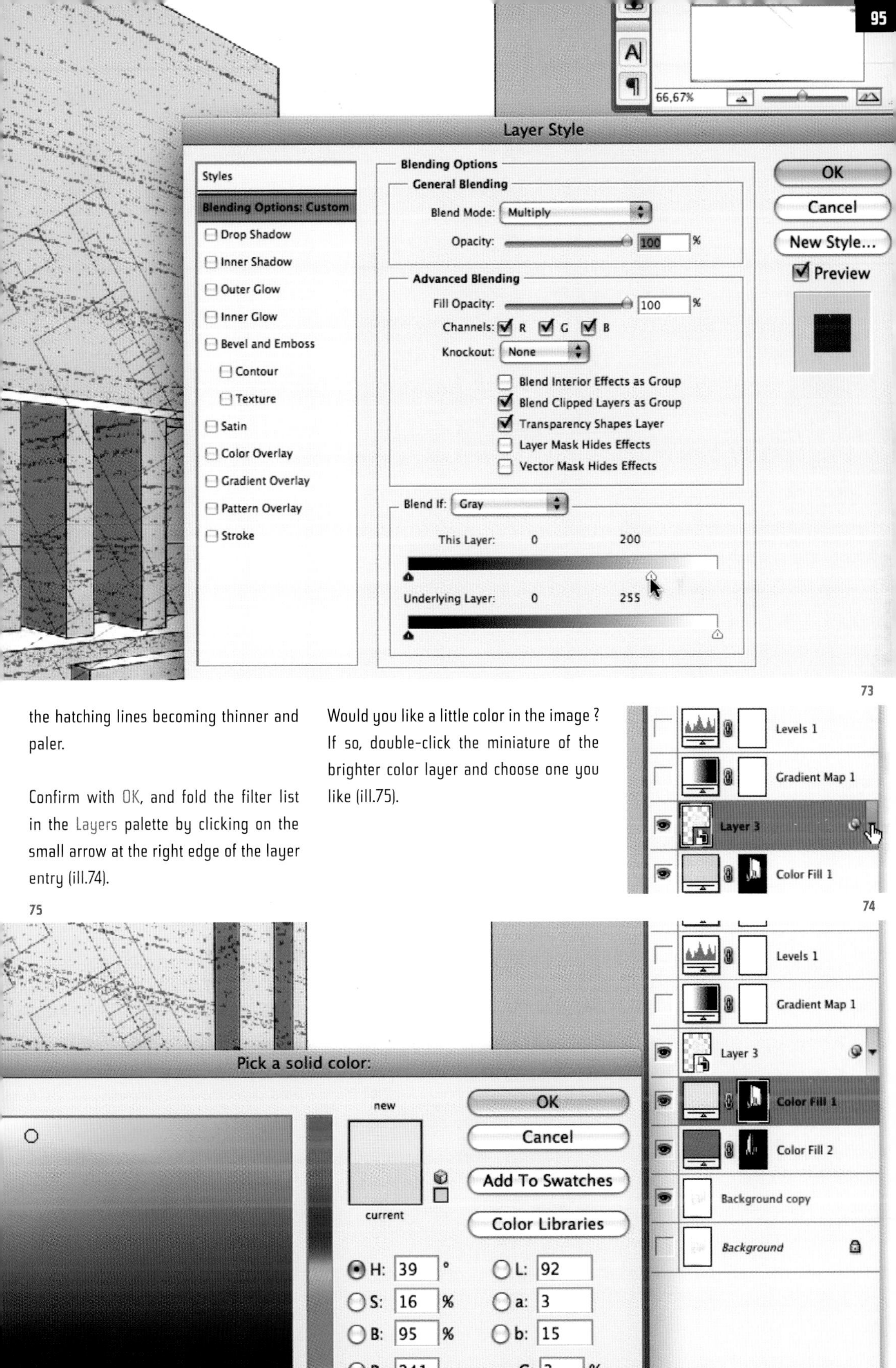

73

the hatching lines becoming thinner and paler.

Confirm with OK, and fold the filter list in the Layers palette by clicking on the small arrow at the right edge of the layer entry (ill.74).

Would you like a little color in the image? If so, double-click the miniature of the brighter color layer and choose one you like (ill.75).

75

74

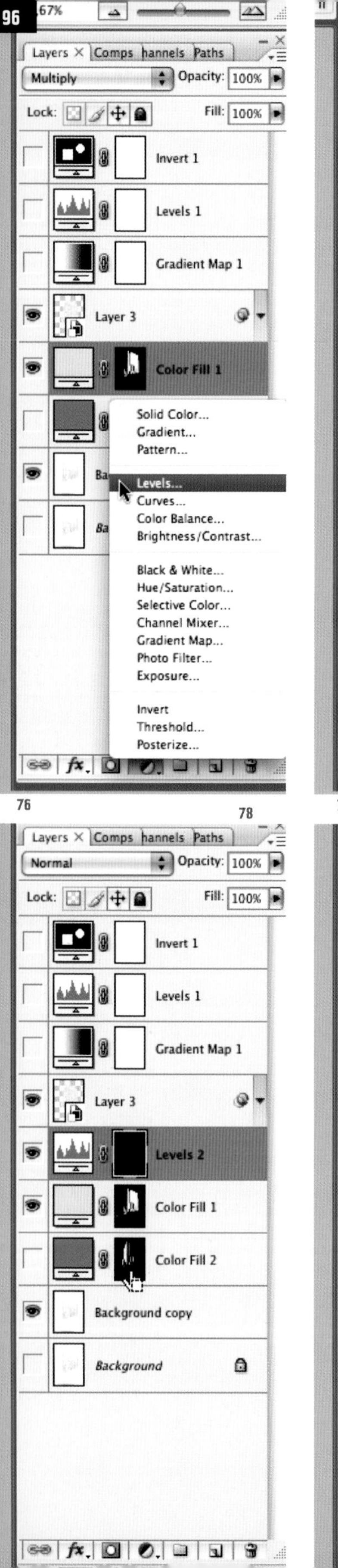

76

78

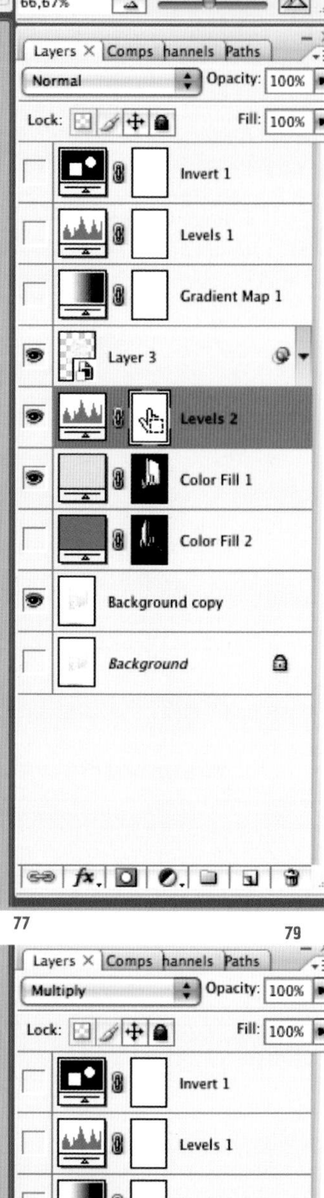

77

79

If you´d now prefer to control the color in such a way that you have a common color layer for all the surfaces that you partially shade with a Levels adjustment, then proceed as follows:

Insert over the brighter color layer (the one you´ve just given a color) a Levels adjustment layer (ill.76). Don´t change anything at the adjustments of the histogram for the moment, and simply confirm with OK.

Fill the mask of the Levels adjustment layer (ill.77) with Black (Alt-Backspace if Black is the foreground color, CTRL-Backspace if Black is the background one).

Bring the mask marking the surfaces pointing left into the image as a selection, by clicking on the mask miniature of the darker color layer with the CTRL key held down (ill.78), click on the black mask miniature of the Levels adjustment layer, and fill the selection area with White (Alt- or CTRL-Backspace, ill.79).

The selection still hovers over your image. Now also click on the mask miniature of the brighter color layer, and here fill the selection area with White too.

Now your drawing is evenly colored, without differences in brightness (ill.80).

80

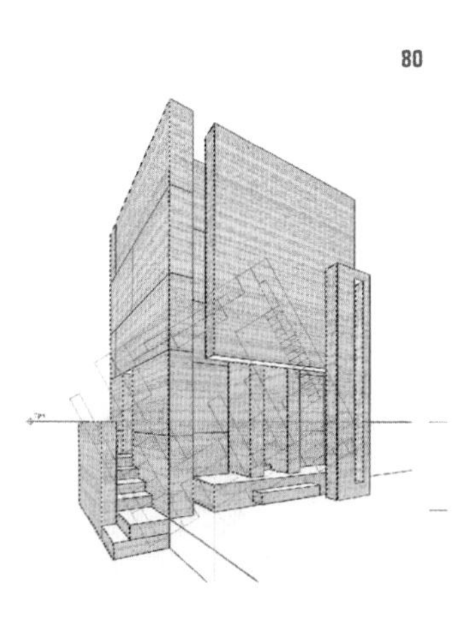

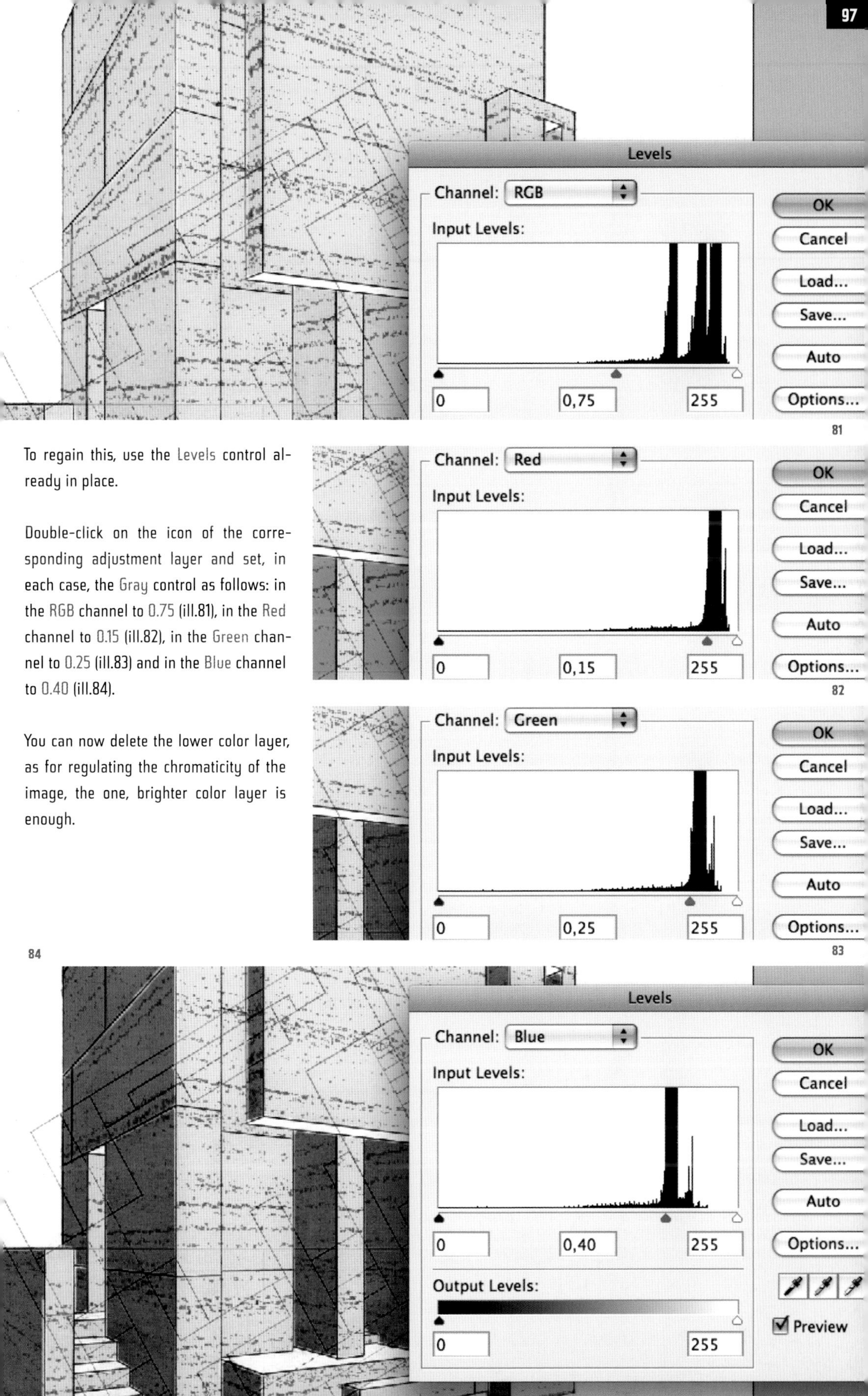

81

To regain this, use the Levels control already in place.

Double-click on the icon of the corresponding adjustment layer and set, in each case, the Gray control as follows: in the RGB channel to 0.75 (ill.81), in the Red channel to 0.15 (ill.82), in the Green channel to 0.25 (ill.83) and in the Blue channel to 0.40 (ill.84).

You can now delete the lower color layer, as for regulating the chromaticity of the image, the one, brighter color layer is enough.

82

83

84

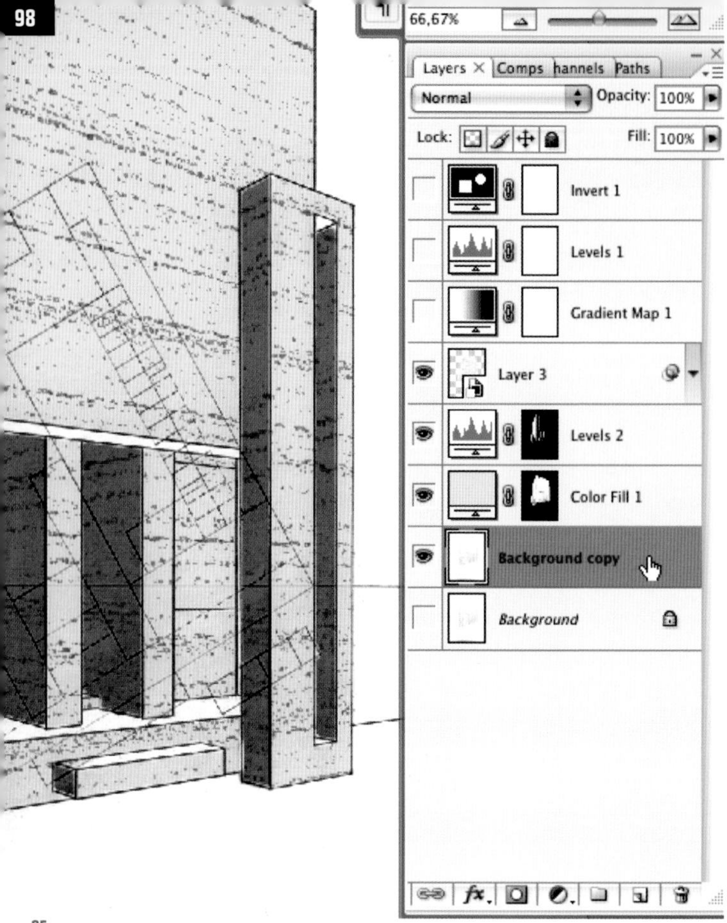

Finally, it can´t do any harm to sharpen the pencil drawing itself too.

Convert the layer containing it into a Smart Object, by right-clicking on the layer entry (ill.85) and selecting the corresponding command (ill.86).

Use the filter Unsharp Mask with the same adjustments as above when creating the hatching (Amount=500%, Radius=0.5 pixels: ill.87; cf. ill.31).

So far, the final result looks quite OK (ill.88). If you want, you may attend to the bottom-view surfaces too.

For that, you´d also have to fill its areas in the mask of the color layer with White, and with the same selection insert a masked Levels adjustment layer, to make the surfaces even darker than the ones pointing left.

85

86

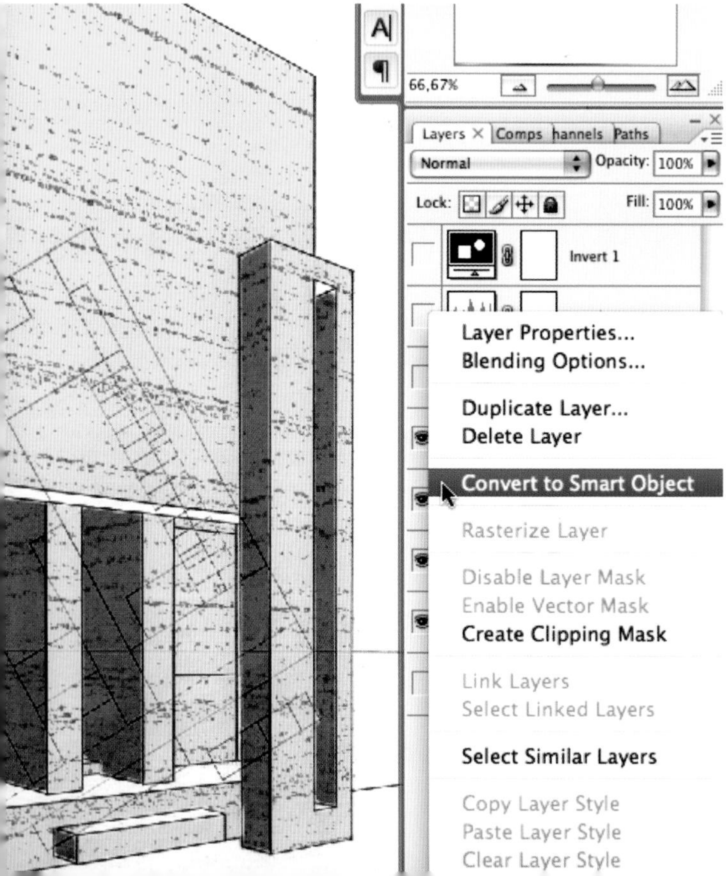

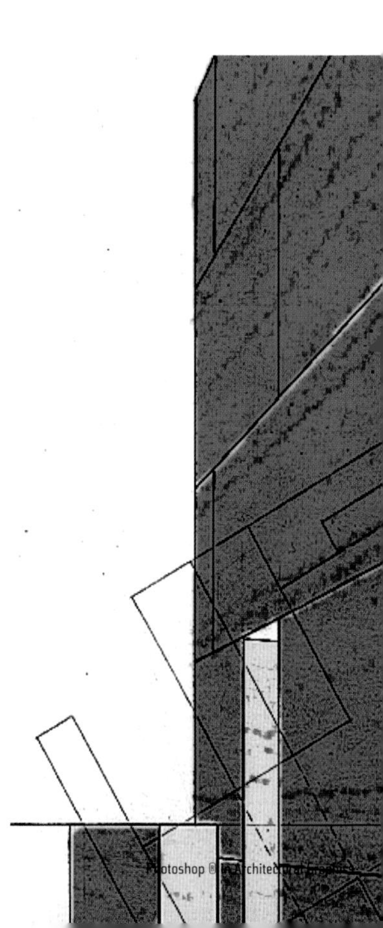

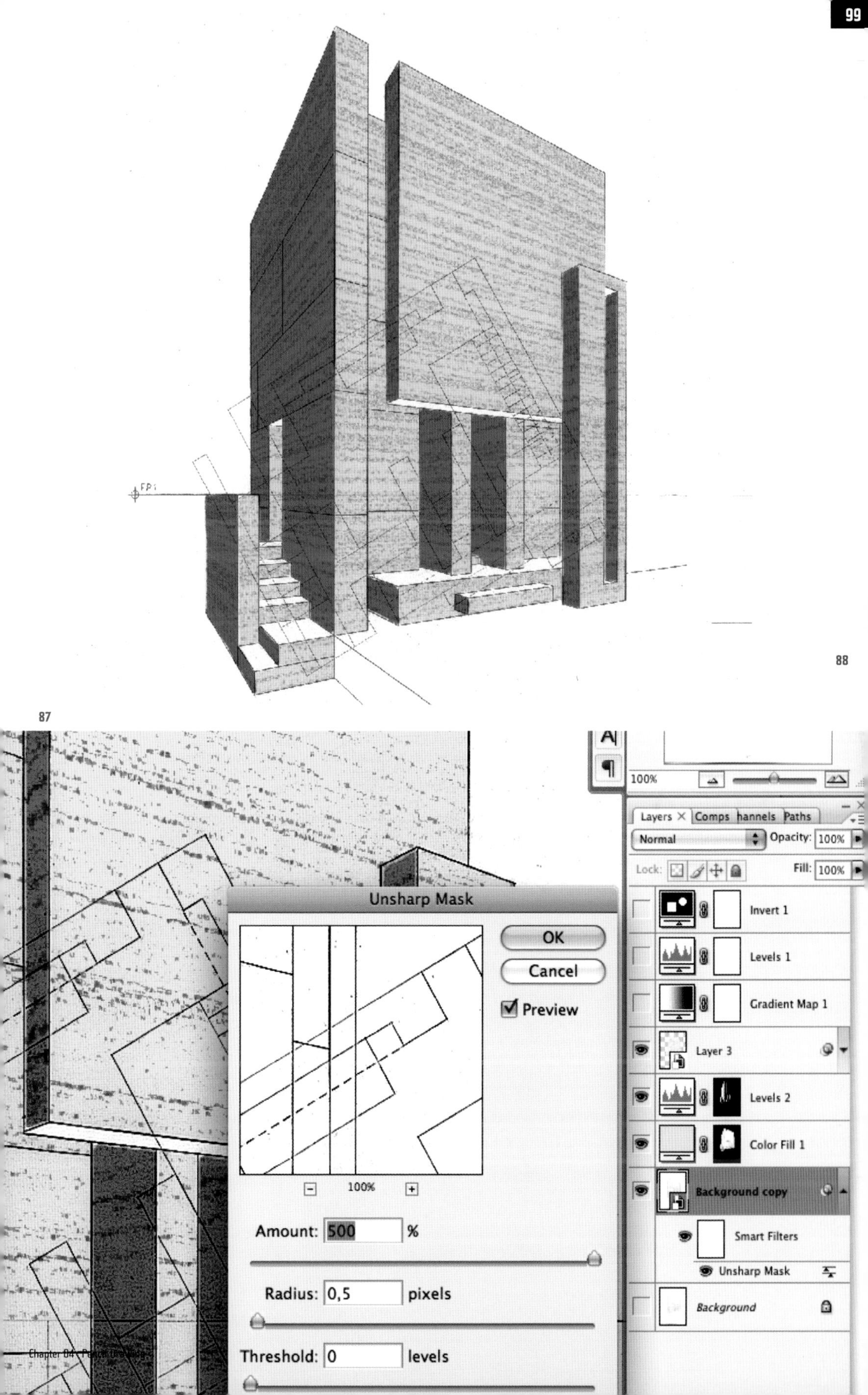
FP1
Unsharp Mask
OK
Cancel
Preview
100%
Amount: 500 %
Radius: 0,5 pixels
Threshold: 0 levels
Layers
Comps
hannels
Paths
Normal
Opacity: 100%
Lock:
Fill: 100%
Invert 1
Levels 1
Gradient Map 1
Layer 3
Levels 2
Color Fill 1
Background copy
Smart Filters
Unsharp Mask
Background

88

87

1

2

Seamless Texture

You need bitmap textures both in Photoshop® and in 3D applications, to map them onto object surfaces.
Using as an example a brick surface I´ve created, I want to show you how to produce such a bitmap texture module.

Take a look at illustrations 1 and 2. The upper illustration shows the assembly of an image module, four times horizontally and three times vertically; the lower illustration shows the original image, in which each brick is placed by hand and no repetitive pattern can be observed (I´ve created this texture for a wall ca. 5 x 3 m in size).

The advantage of a so called tiling like in the first image is that this way you can fill surfaces no matter how big, the disadvantage is, as we know, that the resulting pattern repetition is noticeable from a certain factor.

Of course it helps if the tiling takes place seamlessly, i.e. the right edge of the module in each case attaches itself to the next on the left without any transition, and analogously the lower in each case to the attaching upper edge of the next module.

I´ll show you how to cut out from the large original brick rug a more-or-less square part and work on this in such a way that it can be seamlessly added as a module.

Open the file 05_brick.psd and display the rulers with CTRL-R.

First drag a horizontale guide from the upper ruler into the image so that it runs centered through one of the brick layers (ill.3).
(If you are shown old guides at this point,

select the command Clear Guides from the View menu, and repeat everything.)

Place another horizontal guide so far below the first that 15 complete brick layers lie between the two guides; the second guide should also go centered through a brick layer again (ill.3).

Then insert a first vertical guide so that it intersects the upper horizontal guide in the center of one of the big bricks (ill.3), and place a second vertical so that all of the guides together form a square; the last guide should also cut the horizontals in the center of one of the big bricks (ill.3).

If you´re happy with the position of the guides, pick the Crop tool (C, ill.4).

Make sure that up in the Options palette no crop dimensions are entered; if necessary click at the very right on the Clear button.

3

4

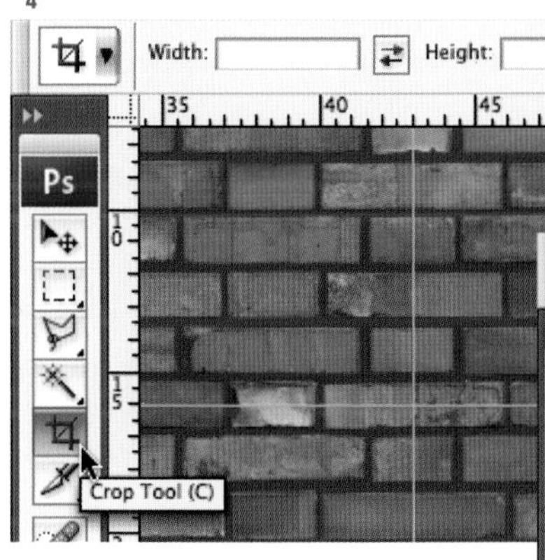

Now trace your guides square with the Crop tool (as you see, the tool snaps to the guides). When you´re finished, the rest of the image is at first shown darkened (ill.5).

Be absolutely sure that now, in the Options palette, Delete is checked for the Cropped Area.

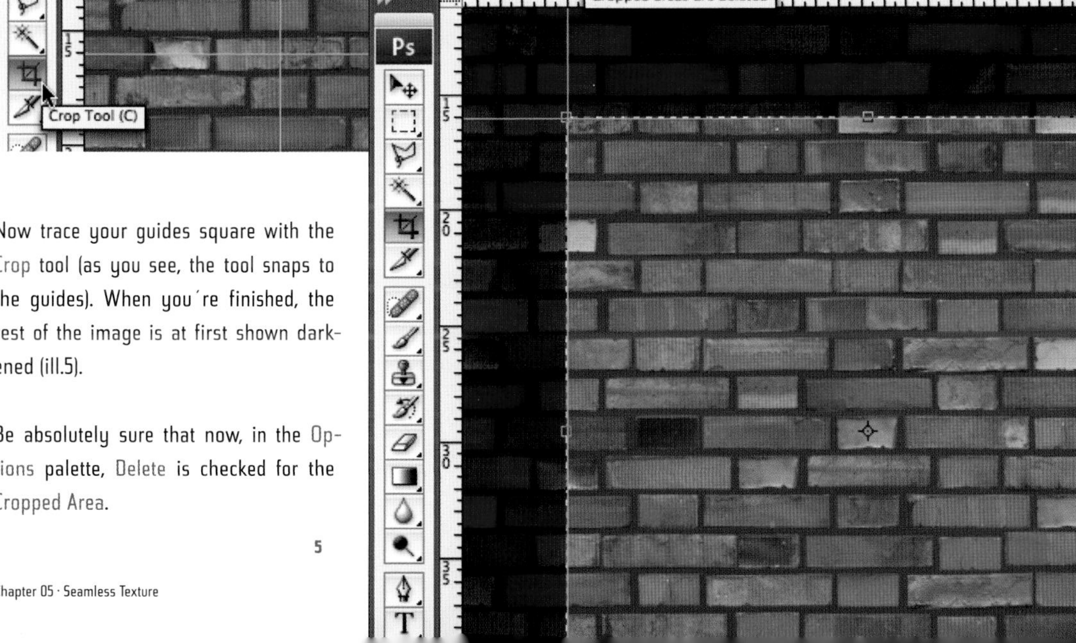

5

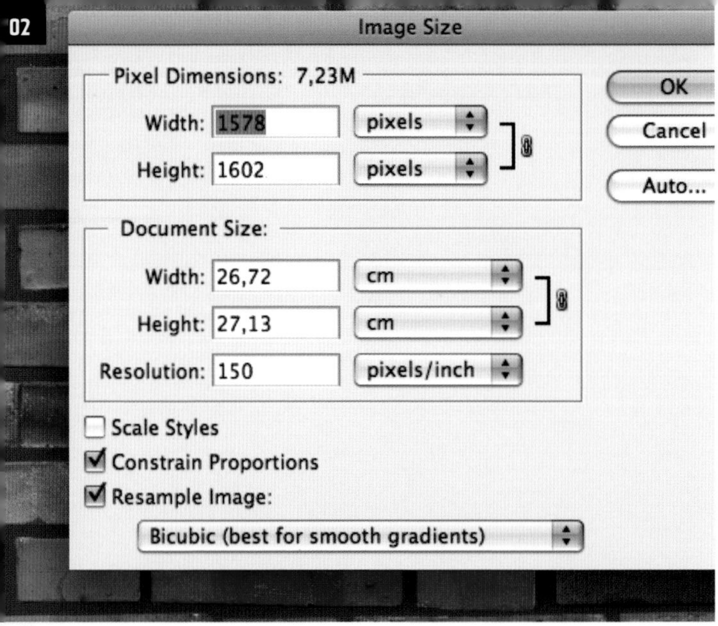

7

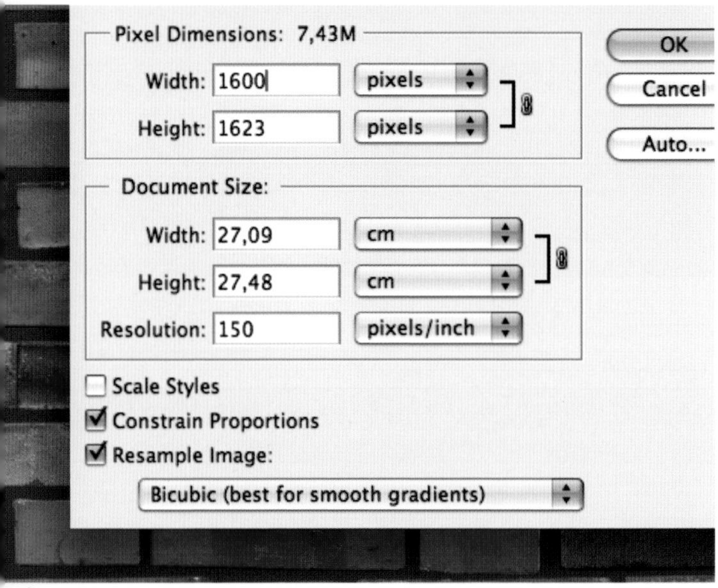

8

9

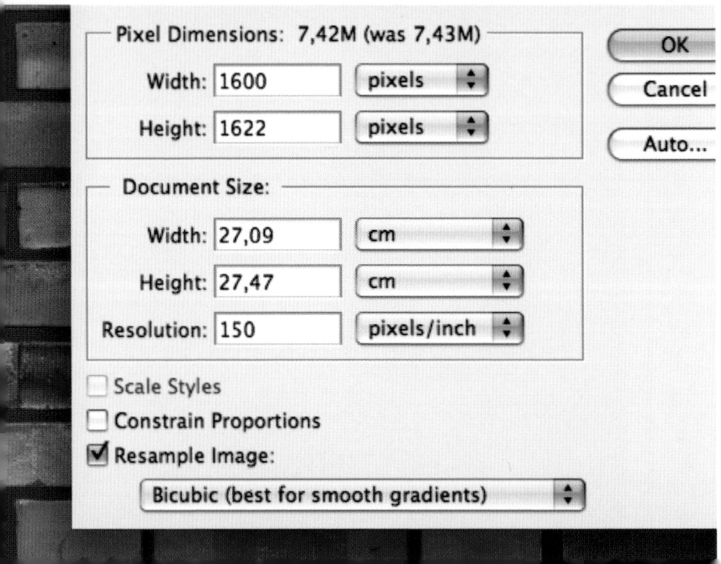

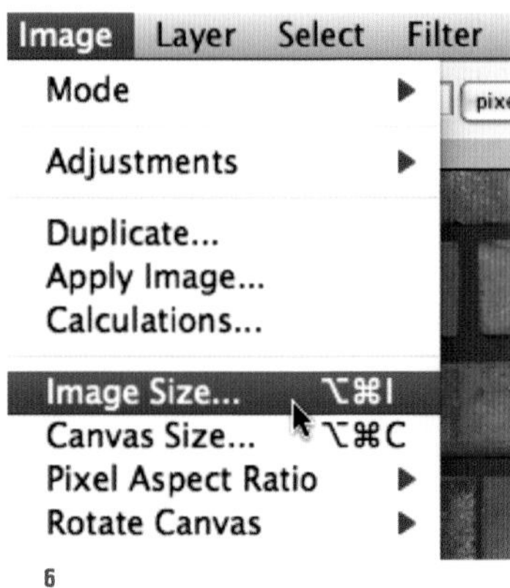

6

Press Return to complete the cropping. Then select the command Image Size (from the Image menu, ill.6), where the Pixel Dimensions of the resulting image are displayed (ill.7).

Check that the options Resample Image and Constrain Proportions are activated, and now enter for Width the value 1600 pixels (ill.8).

For later working it´s essential that the pixel amounts for both dimensions are even numbers, so now deactivate the option Constrain Proportions, and then in addition change the pixel value for the Height to 1622 (ill.9). Confirm with OK.

Now to the essentials. You´ll use a filter which swaps the right and left halves of the image, and also the upper and lower halves; the middle axes thus become borders of the module, which enables a seamless addition of the module.
Make sure the image layer brick is ac-

10

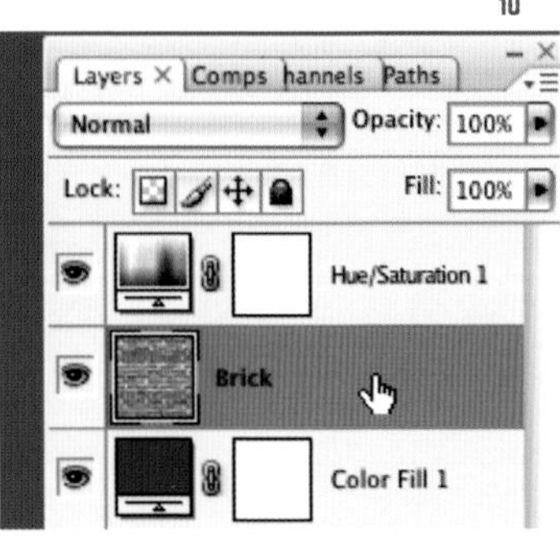

tivated (ill.10), and select the filter Offset (Other filters from the Filter menu, ill.11).

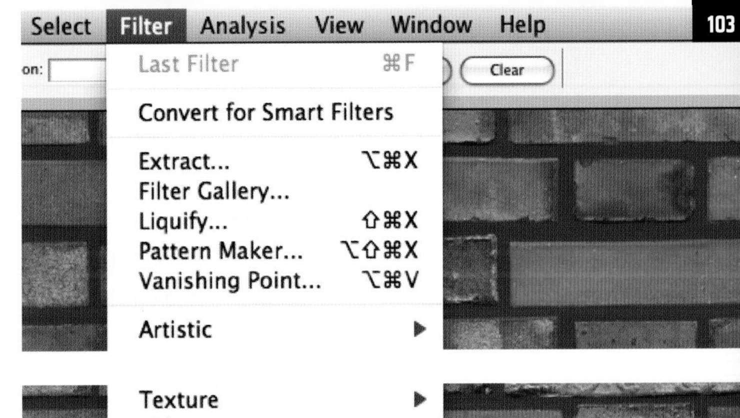

In the adjustment dialog, enter for the offset in each case half of the pixel dimensions of the image: Horizontal 800, Vertical 811 pixels (ill.12).

For the Undefined Areas (which become free when they´re moved) select the option Wrap Around.
With Preview switched on, you can see the image components move- the left border area now shows the continuation of the right, so to say, and the upper border area the continuation of the lower.

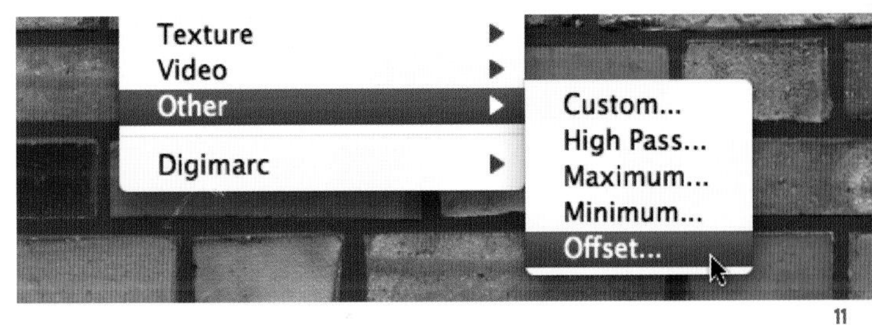

11

The "problem" has now moved from the edge into the middle; the bricks are disconnected along the middle axes and should be replaced by intact ones.

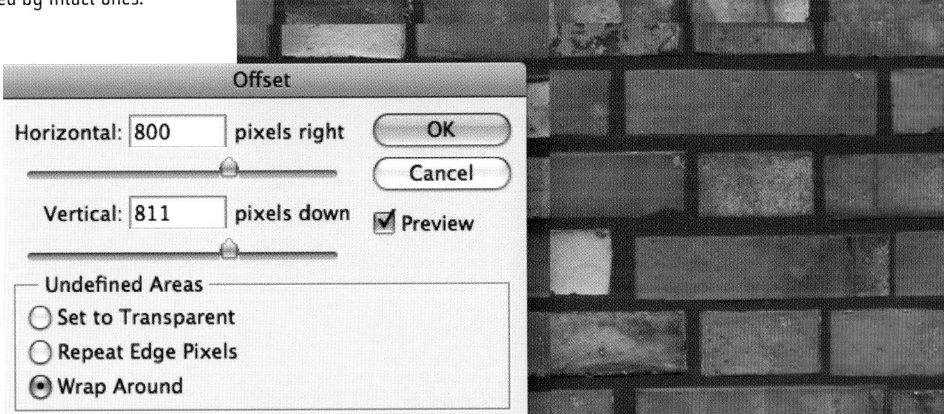

12

13

For this, first remove the wrongly connected bricks lying in the vertical middle axis from the image (except for the uppermost and lowest bisected bricks), by selecting them first.

Use the Rectangular Marquee tool for this - you can add the selections of the individual bricks by pressing the Shift key (ill.13; here the selection is shown in mask mode, using Q).

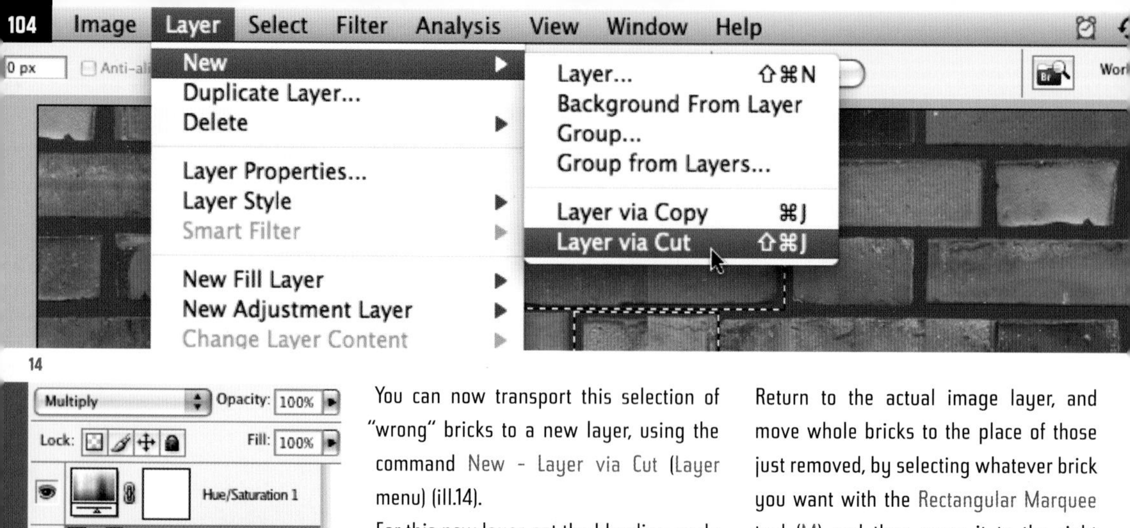

14

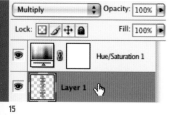

15

You can now transport this selection of "wrong" bricks to a new layer, using the command New - Layer via Cut (Layer menu) (ill.14).
For this new layer, set the blending mode to Multiply (ill.15).

Return to the actual image layer, and move whole bricks to the place of those just removed, by selecting whatever brick you want with the Rectangular Marquee tool (M) and then move it to the right place with the Move tool (V) and the Alt key held down (so it becomes a copy, ill.16).
Make sure you don´t use bricks in the immediate vicinity, so that you´re not caught on too quickly.

Continue in this way, checking the provisional result from time to time by hiding the layer with the removed bricks (ill.17).

Now attend to the horizontal middle axis. Select all the bricks except those lying at the left or right edge and in the middle (ill.18), also create a new layer (Layer menu: New - Layer via Cut), and also set the blending mode of this new layer to Multiply.
On the brick layer, again move new, whole bricks to the emptied areas, as you´ve already done for the vertical middle axis (see above: select and Alt-move).

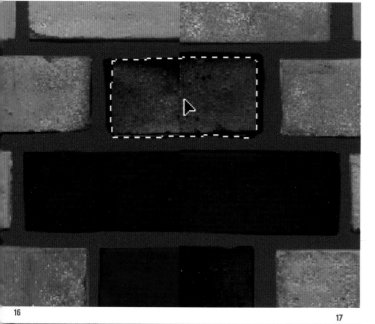

16

17

18

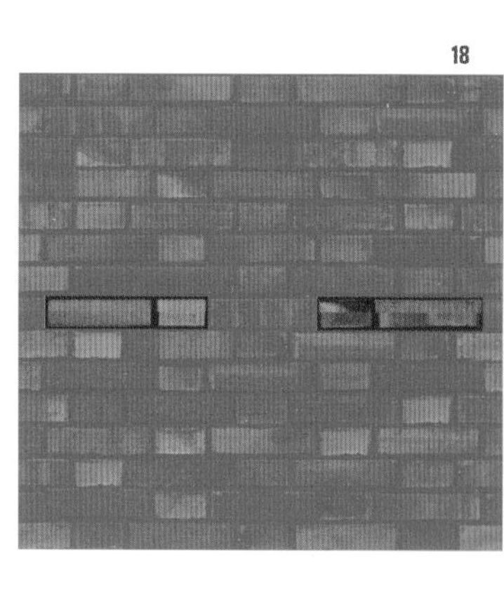

Now to the four last problem cases: at the ends of the middle axes, bisected bricks rather than whole ones have to be inserted (ill.19).

First remove, as before, the four existing "wrong" bricks from the image layer, and set their new layer to Multiply too.

For the left and right bisected bricks select in the image layer brick a complete example and copy it onto a new layer (Layer menu: New – Layer via Copy, ill.20).

Now show only this new layer and the colored background layer, and then with the Rectangular Marquee tool select the right half of the copied brick.

Transport this selection to a new layer, as before with the command New – Layer via Cut (Layer menu, ill.21).

19

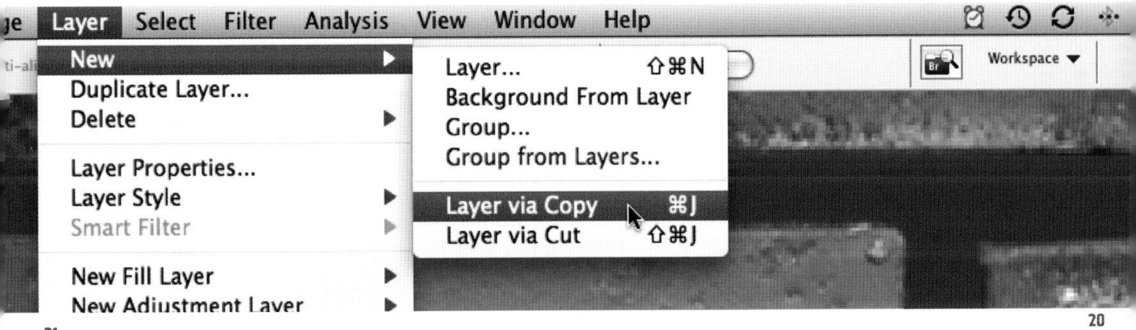

ge Layer Select Filter Analysis View Window Help

Workspace ▼

New ▶
Duplicate Layer...
Delete ▶
Layer Properties...
Layer Style ▶
Smart Filter ▶
New Fill Layer ▶
New Adjustment Layer ▶

Layer... ⇧⌘N
Background From Layer
Group...
Group from Layers...
Layer via Copy ⌘J
Layer via Cut ⇧⌘J

20

21

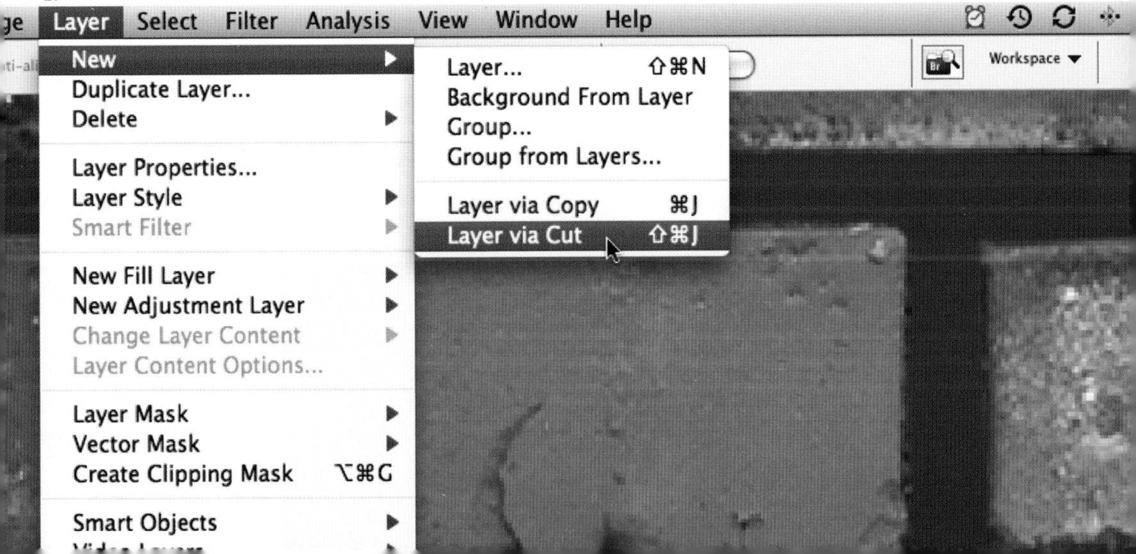

ge Layer Select Filter Analysis View Window Help

Workspace ▼

New ▶
Duplicate Layer...
Delete ▶
Layer Properties...
Layer Style ▶
Smart Filter ▶
New Fill Layer ▶
New Adjustment Layer ▶
Change Layer Content ▶
Layer Content Options...
Layer Mask ▶
Vector Mask ▶
Create Clipping Mask ⌥⌘G
Smart Objects ▶

Layer... ⇧⌘N
Background From Layer
Group...
Group from Layers...
Layer via Copy ⌘J
Layer via Cut ⇧⌘J

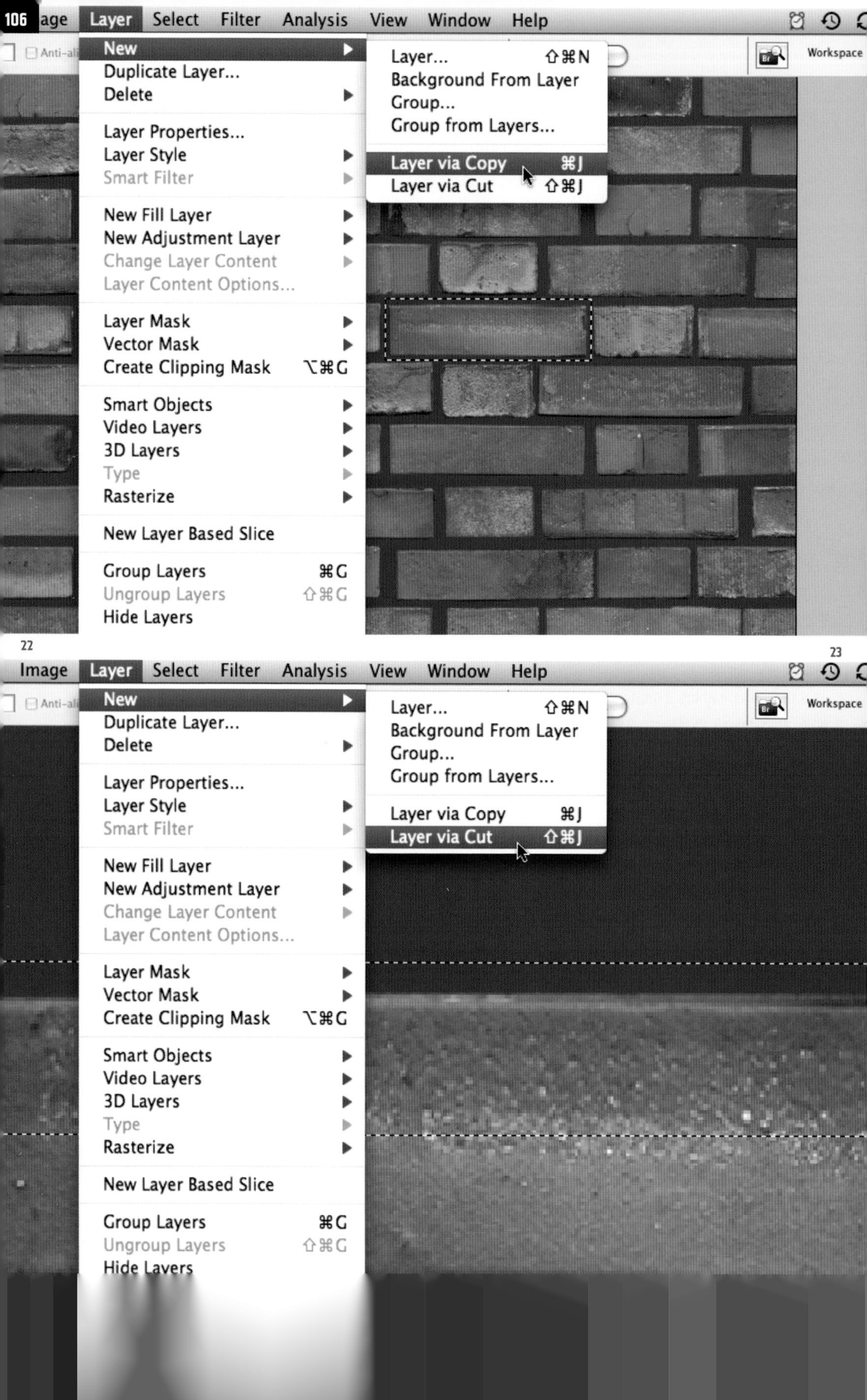
age Layer Select Filter Analysis View Window Help
Anti-ali
Workspace
New
Duplicate Layer...
Delete
Layer Properties...
Layer Style
Smart Filter
New Fill Layer
New Adjustment Layer
Change Layer Content
Layer Content Options...
Layer Mask
Vector Mask
Create Clipping Mask ⌥⌘G
Smart Objects
Video Layers
3D Layers
Type
Rasterize
New Layer Based Slice
Group Layers ⌘G
Ungroup Layers ⇧⌘G
Hide Layers
Layer... ⇧⌘N
Background From Layer
Group...
Group from Layers...
Layer via Copy ⌘J
Layer via Cut ⇧⌘J
Image Layer Select Filter Analysis View Window Help
Anti-ali
Workspace
New
Duplicate Layer...
Delete
Layer Properties...
Layer Style
Smart Filter
New Fill Layer
New Adjustment Layer
Change Layer Content
Layer Content Options...
Layer Mask
Vector Mask
Create Clipping Mask ⌥⌘G
Smart Objects
Video Layers
3D Layers
Type
Rasterize
New Layer Based Slice
Group Layers ⌘G
Ungroup Layers ⇧⌘G
Hide Layers
Layer... ⇧⌘N
Background From Layer
Group...
Group from Layers...
Layer via Copy ⌘J
Layer via Cut ⇧⌘J

22

23

Now you have two new layers, each showing half of a small brick. Activate them, and drag their contents with the Move tool to the right place: the left half to the right, and the right half to the left, respectively.

Repeat all this for the upper and lower half-brick: select a suitable example, copy it onto a new layer (ill.22), draw a selection marquee round its upper half and deposit this via Cut on a further layer (ill.23).

Also move these two halves to the right place, the lower half upwards and the upper downwards.
Again, use the Move tool on the corresponding layer. When you´re finished with that, take a look at the four layers with the half-bricks. It should look like in illustration 24.

As you now have nothing more to move, you can combine all the layers showing the "right" bricks into one.

Show only the layer brick and the four layers containing the moved half-bricks, activate at least one of them (ill.25) and select the command Merge Visible from the palette menu (ill.26).

Delete the layer with the cut-out, wrongly assembled bricks.

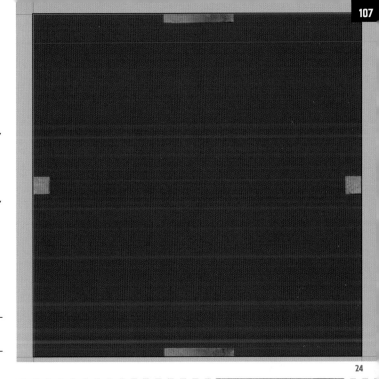

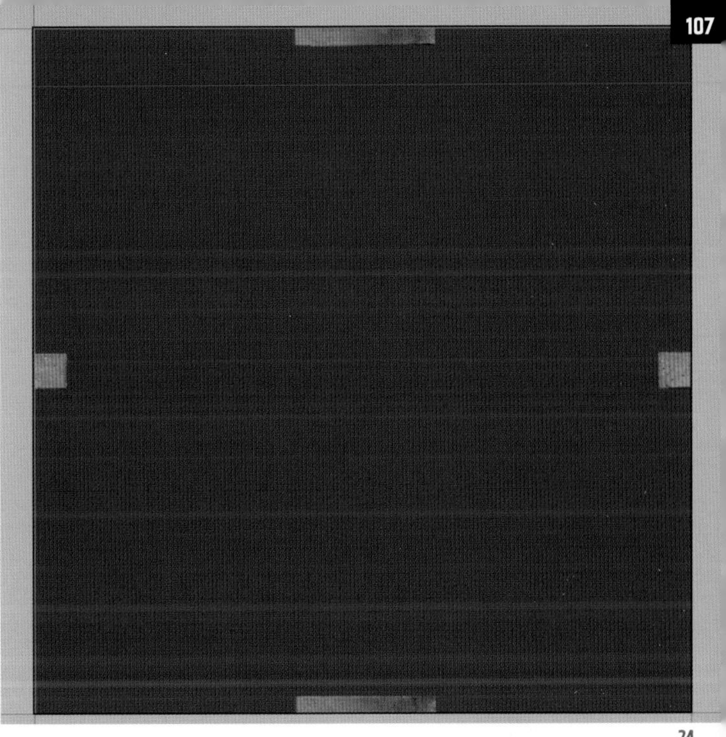

24

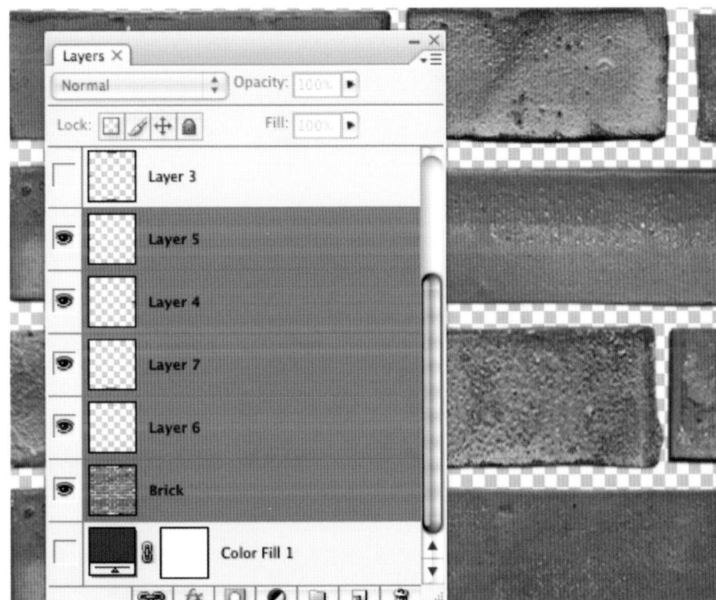

25

26

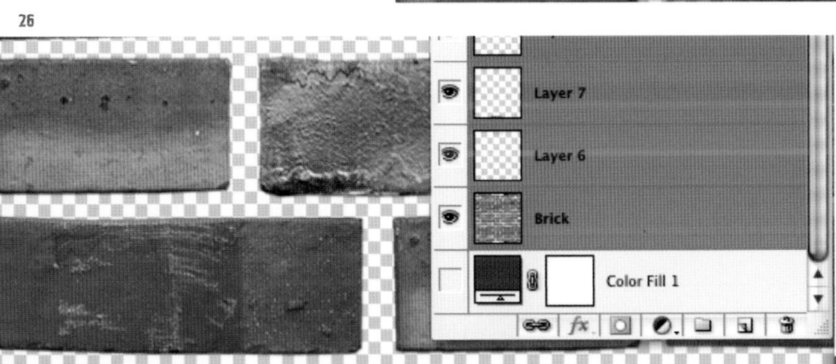

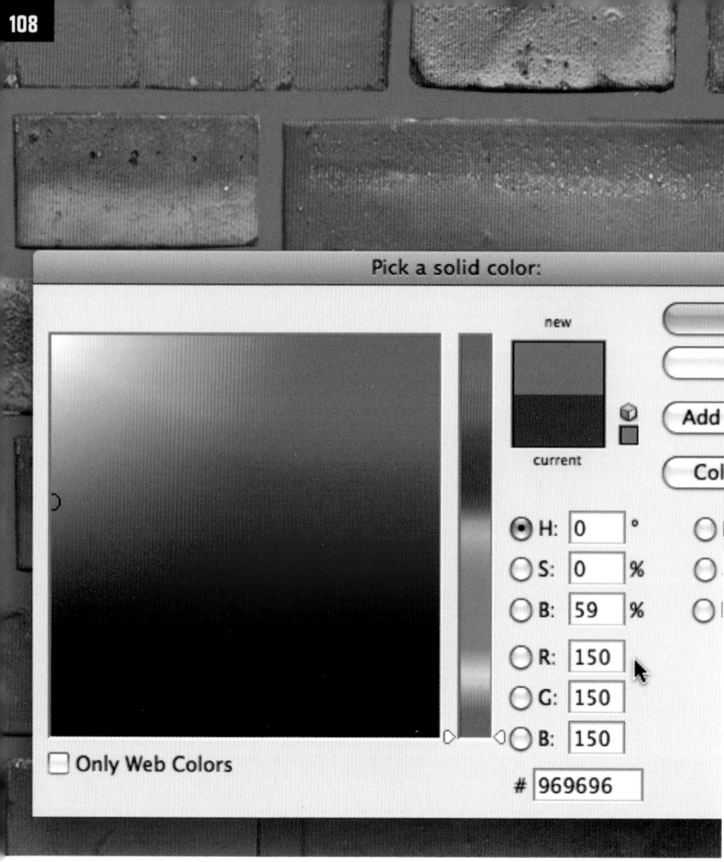

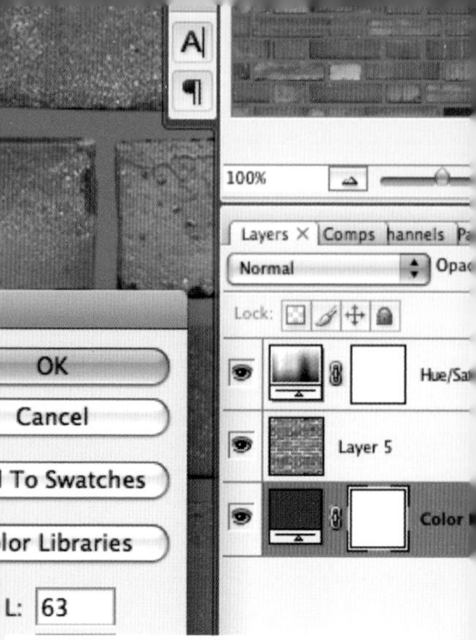

27

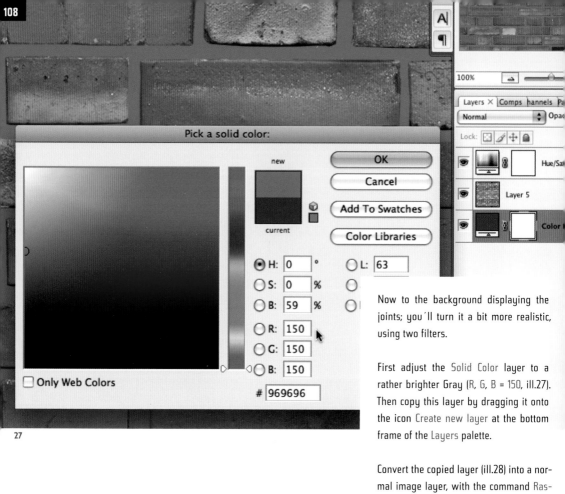

Now to the background displaying the joints; you´ll turn it a bit more realistic, using two filters.

First adjust the Solid Color layer to a rather brighter Gray (R, G, B = 150, ill.27). Then copy this layer by dragging it onto the icon Create new layer at the bottom frame of the Layers palette.

Convert the copied layer (ill.28) into a normal image layer, with the command Rasterize Layer from the context menu (right mouse click on the layer entry, ill.29).

To be able to use the filter losslessly, convert the layer just rasterized into a Smart Object, with the corresponding command from the same context menu (ill.30).

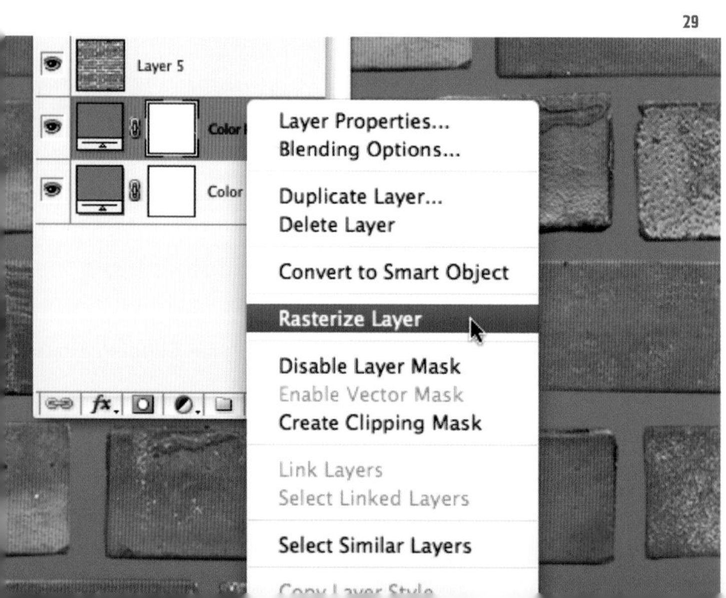

29

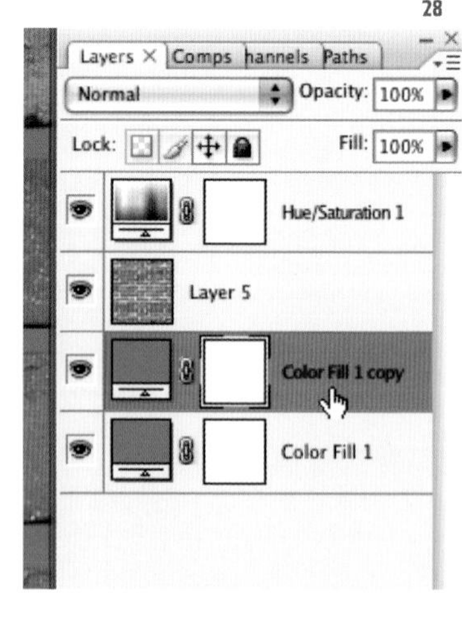

28

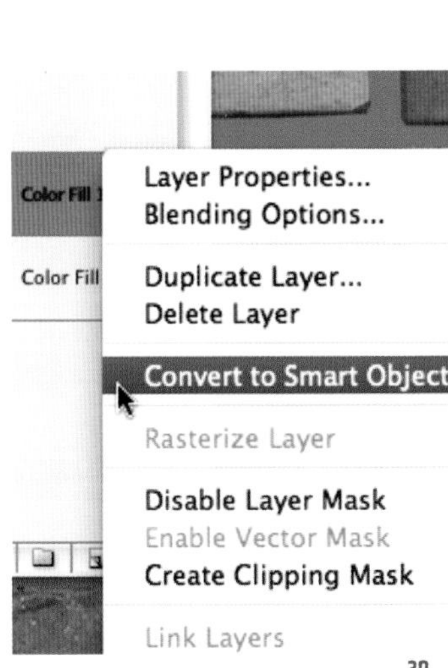

30

Check that your new Smart layer is activated and that the foreground color is Black and the background color White (if necessary, press D and then X).

Now select the Texture filter Grain from the Filter menu (ill.31). Choose the Grain type Stippled, set the Intensity to 100 and the Contrast to 50 (ill.32).

Now set the blending mode of the layer to Multiply, and you´ll see the filtered layer mix with the color layer below it (ill.33).

To soften the filter effect a bit, reduce the new layer's Opacity to 35%.

Now use a further filter on this layer, the Distort filter Ripple (Filter menu, ill.34).

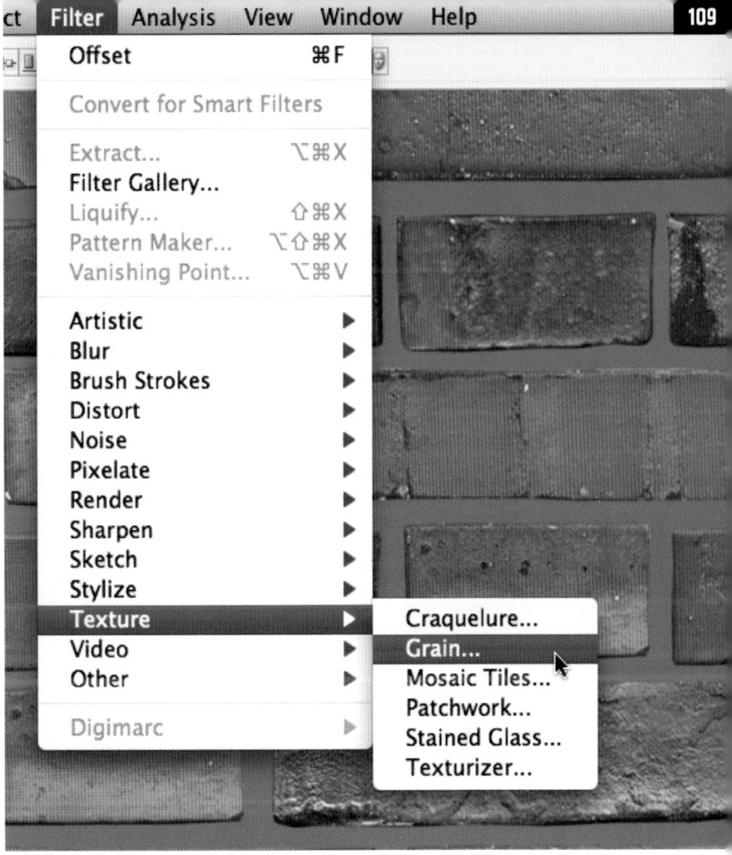

31

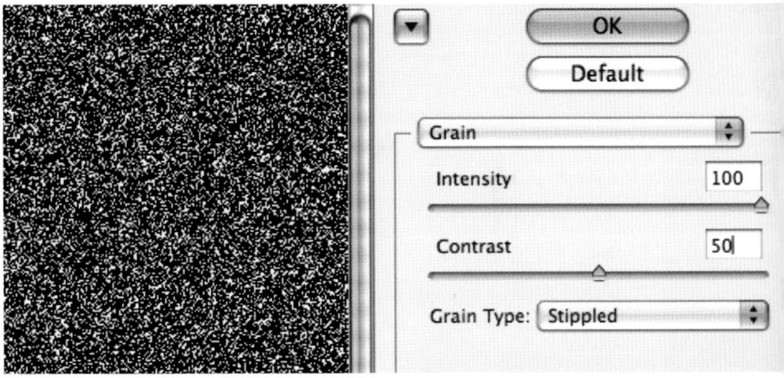

32

33

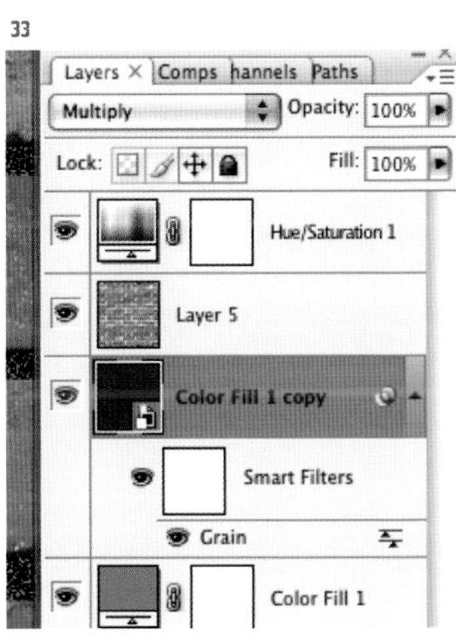

34

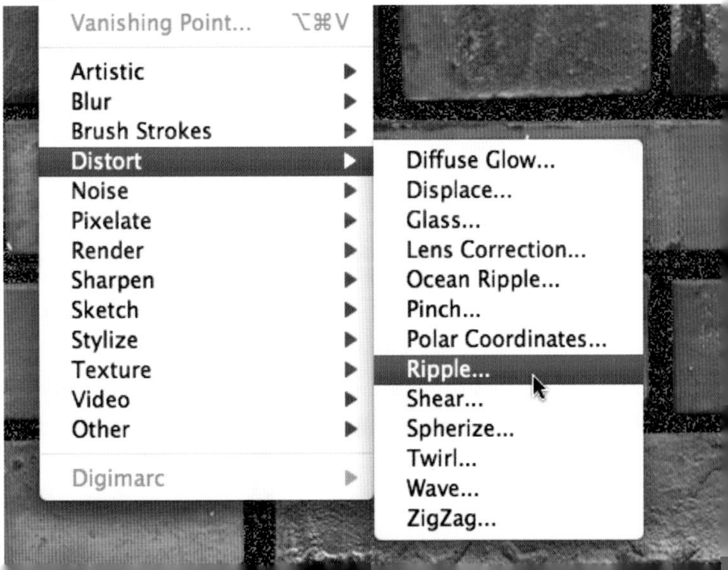

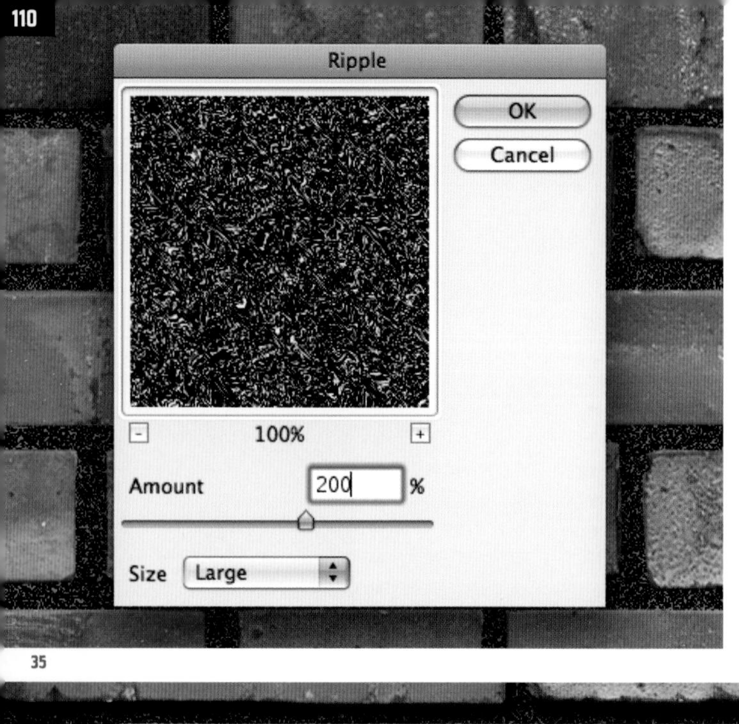

35

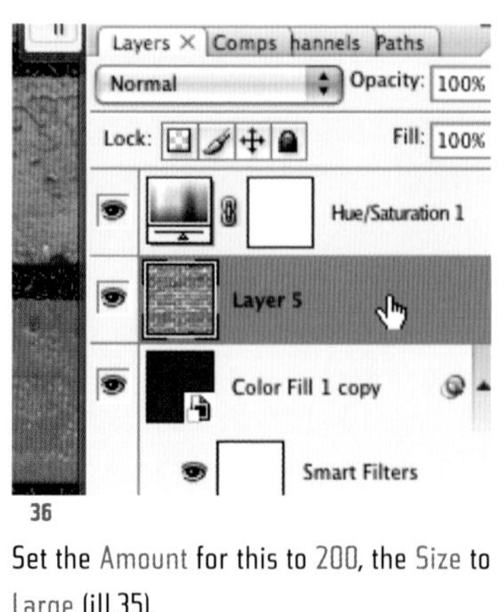

36

Set the Amount for this to 200, the Size to Large (ill.35).
Confirm with OK, and as you see, the grainy surface is modulated additionally by this filter.

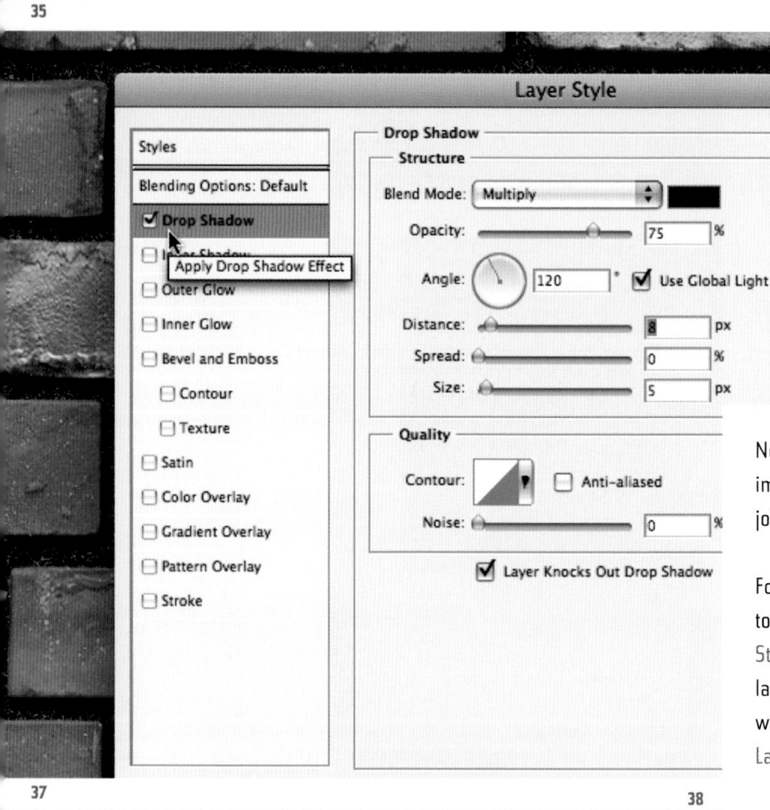

37

38

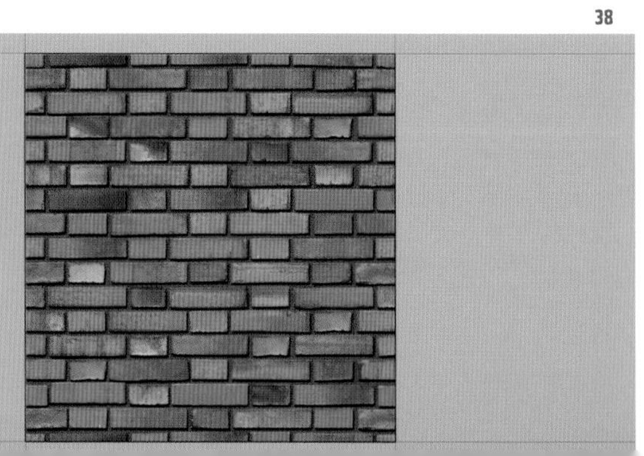

Now you can insert cast shadow into the image, to simulate some depth for the joints surface.

For this you´ll use the brick layer itself, to which you´ll allocate a so called Layer Style. Double-click on the entry of the layer in the Layers palette (ill.36), and a window opens in which you can attend to Layer Styles (ill.37).

Here, click left in the list on the entry Drop Shadow, then this effect is activated and you can carry out adjustments for it on the right.

Just play around a little with it, and note the effects in the image (should you not see any changes, then presumably the option Preview is deactivated). If you´d like to have the default settings again, just press the Alt key and click on the Cancel button, which is now called Reset (under the OK button).

Compared to the presets, I´ve undertaken only one differing adaptation, raising the Distance to 8.

Your brick module is now finished (ill.38); all that's left to do now is to save it as a pattern.

But first of all I want to show you how to process the file so that you can also use it as a texture in a 3D application like Cinema 4D®. For this it´s helpful if you define layers that can be useful when texturing.

First you need, for simple use, a layer that summarizes your composition so far.

Show all the layers, and activate the uppermost (the Hue/Saturation adjustment layer), then press Shift-Alt-CTRL-E to produce a combined copy of all the visible layers, and call it Brick Complete (ill.39).

Then you´d like to have a layer showing the bricks on the gray background without joints and cast shadows, maybe because you´d rather produce these effects in the 3D application – hide the Smart layer with the filters, and also the layer style of the brick layer, by clicking on the eye symbol in front of the name Drop Shadow.

Ensure too that your new layer Brick Complete is hidden.
Then press Shift-Alt-CTRL-E again to get a combination of the layers now shown, and call it No FX.

You´ll now create another Black-and-White mask, with which, in the 3D application, you can clip the bricks of their joint background, so that you can produce a realistic look with the on-board shaders of the 3D application (this mask is also helpful for the joint's relief).

Show only the layer with the bricks, and pick the Magic Wand tool (W, or Shift-W, ill.40). In the Options palette set the Tolerance to 1.

Make sure the brick layer is activated (ill.41), and click somewhere in the transparent area between the bricks.

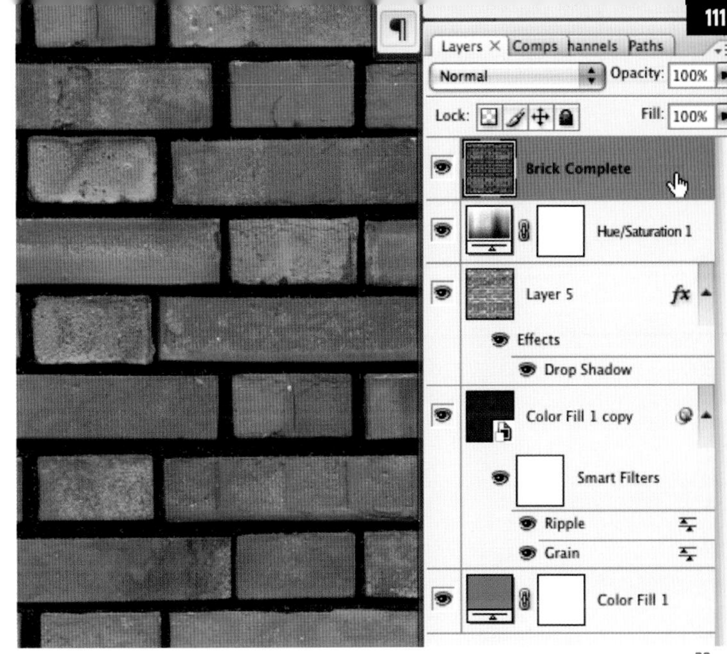

39

40

41

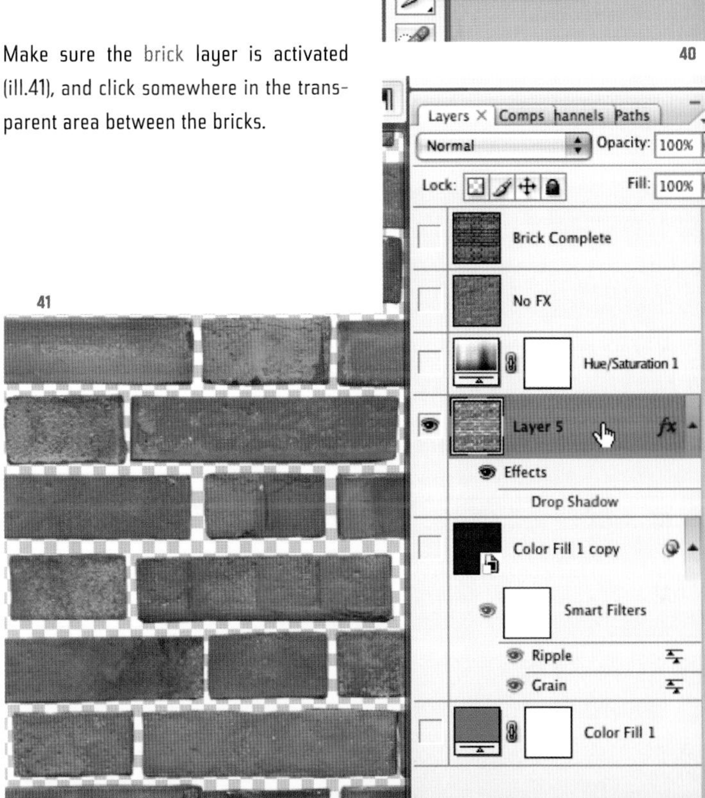

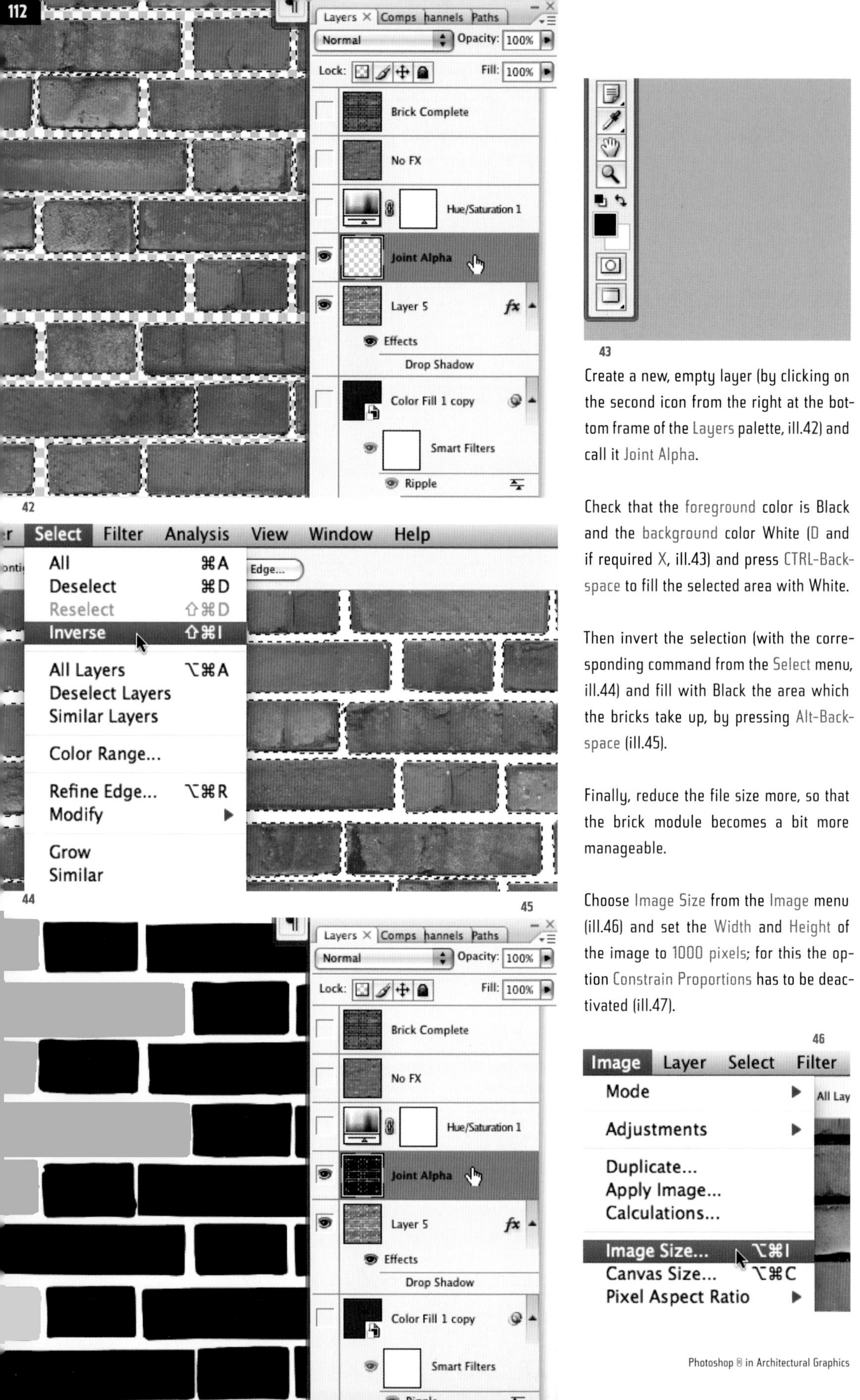

42

43

Create a new, empty layer (by clicking on the second icon from the right at the bottom frame of the Layers palette, ill.42) and call it Joint Alpha.

Check that the foreground color is Black and the background color White (D and if required X, ill.43) and press CTRL-Backspace to fill the selected area with White.

Then invert the selection (with the corresponding command from the Select menu, ill.44) and fill with Black the area which the bricks take up, by pressing Alt-Backspace (ill.45).

Finally, reduce the file size more, so that the brick module becomes a bit more manageable.

44

45

Choose Image Size from the Image menu (ill.46) and set the Width and Height of the image to 1000 pixels; for this the option Constrain Proportions has to be deactivated (ill.47).

46

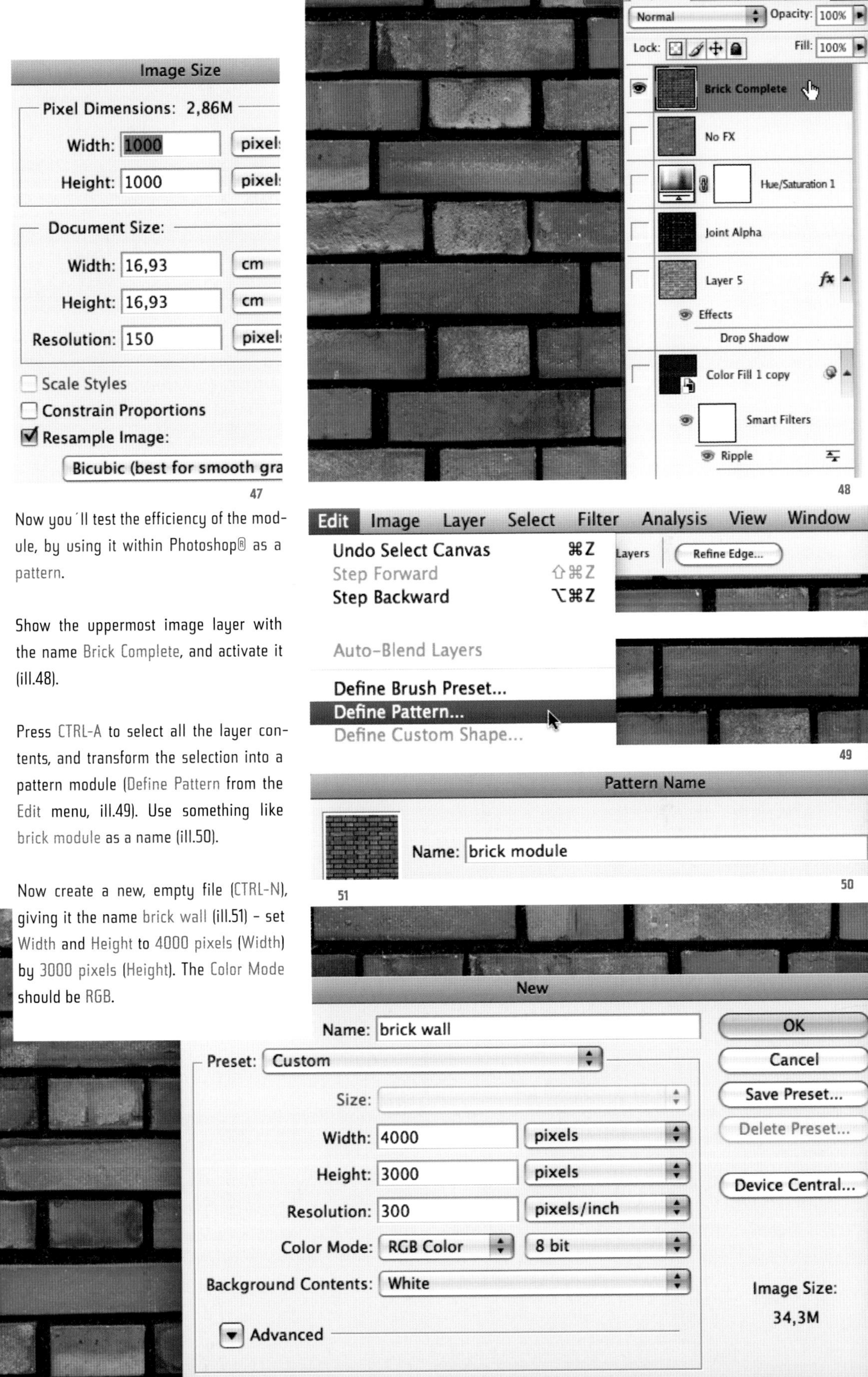

47

48

Now you´ll test the efficiency of the module, by using it within Photoshop® as a pattern.

Show the uppermost image layer with the name Brick Complete, and activate it (ill.48).

Press CTRL-A to select all the layer contents, and transform the selection into a pattern module (Define Pattern from the Edit menu, ill.49). Use something like brick module as a name (ill.50).

49

50

51

Now create a new, empty file (CTRL-N), giving it the name brick wall (ill.51) – set Width and Height to 4000 pixels (Width) by 3000 pixels (Height). The Color Mode should be RGB.

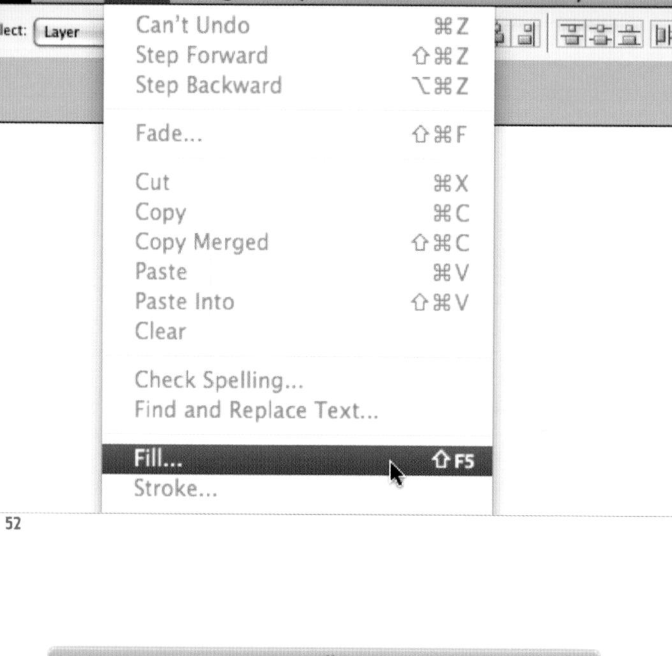

52

Now insert your brick module as a tiled addition, by first choosing the command Fill from the Edit menu (ill.52; you can also press Shift-Backspace).

From the Use popup menu, pick out Pattern, and directly under it click on the menu named Custom Pattern (ill.53).

In the palette with the available patterns which then appears, you can open a menu by clicking on the arrow at the right, from which you can choose the option Large Thumbnail– the pattern miniatures then become a little bit more recognizable.

At the end of the pattern icons, you can spot your brick module, which you of course click on (ill.54).

Confirm with OK, and your image fills with the copies of the brick image you´ve

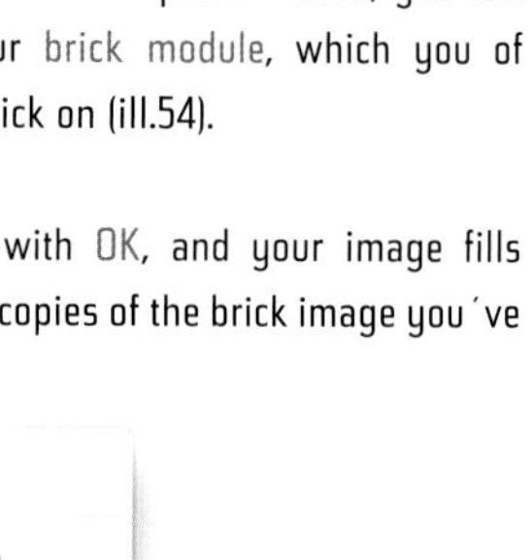

53

54

created (ill.55). And so you´ve achieved your goal: you´ve created a brick module that may be added without all too great peculiarities.

If you want to develop structures that are a bit more abstract, you may well make use of Photoshop´s patterns. Just check in chapter 02, at the very beginning of

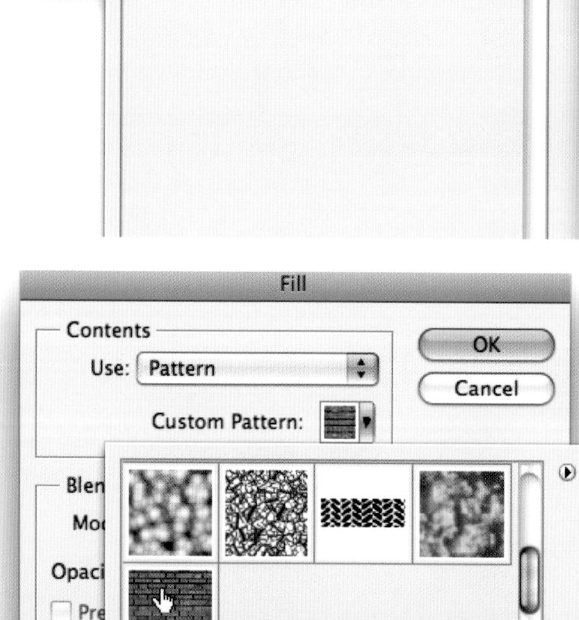

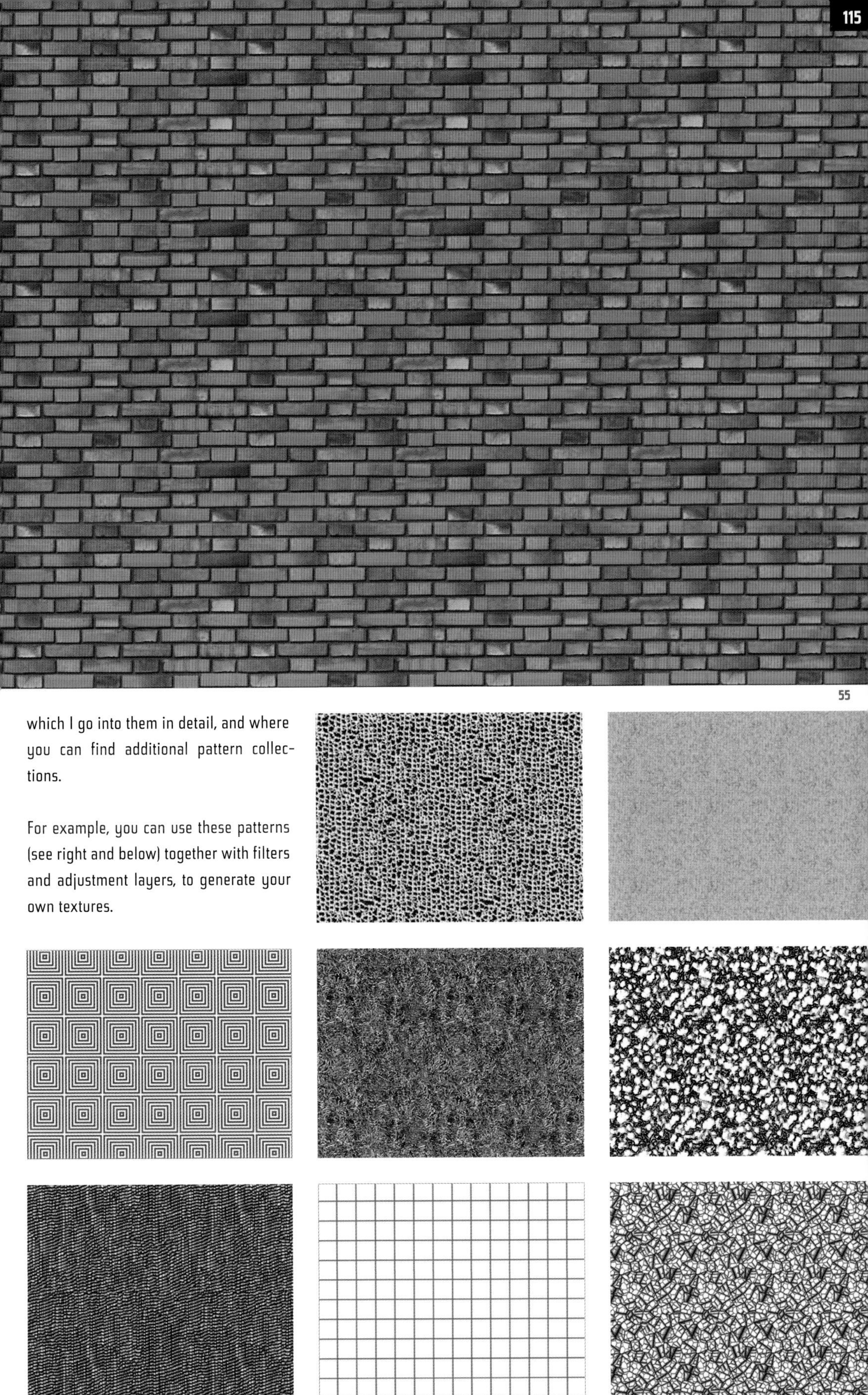

which I go into them in detail, and where you can find additional pattern collections.

For example, you can use these patterns (see right and below) together with filters and adjustment layers, to generate your own textures.

1

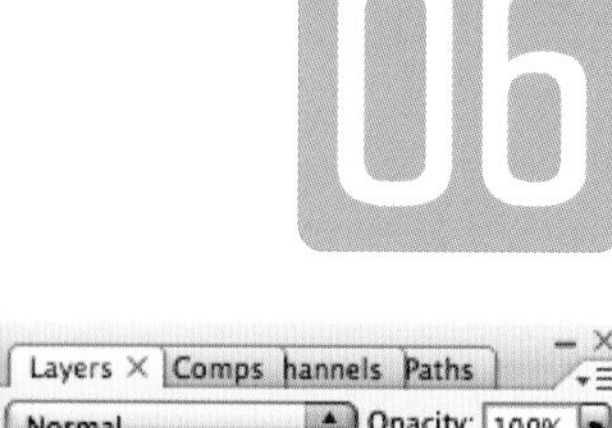

Clipping via Alpha Channel

In this chapter we want to clip a tree (ill.1) from its background, a typical task when processing footage for architectural graphics.

The problem is, the selection tools Photoshop® makes available to us (Rectangular or Elliptical Marquee, Lasso, Magic Wand), can´t be used in this case.

Even the Extract tool from the Filter menu can´t really help us, because the tree motif has all too many "holes".

The way to proceed here is made up of several measures, and we´ll make use of the Color Range selection and the High Pass filter, among others.

Open the file 06_mapletree_start.psd. It was saved in Photoshop® CS3 format.

If you open it in an older version, some of the new functions may not be available.

Be aware the image is not particularly big (CTRL-Alt-I); the small branches will therefore look rather pixelated after clipping.

In a larger image the result would look correspondingly better.

First you´ll try to select most of the tree (the thick parts) using the Color Range selection.

It´s helpful for this purpose if you strengthen the color contrast in the image. First copy the Background layer (CTRL-J, ill.2), and then place an adjustment layer called Selective Color over it (from the corresponding popup menu at the bottom frame of the Layers palette, ill.3).

In the adjustment dialog opening, first choose the Reds from the Colors menu (ill.4), setting the Cyan value to -100% and the Magenta value to +100%, but don´t yet confirm with OK.

Next select the Blues to work on, ad-

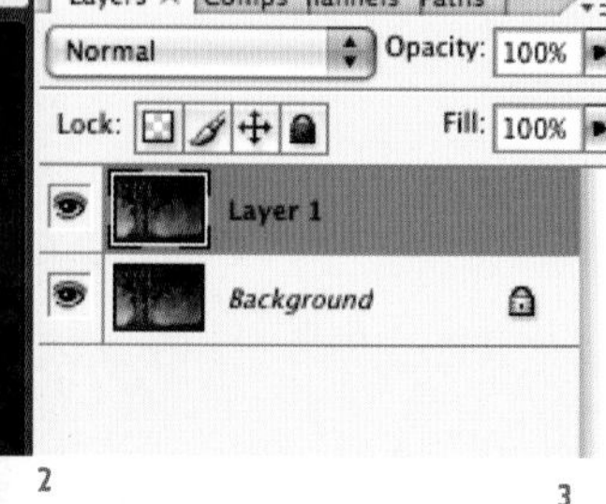

2

3

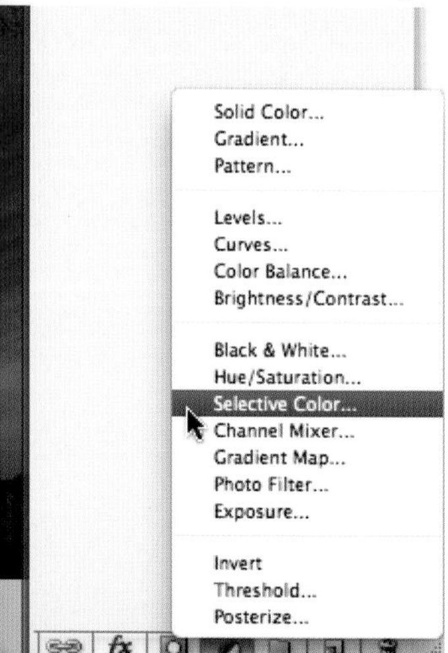

justing Cyan to +100%, Magenta also to +100% and Yellow to -100% (ill.5). Now confirm with OK.

After that, carry out a Hue/Saturation correction; select the adjustment layer with that name from the corresponding menu (ill.6).

For both the Reds and Blues set the Saturation to +100 (ills.7 and 8).

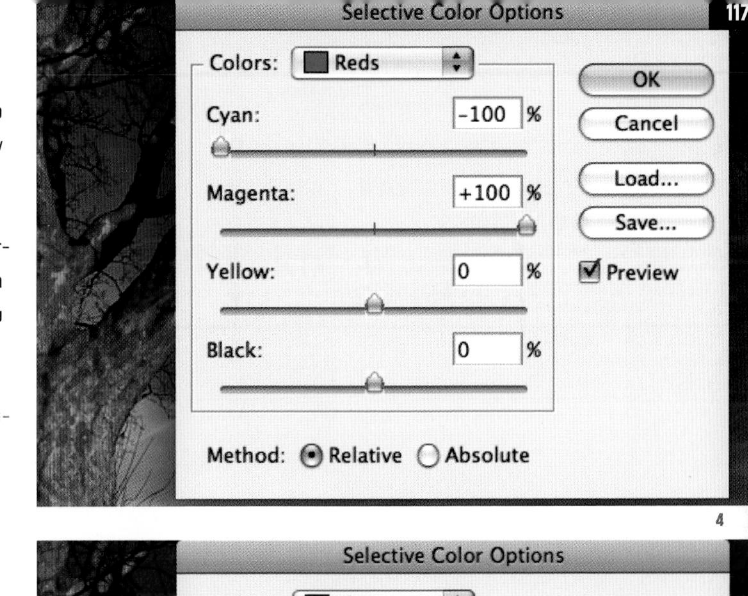

4

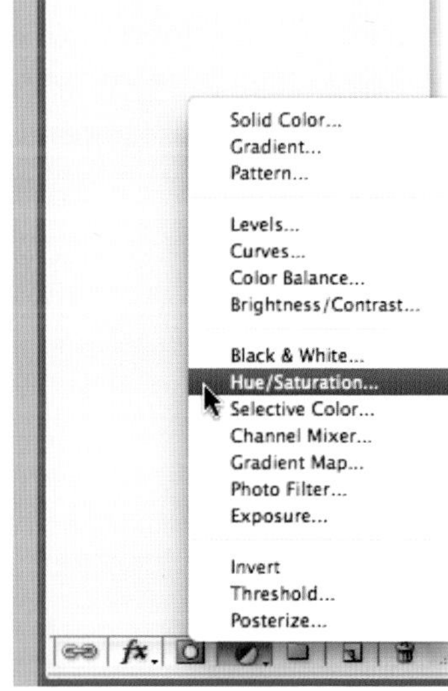

8 6 7 5

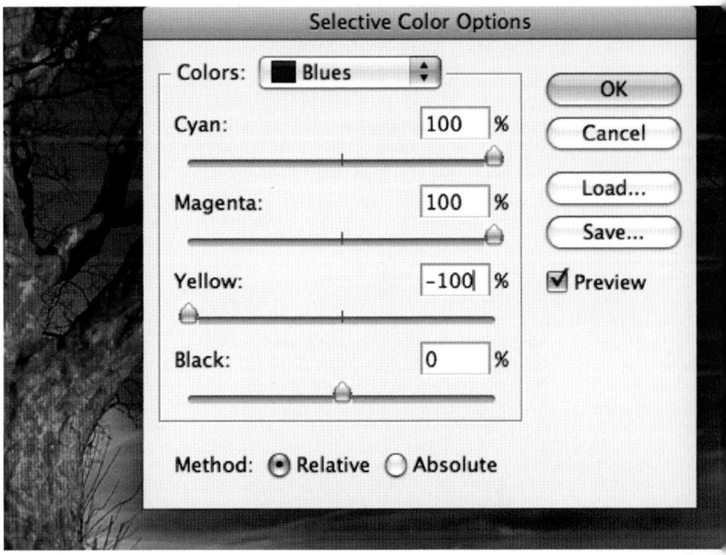

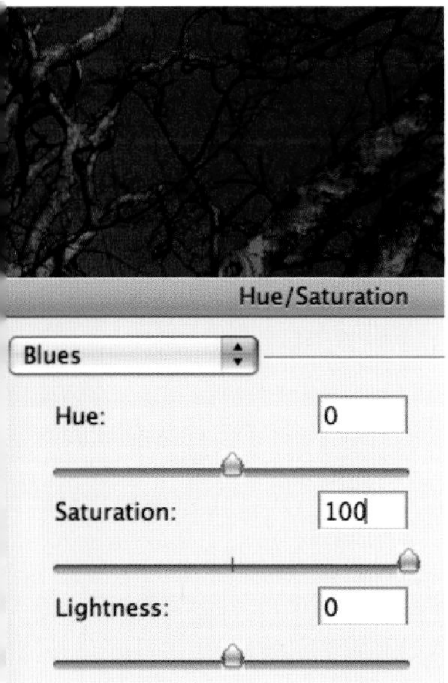

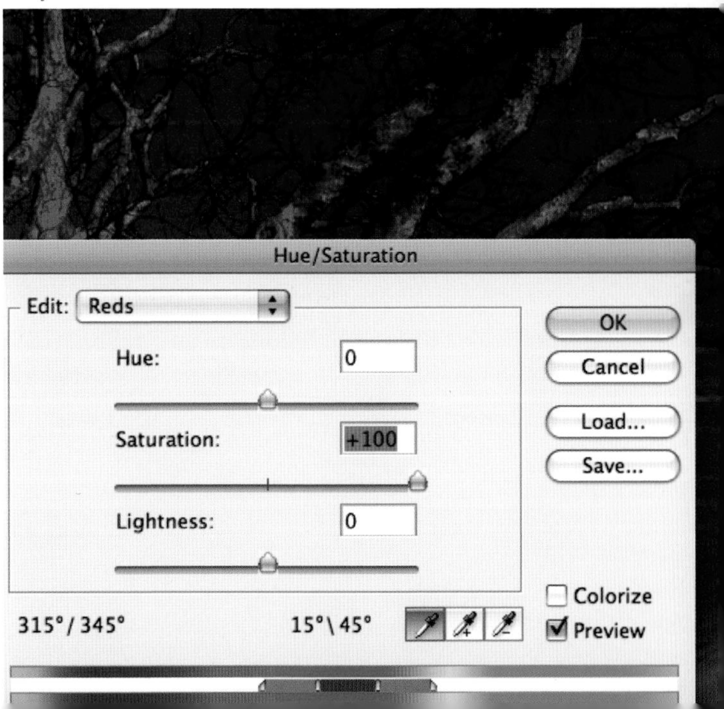

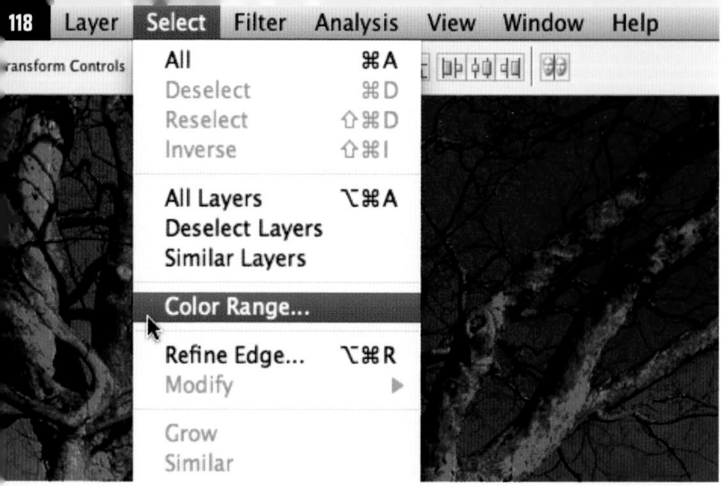

9

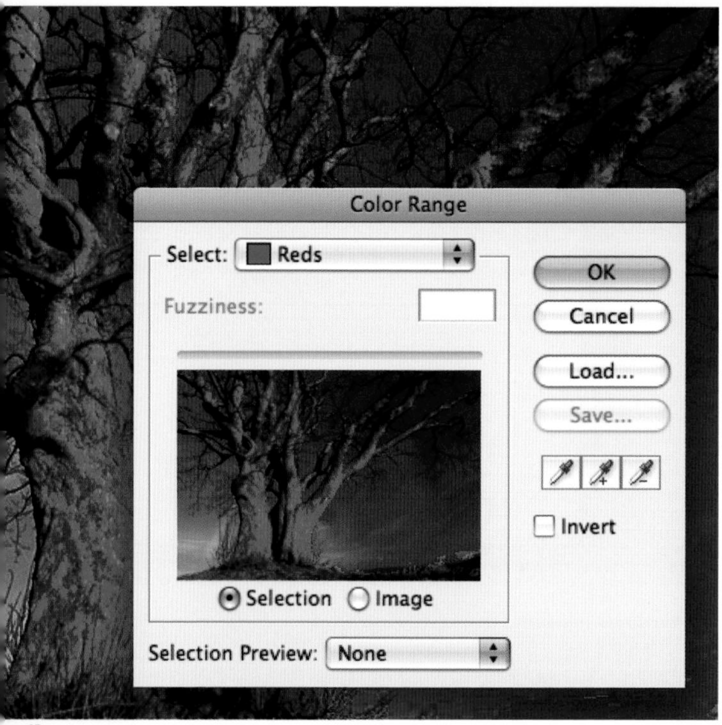

10

12

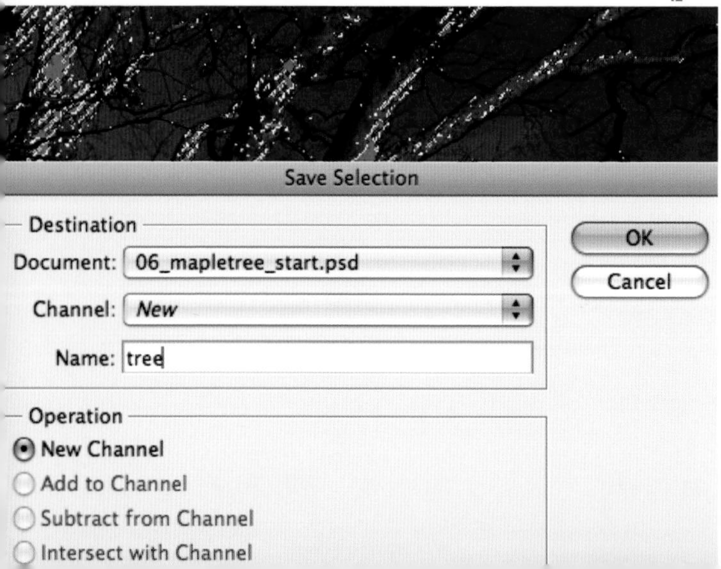

Now you´ll find it easier to select the tree using the Color Range selection.

Navigate to the corresponding command from the Select menu (ill.9), and here too first select the Reds (ill.10).

When you click on OK, you see the unavoidable ants in the image (ill.11).

Save the selection with the corresponding command from the Select menu, and enter tree as the Channel name (ill.12).

Just check up in the Channels palette, and there you´ll find your selection as a grayscale image, at the bottom end of the list. If you click on the entry in the palette, you have it displayed (ill.13).

As you see, the selected parts are black or gray, and the non-selected part is white.

As you can also see, the selection of the tree is clearly not yet complete; the tree seems to consist of more than only the Reds of the Color Range selection tool.

11

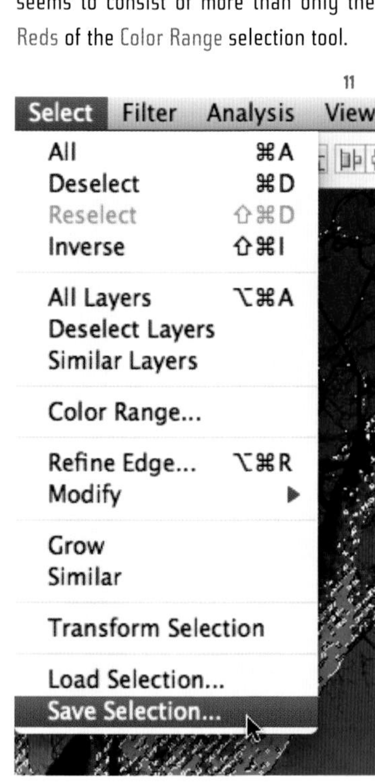

13

Since you want to use this channel later to load it as a selection back into the image, in order to be able to delete the background, you have to invest a little more work in the selection.

Activate the RGB channels before returning to the image (channel tree should again be hidden). It´s enough to click on the entry of the RGB channel (ill.14).

Switch back again to the Layers palette, pick the command Color Range from the Select menu once more, and this time select the Yellows (ill.15).

Confirm with OK, and save this selection too, though not as a new channel but as an addition to the already existing one.

For this, select the already existing Channel tree in the adjustment dialog Save Selection, and activate the option Add to Channel in the lower part (ill.16).

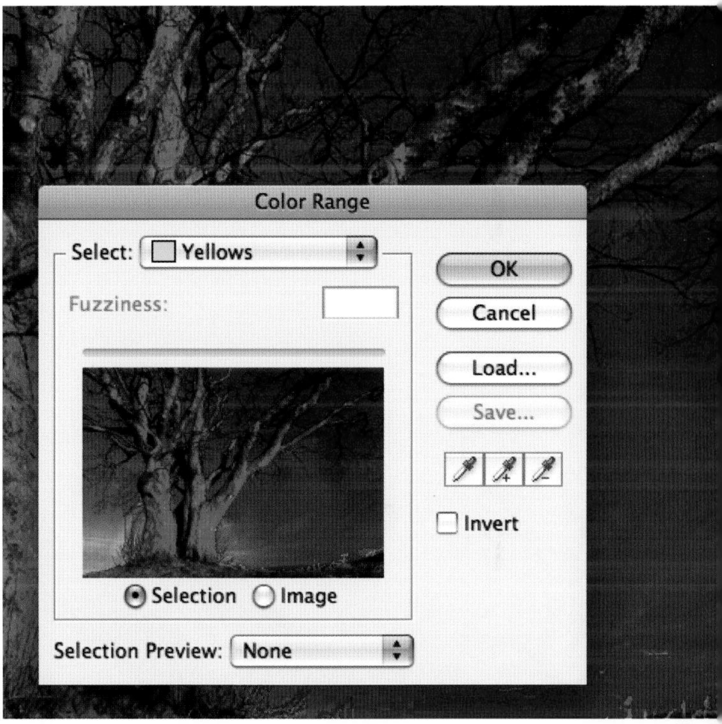

14

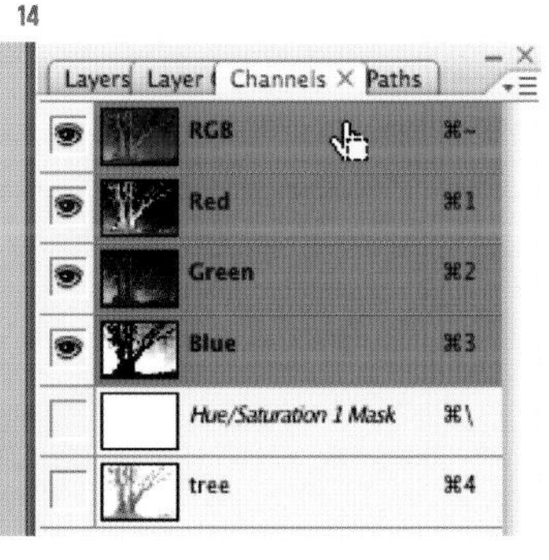

15

16

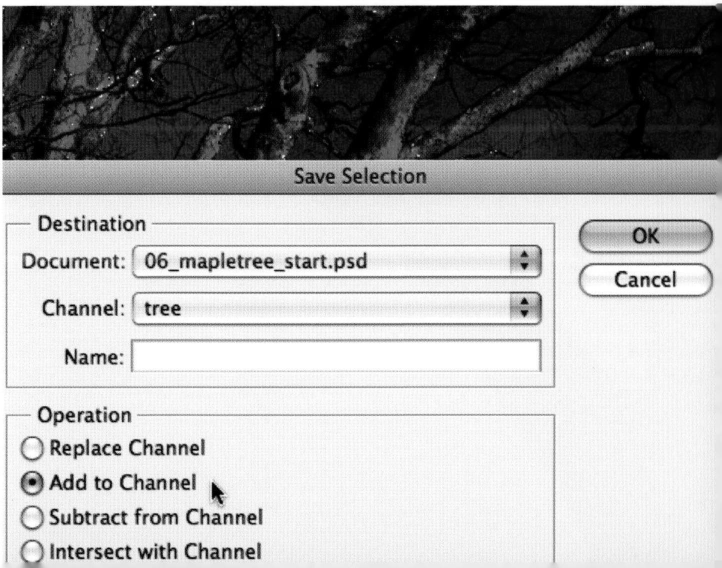

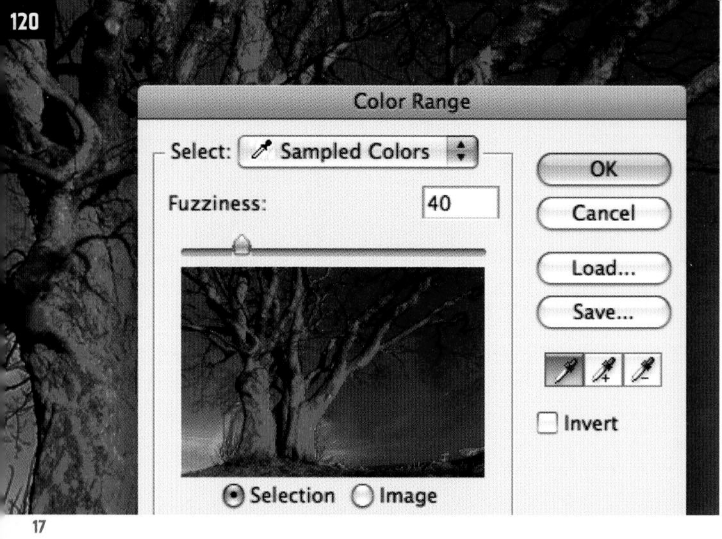

17

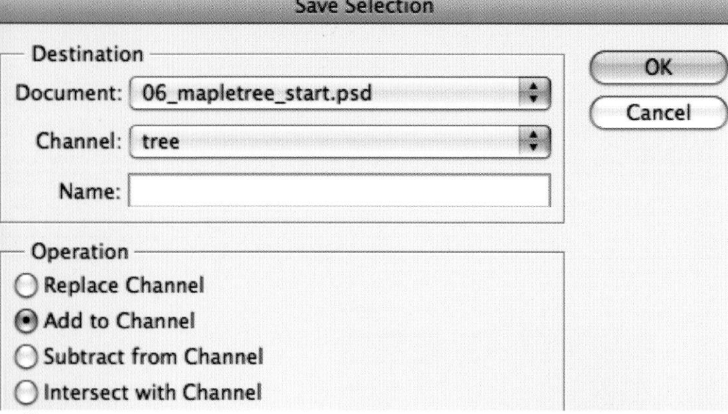

18

19

Check the result in the Channels palette.

To be on the safe side, now select a little bit more. Don´t forget to reactivate the RGB channels, and use the Color Range selection a third time.

This time select the option Sampled Colors from the Select menu of the adjustment dialogs (ill.17) and click around on the tree with the Shift key held down till you feel, on looking at the preview image, that you´ve captured it fully.

Other than shown in ill.17, you'll see the result of your clicking displayed as Black-and-White graphics when the option Selection is checked (under the preview image).

If you´ve accidentally selected parts of the background, click in the corresponding image area with the Alt key held down, then the excess selection is removed again.

Confirm with OK, and save this selection too by adding it to the Channel tree (ill.18).

Now look at the channel again; the tree is already almost totally black in its thicker areas (ill.19).

Since you require a pure Black-and-White mask for later deletion of the background, you can now color black all the parts of the channel that aren´t white.

20

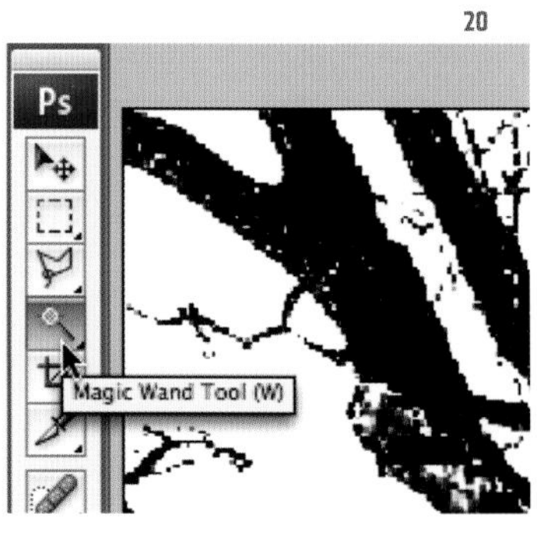

Grab the Magic Wand tool (ill.20); the Tolerance should be set at 1, and the option Contiguous not activated.

Then click somewhere in the white area of the channel and invert the selection (Select - Inverse, ill.21).

21

Press Shift-Backspace to get to the Fill dialog (ill.22); use Black, and confirm with OK.

22

Later in the chapter we´ll deal with the thin branches, which are still largely missing in the selection, using another tool, but first we´ll attempt to complete the existing selection.

For this, we´ll take a small detour, loading the channel as a selection into the image, editing it in mask mode, and then saving it back.
But one step at a time: activate the RGB channels and ensure that the tree channel is again hidden.

24

25

Load the tree channel as a selection into the image (Select -Load Selection, ills.23 and 24) and press the Q key to see the selection as a mask (ill.25).

The non-selected part is colored red, and as you see can, parts of the tree are also affected.

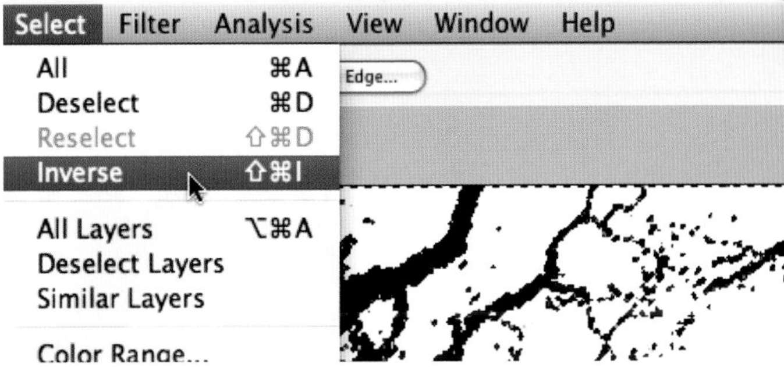

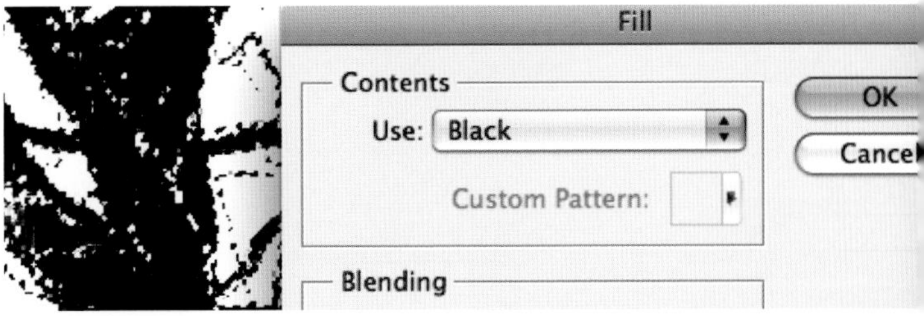

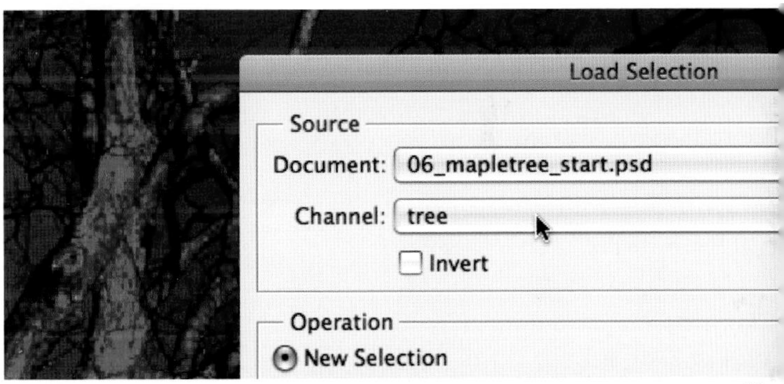

23

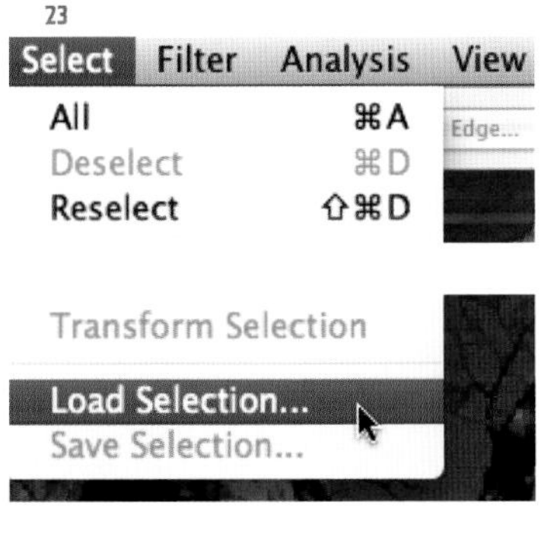

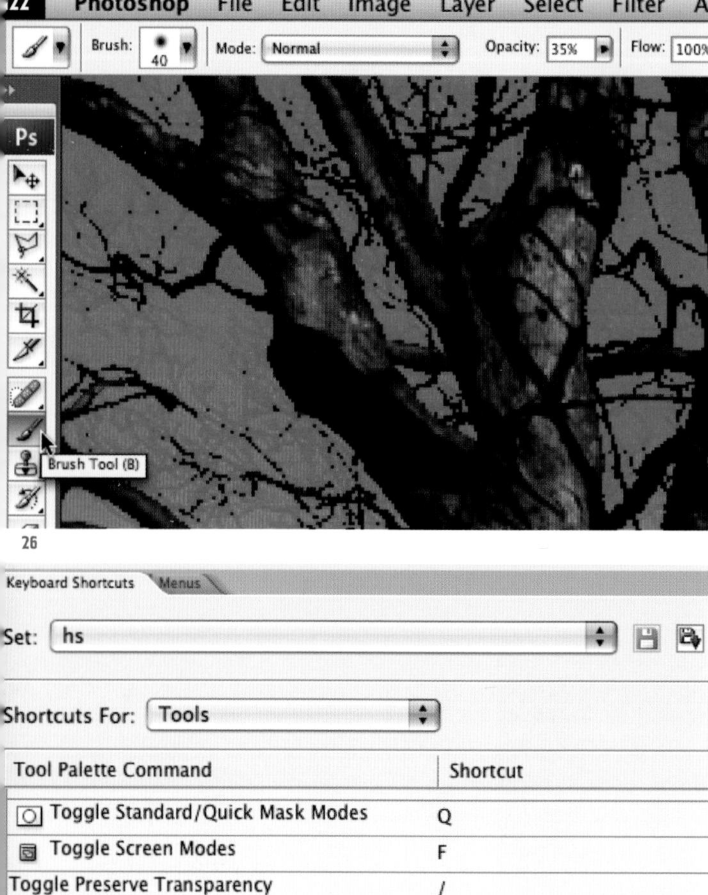

26

28

29

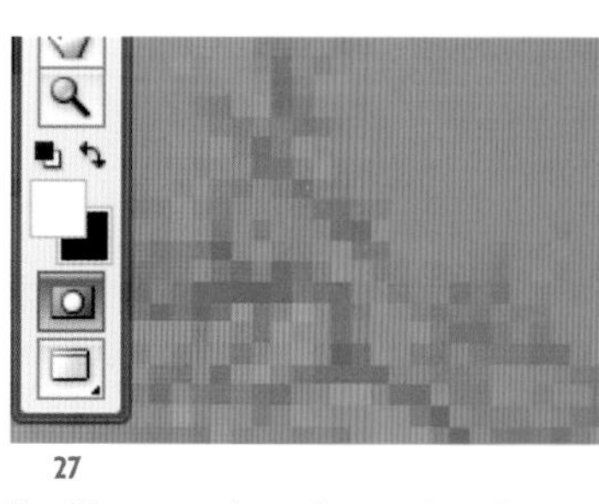

27

You´ll now work on this mask with paint tools. Take the Brush tool (ill.26) and make sure the foreground and background colors are Black and White respectively (ill.27). To play safe, press the D key.

With the brush you should now "paint away" the red mask where it´s visible inside the tree area; for this the foreground color has to be White. Where you´ve removed too much mask color, apply it again; for this the foreground color has to be Black.

Restrict yourself to the tree trunk and its thicker branches; you´ll attend to the thinner ones later.

To use the brush this way, alternately as a paint tool and as an eraser, you just have to swap the foreground and background colors using the X key. You don´t need to change the tool.

Another practical tip: because in the course of your work you continually have to increase or reduce the radius of your brush, you shouldn´t use the controls in the Options palette, which is far too awkward, but your shortcut keys (see Ch.02).

Remember that you can also change the smooth edge of the tool tip this way. I recommend that you work with a very hard brush (also please check up in Ch.02, ill.28).

Also, on no account should you forget while working, that you can zoom into

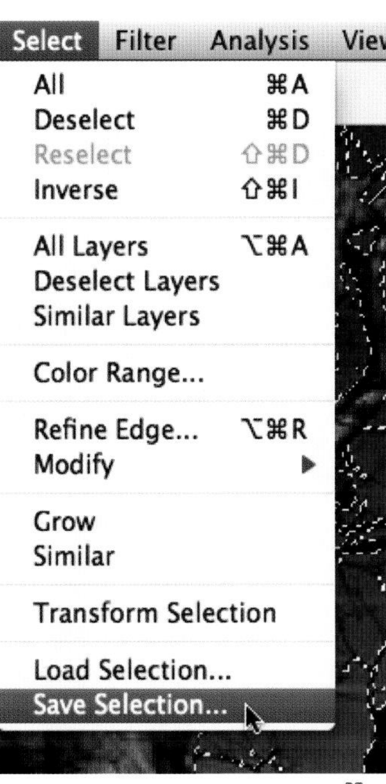

30

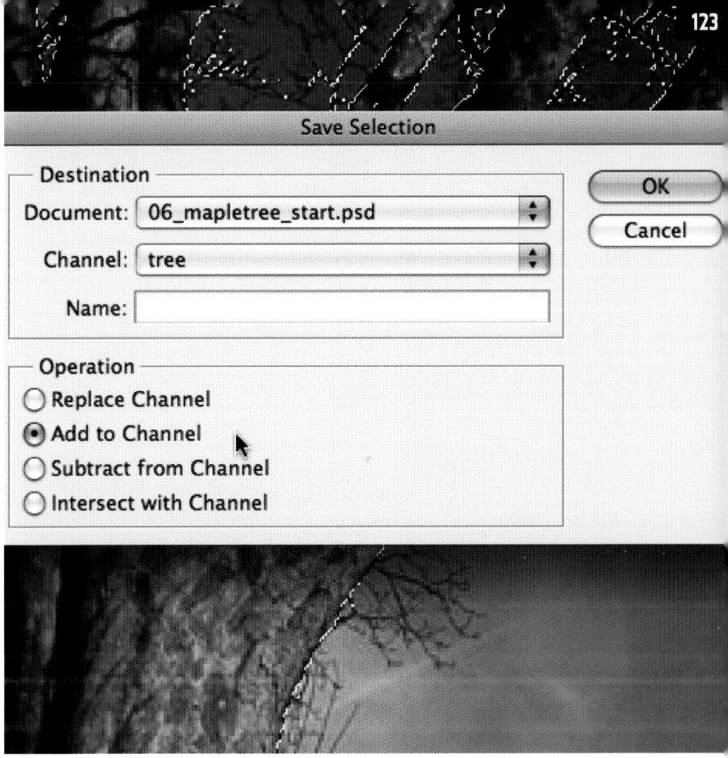

31

the image with CTRL-Space, and out with CTRL-Alt-Space, and that you can move the image in the window with the Space key held down.

During your repair work on the mask, just show the selection ants from time to time with Q, to check your progress. When you´re finished, the whole thing should look roughly like in illustration 29.

Convert the mask into a hovering selection again by pressing Q, and select the command Save Selection (Select menu, ill.30). This time too, add it to the already existing tree channel (ill.31).

32

33

Now take a close look at the channel again. You probably have, as I do, a few leftover selection blurs (ill.32). Just remove them with your brush directly in the channel, by applying White at the critical places.

After you´ve done this too, your tree channel should look something like in illustration 33.

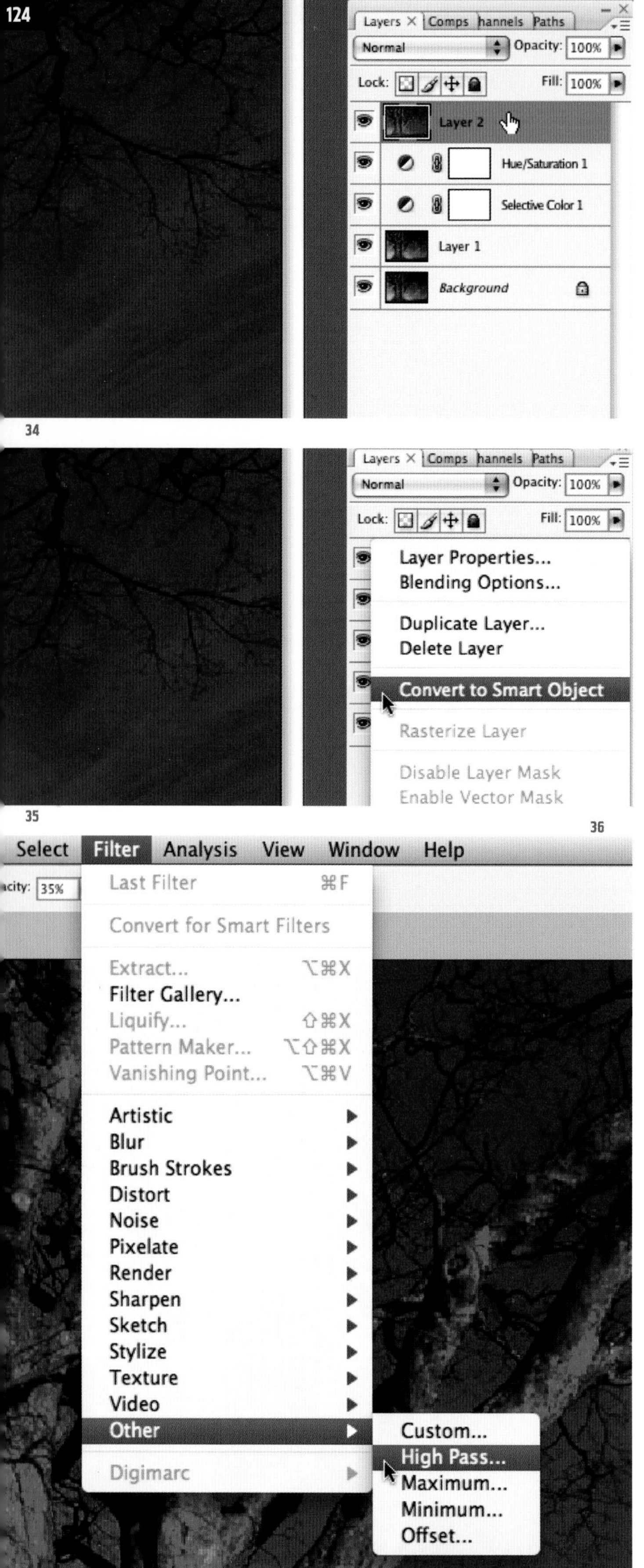

Now for the thin branches. To select them in the same way as the trunk would be a real labor of Sysiphos, and as the thin branches are the same color as the sky in many places, the Color Range selection doesn´t work at all.

That´s why we´ll resort here to another process; there´s a filter that pretty exactly strengthens contours and at the same time can strongly flatten the color surfaces, the so called High Pass.

After working on the image this way, you can fade out the background using a layer style.

Don´t forget to activate the RGB channels in the Channels palette again (by clicking on the RGB Channel), and make sure the tree channel is hidden.

Switch back to the Layers palette, show all the layers, activate the uppermost, and press Shift-Alt-CTRL-E.
You know already that this way you create a new layer which combines all the visible layers into one copy (ill.34; this command only exists in the form of this shortcut.
It´s an extension of the command Merge Visible, Shift-CTRL-E).

You need this copy to use the High Pass filter, which is after all only a means to an end and has nothing to do with the later image.

Convert the new layer into a Smart Object so you can use the filter losslessly (by right-clicking on the layer and selecting the corresponding command from the context menu, ill.35).

Then pick the High Pass from the Other filters (Filter menu, ill.36).
In the adjustment dialog, set a pixels Ra-

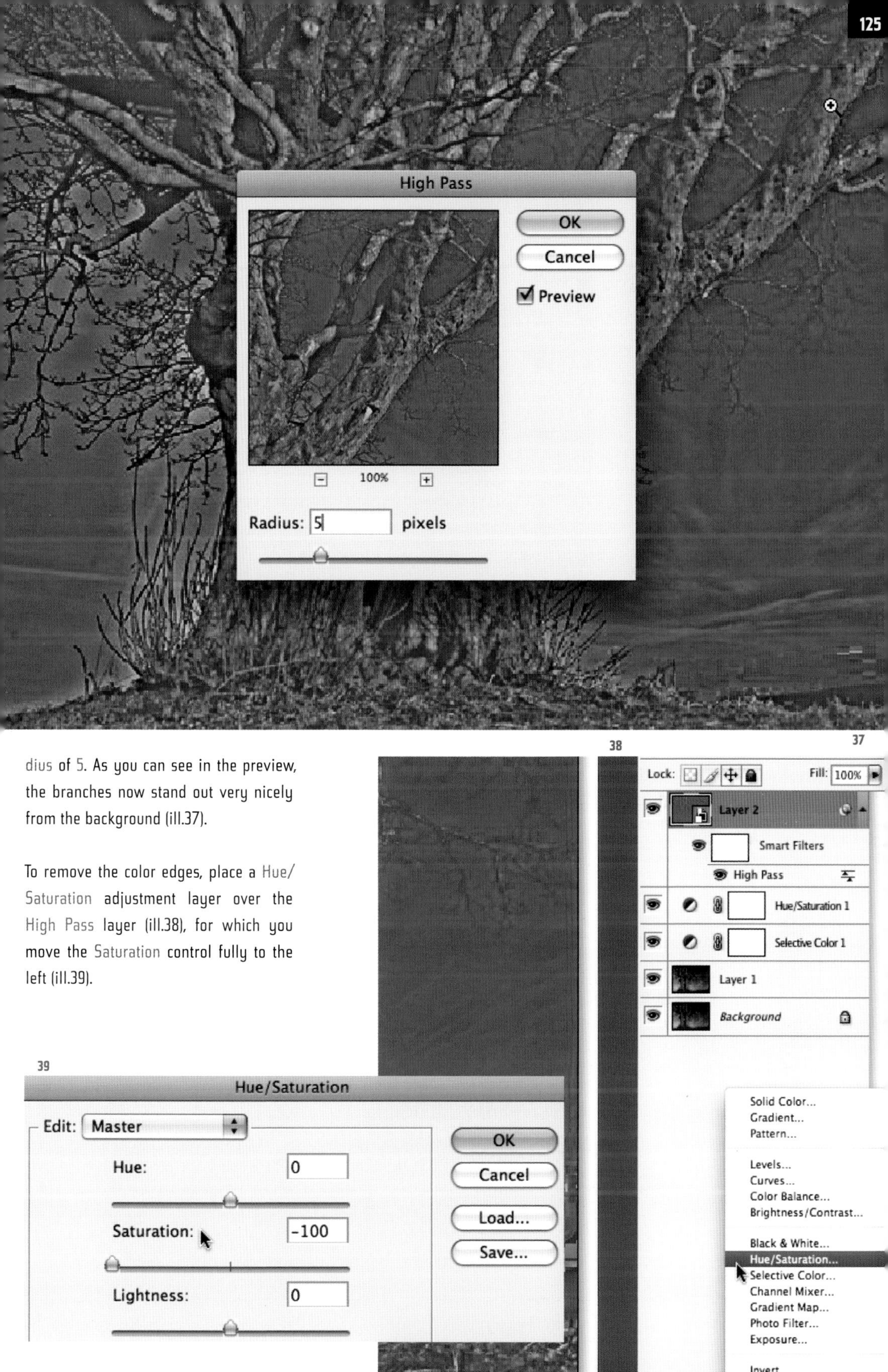

dius of 5. As you can see in the preview, the branches now stand out very nicely from the background (ill.37).

To remove the color edges, place a Hue/Saturation adjustment layer over the High Pass layer (ill.38), for which you move the Saturation control fully to the left (ill.39).

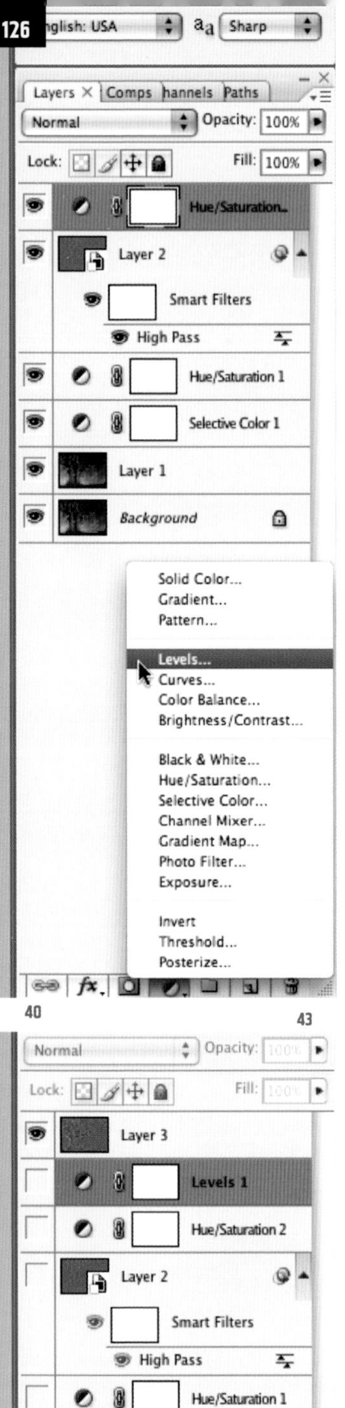

40

43

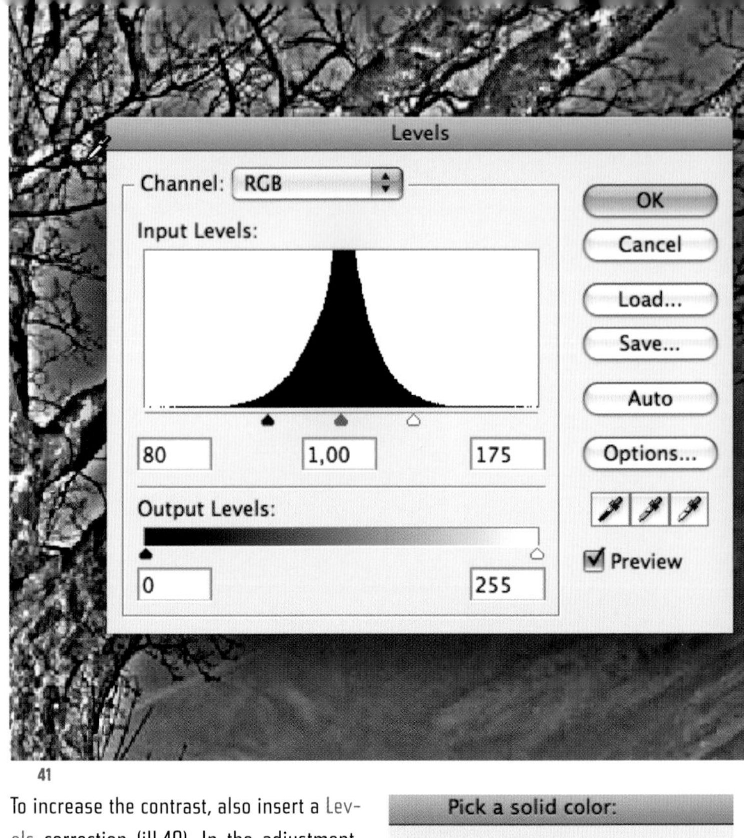

41

To increase the contrast, also insert a Levels correction (ill.40). In the adjustment dialog set the histogram's left control to the value 80, and the right control to 175 (ill.41).

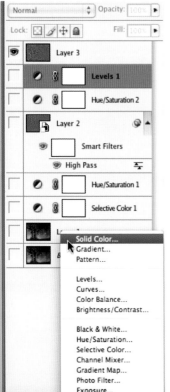

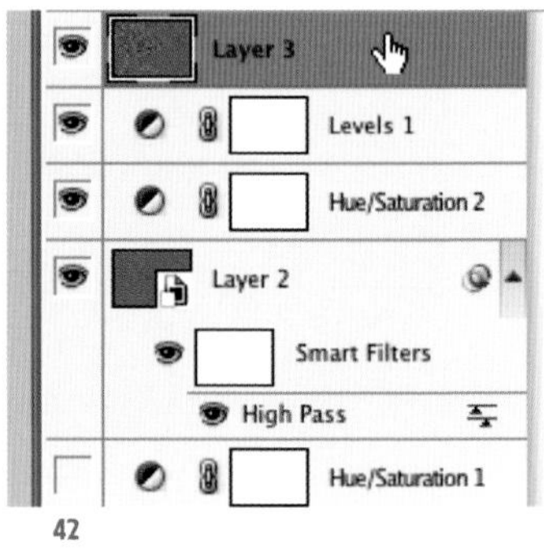

42

Ensure that only your Smart layer and the two adjustment layers just placed are shown, and that the uppermost is activated. Press Shift-Alt-CTRL-E again, to produce a cumulative copy of it too, in which you can then hide the lighter background (layer 3, ill.42).

Now leave only result layer visible, and hide all the other ones.

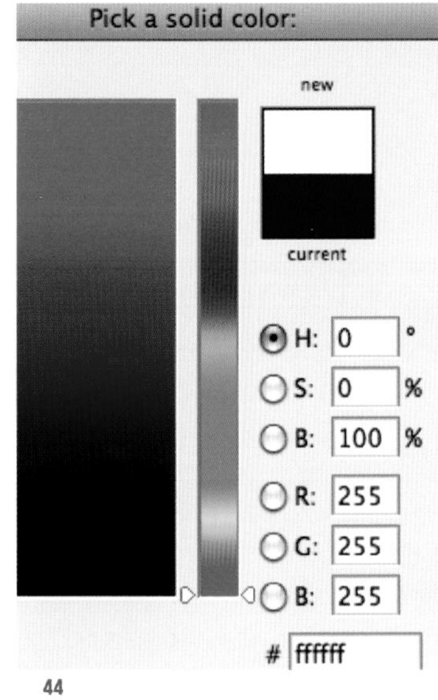

44

Activate the adjustment layer directly under it, without showing it, and select a Solid Color layer from the adjustment layers menu at the bottom frame of the Layers palette (ill.43).

Define pure White as the color (R, G, B = 255, ill.44).

Now double-click on your uppermost layer in the Layers palette, to get to the

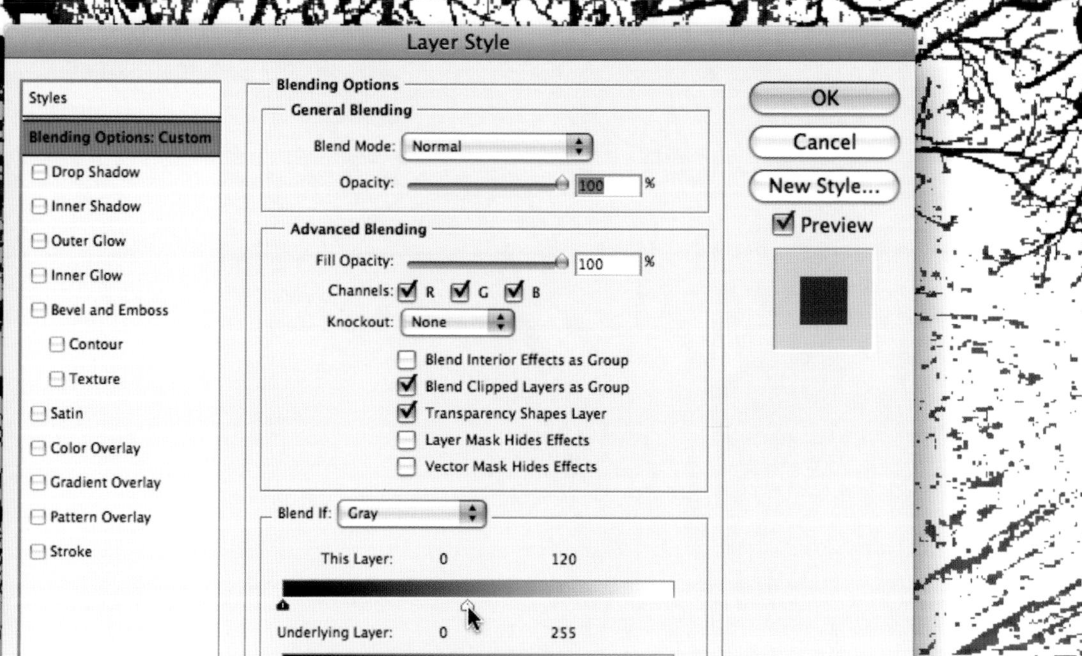

45

adjustments for the Layer Styles (ill.45).

Via this window you can, in the lower area (Blend if: Gray - This Layer), hide parts of this layer, either the bright areas (right control) or the dark ones (left control).

Move the right control to the left till its value is 120.

As you see in the image, the white and light-gray image areas disappear. Admittedly, with the value we´ve chosen there are still a few spots in the area of the background, but all the branches can still be seen.

Now show, in addition to your currently used layer, the color layer under it (ill.46), and select the command Merge Visible from the palette menu (ill.47).

In the combined layer you should now remove the leftover stains in the area of the background.

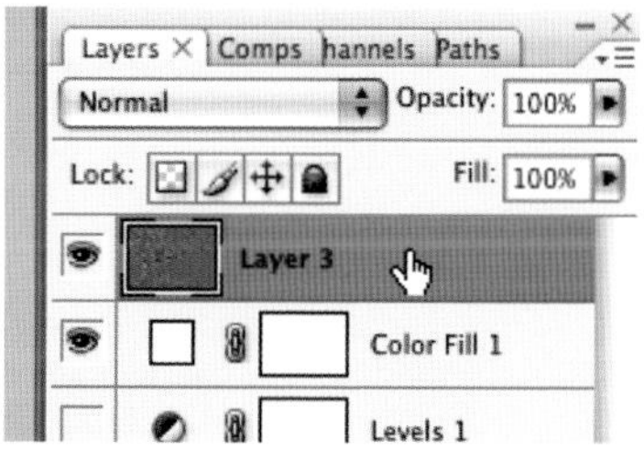

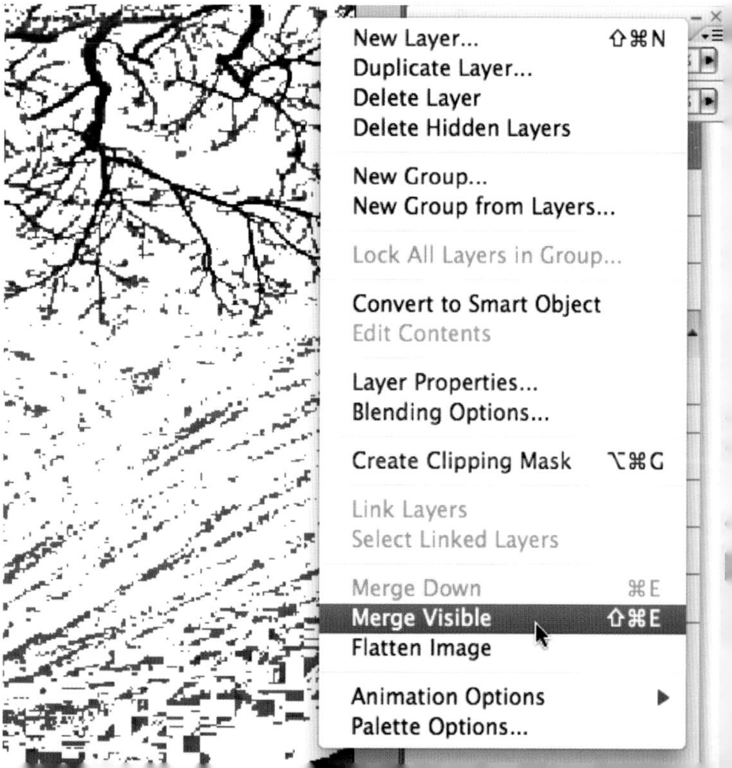

47

46

49

48

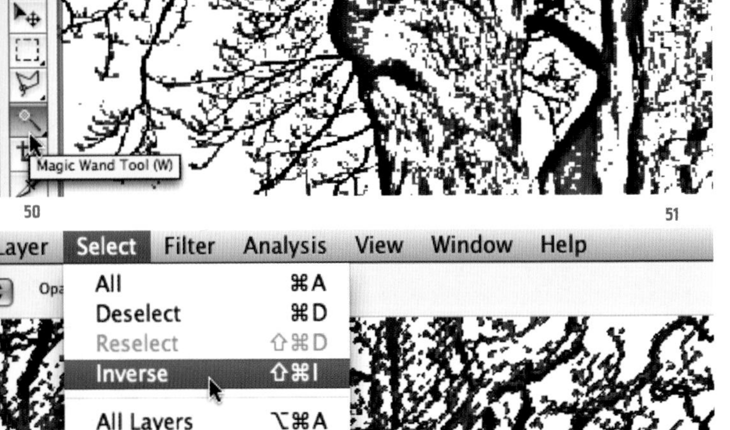

50

51

Use the Brush tool again with the foreground color White (ill.48). When you´re finished, your layer should look like in illustration 49.

Now too you should convert everything that isn´t white into pure Black, so that your delete mask later also works perfectly.
Take the magic wand with Tolerance 1 and the (still) deactivated option Contiguous (ill.50), click somewhere in the white image area, and invert the selection (Select menu, ill.51).

Press Shift-Backspace to get to the adjustment dialog for the command Fill, and select Black for the Use (ill.52). Confirm with OK.

Now you have two Black-and-White images available, showing your tree black on a white background: one in the tree channel showing the trunk and the thicker branches, and one in the form of your layer just completed, also showing the thin branches. You can now combine the two to complete your mask.

Switch to the Channels palette and activate the tree channel (ill.53, press CTRL-A (Select - All) and CTRL-C (Edit - Copy). Activate the RGB channels again and check that the tree channel is hidden (ill.54).

In the Layers palette, activate the uppermost layer and then press CTRL-V for Paste – the Black-and-White graphics of the tree channel are inserted as a layer over your "branch" layer (ill.55).

Set the blending mode of the uppermost layer to Multiply (ill.56), to see the two graphics together (ill.57). Hasn´t it become pretty ?

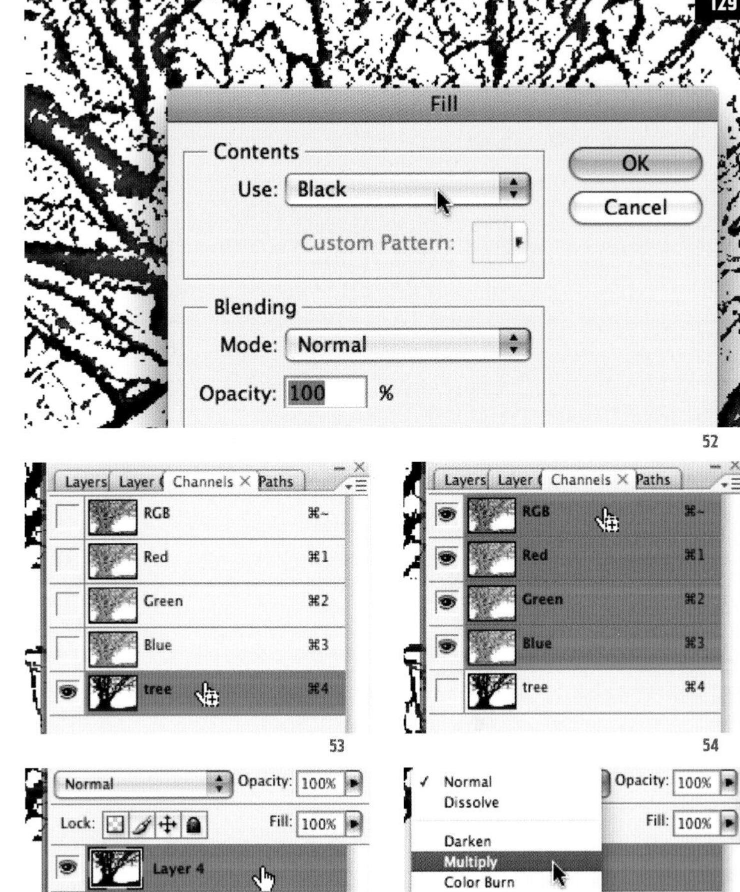

52

53

54

55

56

57

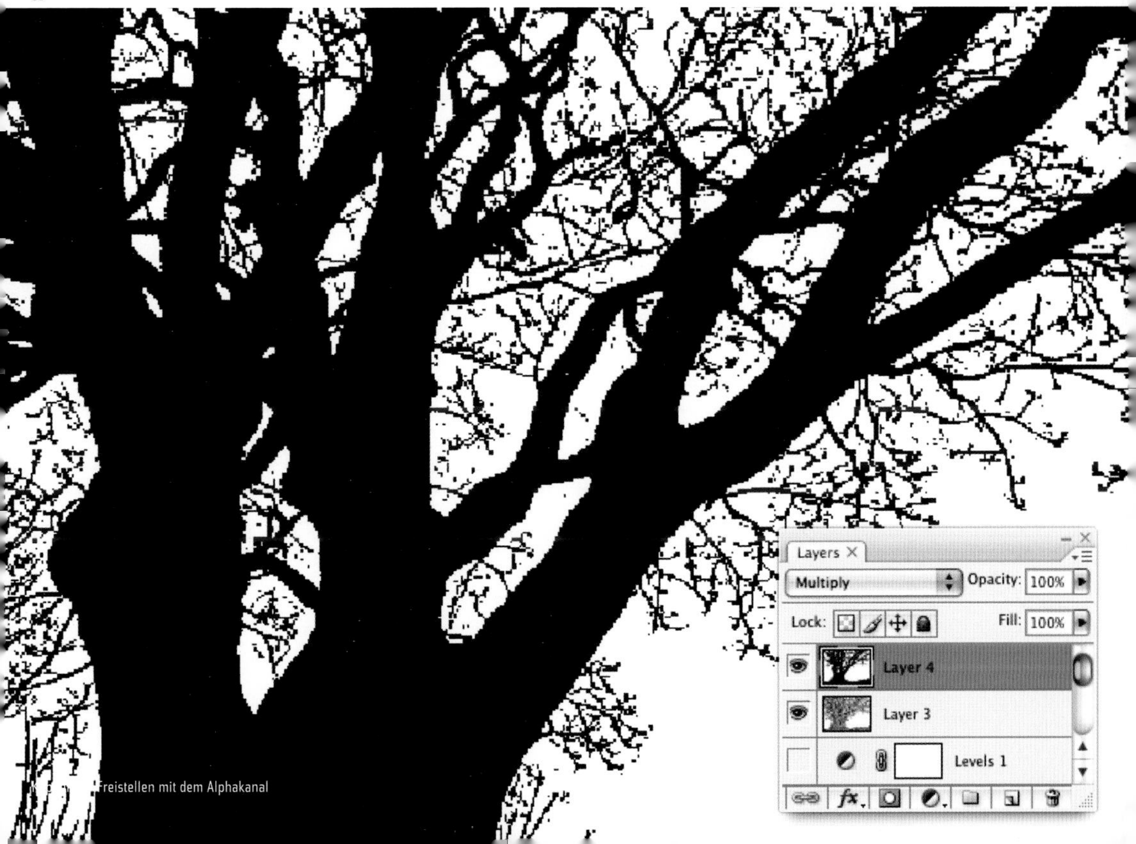

58

You can now also combine the two layers into one. Check that only the two are shown, and again select the command Merge Visible from the Layers palette menu (ill.58).

Press CTRL-A and CTRL-C to copy the layer contents, activate the tree channel in the Channels palette, and insert the image contents with CTRL-V. The channel is now finished and can be consulted as a selection mask (ill.59).

Hide it again and activate the RGB channels once more.

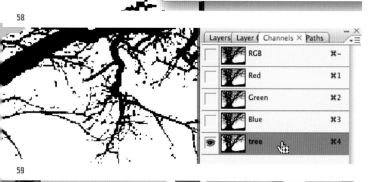

59

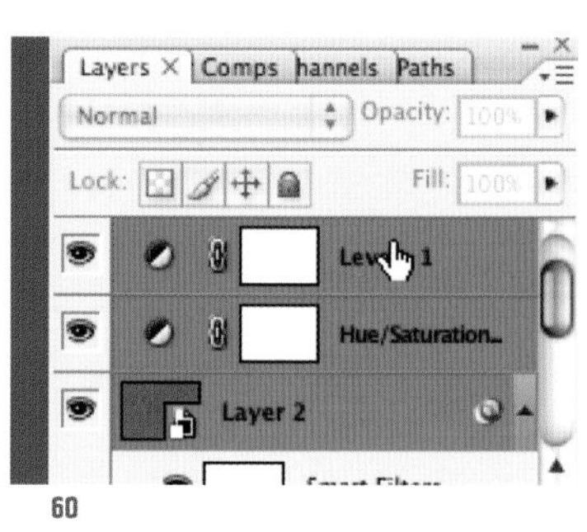

60

Now tidy up a bit in the Layers palette. Show the Smart layer and its two associated adjustment layers, activate all three (with the Shift key held down, ill.60) and combine them into a group (with the command New Group from Layers from the palettes menu, ill.61).

Give the group the name High Pass, and hide it. Actually you no longer need these three layers, but maybe you feel like I do and you don´t want to airily delete anything which has involved quite some work.

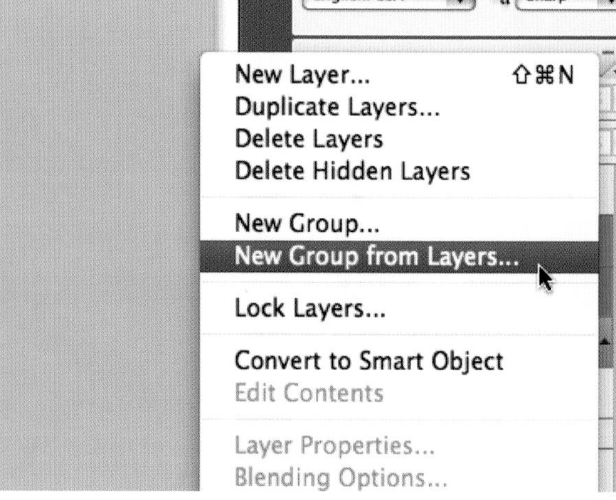

61

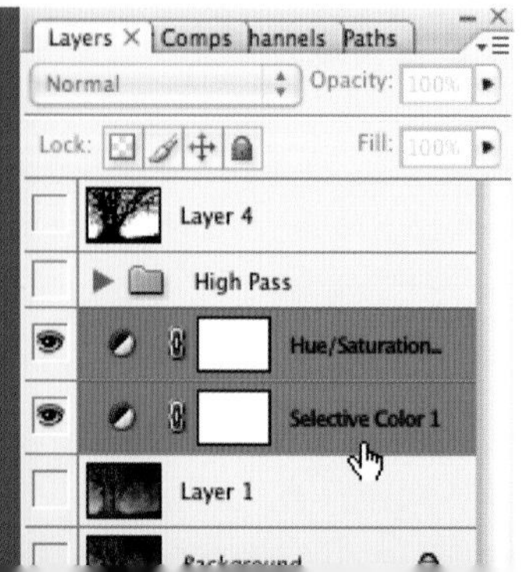

62

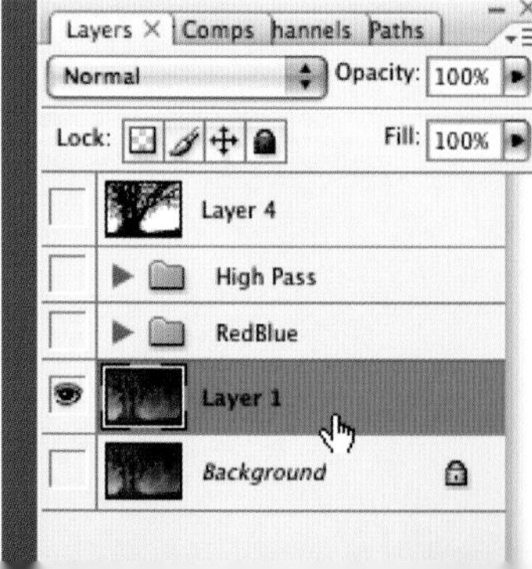

63

Also you no longer need the older adjustment layers, with which you strengthened the color contrast at the beginning.

Combine them into a group, which if you want you can call RedBlue, and hide it too (Ills.62 and 63).

But now to the very aim of our work. Your image still has the background you wanted to delete the whole time, and for which you´ve created such a refined mask.

Activate the image layer with the name Layer 1, and hide the Background layer (ill.63).

Load your tree channel as selection (ill.64), but in the adjustment dialog tick the option Invert (ill.65; after all, you want to delete the background and not the tree).

Press one of your delete buttons to get rid of the background. Then zoom in on the branches you´ve extracted with the High Pass filter.

As I remarked before, they largely have the blue color of the sky (ill.66); you will now remedy this defect.

Insert a Hue/Saturation layer over the image layer (ill.67).

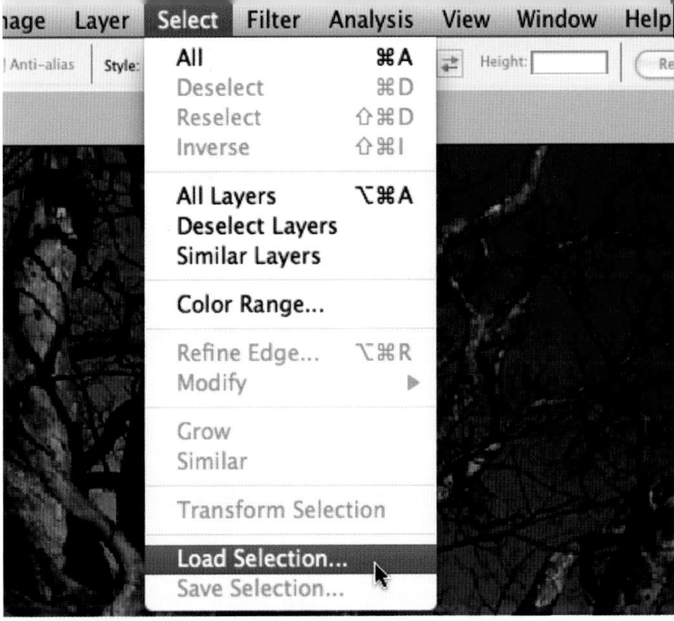

Image Layer Select Filter Analysis View Window Help
Anti-alias Style: Height: Refine Edge
All ⌘A
Deselect ⌘D
Reselect ⇧⌘D
Inverse ⇧⌘I
All Layers ⌥⌘A
Deselect Layers
Similar Layers
Color Range...
Refine Edge... ⌥⌘R
Modify
Grow
Similar
Transform Selection
Load Selection...
Save Selection...

64

Load Selection
Source
Document: 06_mapletree_edit.psd
Channel: tree
Invert
Operation
New Selection
Add to Selection
Subtract from Selection
Intersect with Selection

65

66

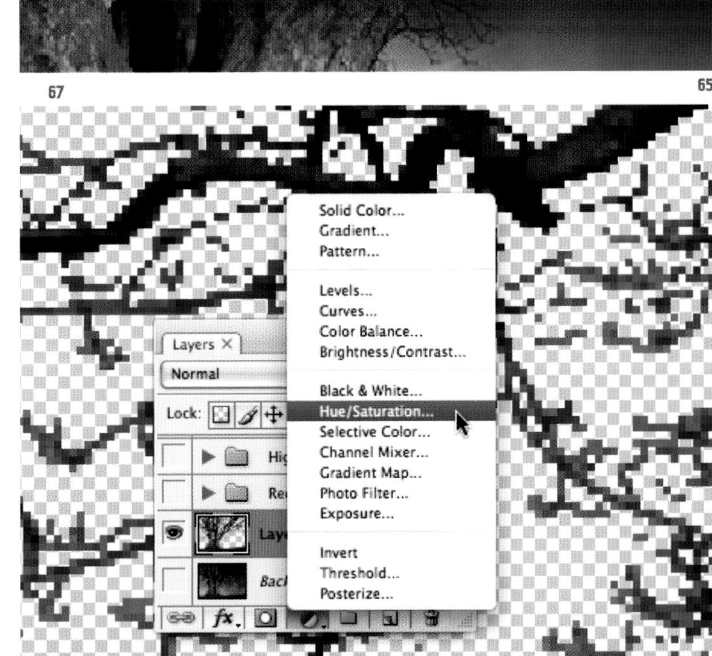

67

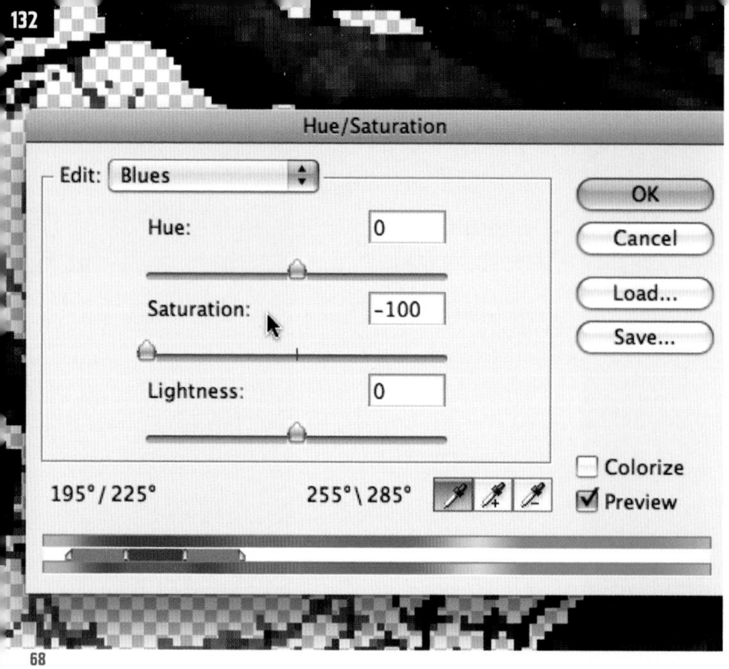

First select the Blues and for them reduce the Saturation to -100 (ill.68), then do the same for the Cyans (ill.69).

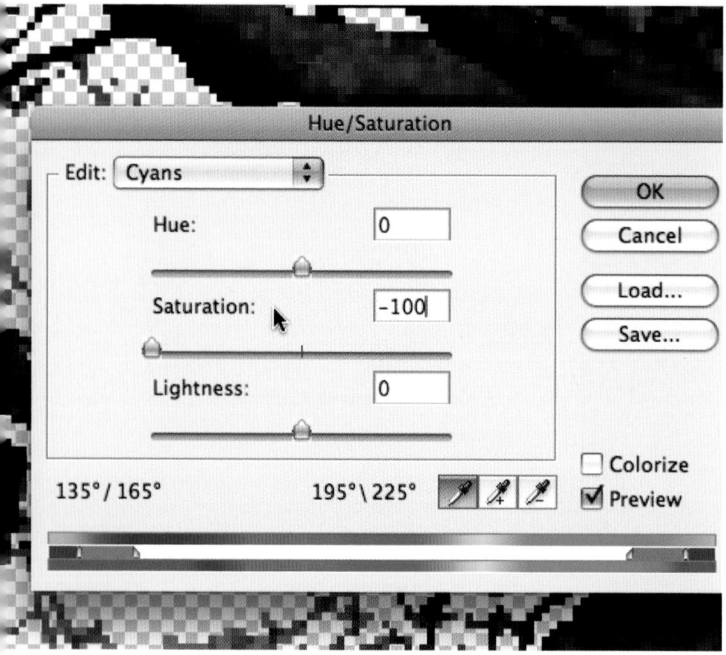

Now the thin branches are discolored, i.e. gray, and you can live very well with that.

Now insert a white color layer under the image layer.
To do this, activate the Background layer, and select the corresponding fill layer from the menu at the bottom frame of the Layers palette (ill.70; White should still be set as the color).

Make sure the image layer, the adjustment layer over it and the color layer under it are all shown (ill.71), and enjoy the sight of your clipped tree motif (ill.72).

68

69

71

70

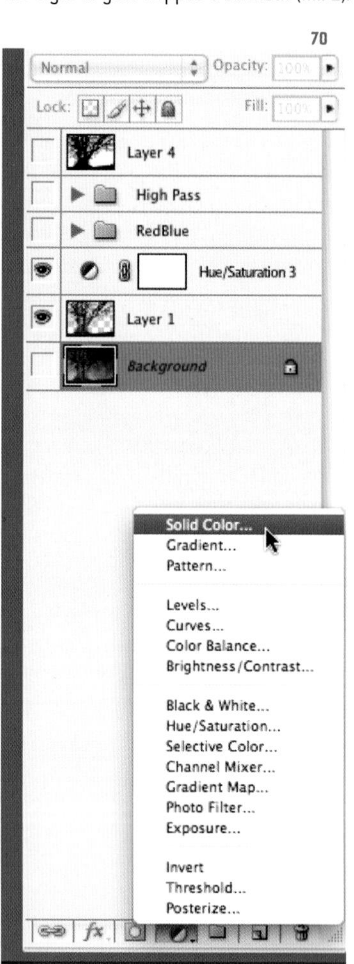

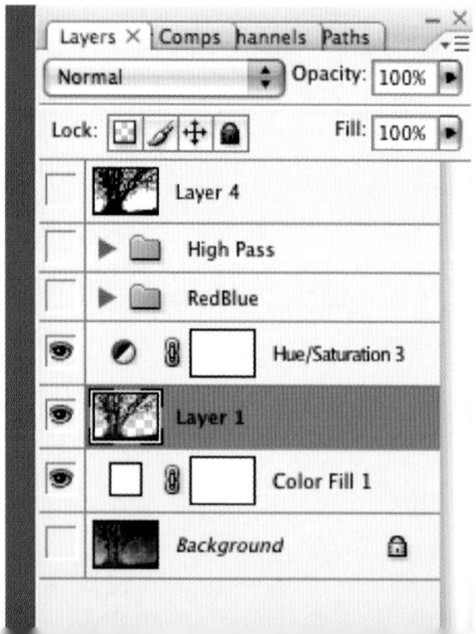

72

Bear in mind that we´re dealing with an image with relatively small resolution, which explains the pixelated structure of the details in the image.

The tree motif can now easily be used in image composings (ill.73).

73

Composing on CAAD-Basis

In this chapter you´ll work on a CAAD drawing in Photoshop®, using again many features which Photoshop® has available for this purpose: adjustment layers, masks, filter, layer groups etc.

First open the file 07_ng_persp_start.psd, to take a look at it (ill.1).

1

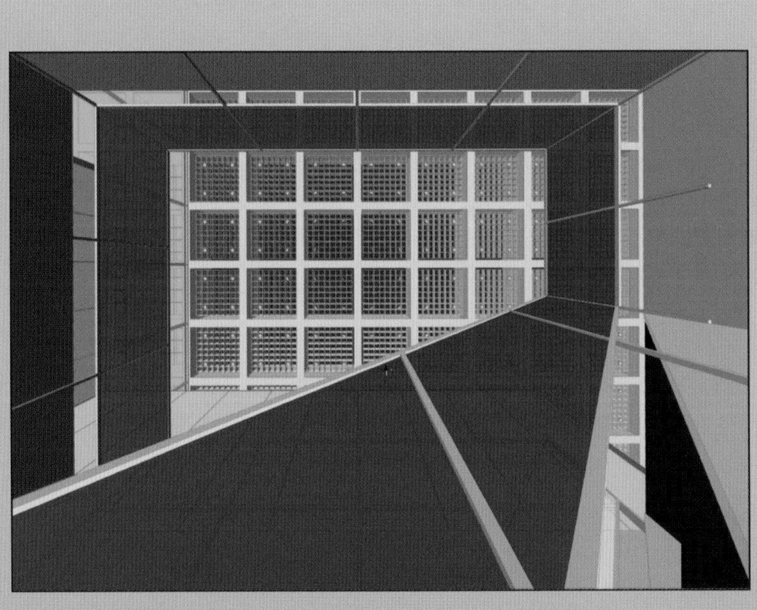

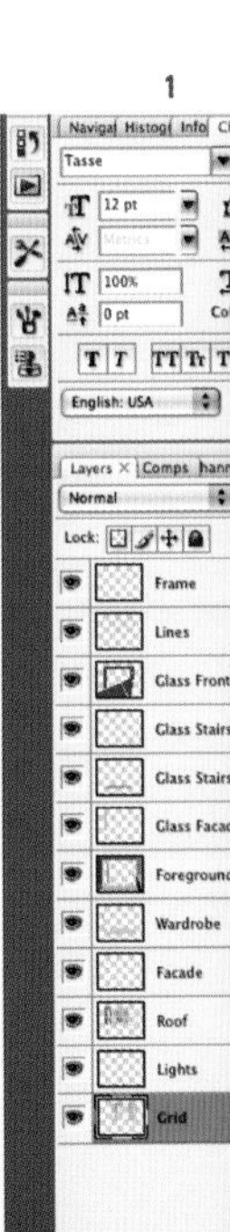

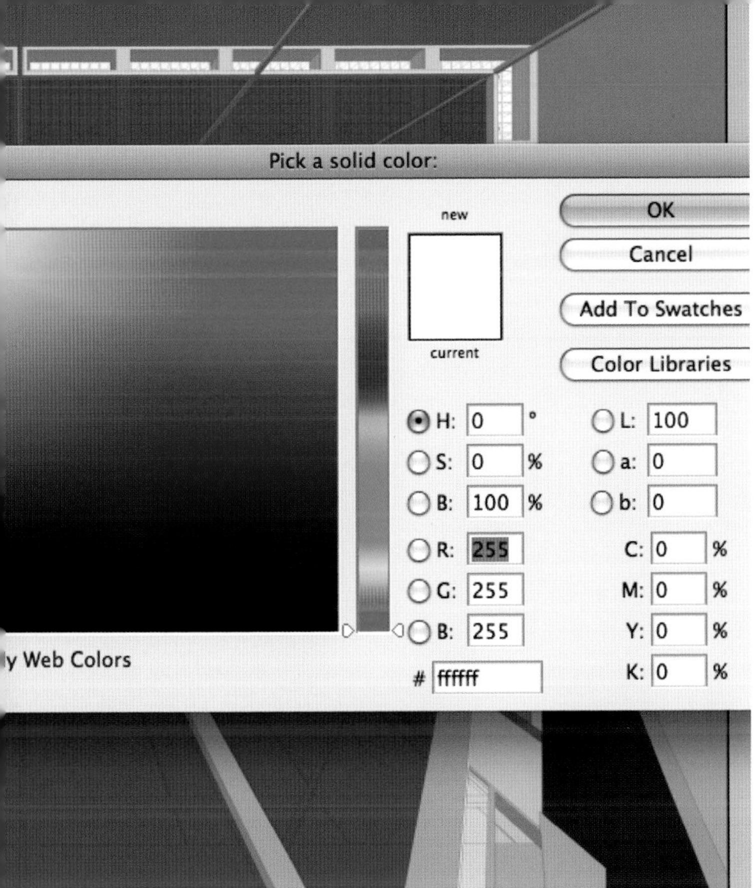

3

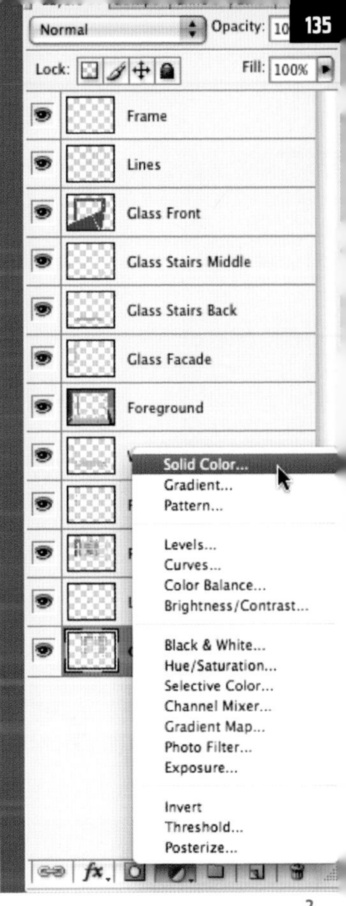

2

The image shows a frontal perspective, a view from the basement of the New National Gallery in Berlin towards the ceiling.

The Export from the CAAD application (in my case ArchiCad®) took place in PDF format, individually for each of the image components, which you now see on layers in the Photoshop® file just opened.

The single PDFs were assembled in Adobe Illustrator®; to have them stacked on one another exactly, all the drawing components had the same frame in common.

Conveniently, when exporting a multi-layer file from Illustrator® in Photoshop®-(.psd-) format all the layers are preserved.

I´ve already dissolved the layer groups for you which Illustrator® created, so that you´re now dealing with a tidied-up, manageable layer structure.

Don´t worry about the colors. In the CAAD application, the job was just to ensure that the colors of contiguous surfaces are clearly different from each other, so they can easily be separated with Photoshop®´s selection tools.

The refinement of the surfaces is reserved for postproduction, in this case in Photoshop®.

So that you can first of all inspect your layers better individually, create a white layer which you place at the very bottom. Of course, use a Solid Color layer for this (ill.2), for which you set all the RGB values to 255 (ill.3).

Confirm with OK, and move the color layer to the very bottom of the Layers palette (ill.4).

4

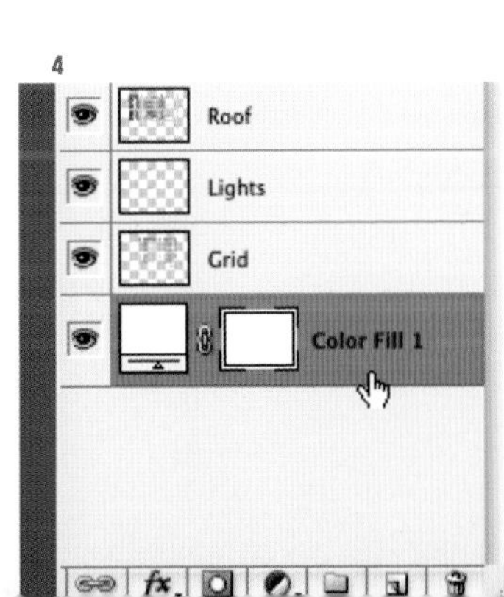

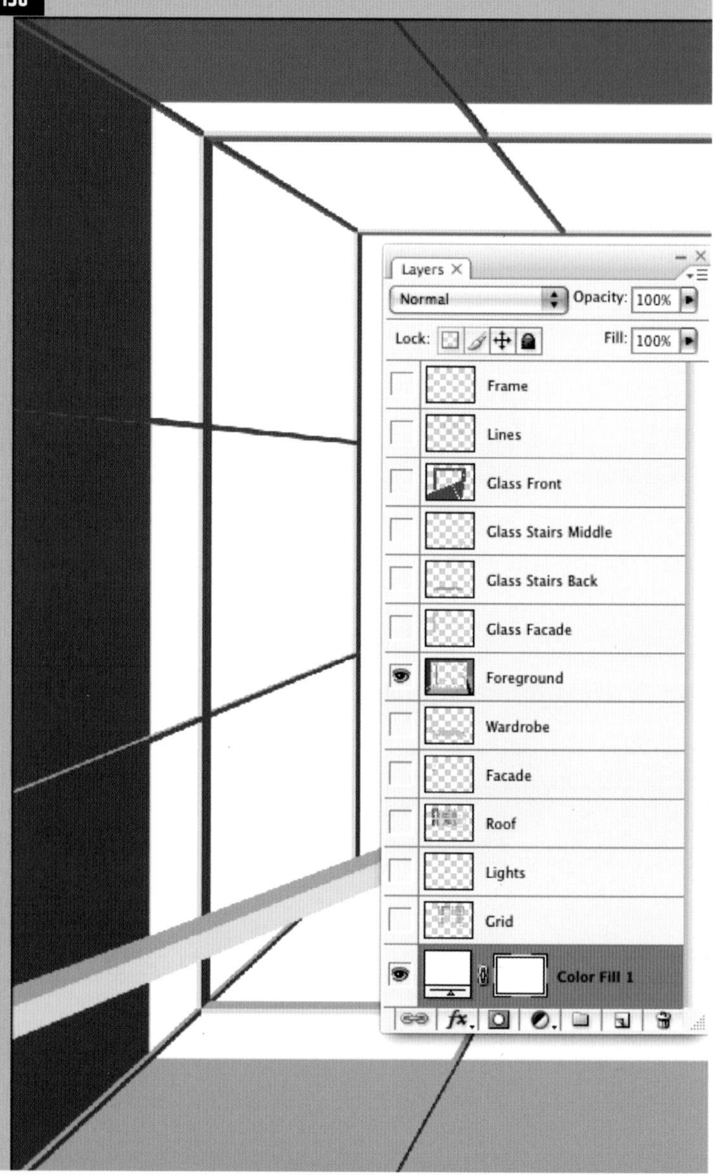

5

Now attend, one by one, to the individual image components. Imagine your image composing as a number of backdrops which you deal with one after the other, and which you give a somewhat realer, spatial look.

First let´s work on the foreground; click on the eye symbol of the layer Foreground with the Alt key held down, so that it´s seen alone at first, and also show the color layer again (ill.5).

So that you know roughly how the metal surfaces of the stairs look in reality, open both the images showing the original situation, one from close-up (07_ng_detail_metal01.psd, ill.6), and one from quite a distance (07_ng_detail_metal02.psd, ill.7).

As a start, you´ll try to recreate this surface characteristic in Photoshop®, first in a separate document.

Since the metal surface has a gray-to-black color, you could create a new document in the Grayscale mode, so it doesn´t need so much disk usage, and so that the texture you create doesn´t appear all too rough after pasting it into your image, select double the size for your new file.

6

A look in the Image Size window of your image file (CTRL-Alt-I) shows that your image is 59.4 x 42.02 cm (ill.8).

So, select the command New from the File menu (ill.9), and for the new document set the size (Width and Height) as 120 x 84 cm, the Resolution 300 pixels/inch and the Color Mode Grayscale (ill.10).

The new document is now at your disposal to create a metal surface which resembles the real one, using Photoshop®´s tools.

Save it as a Photoshop® file with the name 07_ng_metal.psd.

First color the Background layer black. Press D, and if necessary X, so that Black is the foreground color (ill.11), and then Alt-Backspace to fill the layer with Black (ill.12).

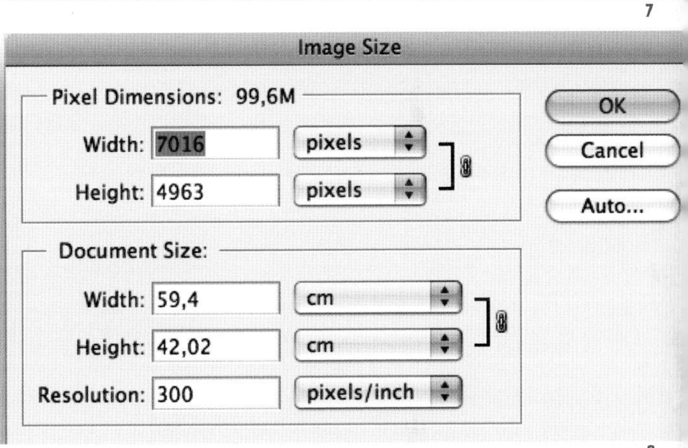

11 12

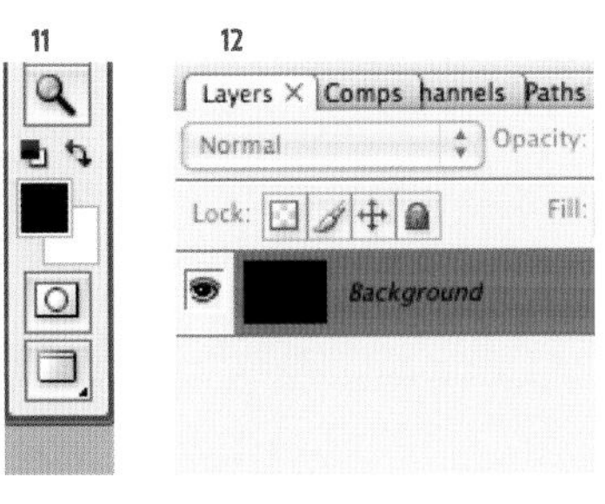

7

Image Size
Pixel Dimensions: 99,6M
Width: 7016 pixels
Height: 4963 pixels
Document Size:
Width: 59,4 cm
Height: 42,02 cm
Resolution: 300 pixels/inch
OK
Cancel
Auto...

8

Photoshop File Edit Image Layer Select Filter Analy
New... ⌘N
Open... ⌘O
Width:

9

10

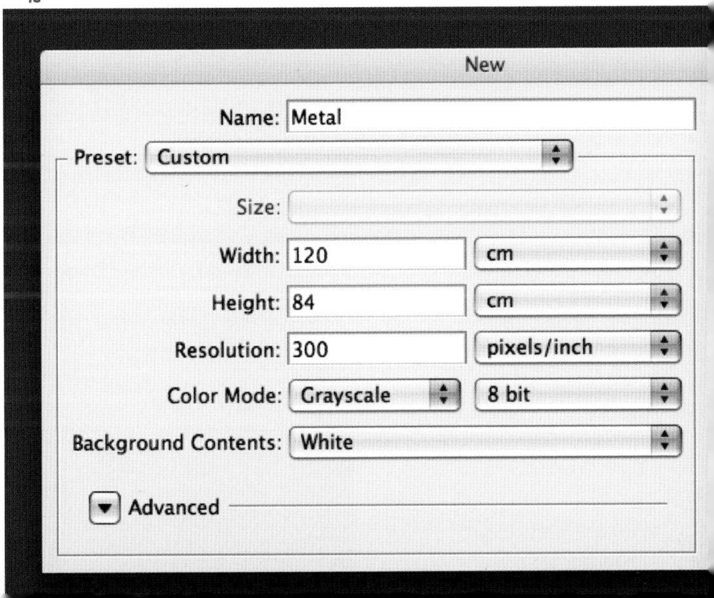

New
Name: Metal
Preset: Custom
Size:
Width: 120 cm
Height: 84 cm
Resolution: 300 pixels/inch
Color Mode: Grayscale 8 bit
Background Contents: White
Advanced

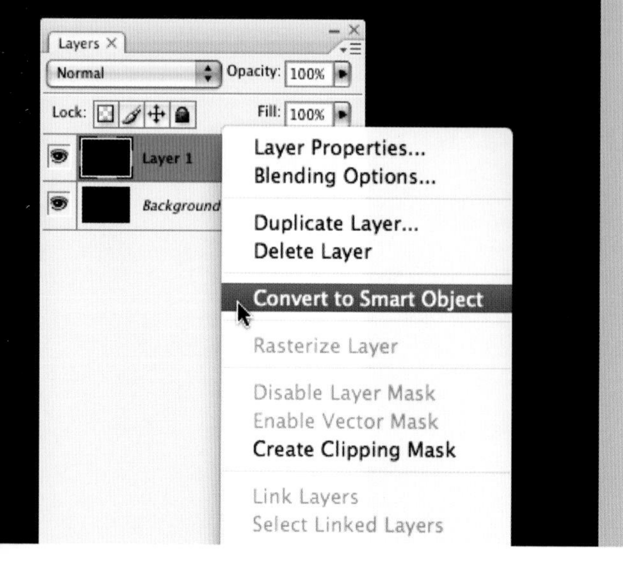

Copy the Background layer, and convert it into a Smart Object (select this option from the context menu that opens after you right-click on the new layer in the Layers palette, ill.13).

You can now reconstruct the real surface you see in the image 07_ng_detail_metal01.psd by means of some filters. As you´re using the filter in such a Smart layer instead of in a normal one, you can losslessly modify the filter adjustments at any time.

To be able to compare your new image with the detailed display of the real situation, first select Standard Screen Mode from the View menu (ill.14; alternatively, you can also press F till you see the familiar window display).

Then zoom the image to 50% display size (first press Alt-CTRL-0, see above ill.15, and then CTRL-- twice; in the window title, the size is indicated in percents (ill.16).

Switch to your image 07_ng_detail_metal01.psd, and zoom it to 100% display size (Alt-CTRL-0, see above).

Close all the other open files (apart from 07_ng_detail_metal01.psd and your new file, of course), and then select the command Arrange – Tile Vertically from the Window menu (ill.17). Both images, the

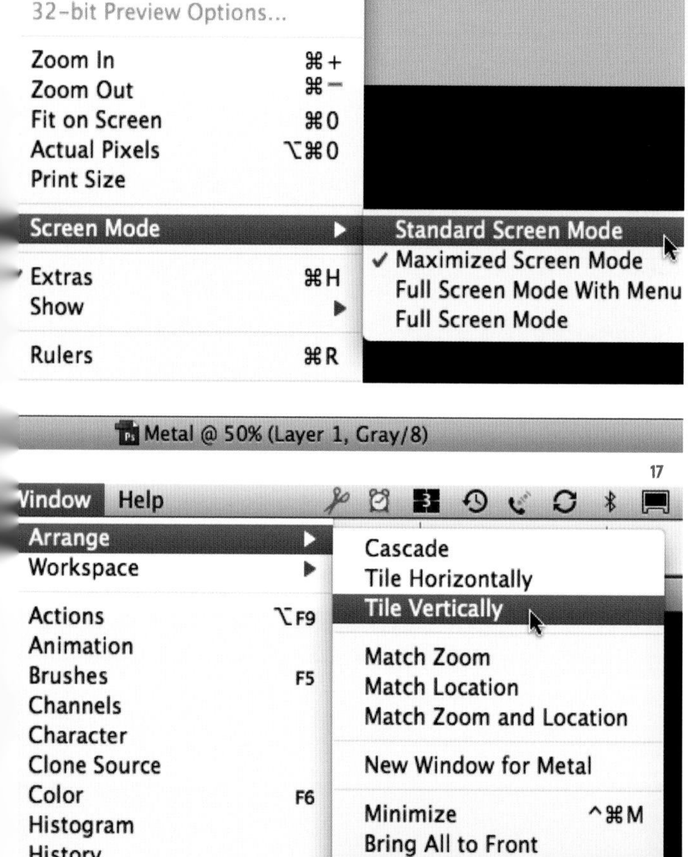

15

View Window Help
Proof Setup
Proof Colors ⌘Y
Gamut Warning ⇧⌘Y
Pixel Aspect Ratio Correction
32-bit Preview Options...
Zoom In ⌘+
Zoom Out ⌘−
Fit on Screen ⌘0
Actual Pixels ⌥⌘0
Print Size

real photo and your new, artificial product, can now be compared well while you work on them, as they´re beside each other.

Your new image is at first created twice as large as is later necessary, thus the display in 50% (ill.18; you´ll see that this large format results from the scaling of the filter you´ll now use).

Make sure your new file is in front, and that you´re in your newly created Smart layer.

Now select the filter Add Noise from the Filter menu (Noise filters, ill.19). In the adjustment dialog that opens,set the Amount to 15% and select Gaussian Distribution (ill.20).

21

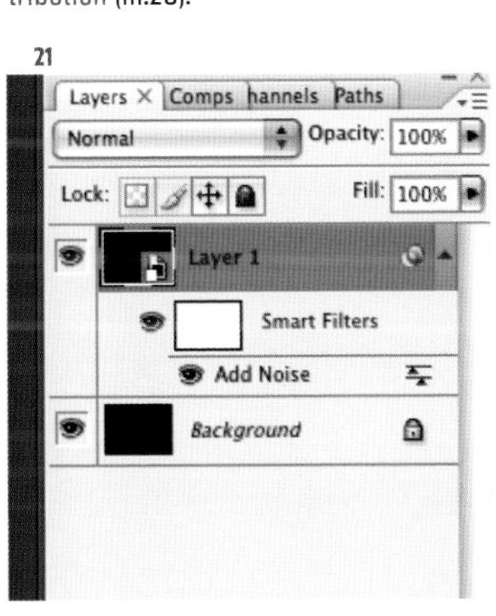

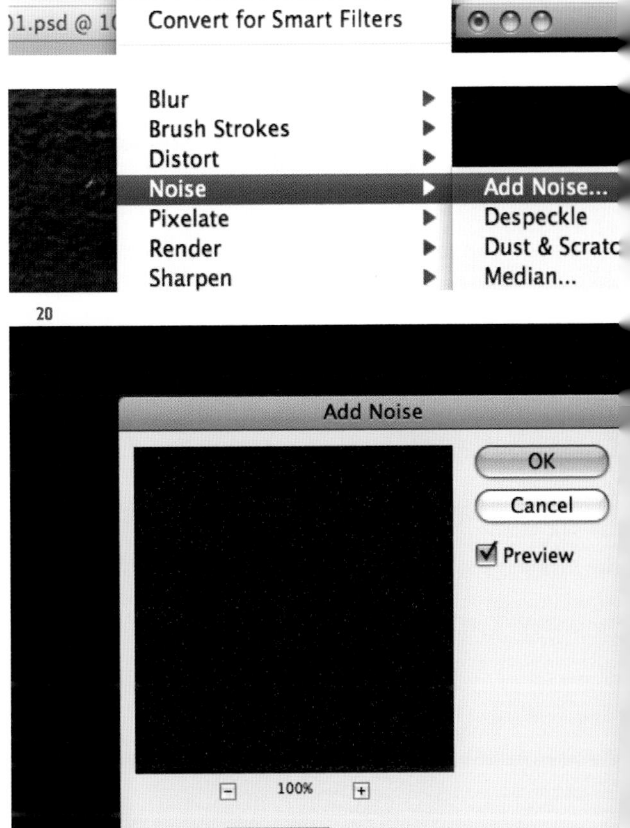

20

Confirm with OK. Your filter is now stacked in the Layers palette and can be opened again at any time for eventual tunings, by double-clicking on its name (ill.21).

Now it´s the turn of the next filter. Your Smart layer is active as before; now select Bas Relief from the Filter menu (Sketch filters, ill.22). This time a rather more ample window opens; for Detail set

22

23

24

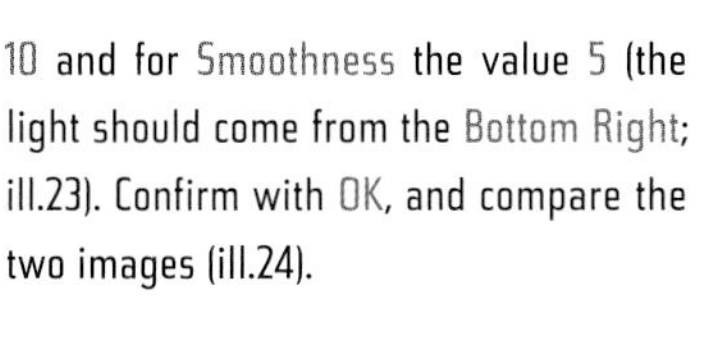

10 and for Smoothness the value 5 (the light should come from the Bottom Right; ill.23). Confirm with OK, and compare the two images (ill.24).

To smooth the whole thing somewhat, use the Emboss filter (Filter – Stylize filters, ill.25). Here set the following values: Angle = -45°, Height = 70 pixels, Amount = 25%, ill.26). Confirm with OK, and compare the two images again (ill.27).

The texture has at first become very similar; now you´ll make everything rather darker.
For this, use the Levels correction, of course as an adjustment layer. Select it from the corresponding menu of the Layers palette (ill.28).

25

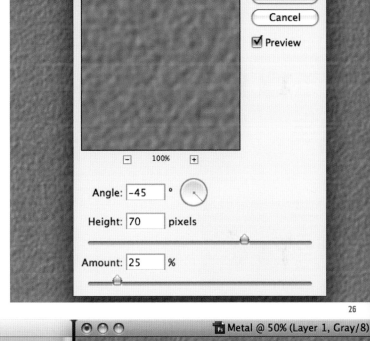

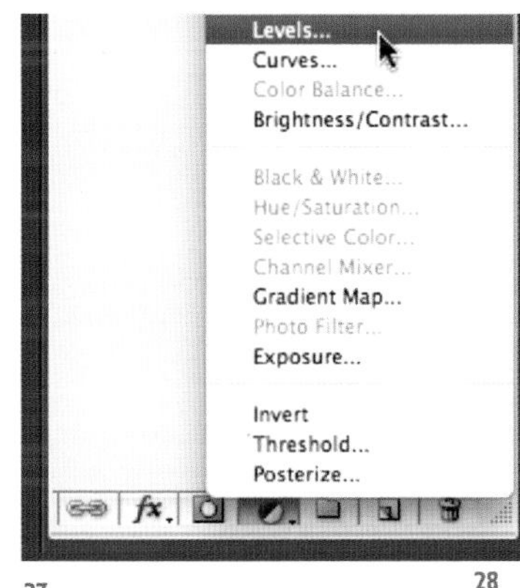

27

28

26

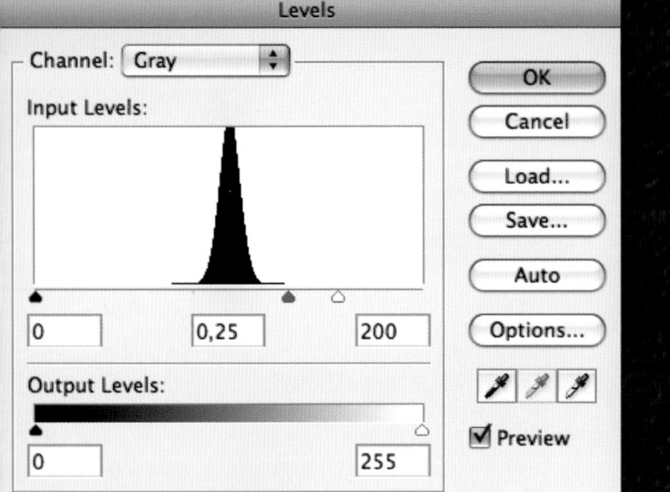

29

07_ng_structure.psd @ 100%

30

31

Set the values below the histogram to 0 - 0,25 - 200 (ill.29); as you see, the artificial image already greatly resembles the real one. Confirm with OK.

Yet, you should modulate the regular structure of your previous filter overlay with an irregular texture, which you obtain from "real", not mathematically generated images.

In your download folder there´s firstly a cloud image, and secondly the scan of a cardboard sheet, which you know as the back of a writing pad.

First open this image (07_ng_structure.psd), and set the display size with Alt CTRL-0 to 100% (ill.30).

To be integrated in your metal composing correctly, the background of your cardboard texture should either be white (then you could insert it in the layer blending mode Multiply), or black (then Linear Dodge would be the right mode).

If you take another close look at the image of the real surface (07_ng_detail_metal01.psd, ill.31), you see small white spots spread over the surface at irregular intervals.
This means that in our case it would be better if the background of our structure image was black, and the spots white.

In order that the small spots on your texture, which are mainly black or dark gray, become white, make a negative from your image.

Select the adjustment layer Invert from the menu at the bottom frame of the Layers palette, and the spots are now bright instead of dark.

To make the background black and to brighten up the spots further, use the Levels correction, also via an adjustment layer (ill.33).

34

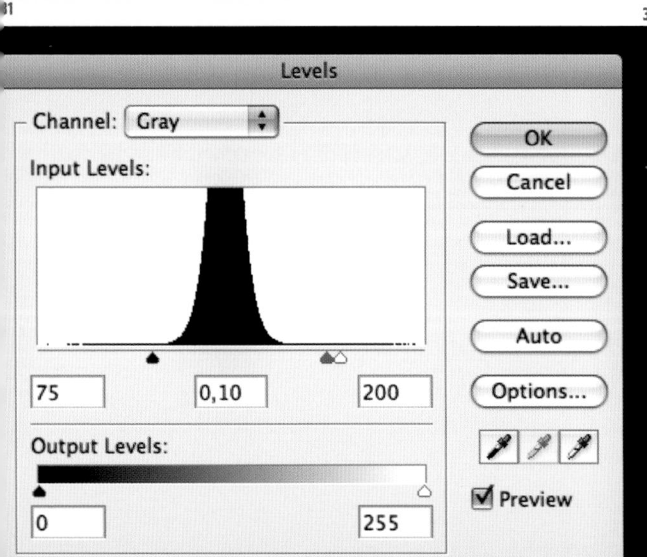

33

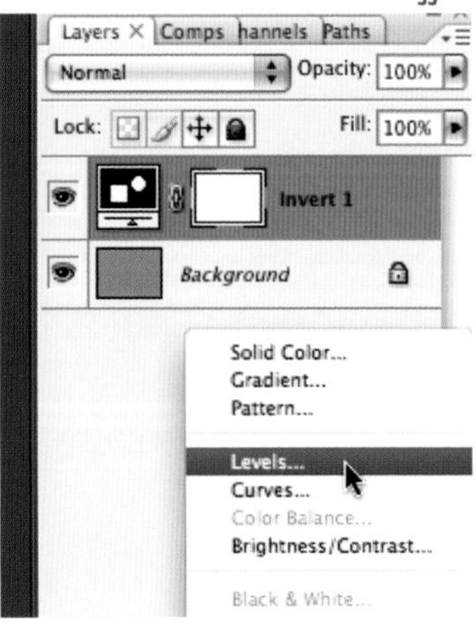

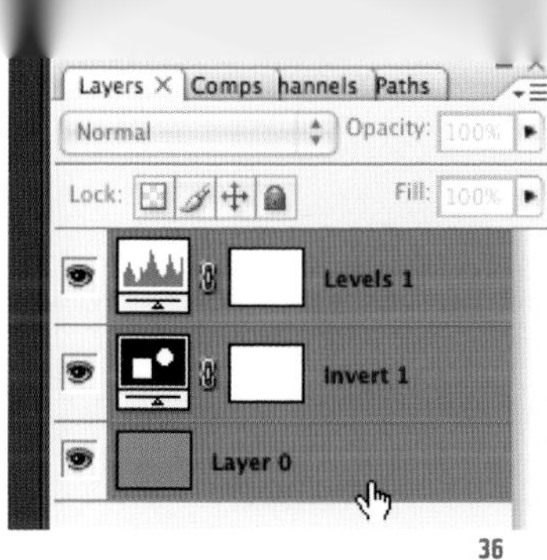

36

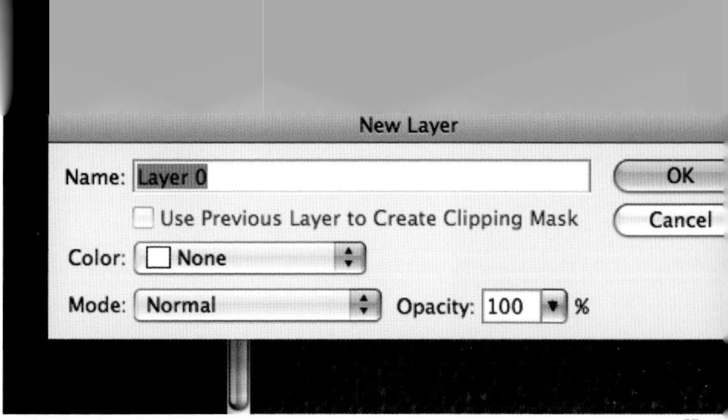

35

Set the values to 75 – 0.10 – 200, and you see everything change as you wanted (ill.34). Confirm with OK.

Reduce and move the window, so that you also see your home-made file again (07_ng_metal.psd).

Still in the file 07_ng_structure.psd, you´ll first group all your layers, so you can insert them in your composing altogether.

For this, first convert the Background layer into a "normal" Photoshop® layer, by double-clicking it in the Layers palette, and confirm the option dialog with OK (ill.35).

Then mark all the layers (Shift-click, ill.36) and from the pulldown menu of the Layers palette (behind the small black arrow top-right) select the command New Group from Layers (ill.37).

In the adjustment dialog, enter Structure 1 as the name, and confirm with OK (ill.38).

So, you now have the image 07_ng_structure.psd in the foreground, but you also see your composing 07_ng_metal.psd; now drag the layer group Structure 1 from the Layers palette into the window of the image 07_ng_metal.psd.

There, move the imported layer group in the Layers palette to the very top if necessary (ill.39).

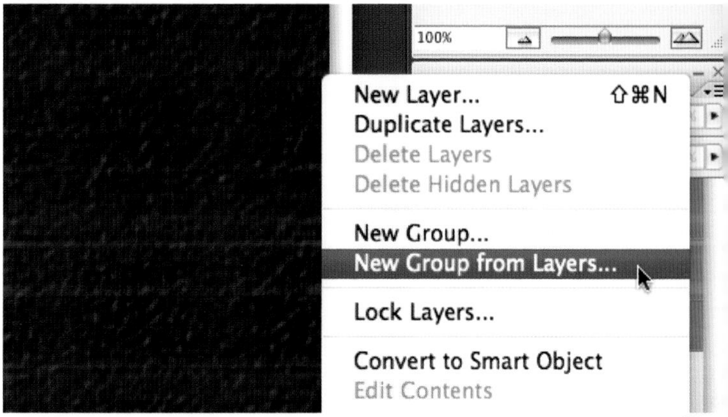

37

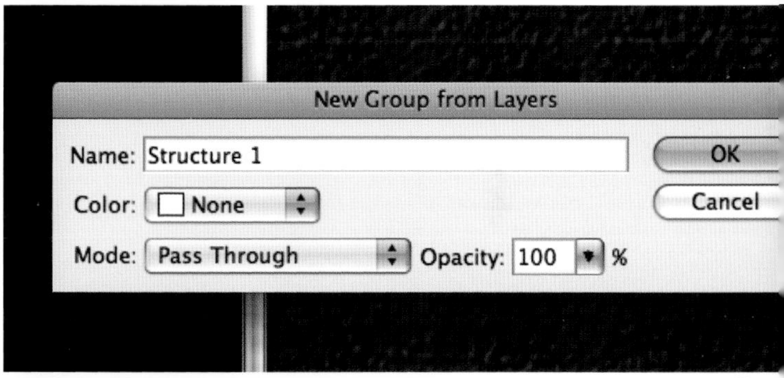

38

39

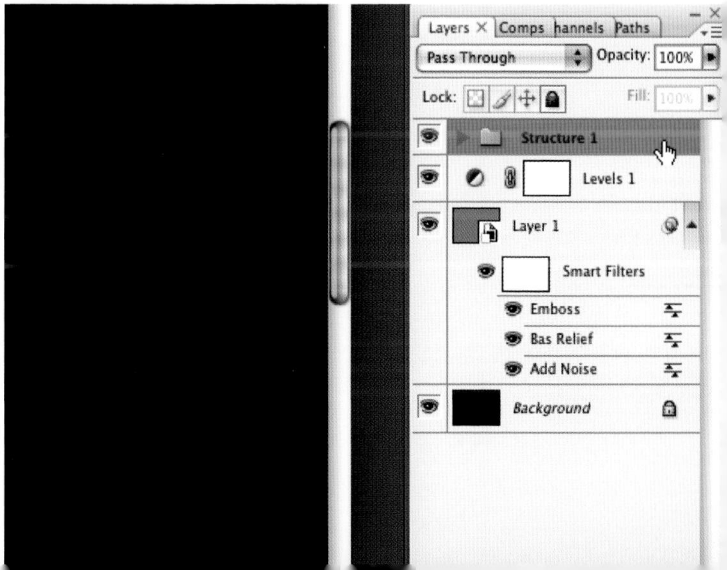

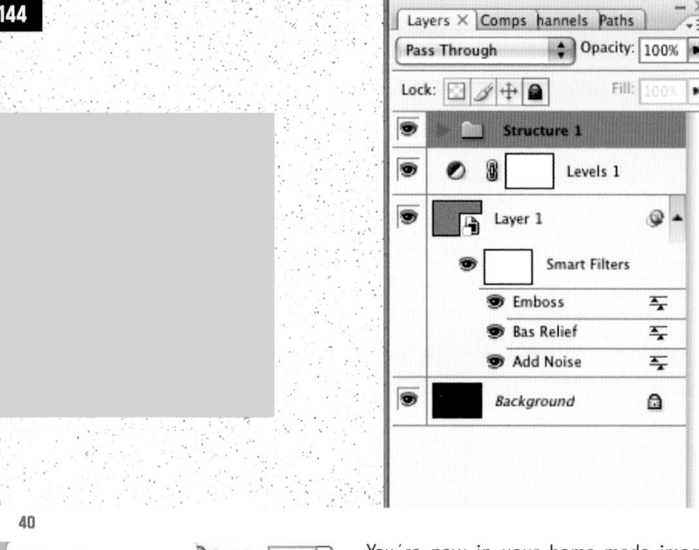

40

42

You´re now in your home-made image 07_ng_metal.psd. again. Press F twice to see it in Full Screen Mode, and then CTRL-0 to gain an overview.

As you see, your imported layer group is a lot smaller than your image (ill.40).

Make sure your imported layer group is activated in the Layers palette, and press

41

CTRL-T to scale it. Just pull it at its corner points, over the edge of the image if you want (ill.41), and finish the scaling with Return.

Set the blending mode of the layer group to Linear Dodge (ill.42), to hide the black background.

Press Alt-CTRL-0, and you see your newly added spots (ill.43). Now save and close the file 07_ng_structure.psd.

43

44

Now we want to lay a further structure over our composing, which we create from a cloud image. Open the file 07_ng_clouds_internet.jpg (it´s taken from the website www.wolkenatlas.de, ill.44).
Crop it to the dimensions 42 x 29.7 cm, selecting a clipping that shows a relatively even cloud texture.

To do this, select the Crop tool (key C, ill.45), and up in the Options palette set the dimensions 42 cm (Width), 29.7 cm

45

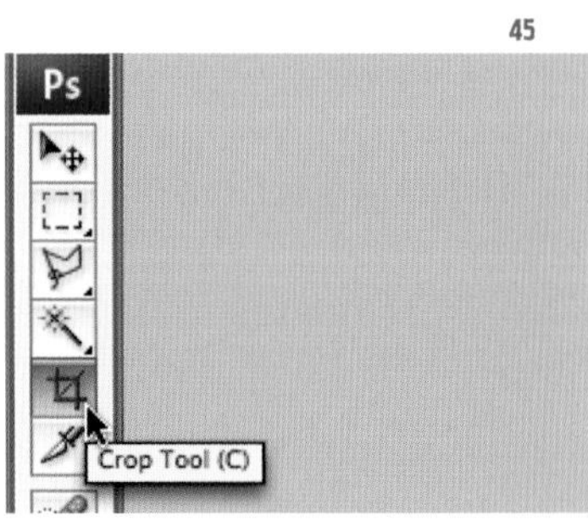

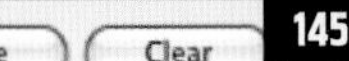

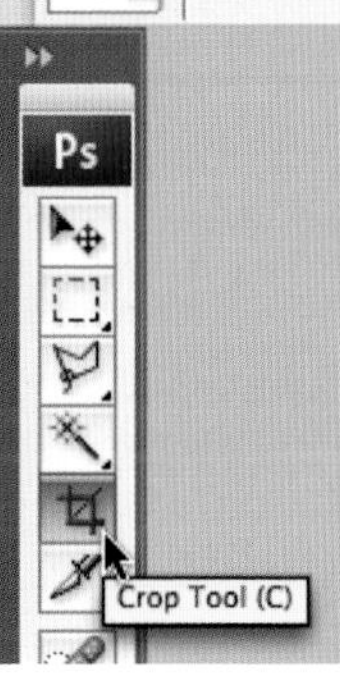

46

(Height) and 300 pixels/inch (Resolution, ill.46; enter the cm for safety´s sake, as you maybe now don´t know by heart which ruler units are being decided in Photoshop® ´s preferences).

Then draw the desired cropping frame. You can move or scale it till it seems right to you (ill.47; I´ve tried to select the part showing a relatively evenly bright cloud pattern).

If you´re satisfied, double-click in the frame or press Return, or Enter.
The image now shows the clipping you´ve chosen, with the dimensions you´ve decided on (ill.48) and so it´s just as big as the image with the cardboard texture.

You require the present image to overlay it with the metal texture you´ve created, as well as the cardboard image you´ve just worked on

So you should convert it into Black-and-White; for this, select the adjustment layer with the name Black & White (ill.49), and in the adjustment dialog, do without a Filter Preset (Without, ill.50).

47

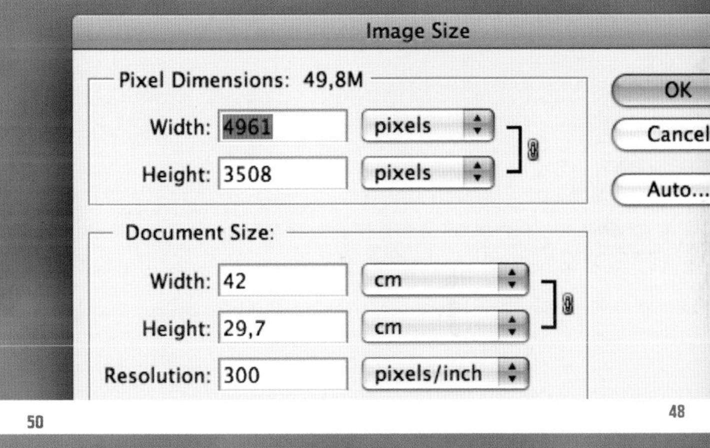

48

49

Solid Color...
Gradient...
Pattern...
Levels...
Curves...
Color Balance...
Brightness/Contrast...
Black & White...
Hue/Saturation...
Selective Color...
Channel Mixer...
Gradient Map...
Photo Filter...
Exposure...
Invert
Threshold...
Posterize...

50

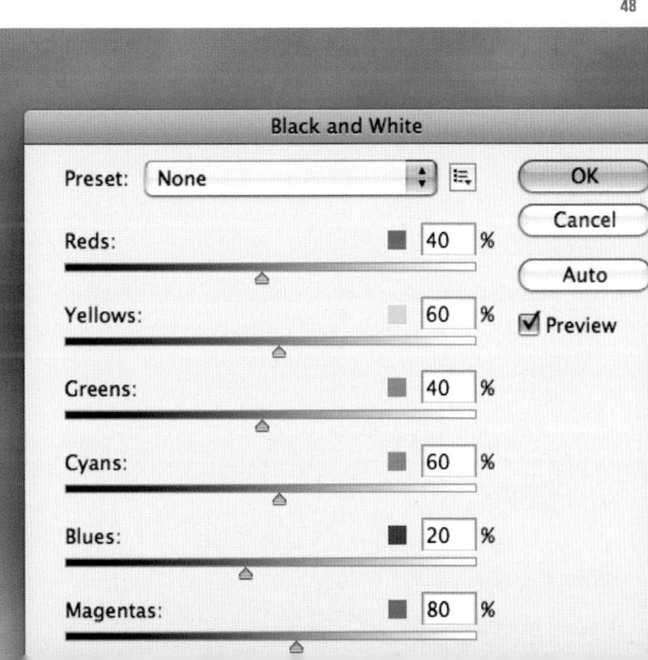

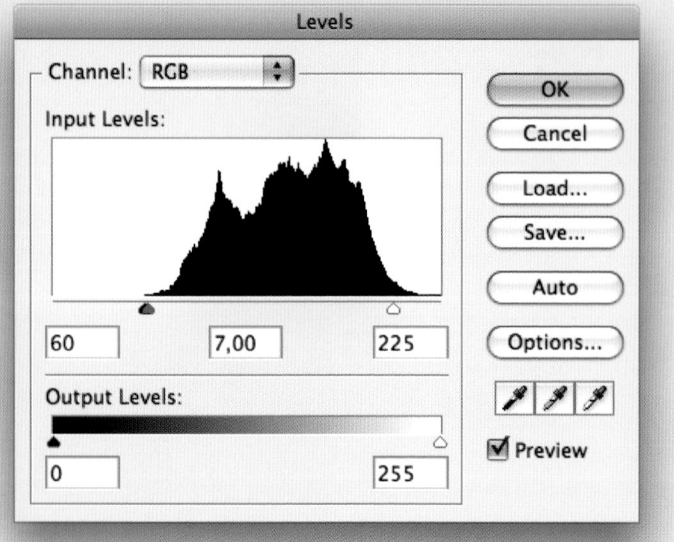

52

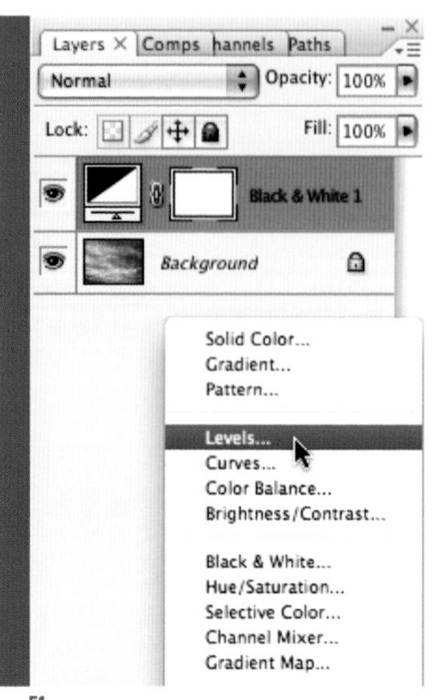

51

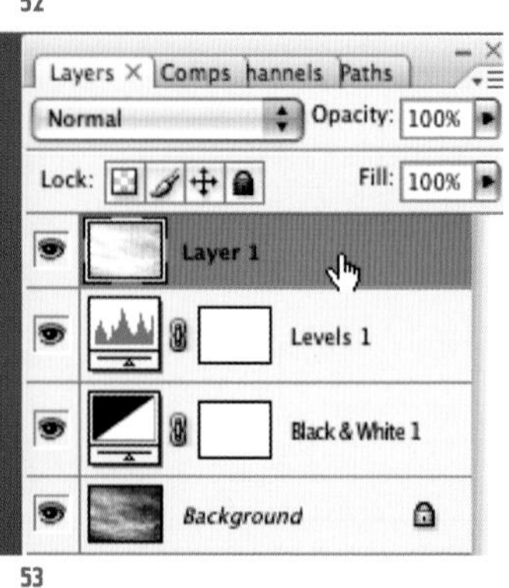

53

So that the later overlay turns out subtle rather than dramatic, greatly brighten the image, but also increase the contrast. Select a Levels adjustment layer (ill.51) and set the values 60 – 7.00 – 225 (ill.52).

Repair the dark part top-right with the Clone Stamp tool.
In order not to damage your original, do it in a copy, preferably in one which shows the result of your corrections so far.

Check that the uppermost layer (the Levels correction) is active, and press Shift-Alt-CTRL-E.

You get a fourth layer (ill.53), on which you can now work with the Clone Stamp tool.

Select it (S), make the tool tip big enough, pick a suitable image area with the Alt key held down, and paint over the dark corner.
After that, your image should resemble a relatively homogeneous impression (ill.54).

Now combine all the layers into one group too.
To do this, first convert the Background layer into a normal one, by double-clicking on the entry in the Layers palette (leave it at the name I´ve suggested, and confirm with OK, ill.55).

As the metal file is in Grayscale mode, your cloud image is converted on importing, because the Black & White adjustment layer doesn´t work in a Grayscale

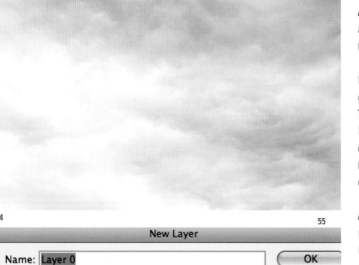

54

55

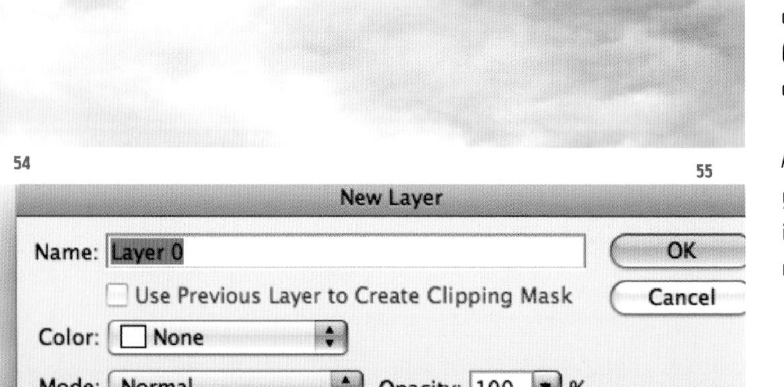

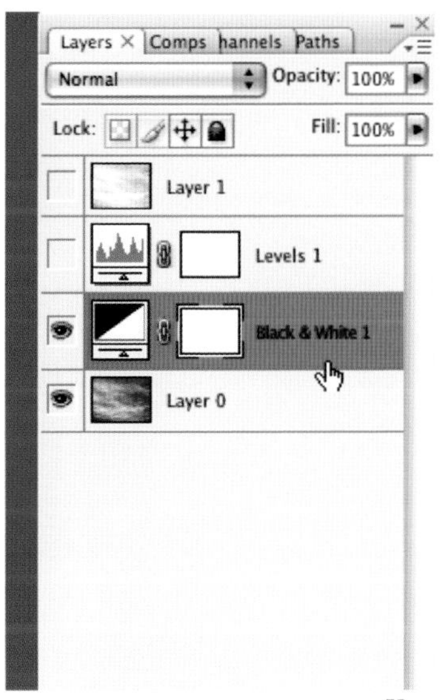

56

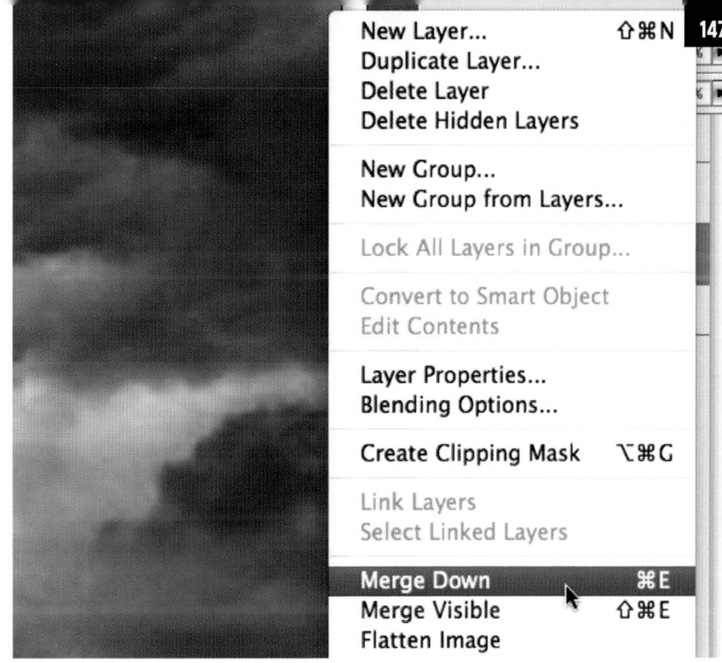

57

file. That´s why you should first combine the colored background layer and this adjustment layer into one.

Hide the two other layers and mark the Black & White one (ill.56).

Then select the command Merge Down from the menu of the Layers palette, or press CTRL-E (ill.57).

Show all the layers again, and also mark them all – then select, again from the menu of the Layers palette, the command New Group from Layers (ill.58).

Call the group Structure 2 (ill.59).

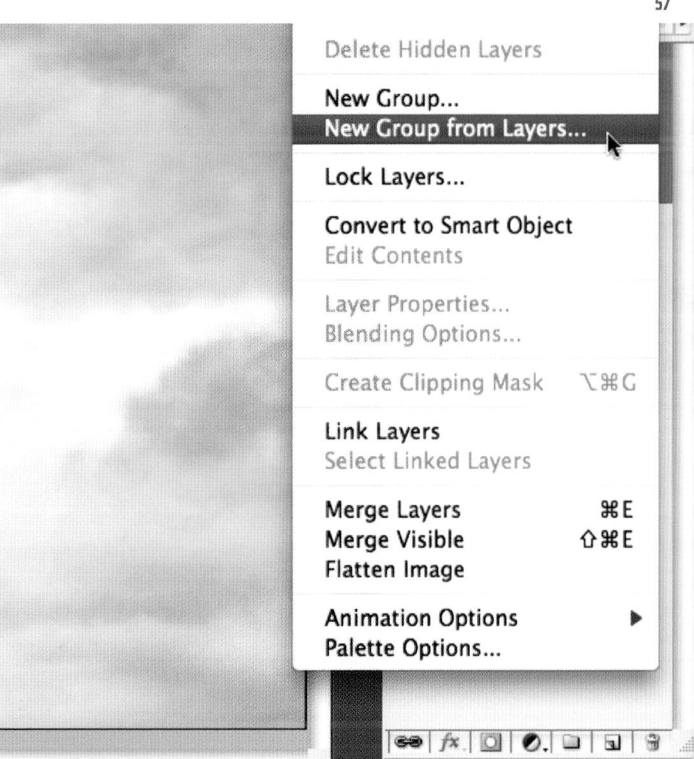

58

59

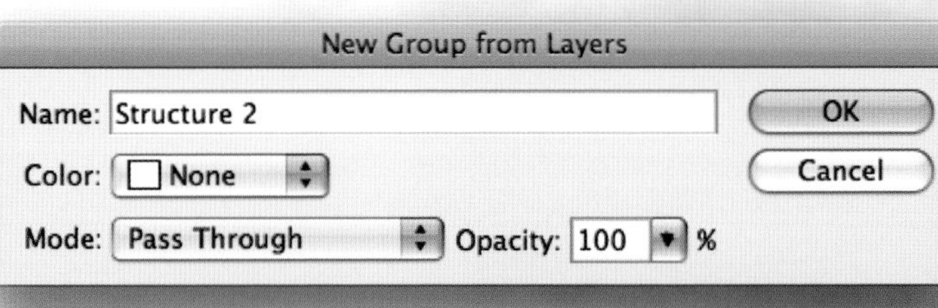

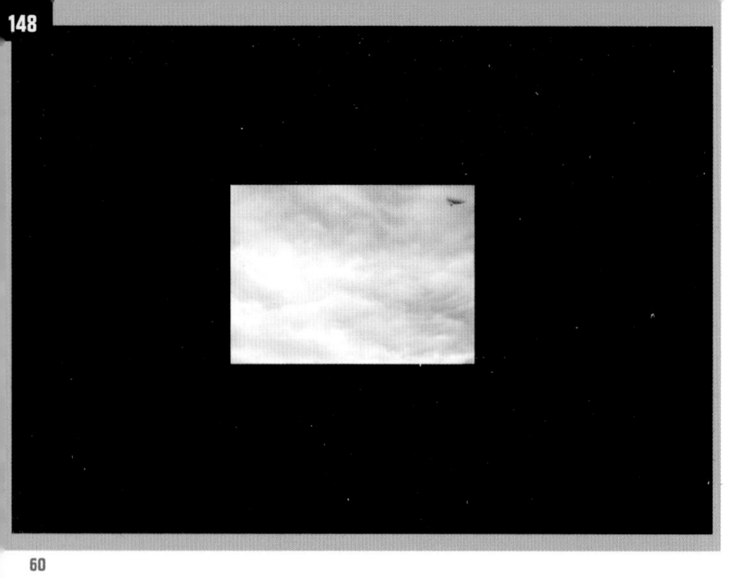

60

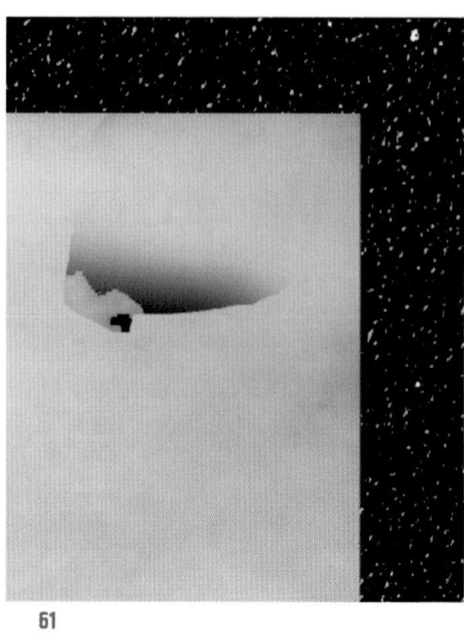

61

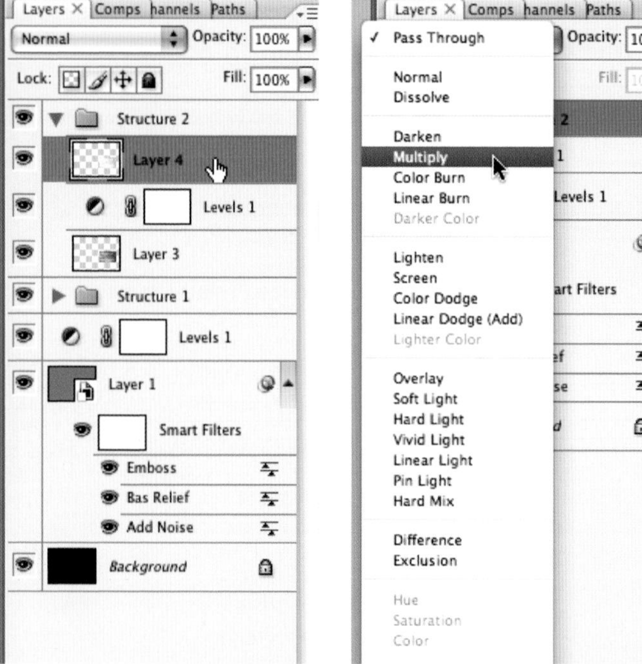

62

63

64

Press F till you see your cloud image in normal window display, and move the Window till you can also see the Window of your metal file.

Then with the Move tool (V) drag the layer group out of the Layers palette in the Window of your metal image.
As you see, this import graphic is smaller than the target file too (ill.60).

On importing, the retouched area in the top-right corner has again got a bit mixed up; this occured when pasting in the Grayscale file (ill.61). Open the new imported layer group Structure 2 in the Layers palette by clicking on the small arrow in front of the group name, and mark the upper layer of the group (ill.62). Repeat once again your touching-up at the critical place.

Now also set the blending mode of the new layer group to Multiply (ill.63). Press CTRL-T, and scale the import image. Now too you can drag a little over the image borders (ill.64).

Now that you can see the cloud texture in the composing of the metal surface, you´ll surely want to use another filter on the cloud image. For this, convert the upper layer of your cloud group into a

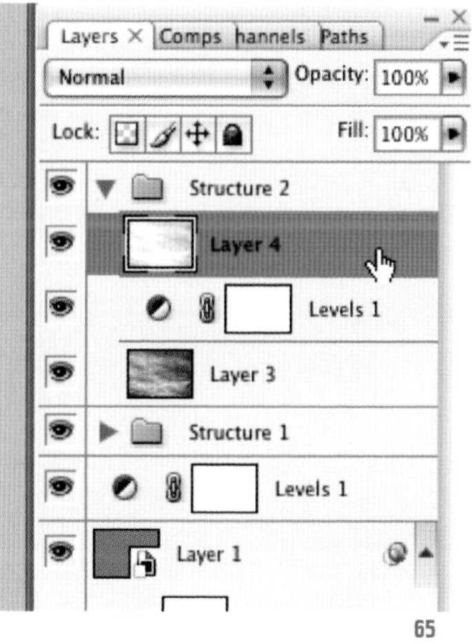

65

66

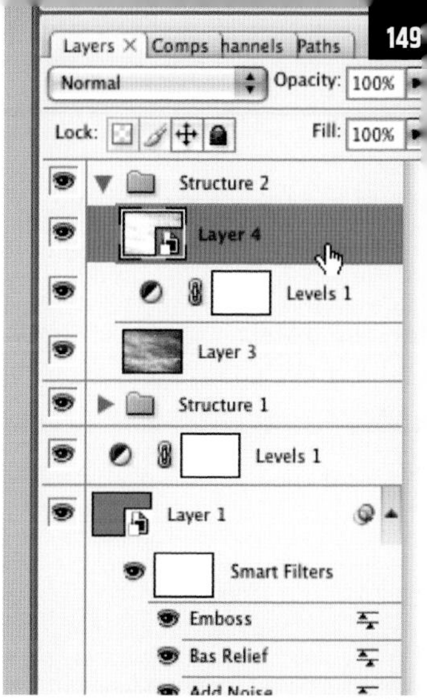

67

Smart Object (the command can be found in the context menu, which you reach by right-clicking on the layer entry, ills.65, 66 and 67).

Then select the Texture filter Grain (Filter menu, ill.68). In the Window of the Filter Gallery which opens, first scale the preview to full image (CTRL-0), and then set the values for Intensity to 16 and for Contrast to 0. Select Horizontal as the Grain Type (ill.69).

Did you know that you can stack the same filter with different adjustments over each other? Look at the lower end of the gallery window, and there you´ll see two small icons. With the one on the left you can insert a second layer inside the filter (ill.70),

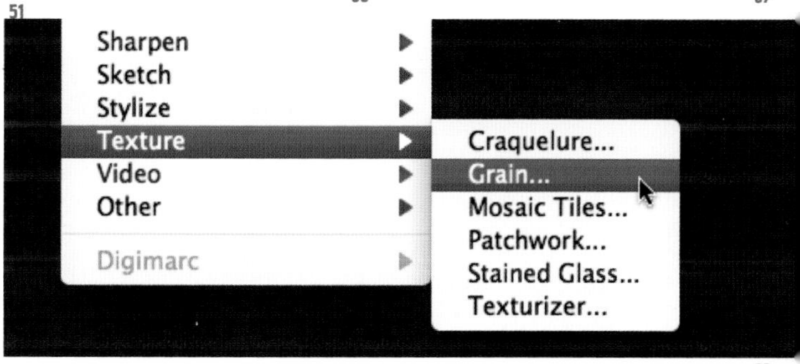

68

70

69

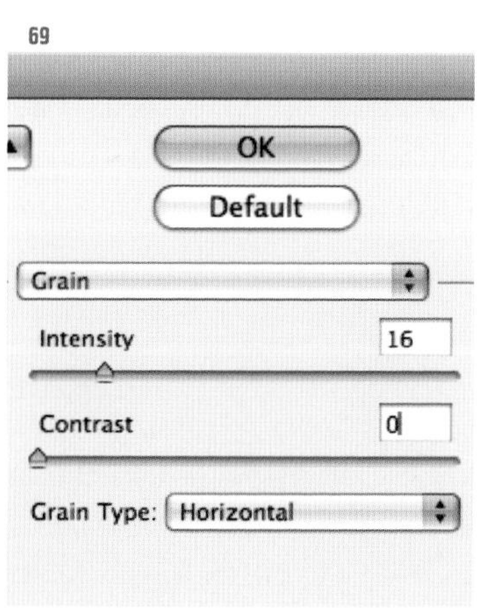

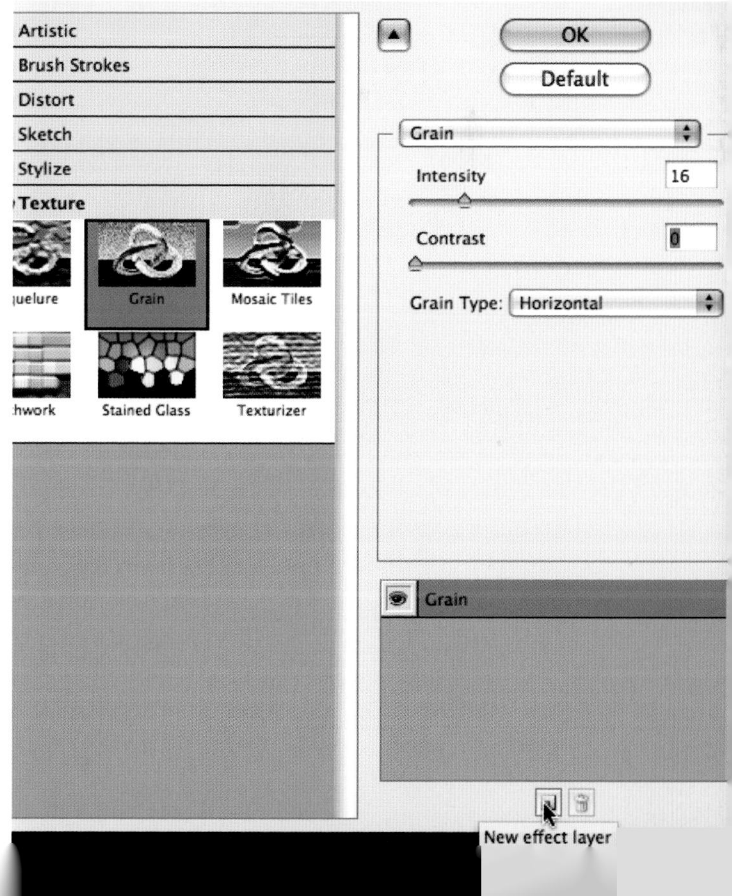

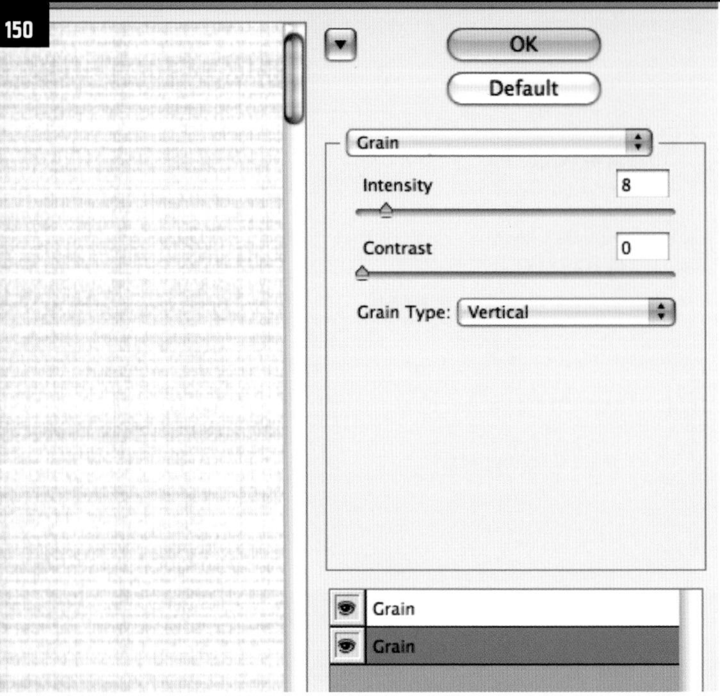

71

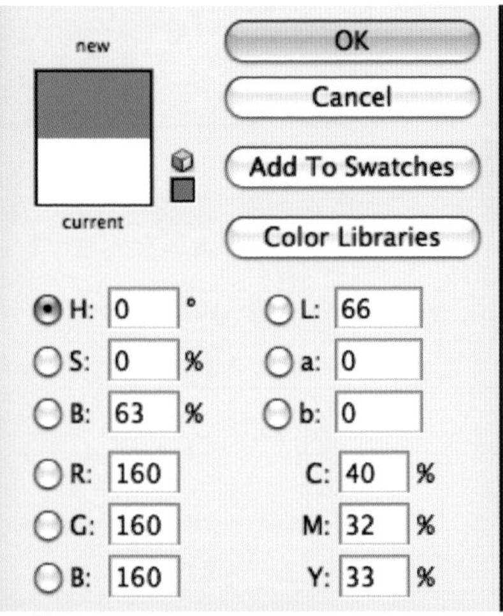

73

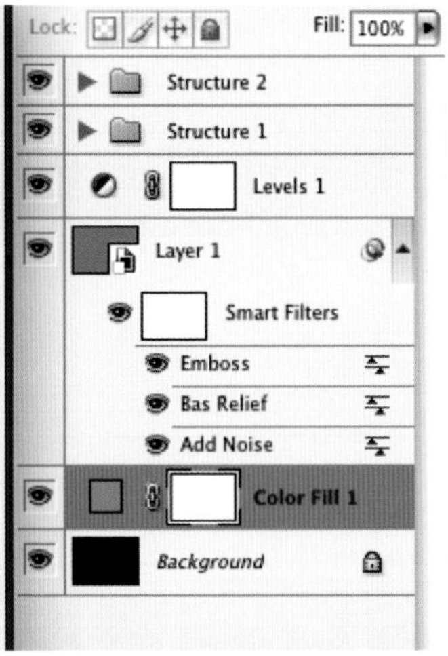

74

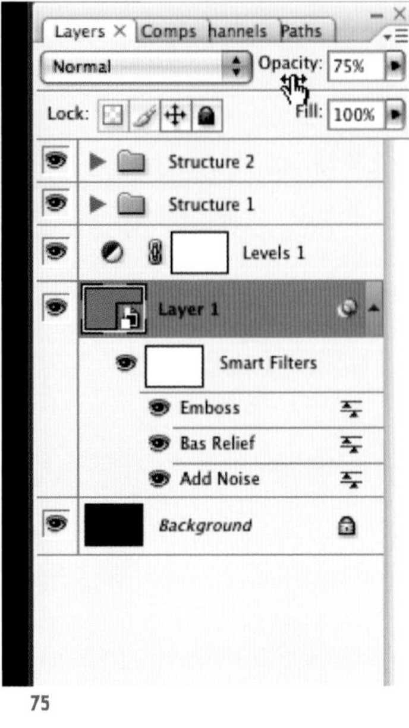

75

which initially takes on the adjustments of the first, already existing one.

Click on one of the two layers, and then change the values of the filter for this layer: Intensity = 8, Contrast = 0, Grain Type Vertical (ill.71). Confirm with OK.

Now open file 07_ng_detail_metal01.psd again, and have a look at it and your current image beside each other.

Still in your own new metal image, reduce slightly the Opacity of the layer with the relief (Opacity 75%, ill.72), and add a Solid Color layer under it, for which you set a midrange Gray value (R, G, B = 160, ill.73).
The original and the reproduction look fairly similar (ill.74).

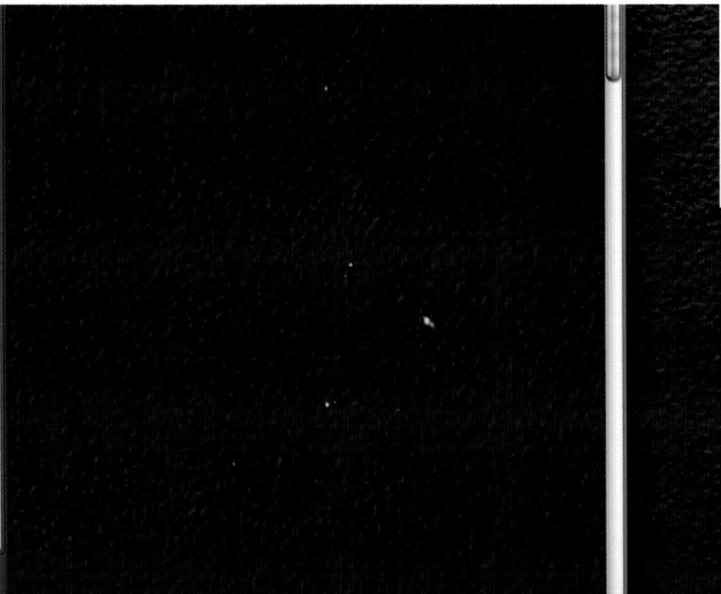

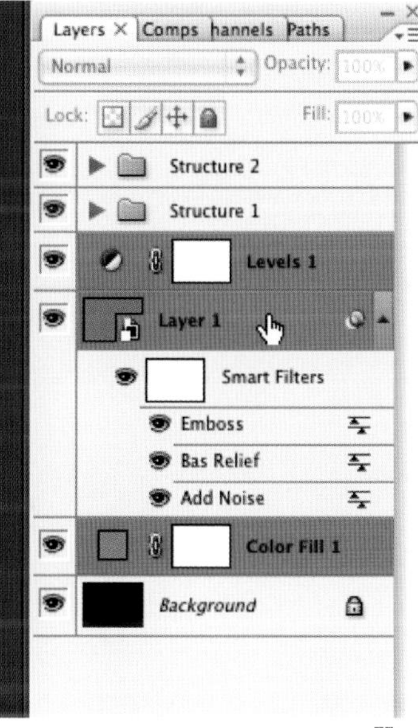

75

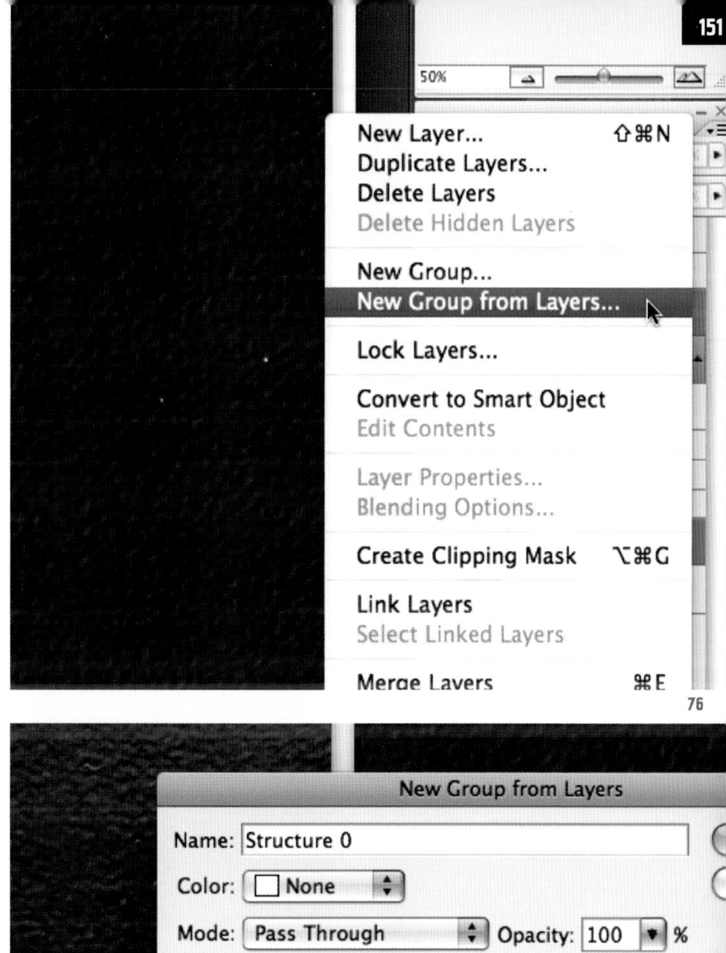

76

77

You can now set to work inserting the metal texture in your image of the National Gallery.

For this, combine the remaining individual layers into one group, apart from the Background layer.
Mark them for this purpose (ill.75), and select again the command New Group from Layers from the Layers palette menu (ill.76); choosing Structure 0 as the name (ill.77).

Release the Background layer by double-clicking and deleting, so that in your composing only the three layer groups are left (ill.78).

I´d like to remind you that you´ll downscale this metal texture in your image of the National Gallery, as the relief otherwise turns out too big.

I pointed out at the beginning that the relief filters have a certain scale which can´t be changed. That´s also why we´ve compared the original image in 100% and the new metal texture image always in 50% display size.

As the filters in your metal texture are still active, because they were used on Smart Objects, they would also be scaled when reducing, which on halving the size of the image would make the relief structure appear proportionately twice as big.

You should therefore first distil a "resulting" layer from all your layers, and only insert this one into the image of the National Gallery. For this, use again the wonderful command Shift-Alt-CTRL-E, which can´t be found in the menus, which combines all the visible layers into one, fortunately as a copy.

So, activate it and you get a new layer showing everything you´ve achieved so far with your many image and adjustment layers, including the Smart filters (ill.79).

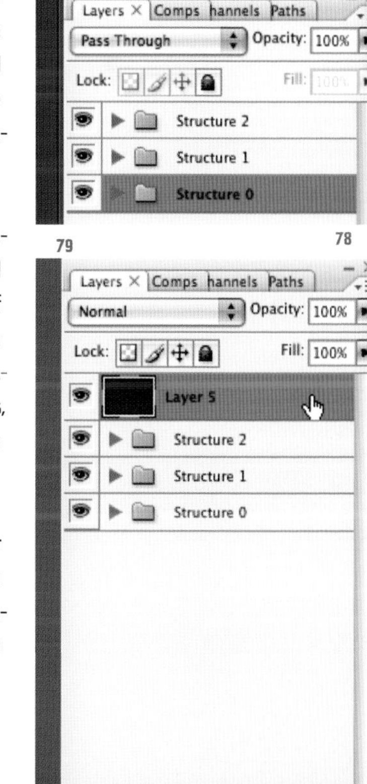

78

79

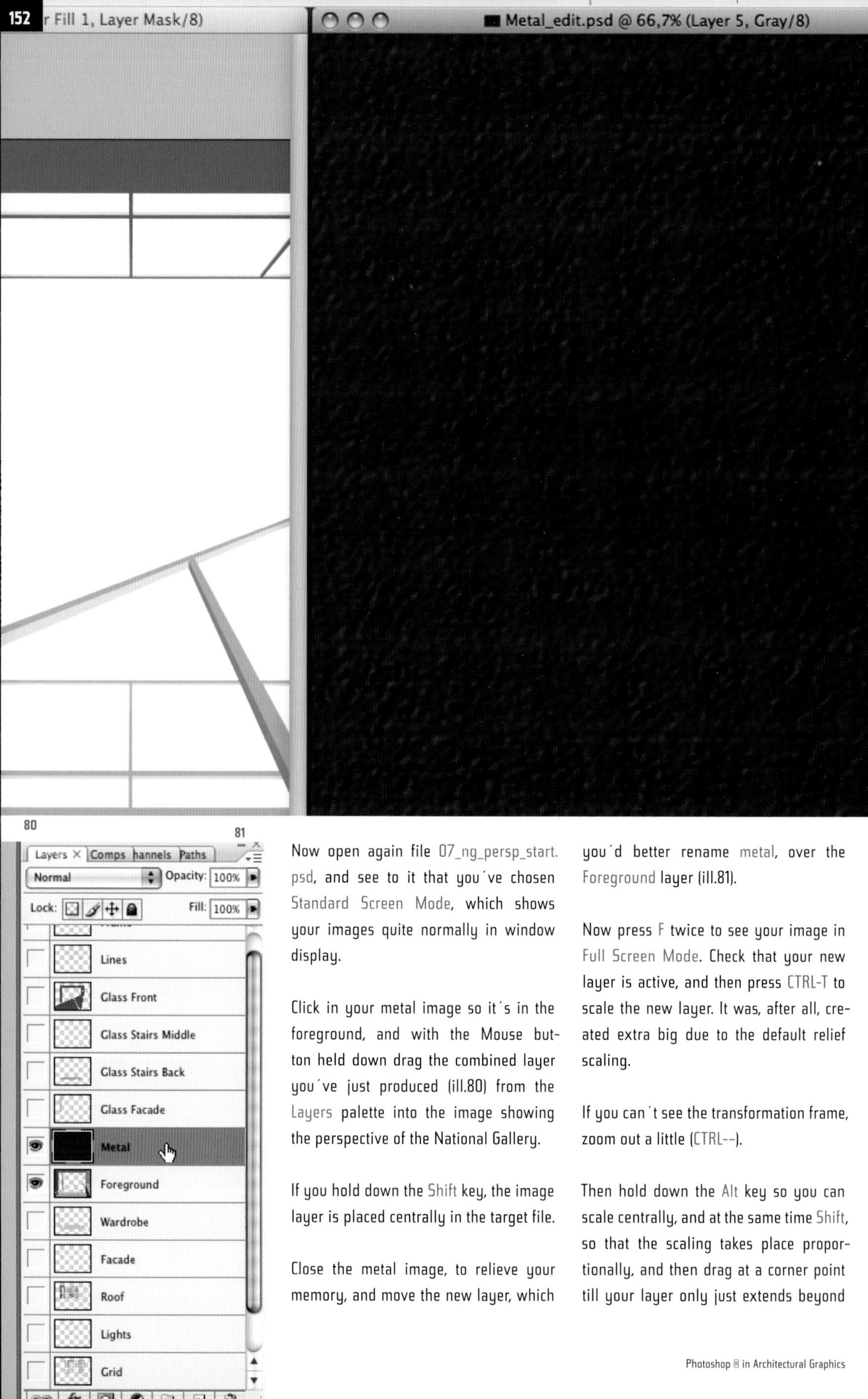

Now open again file 07_ng_persp_start.psd, and see to it that you´ve chosen Standard Screen Mode, which shows your images quite normally in window display.

Click in your metal image so it´s in the foreground, and with the Mouse button held down drag the combined layer you´ve just produced (ill.80) from the Layers palette into the image showing the perspective of the National Gallery.

If you hold down the Shift key, the image layer is placed centrally in the target file.

Close the metal image, to relieve your memory, and move the new layer, which you´d better rename metal, over the Foreground layer (ill.81).

Now press F twice to see your image in Full Screen Mode. Check that your new layer is active, and then press CTRL-T to scale the new layer. It was, after all, created extra big due to the default relief scaling.

If you can´t see the transformation frame, zoom out a little (CTRL--).

Then hold down the Alt key so you can scale centrally, and at the same time Shift, so that the scaling takes place proportionally, and then drag at a corner point till your layer only just extends beyond

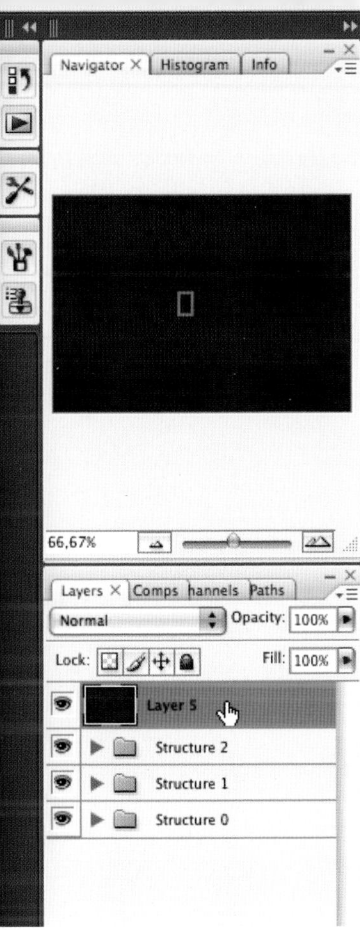

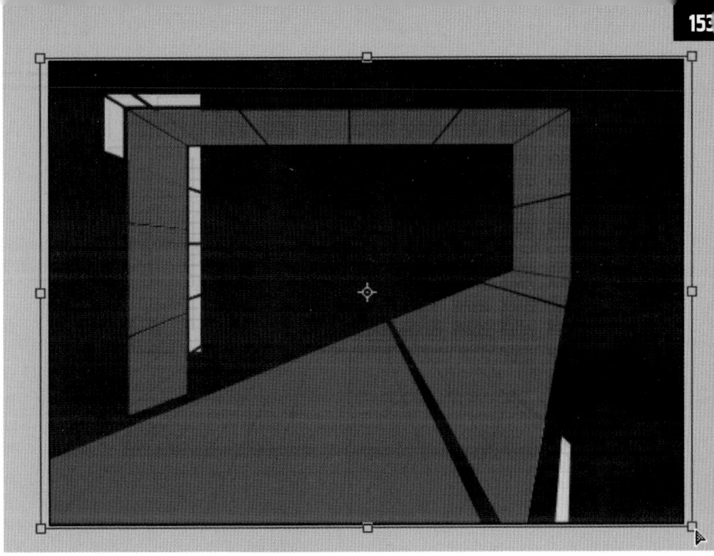

82

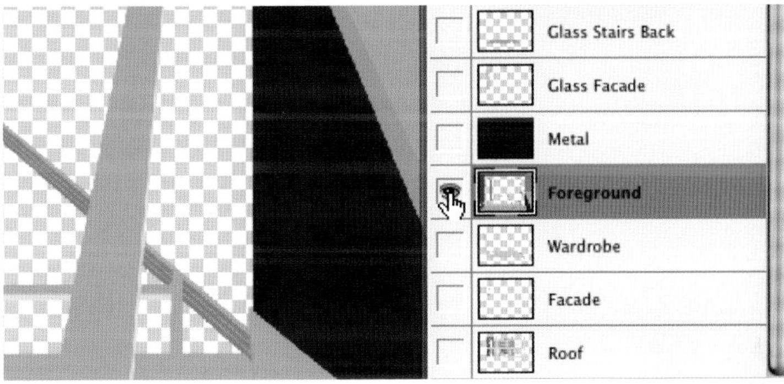

83

the image borders (ill.82). Finish the scaling with Return.
Now you have to crop the metal texture, and then adjust it perspectively to the image area of the Foreground.

To do this, hide all the layers except the Foreground one (it´s easiest with an Alt-click on the eye symbol of this layer, ill.83).

For more accurate working it´s sensible to organize first a few guides, which allow you to align yourself during perspective-transforming.

To set the color of the guides the way we want, select Guides, Grid, Slices & Count from the Preferences (Photoshop -or Edit menu, ill.84).
There set the color you like for the guides (ill.85).

84

85

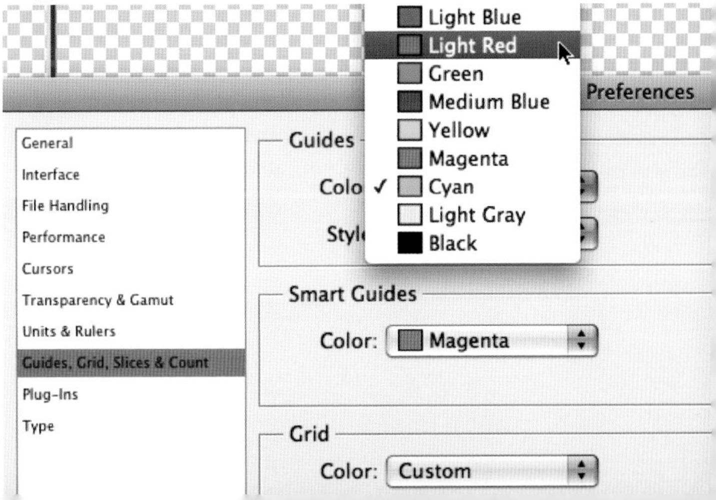

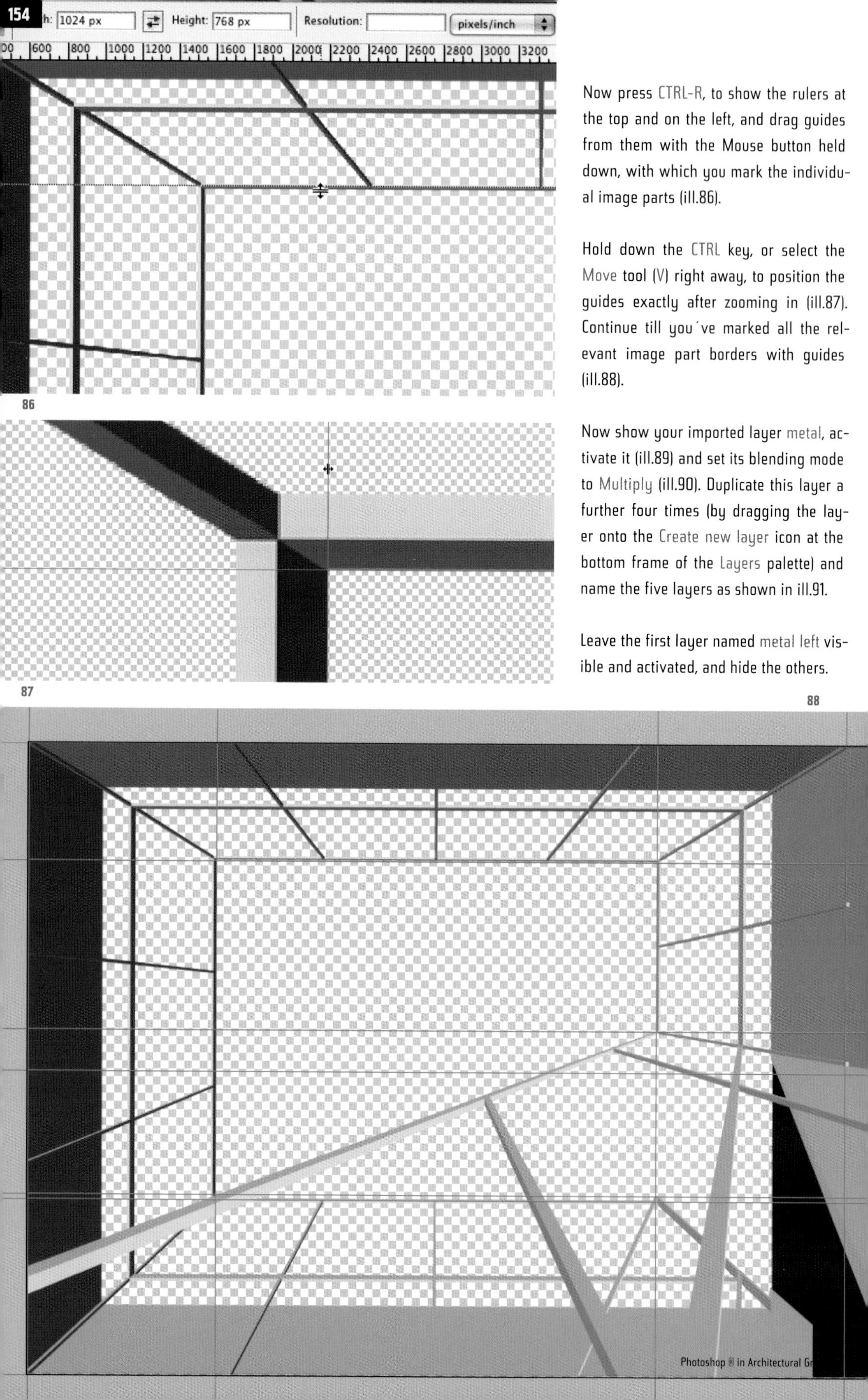

86

87

Now press CTRL-R, to show the rulers at the top and on the left, and drag guides from them with the Mouse button held down, with which you mark the individual image parts (ill.86).

Hold down the CTRL key, or select the Move tool (V) right away, to position the guides exactly after zooming in (ill.87). Continue till you´ve marked all the relevant image part borders with guides (ill.88).

Now show your imported layer metal, activate it (ill.89) and set its blending mode to Multiply (ill.90). Duplicate this layer a further four times (by dragging the layer onto the Create new layer icon at the bottom frame of the Layers palette) and name the five layers as shown in ill.91.

Leave the first layer named metal left visible and activated, and hide the others.

88

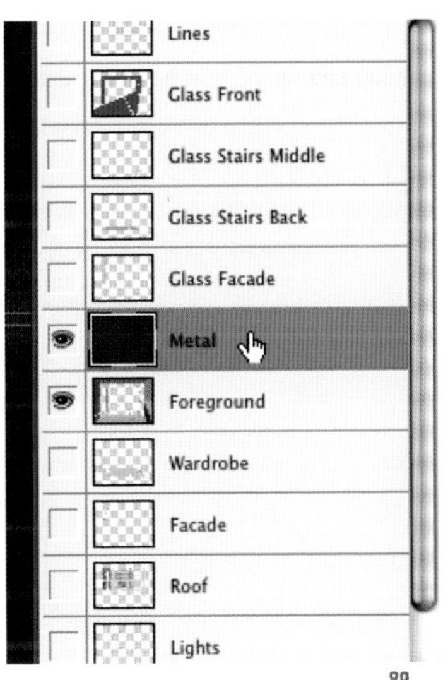

89

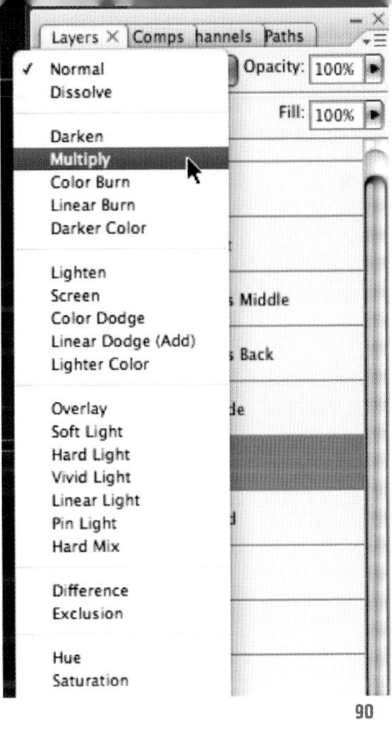

90

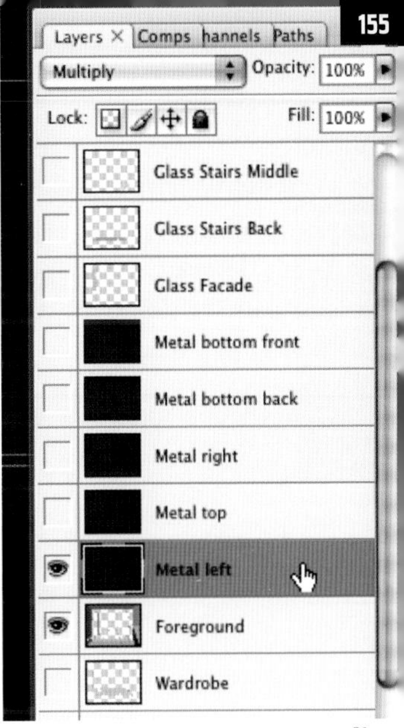

91

To crop the metal surface for the left image area, pick the Rectangular Marquee tool (M, ill.92).

Now select the right part of the layer metal left, i.e. the area you wish to remove (ill.93), and press Delete.

92

93

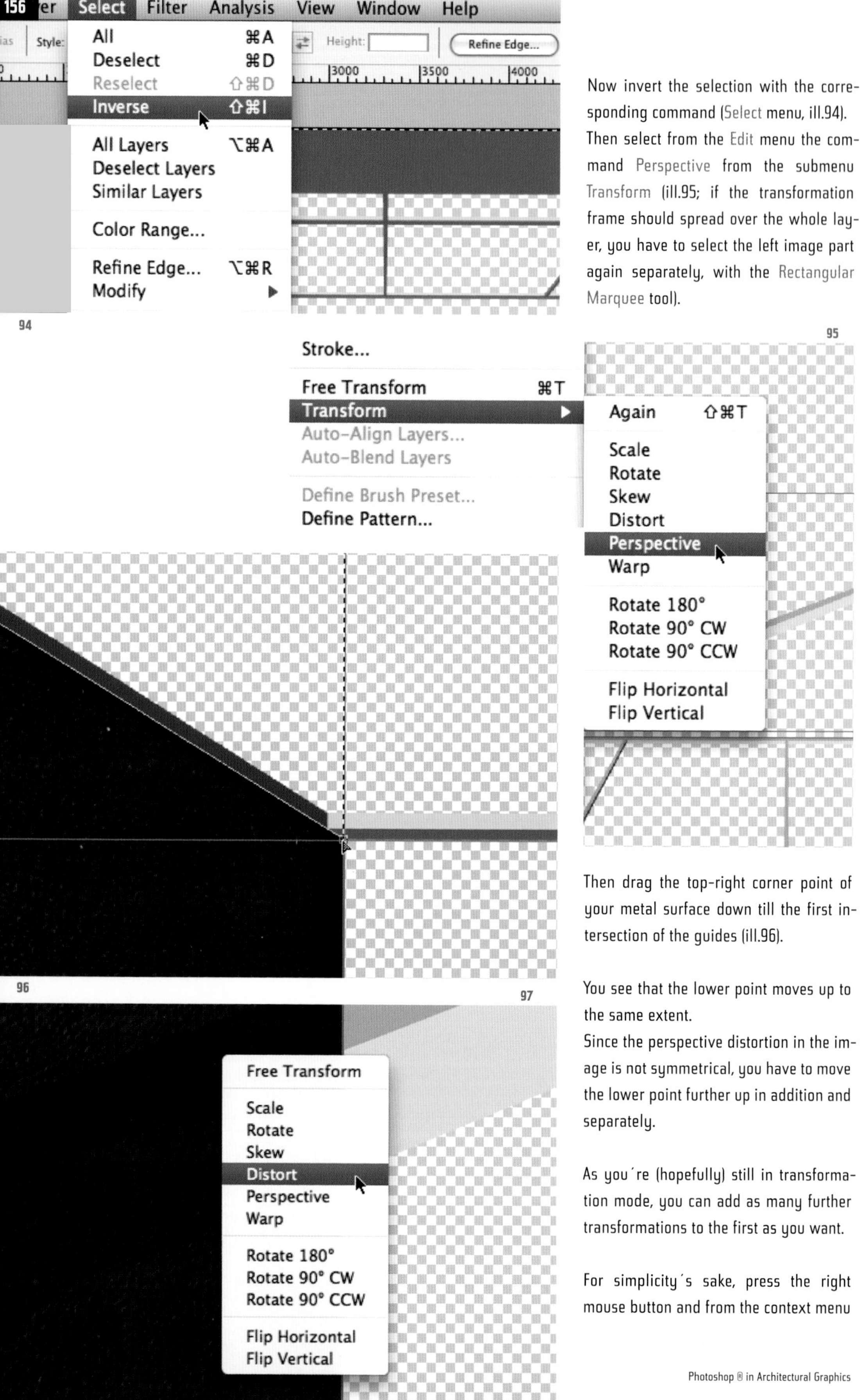

94

95

96

97

Now invert the selection with the corresponding command (Select menu, ill.94). Then select from the Edit menu the command Perspective from the submenu Transform (ill.95; if the transformation frame should spread over the whole layer, you have to select the left image part again separately, with the Rectangular Marquee tool).

Then drag the top-right corner point of your metal surface down till the first intersection of the guides (ill.96).

You see that the lower point moves up to the same extent.
Since the perspective distortion in the image is not symmetrical, you have to move the lower point further up in addition and separately.

As you´re (hopefully) still in transformation mode, you can add as many further transformations to the first as you want.

For simplicity´s sake, press the right mouse button and from the context menu

98

select the command Distort, which allows you to move individual points (ill.97).

Then move the lower point further up to the lower guides intersection (ill.98), and finish the transformation with Return.

Hide the metal left layer, and show the next one with the name metal up, checking that the latter is also activated (ill.99).

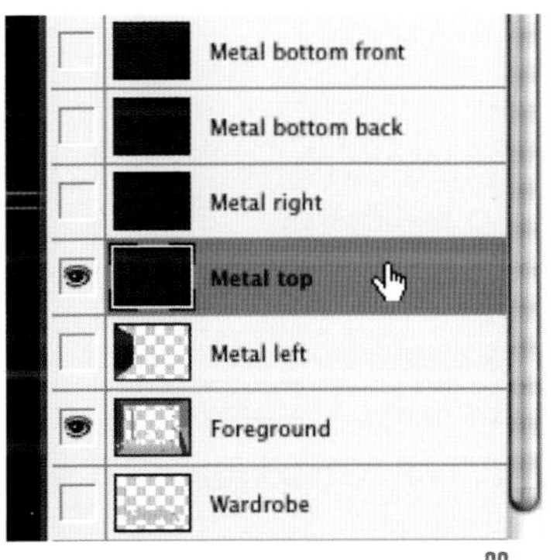

99

Do the same as in the metal left layer, i.e. first select the part you want to remove, delete it, and then invert the selection.

For a change, press CTRL-T once to prepare the transformation, move the right edge of the selection to the left, and then select the command Perspective from the context menu by right-clicking (ill.100).

Modify the perspective of the surface, and now the symmetry should be right (ill.101). Finish with Return.

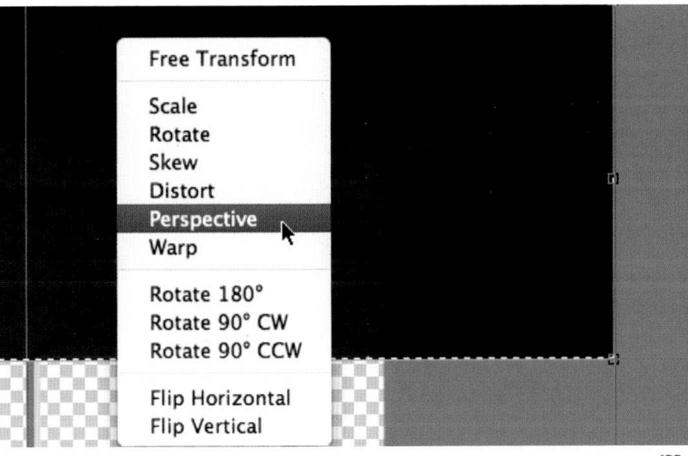

100

101

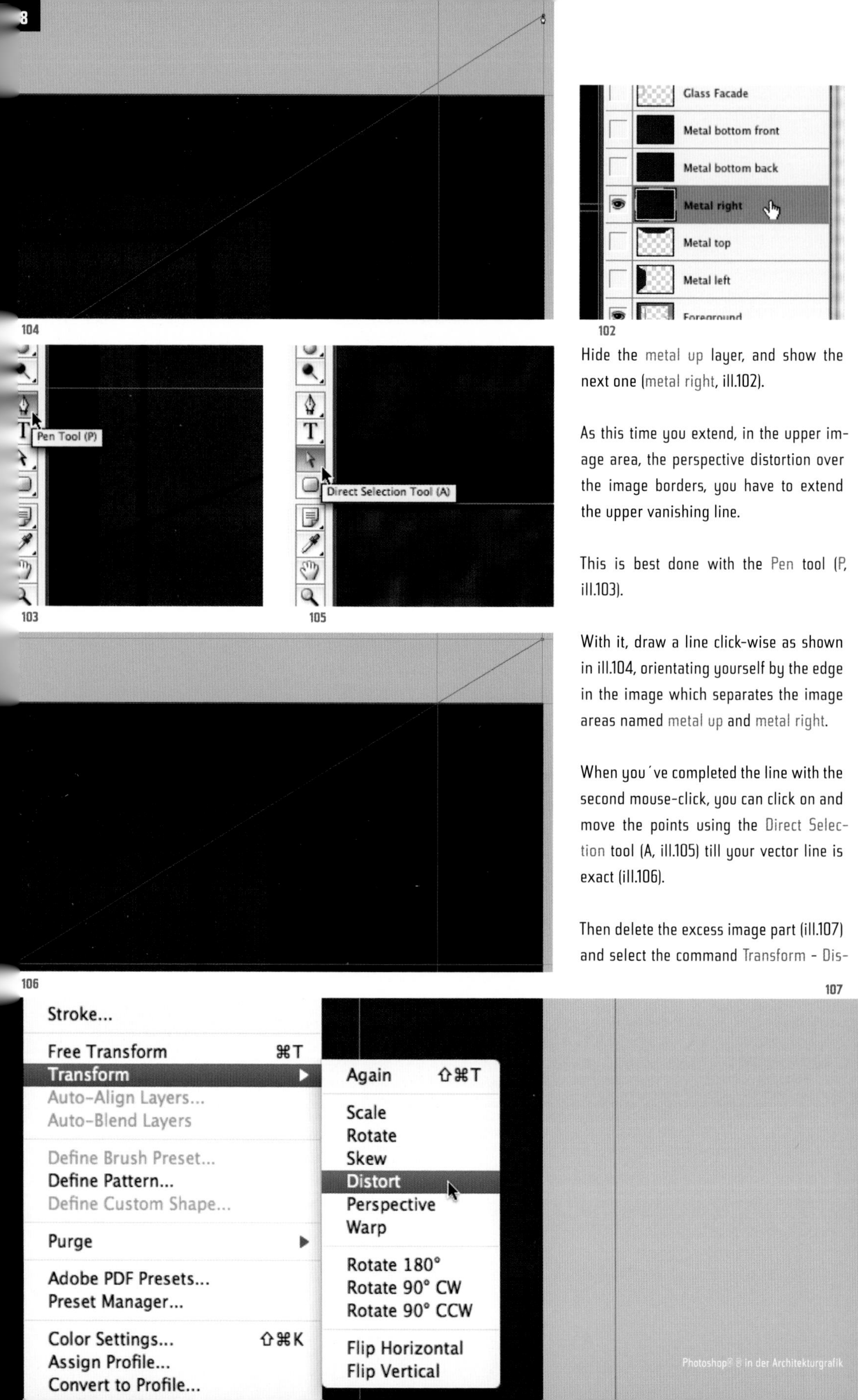

104

103

105

106

102

Hide the metal up layer, and show the next one (metal right, ill.102).

As this time you extend, in the upper image area, the perspective distortion over the image borders, you have to extend the upper vanishing line.

This is best done with the Pen tool (P, ill.103).

With it, draw a line click-wise as shown in ill.104, orientating yourself by the edge in the image which separates the image areas named metal up and metal right.

When you´ve completed the line with the second mouse-click, you can click on and move the points using the Direct Selection tool (A, ill.105) till your vector line is exact (ill.106).

Then delete the excess image part (ill.107) and select the command Transform - Dis-

107

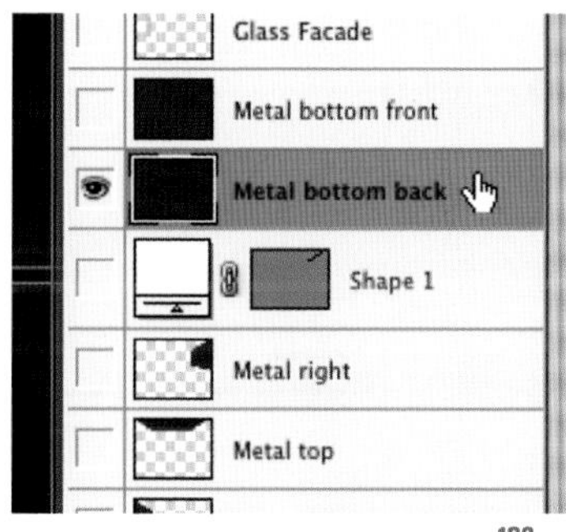

109

tort from the Edit menu. Should the transformation frame spread again over the whole layer, select again the image part to be transformed by hand with the Rectangular Marquee tool.

Then move the points as shown in ill.108, and confirm with Return.

Hide the metal right layer, and show the layer metal down back, making sure it´s also activated (ill.109).

Now proceed as in the layer before, but during this ensure that on the right side at first more remains than you need later (Ills.110 and 111).

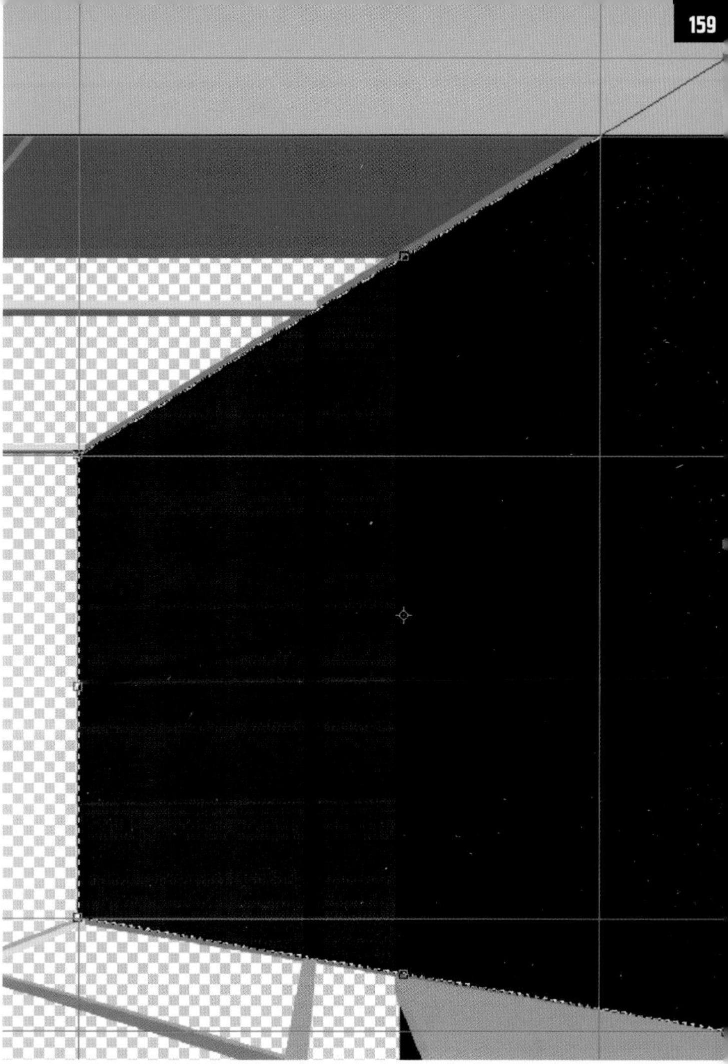

108

110

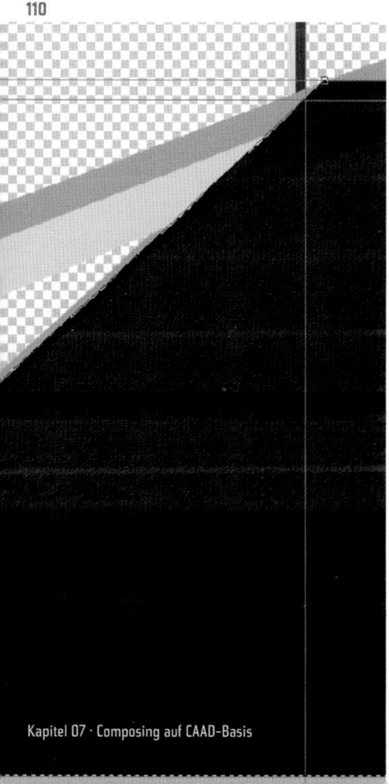

111

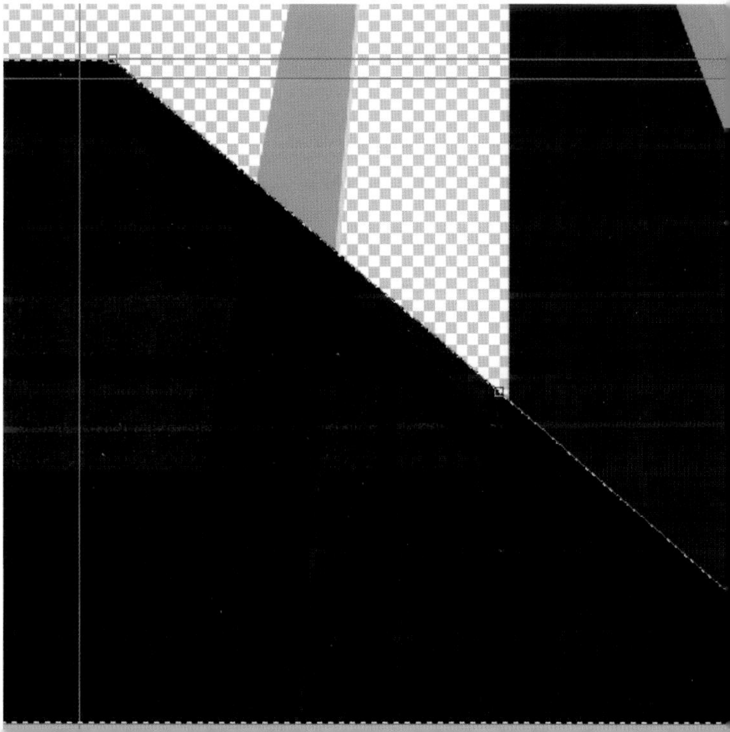

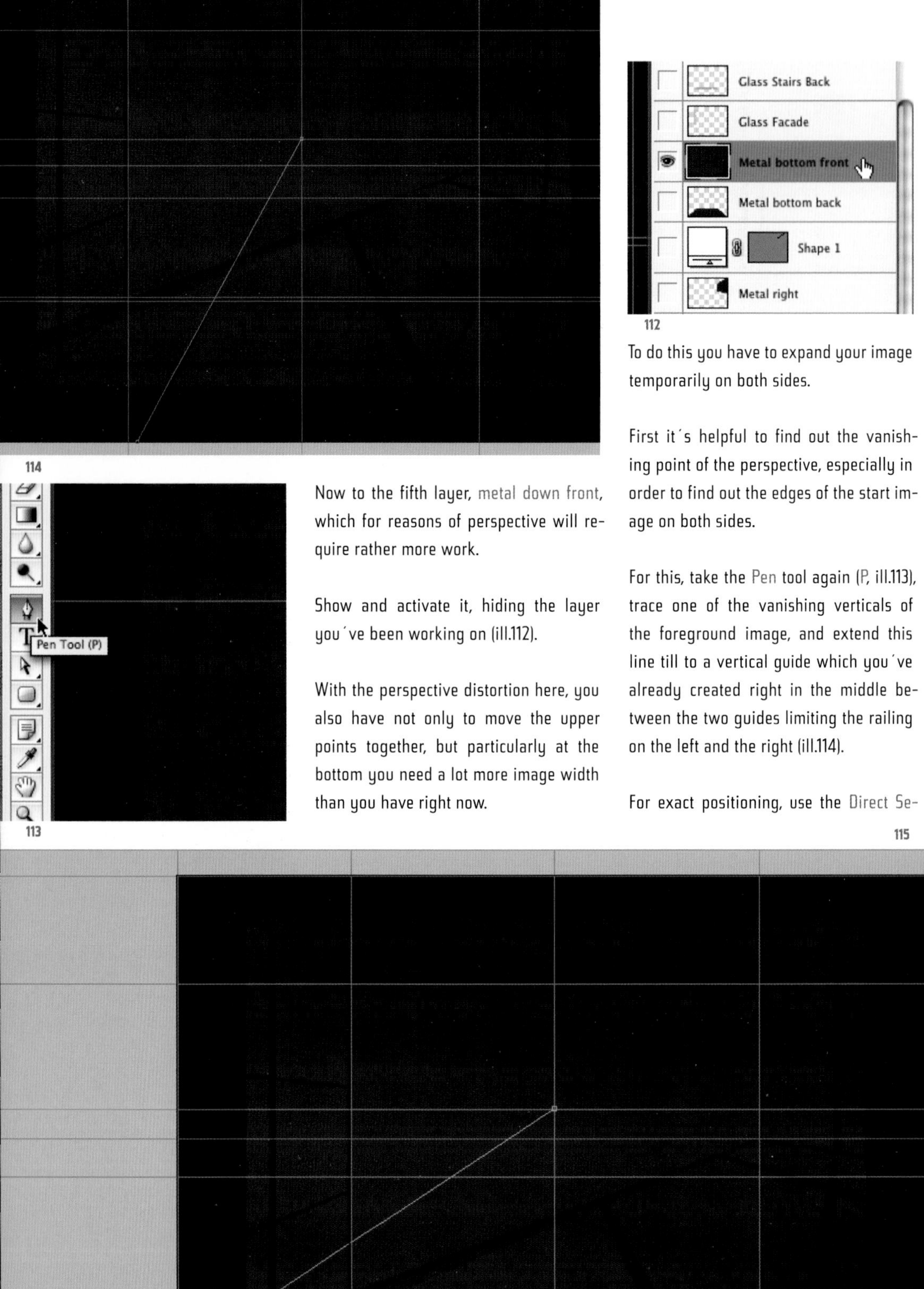

114

112

113

115

Now to the fifth layer, metal down front, which for reasons of perspective will require rather more work.

Show and activate it, hiding the layer you´ve been working on (ill.112).

With the perspective distortion here, you also have not only to move the upper points together, but particularly at the bottom you need a lot more image width than you have right now.

To do this you have to expand your image temporarily on both sides.

First it´s helpful to find out the vanishing point of the perspective, especially in order to find out the edges of the start image on both sides.

For this, take the Pen tool again (P, ill.113), trace one of the vanishing verticals of the foreground image, and extend this line till to a vertical guide which you´ve already created right in the middle between the two guides limiting the railing on the left and the right (ill.114).

For exact positioning, use the Direct Se-

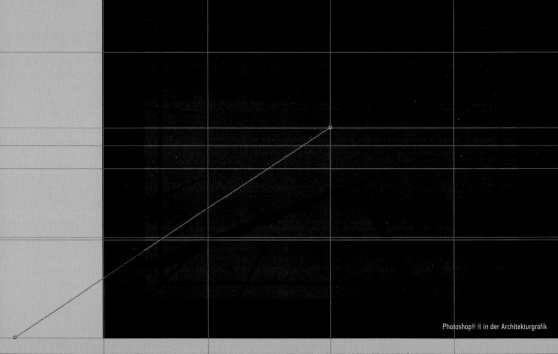

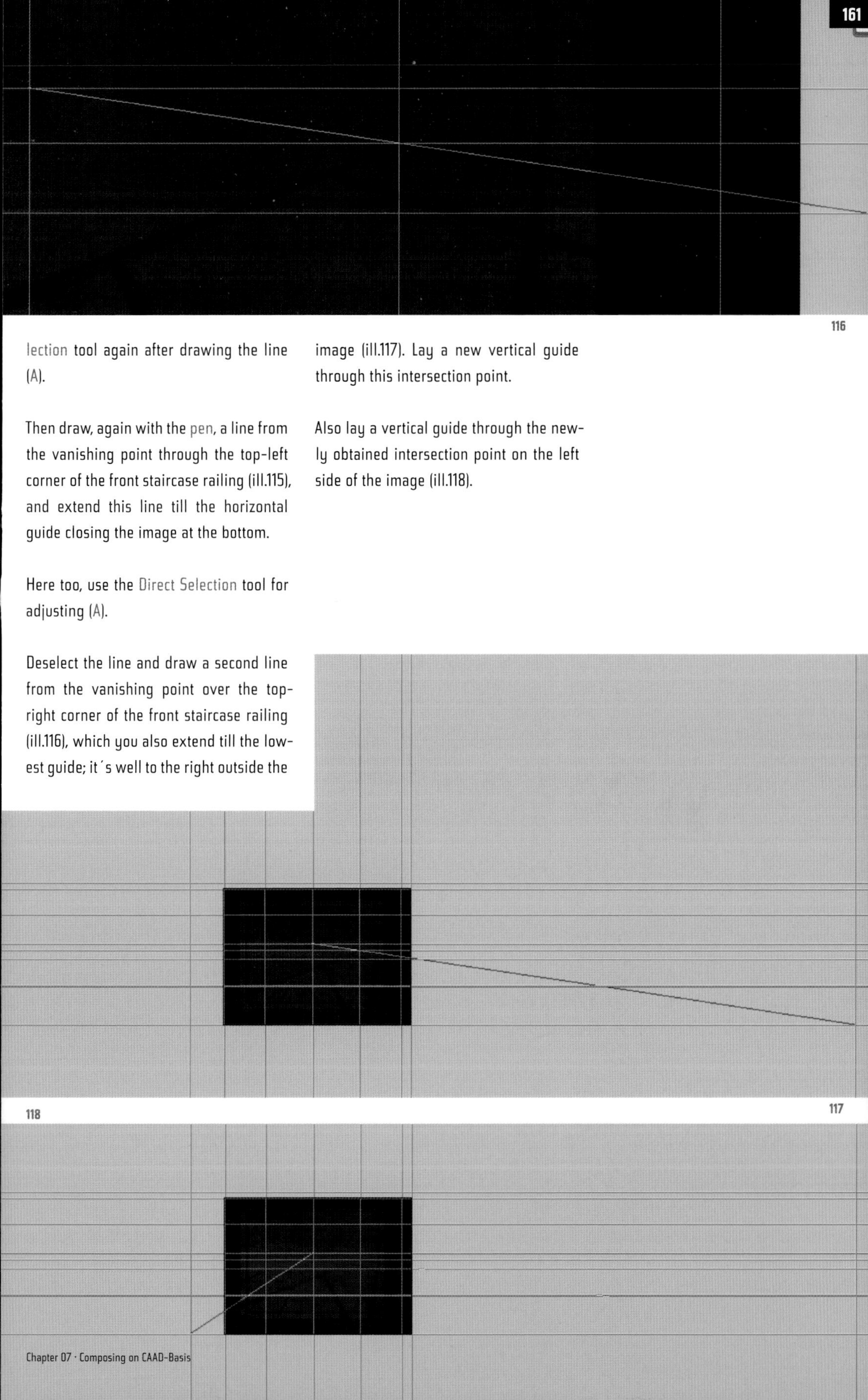

116

lection tool again after drawing the line (A).

Then draw, again with the pen, a line from the vanishing point through the top-left corner of the front staircase railing (ill.115), and extend this line till the horizontal guide closing the image at the bottom.

Here too, use the Direct Selection tool for adjusting (A).

Deselect the line and draw a second line from the vanishing point over the top-right corner of the front staircase railing (ill.116), which you also extend till the lowest guide; it´s well to the right outside the image (ill.117). Lay a new vertical guide through this intersection point.

Also lay a vertical guide through the newly obtained intersection point on the left side of the image (ill.118).

118

117

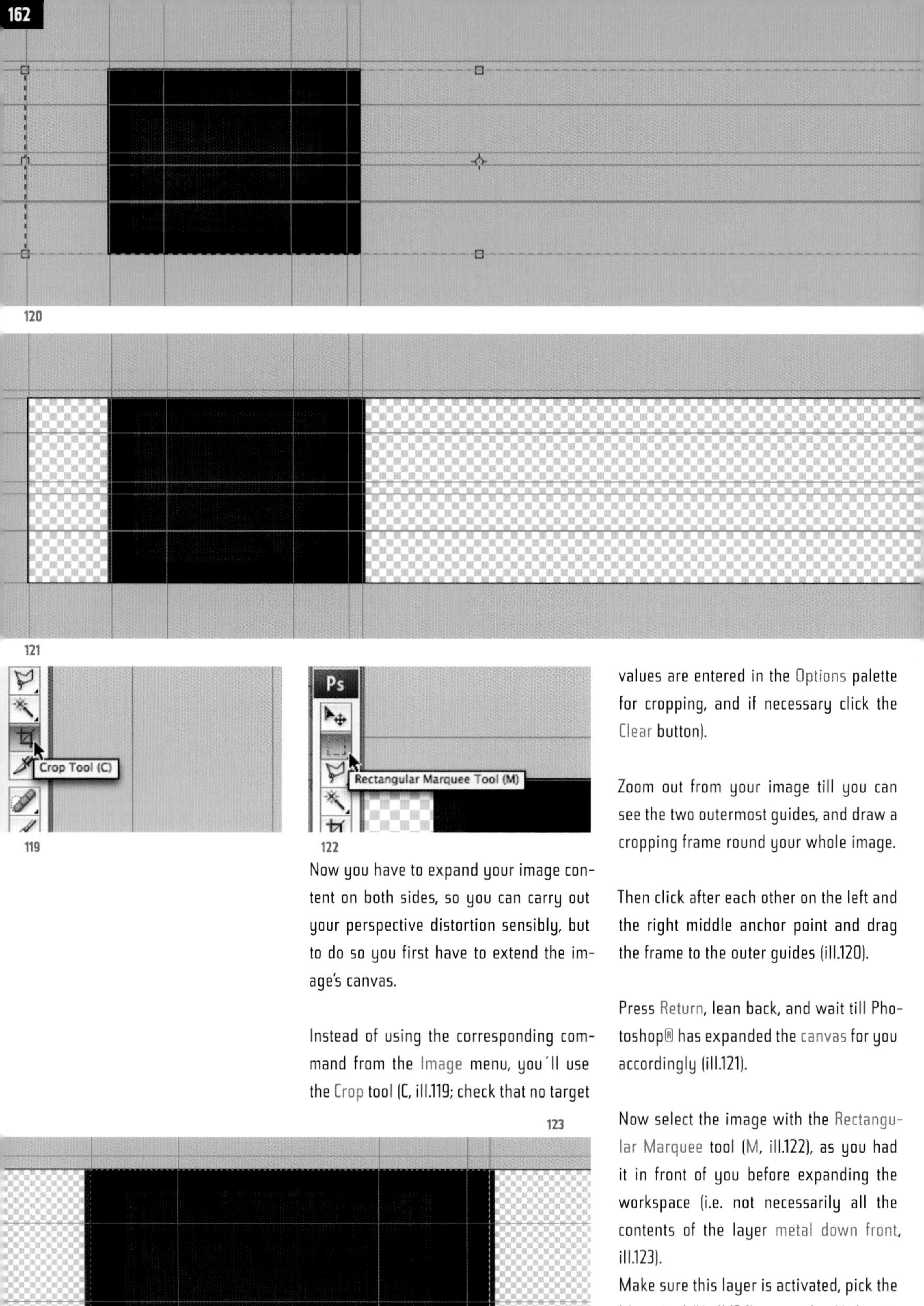

120

121

119

122

123

Now you have to expand your image content on both sides, so you can carry out your perspective distortion sensibly, but to do so you first have to extend the image's canvas.

Instead of using the corresponding command from the Image menu, you´ll use the Crop tool (C, ill.119; check that no target values are entered in the Options palette for cropping, and if necessary click the Clear button).

Zoom out from your image till you can see the two outermost guides, and draw a cropping frame round your whole image.

Then click after each other on the left and the right middle anchor point and drag the frame to the outer guides (ill.120).

Press Return, lean back, and wait till Photoshop® has expanded the canvas for you accordingly (ill.121).

Now select the image with the Rectangular Marquee tool (M, ill.122), as you had it in front of you before expanding the workspace (i.e. not necessarily all the contents of the layer metal down front, ill.123).
Make sure this layer is activated, pick the Move tool (V, ill.124), press the Alt key to produce a copy when moving, and drag the metal selection towards the left with

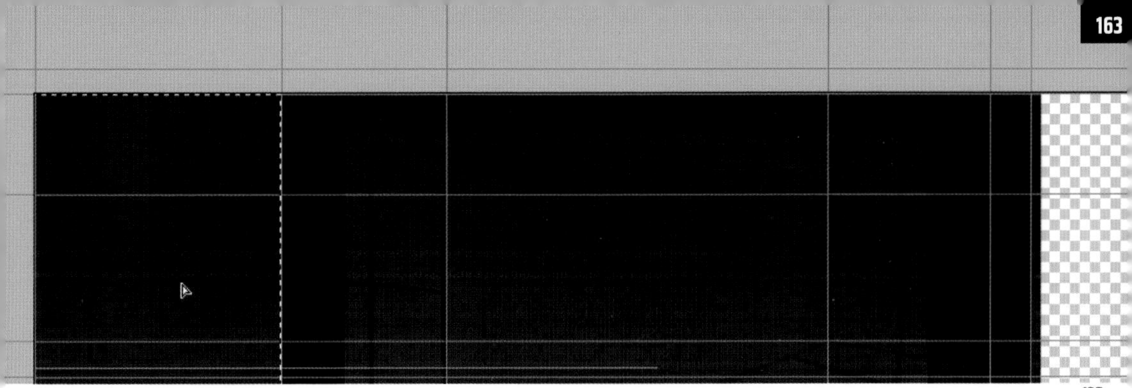

125

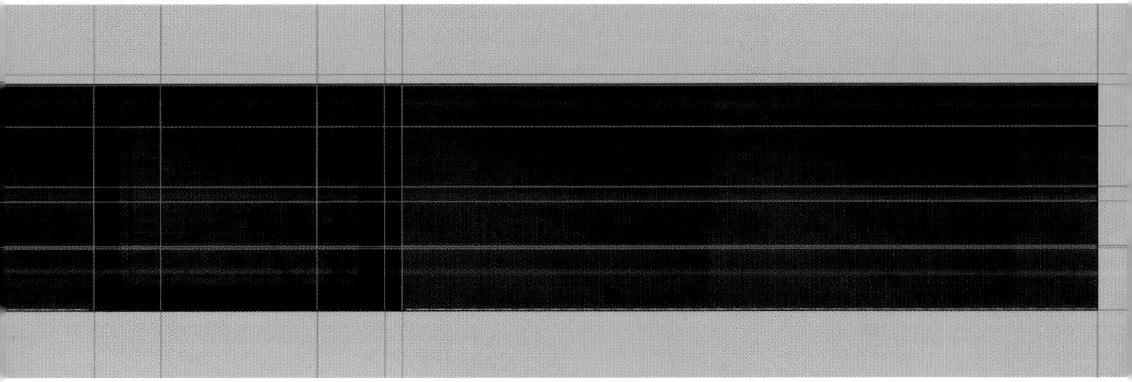

126

the mouse button held down, till with its right edge it connects at the left edge of your image (ill.125).
As long as the selection is still visible, do the same thing another three times on the right side till the canvas is filled completely (ill.126).

Should your selection ants disappear during this due to a wrong click, just chosse Reselect from the Select menu (ill.127).

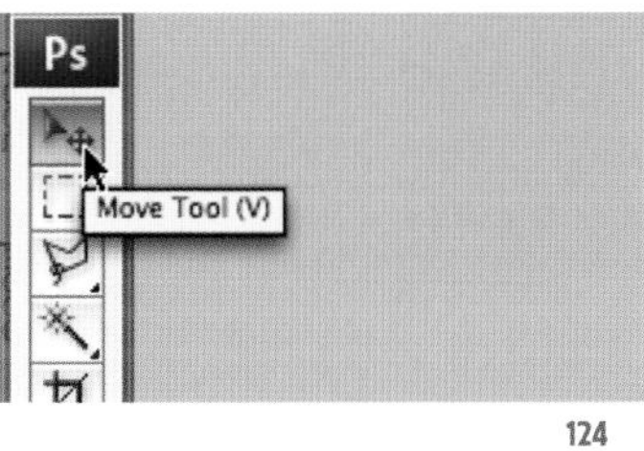

124

Now remove the image part above the horizon (the line your vanishing point is on), using the Rectangular Marquee tool (ill.128).

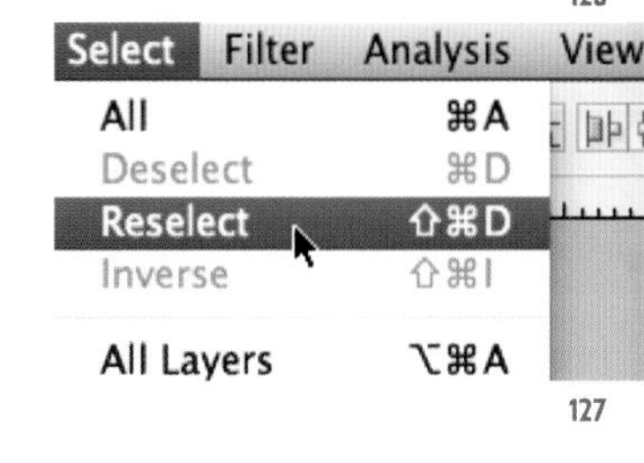

127

128

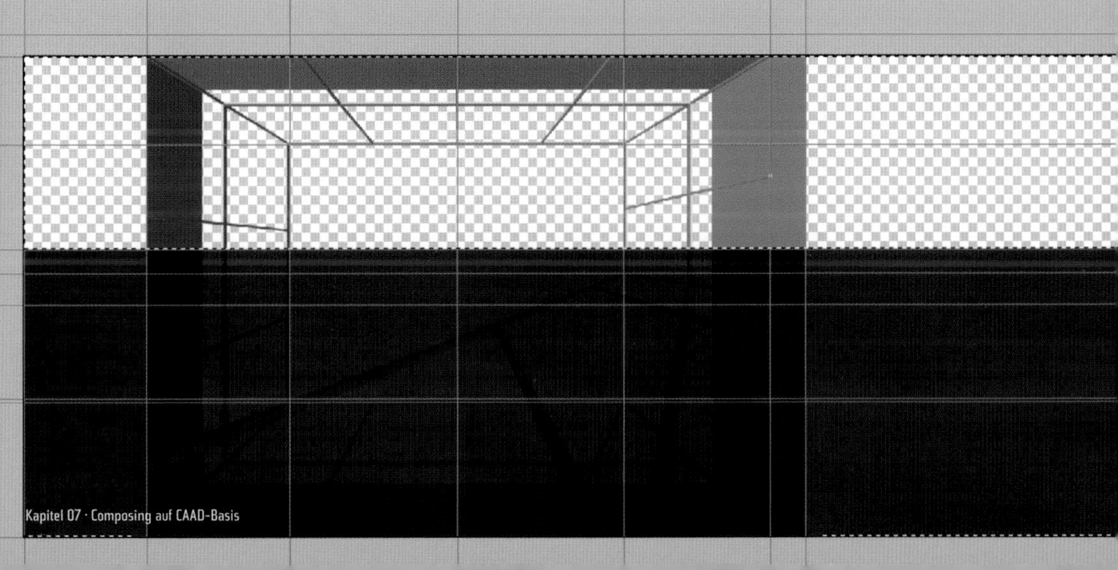

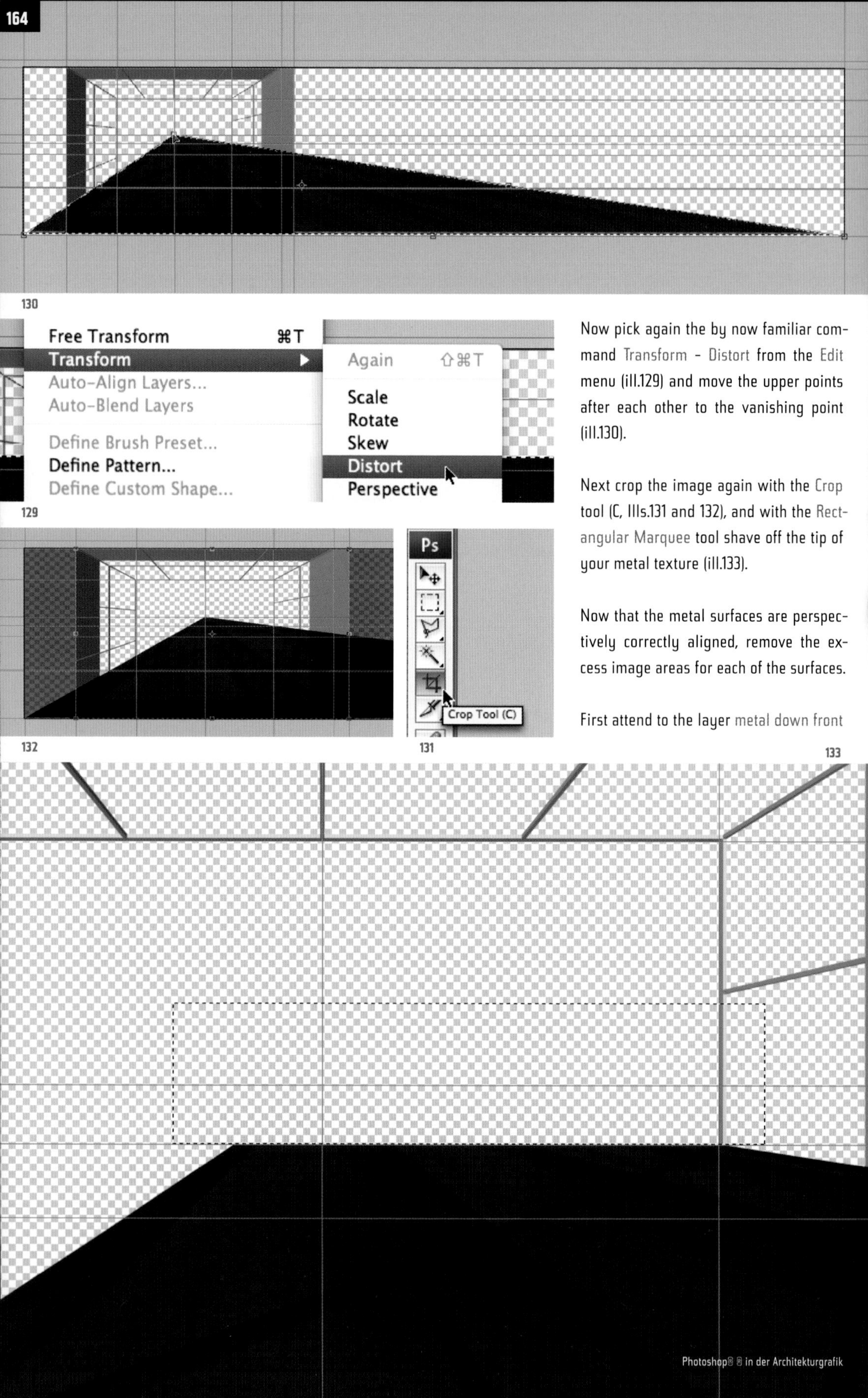

130

129

132

131

133

Now pick again the by now familiar command Transform - Distort from the Edit menu (ill.129) and move the upper points after each other to the vanishing point (ill.130).

Next crop the image again with the Crop tool (C, Ills.131 and 132), and with the Rectangular Marquee tool shave off the tip of your metal texture (ill.133).

Now that the metal surfaces are perspectively correctly aligned, remove the excess image areas for each of the surfaces.

First attend to the layer metal down front

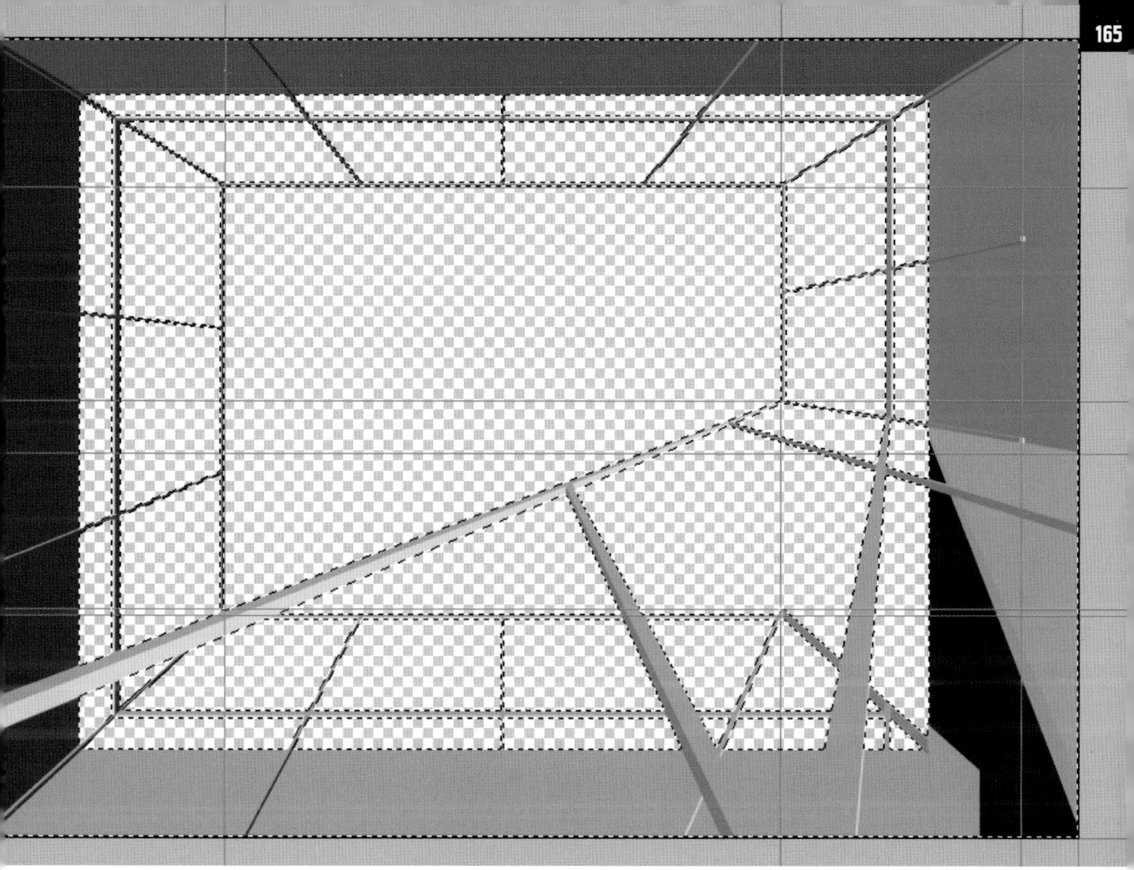

135

you´ve just worked-on, hiding it and activating the layer Foreground (ill.134).

Click on your layer miniature with the CTRL key held down, and as you see, everything visible on this layer is now selected (ill.135).

Next, see that you remove everything in the selection that doesn´t belong to this front railing, first with the polygonal lasso (L, or Shift-L, ill.136).

If you wish to subtract something from an active selection, no matter with which tool, hold down the Alt key for the first click; in our case you see that the polygonal lasso cursor is garnished with a small minus symbol.
Now draw a selection with this, containing everything above the railing. With the last click, which closes the selection, you get a reduced selection area as a result (ill.137).

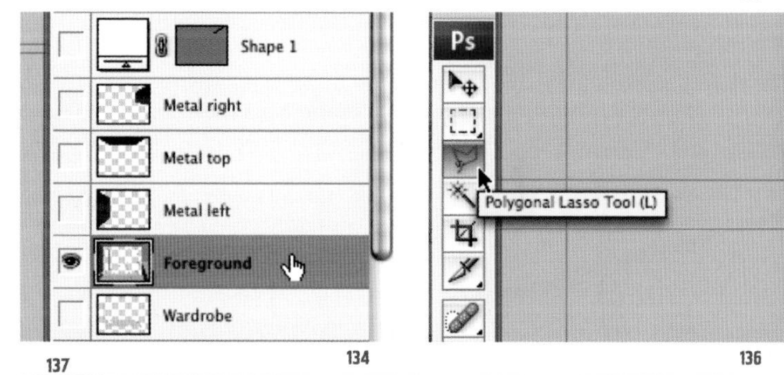

137

134

136

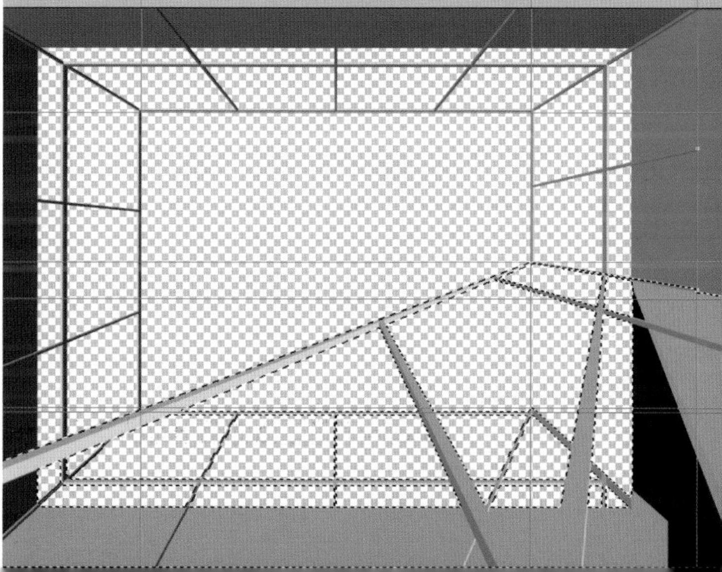

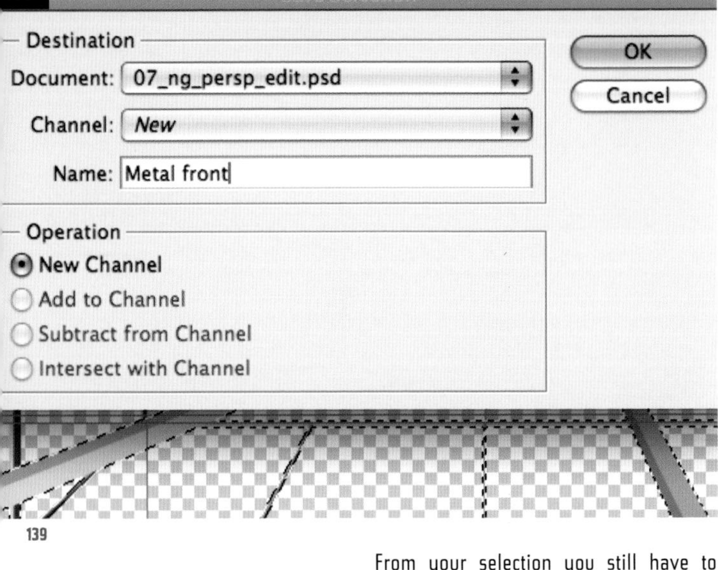

139

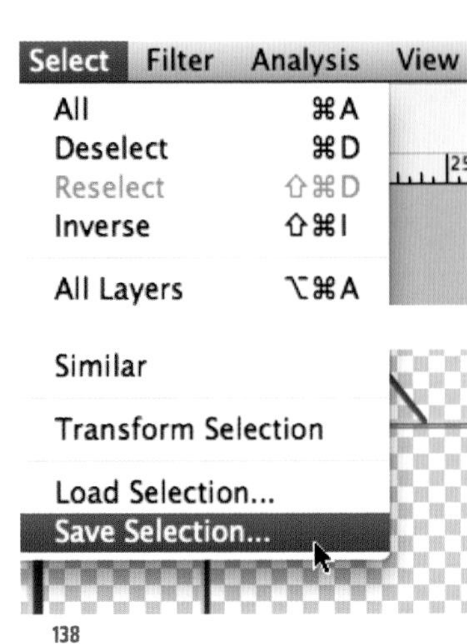

138

From your selection you still have to cut out four parts, three of which can be done as before with the polygonal lasso (for orientation see ill.150; don´t forget to press the Alt key in each case before your first click, otherwise all your selections go down the drain.

In this case you can rescue yourself by means of the History palette).

The second-largest opening in the railing (see ill. 147) can not be selected well with the lasso, as you can´t see the difference in the lower area of the individual surfaces due to the same Gray tone. Here you´ll help yourself with an adjustable path selection.

First, however, save your selection so that you can undisturbedly work with the Pen tool. For this, select the corresponding command from the Select menu (ill.138), and give the new Channel (into which your selection will mutate) the name metal front (ill.139).
Confirm with OK, and in the Channels palette you can now admire your selection as Black-and-White graphics (ill.140). Be aware that you must activate the color channels again to continue working (ill.141), and then switch back to the Layers palette.
Now pick the Pen tool (P, ill.142), and with

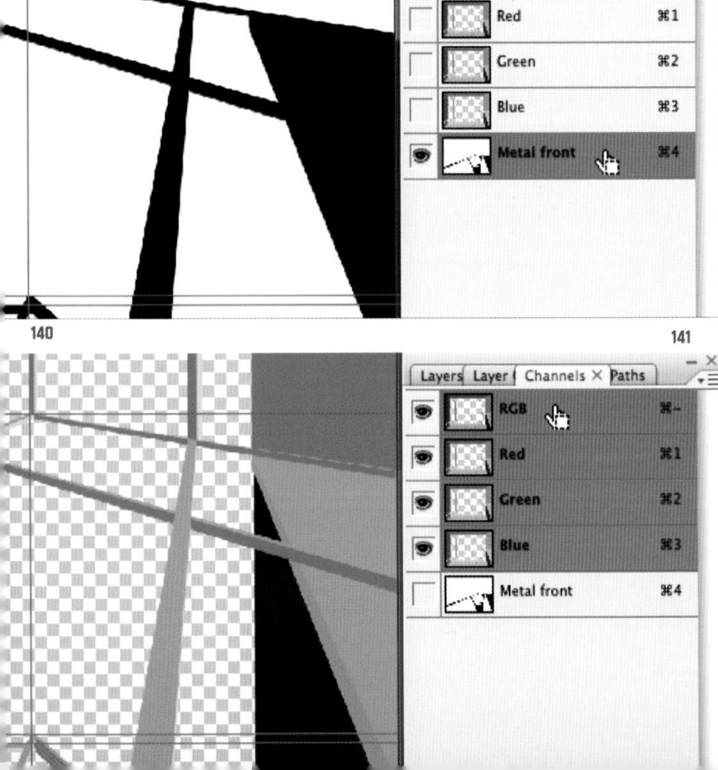

140

141

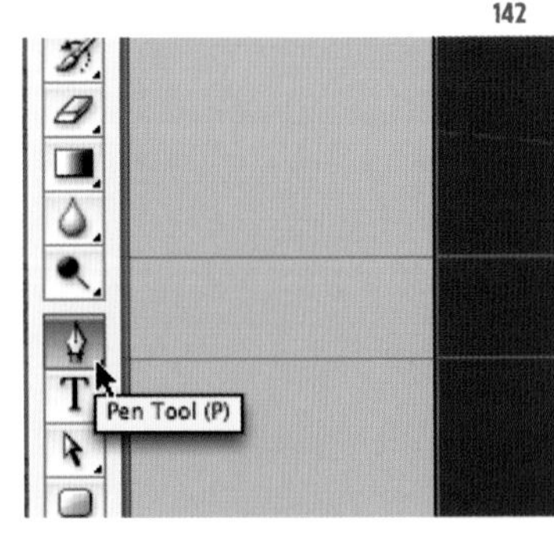

142

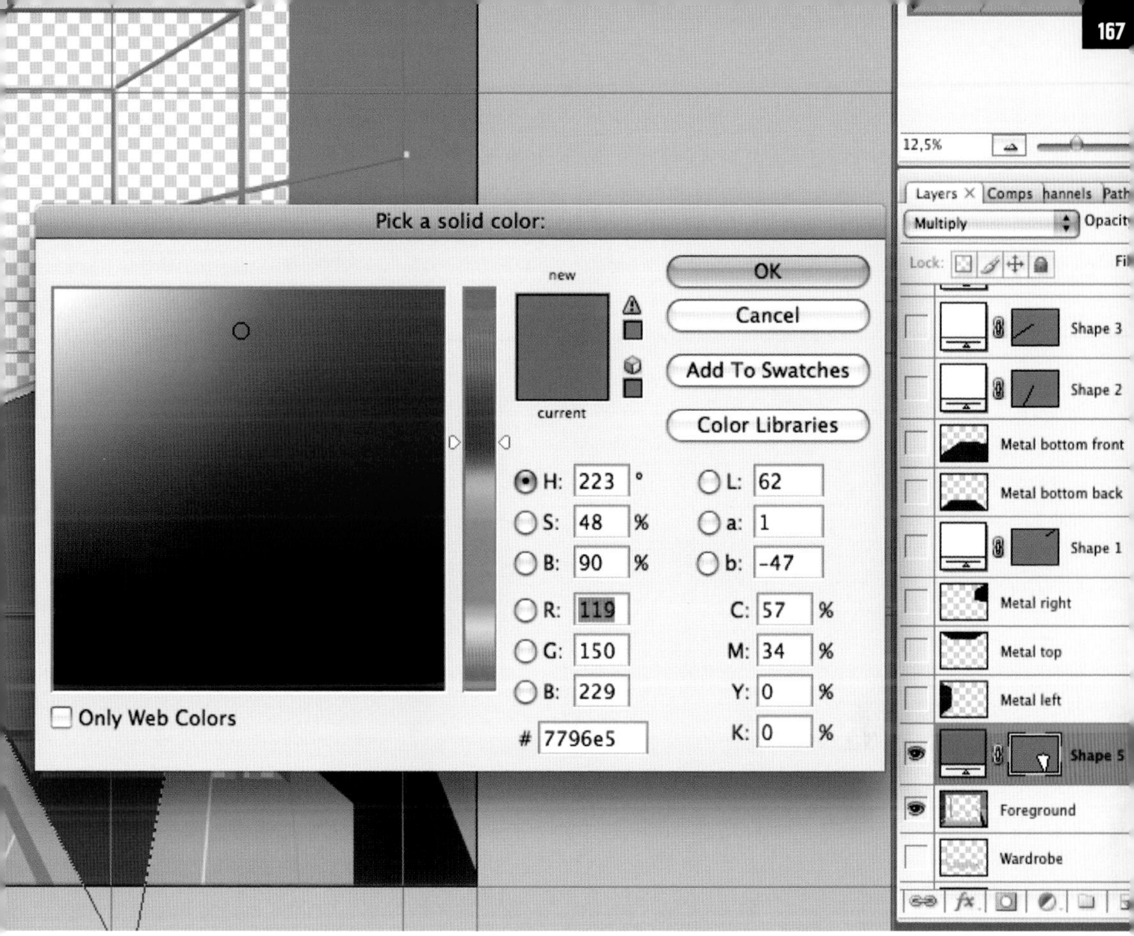

143

it trace the critical opening. You don´t need to work too accurately, because you can adjust the form point-wise afterwards.

Double-click on the miniature of the Shape layer created, and select a bright color (ill.143). Moreover, this layer's blending mode should be switched to Multiply.

With the Direct Selection tool align the corner points (A, ill.144) so that the shape exactly fills the opening (ill.145).

Now click in the mask miniature of the Shape layer with the CTRL key held down (ill.146), and you see a quite familiar ants selection appear over your vector plane (ill.147).

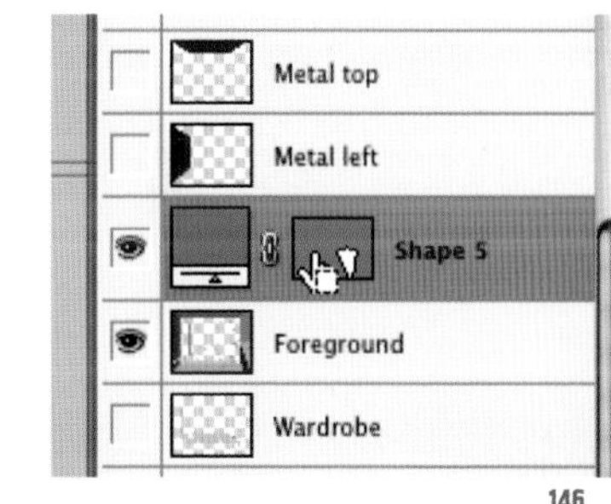

146

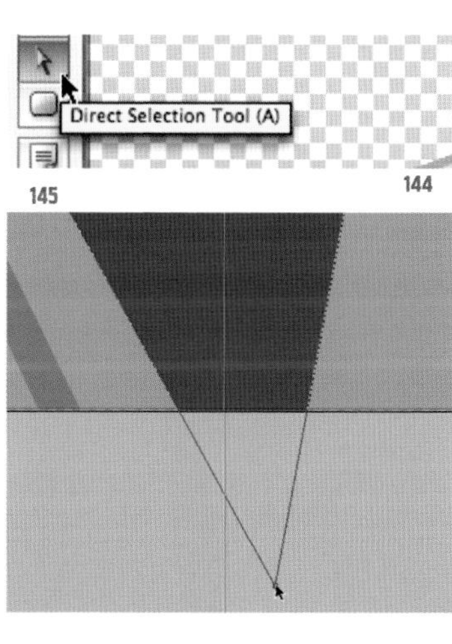

144

145

147

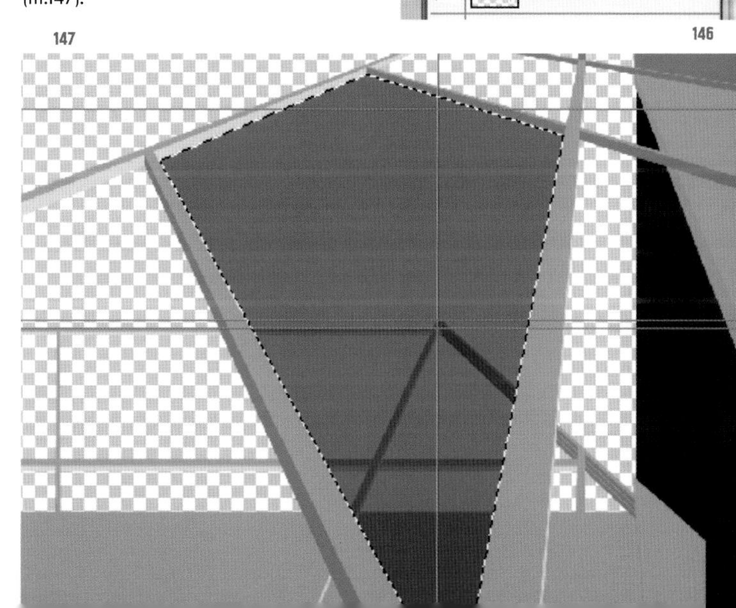

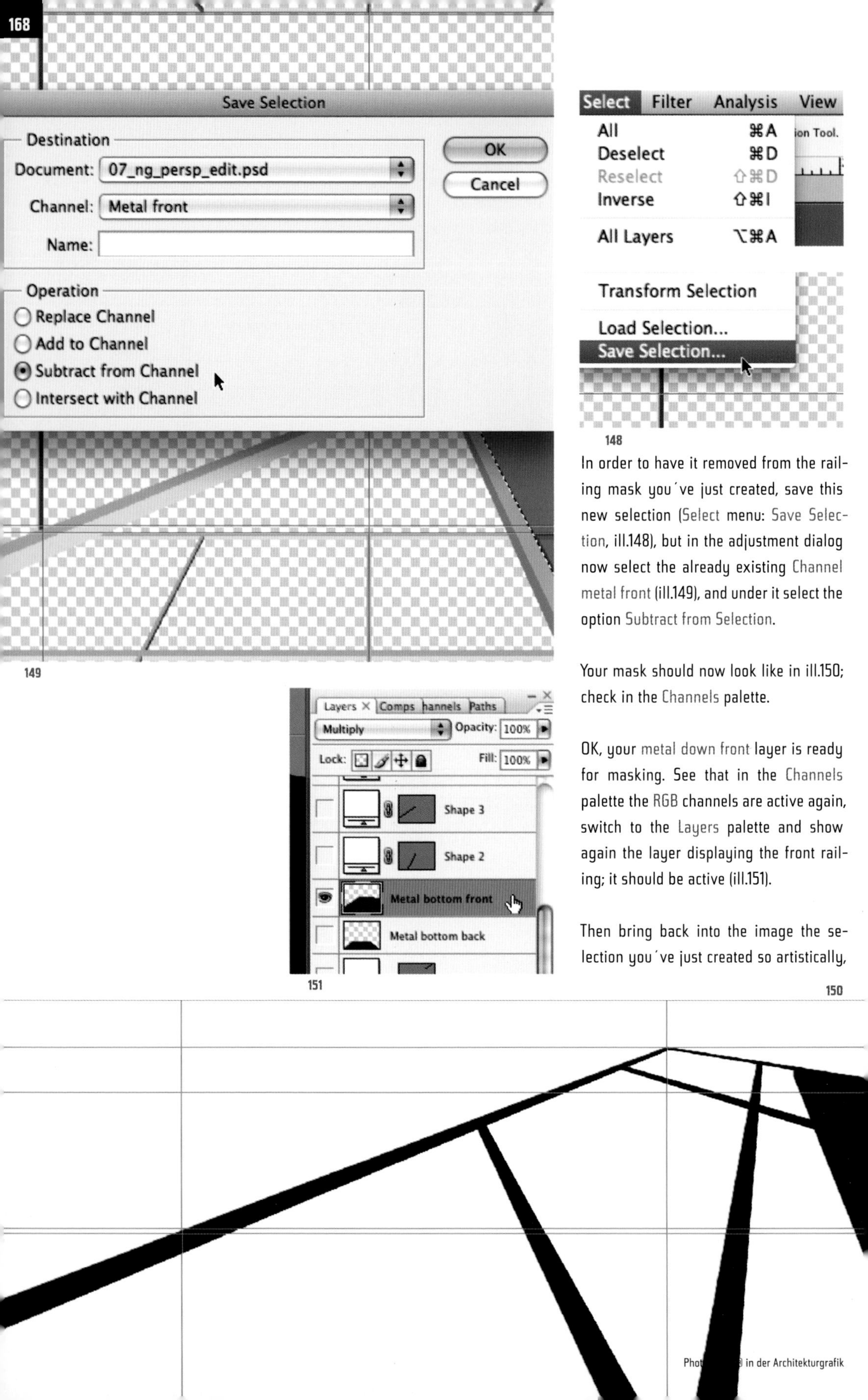

149

151

148

In order to have it removed from the railing mask you´ve just created, save this new selection (Select menu: Save Selection, ill.148), but in the adjustment dialog now select the already existing Channel metal front (ill.149), and under it select the option Subtract from Selection.

Your mask should now look like in ill.150; check in the Channels palette.

OK, your metal down front layer is ready for masking. See that in the Channels palette the RGB channels are active again, switch to the Layers palette and show again the layer displaying the front railing; it should be active (ill.151).

Then bring back into the image the selection you´ve just created so artistically,

150

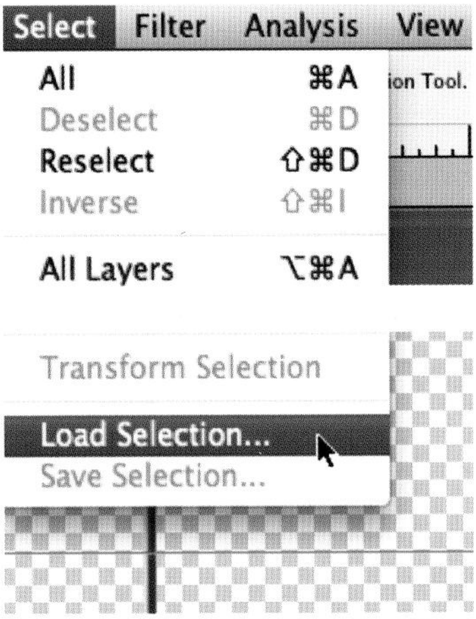

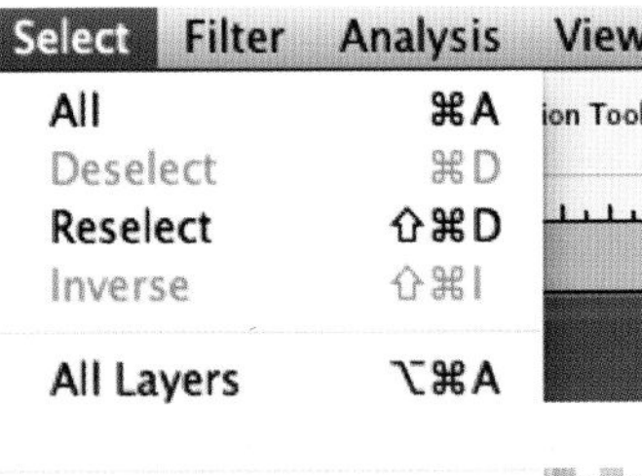

152

153

with the command Load Selection from the Select menu (ill.152).

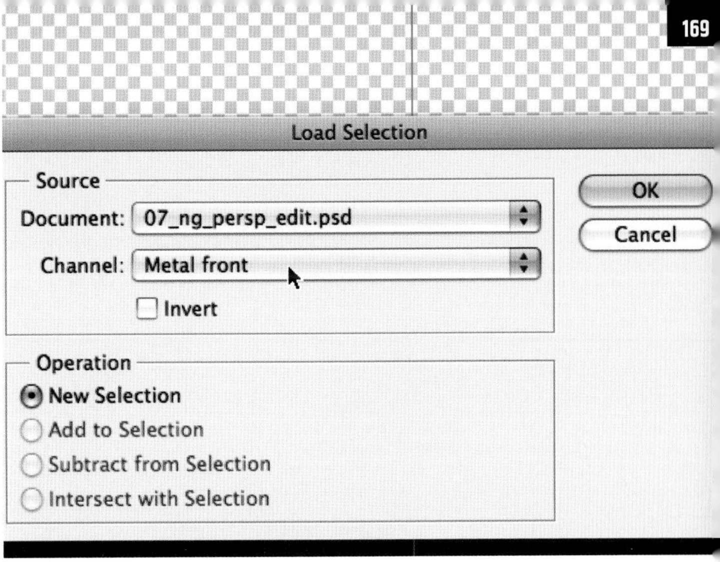

In the adjustment dialog select the channel metal front (ill.153), and click OK. Your selection appears in the form of the familiar ants.

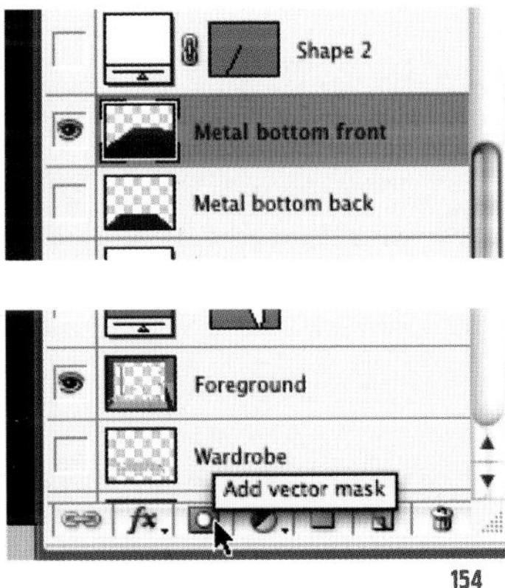

154

155

Now click on the Add layer mask icon at the bottom frame of the Layers palette (ill.154), and lo and behold!, your layer is masked (ill.155).
Please hide it so you can deal with the other layers.

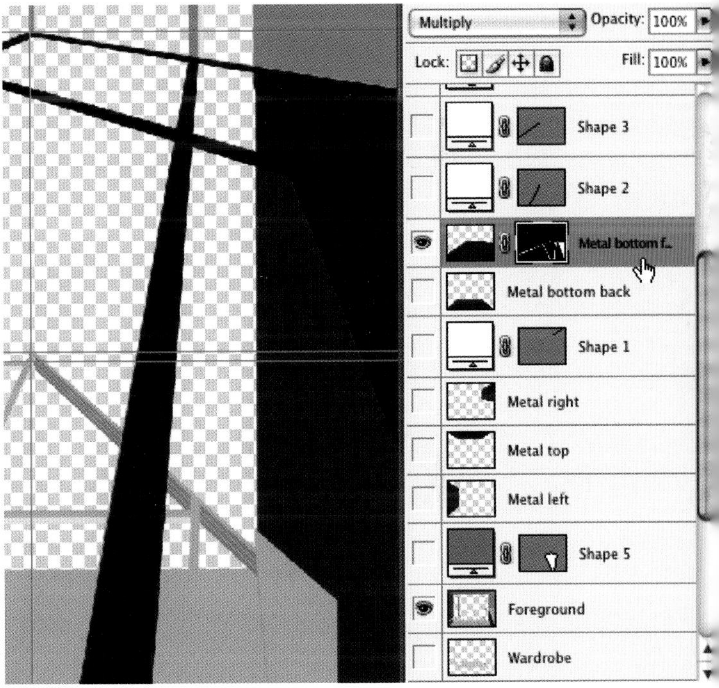

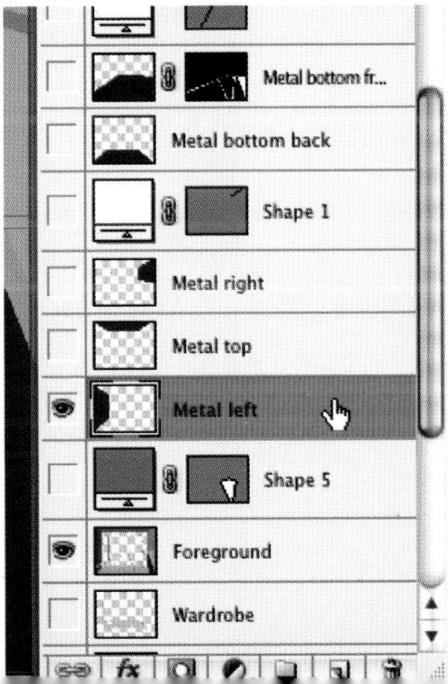

Now show the metal left layer, and click in your layer miniature with the CTRL key held down, to select its contents (ill.156).

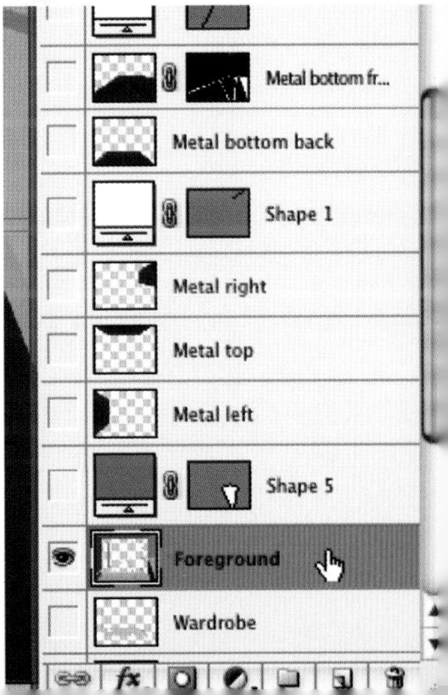

156

157

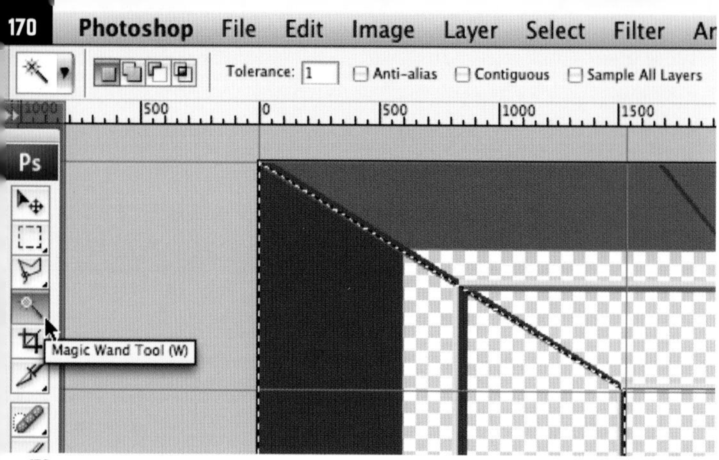

158

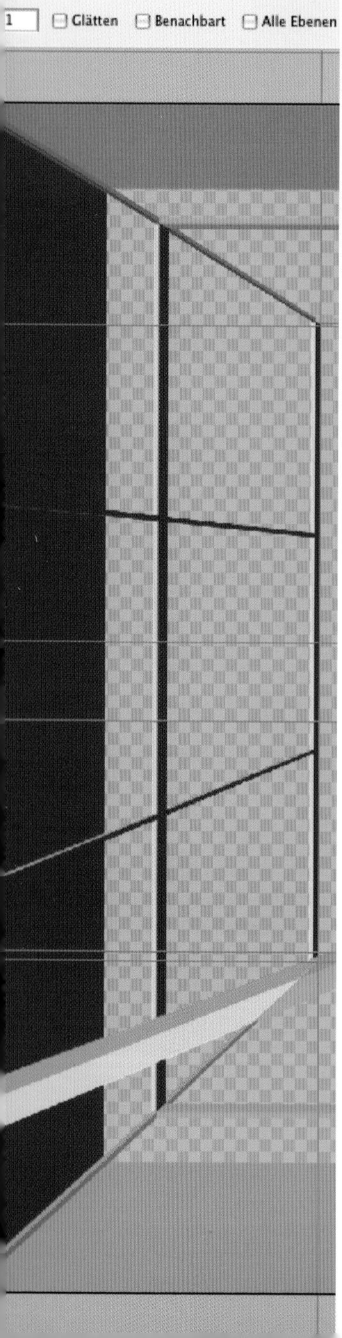

159

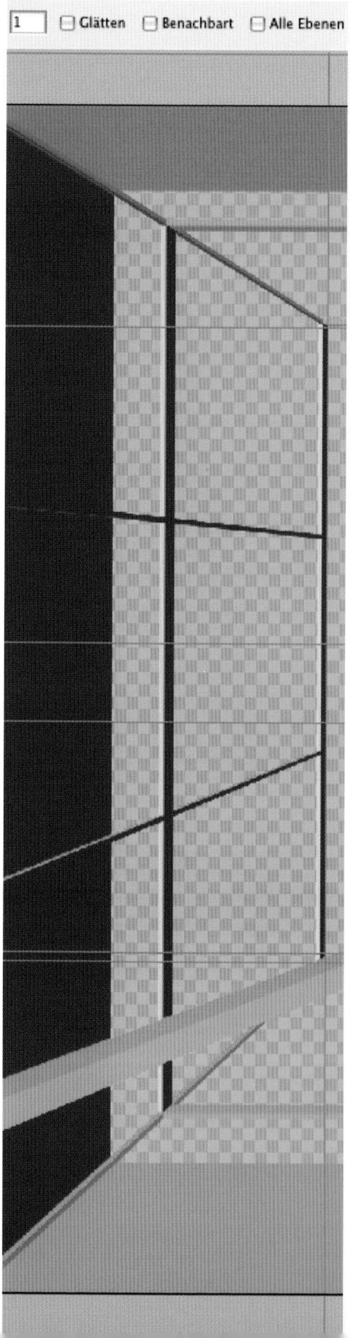

161

To remove from the selection the image parts between the railing profiles, which you can of course only see and select on the Foreground layer, activate that layer (ill.157), and then pick the Magic Wand tool (W, or Shift-W, ill.158).
Check that in the Options palette Tolerance is set to 1 and the Contiguous option is deactivated.

Then click with the Alt key held down in the empty (= transparent) areas between the railing profiles (which only makes sense if the Foreground layer is active).

When you think you´ve finished, press Q to see your selection in mask mode (ill.159).

As you see, the profile of the railing in the foreground of the the selection area still has to be removed.

To do this, use the polygonal lasso (ill.160; don´t forget to press the Alt key before the first click!), and after that check again in mask mode (Q) that everything is right (ill.161).

Switch back to standard mode (Q), so that you see your ants again, and assign the layer metal left a mask too (see above).

With the metal up layer you can proceed likewise, but it´s somewhat easier here, and you only have to subtract a few surfaces with the magic wand.

160

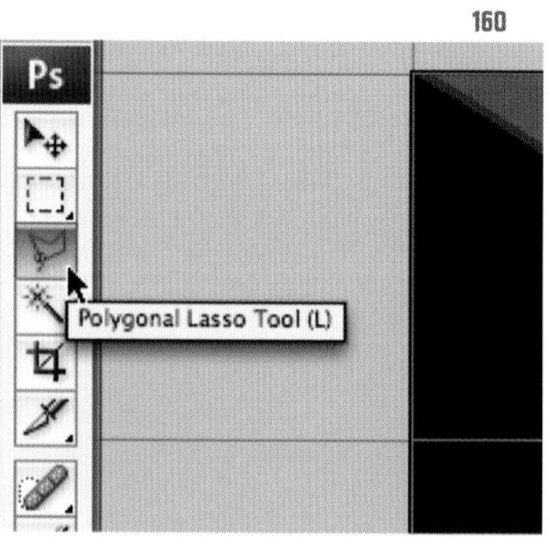

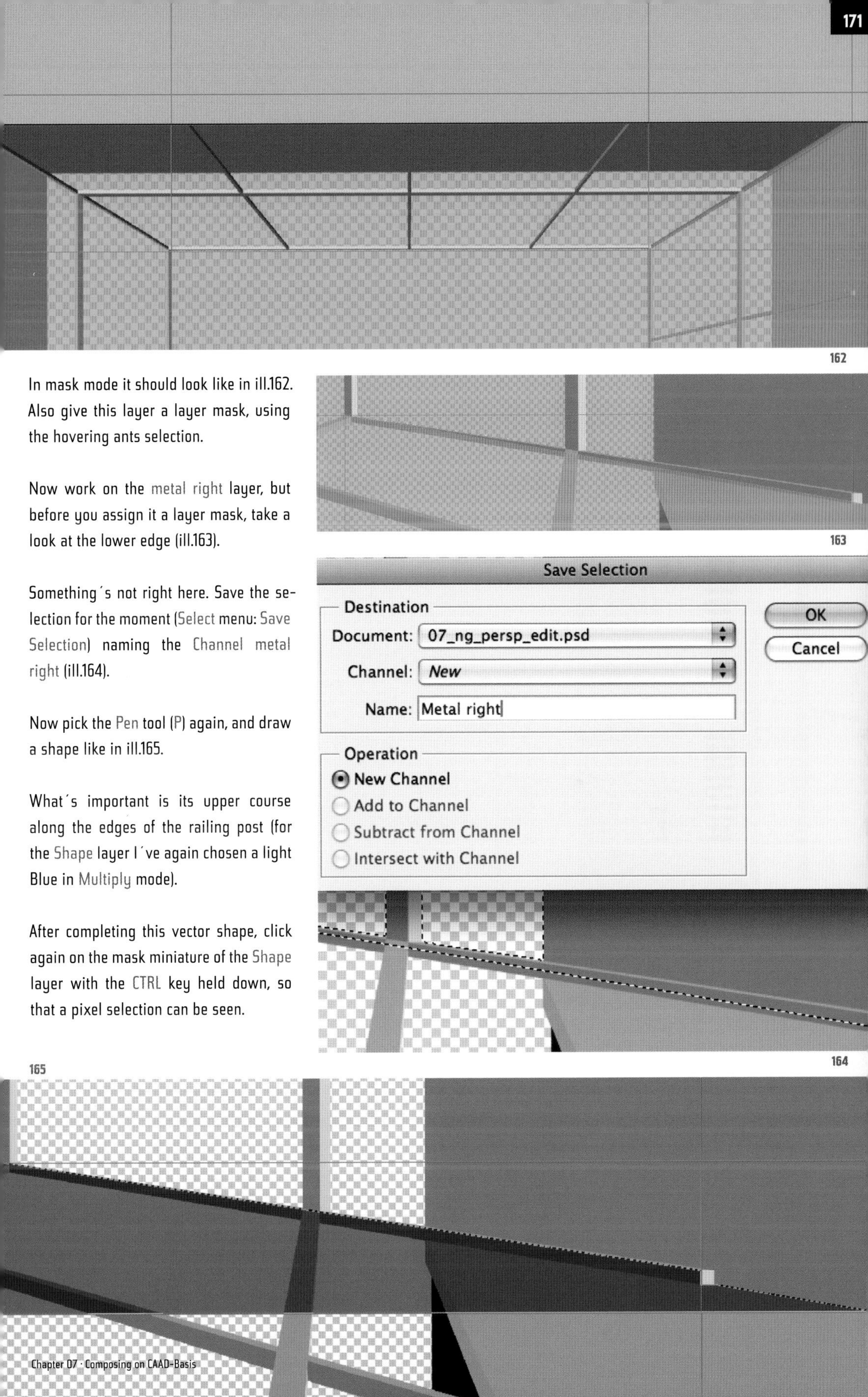

162

In mask mode it should look like in ill.162. Also give this layer a layer mask, using the hovering ants selection.

Now work on the metal right layer, but before you assign it a layer mask, take a look at the lower edge (ill.163).

163

Something´s not right here. Save the selection for the moment (Select menu: Save Selection) naming the Channel metal right (ill.164).

Now pick the Pen tool (P) again, and draw a shape like in ill.165.

What´s important is its upper course along the edges of the railing post (for the Shape layer I´ve again chosen a light Blue in Multiply mode).

After completing this vector shape, click again on the mask miniature of the Shape layer with the CTRL key held down, so that a pixel selection can be seen.

164

165

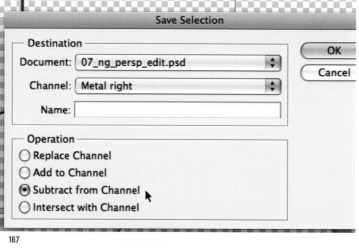

167

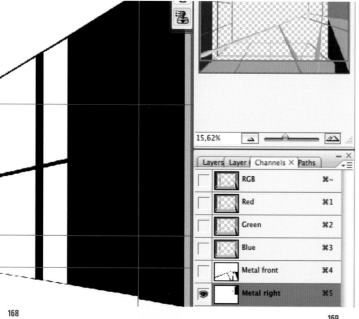

168

169

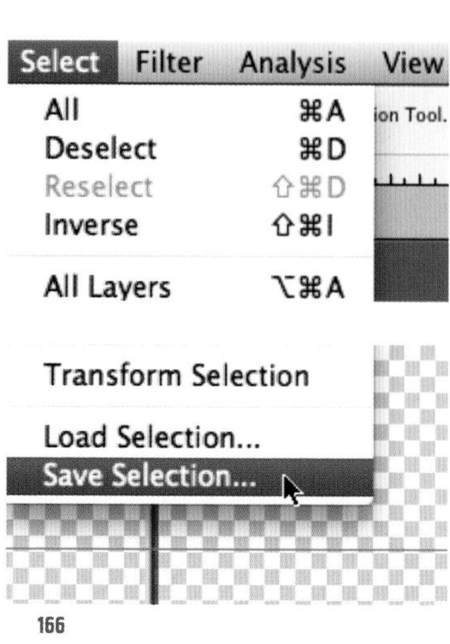

166

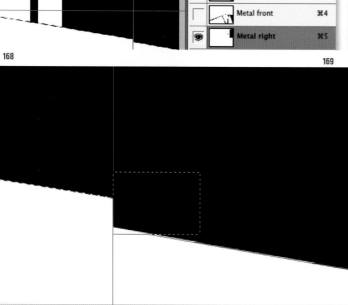

Now subtract this surface from the metal right selection you´ve just saved, by selecting the command Save Selection (Select menu, ill.166).

There pick the Channel metal right and go for the Variant Subtract from Selection (ill.167).
Confirm with OK, and check again in the Channels palette that everything is OK (ill.168). On zooming in closer you see that that´s not the case; a little thing has to be repaired (ill.169).

Take the Rectangular Marquee tool (M), draw a frame as shown, and fill it with Black (your selection has changed into a channel, i.e. a Black-and-White image; all non-selected areas are black).

To do this, either press D to set the foreground and background colors to Black and White respectively, and if required X till Black is the foreground color, and finally Alt-Backspace; or you press Shift-Backspace and select Black from the Use menu.

Switch back to the Layers palette after reactivating the RGB channels, and activate the metal right layer (ill.170). Load the selection with the name metal right (with the command Load Selection from the

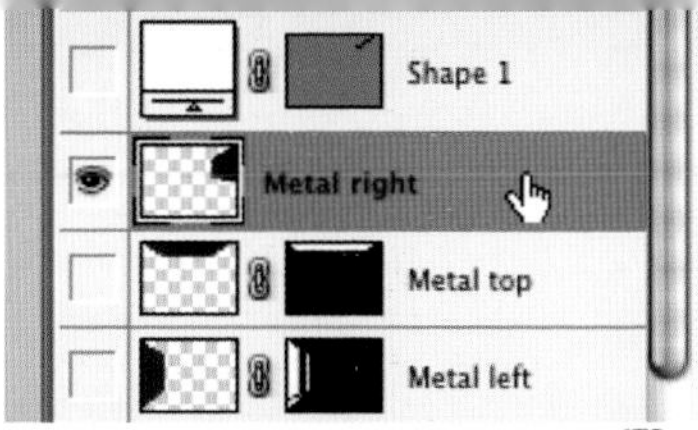

Select menu), and convert it into a layer mask using the corresponding button at the bottom frame of the Layers palette.

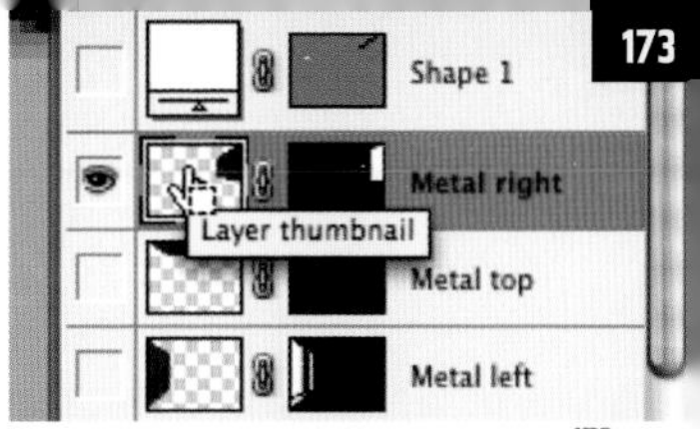

170

172

The defect you´ve just already repaired in the channel also still has to be corrected in the image; just add the missing part with the Clone Stamp tool (ill.171), but make sure that in the Layers palette the image miniature of the layer is marked, which is indicated by the miniature's double edge (ill.172).

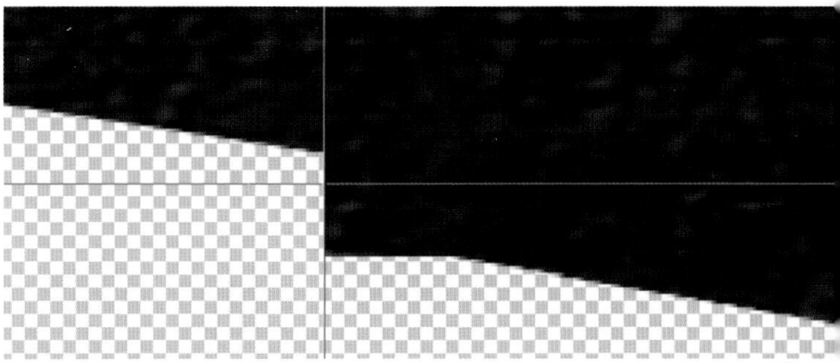

171

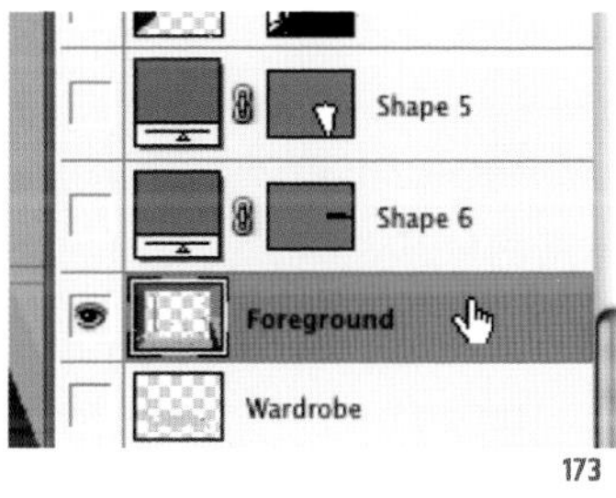

173

Now to the last layer, with the name metal down back.
Click in your miniature with the CTRL key held down, to select its contents, and then activate the Foreground layer again (ill.173).
Delete from the hovering selection the parts which don´t belong to the railing, using the magic wand (W) and the polygonal lasso (L; don´t forget to press the Alt key).

So, here you´ll notice that there are again areas which are better marked with an adjustable vector selection. If you don´t get any further with the magic wand and lasso, first of all save your selection (Channel: metal down back, ill.174).

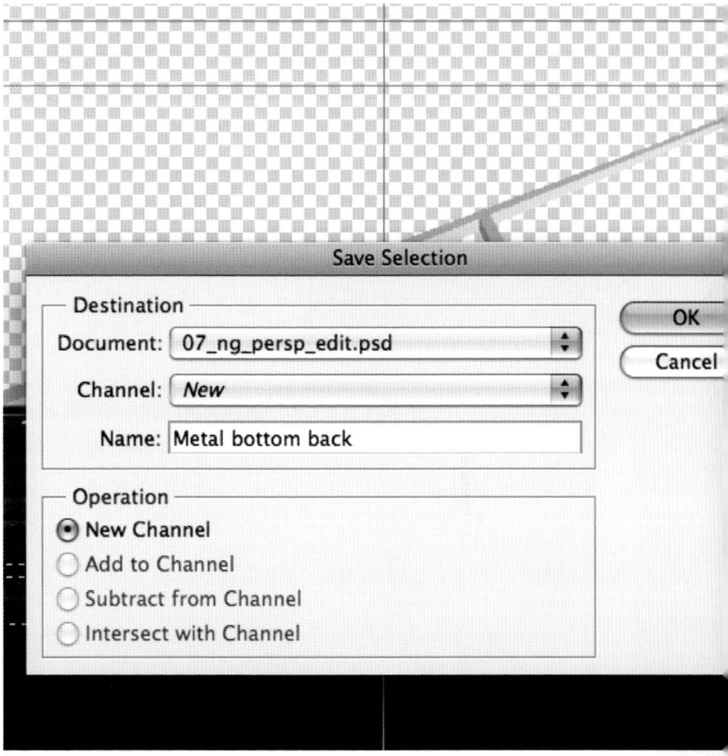

174

Then draw your vector shapes with the Pen tool (P), and convert them into pixel selections by first clicking with the CTRL key held down in the mask miniature of the one, then with Shift-CTRL in the mask miniature of the other Shape layer (ill.175).

175

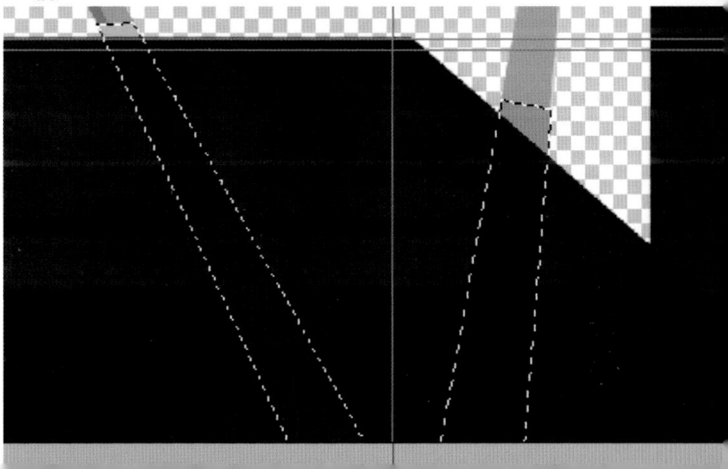

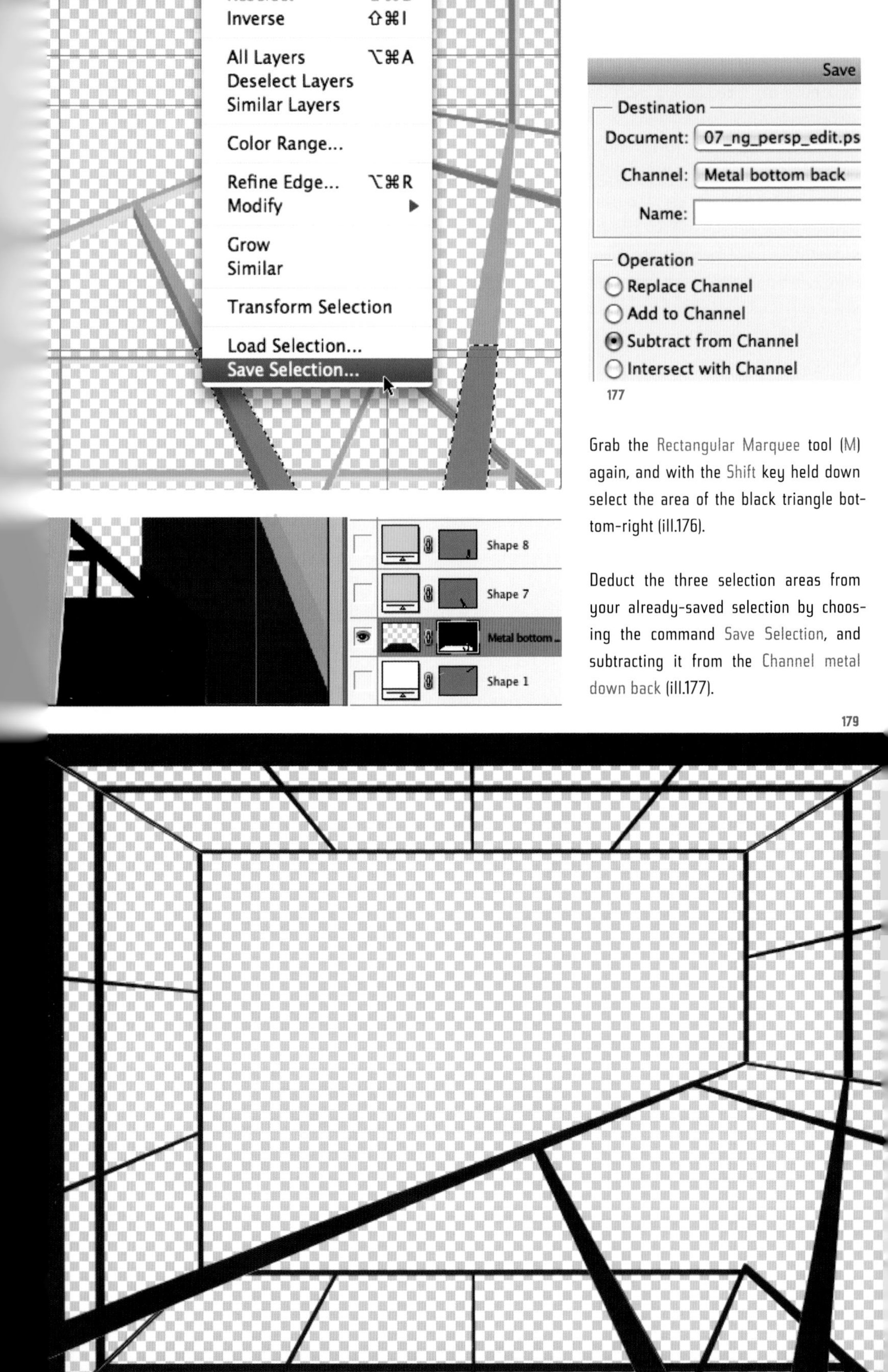

177

Grab the Rectangular Marquee tool (M) again, and with the Shift key held down select the area of the black triangle bottom-right (ill.176).

Deduct the three selection areas from your already-saved selection by choosing the command Save Selection, and subtracting it from the Channel metal down back (ill.177).

179

Load your finished selection, activate the layer metal down back, and convert the selection into a layer mask by clicking on the corresponding button at the bottom frame of the Layers palette (ill.178).

Now it´s done; all the metal surfaces are perspectively aligned and masked. Show them all, and hide the Foreground layer (ill.179).

You surely agree that the work on the metal surfaces isn´t yet done – the brightness differentiation of the individual surfaces is still lacking. For simplicity´s sake we´ll at least combine the four railings behind on one layer, but before that we want to save, for safety´s sake, the individual layer masks as selections, as far as this hasn´t already happened.

For the layer metal left there´s not yet a saved selection, so please click in its mask miniature with the CTRL key held down (ill.180), so that the according selection appears. Then select Save Selection from the Select menu (ill.181), and give the new Channel the name metal left (ill.182).

Next attend to the layer metal up; click first in your mask miniature with the CTRL key held down, to start the selection (ill.183); when saving the selection, logic suggests you select the Channel name metal up (ill.184).

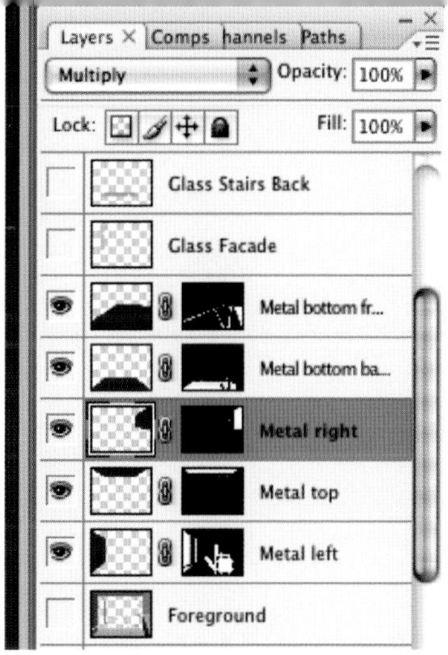

180

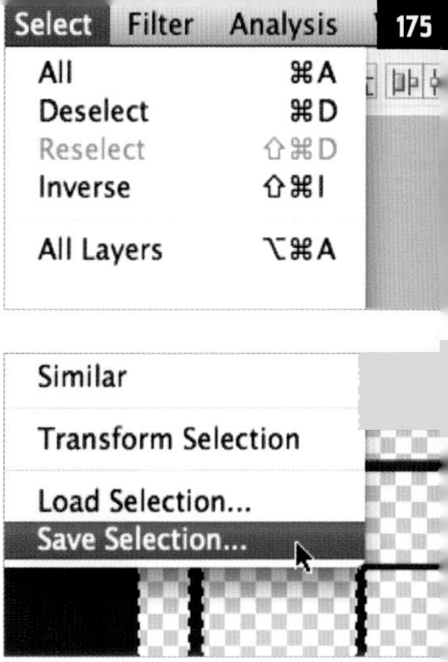

181

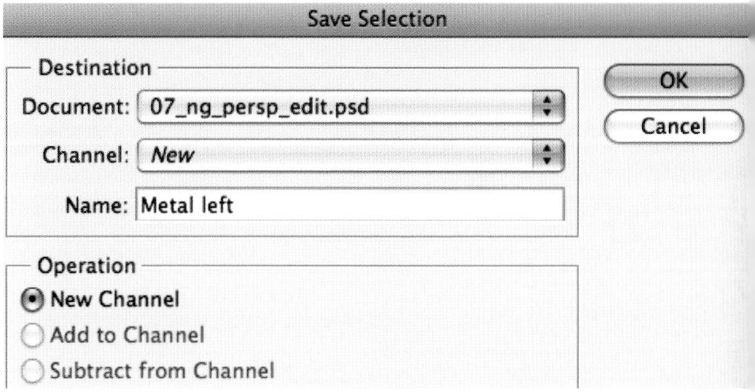

182

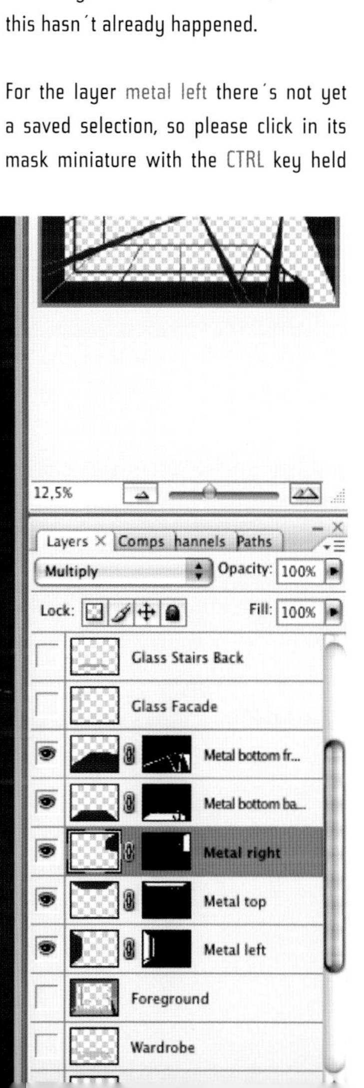

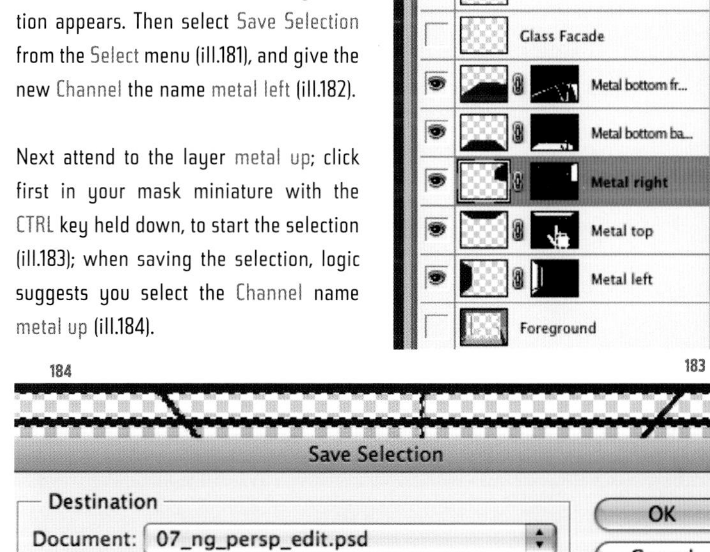

183

184

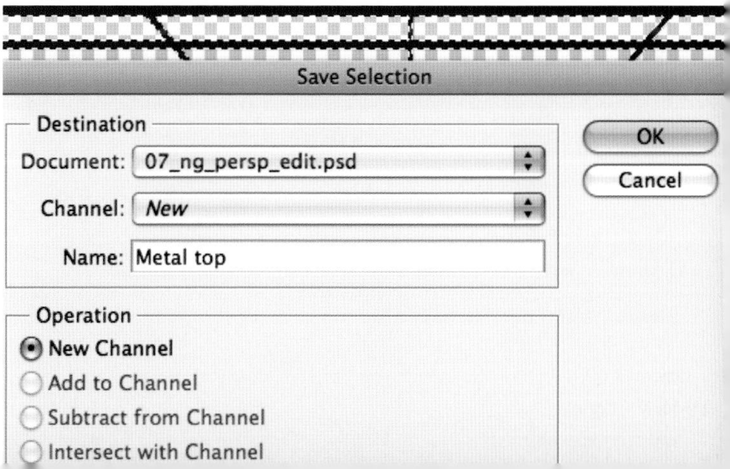

Save Selection
Destination
Document: 07_ng_persp_edit.psd
Channel: New
Name: Metal top
Operation
New Channel
Add to Channel
Subtract from Channel
Intersect with Channel
OK
Cancel

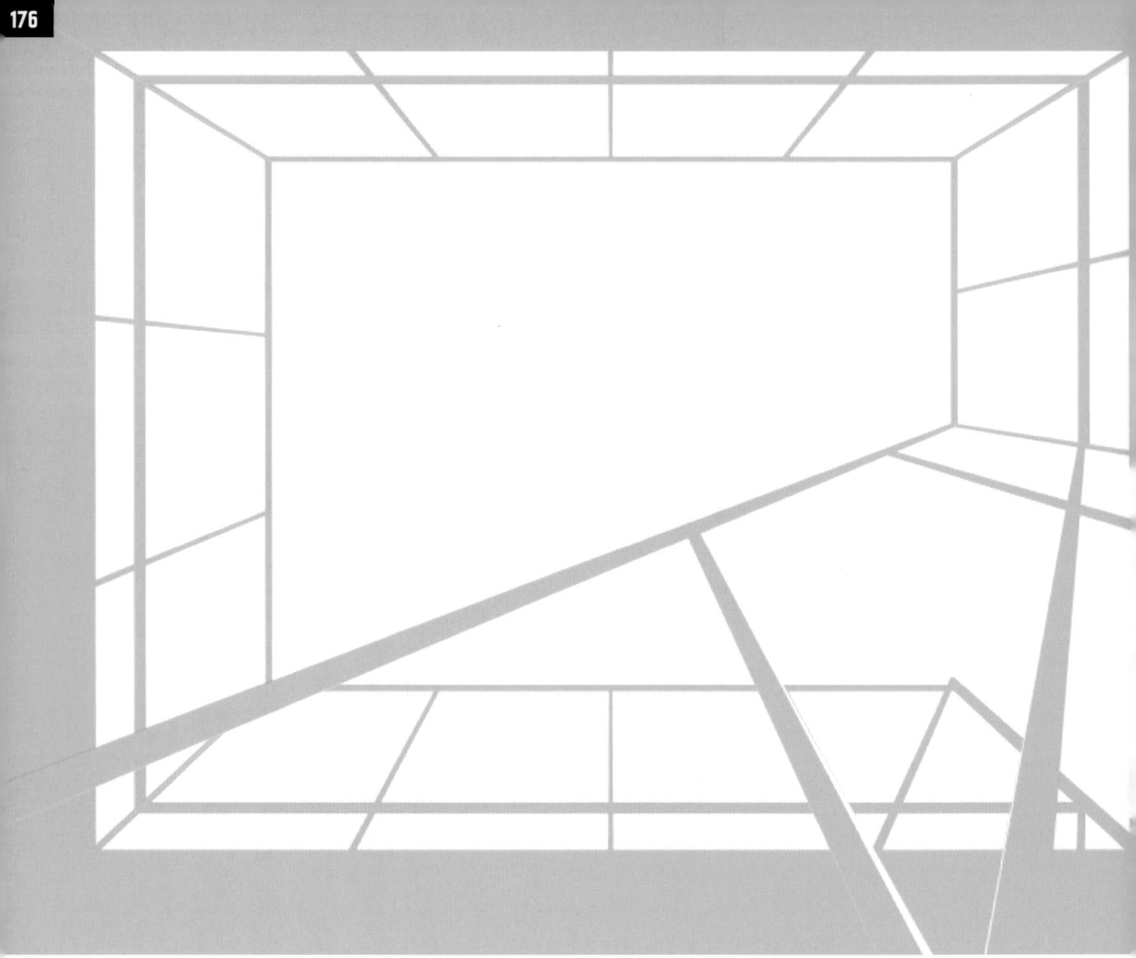

185

In the Channels palette you can now check if all the single planes exist as channels (ill.185, I´ve rearranged the channels a bit, as you can see).

Staying in the Channels palette, we create right away another channel for the four background metal surfaces altogether. Click on the miniature of the first one with the CTRL key held down, and then subsequently with Shift-CTRL on the miniatures of the remaining channels, to create a selection encompassing the four. You can save this too, calling the Channel metal back complete (ill.186).

Reactivate the RGB channels, switch back to the Layers palette and ensure that only the four layers with the metal surfaces behind are shown (ill.187). Then select the

186

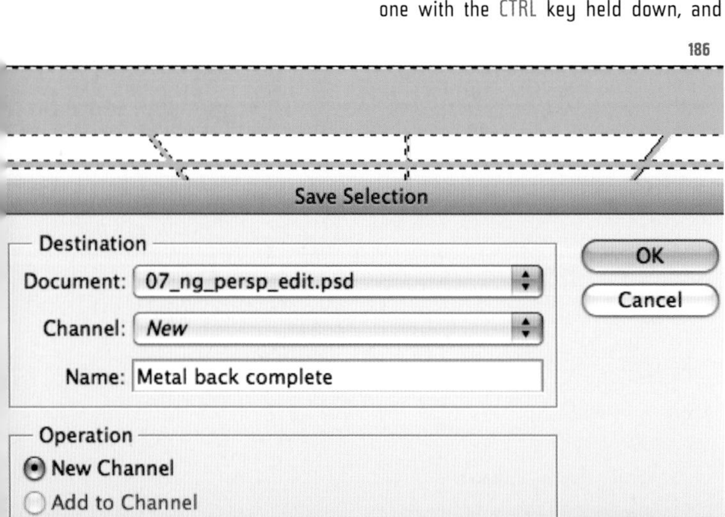

187

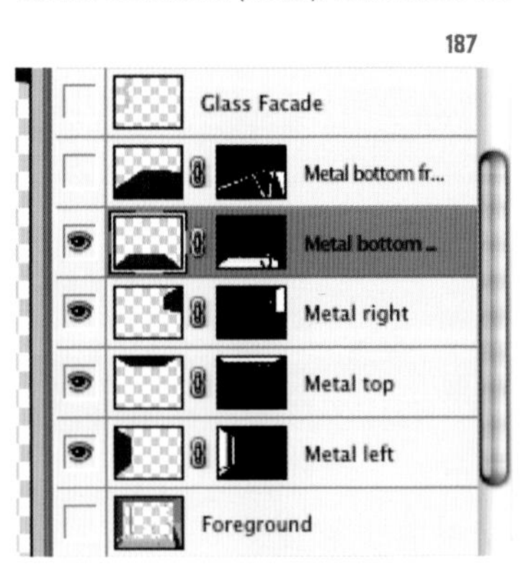

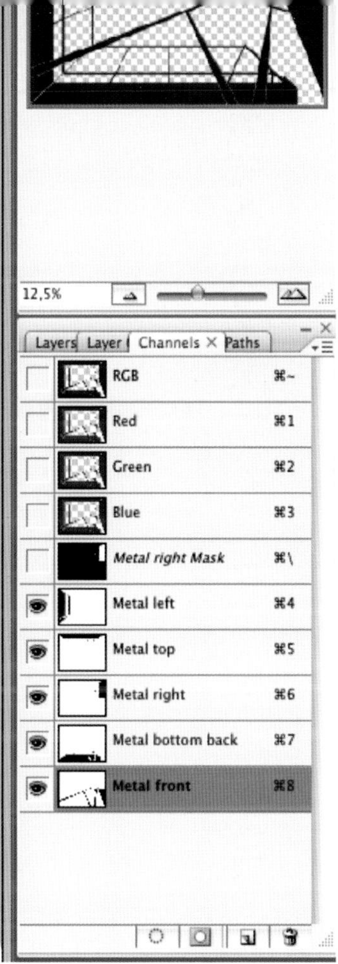

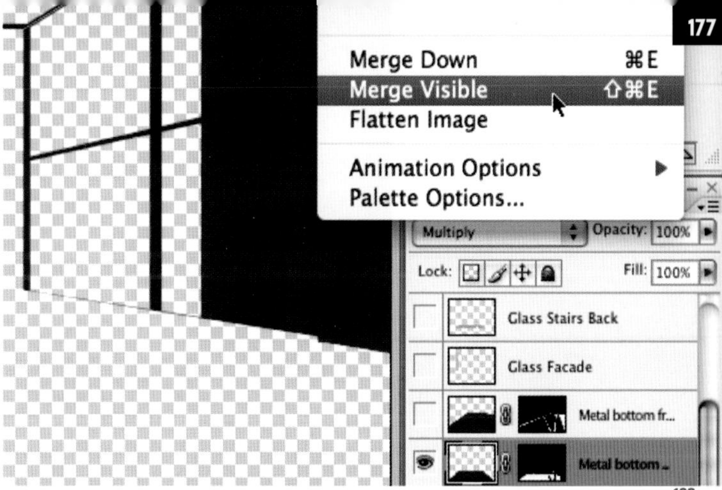

188

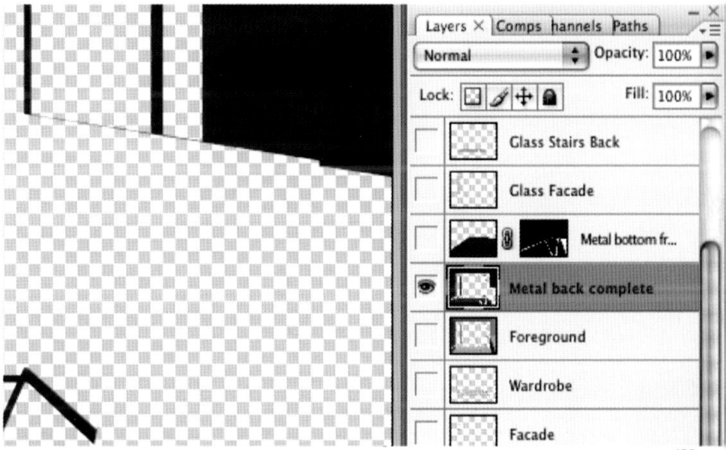

189

command Merge Visible from the menu of the Layers palette (ill.188).

As you see, the four layers are combined into one, and the former masks of the layers are processed into the resulting image (ill.189).

Now to brightness differentiation. Hide the metal layer and show the Foreground one (ill.190). You see that there are several brightness steps for the railing design, depending on the direction of the single planes (ill.191).

You´ll now select the Magic Wand tool (W, ill.192), first with the Tolerance 1 and the option Contiguous deactivated, to select the brightest planes facing downwards. Using this selection you´ll then place a masked Levels adjustment layer over the metal layer.

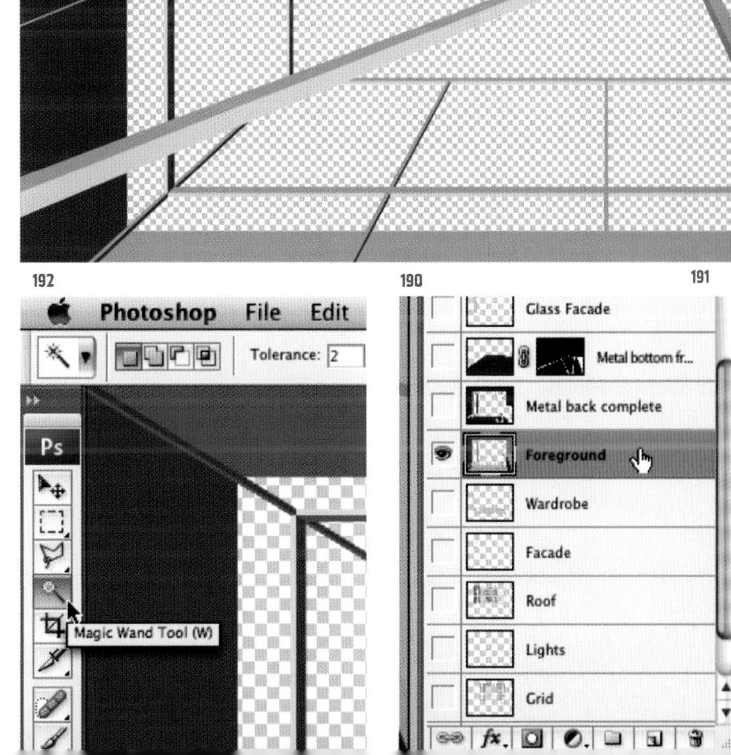

192 190 191

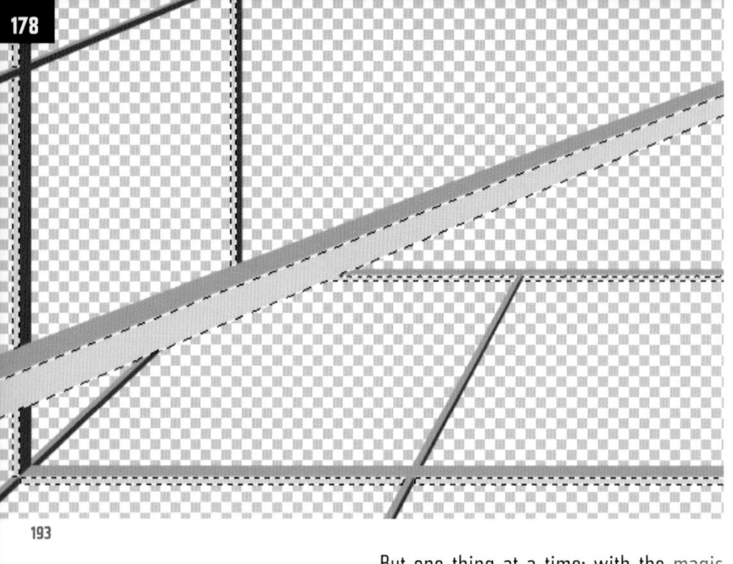

193

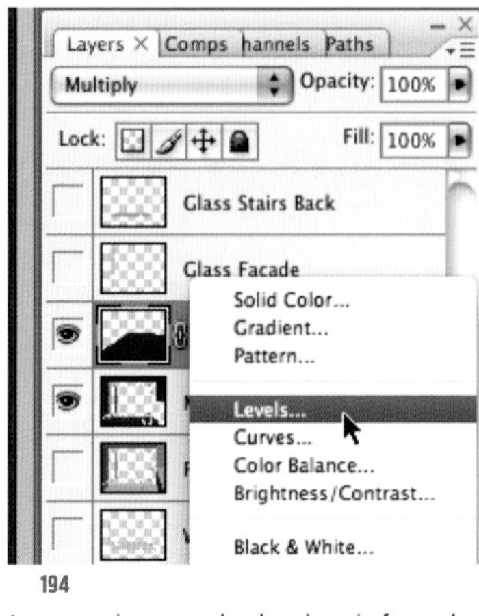

194

But one thing at a time: with the magic wand, click in one of the respective surfaces.

Make sure that for this purpose the Foreground layer is both shown and activated (Ills.190 and 193), then show the metal layer and activate the upper one.

At the bottom frame of the Layers palette, click on the button Create new fill or adjustment layer, and select Levels from the pop-up (ill.194).

In the histogram window that opens, set the Gray control to 5,00 (ill.195).

You can see in the image that the formerly selected image area becomes much brighter.

195

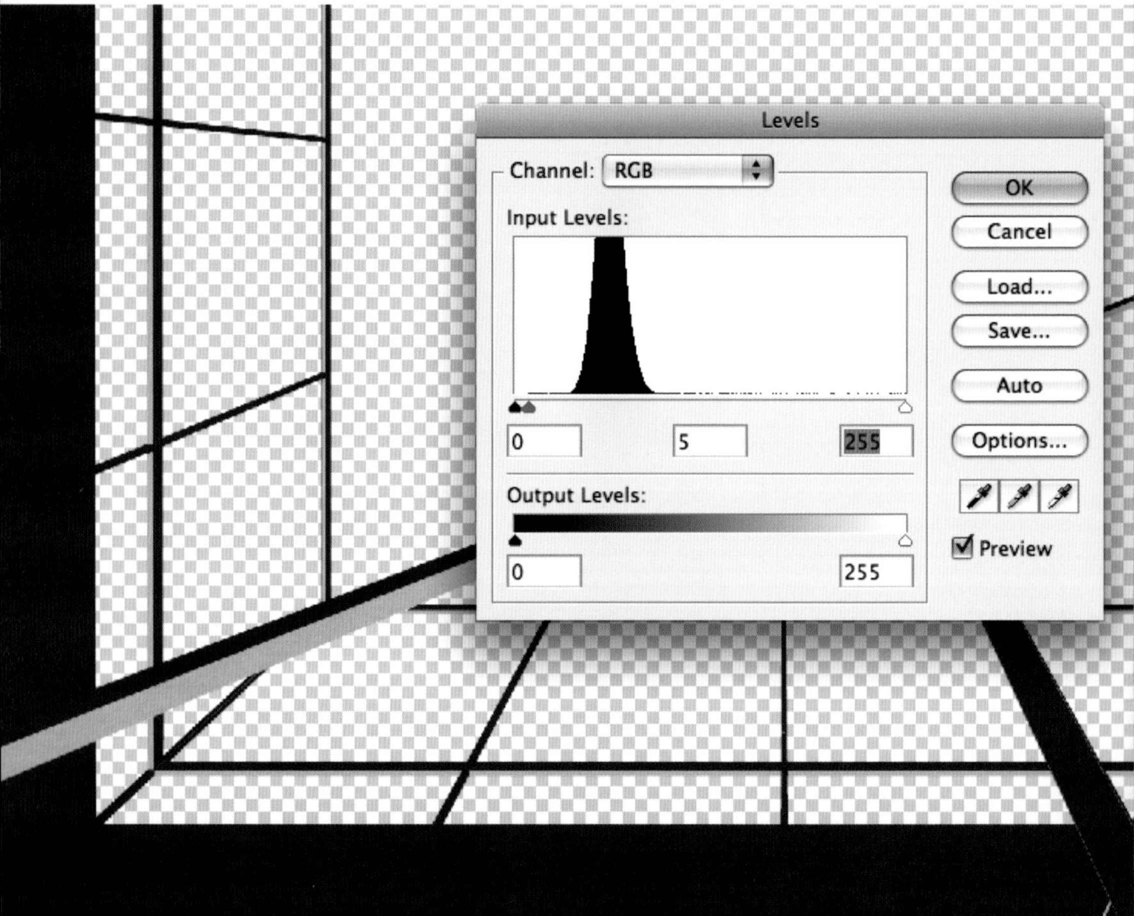

196

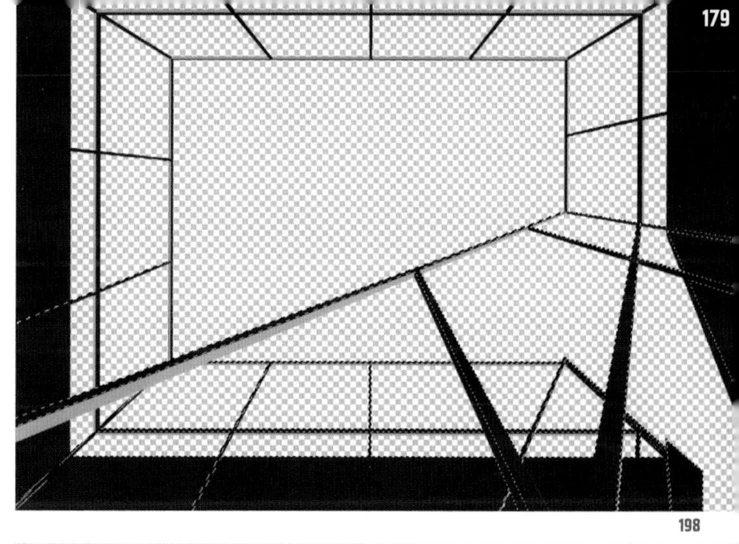

198

Reactivate the Foreground layer, though you no longer need to show it for your further efforts (ill.196), and click with the magic wand in one of the next-brightest front surfaces.

You´ll see that for this it makes more sense to increase the magic wand Tolerance to 2 (Ills.197 and 198).

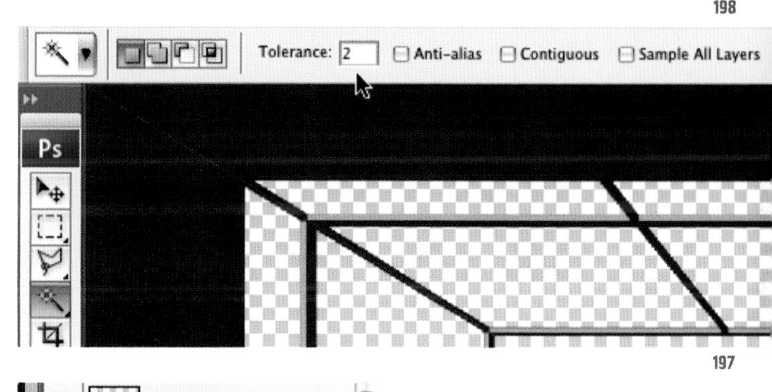

197

Activate the adjustment layer above the metal layer, and then add a second Levels adjustment layer (ill.199), in whose histogram you leave the Gray control at 1.00, i.e. nothing changes (ill.200; yet we need this adjustment layer if we later wish to tune the brightness system of the railing somewhat).

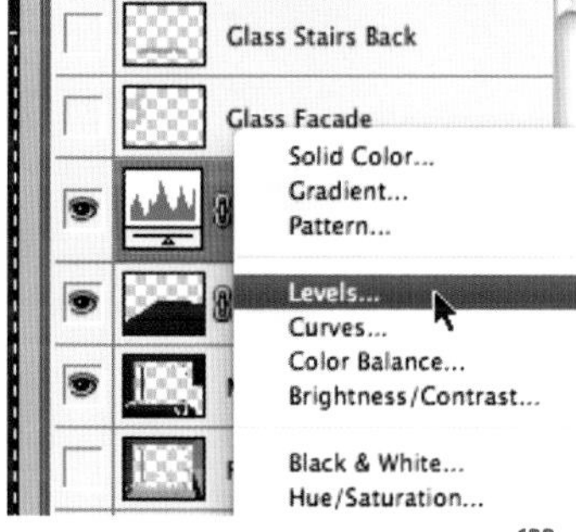

199

200

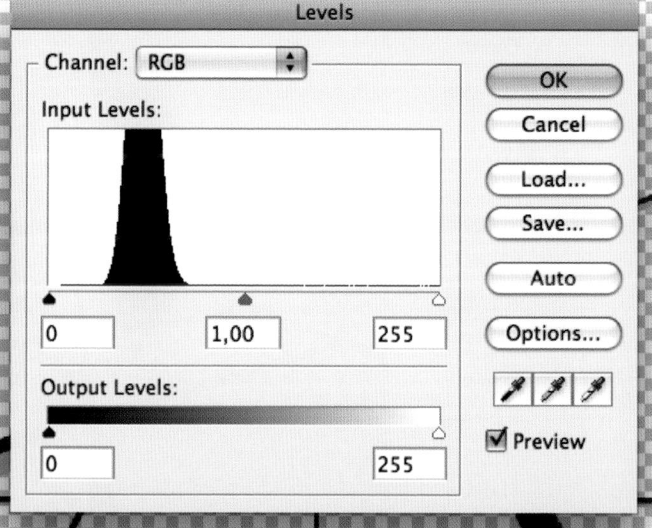

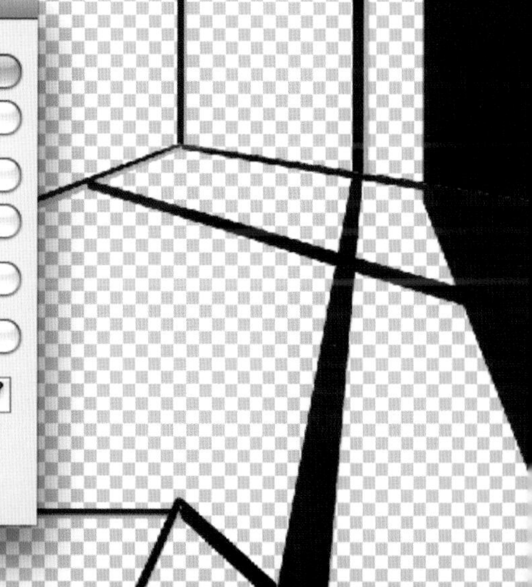

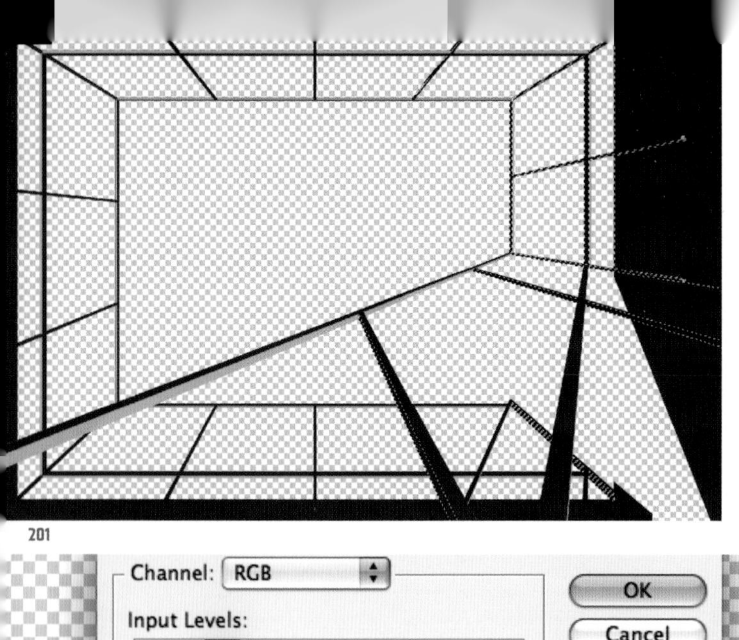

201

Now you will go on like this - to select the surfaces activate the Foreground layer, click into one of the according faces, and insert a new Levels adjustment layer above the one last installed, which will be appropriately masked.

Next do this for the right side-surfaces (ill.201), with the Gray control 0.85 in the Levels histogram (ill.202), then for the upper front-surfaces with the value 0.55 (ill.203) and finally for the left side-

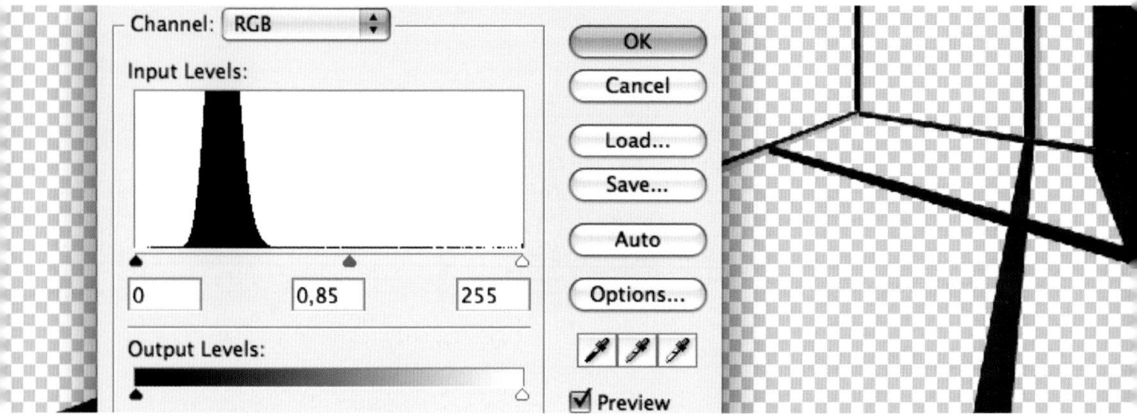

202

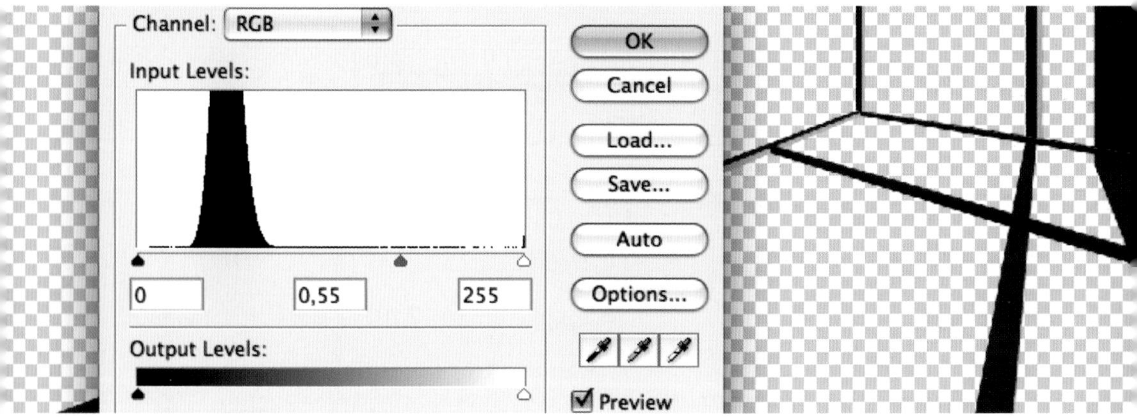

203

204

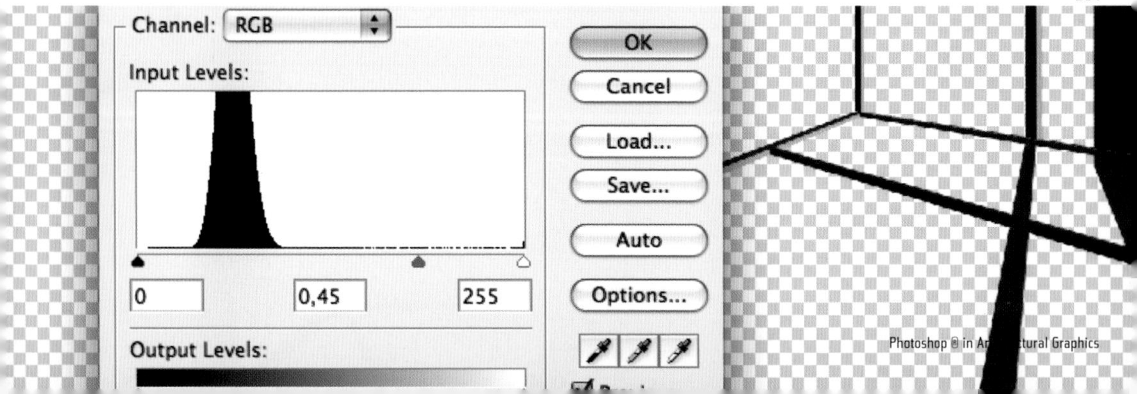

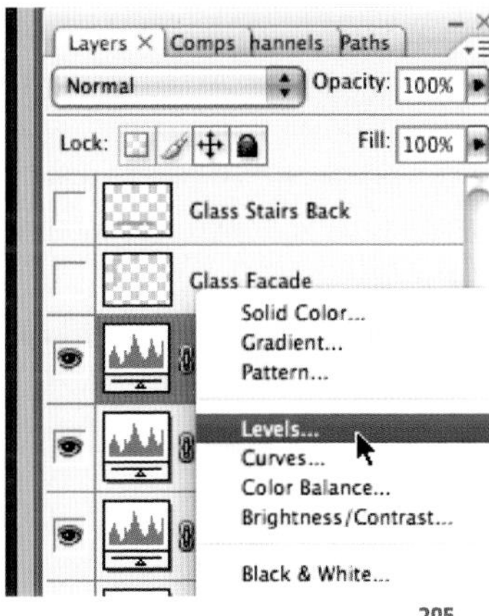

205

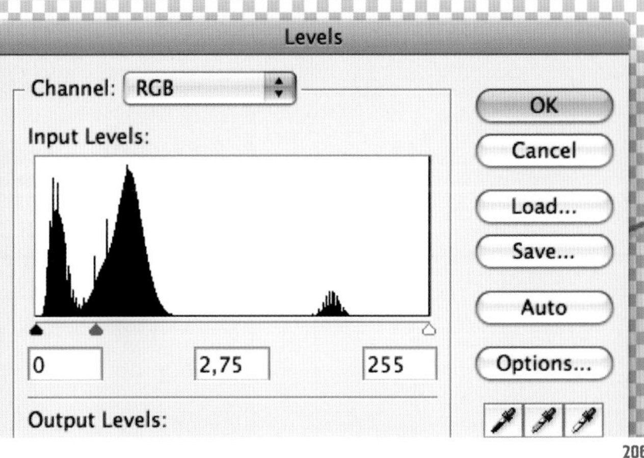

206

surfaces, the darkest ones, with the value 0.45 (ill.204).

Last of all there´s to be an additional brightness gradient on the metal surfaces, becoming darker from the bottom to the top.

To do this, place a further adjustment layer above the previously inserted ones (ill.205) and set the histogram Gray control to 2.75 (ill.206).
You see that the railing complex becomes clearly brighter.

To get your gradient, however, you still have to mask this Levels adjustment layer, for each of the single planes separately, one at a time.
First ensure that your new adjustment layer is active and that your mask miniature is clicked on (ill.207).

To be able to place the Black-and-White gradients accurately, load the saved surface selections one after the other (see ill.187), and in each case paint the gradient inside the hovering selections.

Begin with the command Load Selection from the Select menu (ill.208).

First opt for the Channel metal down back (ill.209) and confirm with OK.

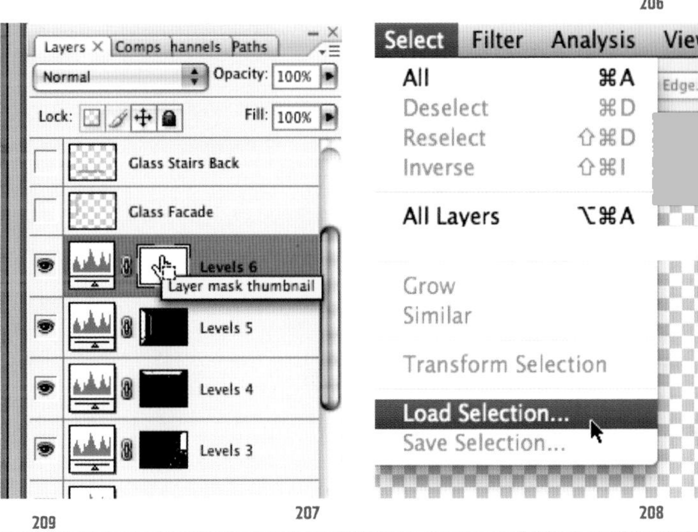

207

208

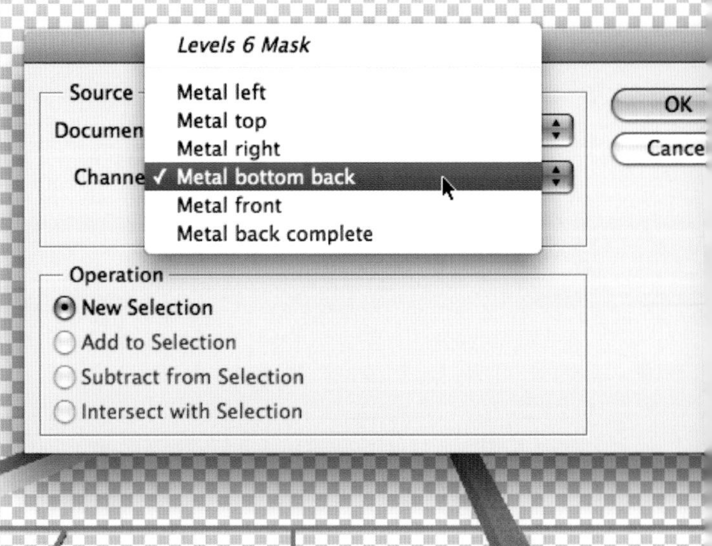

209

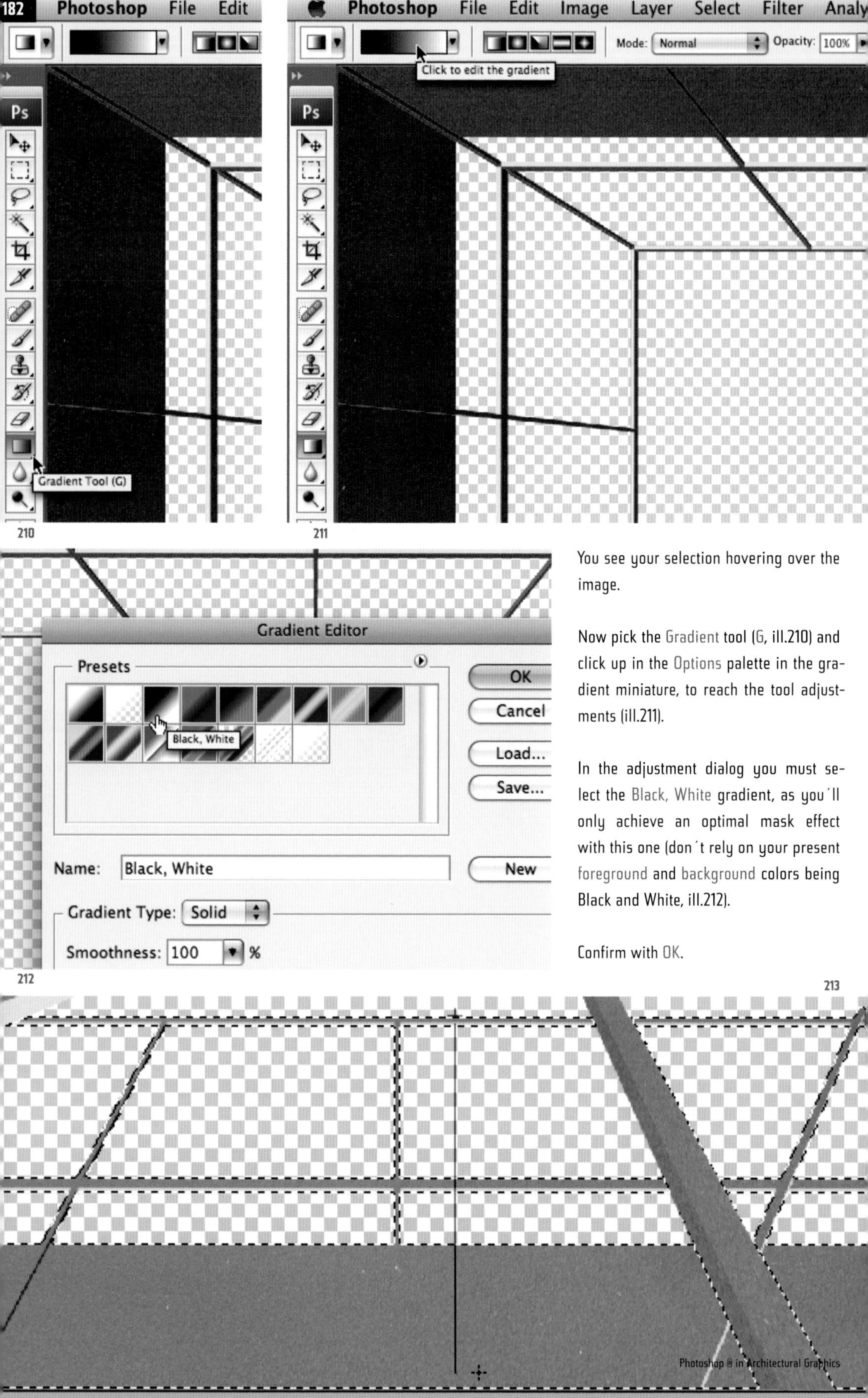

210

211

You see your selection hovering over the image.

Now pick the Gradient tool (G, ill.210) and click up in the Options palette in the gradient miniature, to reach the tool adjustments (ill.211).

In the adjustment dialog you must select the Black, White gradient, as you´ll only achieve an optimal mask effect with this one (don´t rely on your present foreground and background colors being Black and White, ill.212).

Confirm with OK.

212

213

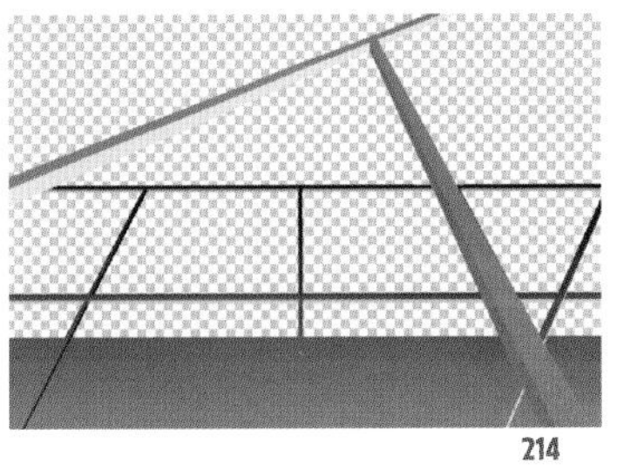

214

So, your selection is still visible; now paint a vertical gradient from the upper to the lower border of your selection (ill.213) and deselect your ants (CTRL-D).

The result is a brightness gradient on the surface formerly selected, with the brightest area at the bottom (ill.214).

Repeat this action for all the other single planes, beginning with the channel metal left (ill.215), then metal up (ill.216) and finally metal right (ill.217).

With the Alt key held down, click in the mask miniature, and you can see the mask as a grayscale image (ill.218).

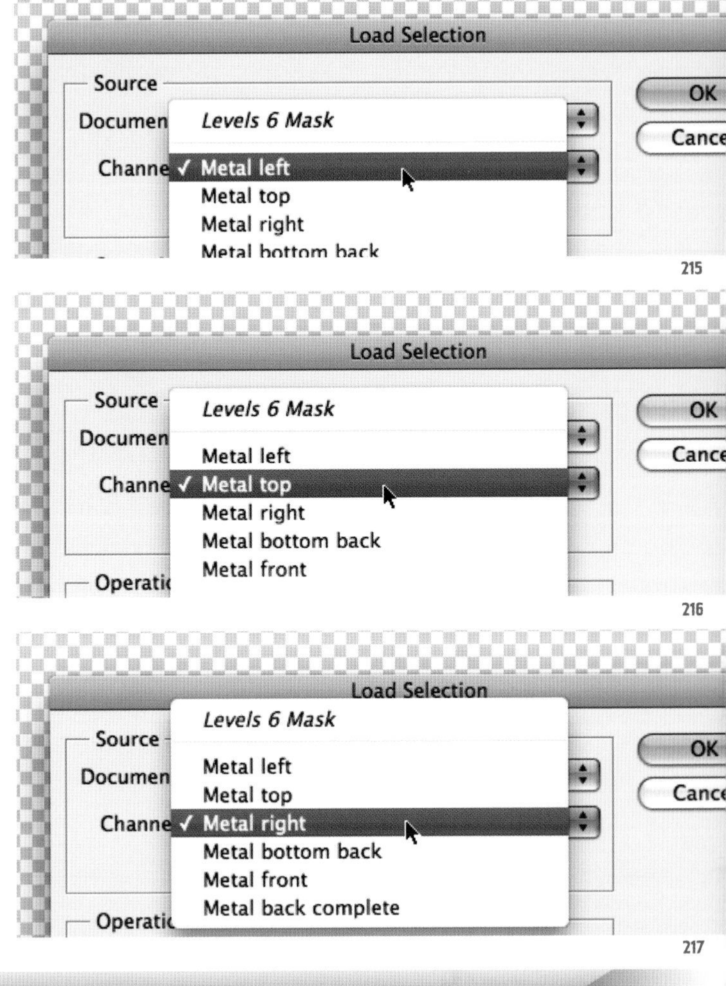

215

216

217

218

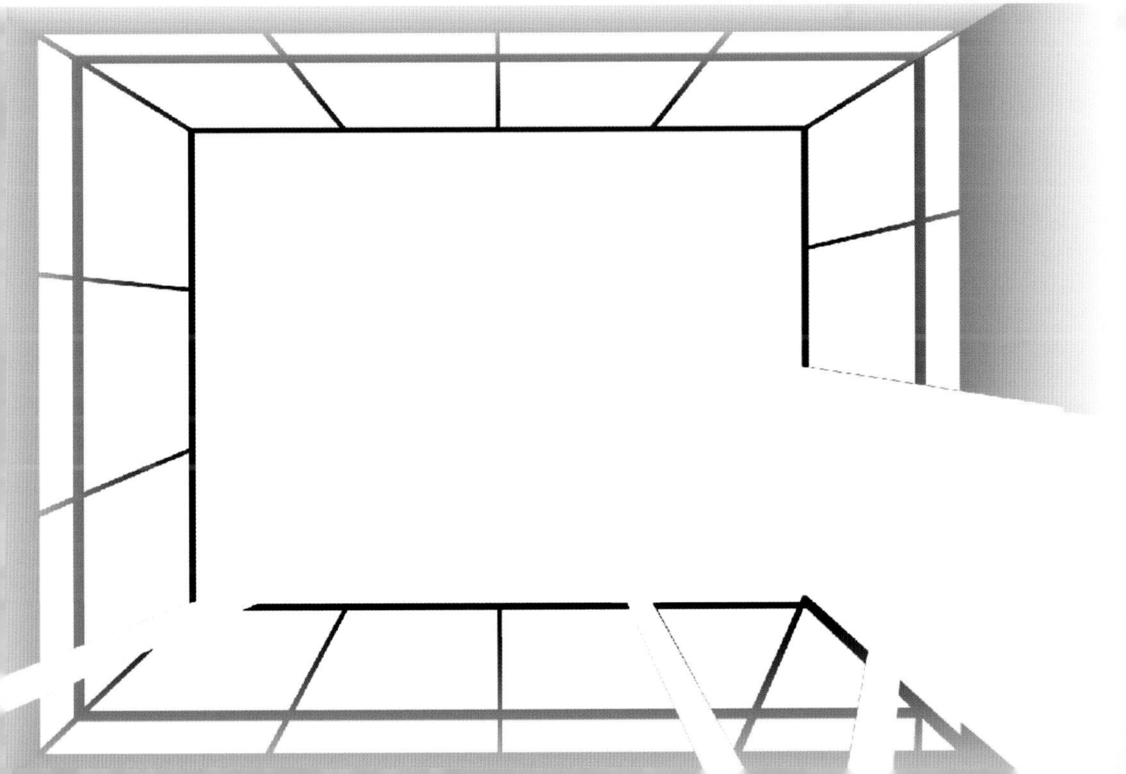

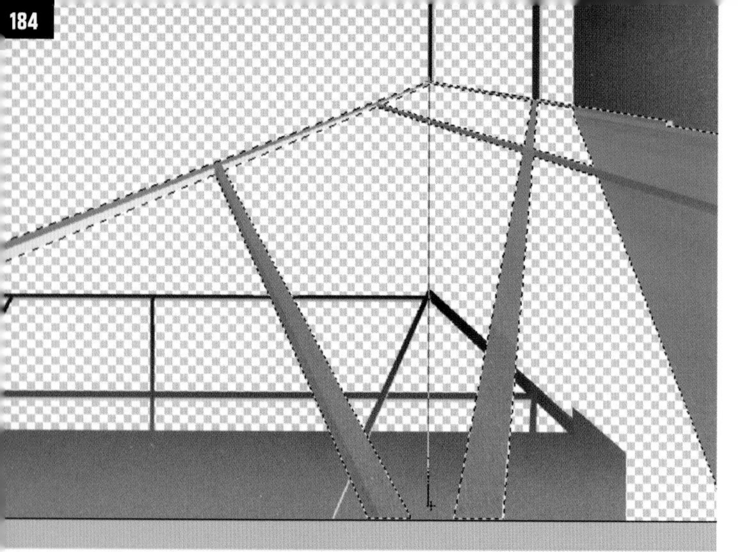

220

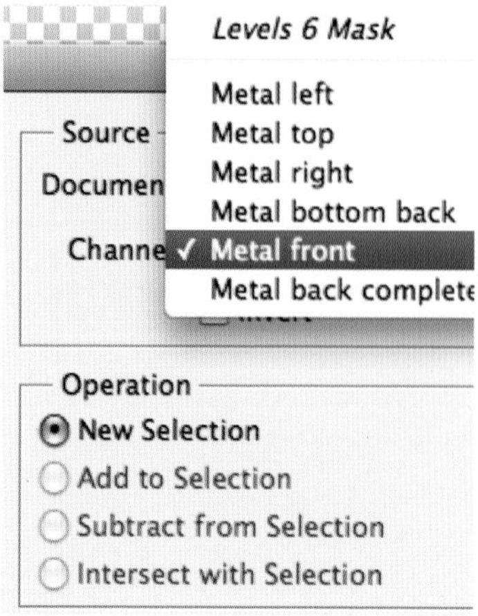

Levels 6 Mask

Source
Document
Channel
Metal left
Metal top
Metal right
Metal bottom back
✓ Metal front
Metal back complete

Operation
New Selection
Add to Selection
Subtract from Selection
Intersect with Selection

219

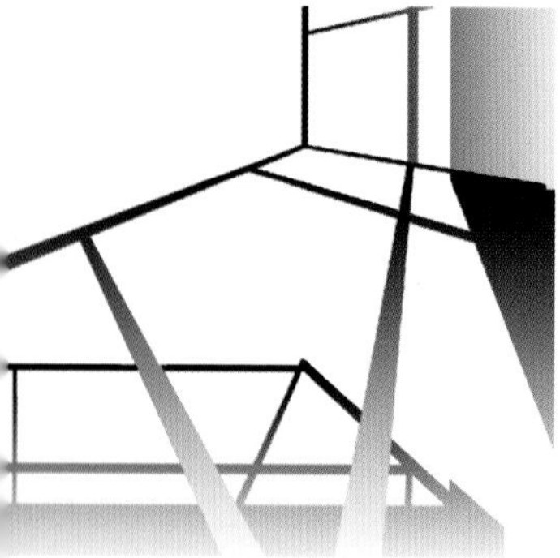

221

Alt-click again in the mask miniature, to see your image once more. Now complement your mask with a gradient for the front railing layer.

To do this, load the selection metal front (ill.219), and paint your gradient into it too, making quite sure you do it vertically, down from the upper to the lower selection border (ill.220).

Now too check the result by Alt-clicking on the mask miniature (ill.221).

Switch back to the image display and show the remaining image layers, to get a foretaste of how the railing looks in relation to the complete image (ill.222).

You may later still have to adjust the brightness differentiation of the fore-

222

223

ground, and you´ll definitely want to use another filter on the surfaces (also with a mask gradient), but now let´s attend to other parts of the image.

Close your image for the moment so your memory can recover, and open the file 07_ng_detail_wood.jpg (ill.223).

From this real photo you´ll assemble a wood surface that you can use in your composing.

First convert the Background layer into a normal one by double-clicking it in the Layers palette. You may stay with the suggested name Layer 0 (ill.224).

224

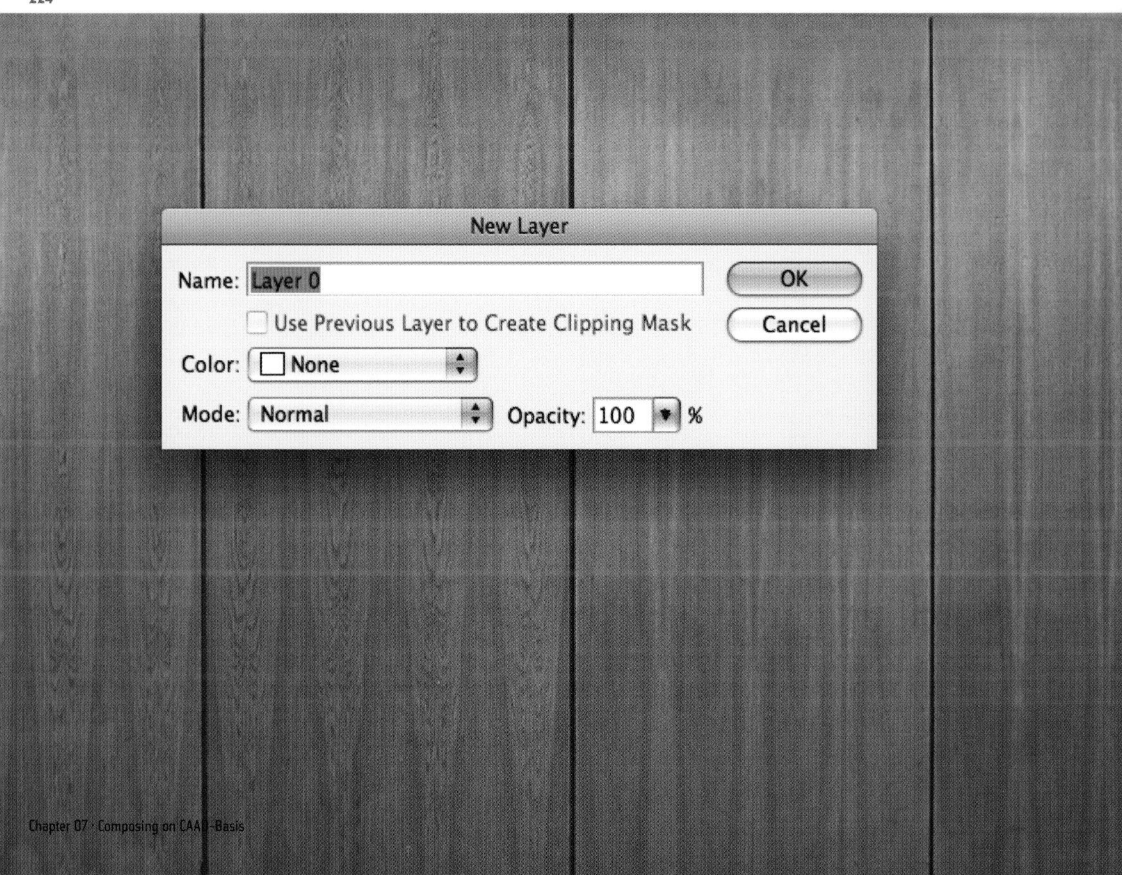

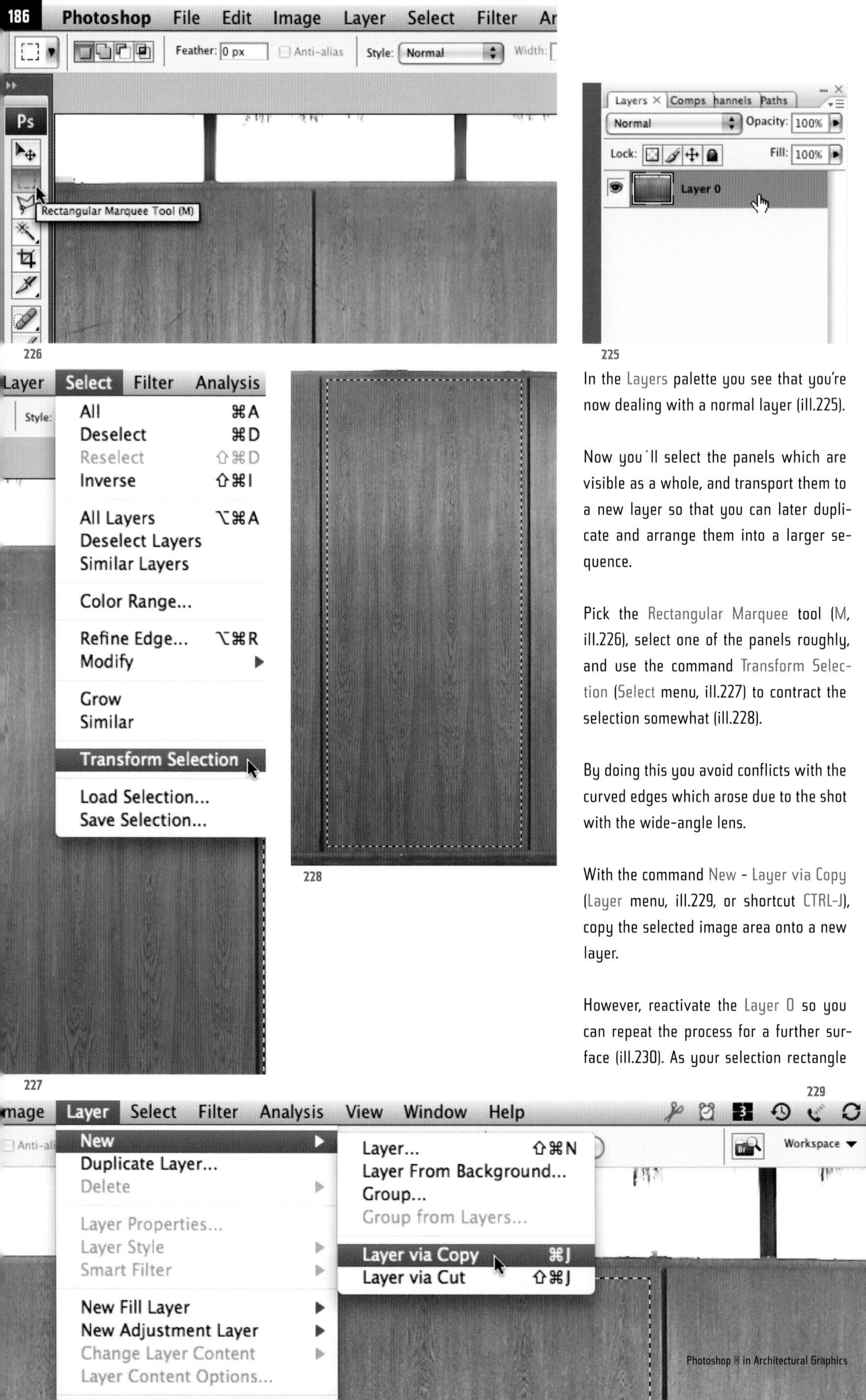

226

225

227

228

229

In the Layers palette you see that you're now dealing with a normal layer (ill.225).

Now you´ll select the panels which are visible as a whole, and transport them to a new layer so that you can later duplicate and arrange them into a larger sequence.

Pick the Rectangular Marquee tool (M, ill.226), select one of the panels roughly, and use the command Transform Selection (Select menu, ill.227) to contract the selection somewhat (ill.228).

By doing this you avoid conflicts with the curved edges which arose due to the shot with the wide-angle lens.

With the command New - Layer via Copy (Layer menu, ill.229, or shortcut CTRL-J), copy the selected image area onto a new layer.

However, reactivate the Layer 0 so you can repeat the process for a further surface (ill.230). As your selection rectangle

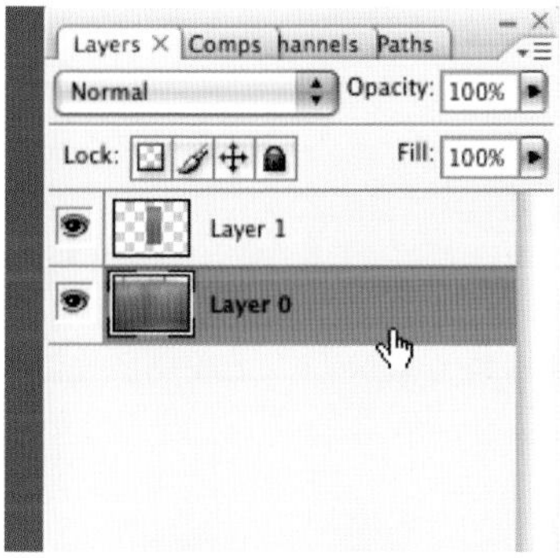

230

can still be seen, just move it onto the next selected panel (with the Rectangular Marquee tool still active, ill.231).

In this way the next selection is sure to be just as big as the one before.

When the selection is positioned correctly, press CTRL-J again to lay this image part too onto a separate layer.

Repeat all this a further time, to also copy the third fully visible wood panel. When you´re finished, you should have three new layers, on which in each case lies a different panel face (ill.232). Hide Layer 0.

231

232

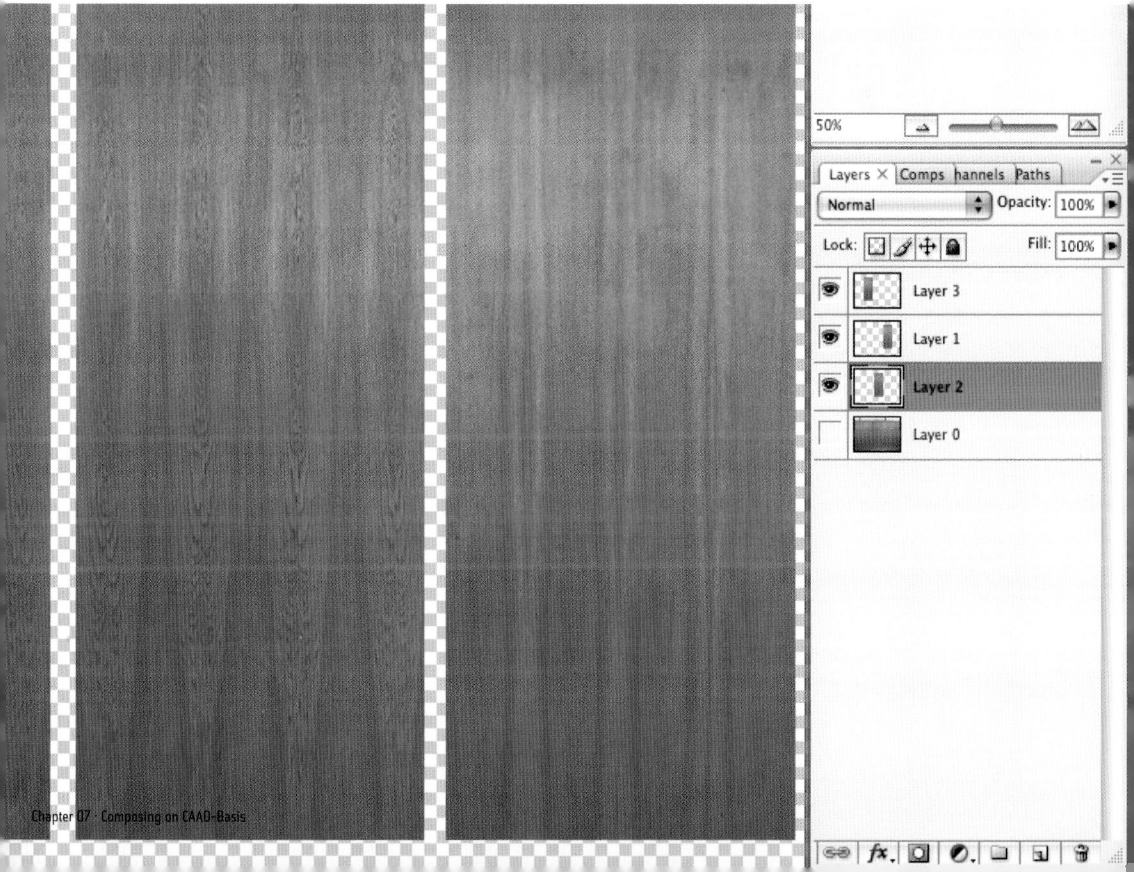

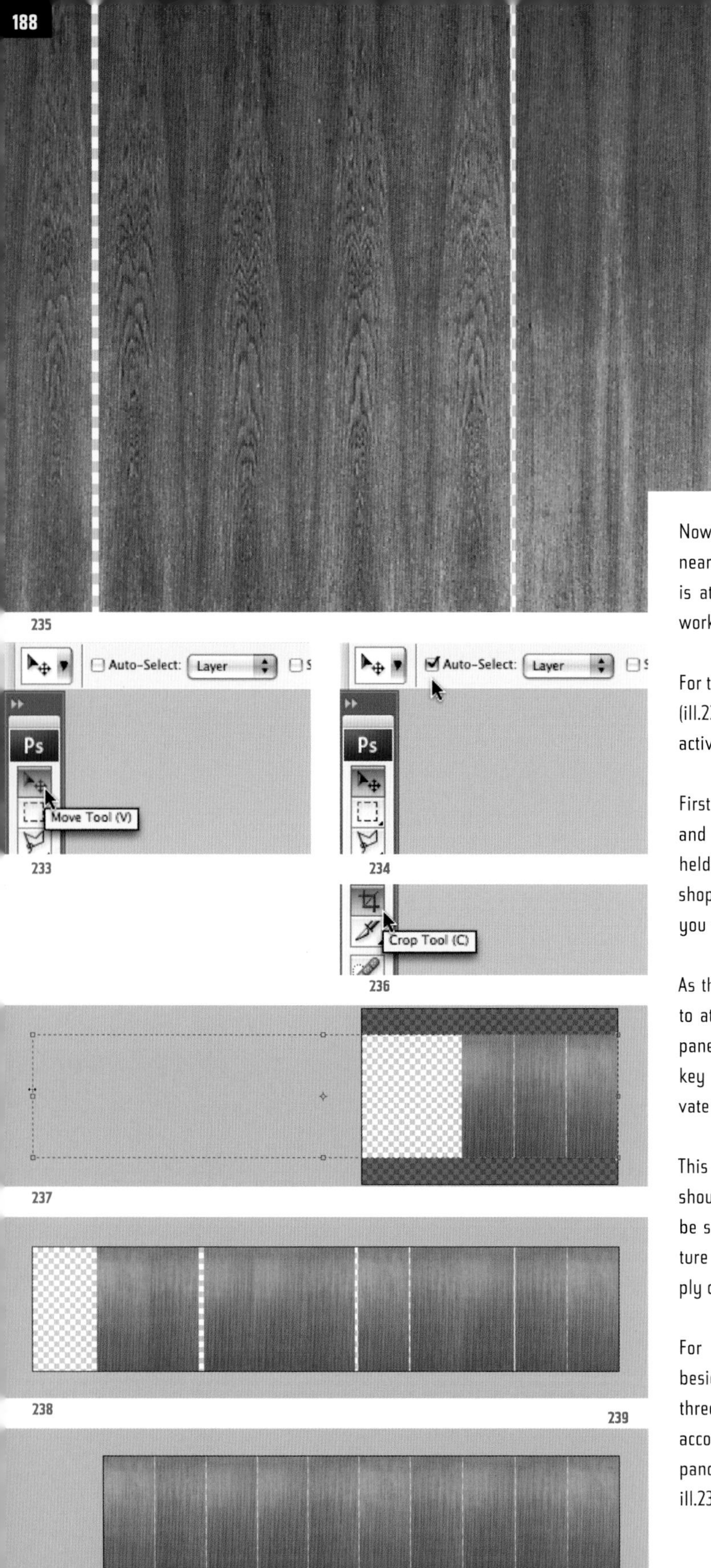

235

233

234

236

237

238

239

Now you´ll move the individual surfaces nearer to each other, so that one of them is at the very right, at the edge of the workspace.

For this, of course, you take the Move tool (ill.233) with the option Auto-Select: Layer activated (ill.234).

First click on the face you want to move and then drag it, with the mouse button held down, to the place desired; Photoshop® helps with horizontal guides while you work (ill.235).

As the image components you move like to attach themselves to the neighboring panels, you should hold down the CTRL key when you get near them, to deactivate this "magnetism".

This is because the individual surfaces shouldn´t directly touch each other but be slightly apart (like in the original picture too), the gap's distance you may simply decide upon approximately.

For composing, you require 10 panels beside each other; so far you only have three, and also not enough workspace to accommodate the missing seven. To expand the workspace, use the Crop tool (C, ill.236).

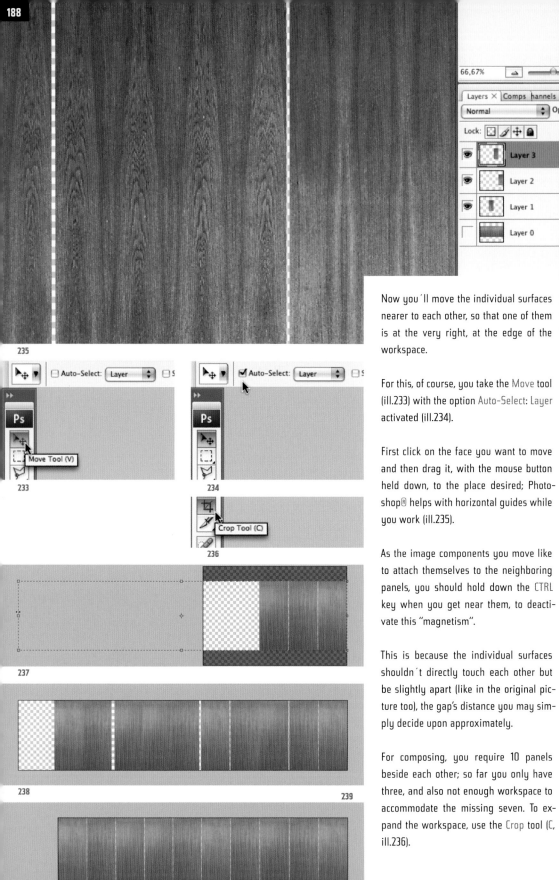

Check that in the Options palette no target dimensions are entered for cropping, and if necessary click on the Clear button. Now first draw a cropping frame round your wood panels (Photoshop® helps you again, as the tool attaches itself to the image borders), and then expand the frame generously to the left (ill.237).

Double-click or press Return, and your workspace is big enough.

For copying, take the Move tool again, only this time press the Alt key before the first click on a panel, so that Photoshop® creates a copy during the move. Distribute the panels in such a way that the same ones won´t lie beside each other (ill.238).

The position doesn´t need to be exact, as you´ll deal with that next, but make sure the move always takes place horizontally; Photoshop®´s guides help you here.

Now zoom in on each of the gaps, and move the wood panels to their final position. For this you can also use the arrow keys, with the Move tool active and after a click on the panel to be moved (ill.239).

When you´re finished, clip your image again with the Crop tool (C, again without using target dimensions).

Vary the panel assembly a little more by mirroring some of the faces.

Click on the panel desired with the Move tool, to select the corresponding layer (ill.240), and then select the command Transform - Flip Horizontal from the Edit menu (ill.241).

Yet, you´ll have to remove the light reflections on the wood surfaces, as well as you can. To do this, use the Levels correction, again of course as an adjustment layer, with a gradient mask.

First activate the upper layer and then select the Levels from the popup menu of the adjustment layers (ill.242).

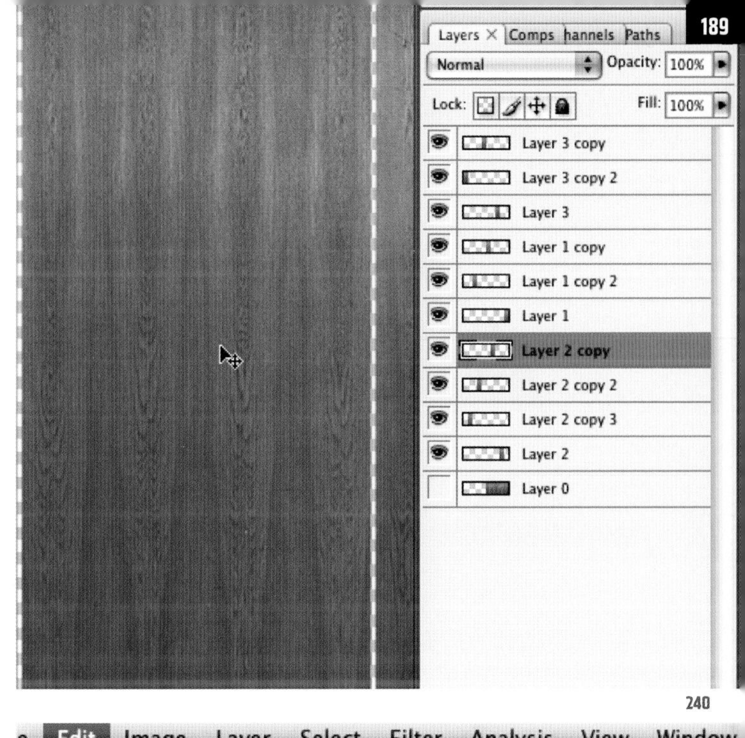

240

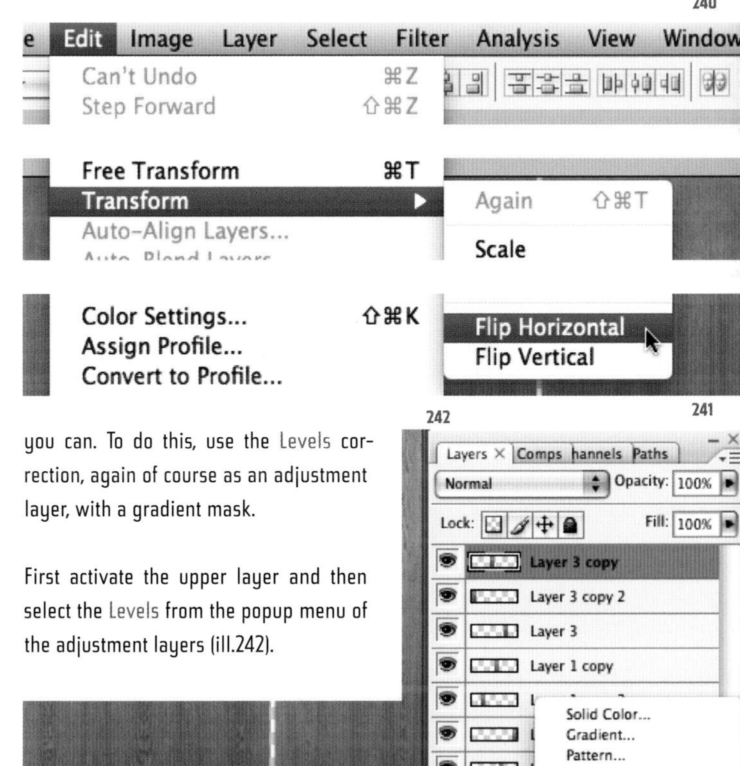

241

242

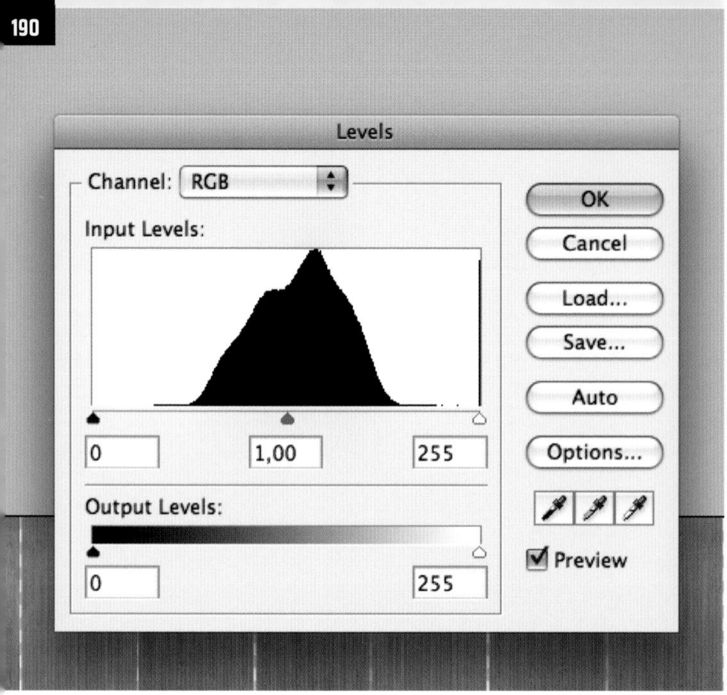

243

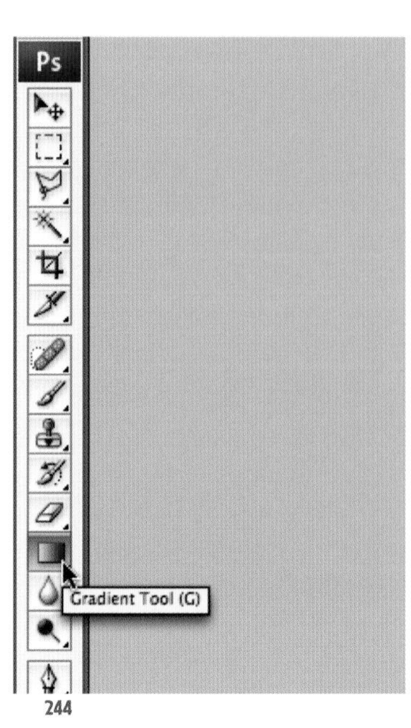

244

245

246

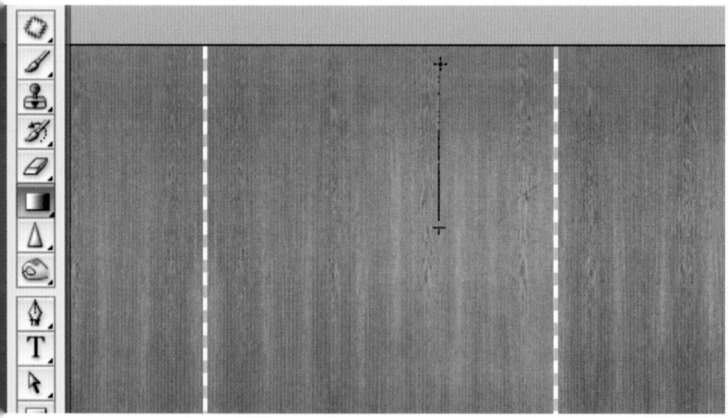

247

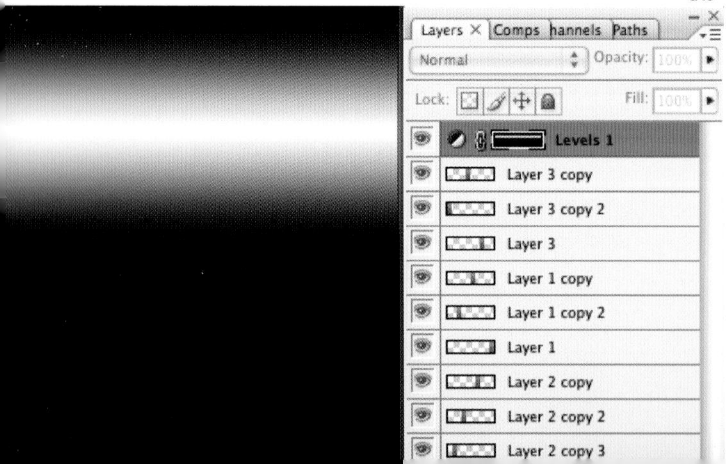

248

Leave the histogram adjustments unchanged for the moment (ill.243). After clicking on OK your adjustment layer is installed and your mask is available to work on.

Now pick the Gradient tool (G, ill.244), select the Reflected Gradient as type (ill.245), and reverse it so that it starts with White and ends with Black (ill.246; assuming of course that you still have the Black, White gradient in use).

Then draw a gradient vector from the lightest spot upwards, to roughly where the reflection on the wood surface ends (ill.247).

Click once in the mask miniature of the adjustment layer with the Alt key held down, to check the result (ill.248), and then switch back to the normal image display with a further Alt-click.

Now double-click in the layer miniature to get to the Levels adjustments again, and move the Gray control under the histogram to the right, till about the value 0.75 (ill.249).

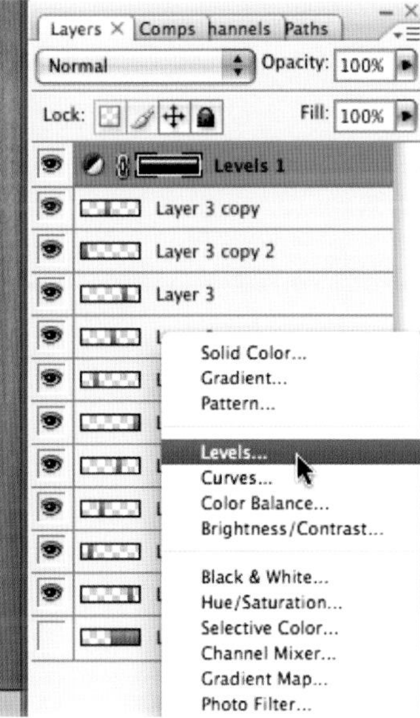

250

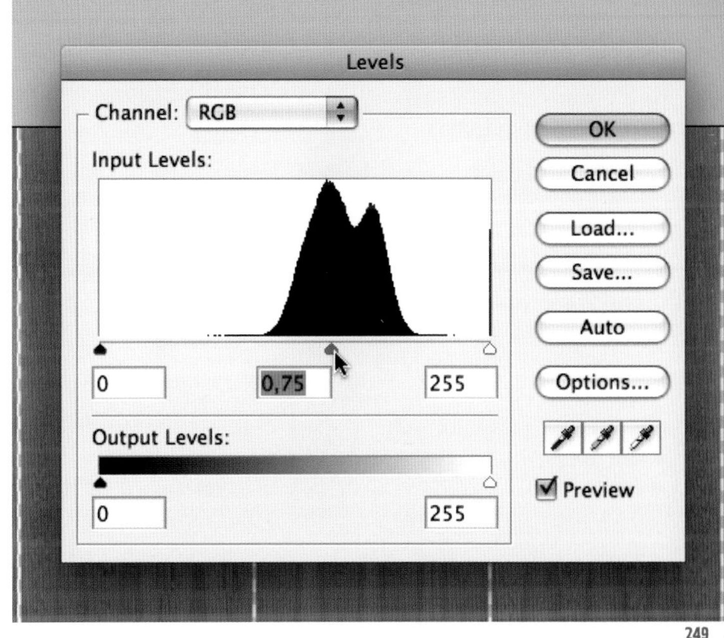

249

In the image you can at the same time follow how the brightness homogenizes on the surfaces.

Should you still not be happy with the result, you can change the gradient. Always start at the same place, but vary the length of the gradient vector.

Now add a further Levels adjustment layer over this one (ill.250), to enhance the contrast in the entire image.

Set the left control of the histogram to 0.50, and the right one to 210 (ill.251).

In addition to the single panels you require a further layer, on which a large wood surface the size of the entire image is visible.

You will later need it for the background. First combine your layers created so far into one group, by marking them (ill.252), and then select the command New Group from Layers from the Layer menu (ill.253).

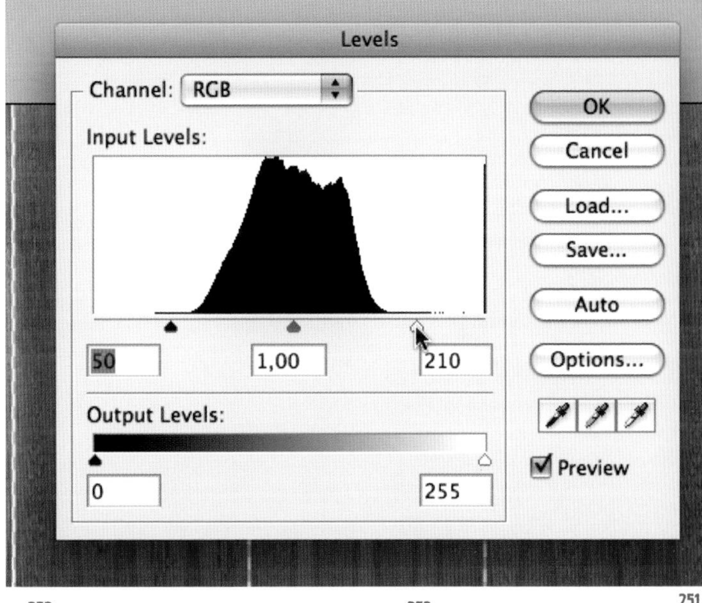

251

252

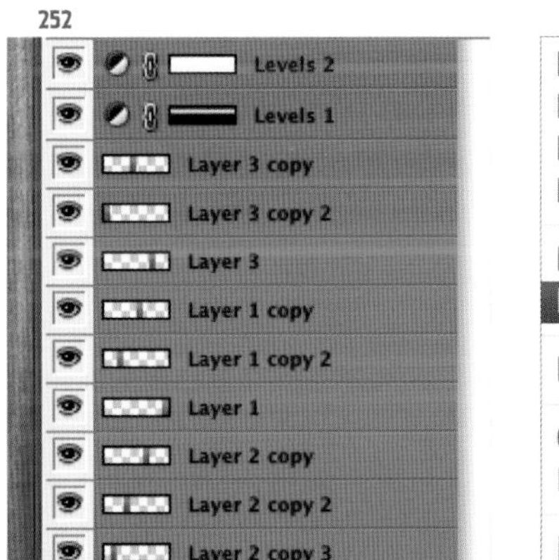

253

New Layer... ⇧⌘N
Duplicate Layers...
Delete Layers
Delete Hidden Layers
New Group...
New Group from Layers...
Lock Layers...
Convert to Smart Object
Edit Contents
Layer Properties...
Blending Options...
Create Clipping Mask ⌥⌘G

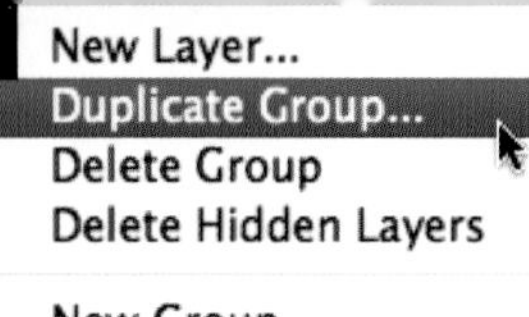

254

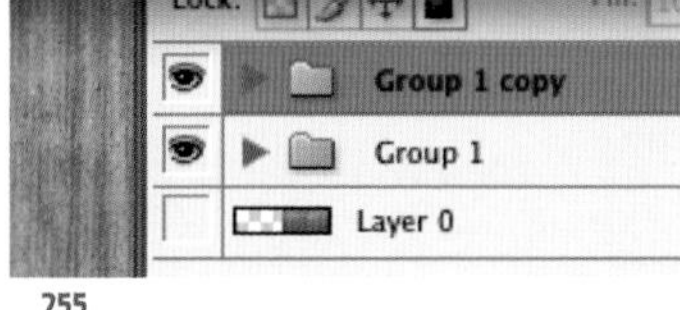

255

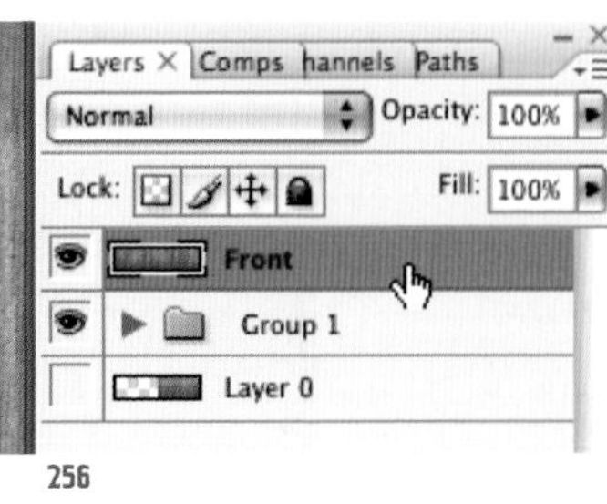

256

Then duplicate this group for the background image (Duplicate Group from the same menu, ill.254).

You can now reduce one of the two groups to one layer, to simplify the later import into your image of the National Gallery, and also because there´s nothing more to do on the individual layers.
The corresponding command is called Merge Group (ill.255). Call the new layer front (ill.256).

Now move together the individual panels, which are still on the layers of the remaining group, with the Move tool (V), so that there´s no longer a gap between them.

This admittedly makes the background surface rather smaller than you need later, but you can compensate for this during composing, by scaling (ill.257).

When you´re finished, also combine these layers into one, again using the command Merge Group (ill.258). Call the new layer back (ill.259).

257

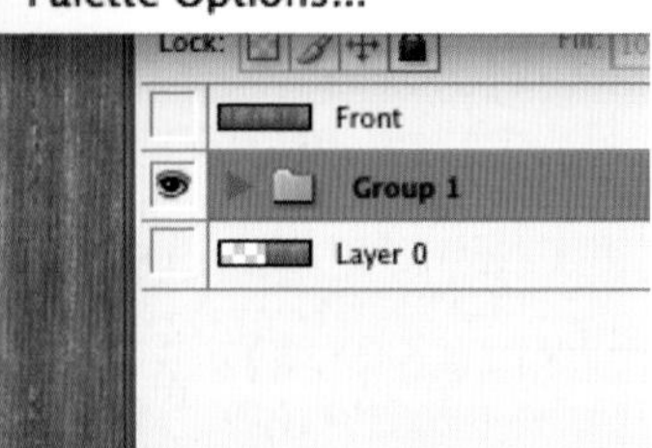

258

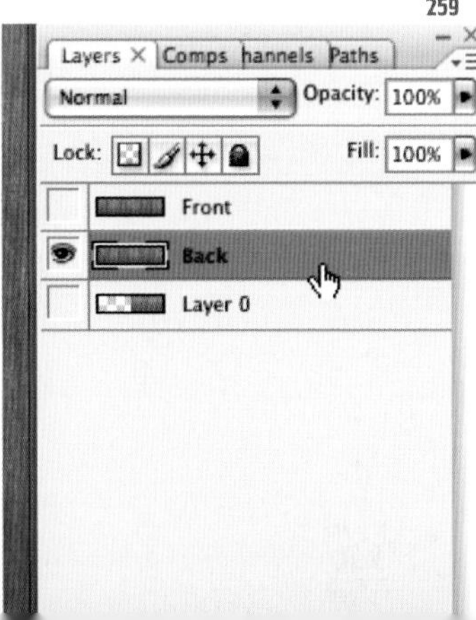

259

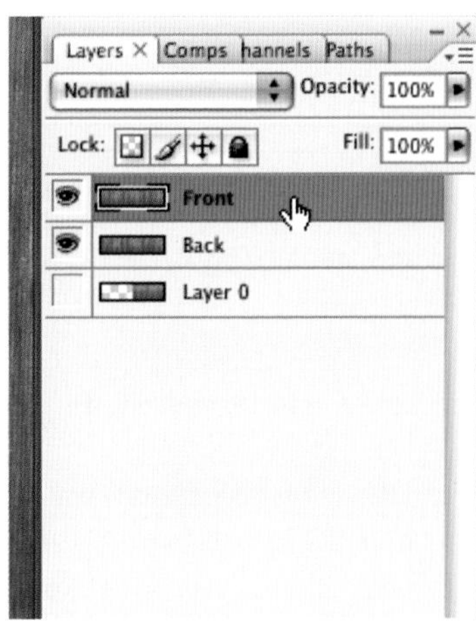

260

As the brightness on the front panels isn´t totally homogeneous, despite your processing further up, rotate it 180° so that the reflection spots are in the bottom range, where later they won´t be so conspicuous in the image.

Activate the layer front (ill.260) and select Transform - Rotate 180° from the Edit

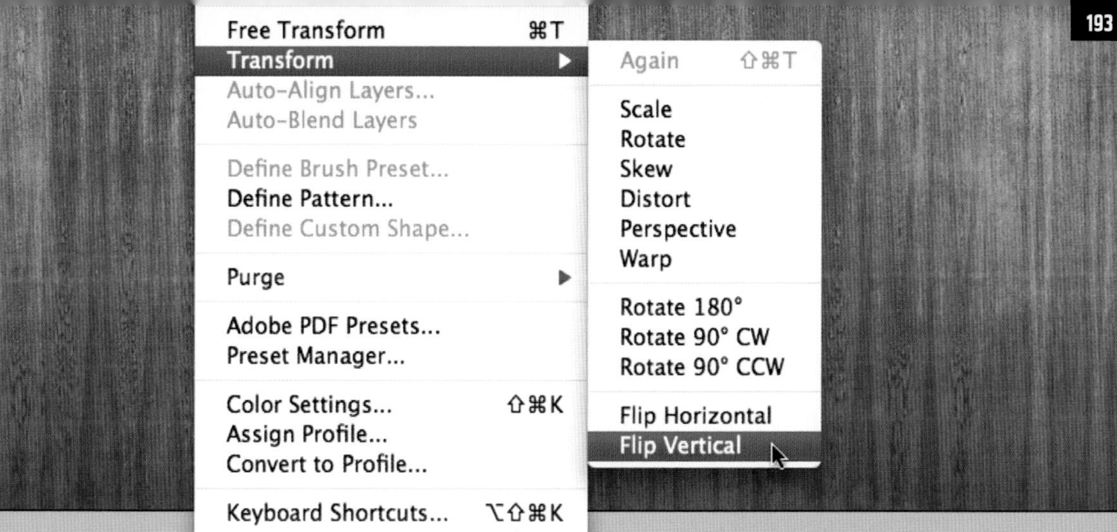

261

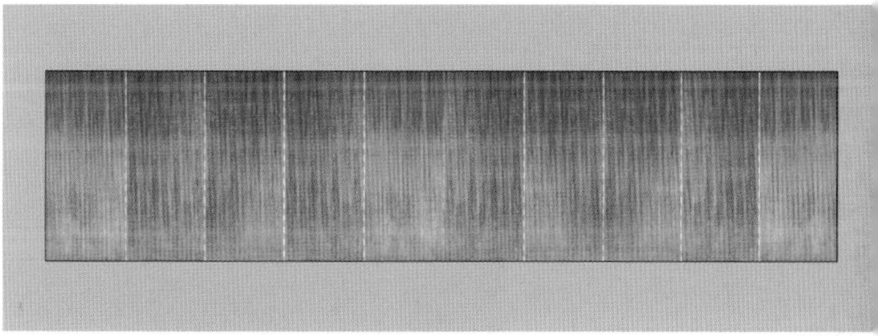

menu (ills.261 and 262). Your wood panel texture is now finished and can be inserted into your large image, so leave the current file open.

Open your large image file 07_ng_persp_edit.psd again, and press F till you can see it in the "classical" window. (You require this to be able to drag image components from one file to another).
Bring your newly processed wood image forward and activate the layer front in the Layers palette (ill.263).

Then with your mouse, drag this layer directly from the Layers palette into your large image of the National Gallery. There it´s inserted as a new layer, which you can move in the Layers palette in such a way that it lies directly over the layer Wardrobe (ill.264). Rename it wood front.

262

263

264

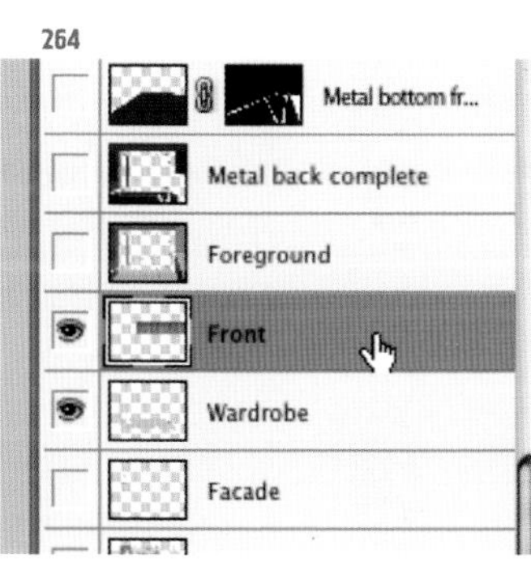

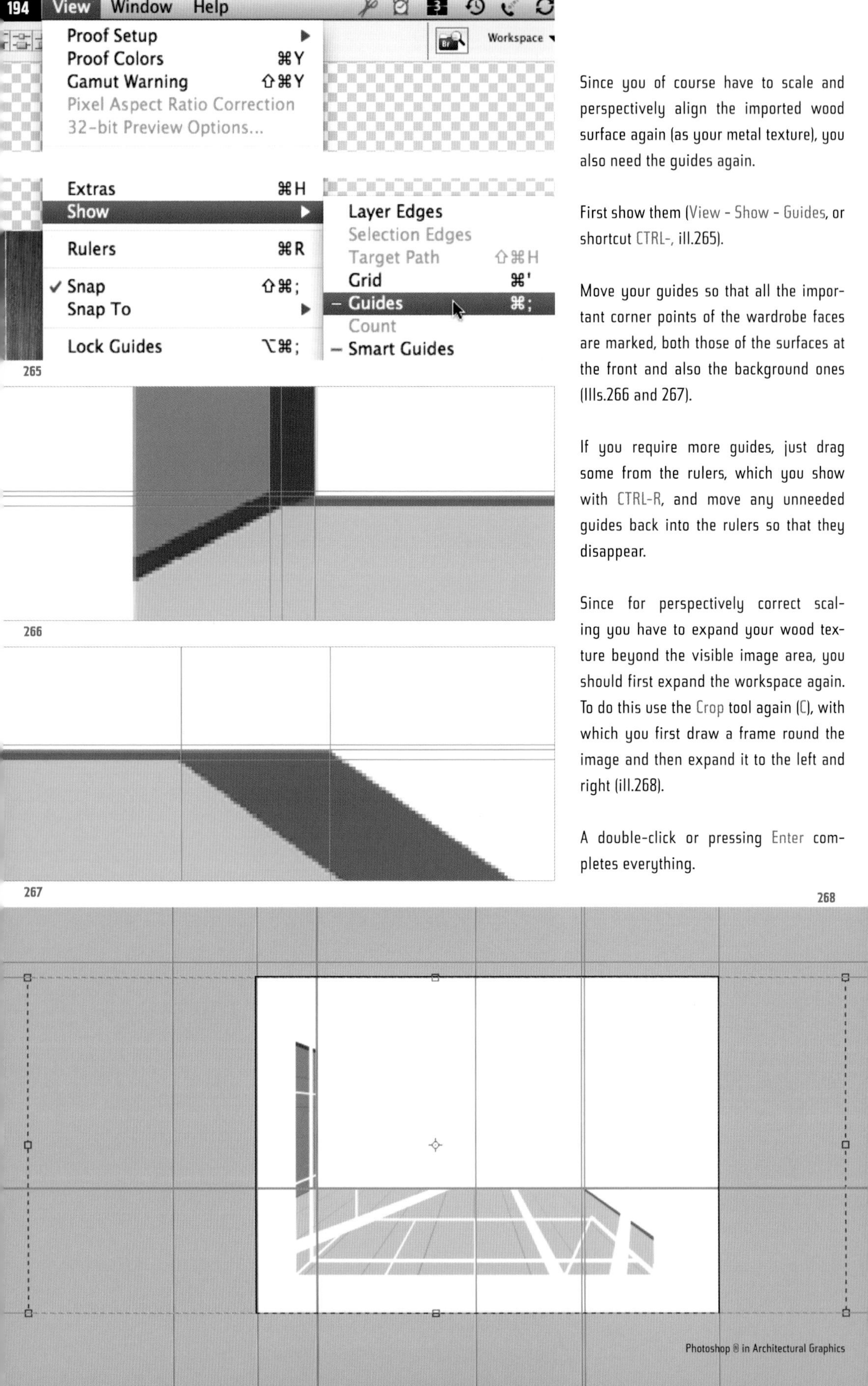

265

266

267

268

Since you of course have to scale and perspectively align the imported wood surface again (as your metal texture), you also need the guides again.

First show them (View - Show - Guides, or shortcut CTRL-, ill.265).

Move your guides so that all the important corner points of the wardrobe faces are marked, both those of the surfaces at the front and also the background ones (Ills.266 and 267).

If you require more guides, just drag some from the rulers, which you show with CTRL-R, and move any unneeded guides back into the rulers so that they disappear.

Since for perspectively correct scaling you have to expand your wood texture beyond the visible image area, you should first expand the workspace again. To do this use the Crop tool again (C), with which you first draw a frame round the image and then expand it to the left and right (ill.268).

A double-click or pressing Enter completes everything.

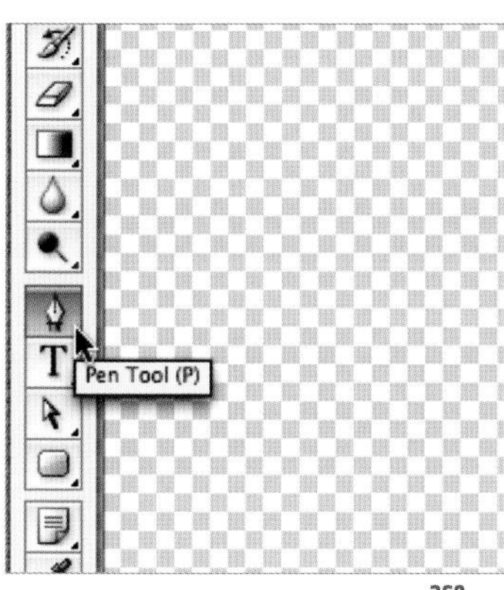

269

270

To find out how big the wood texture has to be before the perspective distortion, you should trace the laterally vanishing edges of the corresponding image parts.

As Photoshop® only offers vertical and horizontal guides, you have to make use of the Pen tool again (P, ill.269).

First deal with the front surfaces in the foreground; draw a line from your upper right corner along your side edge to the lower image border.

Zoom in just close enough to the upper right corner - you'll see that when placing your first point it snaps to the intersection point of the guides

As to the lower point: set it first, and then correct it using the Direct Selection tool (A, ill.270).

Place a horizontal guide somewhere between the lower edge of the color surface depicting the frontal wood surface, and the lower image border.

Then lay a vertical guide through the intersection point which this forms with your newly drawn vanishing line (ill.271).

Do the same on the left side. As you´ve now already decided on your lower image border, draw the vanishing line only to this horizontal guide (ill.272).

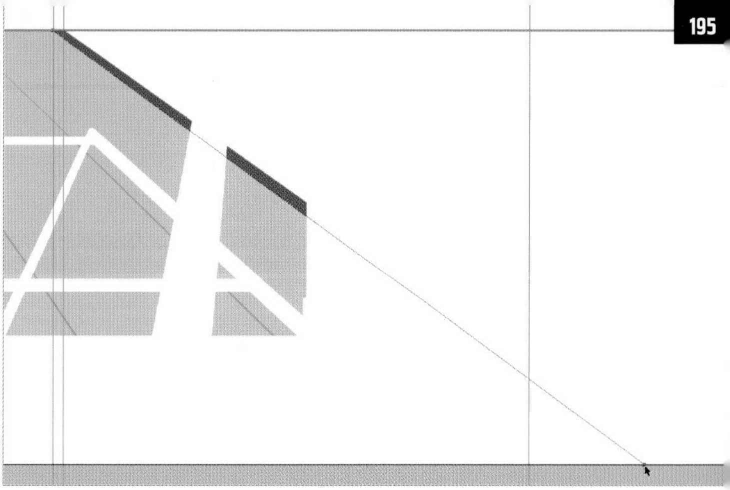

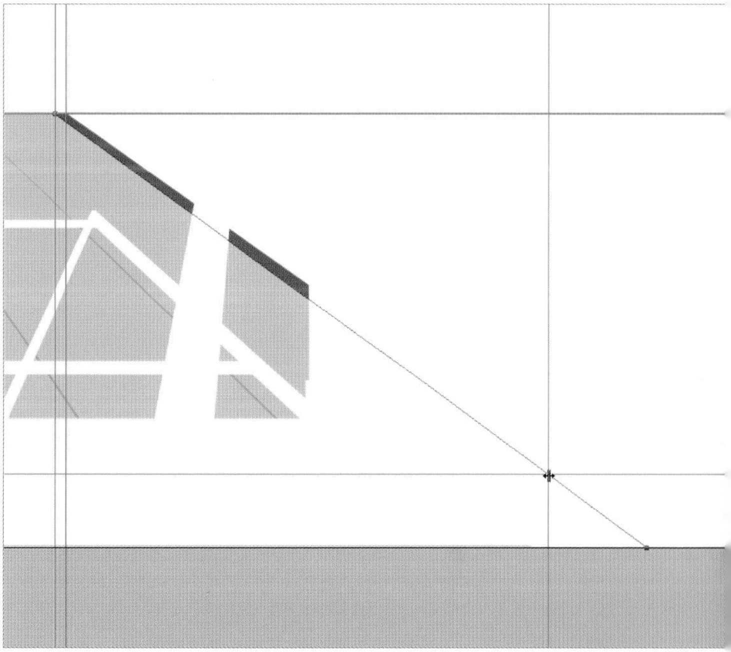

271

272

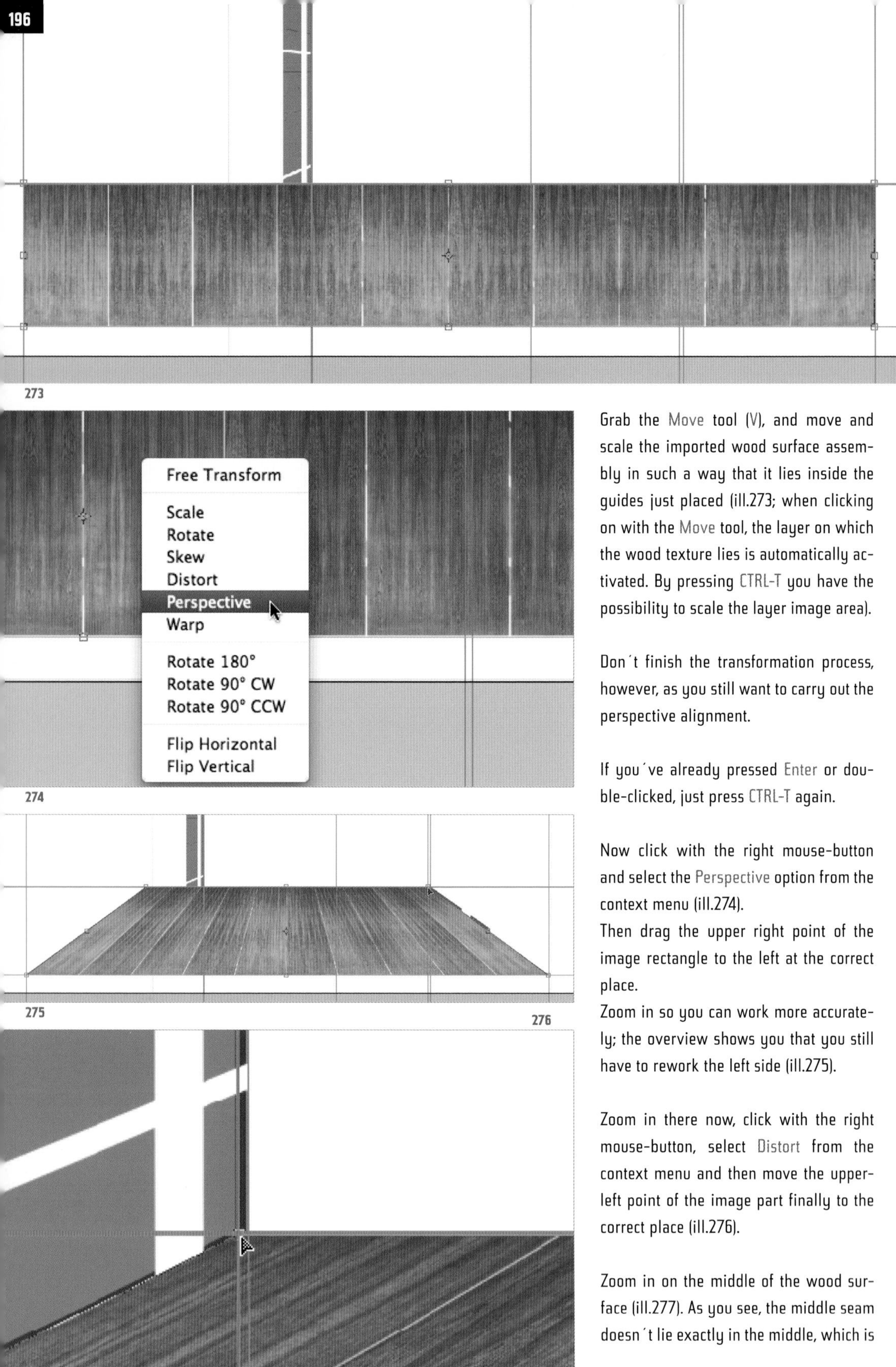

273

274

275

276

Grab the Move tool (V), and move and scale the imported wood surface assembly in such a way that it lies inside the guides just placed (ill.273; when clicking on with the Move tool, the layer on which the wood texture lies is automatically activated. By pressing CTRL-T you have the possibility to scale the layer image area).

Don´t finish the transformation process, however, as you still want to carry out the perspective alignment.

If you´ve already pressed Enter or double-clicked, just press CTRL-T again.

Now click with the right mouse-button and select the Perspective option from the context menu (ill.274).
Then drag the upper right point of the image rectangle to the left at the correct place.
Zoom in so you can work more accurately; the overview shows you that you still have to rework the left side (ill.275).

Zoom in there now, click with the right mouse-button, select Distort from the context menu and then move the upper-left point of the image part finally to the correct place (ill.276).

Zoom in on the middle of the wood surface (ill.277). As you see, the middle seam doesn´t lie exactly in the middle, which is displayed by a guide (if you don´t have a guide there, switch your wood front layer into the blending mode Multiply, then you see your CAAD faces under it).

To get the seam in the middle, tug at the four corner points of your transformation frame till the middle seam lies exactly in the middle and is vertically aligned (ill.278).

As you´ve thus dragged your image at the sides beyond the border of the wardrobe area, it´s worth masking the image at the end, but first close the transformation by double-clicking or pressing the Enter key, then select the polygonal lasso (L, or Shift-L, ill.279).

"Trace" the framing of the wardrobe surface with it.

This is best done by hiding the wood layer and leaving only the CAAD layer Wardrobe visible (ill.280; after pressing Q the selection is depicted here as a mask).

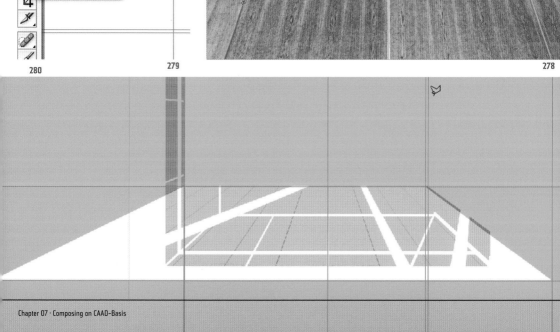

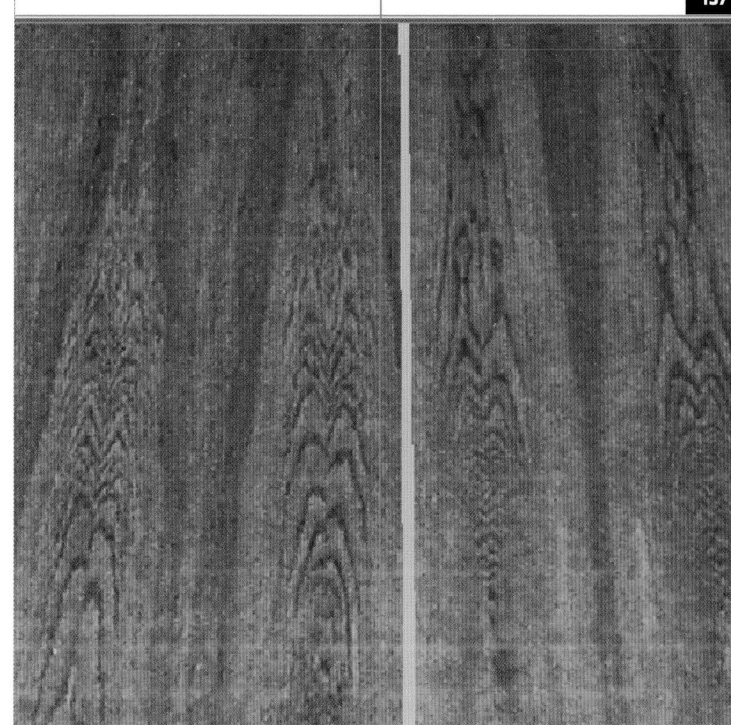

277

278

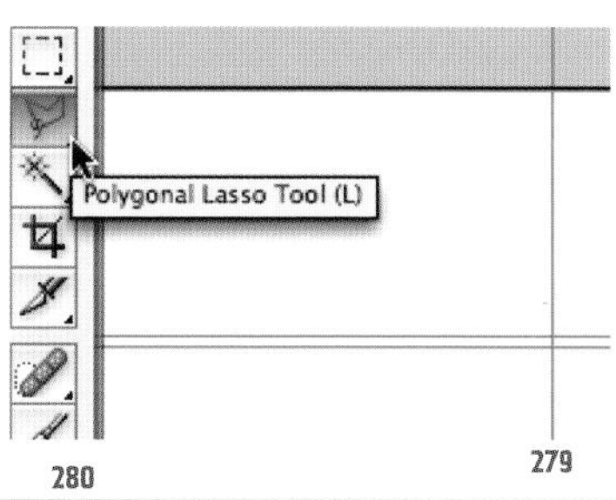

279

280

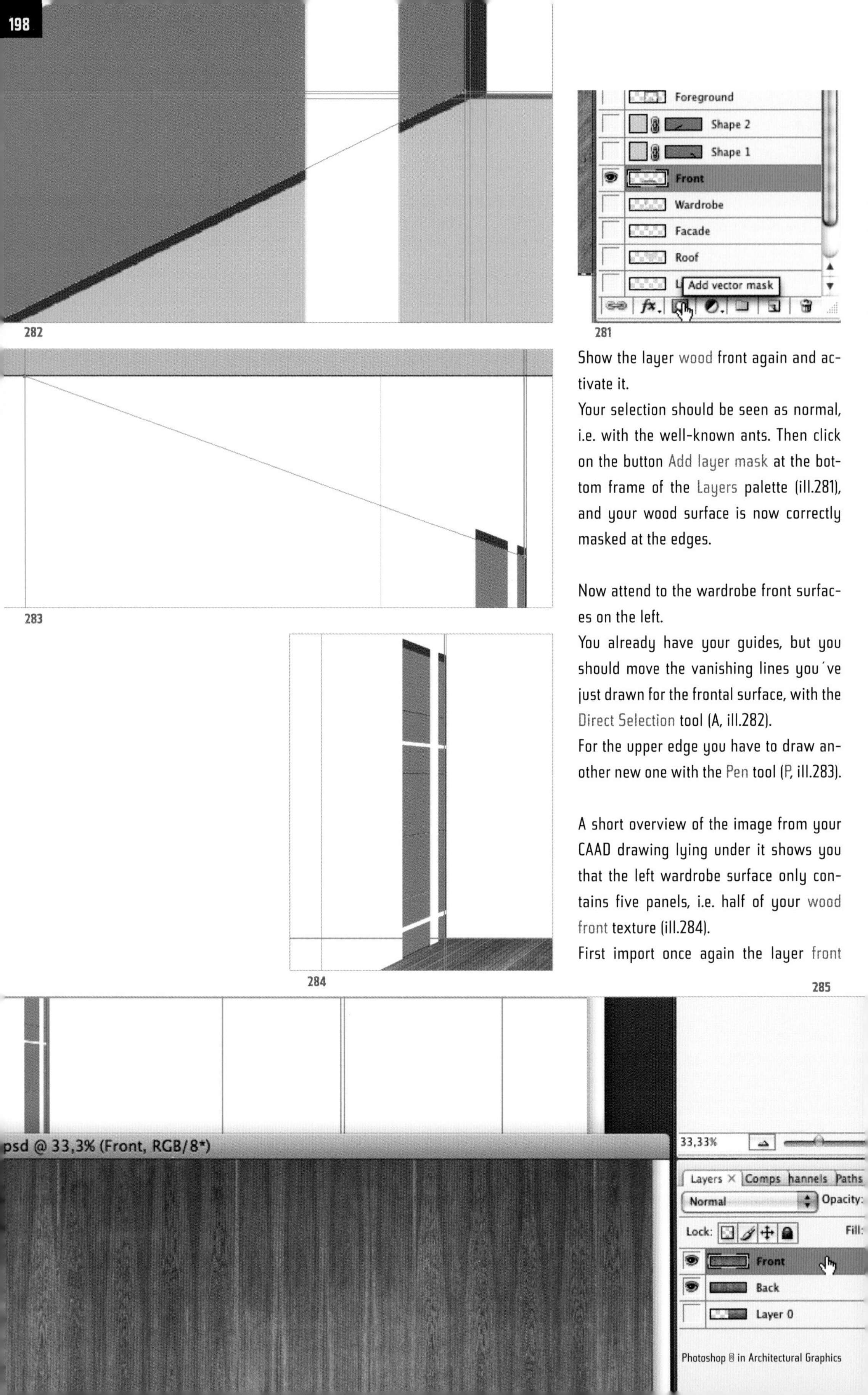

282

283

284

281

Show the layer wood front again and activate it.

Your selection should be seen as normal, i.e. with the well-known ants. Then click on the button Add layer mask at the bottom frame of the Layers palette (ill.281), and your wood surface is now correctly masked at the edges.

Now attend to the wardrobe front surfaces on the left.

You already have your guides, but you should move the vanishing lines you´ve just drawn for the frontal surface, with the Direct Selection tool (A, ill.282).

For the upper edge you have to draw another new one with the Pen tool (P, ill.283).

A short overview of the image from your CAAD drawing lying under it shows you that the left wardrobe surface only contains five panels, i.e. half of your wood front texture (ill.284).

First import once again the layer front

285

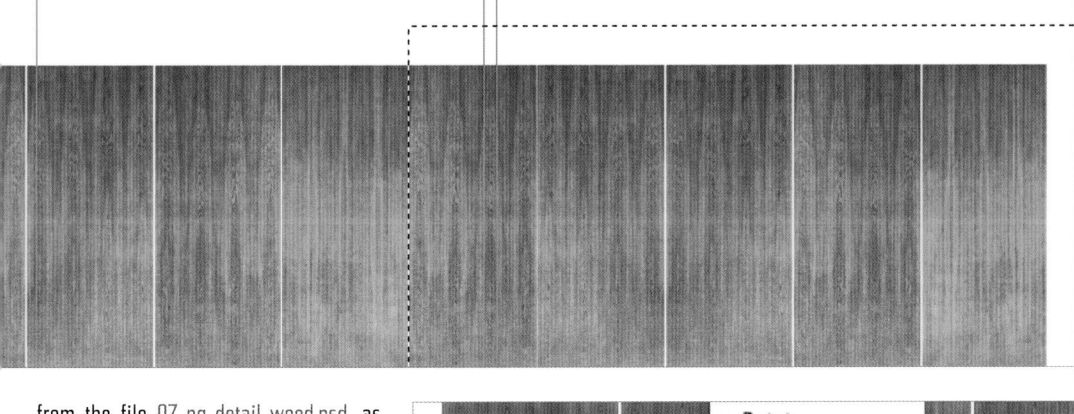

286

from the file 07_ng_detail_wood.psd, as you´ve already done once before (ill.285; for this you again have to temporarily see your picture files in the normal window display.
Press F several times if necessary).

After importing, press F twice again to see your image of the National Gallery on the gray background.
Then select half of the newly imported wood texture with the Rectangular Marquee tool (M, ill.286), making sure the transparent strip on the left side is also fully selected. If required, zoom in and move your ant rectangle by means of the arrow keys, then delete the part selected.

Activate the transformation mode for the new wood texture (CTRL-T), and after a right-click select the Rotate option from the context menu (ill.287).
Rotate the texture using the Shift key so that the rotation is exactly 90°.

Move the texture in such a way that one of your corner points lies on an intersection point of the corresponding guides. You don´t have to take the Move tool for this, as in the transformation mode you can just drag image parts with the mouse.

Having moved it to the right place, select the option Scale from the context menu (ill.288), and then enlarge the texture so that it fills the corresponding guides rectangle (ill.289).

Rotate
Skew
Distort
Perspective
Warp
Rotate 180°
Rotate 90° CW
Rotate 90° CCW
Flip Horizontal
Flip Vertical

287

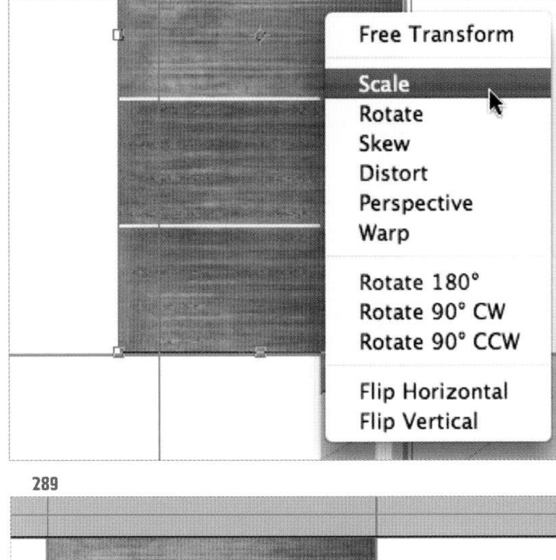

288

289

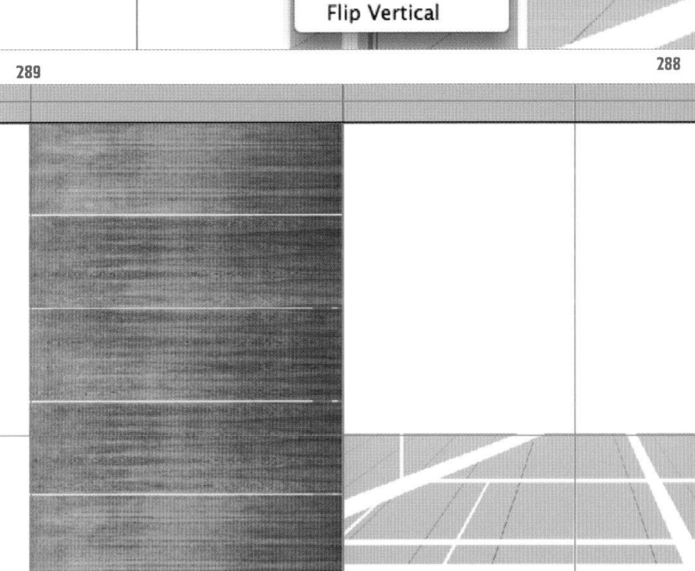

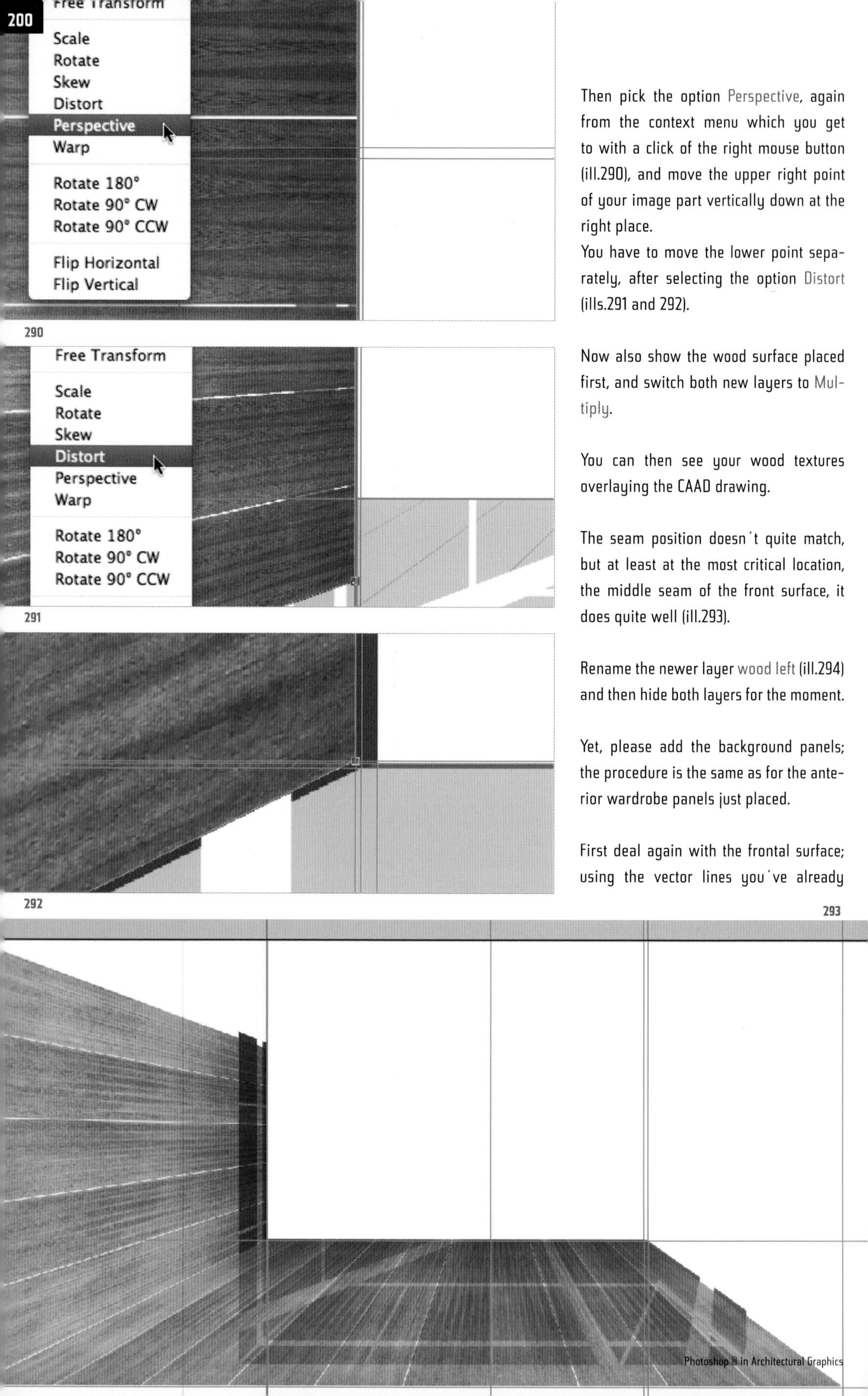

290

291

292

Then pick the option Perspective, again from the context menu which you get to with a click of the right mouse button (ill.290), and move the upper right point of your image part vertically down at the right place.
You have to move the lower point separately, after selecting the option Distort (ills.291 and 292).

Now also show the wood surface placed first, and switch both new layers to Multiply.

You can then see your wood textures overlaying the CAAD drawing.

The seam position doesn´t quite match, but at least at the most critical location, the middle seam of the front surface, it does quite well (ill.293).

Rename the newer layer wood left (ill.294) and then hide both layers for the moment.

Yet, please add the background panels; the procedure is the same as for the anterior wardrobe panels just placed.

First deal again with the frontal surface; using the vector lines you´ve already

293

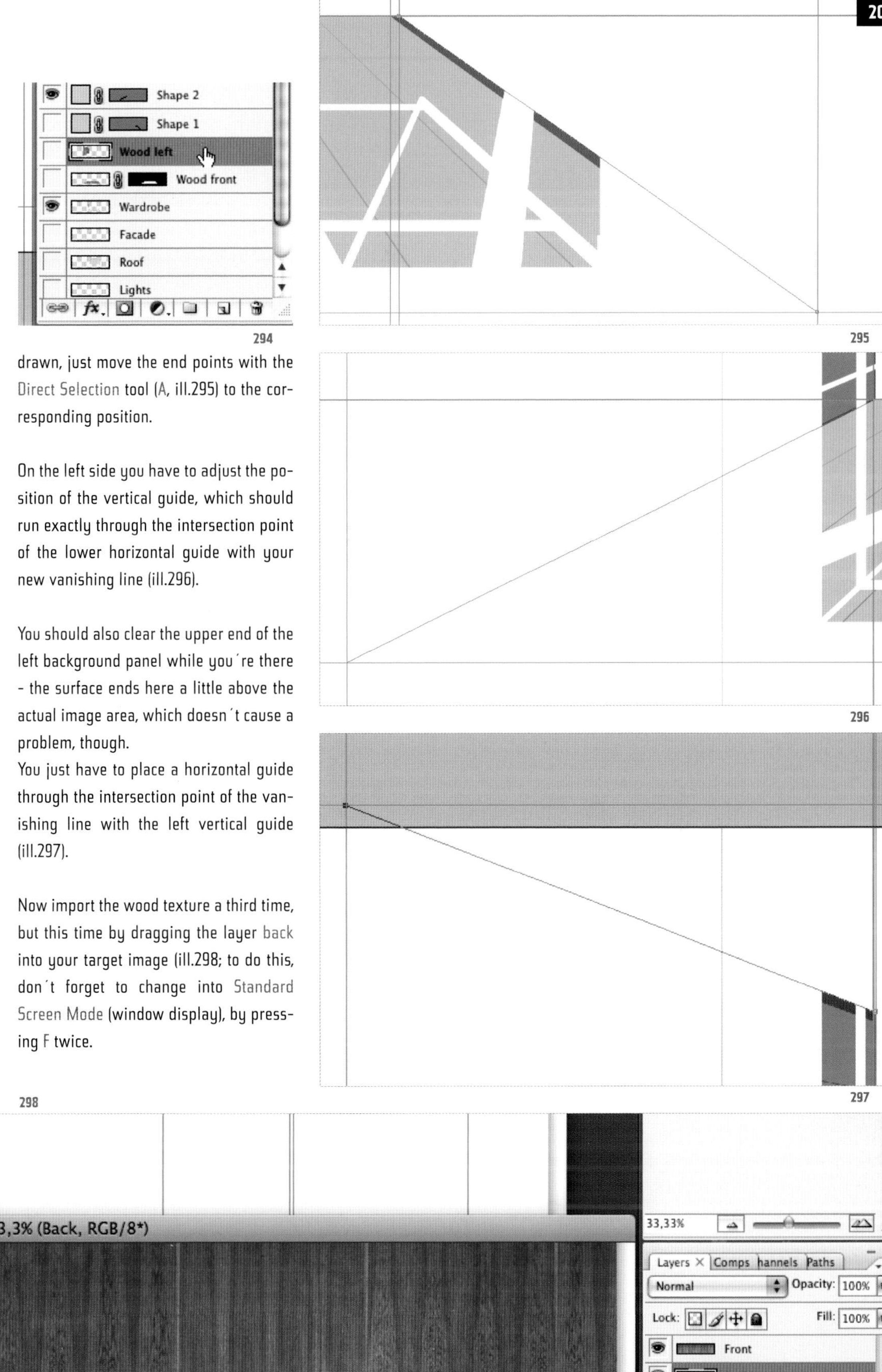

294

295

drawn, just move the end points with the Direct Selection tool (A, ill.295) to the corresponding position.

On the left side you have to adjust the position of the vertical guide, which should run exactly through the intersection point of the lower horizontal guide with your new vanishing line (ill.296).

296

You should also clear the upper end of the left background panel while you´re there - the surface ends here a little above the actual image area, which doesn´t cause a problem, though.
You just have to place a horizontal guide through the intersection point of the vanishing line with the left vertical guide (ill.297).

Now import the wood texture a third time, but this time by dragging the layer back into your target image (ill.298; to do this, don´t forget to change into Standard Screen Mode (window display), by pressing F twice.

297

298

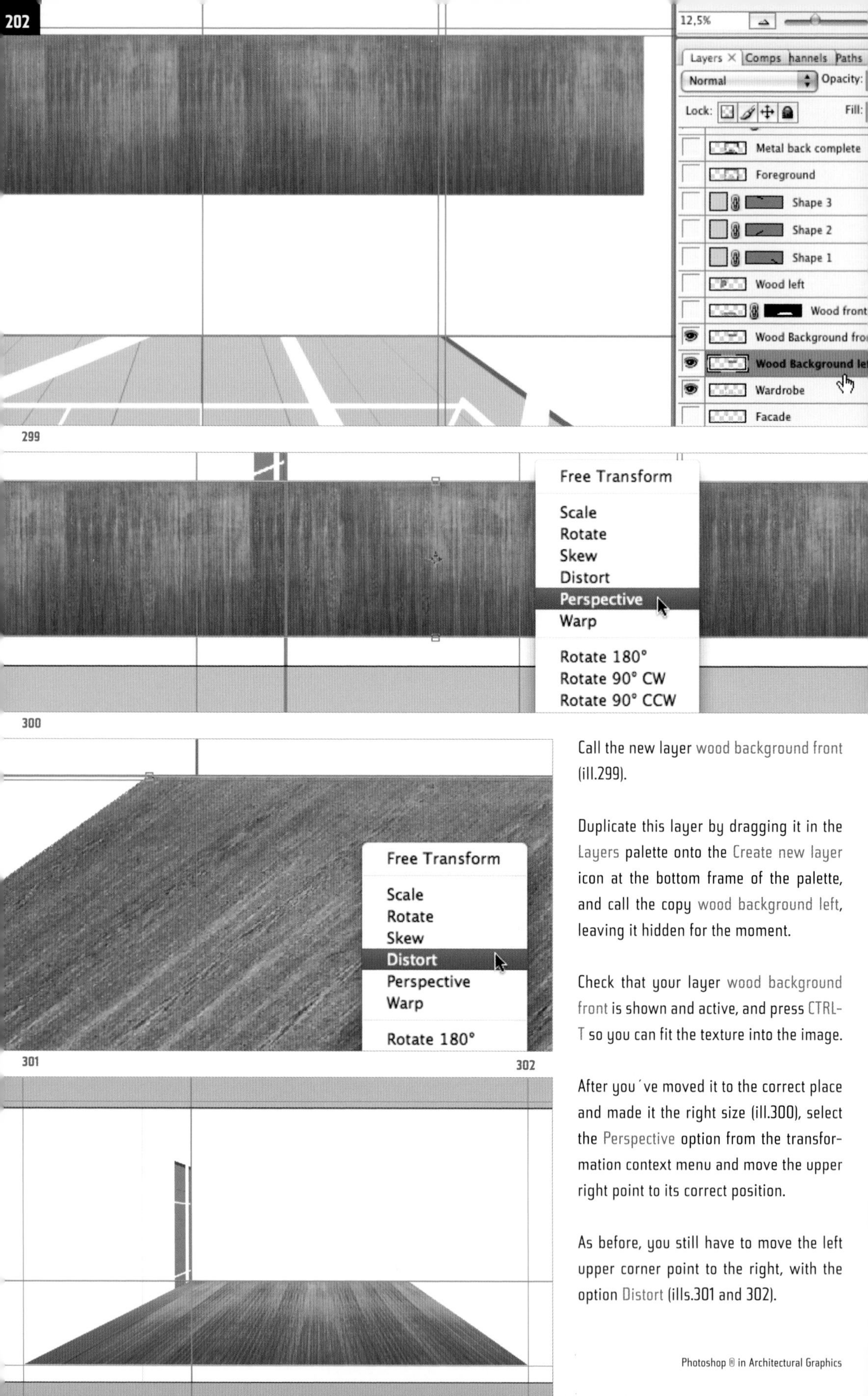

299

300

301

302

Call the new layer wood background front (ill.299).

Duplicate this layer by dragging it in the Layers palette onto the Create new layer icon at the bottom frame of the palette, and call the copy wood background left, leaving it hidden for the moment.

Check that your layer wood background front is shown and active, and press CTRL-T so you can fit the texture into the image.

After you´ve moved it to the correct place and made it the right size (ill.300), select the Perspective option from the transformation context menu and move the upper right point to its correct position.

As before, you still have to move the left upper corner point to the right, with the option Distort (ills.301 and 302).

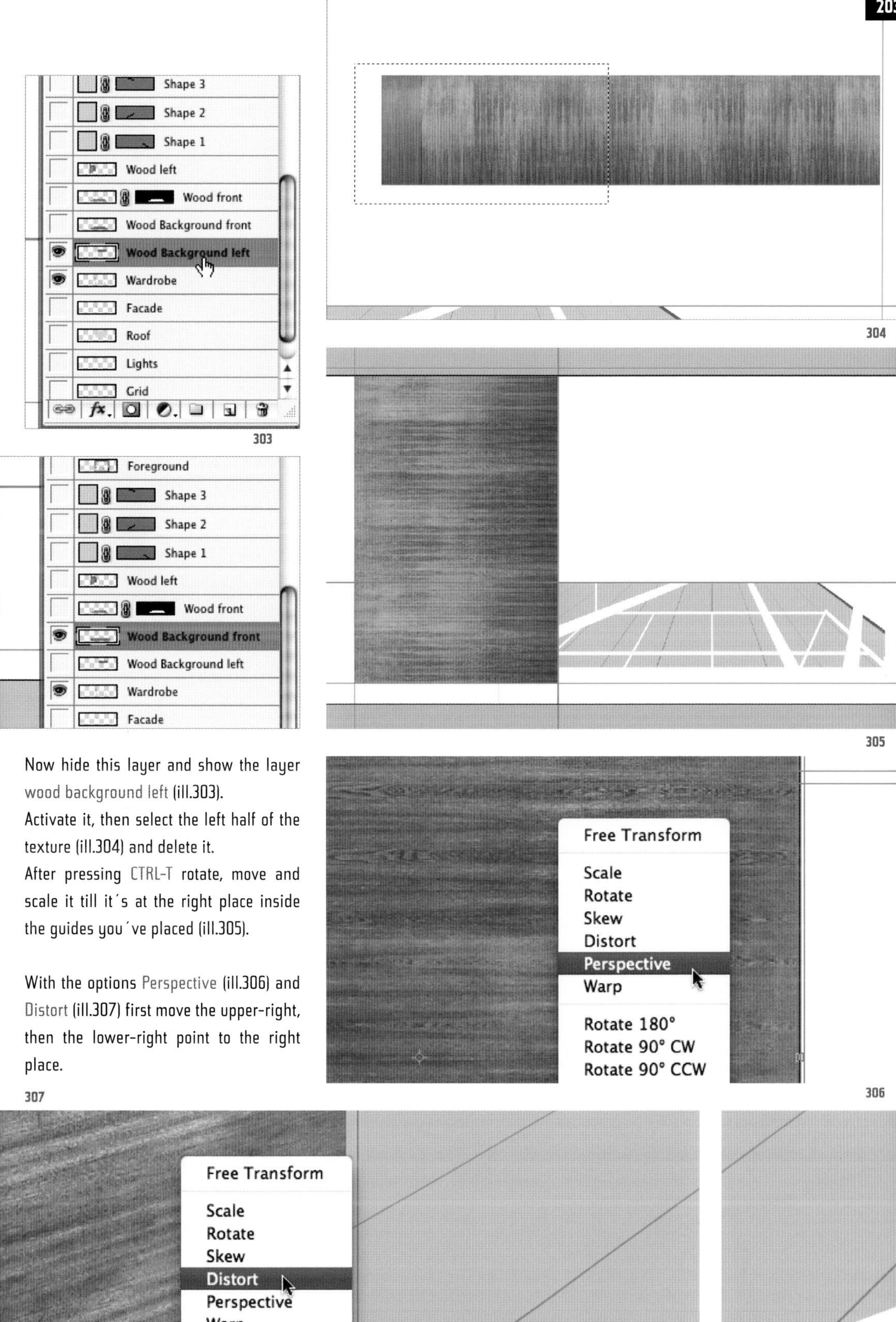

303

304

305

Now hide this layer and show the layer wood background left (ill.303).
Activate it, then select the left half of the texture (ill.304) and delete it.
After pressing CTRL-T rotate, move and scale it till it´s at the right place inside the guides you´ve placed (ill.305).

With the options Perspective (ill.306) and Distort (ill.307) first move the upper-right, then the lower-right point to the right place.

306

307

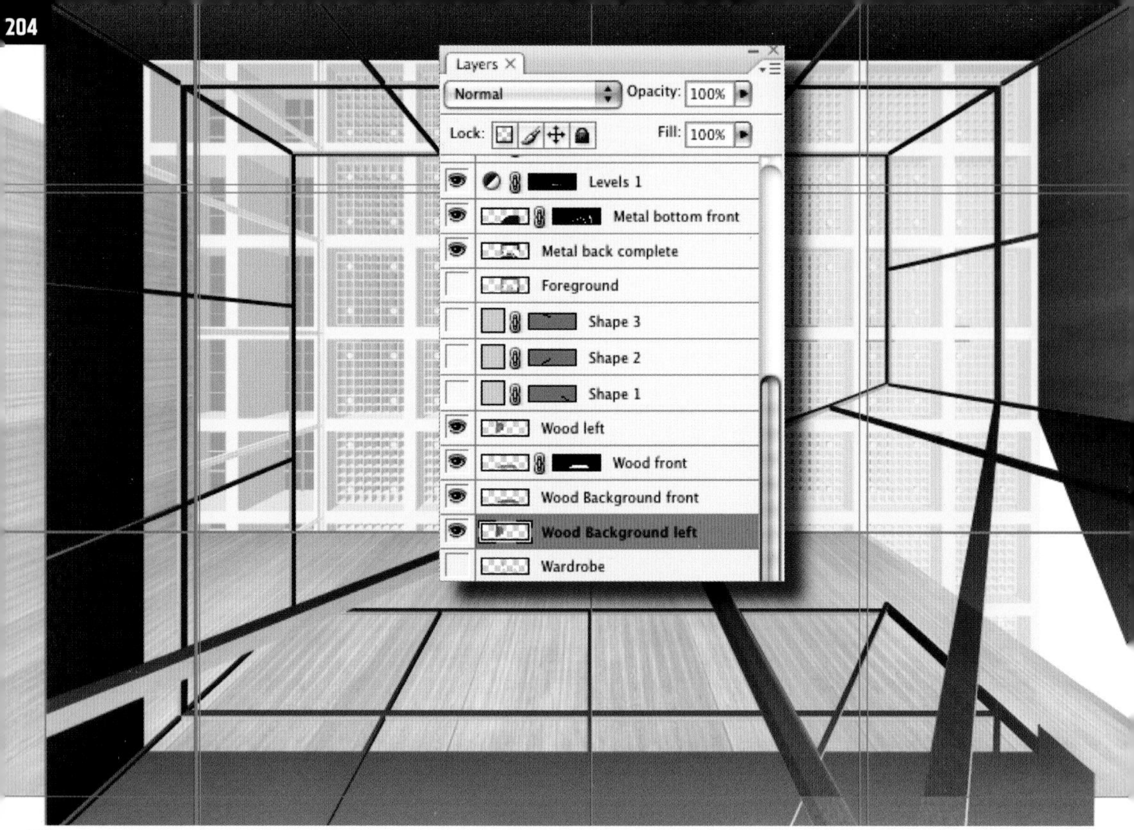

308

309

310

Now show all four new wood layers, and hide the Wardrobe layer. Show all the other image layers too, to get an overview of what you´ve achieved so far (ill.308).

Before continuing crop the image again, however, with the Crop tool (C).

Hide the rulers with CTRL-R, and the guides with CTRL-, (ill.309).

You no longer need the three Shape layers created when drawing the vanishing lines with the Pen tool, so select them with the Shift key held down (ill.310), and drag them to the trash of the Layers palette to delete them.

Now it´s slowly but surely time to attend a little to clarity and an overview in the Layers palette. In the meantime there´s quite a mess, which may also lead to unwanted effects.
It makes sense that the metal surfaces lie over the wood surfaces, but it's no use

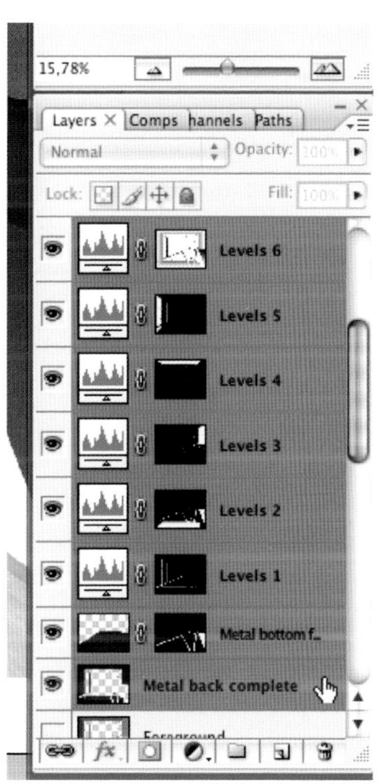

311

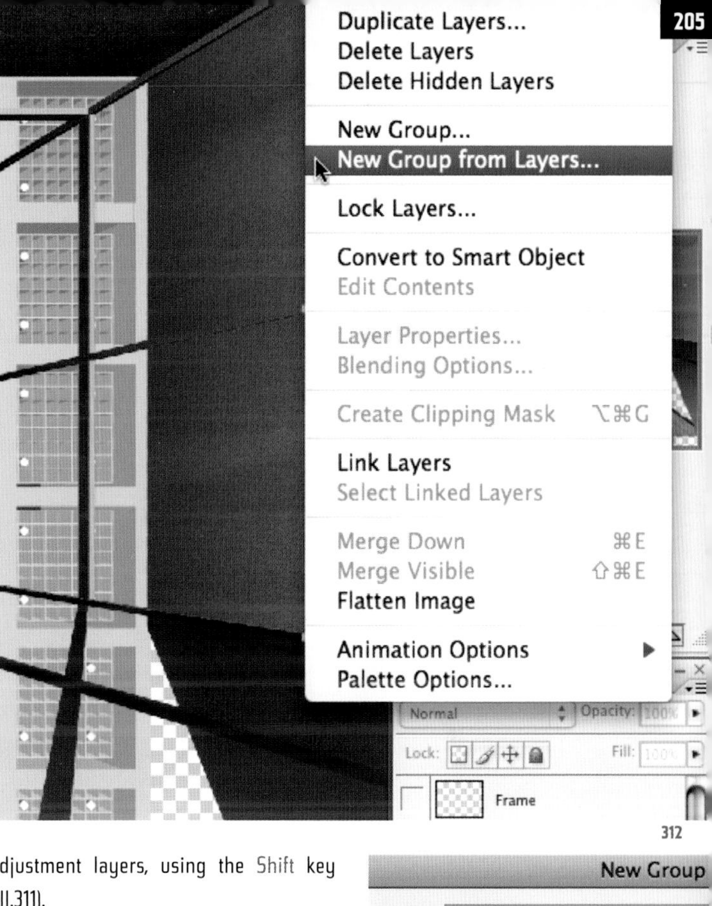

312

their Levels adjustments brighten up our wood surfaces too.

You could group the corresponding adjustment layers with one of the metal layers to avoid this, but for that you´d then have to combine both metal layers into one, which you again would rather not do.

The best way, due to the desired overview, is that you create layer groups for your image file, first for the metal surfaces.

To do this, mark the two corresponding layers and all the associated Levels adjustment layers, using the Shift key (ill.311).

Then select the command New Group from Layers from the popup menu of the Layers palette (ill.312), and in the adjustment dialog for the new group select the name metal. Change the blending mode to Normal (ill.313).

After pressing the OK button, you see the image change.

The metal surfaces´ brightness is differentiated as before, but the wood surfaces are not affected any more (ill.314).

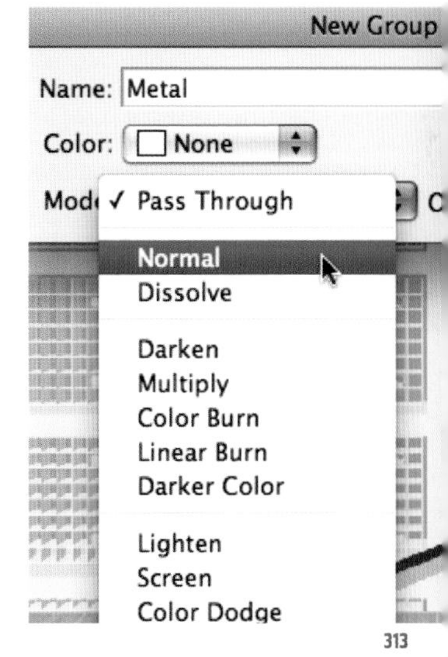

313

314

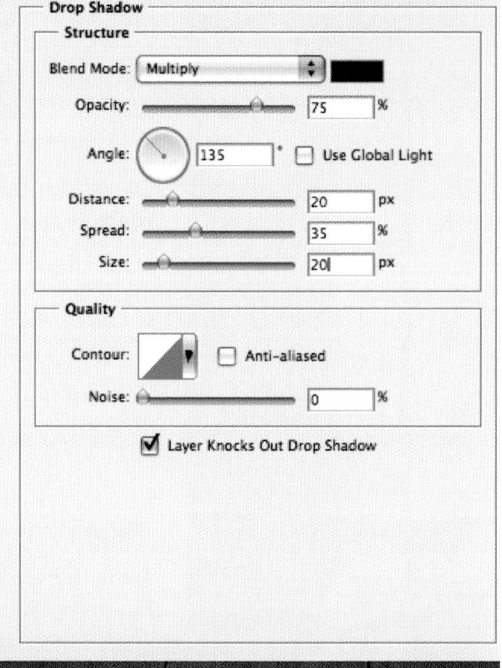

316

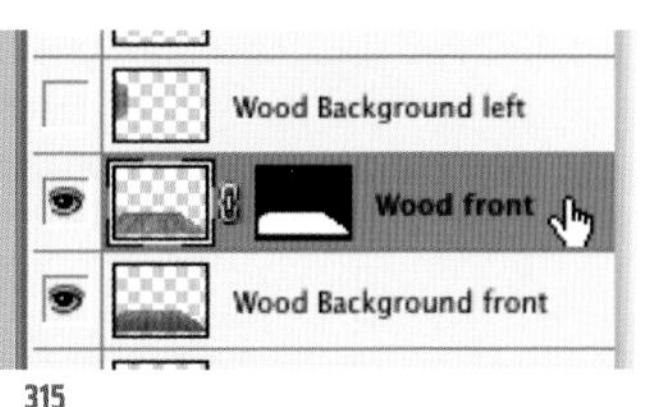

315

317

318

Obviously the effect of adjustment layers is limited to the image layers stacked in the same group when the blending mode of the group is set at Normal.

Before you also combine the wood layer into one group, we want to allocate another brightness gradient to it. Moreover, you can make the surfaces look a little bit more 3D with a simple trick, by using the Layer Style Drop Shadow on the two layers showing the respective foreground panels.

Concentrate first on the two frontal surfaces on the layer wood front and wood background front. Leave only these two shown, and if you want, the white background layer.
Then double-click in the Layers palette on the layer wood front, in the area to the right beside the layer mask miniature (ill.315).

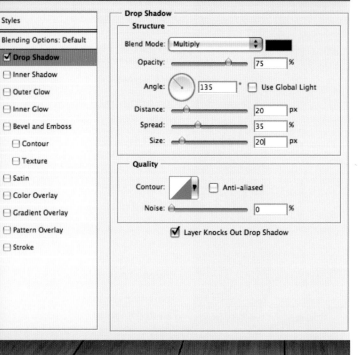

An adjustment dialog opens, in which you can decide on one or several styles for this layer.

Click on the entry Drop Shadow in the left column at the top (directly on the word, ill.316).
This effect is then activated, and you can carry out on the right side the apt adjustments.

First deactivate the Use Global Light option, so that you are allowed to choose an individual light direction for each of the foreground wood layers.
Now please set the Angle to 135°, the Distance to 20 px, Spread to 35 px and the Size again to 20 px, leaving the other values as they are.

In the preview you see the result, a soft cast shadow, which causes the front panels appear a little detached from their background.

Confirm with OK and check in the Layers palette. There you see your effect displayed under the actual layer entry, whose adjustments you can, by the way, tune at any time by a double-click on its name.

As you´re satisfied, however, and want order in the Layers palette, click on the right on the small arrow beside the layer style symbol (ill.317), so that the effect list collapses.

Repeat all this for the left wood surfaces, showing them and hiding the ones you´ve just worked on, and then double-click in the entry of the layer wood left (ill.318).

In the adjustment dialog for the layer style, select again the Drop Shadow (click directly on the words Drop Shadow) and as before set the Distance to 20 px, Spread to 35 px and the Size to 20 px.

As the Use Global Light option is deactivated (or should be), you can now enter another Angle at this place, namely 45° (ill.319).

Confirm with OK, and also now fold the effect entry in the Layers palette by clicking on the small arrow on the right beside the effect symbol of the layer wood left (ill.320).

Now you´ll attend to a nice brightness gradient on the wood surfaces, separately for the front and the left wood surface.

In each case you´ll use for this a Levels adjustment layer, whose mask you give a gradient. You save work if you mask the Levels correction before pasting the gradient onto one of the two wood surfaces. First deal with the front part.

For "instant"-masking your first Levels adjustment layer, you need a selection of the front wood surface.

For simplicity´s sake, click in the layer miniature of the layer wood background front with the CTRL key held down; in the image you see the selection.

Now ensure that your uppermost wood layer is activated, and select the Levels from the adjustment layer menu of the Layers palette (ill.321).

In the histogram, set the Gray control to 2.00, which at first greatly brightens up the frontal wood surfaces (ill.322).

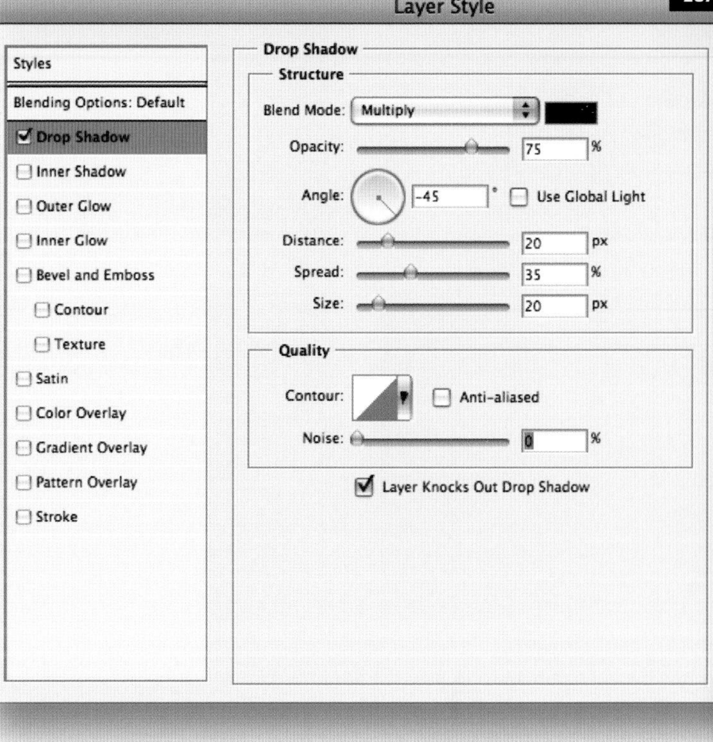

319

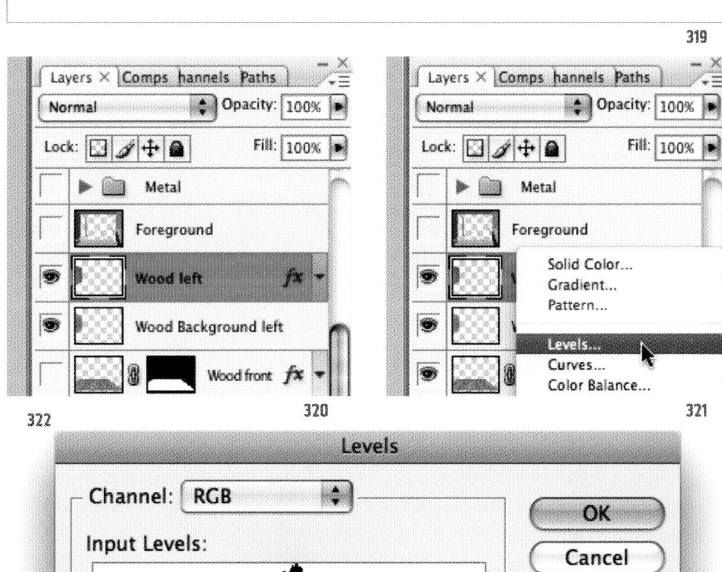

322 320 321

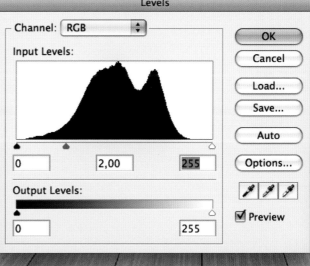

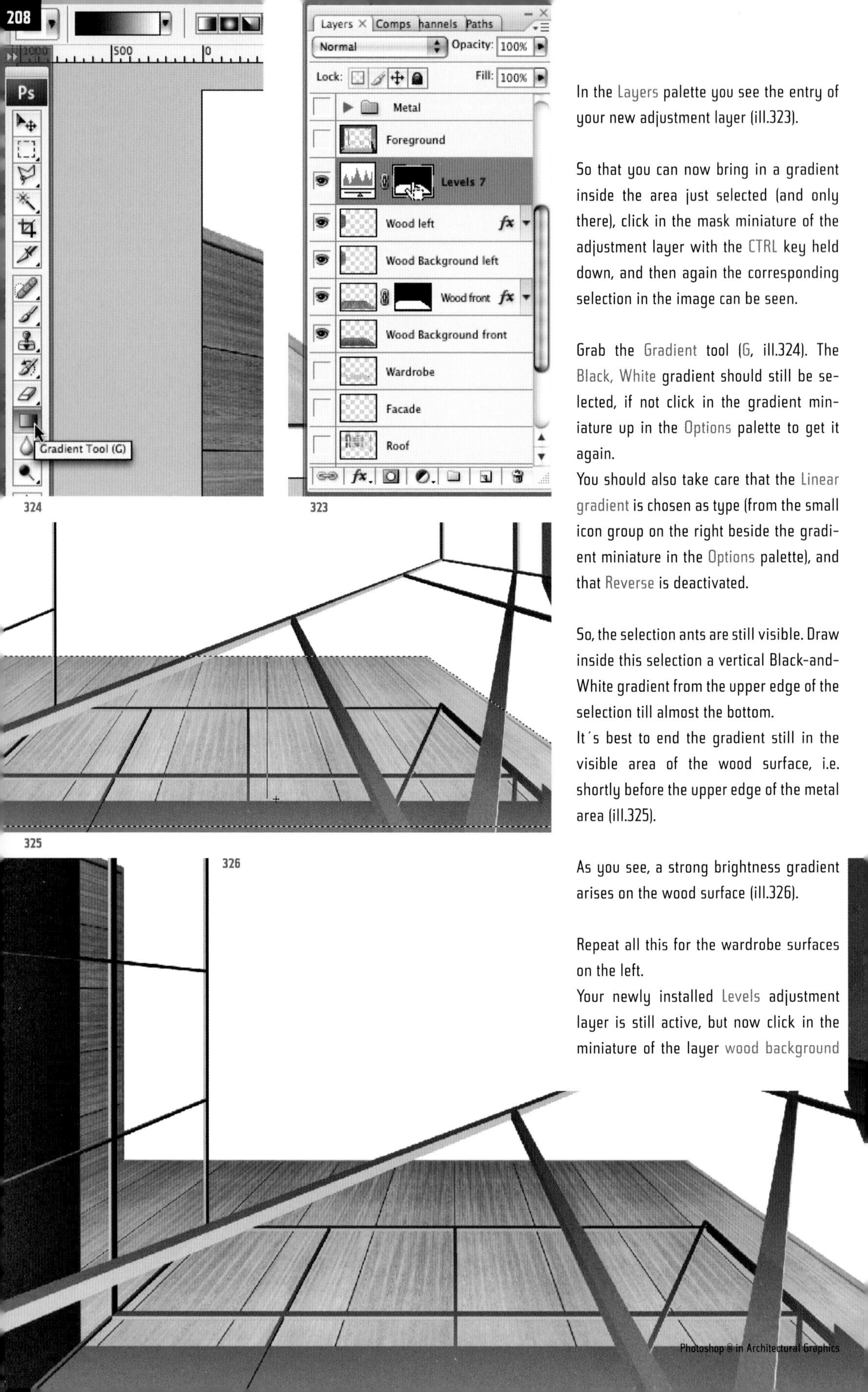

324

323

In the Layers palette you see the entry of your new adjustment layer (ill.323).

So that you can now bring in a gradient inside the area just selected (and only there), click in the mask miniature of the adjustment layer with the CTRL key held down, and then again the corresponding selection in the image can be seen.

Grab the Gradient tool (G, ill.324). The Black, White gradient should still be selected, if not click in the gradient miniature up in the Options palette to get it again.
You should also take care that the Linear gradient is chosen as type (from the small icon group on the right beside the gradient miniature in the Options palette), and that Reverse is deactivated.

So, the selection ants are still visible. Draw inside this selection a vertical Black-and-White gradient from the upper edge of the selection till almost the bottom.
It´s best to end the gradient still in the visible area of the wood surface, i.e. shortly before the upper edge of the metal area (ill.325).

325

As you see, a strong brightness gradient arises on the wood surface (ill.326).

326

Repeat all this for the wardrobe surfaces on the left.
Your newly installed Levels adjustment layer is still active, but now click in the miniature of the layer wood background

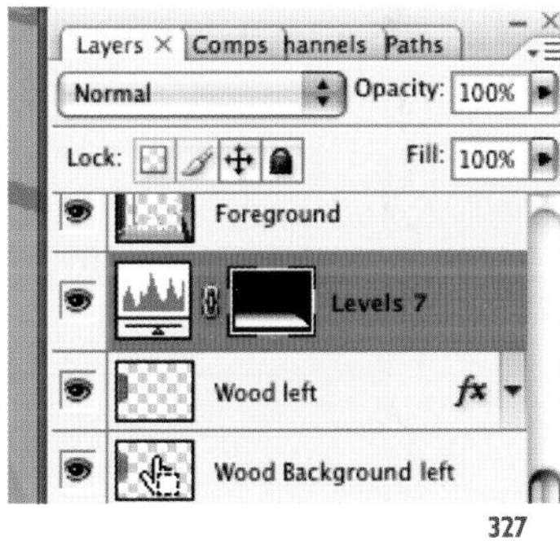

327

left with the CTRL key held down (ill.327), to produce a corresponding selection.

Place a further Levels adjustment layer (from the adjustment layer menu at the bottom frame of the Layers palette), for whose histogram you also set the Gray control to 2.00 (ill.328).

Now the gradient also comes into play here.

Click in the mask miniature of the new adjustment layer with the CTRL key held down (ill.329), and draw with the Gradient tool (which actually should still be active) a horizontal gradient from the right edge of the selection till just before your left edge (ill.330; this time don´t end in front of the metal area, but draw the gradient longer, so that the brightness gradient on the left matches the one on the front wardrobe surface.

The left surface should get some extra shading to differentiate it from the front one, so place a third Levels adjustment layer over the other two, but before that select again the left surface by a CTRL-click on the miniature of the layer wood background left, so that the adjustment layer will be masked accordingly.

In the histogram, move the Gray control to the right, to the value 0.70 (ill.331), to clearly differentiate the left surface from the front one.

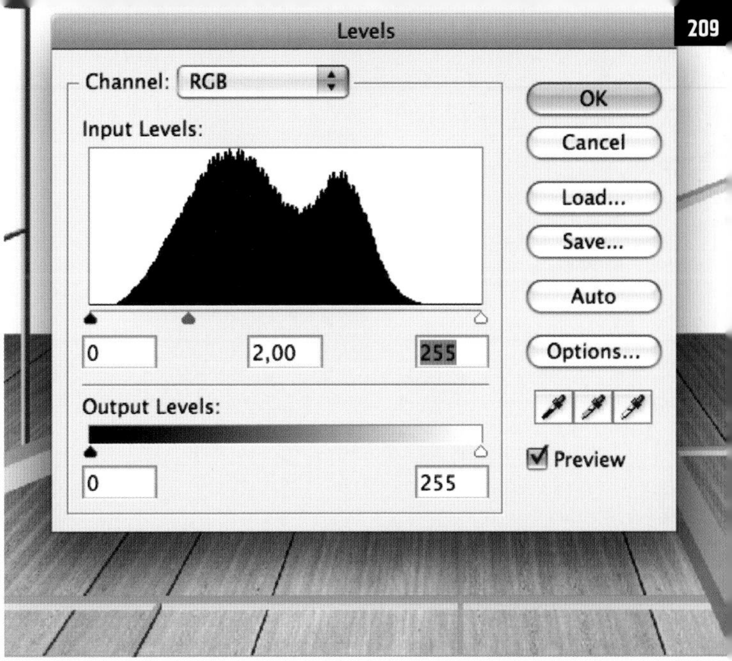

328

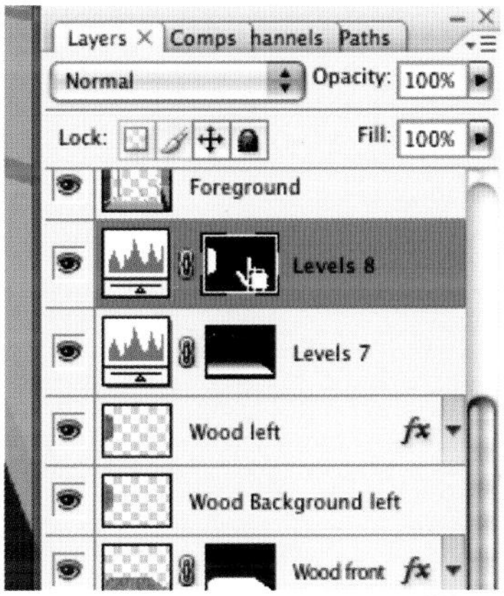

331

329

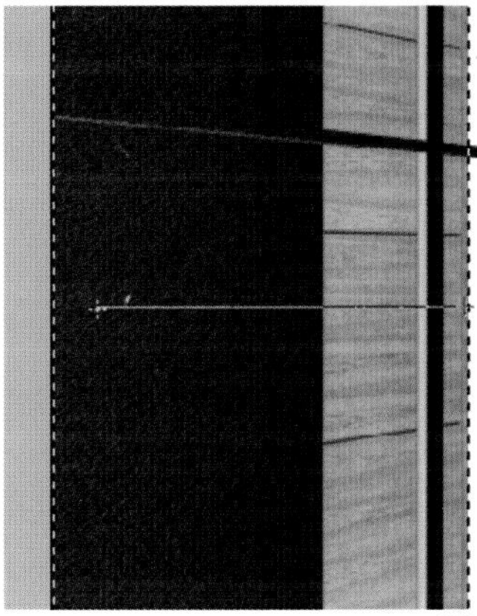

330

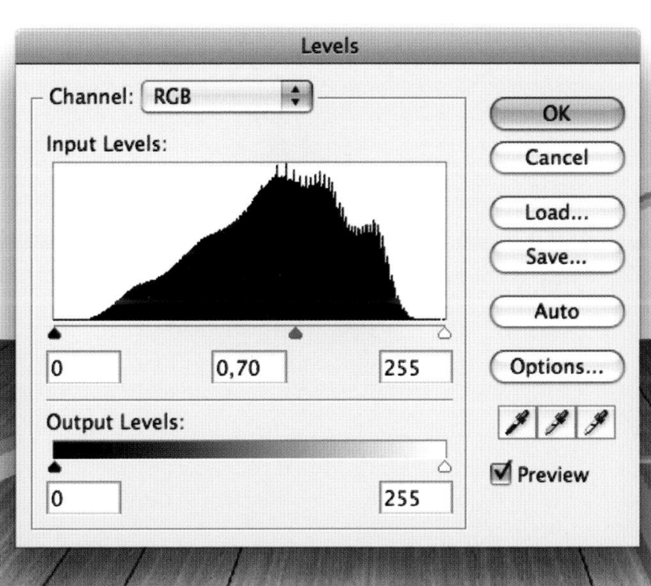

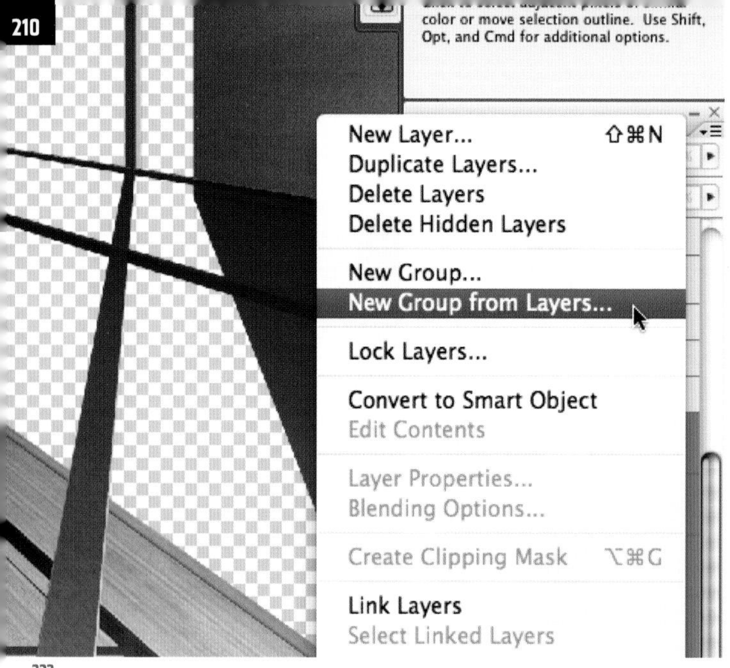

333

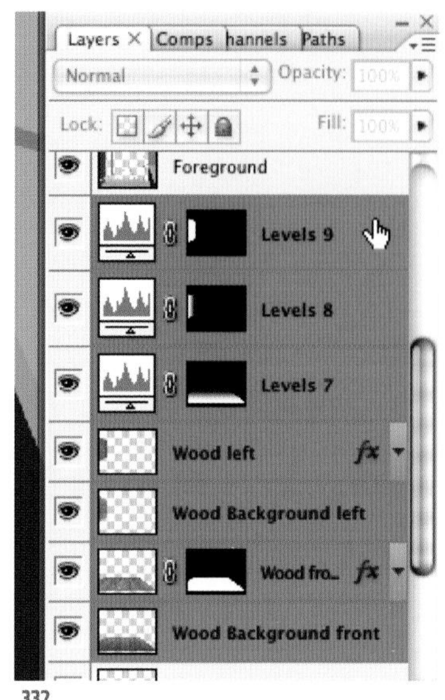

332

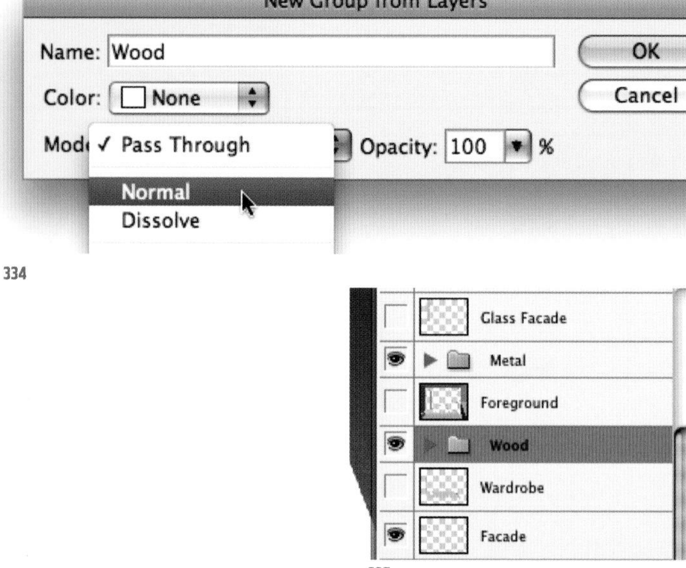

334

335

336

So, now you´ve completed your wardrobe for the moment, and so it´s time to tidy up a little in the Layers palette.

Activate the four wood and the three adjustment layers (ill.332) and then select the command New Group from Layers from the menu of the Layers palette (ill.333).

Call the group wood, and as the blending mode decide on Normal, as you´ve already done with the metal group, so that the Levels adjustment only has an effect inside the group (ill.334).

Show the other image layers (except the CAAD layers Foreground and Wardrobe, ill.335), to allow yourself an impression of your progress regarding the overall picture (ill.336).

Before we turn to working on the ceiling, we´ll yet close some uncharted territory in the foreground in which we should rather see the front faces of two steps (see end result, ill.353).

For this I have actually provided an image that I put together some time ago from

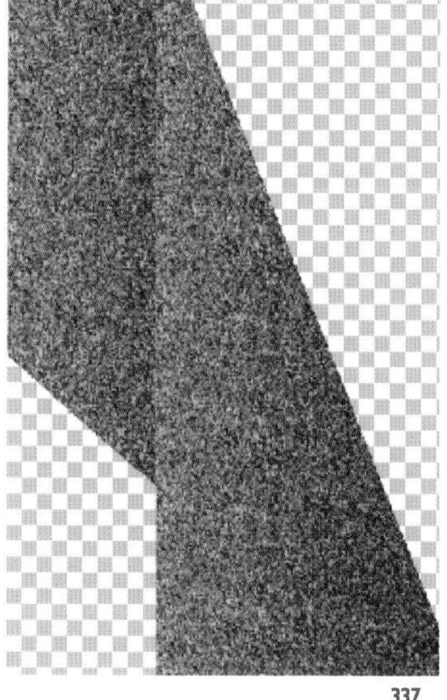

337

338

real photos (ill.337), but as it doesn´t quite fit I´ve taken the liberty of generating a separate granite texture, which you can admire in file 07_ng_granite.psd (ill.338).

Take a cool look at it. The characteristic stone texture was produced only by using filters applied to a monochromatic canvas, plus two correction tools (Levels and Hue/Saturation).

On top lies a layer showing a summary of all the layers beneath (produced by Shift-Alt-CTRL-E), and which will serve for importing into our image.

Switch again to conventional window display (by pressing F till you see your images in normal windows, making sure the file with the granite texture is in the foreground.Then mouse-drag the layer Export into the image of the National Gallery (ill.339).

There place the new layer directly under the metal group and rename it granite (ill.340).

Press CTRL-T, and move and scale the granite tatter in such a way that it just fits in the clipping (ill.341).

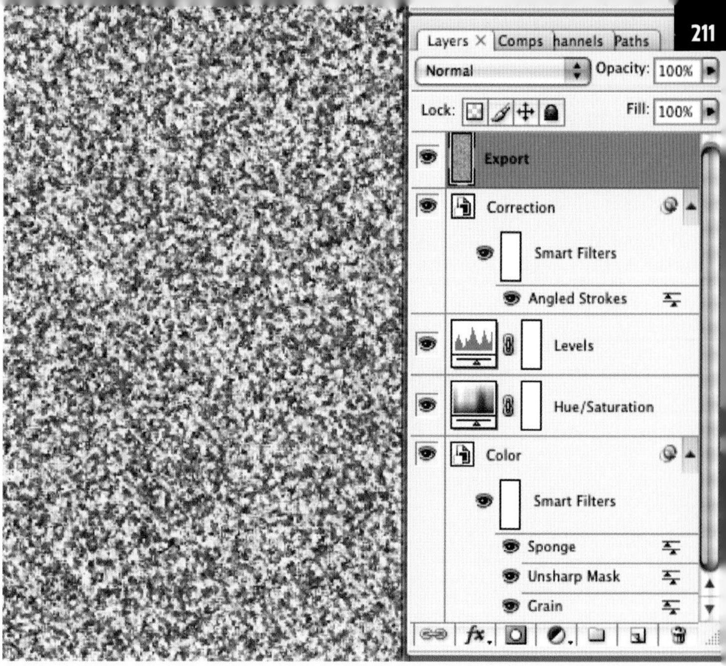

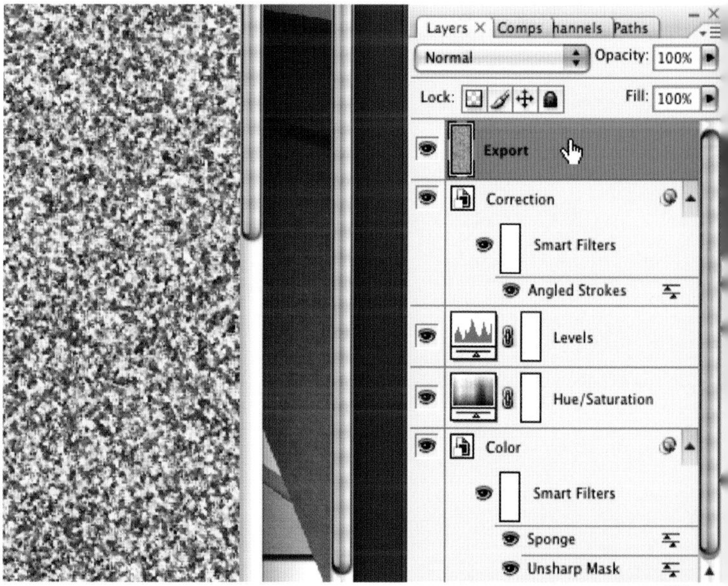

339

340

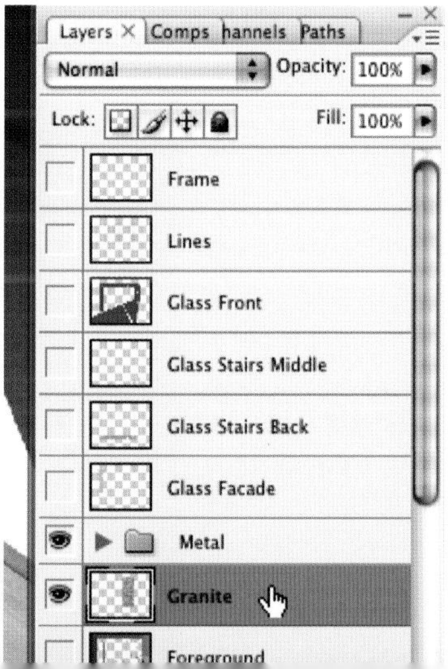

341

342

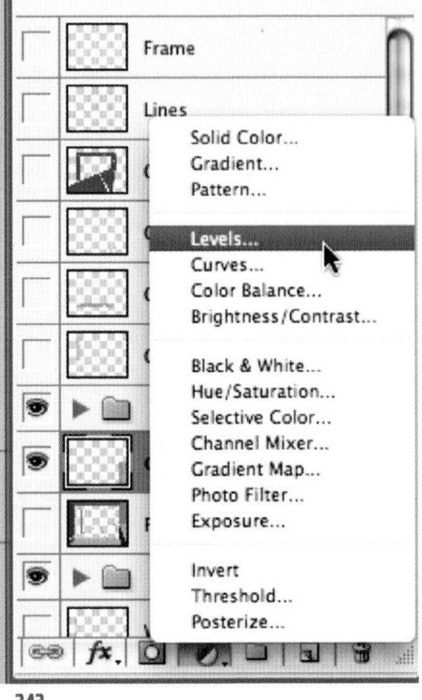

343

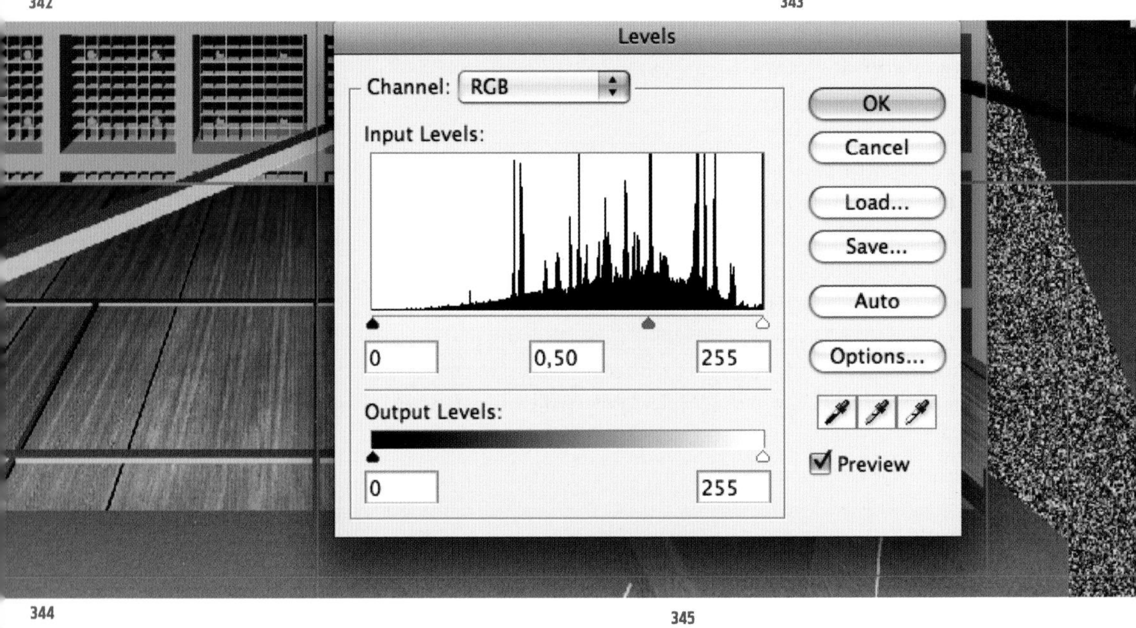

344

345

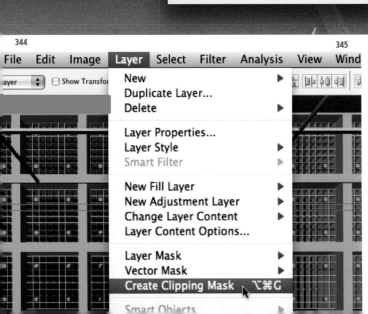

Show the rulers and guides (CTRL-R for the rulers, CTRL-, for the guides, ill.342), and lay vertical guides through the later step edges.

Place a Levels adjustment layer over the layer granite (ill.343), and set the middle histogram control for the Channel RGB to 0.50 (ill.344).

Group the adjustment layer and the granite layer under it so that the Levels cor-

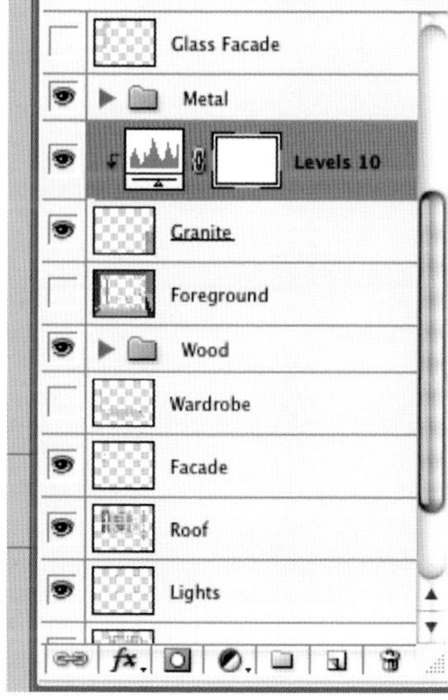

346

347

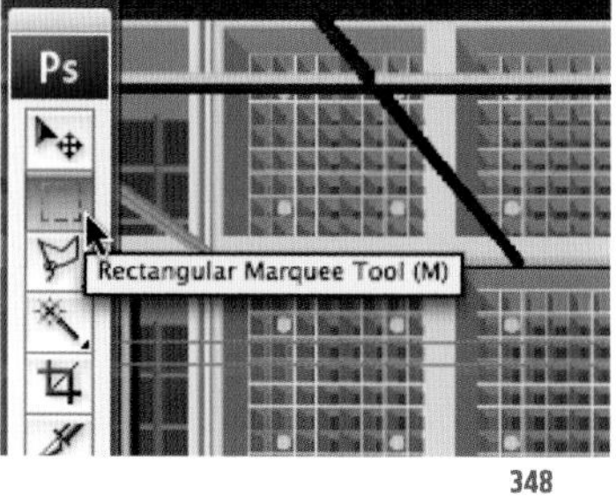

348

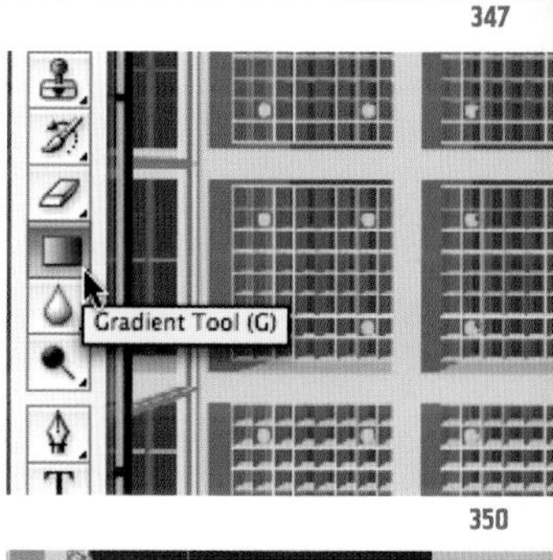

350

349

rection only affects the stone surface, not by making a group from it (that comes later), but first by using the command Create Clipping Mask from the Layer menu (ill.345; alternatively click, with the Alt key held down, in the Layers palette on the line between the two layers).

In the Layers palette you see that the adjustment layer is indented (ill.346), a sign that the Levels correction now only affects the image layer under it.

Leave the adjustment layer activated so you can create a mask, since this time too there´s to be a brightness gradient on the step surfaces.

First fill the mask with Black by pressing Shift-Backspace, and use Black (ill.347).

As now both step faces are to get a gradient, select each of them, with the Rectangular Marquee tool (M, ill.348).

First draw a selection frame round the step on the right (ill.349).

Now grab the Gradient tool yet again (G, ill.350); the Black, White gradient should still be selected, as well as the option Linear gradient in the Options palette. The option Reverse should be deactivated.

Now draw a horizontal gradient from the left to the right selection border (ill.351).

Repeat all this for the step on the left (draw a selection first and then a gradient inside it), but draw the gradient starting at the left selection border just as far to the right as in the first step, beyond the right-hand selection border (ill.352).

351

352

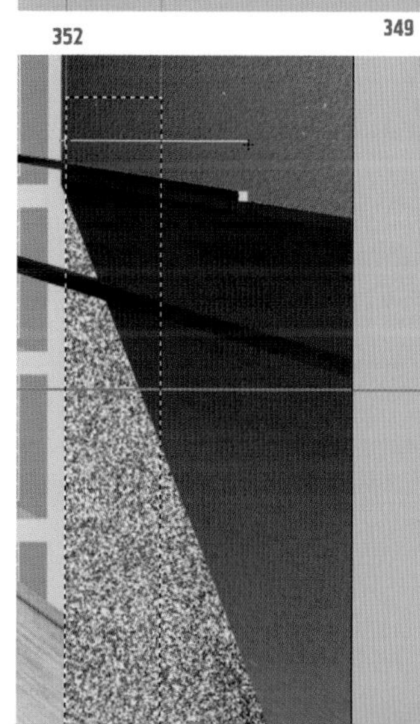

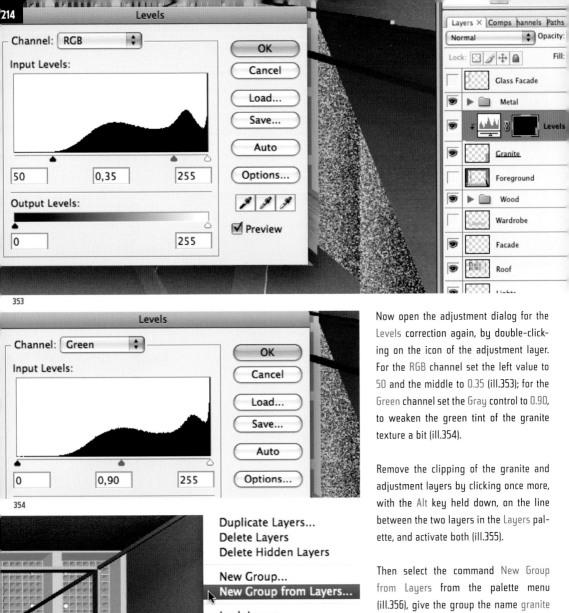

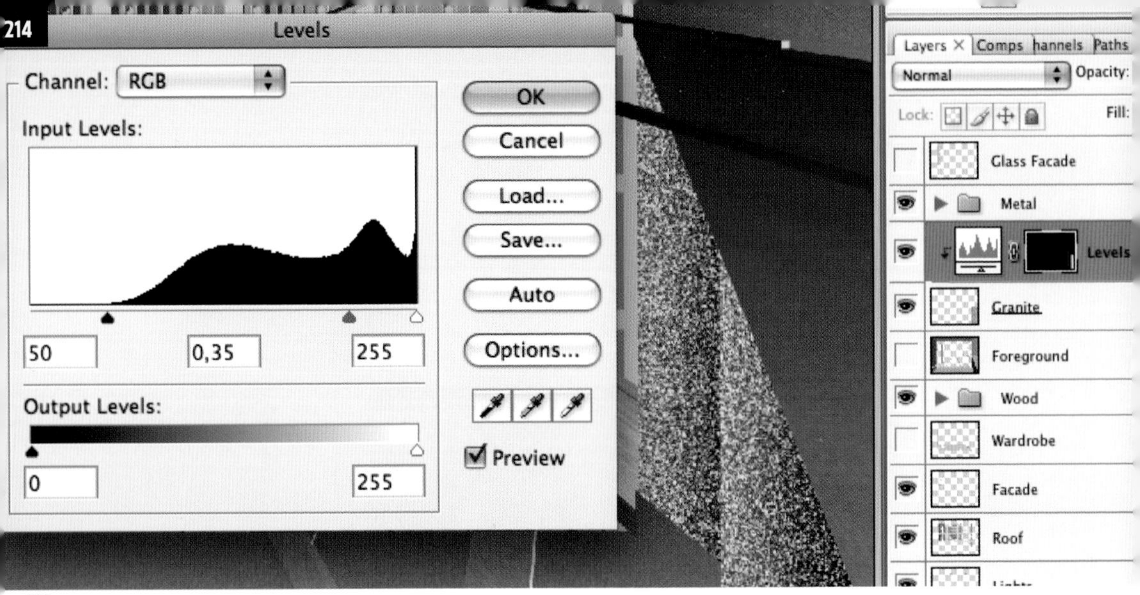

353

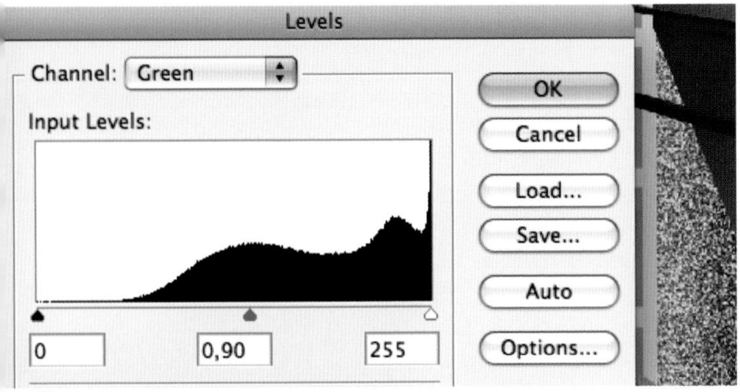

354

Now open the adjustment dialog for the Levels correction again, by double-clicking on the icon of the adjustment layer. For the RGB channel set the left value to 50 and the middle to 0.35 (ill.353); for the Green channel set the Gray control to 0.90, to weaken the green tint of the granite texture a bit (ill.354).

Remove the clipping of the granite and adjustment layers by clicking once more, with the Alt key held down, on the line between the two layers in the Layers palette, and activate both (ill.355).

Then select the command New Group from Layers from the palette menu (ill.356), give the group the name granite and set the layer blending mode to Normal (ill.357; you know already that this way the Levels correction only affects the image layer under it, which is also in the group).

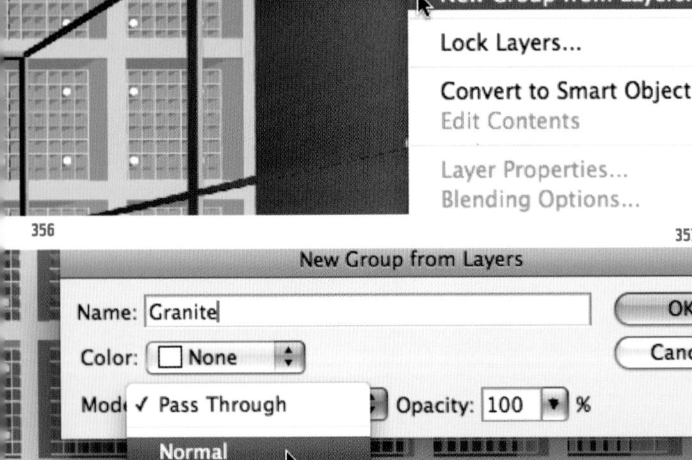

356

357

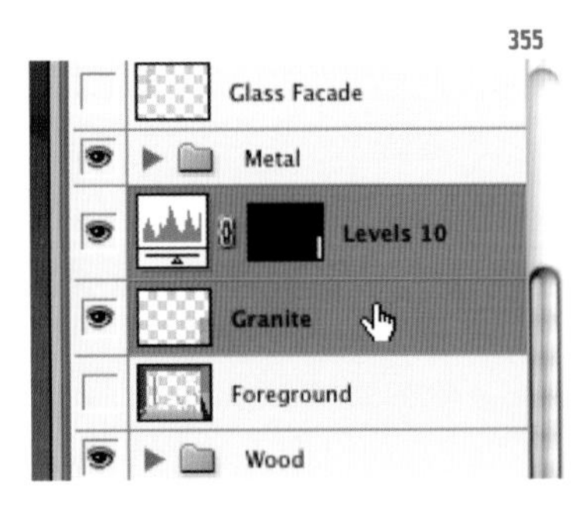

355

358

359

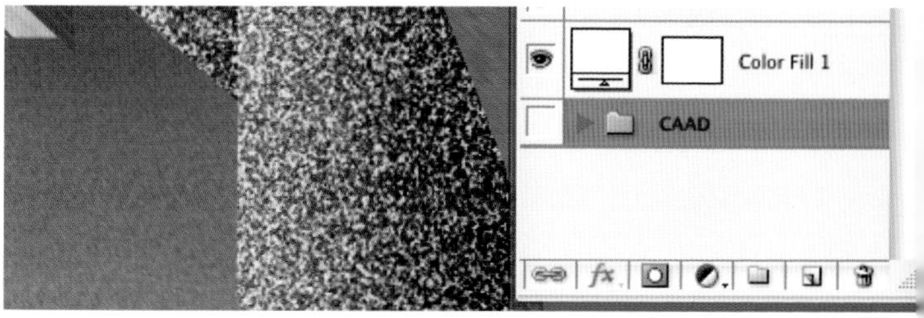

360

To tidy up a little more in the Layers palette, select the two CAAD layers Foreground and Wardrobe (the second with the Shift key held down, ill.358), and combine these two into a group as well.

Call it CAAD (ill.359), move it to the very bottom in the Layers palette, and hide it (ill.360).

Now to the ceiling. As you may know, the roof structure of the New National Gallery is painted completely black, just like the railing in the image foreground.
However, since the ceiling is away in the background, you don´t require a special texture for it; it´s enough if you color it black or gray.

First hide all the layers you´ve already processed, and show the three layers Facade, Roof and Grid (ill.361); the image still dazzles in the colors of the CAAD file.

361

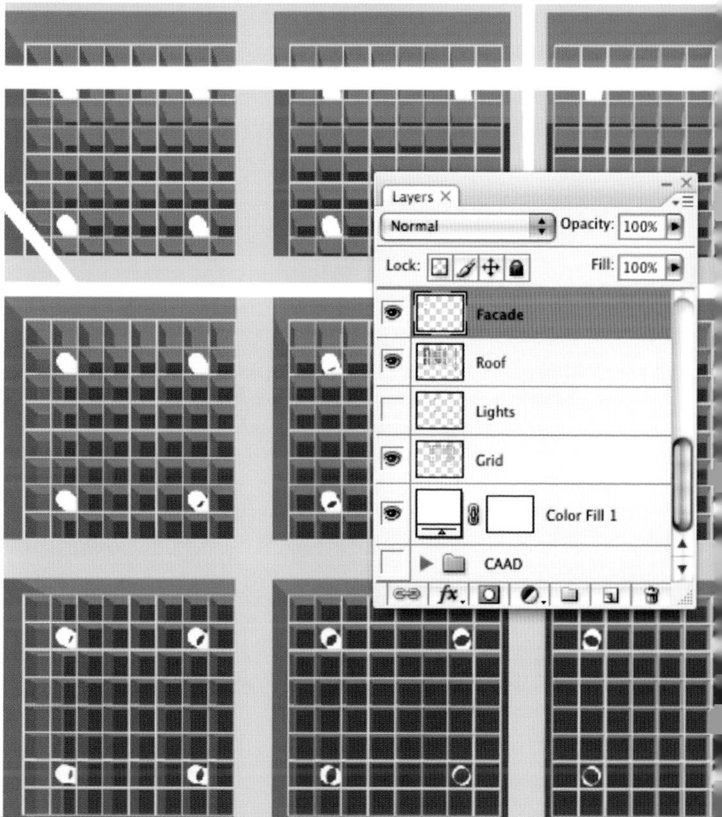

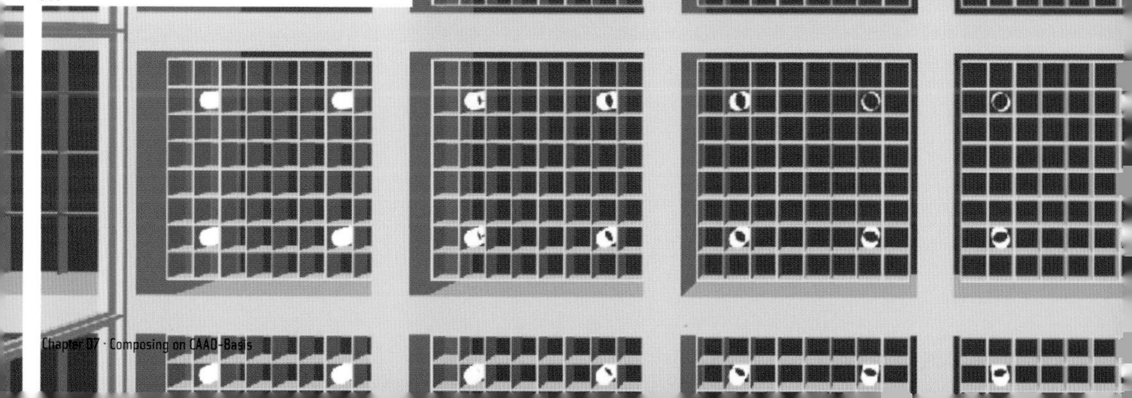

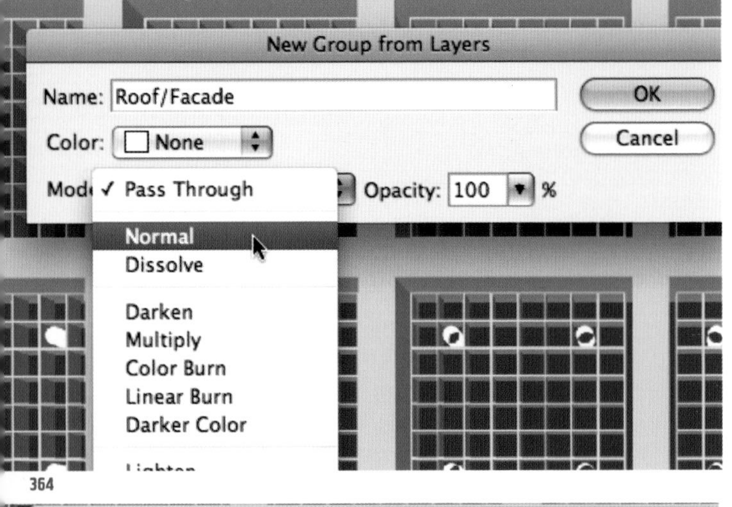

364

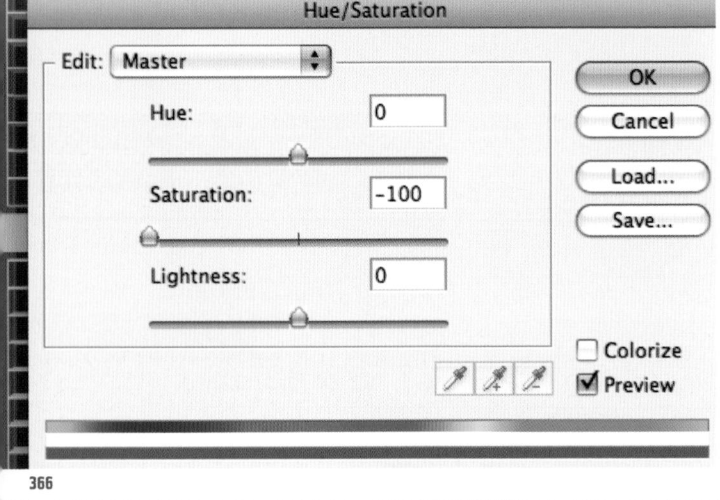

366

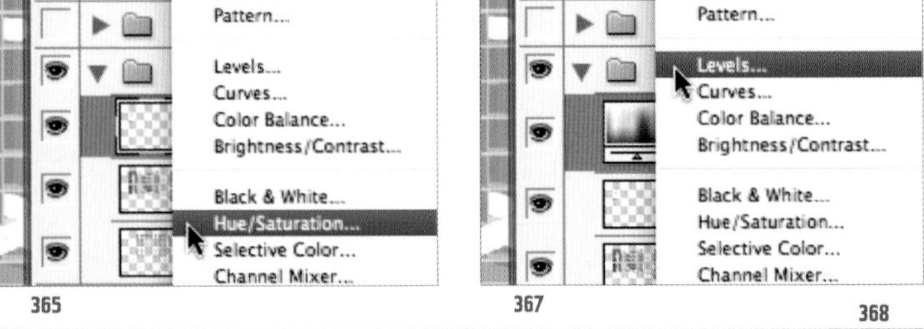

365 367

368

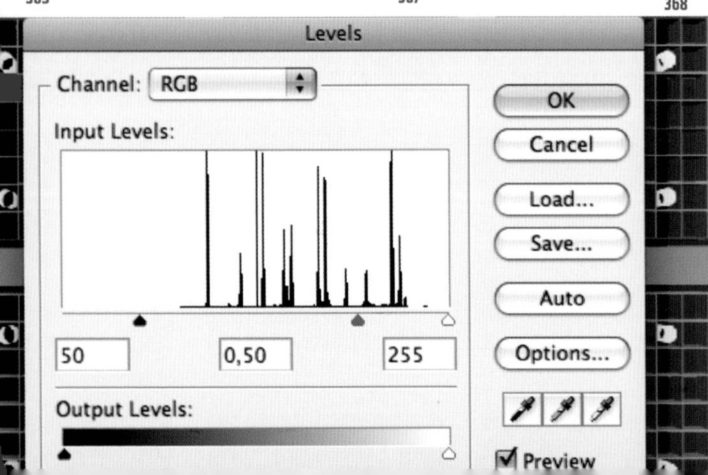

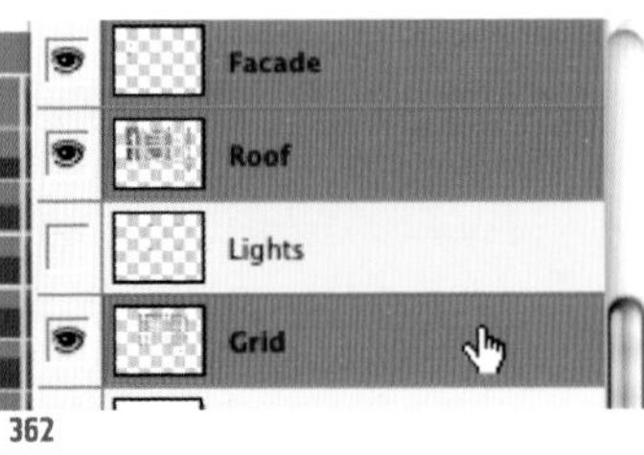

362

Delete Layers
Delete Hidden Layers

New Group...
New Group from Layers...

Lock Layers...

363

Activate all three (ill.362) and combine them into a group (ill.363). Call the new group roof/facade, and set the blending mode to Normal again (ill.364).

Keep the group open in the Layers palette, and activate the uppermost layer (Facade). Then select Hue/Saturation from the adjustment layers popup menu of the Layers palette (ill.365).

In the adjustment dialog, move the Saturation control fully to the left, to decolor the visible image area completely (ill.366). Confirm with OK; the Hue/Saturation correction is finished and the adjustment layer is active.

Now place a further adjustment layer for a Levels correction (ill.367). Set the left control of the histogram to the value 50, the middle one to 0.50 (ill.368).

Basically your roof and facade structure is so darkened by this that its brightness spectrum matches that of the railing in the foreground.

Yet what we´d still like is a brightness gradient on the downward surface of the roof, extending from the left side (bright) to the very right, the middle of the room (dark).

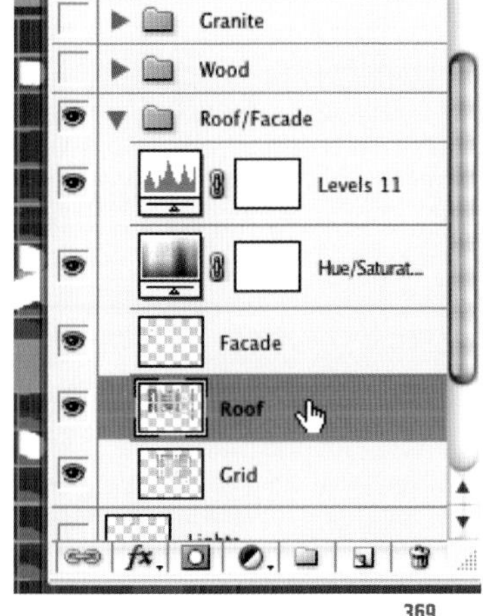
369

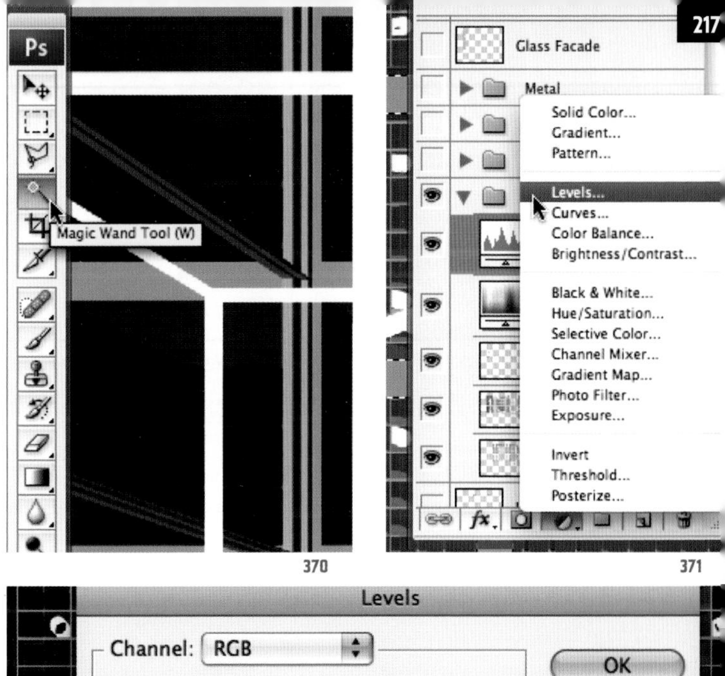
370

371

So that later you can control the brightness gradient optimally, you´ll insert two further Levels adjustment layers, with which you can control both the brightest and the darkest part separately.

In order that the Levels control is only used on the bottom surface, first select the latter.

To do this, activate the layer Roof (ill.369), grab the Magic Wand tool (W, ill.370; set the value for the Tolerance up in the Options palette to 1), and click on some point of the bottom surface.

When the selection is on, activate the uppermost layer of your roof group, and select a further Levels control from the adjustment layer menu of the Layers palette (ill.371).
Set the middle value of the histogram to 3.50 (ill.372 - thanks to your selection the brightening is limited to the desired image area).

After confirming with OK, your selection is still active, and you can place the second Levels adjustment layer (if your ants have disappeared, just choose Reselect from the Select menu, ill.373). Set the Gray control of the second Levels histogram to 0.25 (ill.374).

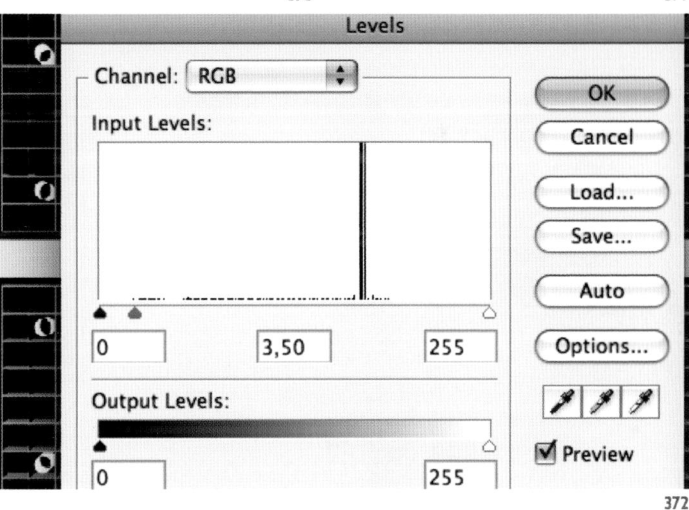
372

373

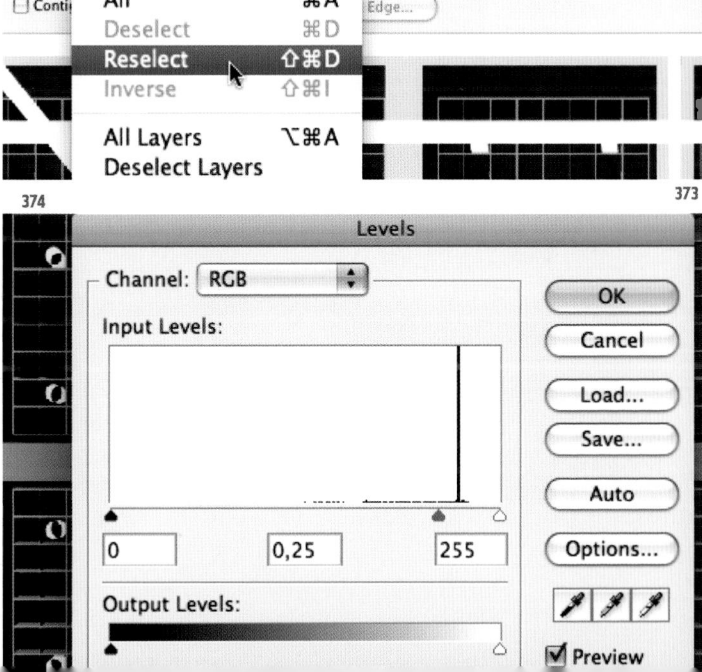
374

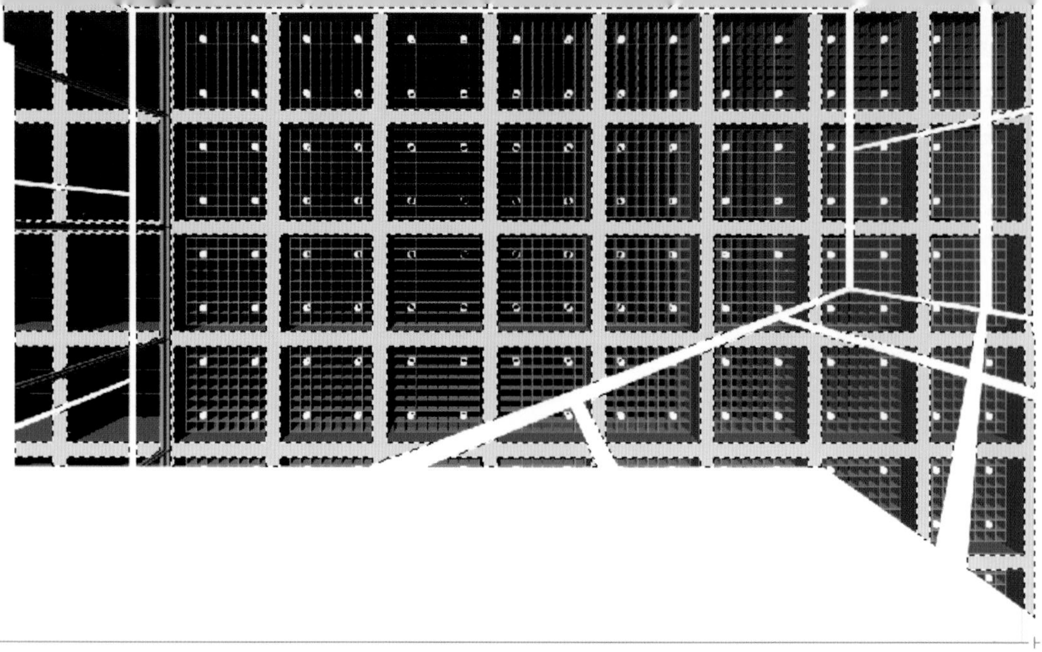

377

375

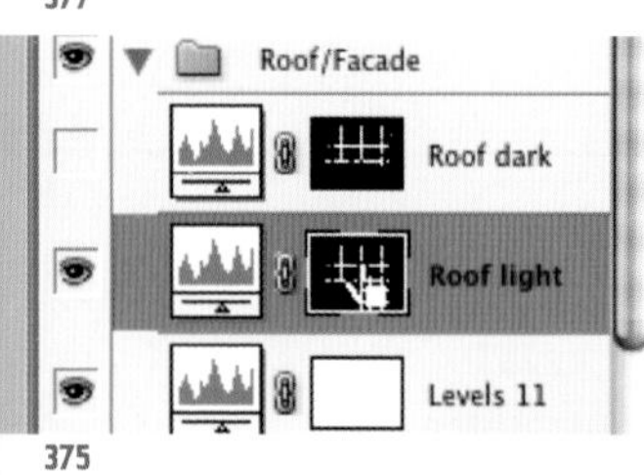

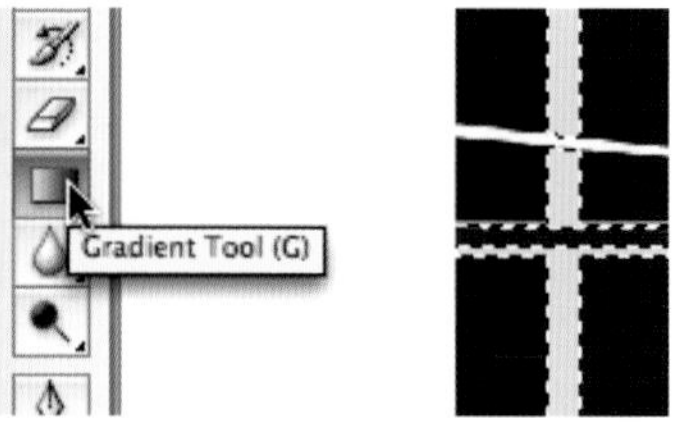

376

For better orientation, call the upper adjustment layer roof dark, and the one under it roof light.

Now to the gradients: first hide the adjustment layer roof dark, and activate roof light.
Click in the mask miniature of the layer with the CTRL key held down, to produce the selection of the bottom surface again (ill.375).

Grab the Gradient tool (G, ill.376; it should still offer a Black-and-White gradient), and draw a horizontal line from the right to the left edge of the selection (ill.377).

Now for a start you already have a gradient from very bright on the left side to the original brightness on the right.

Now activate the adjustment layer roof dark. Your selection should still be active - if not, click in the mask miniature of the layer with the CTRL key held down (ill.378).

Now draw with the Gradient tool, which should still be active, a horizontal line from the left to the right edge of the selection (ill.379).

Show the foreground layer groups again (metal, granite, wood), and check how the roof and facade structures fit into the overall picture (ill.380).

Look in the Layers palette again; the layer Lights also belongs to the complex of the roof structure, which means you should transport this layer into this group too.

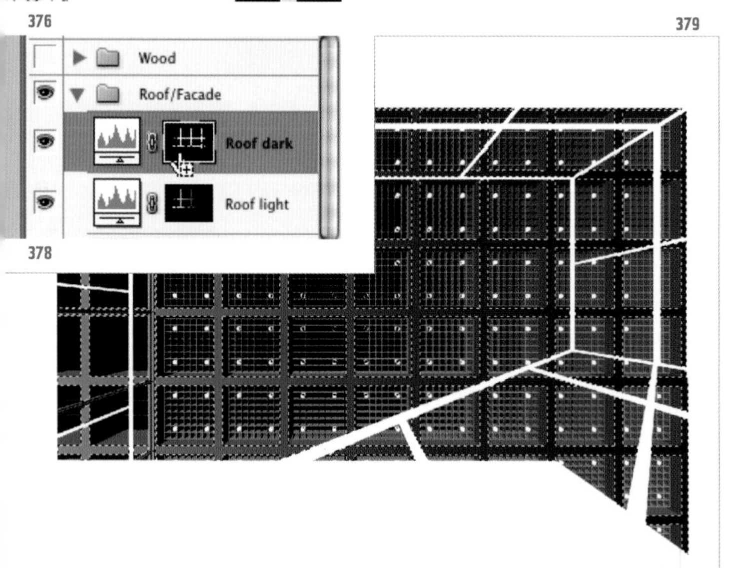

378

379

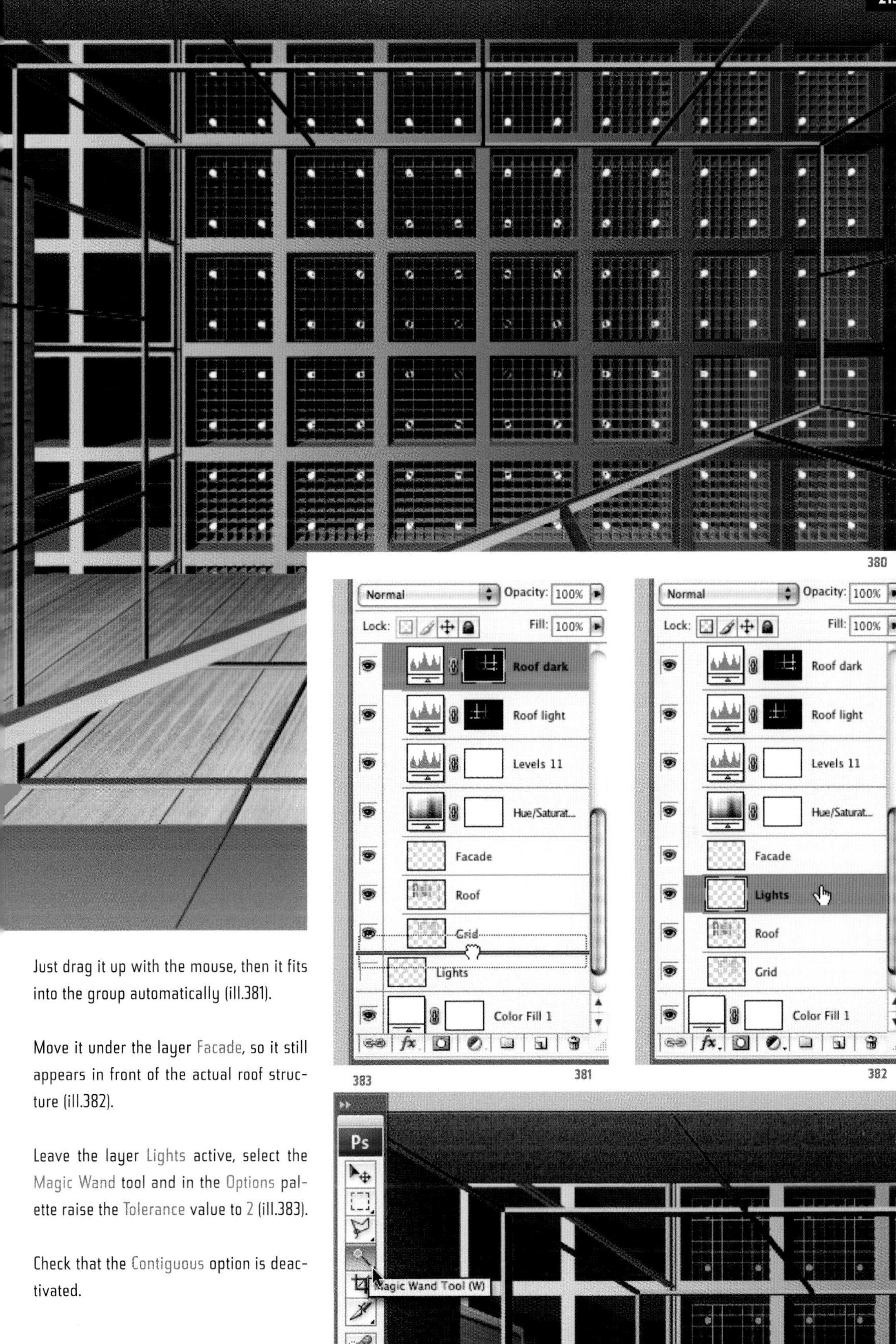

380

381

382

383

Just drag it up with the mouse, then it fits into the group automatically (ill.381).

Move it under the layer Facade, so it still appears in front of the actual roof structure (ill.382).

Leave the layer Lights active, select the Magic Wand tool and in the Options palette raise the Tolerance value to 2 (ill.383).

Check that the Contiguous option is deactivated.

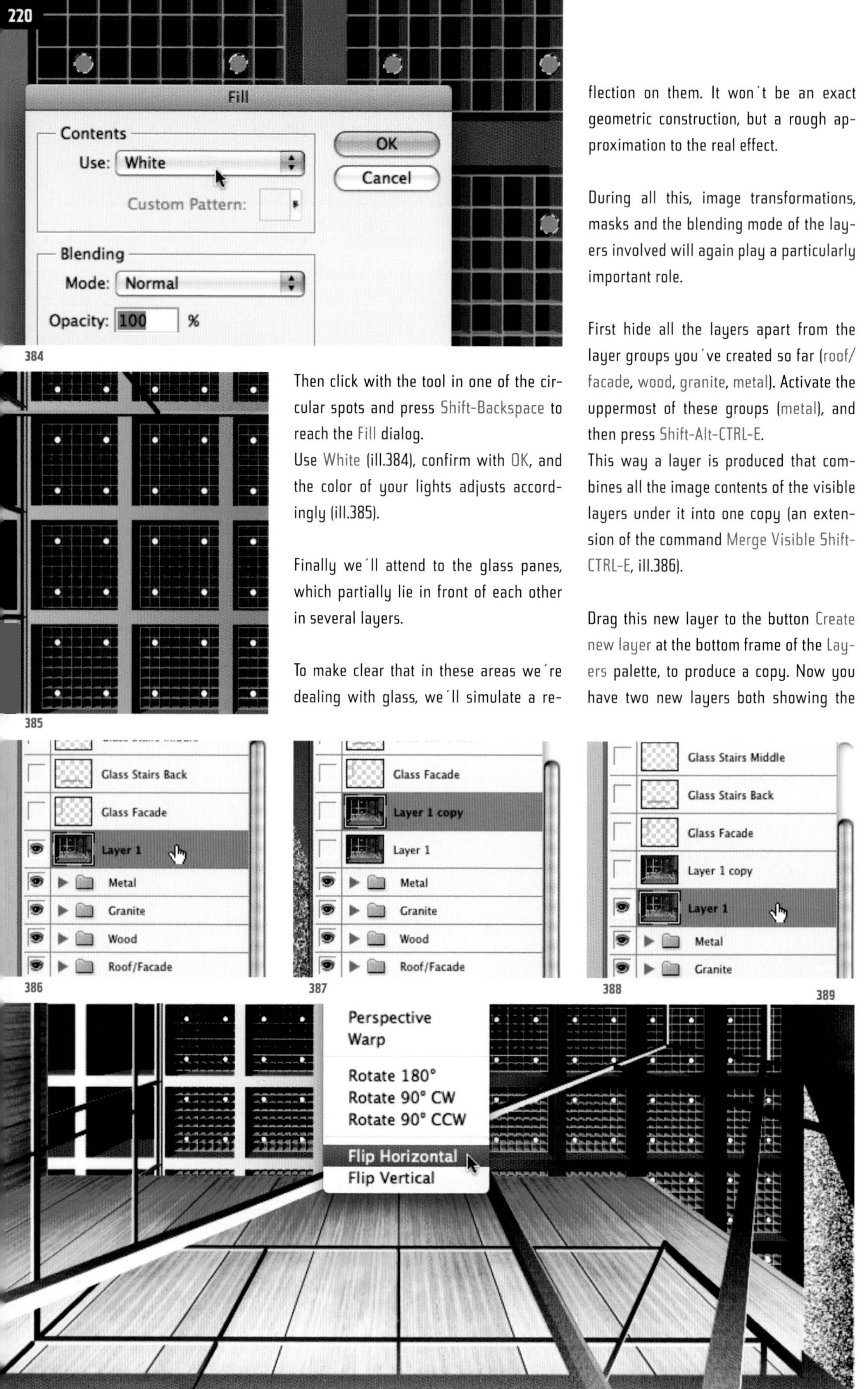

384

385

386

387

388

389

Then click with the tool in one of the circular spots and press Shift-Backspace to reach the Fill dialog.
Use White (ill.384), confirm with OK, and the color of your lights adjusts accordingly (ill.385).

Finally we´ll attend to the glass panes, which partially lie in front of each other in several layers.

To make clear that in these areas we´re dealing with glass, we´ll simulate a reflection on them. It won´t be an exact geometric construction, but a rough approximation to the real effect.

During all this, image transformations, masks and the blending mode of the layers involved will again play a particularly important role.

First hide all the layers apart from the layer groups you´ve created so far (roof/facade, wood, granite, metal). Activate the uppermost of these groups (metal), and then press Shift-Alt-CTRL-E.
This way a layer is produced that combines all the image contents of the visible layers under it into one copy (an extension of the command Merge Visible Shift-CTRL-E, ill.386).

Drag this new layer to the button Create new layer at the bottom frame of the Layers palette, to produce a copy. Now you have two new layers both showing the

390

same thing (ill.387). From them you´ll create the reflection image for the glass panes of the staircase railing that are at the front.

First set the blending mode of both layers to Overlay, show one of them and activate it (ill.388).

Press CTRL-T so you can transform the contents of this layer, and the familiar transformation frame with the handles appears.

Click in it with the right mouse button and select the command Flip Horizontal from the context menu (ill.389). Press Return to conclude the transformation; the mirrored image appears transparent in front of the image contents under it, because the layer blending mode is set at Overlay (ill.390).

You do almost the same with the second layer: show it (its blending mode should be set at Overlay too) and activate it (ill.391).

After starting the transformation mode with CTRL-T, select the command Flip Vertical from the right-click context menu, for a change (ill.392).

The result looks a bit mazy (ill.393), but don´t worry, in the course of your work it´ll mutate into a beautiful (even if wrong) reflection image.

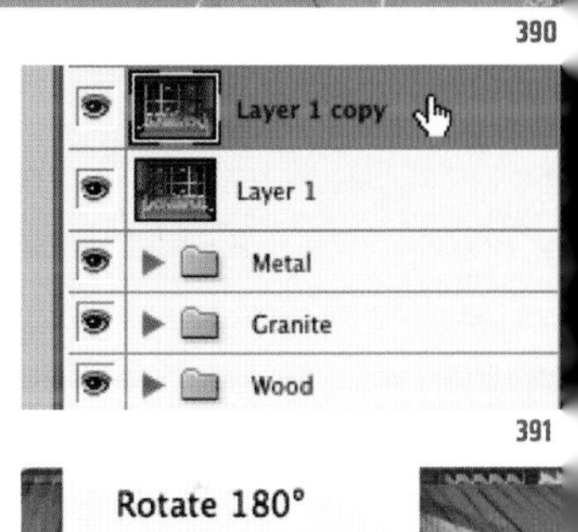

391

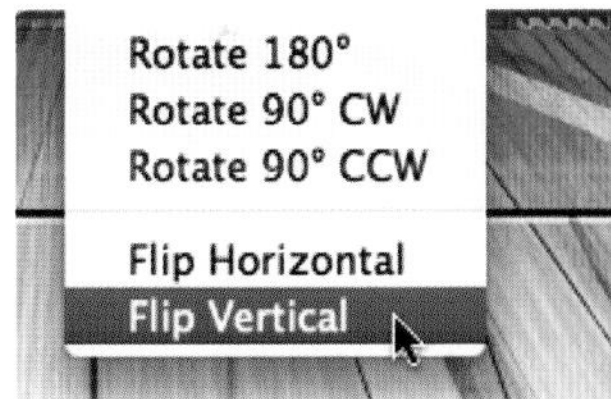

392

393

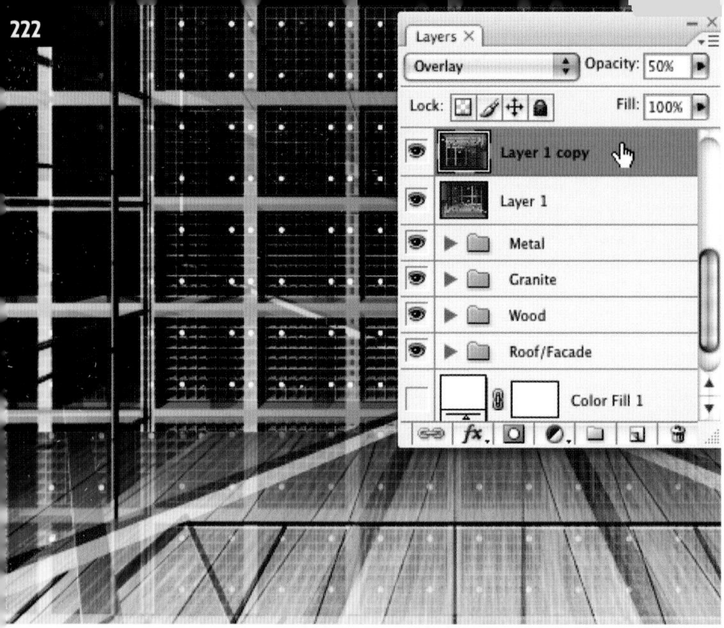

394

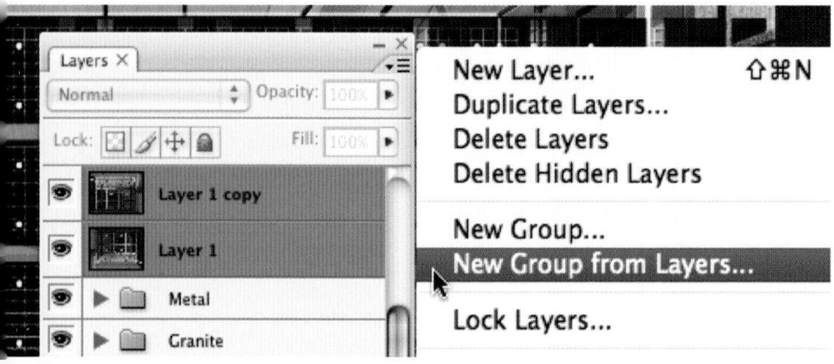

395

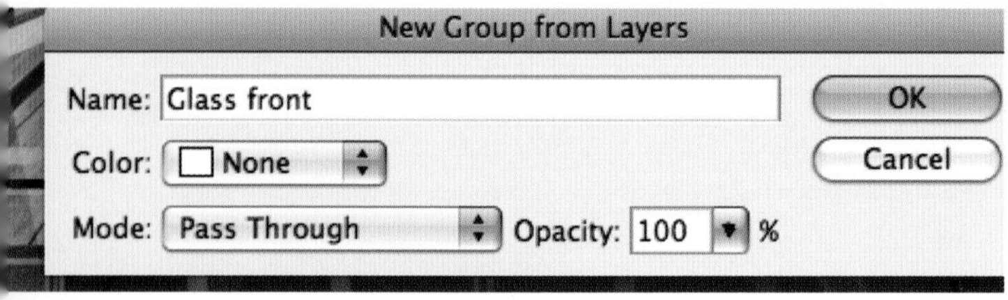

396

398

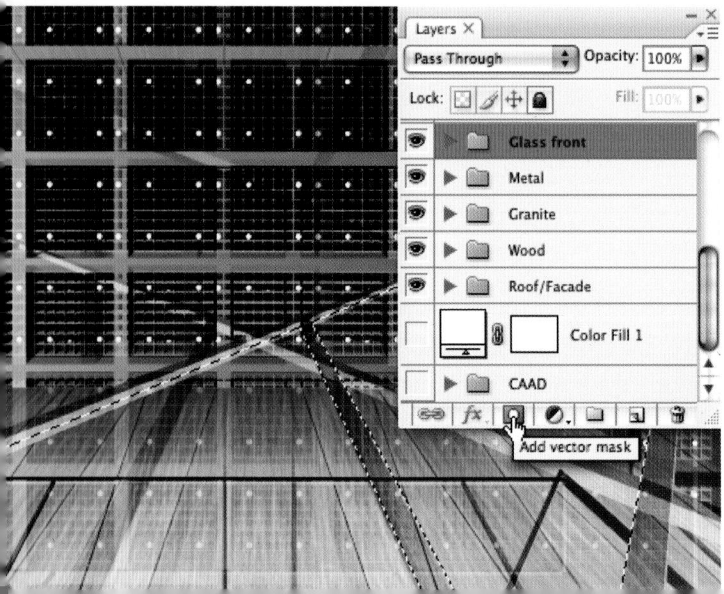

Turn down the Opacity of one of the two layers to 50%, so that one of the reflections is less dominant than the other (ill.394).

In principle you now have everything together to fake the reflection on the front glass panes; you only still have to fine-tune a little and in particular mask the "reflection" images.

First combine the two layers into a group, by first activating both (click with the Shift key held down) and select the command New Group from Layers from the menu of the Layers palette (ill.395).
Give the group the name glass front, leaving its blending mode at Pass Through for the moment (ill.396).

Now mask the layer group, clicking on the miniature of the CAAD layer glass front with the CTRL key held down (it doesn´t need to be shown or activated, ill.397), and the familiar selection ants appear.
Make sure your new layer group glass front is activated, and click on the button Add layer mask at the bottom frame of the Layers palette (ill.398).

Your two layers are now masked altogether (ill.399). Set the blending mode of each of the two back to Normal, and you´ll now regulate the blending with the image beneath via the group's blending mode.
Set this to Linear Dodge (ill.400), reduce the Opacity of the group to 50% and show the layer groups under it again.

397

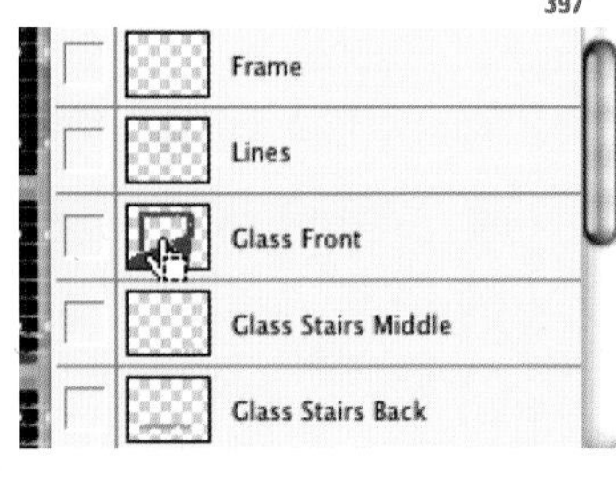

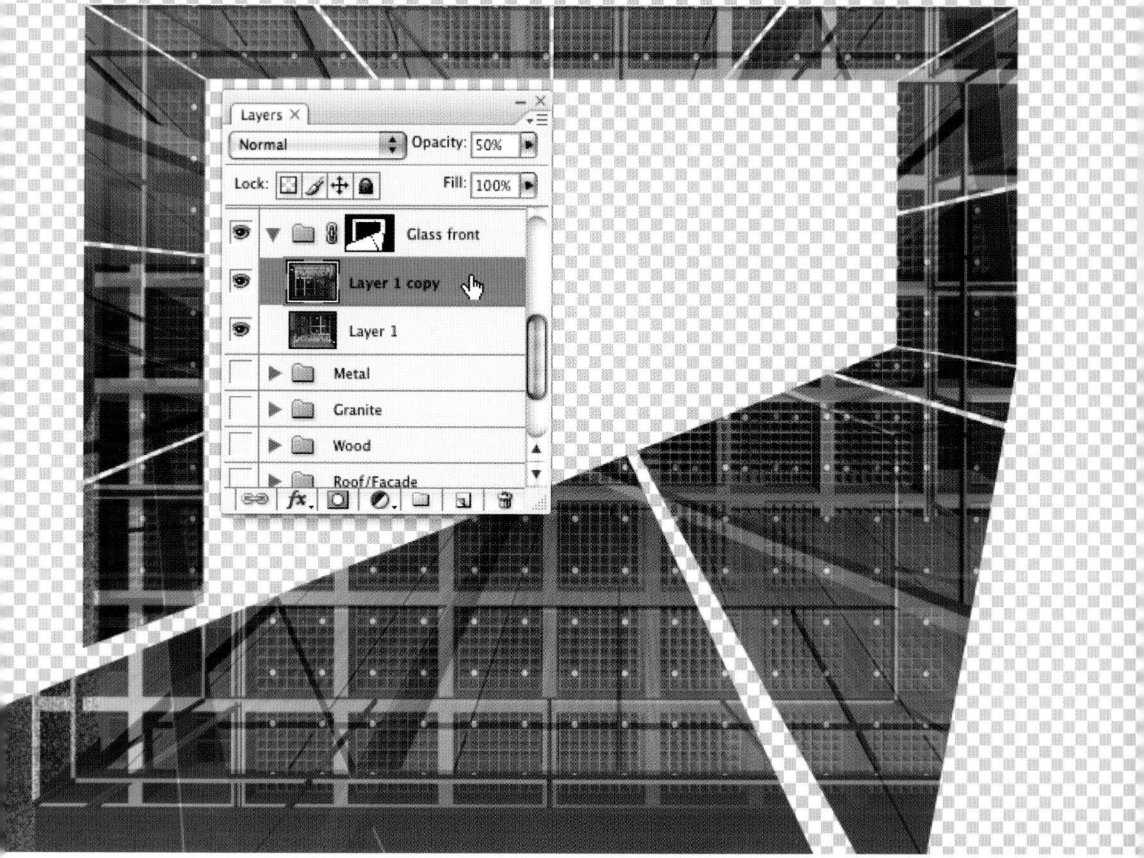
Layers
Normal
Opacity: 50%
Lock:
Fill: 100%
Glass front
Layer 1 copy
Layer 1
Metal
Granite
Wood
Roof/Facade

Layers
Linear Dodge (Add)
Opacity: 50%
Lock:
Fill: 100%
Glass front
Layer 1 copy
Layer 1
Metal
Granite
Wood
Roof/Facade

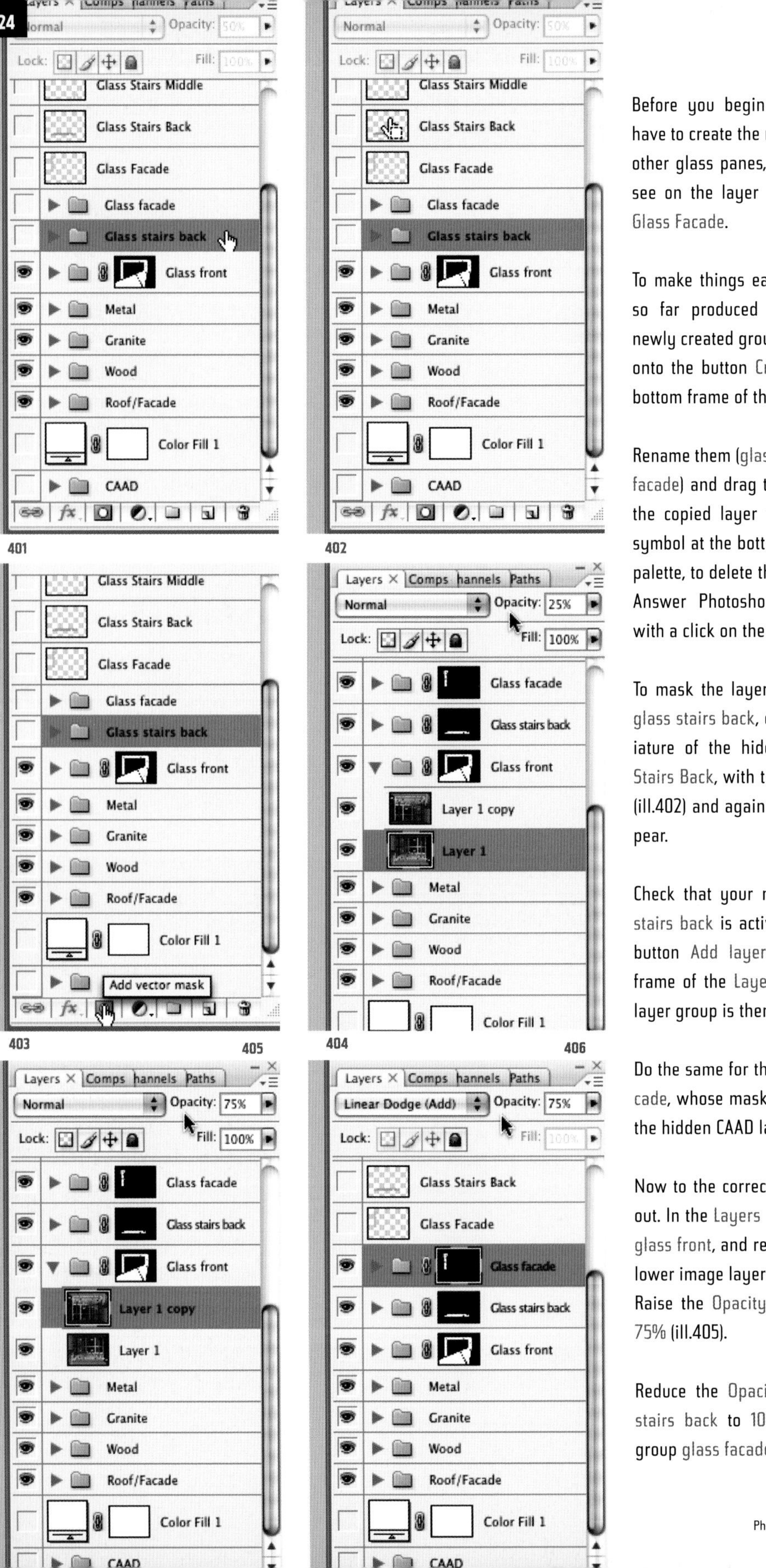

Before you begin fine-tuning, you still have to create the reflection image for the other glass panes, at least for those you see on the layer Glass Stairs Back and Glass Facade.

To make things easy, copy what you´ve so far produced on the subject, your newly created group, by dragging it twice onto the button Create new layer at the bottom frame of the Layers palette.

Rename them (glass stairs back and glass facade) and drag the mask miniatures of the copied layer groups onto the trash symbol at the bottom frame of the Layers palette, to delete them.
Answer Photoshop´s careful questions with a click on the Delete button (ill.401).

To mask the layer group with the name glass stairs back, click in the image miniature of the hidden CAAD layer Glass Stairs Back, with the CTRL key held down (ill.402) and again the notorious ants appear.

Check that your new layer group glass stairs back is activated, and click on the button Add layer mask at the bottom frame of the Layers palette (ill.403). The layer group is then correctly masked.

Do the same for the layer group glass facade, whose mask you logically get from the hidden CAAD layer Glass Facade.

Now to the corrections we want to carry out. In the Layers palette, open the group glass front, and reduce the Opacity of the lower image layer to 25% (ill.404).
Raise the Opacity of the upper layer to 75% (ill.405).

Reduce the Opacity of the group glass stairs back to 10%, raising that of the group glass facade to 75% (ill.406).

But by all means feel free to play around with the Opacity values a little yourself.

The reflection effect has turned out quite OK.

What is rather disturbing in the meantime is the strong color shade of the wood surfaces (ill.407).
We´ll finally remedy this, with a Hue/Saturation correction in the layer group wood.

Open it, activate the uppermost layer in it and add a new adjustment layer for Hue/Saturation (ill.408).

In the adjustment dialog, turn down the Saturation to the value -25 (ill.409), and confirm with OK.

With that, our gigantic composing is finished for the moment (ill.410).

Compared with the tasks in the other chapters it was a real marathon. But perhaps you´ve learned how to get to attractive graphics independent of a render application, and at the same time had pretty good practice in using Photoshop®´s most important tools.

407

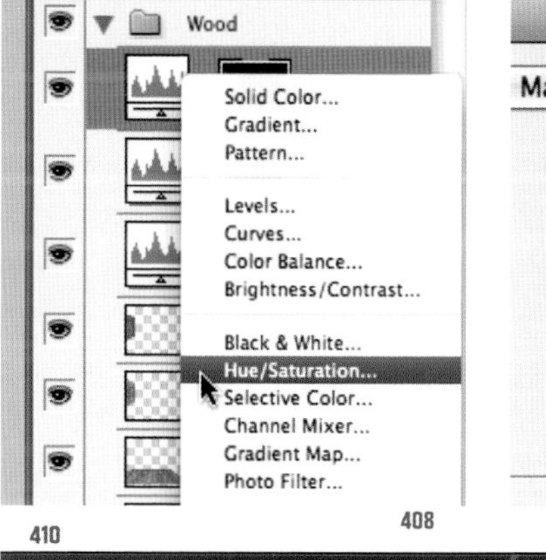

408

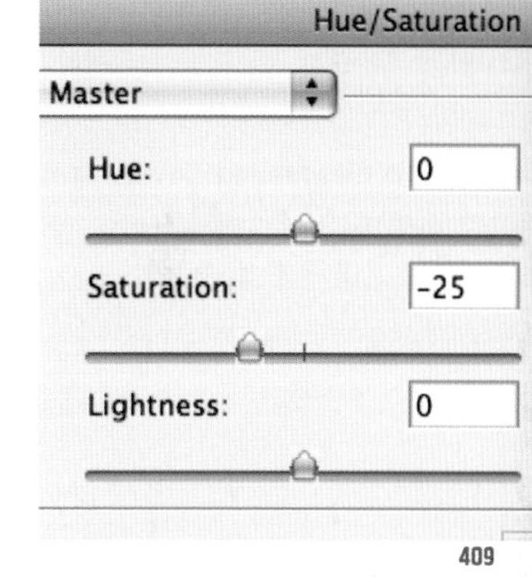

409

410

1

08

Lens and Color Correction

In this chapter I´ll finally, and briefly, deal with a typical correction procedure for digital photos.

Basically it´s just a question of removing geometric aberrations, and improving both the color and the contrast of the image (final result see ill.2).

The present case concerns a photo shot with a Nikon camera in RAW format.

When we were dealing with a normal TIFF or even a JPEG image, only the first step would be omitted, where Photoshop® allows you to undertake lossless corrections of the RAW image (see Ch.01).

So, please open the picture with the name 08_start.NEF, which as I say was photographed with a Nikon (ill.1).

As it´s in RAW format, first a window opens in Photoshop®, in which you can carry out the first image corrections (ill.3). Concerning these, we´ll confine ourselves to a minimum at this point, as we prefer to do the essential repair work with Photoshop®´s trusty tools.

Please change the preset values as follows: White Balance Daylight, Exposure + 1.00, Recovery 10 (you may well leave the remaining parameters).
Then click on the Open Image button (ill.4).

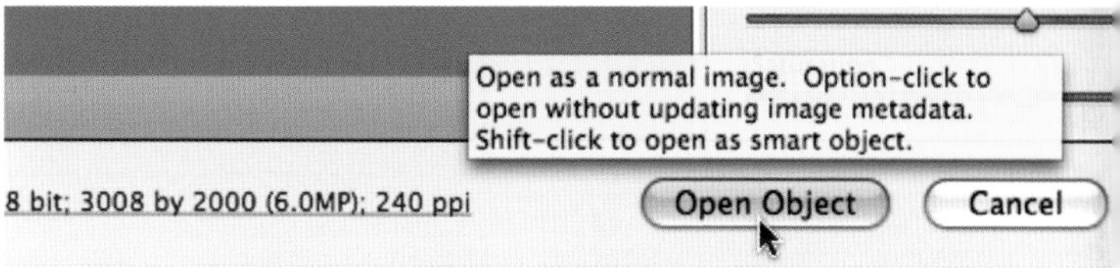

2

Open as a normal image. Option-click to open without updating image metadata. Shift-click to open as smart object.
8 bit; 3008 by 2000 (6.0MP); 240 ppi
Open Object
Cancel

3

4

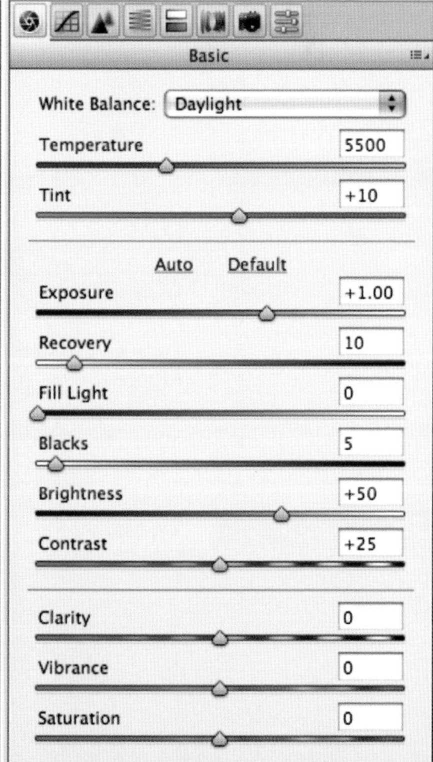

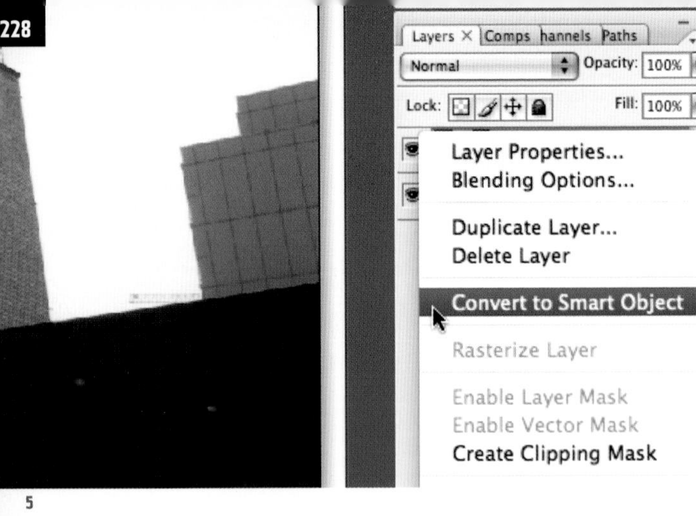

5

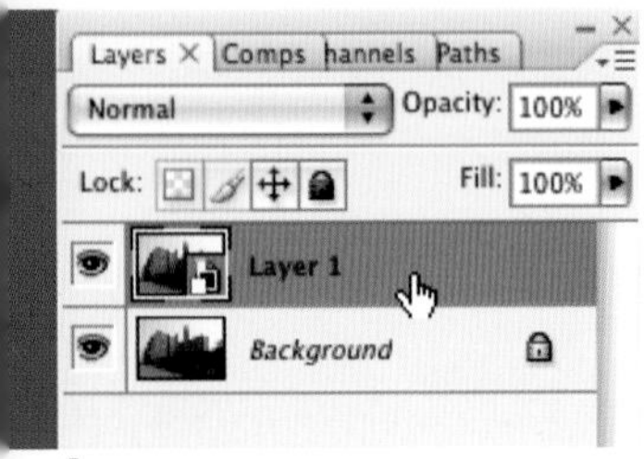

6

When the image is on hand, opened quite normally in Photoshop®, first of all copy the Background layer with CTRL-J (which corresponds to the menu command New – Layer via Copy from the Layer menu).

Apart from the rather floppy chromaticity of the image, the image geometry is particularly problematic.

The verticals converge strongly, as the camera was held at an angle, and moreover the straight lines neighboring the image borders are slightly bent.
The latter effect can, incidentally, occur much more strongly with worse lenses.

We´ll conduct the geometric repair with a filter, so we´ll again make use of Photoshop®´s ability to filter losslessly in a Smart layer.

Click with the right-hand mouse button on the entry of the new layer, and select the command Convert to Smart Object from the context menu (ill.5; if you need

7

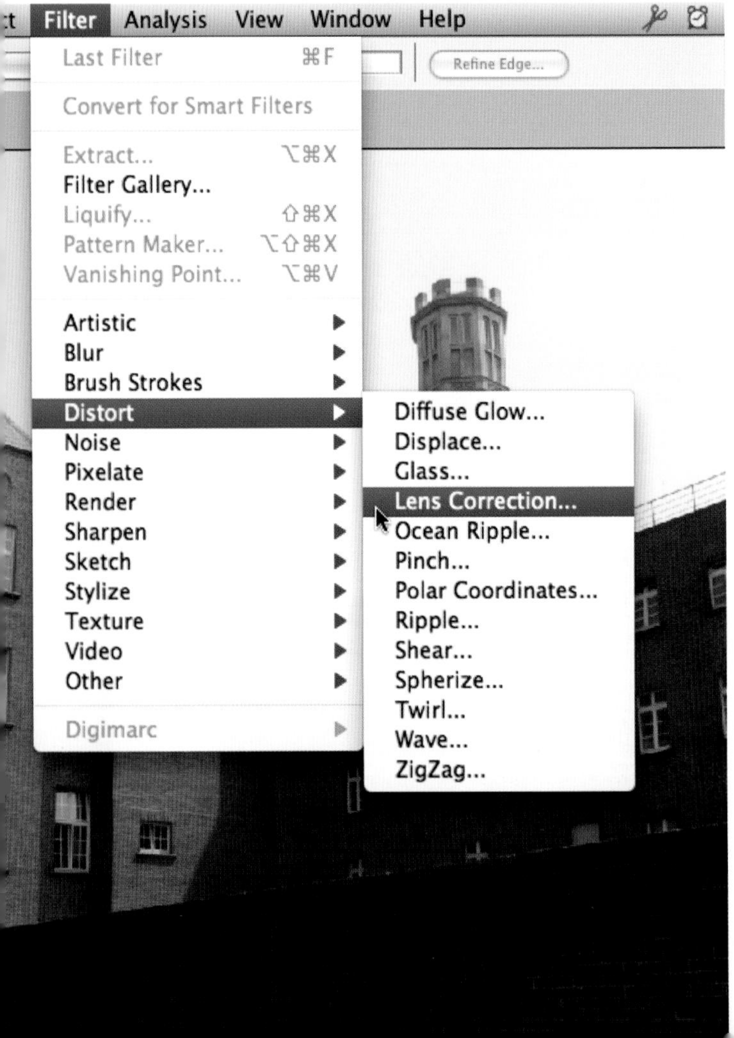

this function regularly, you can also note the shortcut Alt-CTRL-S).

You´ll recognize from the slightly altered layer miniature that the conversion has worked (ill.6).

Pick the Distort filter Lens Correction from the Filter menu (ill.7).

In the adjustment dialog you first see your image again; on the right side you can carry out adjustments to repair eventual flaws.

I recommend that you first of all hide the grid, by deactivating the corresponding option at the bottom edge of the window (ill.8).

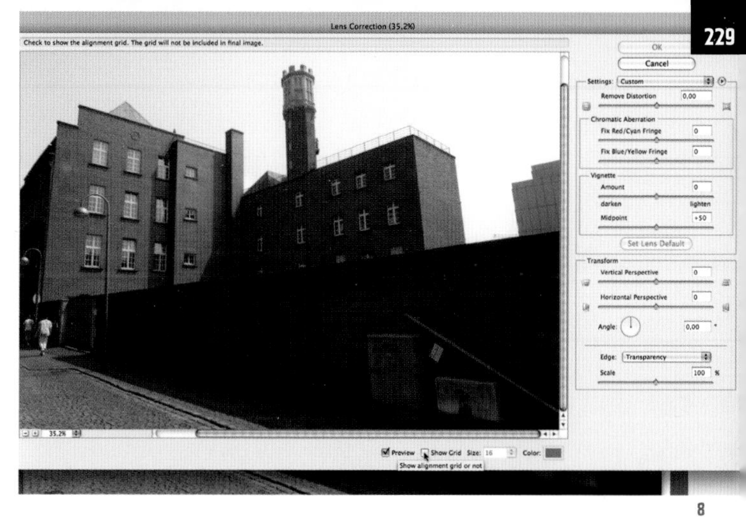

8

Then please tune the following values: Remove Distortion +2.00, Vertical Perspective -30, Angle -1.45 (ill.9).

As you see in the preview left, your image changes accordingly. Confirm with OK.

9

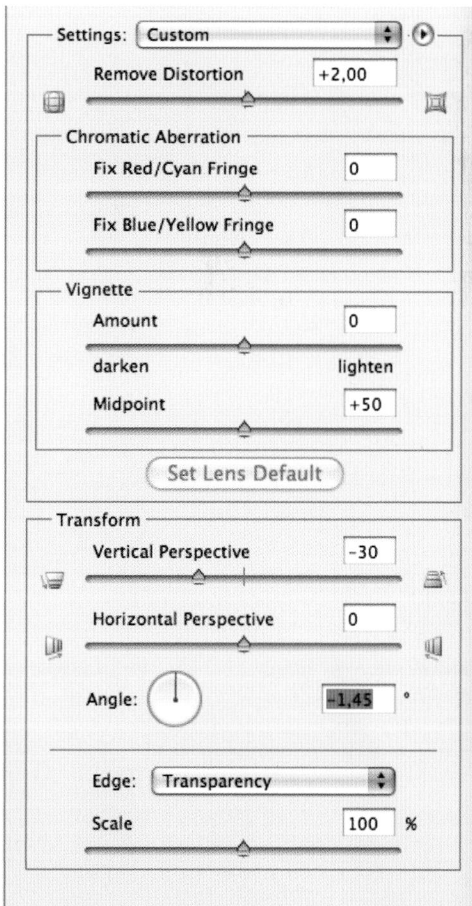

10

Now hide your Background layer, to be able to see the deskewed image clipping alone (ill.10).

Of course, you have to crop the image now, so it gets a "normal", rectangular format again.

Grab the Crop tool (C, ill.11), and check that up in the Options palette no target dimensions for Width and Height are given.
If necessary, click the Clear button at the very right in the Options palette.

With this tool, draw a frame inside the

12

11

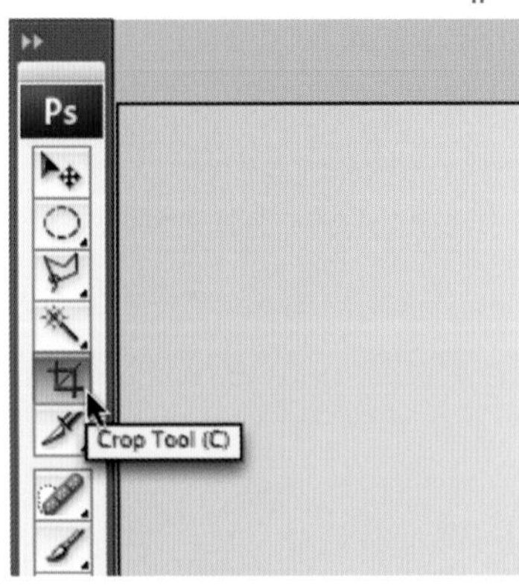

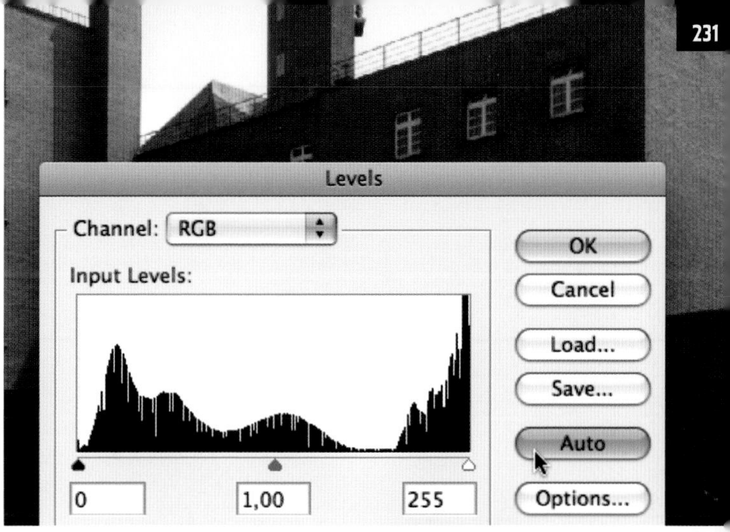

visible image area. You can do this very roughly at first, and then adjust the frame by pulling on the handles (ill.12).

Remember that Photoshop® likes to snap at the border of the image window and meanwhile also at image area borders.

If this bothers you, press the CTRL key when adapting, and the snap feature is deactivated.

When the frame is OK, press Return or double-click inside the frame, then the image is cropped.

Now that the geometric image correction is finished, attend to the levels adjustment and to improving the contrast in the image, which was shot at midday in strong sunshine, i.e. not under ideal conditions.

First insert a Levels adjustment layer - make sure your upper layer is activated, and click on the corresponding button at the bottom frame of the Layers palette. From the menu, select the entry Levels (ill.13).

In the adjustment dialog, just click the Auto button (ill.14), and then Photoshop® automatically optimizes the contrast in the individual color channels, without you having to bother about it any more.

You see the difference in ill.15; the lower part shows the optimized copy of the image.

14

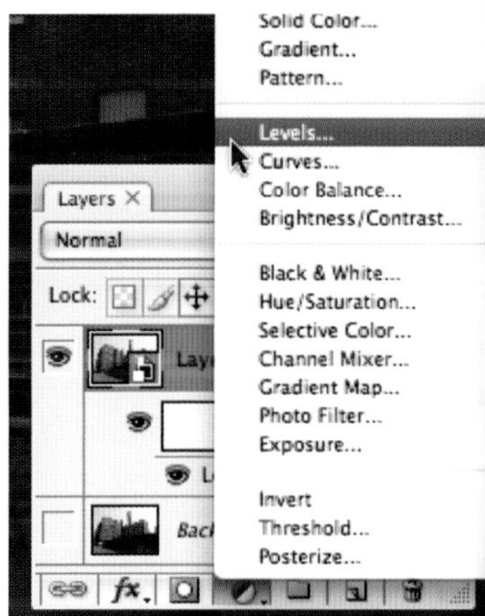

13

15

18

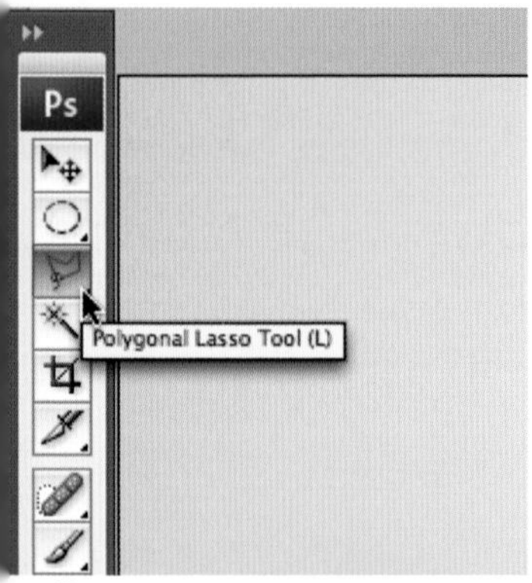

17

As the wall in the foreground and the house wall further behind on the left are in the back light, it makes sense to brighten up this area in addition.
For this you´ll carry out a further Levels correction, again in the form of an adjustment layer which is, however, masked in the whole image area outside the critical surfaces.

To prepare the masking, you´ll now first select the critical area with the polygonal lasso.

Grab the Polygonal Lasso tool (L, or Shift-L, ill.17) and draw click-wise a corresponding selection (ill.18; for clarity´s sake, the selection is shown here in mask mode, after having pressed Q).

Don´t forget that while drawing you can zoom into the image using CTRL-Space, and out using Alt-CTRL-Space.

For using the lasso, it's best to see the image in the so called Full Screen Mode With Menu Bar (View menu - Screen Mode).

When your selection is on, you can insert the new Levels adjustment layer. (Beware that for doing this you should see your selection not in mask but in "ants" mode.)

Ensure that your first adjustment layer is

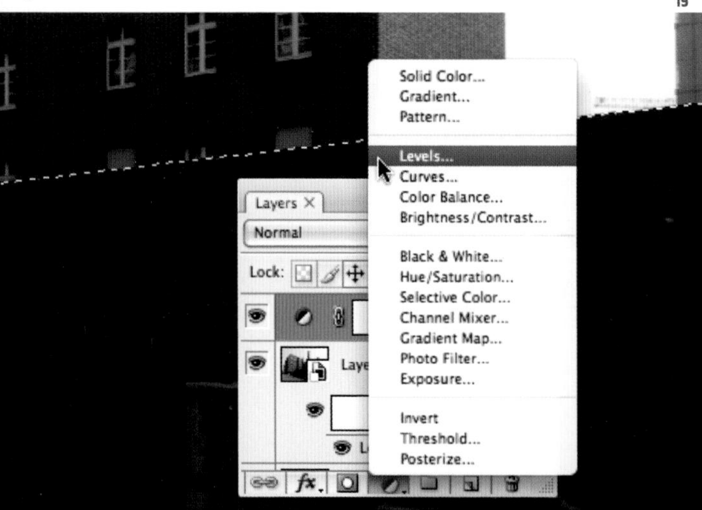

19

active, and select a further one from the same menu as before (ill.19).

In the adjustment dialog, set the White control to 240 (lightening the bright spots in the foreground, ill.20) and move the Gray control to the left, till the value 1.30 is displayed (this makes the foreground generally brighter). Confirm with OK.

During your correction, or at the latest when looking at the Layers palette (ill.21, mask miniature) you see that the second levels correction really is confined to the area selected before.

Now it can´t do any harm to turn the Red of the brick surfaces a bit stronger, so now insert over the latest installed Levels layer an adjustment layer for a Hue/Saturation correction (ill.22).

In the adjustment dialog, select the Reds for editing (ill.23); here you move the Saturation control a little to the right (I´ve chosen the value + 30).

Thus the Gray component within the Reds spectrum of the image is reduced. Confirm with OK.

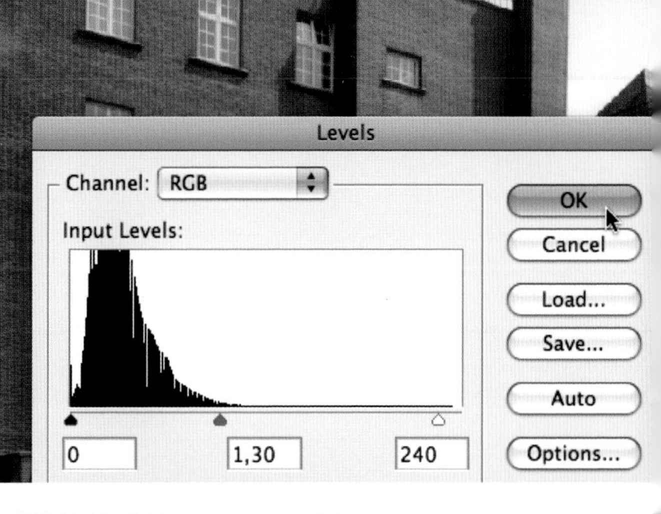

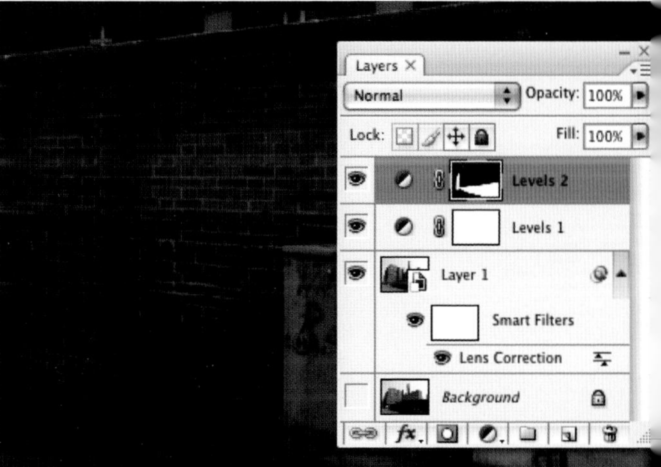

22

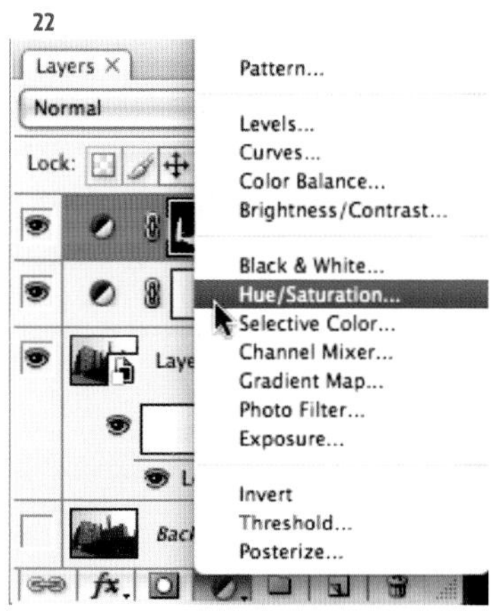

23

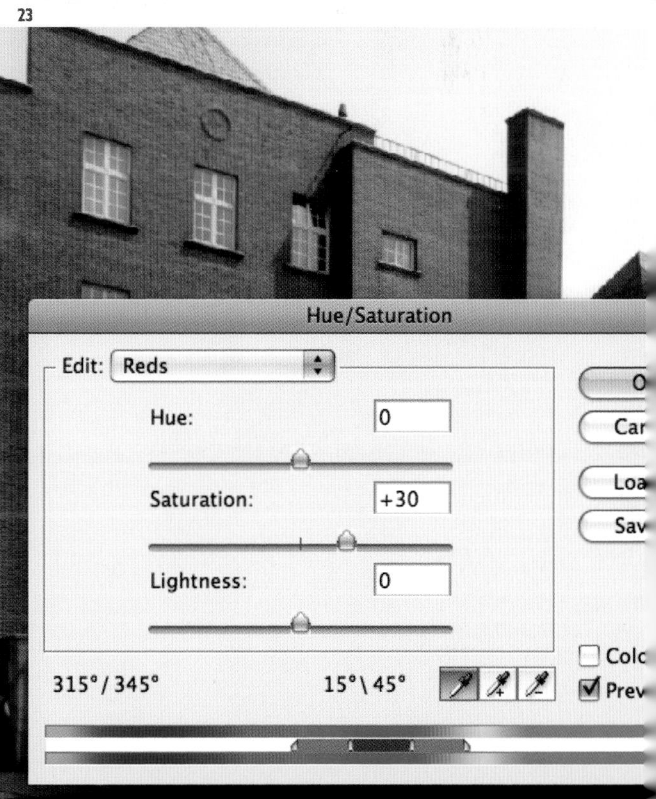

24

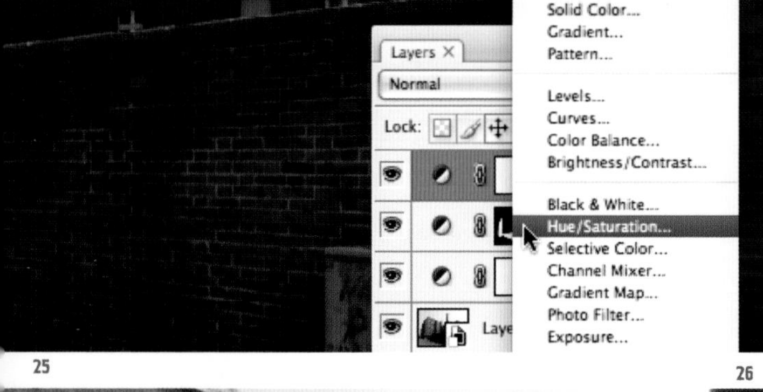

25

26

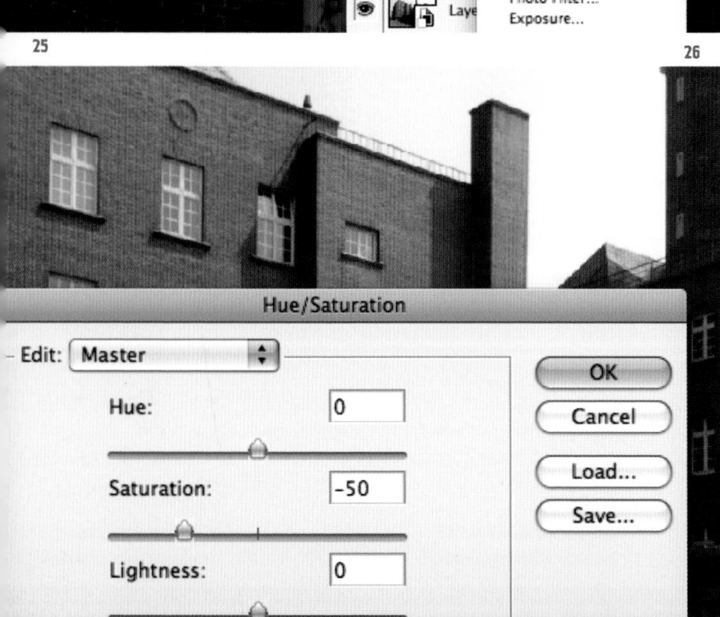

As you can see in the image, after this color refreshment of the facades the street surface has also become more reddish, but for the image contrast it would be good if this color tint was removed again, which speaks for a further Hue/Saturation correction for this area (this time then, however, with a saturation decrease).

For this we´ll proceed exactly as before, at the second Levels correction: first selecting the critical surface and then inserting with the hovering selection a new adjustment layer which is automatically masked.

So, select the area of the street surface with the polygonal lasso (ill.24; here again, for clarity´s sake, the mask mode of the selection is shown).

Your selection is finished; are the ants circling the street surface?
Now insert over the latest installed layer

a further adjustment layer for Hue/Saturation (ill.25).

In the adjustment dialog, stay in the Master department for editing (so that other colors are also removed from the street surface, ill.26), and move the Saturation control to the left, to -50 for example. The street gets a more neutral Gray. Confirm with OK.

Now we have to tidy up in the Layers palette. Activate all four correction layers, by clicking on them one after the other with the Shift key held down (ill.27).

Then select the option New Group from Layers from the menu of the Layers palette (ill.28), and give the group a sensible name (e.g. color correction, ill.29).

With that, you´re finished for the moment (ill.30). Remember that you still have to convert your image into CMYK, if you want to use it in a printing layout (look up chapter 03).

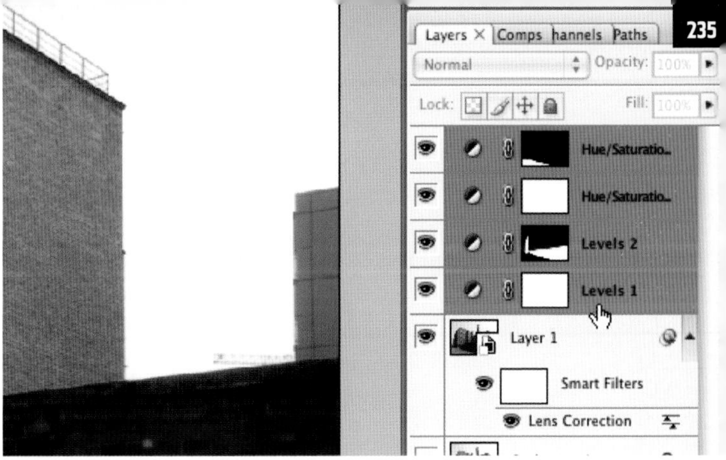

27

28

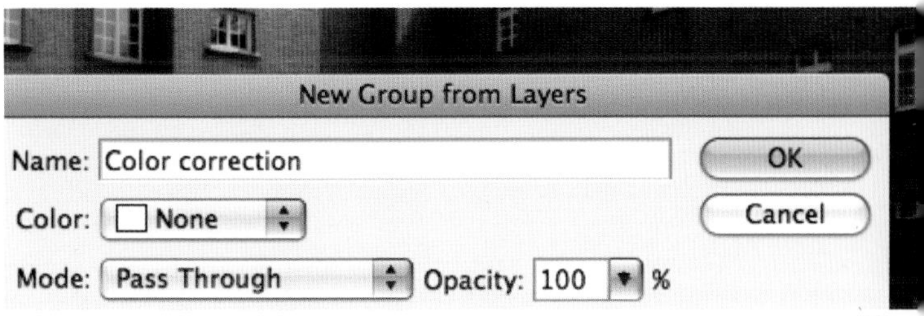

29

30

Software, Tutorial Files

Photoshop®, Bridge®, Illustrator® and InDesign® are registered trademarks of their manufacturer Adobe Systems Incorporated. Bridge® comes along with Photoshop®, which is available as a 30-day free trial version on the Adobe web site:

Photoshop® CS3: http://www.adobe.com/downloads/

The images 02_clouds_internet .jpg (p.49) and 07_ng_clouds_internet.jpg (p.144) come from www.wolkenatlas.de (original name Sc mamma). The image 06_mapletree_start.psd (p.116) comes from http://juergen-huefner.dietestdomain.de (original name gebrueder-ahorn-im-morgenli.jpg). I thank both owners for the right to present these images in my book.

For working yourself through my tutorials, you have to download the according files from my web site:

http://cms.architecturalrendering.de/ps3/english
Name: bella
Password: pittura

You are welcome to use the contact sheet on my site for any questions, remarks, suggestions or criticism.

Work on this book has taken much longer than I thought in the first place. In the beginning, I couldn't make up my mind what to write on Photoshop® that might still be unknown to professionals - in the end, however, so much material has emerged that there is nearly enough for a second volume. During the process of writing, I'm afraid people around me had to suffer from my rather oscillating course of moods.
Thus, and first of all, I want to express my thanks to the editor Springer ViennaNewYork, especially to David Marold, for their enormous patience and helpfulness.

Finally, I would like to pay tribute to Michael, a former friend of mine, who wittily initiated me into the arcane world of computing many years ago, and with whom the strenuous process of learning was so much more joyful. This book is dedicated to him.

Index

Filter

View

Window